Čížek • Härdle • Weron
Statistical Tools for Finance and Insurance

Pavel Čížek • Wolfgang Härdle • Rafał Weron

Statistical Tools for Finance and Insurance

Springer

Pavel Čížek
Tilburg University
Dept. of Econometrics & OR
P.O. Box 90153
5000 LE Tilburg, Netherlands
e-mail: P.Cizek@uvt.nl

Rafał Weron
Wrocław University of Technology
Hugo Steinhaus Center
Wyb. Wyspiańskiego 27
50-370 Wrocław, Poland
e-mail: Rafal.Weron@pwr.wroc.pl

Wolfgang Härdle
Humboldt-Universität zu Berlin
CASE – Center for Applied Statistics and Economics
Institut für Statistik und Ökonometrie
Spandauer Straße 1
10178 Berlin, Germany
e-mail: haerdle@wiwi.hu-berlin.de

This book is also available as e-book on www.i-xplore.de.
Use the licence code at the end of the book to download the e-book.

Library of Congress Control Number: 2005920464

Mathematics Subject Classification (2000): 62P05, 91B26, 91B28

ISBN 3-540-22189-1 Springer Berlin Heidelberg New York

springeronline.com

Printed in Germany

Typesetting by the authors
Production: LE-TEX Jelonek, Schmidt & Vöckler GbR, Leipzig
Cover design: design & production GmbH, Heidelberg
Printed on acid-free paper 46/3142YL – 5 4 3 2 1 0

Contents

Contributors

Noer Azam Achsani Department of Economics, University of Potsdam

Michal Benko Center for Applied Statistics and Economics, Humboldt-Universität zu Berlin

Szymon Borak Center for Applied Statistics and Economics, Humboldt-Universität zu Berlin

Krzysztof Burnecki Hugo Steinhaus Center for Stochastic Methods, Wrocław University of Technology

Pavel Čížek Center for Economic Research, Tilburg University

Kai Detlefsen Center for Applied Statistics and Economics, Humboldt-Universität zu Berlin

Hansjörg Furrer Swiss Life, Zürich

Nicolas Gaussel Société Générale Asset Management, Paris

Wolfgang Härdle Center for Applied Statistics and Economics, Humboldt-Universität zu Berlin

Oliver Holtemöller Department of Economics, RWTH Aachen University

Jan Iwanik Concordia Capital S.A., Poznań

Krzysztof Jajuga Department of Financial Investments and Insurance, Wrocław University of Economics

Seok-Oh Jeong Institut de statistique, Universite catholique de Louvain

Karel Komorád Komerční Banka, Praha

Grzegorz Kukla Towarzystwo Ubezpieczeniowe EUROPA S.A., Wrocław

Heiko Lehmann SAP AG, Walldorf

Zbigniew Michna Department of Mathematics, Wrocław University of Economics

Adam Misiorek Institute of Power Systems Automation, Wrocław

Paweł Miśta Institute of Mathematics, Wrocław University of Technology

Rouslan Moro Center for Applied Statistics and Economics, Humboldt-Universität zu Berlin

Joanna Nowicka-Zagrajek Hugo Steinhaus Center for Stochastic Methods, Wrocław University of Technology

Wojciech Otto Faculty of Economic Sciences, Warsaw University

Daniel Papla Department of Financial Investments and Insurance, Wrocław University of Economics

Dorothea Schäfer Deutsches Institut für Wirtschaftsforschung e.V., Berlin

Rafael Schmidt Department of Statistics, London School of Economics

Hizir Sofyan Mathematics Department, Syiah Kuala University

Julien Tamine Société Générale Asset Management, Paris

David Taylor School of Computational and Applied Mathematics, University of the Witwatersrand, Johannesburg

Aleksander Weron Hugo Steinhaus Center for Stochastic Methods, Wrocław University of Technology

Rafał Weron Hugo Steinhaus Center for Stochastic Methods, Wrocław University of Technology

Agnieszka Wyłomańska Institute of Mathematics, Wrocław University of Technology

Uwe Wystup MathFinance AG, Waldems

Preface

This book is designed for students, researchers and practitioners who want to be introduced to modern statistical tools applied in finance and insurance. It is the result of a joint effort of the Center for Economic Research (CentER), Center for Applied Statistics and Economics (C.A.S.E.) and Hugo Steinhaus Center for Stochastic Methods (HSC). All three institutions brought in their specific profiles and created with this book a wide-angle view on and solutions to up-to-date practical problems.

The text is comprehensible for a graduate student in financial engineering as well as for an inexperienced newcomer to quantitative finance and insurance who wants to get a grip on advanced statistical tools applied in these fields. An experienced reader with a bright knowledge of financial and actuarial mathematics will probably skip some sections but will hopefully enjoy the various computational tools. Finally, a practitioner might be familiar with some of the methods. However, the statistical techniques related to modern financial products, like MBS or CAT bonds, will certainly attract him.

"Statistical Tools for Finance and Insurance" consists naturally of two main parts. Each part contains chapters with high focus on practical applications. The book starts with an introduction to *stable distributions*, which are the standard model for heavy tailed phenomena. Their numerical implementation is thoroughly discussed and applications to finance are given. The second chapter presents the ideas of *extreme value and copula analysis* as applied to multivariate financial data. This topic is extended in the subsequent chapter which deals with *tail dependence*, a concept describing the limiting proportion that one margin exceeds a certain threshold given that the other margin has already exceeded that threshold. The fourth chapter reviews the market in *catastrophe insurance* risk, which emerged in order to facilitate the direct transfer of reinsurance risk associated with natural catastrophes from corporations, insurers, and reinsurers to capital market investors. The next contribution employs *functional data analysis* for the estimation of smooth implied volatility surfaces. These surfaces are a result of using an oversimplified market benchmark model – the Black-Scholes formula – to real data. An attractive approach to overcome this problem is discussed in chapter six, where *implied trinomial trees* are applied to modeling implied volatilities and the corresponding state-price densities. An alternative route to tackling the implied volatility smile has led researchers to develop stochastic volatility models. The relative simplicity and the direct link of model parameters to the market makes *Heston's model* very attractive to front office users. Its application to FX option markets is covered in chapter seven. The following chapter shows how the computational complexity of stochastic volatility models can be overcome with the help of the *Fast Fourier Transform.* In chapter nine the valuation of *Mortgage Backed Securities* is discussed. The optimal prepayment policy is obtained via optimal stopping techniques. It is followed by a very innovative topic of predicting corporate bankruptcy with *Support Vector Machines.* Chapter eleven presents a novel approach to *money-demand modeling* using fuzzy clustering techniques. The first part of the book closes with *productivity analysis* for cost and frontier estimation. The nonparametric Data Envelopment Analysis is applied to efficiency issues of insurance agencies.

The insurance part of the book starts with a chapter on *loss distributions.* The basic models for claim severities are introduced and their statistical properties are thoroughly explained. In chapter fourteen, the methods of simulating and visualizing the *risk process* are discussed. This topic is followed by an overview of the approaches to *approximating the ruin probability* of an insurer. Both finite and infinite time approximations are presented. Some of these methods are extended in chapters sixteen and seventeen, where classical and anomalous *diffusion approximations* to ruin probability are discussed and extended to cases when the risk process exhibits *good and bad periods.* The last three chapters are related to one of the most important aspects of the insurance business – *premium calculation.* Chapter eighteen introduces the basic concepts including the pure risk premium and various safety loadings under different loss distributions. Calculation of a joint premium for a portfolio of insurance policies in the individual and collective risk models is discussed as well. The inclusion of *deductibles* into premium calculation is the topic of the following contribution. The last chapter of the insurance part deals with setting the appropriate level of insurance premium within a broader context of business decisions, including risk transfer through *reinsurance* and the rate of return on capital required to ensure solvability.

Our e-book offers a complete PDF version of this text and the corresponding HTML files with links to algorithms and quantlets. The reader of this book may therefore easily reconfigure and recalculate all the presented examples and methods via the enclosed XploRe Quantlet Server (XQS), which is also available from www.xplore-stat.de and www.quantlet.com. A tutorial chapter explaining how to setup and use XQS can be found in the third and final part of the book.

We gratefully acknowledge the support of Deutsche Forschungsgemeinschaft (SFB 373 Quantifikation und Simulation Ökonomischer Prozesse, SFB 649 Ökonomisches Risiko) and Komitet Badań Naukowych (PBZ-KBN 016/P03/99 Mathematical models in analysis of financial instruments and markets in Poland). A book of this kind would not have been possible without the help of many friends, colleagues, and students. For the technical production of the e-book platform and quantlets we would like to thank Zdeněk Hlávka, Sigbert Klinke, Heiko Lehmann, Adam Misiorek, Piotr Uniejewski, Qingwei Wang, and Rodrigo Witzel. Special thanks for careful proofreading and supervision of the insurance part go to Krzysztof Burnecki.

Pavel Čížek, Wolfgang Härdle, and Rafał Weron

Tilburg, Berlin, and Wrocław, February 2005

Part I

Finance

1 Stable Distributions

Szymon Borak, Wolfgang Härdle, and Rafał Weron

1.1 Introduction

Many of the concepts in theoretical and empirical finance developed over the past decades – including the classical portfolio theory, the Black-Scholes-Merton option pricing model and the RiskMetrics variance-covariance approach to Value at Risk (VaR) – rest upon the assumption that asset returns follow a normal distribution. However, it has been long known that asset returns are not normally distributed. Rather, the empirical observations exhibit fat tails. This heavy tailed or leptokurtic character of the distribution of price changes has been repeatedly observed in various markets and may be quantitatively measured by the kurtosis in excess of 3, a value obtained for the normal distribution (Bouchaud and Potters, 2000; Carr et al., 2002; Guillaume et al., 1997; Mantegna and Stanley, 1995; Rachev, 2003; Weron, 2004).

It is often argued that financial asset returns are the cumulative outcome of a vast number of pieces of information and individual decisions arriving almost continuously in time (McCulloch, 1996; Rachev and Mittnik, 2000). As such, since the pioneering work of Louis Bachelier in 1900, they have been modeled by the Gaussian distribution. The strongest statistical argument for it is based on the Central Limit Theorem, which states that the sum of a large number of independent, identically distributed variables from a finite-variance distribution will tend to be normally distributed. However, as we have already mentioned, financial asset returns usually have heavier tails.

In response to the empirical evidence Mandelbrot (1963) and Fama (1965) proposed the stable distribution as an alternative model. Although there are other heavy-tailed alternatives to the Gaussian law – like Student's t, hyperbolic, normal inverse Gaussian, or truncated stable – there is at least one good reason for modeling financial variables using stable distributions. Namely, they are supported by the generalized Central Limit Theorem, which states that stable laws are the only possible limit distributions for properly normalized and centered sums of independent, identically distributed random variables.

Since stable distributions can accommodate the fat tails and asymmetry, they often give a very good fit to empirical data. In particular, they are valuable models for data sets covering extreme events, like market crashes or natural catastrophes. Even though they are not universal, they are a useful tool in the hands of an analyst working in finance or insurance. Hence, we devote this chapter to a thorough presentation of the computational aspects related to stable laws. In Section 1.2 we review the analytical concepts and basic characteristics. In the following two sections we discuss practical simulation and estimation approaches. Finally, in Section 1.5 we present financial applications of stable laws.

1.2 Definitions and Basic Characteristics

Stable laws – also called α-stable, stable Paretian or Lévy stable – were introduced by Levy (1925) during his investigations of the behavior of sums of independent random variables. A sum of two independent random variables having an α-stable distribution with index α is again α-stable with the same index α. This invariance property, however, does not hold for different α's.

The α-stable distribution requires four parameters for complete description: an index of stability $\alpha \in (0, 2]$ also called the tail index, tail exponent or characteristic exponent, a skewness parameter $\beta \in [-1, 1]$, a scale parameter $\sigma > 0$ and a location parameter $\mu \in \mathbb{R}$. The tail exponent α determines the rate at which the tails of the distribution taper off, see the left panel in Figure 1.1. When $\alpha = 2$, the Gaussian distribution results. When $\alpha < 2$, the variance is infinite and the tails are asymptotically equivalent to a Pareto law, i.e. they exhibit a power-law behavior. More precisely, using a central limit theorem type argument it can be shown that (Janicki and Weron, 1994; Samorodnitsky and Taqqu, 1994):

$$\begin{cases} \lim_{x\to\infty} x^\alpha \mathrm{P}(X > x) = C_\alpha(1+\beta)\sigma^\alpha, \\ \lim_{x\to\infty} x^\alpha \mathrm{P}(X < -x) = C_\alpha(1+\beta)\sigma^\alpha, \end{cases} \tag{1.1}$$

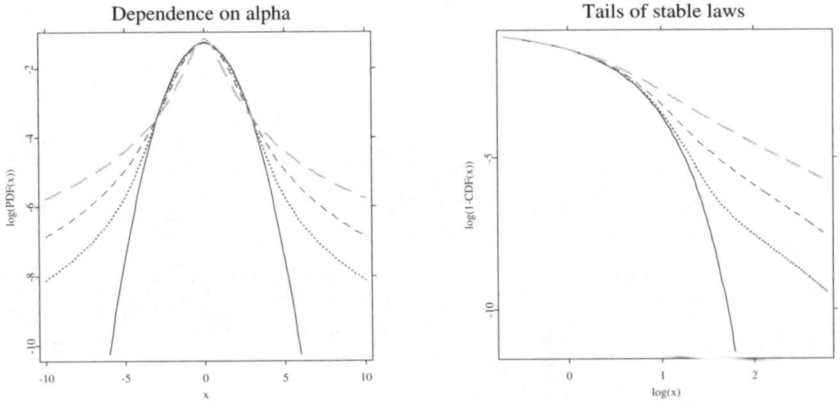

Figure 1.1: *Left panel*: A semilog plot of symmetric ($\beta = \mu = 0$) α-stable probability density functions (pdfs) for $\alpha = 2$ (black solid line), 1.8 (red dotted line), 1.5 (blue dashed line) and 1 (green long-dashed line). The Gaussian ($\alpha = 2$) density forms a parabola and is the only α-stable density with exponential tails. *Right panel*: Right tails of symmetric α-stable cumulative distribution functions (cdfs) for $\alpha = 2$ (black solid line), 1.95 (red dotted line), 1.8 (blue dashed line) and 1.5 (green long-dashed line) on a double logarithmic paper. For $\alpha < 2$ the tails form straight lines with slope $-\alpha$.

`STFstab01.xpl`

where:

$$C_\alpha = \left(2\int_0^\infty x^{-\alpha}\sin(x)dx\right)^{-1} = \frac{1}{\pi}\Gamma(\alpha)\sin\frac{\pi\alpha}{2}.$$

The convergence to a power-law tail varies for different α's and, as can be seen in the right panel of Figure 1.1, is slower for larger values of the tail index. Moreover, the tails of α-stable distribution functions exhibit a crossover from an approximate power decay with exponent $\alpha > 2$ to the true tail with exponent α. This phenomenon is more visible for large α's (Weron, 2001).

When $\alpha > 1$, the mean of the distribution exists and is equal to μ. In general, the pth moment of a stable random variable is finite if and only if $p < \alpha$. When the skewness parameter β is positive, the distribution is skewed to the right,

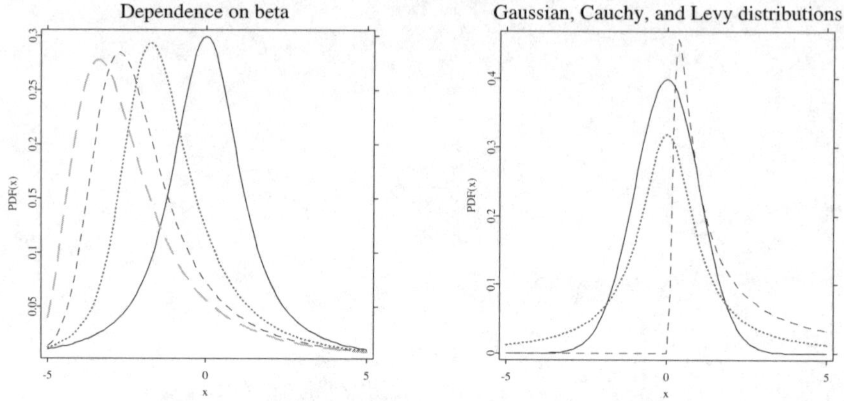

Figure 1.2: *Left panel*: Stable pdfs for $\alpha = 1.2$ and $\beta = 0$ (black solid line), 0.5 (red dotted line), 0.8 (blue dashed line) and 1 (green long-dashed line). *Right panel*: Closed form formulas for densities are known only for three distributions – Gaussian ($\alpha = 2$; black solid line), Cauchy ($\alpha = 1$; red dotted line) and Levy ($\alpha = 0.5, \beta = 1$; blue dashed line). The latter is a totally skewed distribution, i.e. its support is $\mathbb{R}_+$. In general, for $\alpha < 1$ and $\beta = 1$ (-1) the distribution is totally skewed to the right (left).

STFstab02.xpl

i.e. the right tail is thicker, see the left panel of Figure 1.2. When it is negative, it is skewed to the left. When $\beta = 0$, the distribution is symmetric about μ. As α approaches 2, β loses its effect and the distribution approaches the Gaussian distribution regardless of β. The last two parameters, σ and μ, are the usual scale and location parameters, i.e. σ determines the width and μ the shift of the mode (the peak) of the density. For $\sigma = 1$ and $\mu = 0$ the distribution is called standard stable.

1.2.1 Characteristic Function Representation

Due to the lack of closed form formulas for densities for all but three distributions (see the right panel in Figure 1.2), the α-stable law can be most

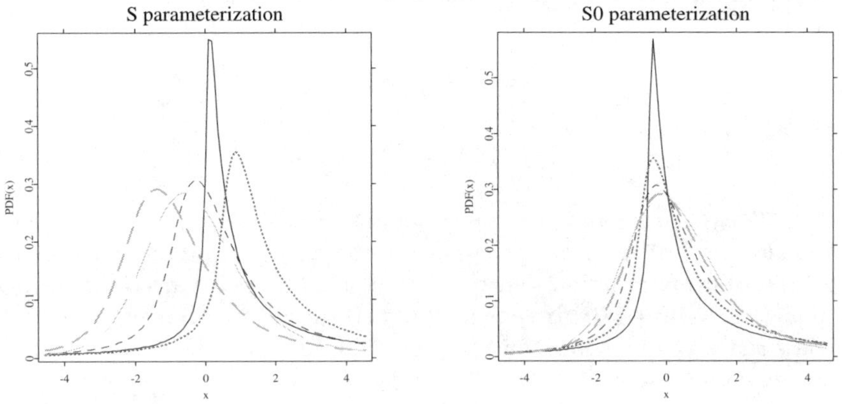

Figure 1.3: Comparison of S and S^0 parameterizations: α-stable pdfs for $\beta = 0.5$ and $\alpha = 0.5$ (black solid line), 0.75 (red dotted line), 1 (blue short-dashed line), 1.25 (green dashed line) and 1.5 (cyan long-dashed line).

STFstab03.xpl

conveniently described by its characteristic function $\phi(t)$ – the inverse Fourier transform of the probability density function. However, there are multiple parameterizations for α-stable laws and much confusion has been caused by these different representations, see Figure 1.3. The variety of formulas is caused by a combination of historical evolution and the numerous problems that have been analyzed using specialized forms of the stable distributions. The most popular parameterization of the characteristic function of $X \sim S_\alpha(\sigma, \beta, \mu)$, i.e. an α-stable random variable with parameters α, σ, β, and μ, is given by (Samorodnitsky and Taqqu, 1994; Weron, 2004):

$$\ln \phi(t) = \begin{cases} -\sigma^\alpha |t|^\alpha \{1 - i\beta \text{sign}(t) \tan \frac{\pi\alpha}{2}\} + i\mu t, & \alpha \neq 1, \\ \\ -\sigma|t|\{1 + i\beta \text{sign}(t) \frac{2}{\pi} \ln |t|\} + i\mu t, & \alpha = 1. \end{cases} \tag{1.2}$$

For numerical purposes, it is often advisable to use Nolan's (1997) parameterization:

$$\ln \phi_0(t) = \begin{cases} -\sigma^\alpha |t|^\alpha \{1 + i\beta \text{sign}(t) \tan \frac{\pi\alpha}{2}[(\sigma|t|)^{1-\alpha} - 1]\} + i\mu_0 t, & \alpha \neq 1, \\ \\ -\sigma|t|\{1 + i\beta \text{sign}(t) \frac{2}{\pi} \ln(\sigma|t|)\} + i\mu_0 t, & \alpha = 1. \end{cases} \tag{1.3}$$

The $S^0_\alpha(\sigma, \beta, \mu_0)$ parameterization is a variant of Zolotariev's (M)-parameterization (Zolotarev, 1986), with the characteristic function and hence the density and the distribution function jointly continuous in all four parameters, see the right panel in Figure 1.3. In particular, percentiles and convergence to the power-law tail vary in a continuous way as α and β vary. The location parameters of the two representations are related by $\mu = \mu_0 - \beta\sigma \tan \frac{\pi\alpha}{2}$ for $\alpha \neq 1$ and $\mu = \mu_0 - \beta\sigma \frac{2}{\pi} \ln \sigma$ for $\alpha = 1$. Note also, that the traditional scale parameter σ_G of the Gaussian distribution defined by:

$$f_G(x) = \frac{1}{\sqrt{2\pi}\sigma_G} \exp\left\{-\frac{(x-\mu)^2}{2\sigma_G^2}\right\}, \tag{1.4}$$

is not the same as σ in formulas (1.2) or (1.3). Namely, $\sigma_G = \sqrt{2}\sigma$.

1.2.2 Stable Density and Distribution Functions

The lack of closed form formulas for most stable densities and distribution functions has negative consequences. For example, during maximum likelihood estimation computationally burdensome numerical approximations have to be used. There generally are two approaches to this problem. Either the fast Fourier transform (FFT) has to be applied to the characteristic function (Mittnik, Doganoglu, and Chenyao, 1999) or direct numerical integration has to be utilized (Nolan, 1997, 1999).

For data points falling between the equally spaced FFT grid nodes an interpolation technique has to be used. Taking a larger number of grid points increases accuracy, however, at the expense of higher computational burden. The FFT based approach is faster for large samples, whereas the direct integration method favors small data sets since it can be computed at any arbitrarily chosen point. Mittnik, Doganoglu, and Chenyao (1999) report that for $N = 2^{13}$ the FFT based method is faster for samples exceeding 100 observations and slower for smaller data sets. Moreover, the FFT based approach is less universal – it is efficient only for large α's and only for pdf calculations. When computing the cdf the density must be numerically integrated. In contrast, in the direct integration method Zolotarev's (1986) formulas either for the density or the distribution function are numerically integrated.

Set $\zeta = -\beta \tan \frac{\pi\alpha}{2}$. Then the density $f(x;\alpha,\beta)$ of a standard α-stable random variable in representation S^0, i.e. $X \sim S^0_\alpha(1,\beta,0)$, can be expressed as (note, that Zolotarev (1986, Section 2.2) used yet another parametrization):

- when $\alpha \neq 1$ and $x > \zeta$:

$$f(x;\alpha,\beta) = \frac{\alpha(x-\zeta)^{\frac{1}{\alpha-1}}}{\pi \mid \alpha - 1 \mid} \int_{-\xi}^{\frac{\pi}{2}} V(\theta;\alpha,\beta) \exp\left\{-(x-\zeta)^{\frac{\alpha}{\alpha-1}} V(\theta;\alpha,\beta)\right\} d\theta, \tag{1.5}$$

- when $\alpha \neq 1$ and $x = \zeta$:

$$f(x;\alpha,\beta) = \frac{\Gamma(1+\frac{1}{\alpha})\cos(\xi)}{\pi(1+\zeta^2)^{\frac{1}{2\alpha}}},$$

- when $\alpha \neq 1$ and $x < \zeta$:

$$f(x;\alpha,\beta) = f(-x;\alpha,-\beta),$$

- when $\alpha = 1$:

$$f(x;1,\beta) = \begin{cases} \frac{1}{2|\beta|} e^{-\frac{\pi x}{2\beta}} \int_{-\frac{\pi}{2}}^{\frac{\pi}{2}} V(\theta;1,\beta) \exp\left\{-e^{-\frac{\pi x}{2\beta}} V(\theta;1,\beta)\right\} d\theta, & \beta \neq 0, \\ \frac{1}{\pi(1+x^2)}, & \beta = 0, \end{cases}$$

where

$$\xi = \begin{cases} \frac{1}{\alpha}\arctan(-\zeta), & \alpha \neq 1, \\ \frac{\pi}{2}, & \alpha = 1, \end{cases}$$

and

$$V(\theta;\alpha,\beta) = \begin{cases} (\cos\alpha\xi)^{\frac{1}{\alpha-1}} \left(\frac{\cos\theta}{\sin\alpha(\xi+\theta)}\right)^{\frac{\alpha}{\alpha-1}} \frac{\cos\{\alpha\xi+(\alpha-1)\theta\}}{\cos\theta}, & \alpha \neq 1, \\ \frac{2}{\pi}\left(\frac{\frac{\pi}{2}+\beta\theta}{\cos\theta}\right) \exp\left\{\frac{1}{\beta}(\frac{\pi}{2}+\beta\theta)\tan\theta\right\}, & \alpha = 1, \beta \neq 0. \end{cases}$$

The distribution $F(x;\alpha,\beta)$ of a standard α-stable random variable in representation S^0 can be expressed as:

- when $\alpha \neq 1$ and $x > \zeta$:

$$F(x;\alpha,\beta) = c_1(\alpha,\beta) + \frac{\text{sign}(1-\alpha)}{\pi} \int_{-\xi}^{\frac{\pi}{2}} \exp\left\{-(x-\zeta)^{\frac{\alpha}{\alpha-1}} V(\theta;\alpha,\beta)\right\} d\theta,$$

where

$$c_1(\alpha,\beta) = \begin{cases} \frac{1}{\pi}\left(\frac{\pi}{2} - \xi\right), & \alpha < 1, \\ 1, & \alpha > 1, \end{cases}$$

- when $\alpha \neq 1$ and $x = \zeta$:

$$F(x;\alpha,\beta) = \frac{1}{\pi}\left(\frac{\pi}{2} - \xi\right),$$

- when $\alpha \neq 1$ and $x < \zeta$:

$$F(x;\alpha,\beta) = 1 - F(-x;\alpha,-\beta),$$

- when $\alpha = 1$:

$$F(x;1,\beta) = \begin{cases} \frac{1}{\pi}\int_{-\frac{\pi}{2}}^{\frac{\pi}{2}} \exp\left\{-e^{-\frac{\pi x}{2\beta}} V(\theta;1,\beta)\right\} d\theta, & \beta > 0, \\ \frac{1}{2} + \frac{1}{\pi}\arctan x, & \beta = 0, \\ 1 - F(x,1,-\beta), & \beta < 0. \end{cases}$$

Formula (1.5) requires numerical integration of the function $g(\cdot)\exp\{-g(\cdot)\}$, where $g(\theta;x,\alpha,\beta) = (x-\zeta)^{\frac{\alpha}{\alpha-1}} V(\theta;\alpha,\beta)$. The integrand is 0 at $-\xi$, increases monotonically to a maximum of $\frac{1}{e}$ at point θ^* for which $g(\theta^*;x,\alpha,\beta) = 1$, and then decreases monotonically to 0 at $\frac{\pi}{2}$ (Nolan, 1997). However, in some cases the integrand becomes very peaked and numerical algorithms can miss the spike and underestimate the integral. To avoid this problem we need to find the argument θ^* of the peak numerically and compute the integral as a sum of two integrals: one from $-\xi$ to θ^* and the other from θ^* to $\frac{\pi}{2}$.

1.3 Simulation of α-stable Variables

The complexity of the problem of simulating sequences of α-stable random variables results from the fact that there are no analytic expressions for the inverse F^{-1} of the cumulative distribution function. The first breakthrough was made by Kanter (1975), who gave a direct method for simulating $S_\alpha(1,1,0)$ random variables, for $\alpha < 1$. It turned out that this method could be easily adapted to the general case. Chambers, Mallows, and Stuck (1976) were the first to give the formulas.

The algorithm for constructing a standard stable random variable $X \sim S_\alpha(1,\beta,0)$, in representation (1.2), is the following (Weron, 1996):

- generate a random variable V uniformly distributed on $(-\frac{\pi}{2},\frac{\pi}{2})$ and an independent exponential random variable W with mean 1;
- for $\alpha \neq 1$ compute:

$$X = S_{\alpha,\beta} \cdot \frac{\sin\{\alpha(V+B_{\alpha,\beta})\}}{\{\cos(V)\}^{1/\alpha}} \cdot \left[\frac{\cos\{V-\alpha(V+B_{\alpha,\beta})\}}{W}\right]^{(1-\alpha)/\alpha}, \quad (1.6)$$

  where

$$B_{\alpha,\beta} = \frac{\arctan(\beta \tan\frac{\pi\alpha}{2})}{\alpha},$$
$$S_{\alpha,\beta} = \left\{1+\beta^2\tan^2\left(\frac{\pi\alpha}{2}\right)\right\}^{1/(2\alpha)};$$

- for $\alpha = 1$ compute:

$$X = \frac{2}{\pi}\left\{\left(\frac{\pi}{2}+\beta V\right)\tan V - \beta\ln\left(\frac{\frac{\pi}{2}W\cos V}{\frac{\pi}{2}+\beta V}\right)\right\}. \quad (1.7)$$

Given the formulas for simulation of a standard α-stable random variable, we can easily simulate a stable random variable for all admissible values of the parameters α, σ, β and μ using the following property: if $X \sim S_\alpha(1,\beta,0)$ then

$$Y = \begin{cases} \sigma X + \mu, & \alpha \neq 1, \\ \sigma X + \frac{2}{\pi}\beta\sigma\ln\sigma + \mu, & \alpha = 1, \end{cases} \quad (1.8)$$

is $S_\alpha(\sigma,\beta,\mu)$. It is interesting to note that for $\alpha = 2$ (and $\beta = 0$) the Chambers-Mallows-Stuck method reduces to the well known Box-Muller algorithm for generating Gaussian random variables (Janicki and Weron, 1994). Although many other approaches have been proposed in the literature, this method is regarded as the fastest and the most accurate (Weron, 2004).

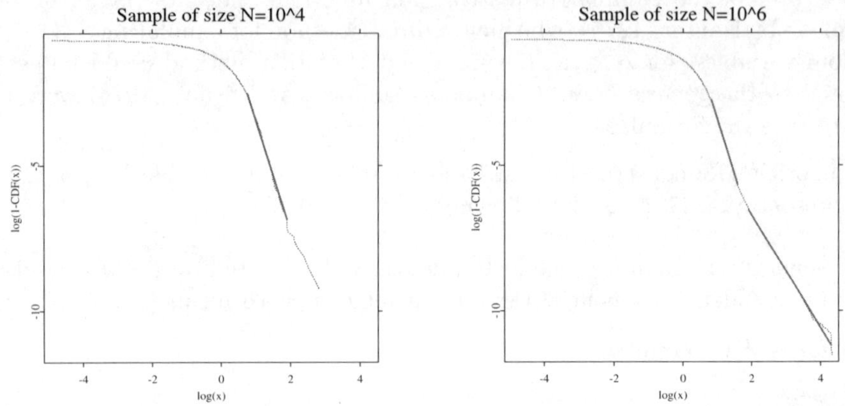

Figure 1.4: A double logarithmic plot of the right tail of an empirical symmetric 1.9-stable distribution function for a sample of size $N = 10^4$ (*left panel*) and $N = 10^6$ (*right panel*). Thick red lines represent the linear regression fit. The tail index estimate ($\hat{\alpha} = 3.7320$) obtained for the smaller sample is close to the initial power-law like decay of the larger sample ($\hat{\alpha} = 3.7881$). The far tail estimate $\hat{\alpha} = 1.9309$ is close to the true value of α.

`STFstab04.xpl`

1.4 Estimation of Parameters

Like simulation, the estimation of stable law parameters is in general severely hampered by the lack of known closed-form density functions for all but a few members of the stable family. Either the pdf has to be numerically integrated (see the previous section) or the estimation technique has to be based on a different characteristic of stable laws.

All presented methods work quite well assuming that the sample under consideration is indeed α-stable. However, if the data comes from a different distribution, these procedures may mislead more than the Hill and direct tail estimation methods. Since the formal tests for assessing α-stability of a sample are very time consuming we suggest to first apply the "visual inspection" tests to see whether the empirical densities resemble those of α-stable laws.

1.4.1 Tail Exponent Estimation

The simplest and most straightforward method of estimating the tail index is to plot the right tail of the empirical cdf on a double logarithmic paper. The slope of the linear regression for large values of x yields the estimate of the tail index α, through the relation $\alpha = -\text{slope}$.

This method is very sensitive to the size of the sample and the choice of the number of observations used in the regression. For example, the slope of about -3.7 may indicate a non-α-stable power-law decay in the tails or the contrary – an α-stable distribution with $\alpha \approx 1.9$. This is illustrated in Figure 1.4. In the left panel a power-law fit to the tail of a sample of $N = 10^4$ standard symmetric ($\beta = \mu = 0$, $\sigma = 1$) α-stable distributed variables with $\alpha = 1.9$ yields an estimate of $\hat{\alpha} = 3.732$. However, when the sample size is increased to $N = 10^6$ the power-law fit to the extreme tail observations yields $\hat{\alpha} = 1.9309$, which is fairly close to the original value of α.

The true tail behavior (1.1) is observed only for very large (also for very small, i.e. the negative tail) observations, after a crossover from a temporary power-like decay (which surprisingly indicates $\alpha \approx 3.7$). Moreover, the obtained estimates still have a slight positive bias, which suggests that perhaps even larger samples than 10^6 observations should be used. In Figure 1.4 we used only the upper 0.15% of the records to estimate the true tail exponent. In general, the choice of the observations used in the regression is subjective and can yield large estimation errors, a fact which is often neglected in the literature.

A well known method for estimating the tail index that does not assume a parametric form for the entire distribution function, but focuses only on the tail behavior was proposed by Hill (1975). The Hill estimator is used to estimate the tail index α, when the upper (or lower) tail of the distribution is of the form: $1 - F(x) = Cx^{-\alpha}$, see Figure 1.5. Like the log-log regression method, the Hill estimator tends to overestimate the tail exponent of the stable distribution if α is close to two and the sample size is not very large. For a review of the extreme value theory and the Hill estimator see Härdle, Klinke, and Müller (2000, Chapter 13) or Embrechts, Klüppelberg, and Mikosch (1997).

These examples clearly illustrate that the true tail behavior of α-stable laws is visible only for extremely large data sets. In practice, this means that in order to estimate α we must use high-frequency data and restrict ourselves to the most "outlying" observations. Otherwise, inference of the tail index may be strongly misleading and rejection of the α-stable regime unfounded.

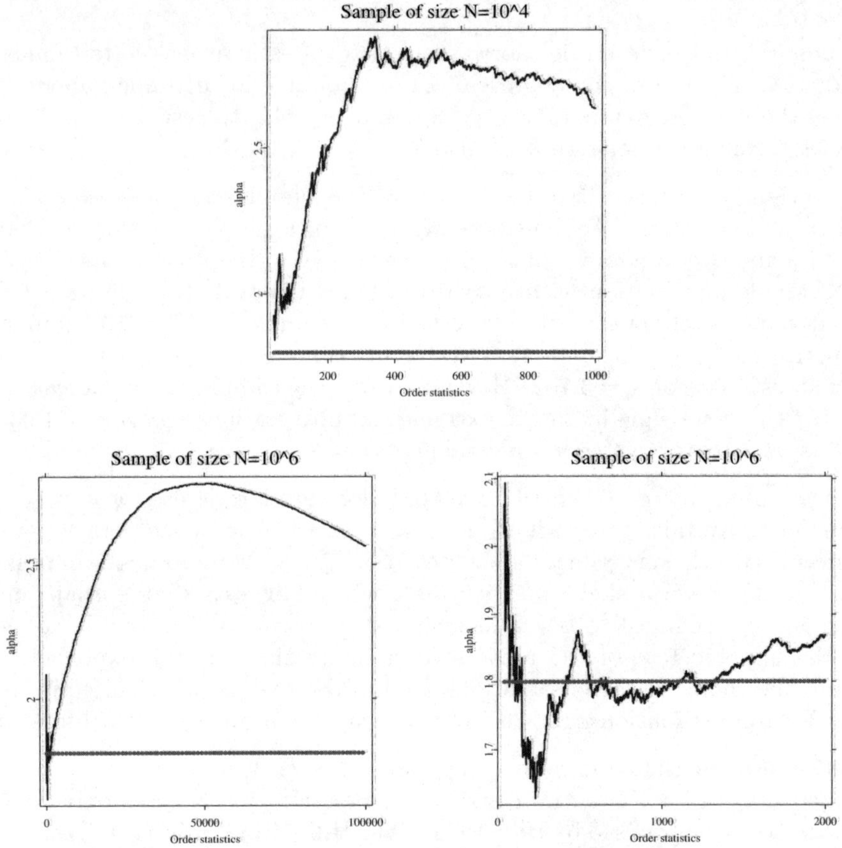

Figure 1.5: Plots of the Hill statistics $\hat{\alpha}_{n,k}$ vs. the maximum order statistic k for 1.8-stable samples of size $N = 10^4$ (*top panel*) and $N = 10^6$ (*left and right panels*). Red horizontal lines represent the true value of α. For better exposition, the right panel is a magnification of the left panel for small k. A close estimate is obtained only for $k = 500, ..., 1300$ (i.e. for $k < 0.13\%$ of sample size).

`STFstab05.xpl`

We now turn to the problem of parameter estimation. We start the discussion with the simplest, fastest and ... least accurate quantile methods, then develop the slower, yet much more accurate sample characteristic function methods and, finally, conclude with the slowest but most accurate maximum likelihood approach. Given a sample $x_1, ..., x_n$ of independent and identically distributed $S_\alpha(\sigma, \beta, \mu)$ observations, in what follows, we provide estimates $\hat{\alpha}$, $\hat{\sigma}$, $\hat{\beta}$, and $\hat{\mu}$ of all four stable law parameters.

1.4.2 Quantile Estimation

Already in 1971 Fama and Roll provided very simple estimates for parameters of symmetric ($\beta = 0, \mu = 0$) stable laws when $\alpha > 1$. McCulloch (1986) generalized and improved their method. He analyzed stable law quantiles and provided consistent estimators of all four stable parameters, with the restriction $\alpha \geq 0.6$, while retaining the computational simplicity of Fama and Roll's method. After McCulloch define:

$$v_\alpha = \frac{x_{0.95} - x_{0.05}}{x_{0.75} - x_{0.25}}, \tag{1.9}$$

which is independent of both σ and μ. In the above formula x_f denotes the f-th population quantile, so that $S_\alpha(\sigma, \beta, \mu)(x_f) = f$. Let $\hat{v}_\alpha$ be the corresponding sample value. It is a consistent estimator of v_α. Now, define:

$$v_\beta = \frac{x_{0.95} + x_{0.05} - 2x_{0.50}}{x_{0.95} - x_{0.05}}, \tag{1.10}$$

and let $\hat{v}_\beta$ be the corresponding sample value. v_β is also independent of both σ and μ. As a function of α and β it is strictly increasing in β for each α. The statistic $\hat{v}_\beta$ is a consistent estimator of v_β.

Statistics v_α and v_β are functions of α and β. This relationship may be inverted and the parameters α and β may be viewed as functions of v_α and v_β:

$$\alpha = \psi_1(v_\alpha, v_\beta), \ \beta = \psi_2(v_\alpha, v_\beta). \tag{1.11}$$

Substituting v_α and v_β by their sample values and applying linear interpolation between values found in tables provided by McCulloch (1986) yields estimators $\hat{\alpha}$ and $\hat{\beta}$.

Scale and location parameters, σ and μ, can be estimated in a similar way. However, due to the discontinuity of the characteristic function for $\alpha = 1$ and $\beta \neq 0$ in representation (1.2), this procedure is much more complicated. We refer the interested reader to the original work of McCulloch (1986).

1.4.3 Characteristic Function Approaches

Given a sample $x_1, ..., x_n$ of independent and identically distributed (i.i.d.) random variables, define the sample characteristic function by

$$\hat{\phi}(t) = \frac{1}{n} \sum_{j=1}^{n} e^{itx_j}. \quad (1.12)$$

Since $|\hat{\phi}(t)|$ is bounded by unity all moments of $\hat{\phi}(t)$ are finite and, for any fixed t, it is the sample average of i.i.d. random variables $\exp(itx_j)$. Hence, by the law of large numbers, $\hat{\phi}(t)$ is a consistent estimator of the characteristic function $\phi(t)$.

Press (1972) proposed a simple estimation method, called the method of moments, based on transformations of the characteristic function. The obtained estimators are consistent since they are based upon estimators of $\phi(t)$, $\mathrm{Im}\{\phi(t)\}$ and $\mathrm{Re}\{\phi(t)\}$, which are known to be consistent. However, convergence to the population values depends on a choice of four points at which the above functions are evaluated. The optimal selection of these values is problematic and still is an open question. The obtained estimates are of poor quality and the method is not recommended for more than preliminary estimation.

Koutrouvelis (1980) presented a regression-type method which starts with an initial estimate of the parameters and proceeds iteratively until some prespecified convergence criterion is satisfied. Each iteration consists of two weighted regression runs. The number of points to be used in these regressions depends on the sample size and starting values of α. Typically no more than two or three iterations are needed. The speed of the convergence, however, depends on the initial estimates and the convergence criterion.

The regression method is based on the following observations concerning the characteristic function $\phi(t)$. First, from (1.2) we can easily derive:

$$\ln(-\ln|\phi(t)|^2) = \ln(2\sigma^\alpha) + \alpha \ln|t|. \quad (1.13)$$

The real and imaginary parts of $\phi(t)$ are for $\alpha \neq 1$ given by

$$\Re\{\phi(t)\} = \exp(-|\sigma t|^\alpha) \cos\left[\mu t + |\sigma t|^\alpha \beta \mathrm{sign}(t) \tan\frac{\pi\alpha}{2}\right],$$

and

$$\Im\{\phi(t)\} = \exp(-|\sigma t|^\alpha) \sin\left[\mu t + |\sigma t|^\alpha \beta \mathrm{sign}(t) \tan\frac{\pi\alpha}{2}\right].$$

The last two equations lead, apart from considerations of principal values, to

$$\arctan\left(\frac{\Im\{\phi(t)\}}{\Re\{\phi(t)\}}\right) = \mu t + \beta\sigma^\alpha \tan\frac{\pi\alpha}{2}\text{sign}(t)|t|^\alpha. \tag{1.14}$$

Equation (1.13) depends only on α and σ and suggests that we estimate these parameters by regressing $y = \ln(-\ln|\phi_n(t)|^2)$ on $w = \ln|t|$ in the model

$$y_k = m + \alpha w_k + \epsilon_k, \quad k = 1, 2, ..., K, \tag{1.15}$$

where t_k is an appropriate set of real numbers, $m = \ln(2\sigma^\alpha)$, and ϵ_k denotes an error term. Koutrouvelis (1980) proposed to use $t_k = \frac{\pi k}{25}, k = 1, 2, ..., K$; with K ranging between 9 and 134 for different estimates of α and sample sizes.

Once $\hat{\alpha}$ and $\hat{\sigma}$ have been obtained and α and σ have been fixed at these values, estimates of β and μ can be obtained using (1.14). Next, the regressions are repeated with $\hat{\alpha}$, $\hat{\sigma}$, $\hat{\beta}$ and $\hat{\mu}$ as the initial parameters. The iterations continue until a prespecified convergence criterion is satisfied.

Kogon and Williams (1998) eliminated this iteration procedure and simplified the regression method. For initial estimation they applied McCulloch's (1986) method, worked with the continuous representation (1.3) of the characteristic function instead of the classical one (1.2) and used a fixed set of only 10 equally spaced frequency points t_k. In terms of computational speed their method compares favorably to the original method of Koutrouvelis (1980). It has a significantly better performance near $\alpha = 1$ and $\beta \neq 0$ due to the elimination of discontinuity of the characteristic function. However, it returns slightly worse results for very small α.

1.4.4 Maximum Likelihood Method

The maximum likelihood (ML) estimation scheme for α-stable distributions does not differ from that for other laws, at least as far as the theory is concerned. For a vector of observations $x = (x_1, ..., x_n)$, the ML estimate of the parameter vector $\theta = (\alpha, \sigma, \beta, \mu)$ is obtained by maximizing the log-likelihood function:

$$L_\theta(x) = \sum_{i=1}^{n} \ln \tilde{f}(x_i; \theta), \tag{1.16}$$

where $\tilde{f}(\cdot; \theta)$ is the stable pdf. The tilde denotes the fact that, in general, we do not know the explicit form of the density and have to approximate it numerically. The ML methods proposed in the literature differ in the choice of the approximating algorithm. However, all of them have an appealing common feature – under certain regularity conditions the maximum likelihood estimator is asymptotically normal.

Modern ML estimation techniques either utilize the FFT-based approach for approximating the stable pdf (Mittnik et al., 1999) or use the direct integration method (Nolan, 2001). Both approaches are comparable in terms of efficiency. The differences in performance result from different approximation algorithms, see Section 1.2.2.

Simulation studies suggest that out of the five described techniques the method of moments yields the worst estimates, well outside any admissible error range (Stoyanov and Racheva-Iotova, 2004; Weron, 2004). McCulloch's method comes in next with acceptable results and computational time significantly lower than the regression approaches. On the other hand, both the Koutrouvelis and the Kogon-Williams implementations yield good estimators with the latter performing considerably faster, but slightly less accurate. Finally, the ML estimates are almost always the most accurate, in particular, with respect to the skewness parameter. However, as we have already said, maximum likelihood estimation techniques are certainly the slowest of all the discussed methods. For example, ML estimation for a sample of a few thousand observations using a gradient search routine which utilizes the direct integration method is slower by 4 orders of magnitude than the Kogon-Williams algorithm, i.e. a few minutes compared to a few hundredths of a second on a fast PC! Clearly, the higher accuracy does not justify the application of ML estimation in many real life problems, especially when calculations are to be performed on-line.

1.5 Financial Applications of Stable Laws

Many techniques in modern finance rely heavily on the assumption that the random variables under investigation follow a Gaussian distribution. However, time series observed in finance – but also in other applications – often deviate from the Gaussian model, in that their marginal distributions are heavy-tailed and, possibly, asymmetric. In such situations, the appropriateness of the commonly adopted normal assumption is highly questionable.

It is often argued that financial asset returns are the cumulative outcome of a vast number of pieces of information and individual decisions arriving almost continuously in time. Hence, in the presence of heavy-tails it is natural

Table 1.1: Fits to 2000 Dow Jones Industrial Average (DJIA) index returns from the period February 2, 1987 – December 29, 1994. Test statistics and the corresponding p-values based on 1000 simulated samples (in parentheses) are also given.

Parameters:	α	σ	β	μ
α-stable fit	1.6411	0.0050	-0.0126	0.0005
Gaussian fit		0.0111		0.0003

Tests:	Anderson-Darling	Kolmogorov
α-stable fit	0.6441	0.5583
	(0.020)	(0.500)
Gaussian fit	$+\infty$	4.6353
	(<0.005)	(<0.005)

STFstab06.xpl

to assume that they are approximately governed by a stable non-Gaussian distribution. Other leptokurtic distributions, including Student's t, Weibull, and hyperbolic, lack the attractive central limit property.

Stable distributions have been successfully fit to stock returns, excess bond returns, foreign exchange rates, commodity price returns and real estate returns (McCulloch, 1996; Rachev and Mittnik, 2000). In recent years, however, several studies have found, what appears to be strong evidence against the stable model (Gopikrishnan et al., 1999; McCulloch, 1997). These studies have estimated the tail exponent directly from the tail observations and commonly have found α that appears to be significantly greater than 2, well outside the stable domain. Recall, however, that in Section 1.4.1 we have shown that estimating α only from the tail observations may be strongly misleading and for samples of typical size the rejection of the α-stable regime unfounded. Let us see ourselves how well the stable law describes financial asset returns.

In this section we want to apply the discussed techniques to financial data. Due to limited space we chose only one estimation method – the regression approach of Koutrouvelis (1980), as it offers high accuracy at moderate computational time. We start the empirical analysis with the most prominent example – the Dow Jones Industrial Average (DJIA) index, see Table 1.1. The data set covers the period February 2, 1987 – December 29, 1994 and comprises 2000

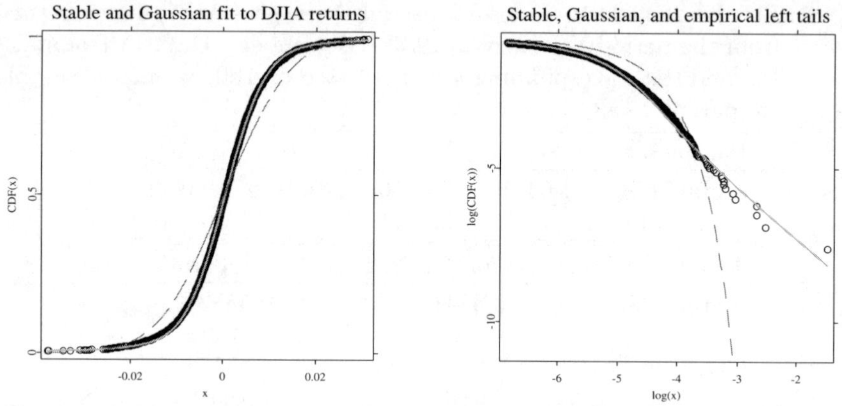

Figure 1.6: Stable (cyan) and Gaussian (dashed red) fits to the DJIA returns (black circles) empirical cdf from the period February 2, 1987 – December 29, 1994. Right panel is a magnification of the left tail fit on a double logarithmic scale clearly showing the superiority of the 1.64-stable law.

STFstab06.xpl

daily returns. Recall, that it includes the largest crash in Wall Street history – the Black Monday of October 19, 1987. Clearly the 1.64-stable law offers a much better fit to the DJIA returns than the Gaussian distribution. Its superiority, especially in the tails of the distribution, is even better visible in Figure 1.6.

To make our statistical analysis more sound, we also compare both fits through Anderson-Darling and Kolmogorov test statistics (D'Agostino and Stephens, 1986). The former may be treated as a weighted Kolmogorov statistics which puts more weight to the differences in the tails of the distributions. Although no asymptotic results are known for the stable laws, approximate p-values for these goodness-of-fit tests can be obtained via the Monte Carlo technique, for details see Chapter 13. First the parameter vector is estimated for a given sample of size n, yielding $\hat{\theta}$, and the test statistics is calculated assuming that the sample is distributed according to $F(x;\hat{\theta})$, returning a value of d. Next, a sample of size n of $F(x;\hat{\theta})$-distributed variates is generated. The parameter

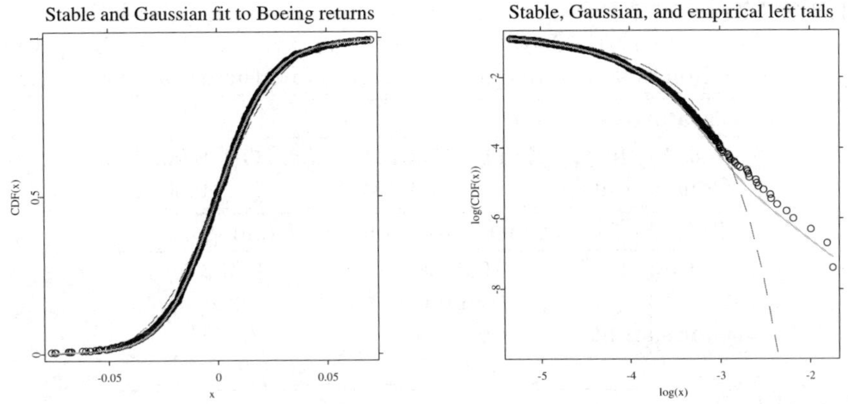

Figure 1.7: Stable (cyan) and Gaussian (dashed red) fits to the Boeing stock returns (black circles) empirical cdf from the period July 1, 1997 – December 31, 2003. Right panel is a magnification of the left tail fit on a double logarithmic scale clearly showing the superiority of the 1.78-stable law.

STFstab07.xpl

vector is estimated for this simulated sample, yielding $\hat{\theta}_1$, and the test statistics is calculated assuming that the sample is distributed according to $F(x; \hat{\theta}_1)$. The simulation is repeated as many times as required to achieve a certain level of accuracy. The estimate of the p-value is obtained as the proportion of times that the test quantity is at least as large as d.

For the α-stable fit of the DJIA returns the values of the Anderson-Darling and Kolmogorov statistics are 0.6441 and 0.5583, respectively. The corresponding approximate p-values based on 1000 simulated samples are 0.02 and 0.5 allowing us to accept the α-stable law as a model of DJIA returns. The values of the test statistics for the Gaussian fit yield p-values of less than 0.005 forcing us to reject the Gaussian law, see Table 1.1.

Next, we apply the same technique to 1635 daily returns of Boeing stock prices from the period July 1, 1997 – December 31, 2003. The 1.78-stable distribution fits the data very well, yielding small values of the Anderson-Darling (0.3756) and Kolmogorov (0.4522) test statistics, see Figure 1.7 and Table 1.2. The

Table 1.2: Fits to 1635 Boeing stock price returns from the period July 1, 1997 – December 31, 2003. Test statistics and the corresponding p-values based on 1000 simulated samples (in parentheses) are also given.

Parameters:	α	σ	β	μ
α-stable fit	1.7811	0.0141	0.2834	0.0009
Gaussian fit		0.0244		0.0001

Tests:	Anderson-Darling	Kolmogorov
α-stable fit	0.3756	0.4522
	(0.18)	(0.80)
Gaussian fit	9.6606	2.1361
	(<0.005)	(<0.005)

`STFstab07.xpl`

approximate p-values based, as in the previous example, on 1000 simulated samples are 0.18 and 0.8, respectively, allowing us to accept the α-stable law as a model of Boeing returns. On the other hand, the values of the test statistics for the Gaussian fit yield p-values of less than 0.005 forcing us to reject the Gaussian distribution.

The stable law seems to be tailor-cut for the DJIA index and Boeing stock price returns. But does it fit other asset returns as well? Unfortunately, not. Although, for most asset returns it does provide a better fit than the Gaussian law, in many cases the test statistics and p-values suggest that the fit is not as good as for these two data sets. This can be seen in Figure 1.8 and Table 1.3, where the calibration results for 4444 daily returns of the Japanese yen against the US dollar (JPY/USD) exchange rate from December 1, 1978 to January 31, 1991 are presented. The empirical distribution does not exhibit power-law tails and the extreme tails are largely overestimated by the stable distribution. For a risk manager who likes to play safe this may not be a bad idea, as the stable law overestimates the risks and thus provides an upper limit of losses. However, from a calibration perspective other distributions, like the hyperbolic or truncated stable, may be more appropriate for many data sets (Weron, 2004).

Table 1.3: Fits to 4444 JPY/USD exchange rate returns from the period December 1, 1978 – January 31, 1991. Test statistics and the corresponding p-values (in parentheses) are also given.

Parameters:	α	σ	β	μ
α-stable fit	1.3274	0.0020	-0.1393	-0.0003
Gaussian fit		0.0049		-0.0001

Tests:	Anderson-Darling	Kolmogorov
α-stable fit	4.7833	1.4520
	(<0.005)	(<0.005)
Gaussian fit	91.7226	6.7574
	(<0.005)	(<0.005)

STFstab08.xpl

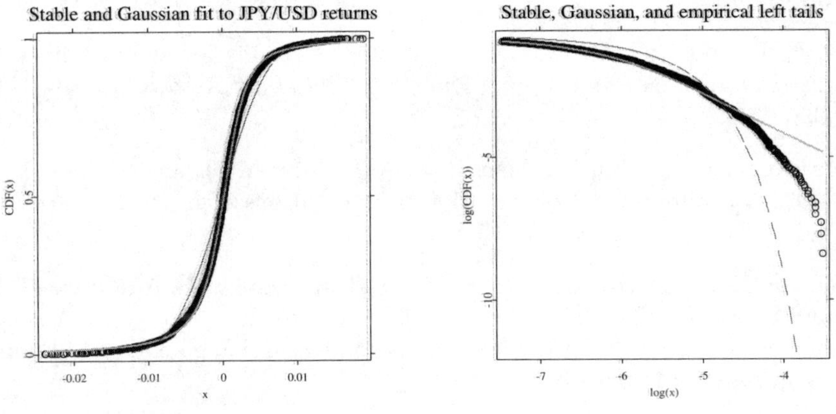

Figure 1.8: Stable (cyan) and Gaussian (dashed red) fits to the JPY/USD exchange rate returns (black circles) empirical cdf from the period December 1, 1978 – January 31, 1991. Right panel is a magnification of the left tail fit on a double logarithmic scale. The extreme returns are largely overestimated by the stable law.

STFstab08.xpl

Bibliography

Bouchaud, J.-P. and Potters, M. (2000). *Theory of Financial Risk*, Cambridge University Press, Cambridge.

Carr, P., Geman, H., Madan, D. B., and Yor, M. (2002). The fine structure of asset returns: an empirical investigation, *Journal of Business* **75**: 305–332.

Chambers, J. M., Mallows, C. L., and Stuck, B. W. (1976). A method for simulating stable random variables, *Journal of the American Statistical Association* **71**: 340–344.

D'Agostino, R. B. and Stephens, M. A. (1986). *Goodness-of-Fit Techniques*, Marcel Dekker, New York.

Embrechts, P., Kluppelberg, C., and Mikosch, T. (1997). *Modelling Extremal Events for Insurance and Finance*, Springer.

Fama, E. F. (1965). The behavior of stock market prices, *Journal of Business* **38**: 34–105.

Fama, E. F. and Roll, R. (1971). Parameter estimates for symmetric stable distributions, *Journal of the American Statistical Association* **66**: 331–338.

Gopikrishnan, P., Plerou, V., Amaral, L. A. N., Meyer, M. and Stanley, H. E. (1999). Scaling of the distribution of fluctuations of financial market indices, *Physical Review E* **60(5)**: 5305–5316.

Guillaume, D. M., Dacorogna, M. M., Dave, R. R., Müller, U. A., Olsen, R. B., and Pictet, O. V. (1997). From the birds eye to the microscope: A survey of new stylized facts of the intra-daily foreign exchange markets, *Finance & Stochastics* **1**: 95–129.

Härdle, W., Klinke, S., and Müller, M. (2000). *XploRe Learning Guide*, Springer.

Hill, B. M. (1975). A simple general approach to inference about the tail of a distribution, *Annals of Statistics* **3**: 1163–1174.

Janicki, A. and Weron, A. (1994). *Simulation and Chaotic Behavior of α-Stable Stochastic Processes*, Marcel Dekker.

Kanter, M. (1975). Stable densities under change of scale and total variation inequalities, *Annals of Probability* **3**: 697–707.

Koutrouvelis, I. A. (1980). Regression-type estimation of the parameters of stable laws, *Journal of the American Statistical Association* **75**: 918–928.

Kogon, S. M. and Williams, D. B. (1998). Characteristic function based estimation of stable parameters, *in* R. Adler, R. Feldman, M. Taqqu (eds.), *A Practical Guide to Heavy Tails*, Birkhauser, pp. 311–335.

Levy, P. (1925). *Calcul des Probabilites*, Gauthier Villars.

Mandelbrot, B. B. (1963). The variation of certain speculative prices, *Journal of Business* **36**: 394–419.

Mantegna, R. N. and Stanley, H. E. (1995). Scaling behavior in the dynamics of an economic index, *Nature* **376**: 46–49.

McCulloch, J. H. (1986). Simple consistent estimators of stable distribution parameters, *Communications in Statistics – Simulations* **15**: 1109–1136.

McCulloch, J. H. (1996). Financial applications of stable distributions, *in* G. S. Maddala, C. R. Rao (eds.), *Handbook of Statistics, Vol. 14*, Elsevier, pp. 393–425.

McCulloch, J. H. (1997). Measuring tail thickness to estimate the stable index α: A critique, *Journal of Business & Economic Statistics* **15**: 74–81.

Mittnik, S., Doganoglu, T., and Chenyao, D. (1999). Computing the probability density function of the stable Paretian distribution, *Mathematical and Computer Modelling* **29**: 235–240.

Mittnik, S., Rachev, S. T., Doganoglu, T. and Chenyao, D. (1999). Maximum likelihood estimation of stable Paretian models, *Mathematical and Computer Modelling* **29**: 275–293.

Nolan, J. P. (1997). Numerical calculation of stable densities and distribution functions, *Communications in Statistics – Stochastic Models* **13**: 759–774.

Nolan, J. P. (1999). An algorithm for evaluating stable densities in Zolotarev's (M) parametrization, *Mathematical and Computer Modelling* **29**: 229–233.

Nolan, J. P. (2001). Maximum likelihood estimation and diagnostics for stable distributions, *in* O. E. Barndorff-Nielsen, T. Mikosch, S. Resnick (eds.), *Lévy Processes*, Brikhäuser, Boston.

Press, S. J. (1972). Estimation in univariate and multivariate stable distribution, *Journal of the American Statistical Association* **67**: 842–846.

Rachev, S., ed. (2003). *Handbook of Heavy-tailed Distributions in Finance*, North Holland.

Rachev, S. and Mittnik, S. (2000). *Stable Paretian Models in Finance*, Wiley.

Samorodnitsky, G. and Taqqu, M. S. (1994). *Stable Non–Gaussian Random Processes*, Chapman & Hall.

Stoyanov, S. and Racheva-Iotova, B. (2004). Univariate stable laws in the field of finance – parameter estimation, *Journal of Concrete and Applicable Mathematics* **2(4)**, in print.

Weron, R. (1996). On the Chambers-Mallows-Stuck method for simulating skewed stable random variables, *Statistics and Probability Letters* **28**: 165–171. *See also* R. Weron, *Correction to: On the Chambers-Mallows-Stuck method for simulating skewed stable random variables*, Research Report HSC/96/1, Wrocław University of Technology, 1996, http://www.im.pwr.wroc.pl/~hugo/Publications.html.

Weron, R. (2001). Levy-stable distributions revisited: Tail index > 2 does not exclude the Levy-stable regime, *International Journal of Modern Physics C* **12**: 209–223.

Weron, R. (2004). Computationally intensive Value at Risk calculations, *in* J. E. Gentle, W. Härdle, Y. Mori (eds.) *Handbook of Computational Statistics*, Springer, Berlin, 911–950.

Zolotarev, V. M. (1986). *One-Dimensional Stable Distributions*, American Mathematical Society.

2 Extreme Value Analysis and Copulas

Krzysztof Jajuga and Daniel Papla

2.1 Introduction

The analysis of financial data, usually given in the form of financial time series, has recently received a lot of attention of researchers and finance practitioners, in such areas as valuation of derivative instruments, forecasting of financial prices, risk analysis (particularly market risk analysis).

From the practical point of view, multivariate analysis of financial data may be more appropriate than univariate analysis. Most market participants hold portfolios containing more than one financial instrument. Therefore they should perform analysis for all components of a portfolio. There are more and more financial instruments where payoffs depend on several underlyings (e.g. rainbow options). Therefore, to value them one should use multivariate models of underlying vectors of indices. Risk analysis is strongly based on the issue of correlation, or generally speaking dependence, between the returns (or prices) of the components of a portfolio. Therefore multivariate analysis is an appropriate tool to detect these relations.

One of the most important applications of financial time series models is risk analysis, including risk measurement. A significant tendency, observed in the market, is the occurrence of rare events, which very often lead to exceptionally high losses. This has caused a growing interest in the evaluation of the so-called extreme risk. There are two groups of models applied to financial time series: "mean-oriented" models, aiming at modeling the mean (expected value) and the variance of the distribution; and "extreme value" models, aiming at modeling tails (including maximum and minimum) of the distribution.

In this chapter we present some methods of time series analysis, both univariate and multivariate time series. The attention is put on two approaches: extreme value analysis and copula analysis. The presented methods are illustrated by examples coming from the Polish financial market.

2.1.1 Analysis of Distribution of the Extremum

The analysis of the distribution of the extremum is simply the analysis of the random variable, defined as the maximum (or minimum) of a set of random variables. For simplicity we concentrate only on the distribution of the maximum. The most important result is the Fisher-Tippet theorem (Embrechts, Klüppelberg, and Mikosch, 1997). In this theorem one considers the limiting distribution for the normalized maximum:

$$\lim_{n\to\infty} P\left(\frac{X_{n:n}-b_n}{a_n} \leq x\right) = G(x), \tag{2.1}$$

where $X_{n:n} = \max(X_1, X_2, ..., X_n)$. It can be proved that this limiting distribution belongs to the family of the so-called Generalized Extreme Value distributions (GEV), whose distribution function is given as:

$$G(x) = \exp\left\{-\left[1+\xi\left(\frac{x-\mu}{\sigma}\right)\right]^{-1/\xi}\right\}, \qquad 1+\xi\sigma^{-1}(x-\mu) > 0. \tag{2.2}$$

The GEV distribution has three parameters Reiss and Thomas (2000): the location parameter μ, the scale parameter σ, and the shape parameter ξ, which reflects the fatness of tails of the distribution (the higher value of this parameter, the fatter tails).

The family of GEV distributions contains three subclasses: the Fréchet distribution, $\xi > 0$, the Weibull distribution, $\xi < 0$, and the Gumbel distribution, $\xi \to 0$. In financial problems one usually encounters the Fréchet distribution. In this case the underlying observations come from a fat-tailed distribution, such as the Pareto distribution, stable distribution (including Cauchy), etc.

One of the most common methods to estimate the parameters of GEV distributions is maximum likelihood. The method is applied to block maxima, obtained by dividing the set of observations into subsets, called blocks, and taking maximum for each block.

The main weakness of this approach comes from the fact that the maxima for some blocks may not correspond to rare events. On the other hand, in some blocks there may be more than one observation corresponding to rare events. Therefore this approach can be biased by the selection of the blocks.

2.1.2 Analysis of Conditional Excess Distribution

To analyze rare events, another approach can be used. Consider the so-called conditional excess distribution:

$$F_u(y) = P(X - u \le y \,|\, X > u) = \frac{F(u+y) - F(u)}{1 - F(u)}, \tag{2.3}$$

where $0 \le y < x_0 - u$; and $x_0 = \sup(x : F(x) < 1)$. This distribution (also called the conditional tail distribution) is simply the distribution conditional on the underlying random variable taking value from the tail. Of course, this distribution depends on the choice of threshold u.

It can be proved (Embrechts, Klüppelberg, and Mikosch, 1997) that the conditional excess distribution can be approximated by the so-called Generalized Pareto distribution (GPD), which is linked by one parameter to the GEV distribution. The following property is important: the larger the threshold (the further one goes in the direction of the tail), the better the approximation. The distribution function of GPD is given by Franke, Härdle and Hafner (2004) and Reiss and Thomas (2000):

$$F_u(y) = 1 - (1 + \xi y/\beta)^{-1/\xi}, \tag{2.4}$$

where $\beta = \sigma + \xi(u - \mu)$. The shape parameter ξ has the same role as in GEV distributions. The generalized parameter β depends on all three parameters of the GEV distribution, as well as on the threshold u.

The family of GPD contains three types of distributions, the Pareto distribution – $\xi > 0$, the Pareto type II distribution – $\xi < 0$, and the exponential distribution – $\xi \to 0$.

The mean of the conditional excess distribution can be characterized by a linear function of the threshold and of the parameters of GPD:

$$\mathrm{E}(X - u \,|\, X > u) = \frac{\beta u}{1 - \xi} + \frac{\xi}{1 - \xi} u \tag{2.5}$$

for $\xi < 1$. One of the most common methods of estimating the parameters of GPD is maximum likelihood. However, the GPD depends on the choice of the threshold u. The higher the threshold, the better the approximation of the tail by GPD – this is a desired property. Then one has fewer observations to perform maximum likelihood estimation, which weakens the quality of estimation.

To choose the threshold, one can use the procedure, based on the fact that for GPD the mean of the conditional excess distribution is a linear function of the threshold. Therefore, one can use the following function, which is just the arithmetic average of the observations exceeding the threshold:

$$\hat{e}(u) = \frac{\sum_{i=1}^{n} \max\{(x_i - u), 0\}}{\sum_{i=1}^{n} I(x_i > u)}. \tag{2.6}$$

We know that for the observations higher than the threshold this relation should be a linear function. Therefore a graphical procedure can be applied. In this procedure the value of $\hat{e}(u)$ is calculated for different values of the threshold u. Then such a value is selected, that for the values above this value the linear relation can be observed.

2.1.3 Examples

Consider the logarithmic rate of returns for the following stock market indices:

- Four indices of the Warsaw Stock Exchange (WSE): WIG (index of most traded stocks on this exchange), WIG20 (index of 20 stocks with the largest capitalization), MIDWIG (index of 40 mid-cap stocks), and TECHWIG (index of high technology stocks);
- Two US market indices: DJIA and S&P 500;
- Two EU market indices: DAX and FT-SE100.

In addition we studied the logarithmic rates of return for the following exchange rates: USD/PLN, EUR/PLN, EUR/USD.

The financial time series of the logarithmic rates of return come from the period January 2, 1995 – October 3, 2003, except for the case of exchange rates EUR/PLN and EUR/USD, where the period January 1, 1999 – October 3, 2003 was taken into account. Figures 2.1–2.3 show histograms of those time series.

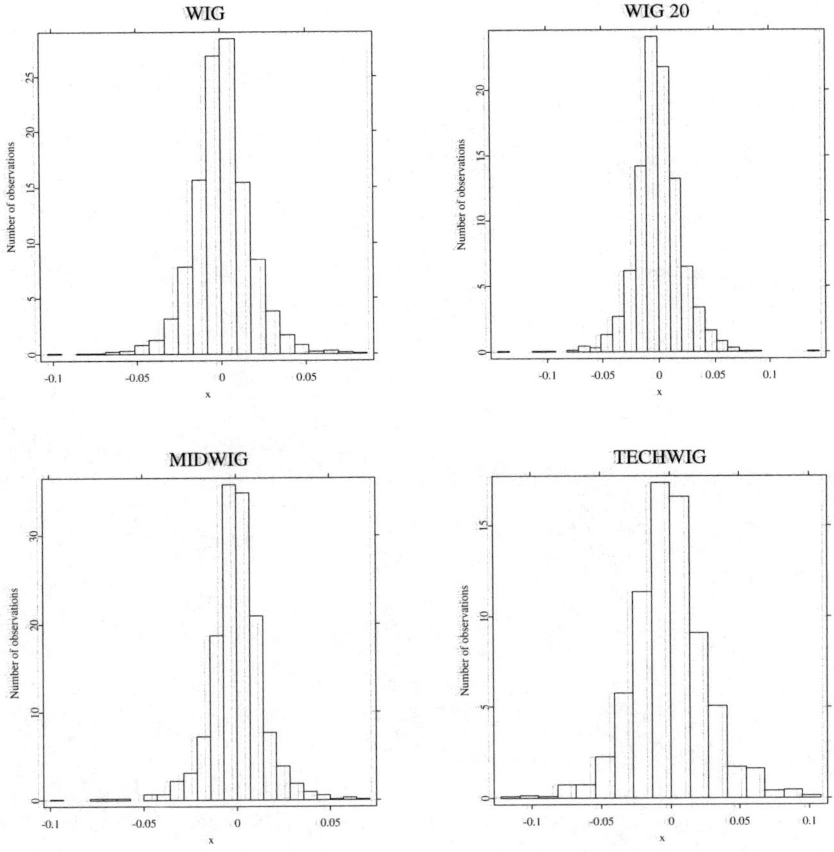

Figure 2.1: Histograms of the logarithmic rates of return for WSE indices
STFeva01.xpl

The most common application of the analysis of the extremum is the estimation of the maximum loss of a portfolio. It can be treated as a more conservative measure of risk than the well-known Value at Risk, defined through a quantile of the loss distribution (rather than the distribution of the maximal loss). The limiting distribution of the maximum loss is the GEV distribution. This, of

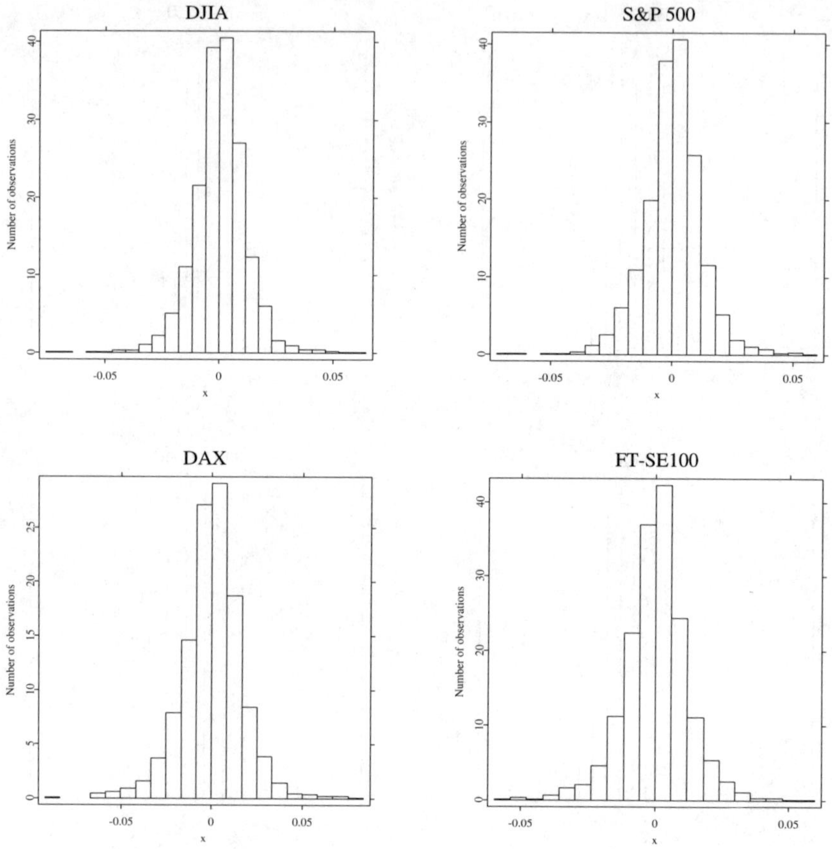

Figure 2.2: Histograms of the logarithmic rates of return for world indices

STFeva01.xpl

course, requires a rather large sample of observations coming from the same underlying distribution. Since most financial data are in the form of time series, the required procedure would call for at least the check of the hypothesis about stationarity of time series by using unit root test e.g. Dickey-Fuller test, (Dickey and Fuller, 1979). The hypothesis of stationarity states that

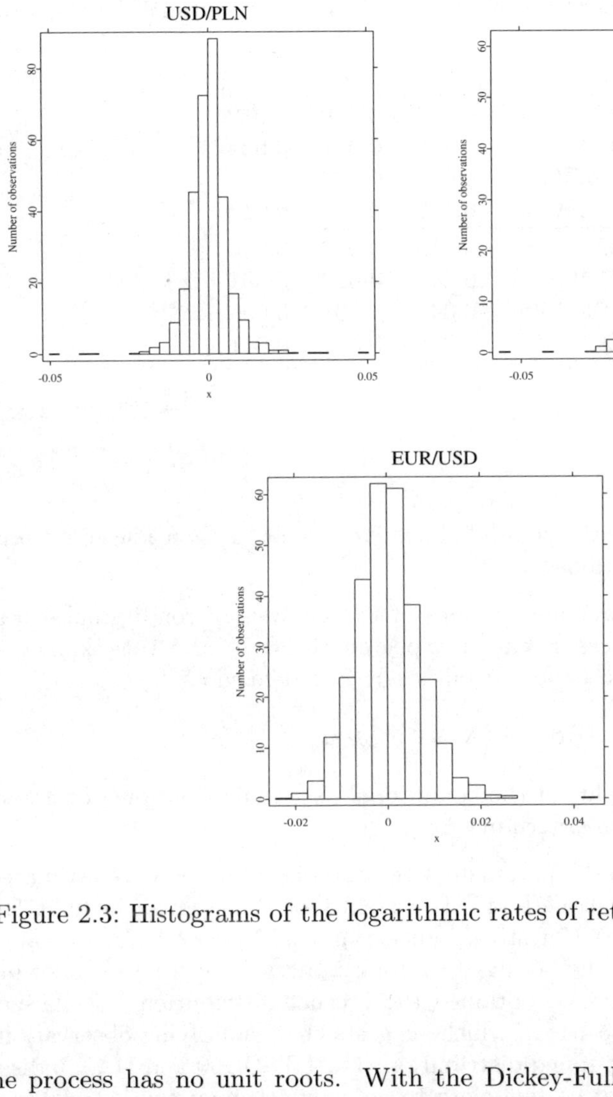

Figure 2.3: Histograms of the logarithmic rates of return for exchange rates
STFeva01.xpl

the process has no unit roots. With the Dickey-Fuller test we test the null hypothesis of a unit root, that is, there is a unit root for the characteristic equation of the AR(1) process. The alternative hypothesis is that the time series is stationary. To verify stationarity hypotheses for each of the considered time series, the augmented Dickey-Fuller test was used. The hypotheses of a

Table 2.1: The estimates of the parameters of GEV distributions, for the stock indices.

Data	ξ	μ	σ
WIG	0.374	0.040	0.012
WIG20	0.450	0.037	0.022
MIDWIG	0.604	0.033	0.011
TECHWIG	0.147	0.066	0.012
DJIA	0.519	0.027	0.006
S&P 500	0.244	0.027	0.007
FT-SE 100	-0.048	0.031	0.006
DAX	-0.084	0.041	0.011

STFeva02.xpl

unit root were rejected with the level of significance lower than 1%, so all time series in question are stationary.

One of the most important applications of the analysis of conditional excess distribution is the risk measure called Expected Shortfall – ES (also known as conditional Value at Risk, expected tail loss). It is defined as:

$$ES = \mathrm{E}(X - u \,|X > u). \tag{2.7}$$

So ES is the expected value of the conditional excess distribution. Therefore the GPD could be used to determine ES.

Then for each time series the parameters of GEV distributions were estimated using maximum likelihood method. The results of the estimation for GEV are presented in Table 2.1 (for stock indices) and in Table 2.2 (for exchange rates). The analysis of the results for stock indices leads to the following conclusions. In most cases we obtained the Fréchet distribution (estimate of the shape parameter is positive), which suggests that underlying observations are characterized by a fat-tailed distribution. For FTSE-100 and DAX indices the estimate of ξ is negative but close to zero, which may suggest either a Weibull distribution or a Gumbel distribution. In the majority of cases, the WSE indices exhibit fatter tails than the other indices. They also have larger estimates of location (related to mean return) and larger estimates of the scale parameter (related to volatility).

Table 2.2: The estimates of the parameters of GEV distributions, for the exchange rates.

Data	ξ	μ	σ
USD/PLN	0.046	0.014	0.005
EUR/PLN	0.384	0.015	0.005
EUR/USD	-0.213	0.014	0.004

STFeva03.xpl

The analysis of the results for the exchange rates leads to the following conclusions. Three different distributions were obtained, for USD/PLN – a Gumbel distribution, for EUR/PLN – a Fréchet distribution, for EUR/USD – a Weibull distribution. This suggests very different behavior of underlying observations. The location and scale parameters are almost the same. The scale parameters are considerably lower for the exchange rates than for the stock indices.

2.2 Multivariate Time Series

2.2.1 Copula Approach

In this section we present the so-called copula approach. It is performed in two steps. In the first step one analyzes the marginal (univariate) distributions. In the second step one analyzes the dependence between components of the random vector. Therefore the analysis of dependence is "independent" from the analysis of marginal distributions. This idea is different from the one present in the classical approach, where multivariate analysis is performed "jointly" for marginal distributions and dependence structure by considering the complete covariance matrix, like e.g. in the MGARCH approach. So one can think that instead of analyzing the whole covariance matrix, where the off diagonal elements contain information about scatter and dependence) one analyzes only the main diagonal (scatter measures) and then the structure of dependence "not contaminated" by scatter parameters.

The fundamental concept of copulas becomes clear by Sklar theorem (Sklar, 1959). The multivariate joint distribution function is represented as a copula function linking the univariate marginal distribution functions:

$$H(x_1, ..., x_n) = C\{F_1(x_1), ..., F_n(x_n)\} \tag{2.8}$$

where H the multivariate distribution function; F_i the distribution function of the i-th marginal distribution; C is a copula. The copula describes the dependence between components of a random vector.

It is worth mentioning some properties of copulas for modeling dependence. The most important ones are the following:

- for independent variables we have:

$$C(u_1, ..., u_n) = C^{\neg}(u_1, ..., u_n) = u_1 u_2 ... u_n$$

- the lower limit for copula function is:

$$C^-(u_1, ..., u_n) = \max\{u_1 + ... + u_n - n + 1; 0\}$$

- the upper limit for copula function is:

$$C^+(u_1, ..., u_n) = \min(u_1, ..., u_n)$$

The lower and upper limits for the copula function have important consequences for modeling the dependence. It can be explained in the simplest, bivariate case. Suppose there are two variables X and Y and there exists a function (not necessarily a linear one), which links these two variables. One speaks about the so-called total positive dependence between X and Y, when $Y = T(X)$ and T is the increasing function. Similarly, one speaks about the so-called total negative dependence between X and Y, when $Y = T(X)$ and T is the decreasing function. Then:

- in the case of total positive dependence the following relation holds:

$$C(u_1, u_2) = C^+(u_1, u_2) = \min(u_1, u_2)$$

- in the case of total negative dependence the following relation holds:

$$C(u_1, u_2) = C^-(u_1, u_2) = \max\{u_1 + u_2 - 1; 0\},$$

The introduction of the copula leads to a natural ordering of the multivariate distributions with respect to the strength and the direction of the dependence. This ordering is given as:

$$C_1(u_1, ..., u_n) \leq C_2(u_1, ..., u_n)$$

and then we have:

$$C^-(u_1, ..., u_n) \leq C^\neg(u_1, ..., u_n) \leq C^+(u_1, ..., u_n).$$

The presented properties are valid for any type of the dependence, not just linear dependence. More facts of copulas is given in Franke, Härdle and Hafner (2004); Rank and Siegl (2002) and Kiesel and Kleinow (2002).

There are very possible copulas. A popular family contains the so-called Archimedean copulas, defined on the base of strictly decreasing and convex function, called generator. In the bivariate case it is given as:

$$C(u_1, u_2) = \psi^{-1}\{\psi(u_1) + \psi(u_2)\}, \tag{2.9}$$

where $\psi : [0;1] \to [0;\infty)$, and $\psi(1) = 0$. The most popular and well-studied Archimedean copulas are:

1. The Clayton copula:

$$\psi(t) = \begin{cases} (t^{-\theta} - 1)/\theta, & \theta \geq -1, \theta \neq 0, \\ -\log(t), & \theta = 0, \end{cases} \quad \theta \in [-1, \infty). \tag{2.10}$$

2. The Frank copula:

$$\psi(t) = \begin{cases} -\log\left(\frac{\exp(-\theta t)-1}{\exp(-\theta)-1}\right) & \theta \neq 0, \\ -\log(t), & \theta = 0. \end{cases} \tag{2.11}$$

3. The Ali-Mikhail-Haq copula:

$$\psi(t) = \log\left(\frac{1 - \theta(1-t)}{t}\right), \theta \in [-1;1]. \tag{2.12}$$

Among other copulas, which do not belong to Archimedean family, it is worth to mention the Farlie-Gumbel-Morgenstern copula, given in the bivariate case as:

$$C_\theta(u,v) = uv + \theta uv(1-u)(1-v), \theta \in [-1;1]. \tag{2.13}$$

In all these copulas there is one parameter, which can be interpreted as dependence parameter. Here the dependence has a more general meaning, presented above and described by a monotonic function.

An often used copula function is the so-called normal (Gaussian) copula, which links the distribution function of multivariate normal distribution with the distribution functions of the univariate normal distributions. This means that:

$$C(u_1, ..., u_n) = \Phi_R^n\{\Phi^{-1}(u_1), ..., \Phi^{-1}(u_n)\} \tag{2.14}$$

The other commonly used example is the Gumbel copula, which for the bivariate case is given as:

$$C(u_1, u_2) = \exp[-\{(-\log u_1)^\delta + (-\log u_2)^\delta\}^{1/\delta}] \tag{2.15}$$

Figure 2.4 presents an example of the shape of the copula function. In this case it is a Frank copula (see (2.11)), with parameters θ taken from results presented in Section 2.2.2. The estimation of the copula parameters can be performed by using maximum likelihood given the distribution function of marginals. As the simplest approach to the distribution function of marginals one can take just the empirical distribution function.

2.2.2 Examples

Consider different pairs of stock market indices and exchange rates, studied in Section 2.1.3. For each pair we fitted a bivariate copula, namely the Clayton, Frank, Ali-Mikhail-Haq, and the Farlie-Gumbel-Morgenstern.

We present here the results obtained for Frank copula. Table 2.3 presents selected results for pairs of exchange rates and Table 2.4 for pairs of stock indices. The important conclusion to be drawn from Table 2.3 is that one pair, namely USD/PLN and EUR/USD, shows negative dependence, whereas the other two show positive dependence. This is particularly important for the entities that are exposed to exchange rate risk and they want to decrease it by appropriate management of assets and liabilities.

There is positive extreme dependence between all stock indices. As could have been expected, there is strong dependence between indices of the WSE and much lower between WSE and the other exchanges, with weaker dependence between WSE and NYSE than between WSE and large European exchanges. The copula approach can be applied in the so-called tail dependence coefficients. The detailed description of tail dependence is given in Chapter 3.

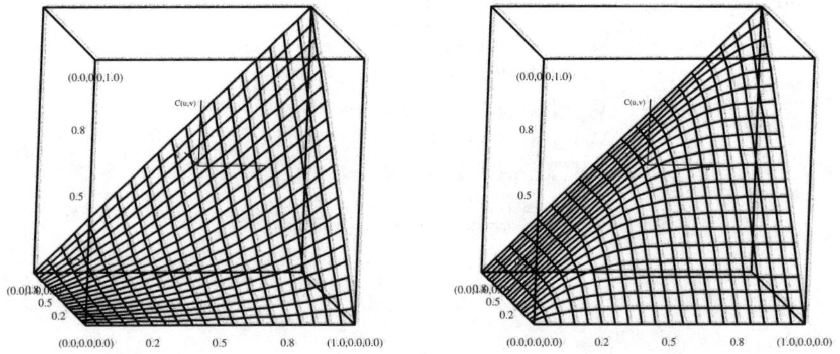

Figure 2.4: Plot of $C(u, v)$ for the Frank copula for $\theta = -2,563$ in left panel, and $\theta = 11.462$ in right panel.

STFeva04.xpl

STFeva05.xpl

Table 2.3: The estimates of the Frank copula for exchange rates.

Bivariate data	θ
USD/PLN and EUR/PLN	2.730
USD/PLN and EUR/USD	-2.563
EUR/PLN and EUR/USD	3.409

STFeva06.xpl

2.2.3 Multivariate Extreme Value Approach

The copula approach also gives the possibility to analyze extreme values in the general multivariate case. This is possible by linking this approach to univariate extreme value analysis. In order to make this possible, we concentrate on the multivariate distribution of extrema, where the extremum is taken for each component of a random vector.

Table 2.4: The estimates of the Frank copula for stock indices.

Bivariate data	θ
WIG and WIG20	11.462
WIG and DJIA	0.943
WIG and FTSE-100	2.021
WIG and DAX	2.086

STFeva07.xpl

The main result in the multivariate extreme value analysis is given for the limiting distribution of normalized maxima:

$$\lim_{n\to\infty} P\left(\frac{X^1_{n:n} - b^1_n}{a^1_n} \le x^1, ..., \frac{X^m_{n:n} - b^m_n}{a^m_n} \le x^m\right) = G(x^1, ..., x^m), \qquad (2.16)$$

It was shown by Galambos (1978) that this limiting distribution can be presented in the following form:

$$G(x^1, ..., x^m) = CG\{G_1(x^1), ..., G_m(x^m)\}. \qquad (2.17)$$

where CG is the so-called Extreme Value Copula (EVC). This is the representation of the multivariate distribution of maxima, called here Multivariate Extreme Value distribution (MEV), in the way it is presented in the Sklar theorem. It is composed of two parts and each part has a special meaning: univariate distributions belong to the family of GEV distributions, therefore they are the Fréchet, Weibull or Gumbel distributions.

Therefore, to obtain the MEV distribution one has to apply the EVC to univariate GEV distributions (Fréchet, Weibull, or Gumbel). Since there are many possible extreme value copulas, we get many possible multivariate extreme value distributions.

The EVC is a copula satisfying the following relation:

$$C(u^t_1, ..., u^t_n) = C^t(u_1, ..., u_n) \text{ for } t > 0. \qquad (2.18)$$

It can be shown that the bivariate extreme value copula can be represented in the following form:

$$C(u_1, u_2) = \exp\{\log(u_1 u_2) A(\log(u_1))/\log(u_1 u_2)\}. \qquad (2.19)$$

Here A is a convex function satisfying the following relations:

$$\begin{aligned} A(0) = A(1) = 1, \\ \max(w, 1-w) \leq A(w) \leq 1. \end{aligned} \tag{2.20}$$

The most common extreme value copulas are:

1. Gumbel copula, where:

$$\begin{aligned} &C(u_1, u_2) = \exp[-\{(\log u_1)^\theta + (\log u_2)^\theta\}^{1/\theta}], \\ &\text{with } A(w) = \{w^\theta + (1-w)^\theta\}^{1/\theta}, \\ &\text{and } \theta \in [1, \infty). \end{aligned} \tag{2.21}$$

2. Gumbel II copula, where:

$$\begin{aligned} &C(u_1, u_2) = u_1 u_2 \exp\{\theta(\log u_1 \log u_2)/(\log u_1 + \log u_2)\}, \\ &\text{with } A(w) = \theta w^2 - \theta w + 1, \\ &\text{and } \theta \in [0, 1]. \end{aligned} \tag{2.22}$$

3. Galambos copula, where:

$$\begin{aligned} &C(u_1, u_2) = u_1 u_2 \exp[\{(\log u_1)^{-\theta} + (\log u_2)^{-\theta}\}^{-1/\theta}], \\ &\text{with } A(w) = 1 - \{w^{-\theta} + (1-w)^{-\theta}\}^{-1/\theta}, \\ &\text{and } \theta \in [0, \infty). \end{aligned} \tag{2.23}$$

All three presented copulas are one parameter functions. This parameter can be interpreted as dependence parameter. The important property is that for these copulas, as well as for other possible extreme value copulas, there is positive dependence between the two components of the random vector.

The main application of multivariate extreme value approach is the estimation of the maximum loss of each component of the portfolio. We get then the limiting distribution of the vector of maximal losses. The limiting distributions for the components are univariate GEV distributions and the relation between the maxima is reflected through extreme value copula.

Table 2.5: The estimates of the Galambos copula for exchange rates.

Bivariate data	θ
USD/PLN and EUR/PLN	34.767
USD/PLN and EUR/USD	2.478
EUR/PLN and EUR/USD	2.973

STFeva08.xpl

2.2.4 Examples

As in Section 2.2.2 we consider different pairs of stock market indices and exchange rates. In the first step we analyze separate components in each pair to get estimates of generalized extreme value distributions. In the second step, we use empirical distribution functions obtained in the first step and estimate three copulas belonging to EVC family: Gumbel, Gumbel II, and Galambos. We present here the results obtained for Galambos copula (Table 2.5) and Gumbel copula (Table 2.6)

It turns out that in the case of exchange rates we obtained the best fit for the Galambos copula, see Table 2.5. In the case of stock indices the best fit was obtained for different copulas. For the comparison we present the results obtained for the Gumbel copula, see Table 2.6. The dependence parameter of the Galambos copula takes only non-negative values. The higher the value of this parameter, the stronger the dependence between maximal losses of respective variables. We see that there is strong extreme dependence between the exchange rates of USD/PLN and EUR/PLN and rather weak dependence between EUR/PLN and EUR/USD as well as for USD/PLN and EUR/USD. The dependence parameter for Gumbel copula takes values higher or equal to 1. The higher the value of this parameter, the stronger the dependence between maximal losses of respective variables. The results given in this table indicate strong dependence (as could have been expected) between stock indices of the Warsaw Stock Exchange. It also shows stronger extreme dependence between WSE and NYSE than between WSE and two large European exchanges.

Table 2.6: The estimates of the Gumbel copula for stock indices.

Bivariate data	θ
WIG and WIG20	21.345
WIG and DJIA	14.862
WIG and FTSE-100	2.275
WIG and DAX	5.562

STFeva09.xpl

2.2.5 Copula Analysis for Multivariate Time Series

One of the basic models applied in the classical (mean-oriented) approach in the analysis of multivariate time series was the multivariate GARCH model (MGARCH) aimed at modeling of conditional covariance matrix. One of the disadvantages of this approach was the joint modeling of volatilities and correlations, as well as relying on the correlation coefficient as a measure of dependence.

In this section we present another approach, where volatilities and dependences in multivariate time series, both conditional, are modeled separately. This is possible due to the application of copula approach directly to univariate time series, being the components of multivariate time series. Our presentation is based on the idea presented by Jondeau and Rockinger (2002), which combines the univariate time series modeling by GARCH type models for volatility with copula analysis. The proposed model is given as:

$$\log(\theta_t) = \sum_{j=1}^{16} d_j I\{(u_{t-1}, v_{t-1}) \in \mathcal{A}_j\}, \tag{2.24}$$

where $\mathcal{A}_j$ is the jth element of the unit-square grid. To each parameter d_j, an area $\mathcal{A}_j$ is associated. For instance, $\mathcal{A}_1 = [0, p_1] \times [0, q_1]$ and $\mathcal{A}_2 = [p_1, p_2] \times [0, q_1]$, where $p_1 = q_1 = 0.15$, $p_2 = q_2 = 0.5$, and $p_3 = q_3 = 0.85$. The choice of 16 subintervals is, according to Jondeau and Rockinger (2002), somewhat arbitrary. Therefore the dependence parameter is conditioned on the lagged values of univariate distribution functions, where the 16 possible sets of pairs of values are taken into account. The larger value of parameter d_j, the stronger dependence on the past values.

Table 2.7: Conditional dependence parameter for time series WIG, WIG20.

	[0, 0.15)	[0.15, 0.5)	[0.5, 0.85)	[0.85, 1]
[0, 0.15)	15.951	4.426	5.010	1.213
[0.15, 0.5)	6.000	18.307	8.704	1.524
[0.5, 0.85)	-0.286	8.409	19.507	5.133
[0.85, 1]	0.000	2.578	1.942	19.202

STFeva10.xpl

We also give the description of the method, which was used in the empirical example. We describe this procedure for the case of bivariate time series. The proposed procedure consists of two steps. In the first step, the models for univariate time series are built for both time series. Here the combined procedure of ARIMA models for conditional mean and GARCH models for conditional variance was used. In the second step, the values of the distribution function for residuals obtained after the application of univariate models were subject to copula analysis.

2.2.6 Examples

In this example we study three pairs of time series, namely WIG and WIG20, WIG and DJIA, USD/PLN and EUR/PLN. First of all, to get the best fit: an AR(10)-GARCH (1,1) model was built for each component of bivariate time series. Then the described procedure of fitting copula and obtaining conditional dependence parameter was applied. In order to do this, the interval [0, 1] of the values of univariate distribution function was divided into 4 subintervals: [0, 0.15), [0.15, 0.5); [0.5, 0.85); [0.85, 1]. Such a selection of subintervals allows us to concentrate on tails of the distributions. Therefore we obtained 16 disjoint areas. For each area the conditional dependence parameter was estimated using different copula function. For the purpose of comparison, we present the results obtained in the case of the Frank copula. These results are given in the Tables 2.7–2.9.

The values on "the main diagonal" of the presented tables correspond to the same subintervals of univariate distribution functions. Therefore, the values for the lowest interval (upper left corner of the table) and highest interval (lower

Table 2.8: Conditional dependence parameter for time series WIG, DJIA.

	[0, 0.15)	[0.15, 0.5)	[0.5, 0.85)	[0.85, 1]
[0, 0.15)	2.182	1.169	0.809	2.675
[0.15, 0.5)	1.868	0.532	0.954	2.845
[0.5, 0.85)	1.454	1.246	0.806	0.666
[0.85, 1]	-0.207	0.493	1.301	1.202

STFeval1.xpl

Table 2.9: Conditional dependence parameter for time series USD/PLN, EUR/PLN.

	[0, 0.15)	[0.15, 0.5)	[0.5, 0.85)	[0.85, 1]
[0, 0.15)	3.012	2.114	2.421	0.127
[0.15, 0.5)	3.887	2.817	2.824	5.399
[0.5, 0.85)	2.432	3.432	2.526	3.424
[0.85, 1]	7.175	3.750	4.534	4.616

STFeval2.xpl

right corner of the table) correspond to the notion of lower tail dependence and upper tail dependence. Also, the higher are values concentrated along "the main diagonal", the stronger conditional dependence is observed.

From the results presented in Tables 2.7–2.9, we can see, that there is a strong conditional dependence between returns on WIG and WIG20; the values of conditional dependence parameter "monotonically decrease with the departure from the main diagonal." This property is not observed in the other two tables, where no significant regular patterns can be identified.

We presented here only some selected non-classical methods of the analysis of financial time series. They proved some usefulness for real data. It seems that the plausible future direction of the research would be the integration of econometric methods, aimed at studying the dynamic properties, with statistical methods, aimed at studying the distributional properties.

Bibliography

Dickey, D. and Fuller, W. (1979). Distribution of the estimators for autoregressive time series with a unit root, *Journal of the American Statistical Association*, **74**: 427–431.

Embrechts, P., Klüppelberg, C. and Mikosch, T. (1997). *Modelling Extremal Events for Insurance and Finance*, Springer.

Franke, J., Härdle, W. and Hafner, C. (2004). *Statistics of Financial Markets*, Springer.

Galambos, J. (1978). *The Asymptotic Theory of Extreme Order Statistics*, Krieger Publishing.

Jondeau, E. and Rockinger, M. (2002). Conditional Dependency of Financial Series: The Copula-GARCH Model, *FAME*, working paper.

Kiesel, R. and Kleinow, T. (2002). Sensitivity analysis of credit portfolio models, in W. Härdle, T. Kleinow, G. Stahl (eds.), *Applied Quantitative Finance*, Springer.

Rank, J. and Siegl, T. (2002). Applications of Copulas for the Calculation of Value-at-Risk, in W. Härdle, T. Kleinow and G. Stahl (eds.), *Applied Quantitative Finance*, Springer.

Reiss, R.-D. and Thomas, M. (2000). Extreme Value Analysis, in W. Härdle, S. Klinke and M. Müller (eds.), *XploRe Learning Guide*, Springer.

Sklar, A. (1959). Fonctions de repartition à n dimensions et leurs marges, *Publications de l'Institut de Statistique de l'Université de Paris*, **8** (1959): 229–231.

3 Tail Dependence

Rafael Schmidt

3.1 Introduction

Tail dependence describes the amount of dependence in the tail of a bivariate distribution. In other words, tail dependence refers to the degree of dependence in the corner of the lower-left quadrant or upper-right quadrant of a bivariate distribution. Recently, the concept of tail dependence has been discussed in financial applications related to market or credit risk, Hauksson et al. (2001) and Embrechts et al. (2003). In particular, tail-dependent distributions are of interest in the context of Value at Risk (VaR) estimation for asset portfolios, since these distributions can model dependence of large loss events (default events) between different assets.

It is obvious that the portfolio's VaR is determined by the risk behavior of each single asset in the portfolio. On the other hand, the general dependence structure, and especially the dependence structure of extreme events, strongly influences the VaR calculation. However, it is not known to most people which are not familiar with extreme value theory, how to measure and model dependence, for example, of large loss events. In other words, the correlation coefficient, which is the most common dependence measure in financial applications, is often insufficient to describe and estimate the dependence structure of large loss events, and therefore frequently leads to inaccurate VaR estimations, Embrechts et al. (1999). The main aim of this chapter is to introduce and to discuss the so-called tail-dependence coefficient as a simple measure of dependence of large loss events.

Kiesel and Kleinow (2002) show empirically that a precise VaR estimation for asset portfolios depends heavily on the proper specification of the tail-dependence structure of the underlying asset-return vector. In their setting, different choices of the portfolio's dependence structure, which is modelled by a copula function, determine the degree of dependence of large loss events. Motivated by their empirical observations, this chapter defines and explores the concept of tail dependence in more detail. First, we define and calculate tail dependence for several classes of distributions and copulae. In our context, tail dependence is characterized by the so-called tail-dependence coefficient (TDC) and is embedded into the general framework of copulae. Second, a parametric and two nonparametric estimators for the TDC are discussed. Finally, we investigate some empirical properties of the implemented TDC estimators and examine an empirical study to show one application of the concept of tail dependence for VaR estimation.

3.2 What is Tail Dependence?

Definitions of tail dependence for multivariate random vectors are mostly related to their bivariate marginal distribution functions. Loosely speaking, tail dependence describes the limiting proportion that one margin exceeds a certain threshold given that the other margin has already exceeded that threshold. The following approach, as provided in the monograph of Joe (1997), represents one of many possible definitions of tail dependence.

Let $X = (X_1, X_2)^\top$ be a two-dimensional random vector. We say that X is (bivariate) *upper tail-dependent* if:

$$\lambda_U \stackrel{\text{def}}{=} \lim_{v \uparrow 1} \mathrm{P}\left\{X_1 > F_1^{-1}(v) \mid X_2 > F_2^{-1}(v)\right\} > 0, \tag{3.1}$$

in case the limit exists. F_1^{-1} and F_2^{-1} denote the generalized inverse distribution functions of X_1 and X_2, respectively. Consequently, we say $X = (X_1, X_2)^\top$ is *upper tail-independent* if λ_U equals 0. Further, we call λ_U the upper tail-dependence coefficient (upper TDC). Similarly, we define the lower tail-dependence coefficient, if it exists, by:

$$\lambda_L \stackrel{\text{def}}{=} \lim_{v \downarrow 0} \mathrm{P}\left\{X_1 \le F_1^{-1}(v) \mid X_2 \le F_2^{-1}(v)\right\}. \tag{3.2}$$

In case $X = (X_1, X_2)^\top$ is standard normally or t-distributed, formula (3.1) simplifies to:

$$\lambda_U = \lim_{v \uparrow 1} \lambda_U(v) \stackrel{\text{def}}{=} \lim_{v \uparrow 1} 2 \cdot \mathrm{P}\left\{X_1 > F_1^{-1}(v) \mid X_2 = F_2^{-1}(v)\right\}. \tag{3.3}$$

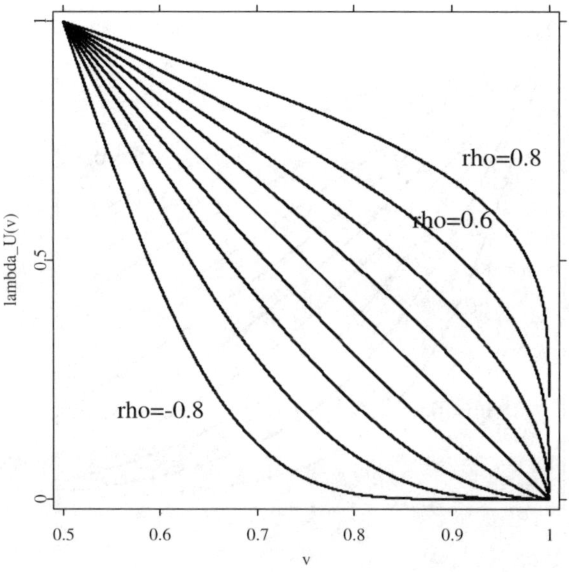

Figure 3.1: The function $\lambda_U(v) = 2 \cdot \mathrm{P}\{X_1 > F_1^{-1}(v) \mid X_2 = F_2^{-1}(v)\}$ for a bivariate normal distribution with correlation coefficients $\rho = -0.8, -0.6, \ldots, 0.6, 0.8$. Note that $\lambda_U = 0$ for all $\rho \in (-1, 1)$.

STFtail01.xpl

A generalization of bivariate tail dependence, as defined above, to multivariate tail dependence can be found in Schmidt and Stadtmüller (2003).

Figures 3.1 and 3.2 illustrate tail dependence for a bivariate normal and t-distribution. Irrespectively of the correlation coefficient ρ, the bivariate normal distribution is (upper) tail independent. In contrast, the bivariate t-distribution exhibits (upper) tail dependence and the degree of tail dependence is affected by the correlation coefficient ρ.

The concept of tail dependence can be embedded within the copula theory. An n-dimensional distribution function $C : [0,1]^n \to [0,1]$ is called a copula if it has one-dimensional margins which are uniformly distributed on the interval $[0,1]$. Copulae are functions that join or "couple" an n-dimensional distribution function F to its corresponding one-dimensional marginal distribution functions

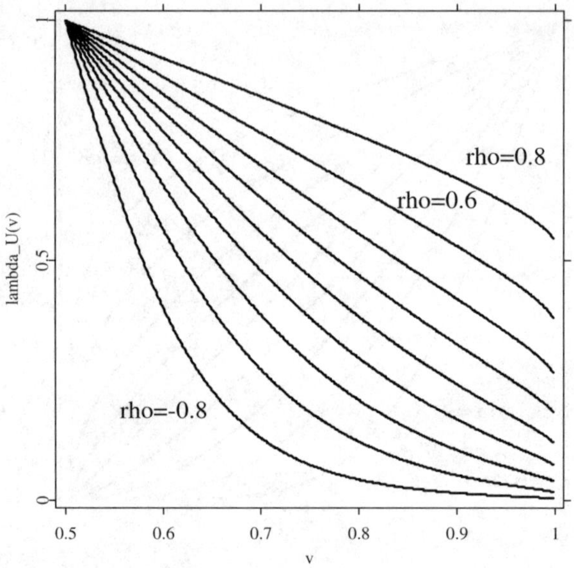

Figure 3.2: The function $\lambda_U(v) = 2 \cdot \mathrm{P}\{X_1 > F_1^{-1}(v) \mid X_2 = F_2^{-1}(v)\}$ for a bivariate t-distribution with correlation coefficients $\rho = -0.8, -0.6, \ldots, 0.6, 0.8$. STFtail02.xpl

F_i, $i = 1, \ldots, n$, in the following way:

$$F(x_1, \ldots, x_n) = C\{F_1(x_1), \ldots, F_n(x_n)\}.$$

We refer the reader to Joe (1997), Nelsen (1999) or Härdle, Kleinow, and Stahl (2002) for more information on copulae. The following representation shows that tail dependence is a copula property. Thus, many copula features transfer to the tail-dependence coefficient such as the invariance under strictly increasing transformations of the margins. If X is a continuous bivariate random vector, then straightforward calculation yields:

$$\lambda_U = \lim_{v \uparrow 1} \frac{1 - 2v + C(v, v)}{1 - v}, \tag{3.4}$$

where C denotes the copula of X. Analogously, $\lambda_L = \lim_{v \downarrow 0} \frac{C(v,v)}{v}$ holds for the lower tail-dependence coefficient.

3.3 Calculation of the Tail-dependence Coefficient

3.3.1 Archimedean Copulae

Archimedean copulae form an important class of copulae which are easy to construct and have good analytical properties. A bivariate Archimedean copula has the form $C(u,v) = \psi^{[-1]}\{\psi(u) + \psi(v)\}$ for some continuous, strictly decreasing, and convex *generator* function $\psi : [0,1] \to [0,\infty]$ such that $\psi(1) = 0$ and the pseudo-inverse function $\psi^{[-1]}$ is defined by:

$$\psi^{[-1]}(t) = \begin{cases} \psi^{-1}(t), & 0 \le t \le \psi(0), \\ 0, & \psi(0) < t \le \infty. \end{cases}$$

We call ψ *strict* if $\psi(0) = \infty$. In that case $\psi^{[-1]} = \psi^{-1}$. Within the framework of tail dependence for Archimedean copulae, the following result can be shown (Schmidt, 2003). Note that the one-sided derivatives of ψ exist, as ψ is a convex function. In particular, $\psi'(1)$ and $\psi'(0)$ denote the one-sided derivatives at the boundary of the domain of ψ. Then:

i) upper tail-dependence implies $\psi'(1) = 0$ and $\lambda_U = 2 - (\psi^{-1} \circ 2\psi)'(1)$,

ii) $\psi'(1) < 0$ implies upper tail-independence,

iii) $\psi'(0) > -\infty$ or a non-strict ψ implies lower tail-independence,

iv) lower tail-dependence implies $\psi'(0) = -\infty$, a strict ψ, and $\lambda_L = (\psi^{-1} \circ 2\psi)'(0)$.

Tables 3.1 and 3.2 list various Archimedean copulae in the same ordering as provided in Nelsen (1999, Table 4.1, p. 94) and in Härdle, Kleinow, and Stahl (2002, Table 2.1, p. 42) and the corresponding upper and lower tail-dependence coefficients (TDCs).

Table 3.1: Various selected Archimedean copulae. The numbers in the first column correspond to the numbers of Table 4.1 in Nelsen (1999), p. 94.

Number & Type		$C(u,v)$	Parameters
(1)	Clayton	$\max\left\{(u^{-\theta}+v^{-\theta}-1)^{-1/\theta},0\right\}$	$\theta\in[-1,\infty)\backslash\{0\}$
(2)		$\max\left[1-\left\{(1-u)^{\theta}+(1-v)^{\theta}\right\}^{1/\theta},0\right]$	$\theta\in[1,\infty)$
(3)	Ali-Mikhail-Haq	$\dfrac{uv}{1-\theta(1-u)(1-v)}$	$\theta\in[-1,1)$
(4)	Gumbel-Hougaard	$\exp\left[-\{(-\log u)^{\theta}+(-\log v)^{\theta}\}^{1/\theta}\right]$	$\theta\in[1,\infty)$
(12)		$\left[1+\left\{(u^{-1}-1)^{\theta}+(v^{-1}-1)^{\theta}\right\}^{1/\theta}\right]^{-1}$	$\theta\in[1,\infty)$
(14)		$\left[1+\left\{(u^{-1/\theta}-1)^{\theta}+(v^{-1/\theta}-1)^{\theta}\right\}^{1/\theta}\right]^{-\theta}$	$\theta\in[1,\infty)$
(19)		$\theta/\log\left(e^{\theta/u}+e^{\theta/v}-e^{\theta}\right)$	$\theta\in(0,\infty)$

3.3.2 Elliptically-contoured Distributions

In this section, we calculate the tail-dependence coefficient for elliptically-contoured distributions (briefly: elliptical distributions). Well-known elliptical distributions are the multivariate normal distribution, the multivariate t-distribution, the multivariate logistic distribution, the multivariate symmetric stable distribution, and the multivariate symmetric generalized-hyperbolic distribution.

Elliptical distributions are defined as follows: Let X be an n-dimensional random vector and $\Sigma\in\mathbb{R}^{n\times n}$ be a symmetric positive semi-definite matrix. If $X-\mu$, for some $\mu\in\mathbb{R}^n$, possesses a characteristic function of the form $\phi_{X-\mu}(t)=\Psi(t^\top\Sigma t)$ for some function $\Psi:\mathbb{R}_0^+\to\mathbb{R}$, then X is said to be el-

Table 3.2: Tail-dependence coefficients (TDCs) and generators ψ_θ for various selected Archimedean copulae. The numbers in the first column correspond to the numbers of Table 4.1 in Nelsen (1999), p. 94.

Number & Type	$\psi_\theta(t)$	Parameter θ	Upper-TDC	Lower-TDC
(1) Pareto	$t^{-\theta}-1$	$[-1,\infty)\backslash\{0\}$	0 for $\theta>0$	$2^{-1/\theta}$ for $\theta>0$
(2)	$(1-t)^\theta$	$[1,\infty)$	$2-2^{1/\theta}$	0
(3) Ali-Mikhail-Haq	$\log\dfrac{1-\theta(1-t)}{t}$	$[-1,1)$	0	0
(4) Gumbel-Hougaard	$(-\log t)^\theta$	$[1,\infty)$	$2-2^{1/\theta}$	0
(12)	$\left(\frac{1}{t}-1\right)^\theta$	$[1,\infty)$	$2-2^{1/\theta}$	$2^{-1/\theta}$
(14)	$\left(t^{-1/\theta}-1\right)^\theta$	$[1,\infty)$	$2-2^{1/\theta}$	$\dfrac{1}{2}$
(19)	$e^{\theta/t}-e^\theta$	$(0,\infty)$	0	1

liptically distributed with parameters μ (location), Σ (dispersion), and Ψ. Let $E_n(\mu,\Sigma,\Psi)$ denote the class of elliptically-contoured distributions with the latter parameters. We call Ψ the *characteristic generator.* The density function, if it exists, of an elliptically-contoured distribution has the following form:

$$f(x)=|\Sigma|^{-1/2}g\{(x-\mu)^\top\Sigma^{-1}(x-\mu)\},\quad x\in\mathbb{R}^n, \tag{3.5}$$

for some function $g:\mathbb{R}_0^+\to\mathbb{R}_0^+$, which we call the *density generator.*

Observe that the name "elliptically-contoured distribution" is related to the elliptical contours of the latter density. For a more detailed treatment of elliptical distributions see the monograph of Fang, Kotz, and Ng (1990) or Cambanis, Huang, and Simon (1981).

In connection with financial applications, Bingham and Kiesel (2002) and Bingham, Kiesel, and Schmidt (2002) propose a semi-parametric approach for elliptical distributions by estimating the *parametric* component (μ, Σ) separately from the density generator g. In their setting, the density generator is estimated by means of a *nonparametric* statistics.

Schmidt (2002b) shows that bivariate elliptically-contoured distributions are upper and lower tail-dependent if the tail of their density generator is regularly varying, i.e. the tail behaves asymptotically like a power function. Further, a necessary condition for tail dependence is given which is more general than regular variation of the latter tail: More precisely, the tail must be O-regularly varying (see Bingham, Goldie, and Teugels (1987) for the definition of O-regular variation). Although the equivalence of tail dependence and regularly-varying density generator has not been shown, all density generators of well-known elliptical distributions possess either a regularly-varying tail or a not O-regularly-varying tail. This justifies a restriction to the class of elliptical distributions with regularly-varying density generator if tail dependence is required. In particular, tail dependence is solely determined by the tail behavior of the density generator (except for completely correlated random variables which are always tail dependent).

The following closed-form expression exists (Schmidt, 2002b) for the upper and lower tail-dependence coefficient of an elliptically-contoured random vector $(X_1, X_2)^\top \in E_2(\mu, \Sigma, \Psi)$ with positive-definite matrix

$$\Sigma = \begin{pmatrix} \sigma_{11} & \sigma_{12} \\ \sigma_{11} & \sigma_{12} \end{pmatrix},$$

having a regularly-varying density generator g with regular variation index $-\alpha/2 - 1 < 0$:

$$\lambda \stackrel{\text{def}}{=} \lambda_U = \lambda_L = \frac{\displaystyle\int_0^{h(\rho)} \frac{u^\alpha}{\sqrt{1-u^2}} du}{\displaystyle\int_0^1 \frac{u^\alpha}{\sqrt{1-u^2}} du}, \tag{3.6}$$

where $\rho = \sigma_{12}/\sqrt{\sigma_{11}\sigma_{22}}$ and $h(\rho) = \left\{1 + \frac{(1-\rho)^2}{1-\rho^2}\right\}^{-1/2}$.

Note that ρ corresponds to the "correlation" coefficient when it exists (Fang, Kotz, and Ng, 1990). Moreover, the upper tail-dependence coefficient λ_U coincides with the lower tail-dependence coefficient λ_L and depends only on the "correlation" coefficient ρ and the regular variation index α, see Figure 3.3.

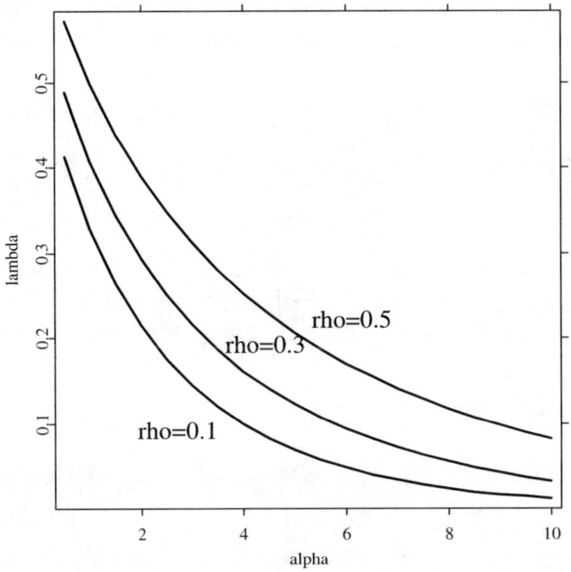

Figure 3.3: Tail-dependence coefficient λ versus regular variation index α for "correlation" coefficients $\rho = 0.5,\ 0.3,\ 0.1$. STFtail03.xpl

Table 3.3 lists various elliptical distributions, the corresponding density generators (here c_n denotes a normalizing constant depending only on the dimension n) and the associated regular variation index α from which one easily derives the tail-dependence coefficient using formula (3.6).

Table 3.3: Tail index α for various density generators g of multivariate elliptical distributions. K_ν denotes the modified Bessel function of the third kind (or Macdonald function).

Number & Type	Density generator g or characteristic generator Ψ	Parameters	α for $n=2$
(23) Normal	$g(u) = c_n \exp(-u/2)$	—	∞
(24) t	$g(u) = c_n \left(1 + \frac{t}{\theta}\right)^{-(n+\theta)/2}$	$\theta > 0$	θ
(25) Symmetric general. hyperbolic	$g(u) = c_n \frac{K_{\lambda - \frac{n}{2}}\{\sqrt{\varsigma(\chi + u)}\}}{(\sqrt{\chi + u})^{\frac{n}{2} - \lambda}}$	$\varsigma, \chi > 0$, $\lambda \in \mathbb{R}$	∞
(26) Symmetric θ-stable	$\Psi(u) = \exp\left\{-\left(\frac{1}{2}u\right)^{\theta/2}\right\}$	$\theta \in (0, 2]$	θ
(27) logistic	$g(u) = c_n \frac{\exp(-u)}{\{1 + \exp(-u)\}^2}$	—	∞

3.3.3 Other Copulae

For many other closed form copulae one can explicitly derive the tail-dependence coefficient. Tables 3.4 and 3.5 list some well-known copula functions and the corresponding lower and upper TDCs.

Table 3.4: Various copulae. Copulae BBx are provided in Joe (1997).

Number & Type	$C(u,v)$	Parameters
(28) Raftery	$g\{\min(u,v),\max(u,v);\theta\}$ with $g\{x,y;\theta\} = x - \frac{1-\theta}{1+\theta}x^{1/(1-\theta)}\left(y^{-\theta/(1-\theta)} - y^{1/(1-\theta)}\right)$	$\theta \in [0,1]$
(29) BB1	$\left[1+\left\{(u^{-\theta}-1)^{\delta}+(v^{-\theta}-1)^{\delta}\right\}^{1/\delta}\right]^{-1/\theta}$	$\theta \in (0,\infty)$ $\delta \in [1,\infty)$
(30) BB4	$\left[u^{-\theta}+v^{-\theta}-1- -\left\{(u^{-\theta}-1)^{-\delta}+(v^{-\theta}-1)^{-\delta}\right\}^{-1/\delta}\right]^{-1/\theta}$	$\theta \in [0,\infty)$ $\delta \in (0,\infty)$
(31) BB7	$1-\left(1-\left[\{1-(1-u)^{\theta}\}^{-\delta}+ +\{1-(1-v)^{\theta}\}^{-\delta}-1\right]^{-1/\delta}\right)^{1/\theta}$	$\theta \in [1,\infty)$ $\delta \in (0,\infty)$
(32) BB8	$\frac{1}{\delta}\left(1-\left[1-\{1-(1-\delta)^{\theta}\}^{-1}\cdot \cdot\{1-(1-\delta u)^{\theta}\}\{1-(1-\delta v)^{\theta}\}\right]^{1/\theta}\right)$	$\theta \in [1,\infty)$ $\delta \in [0,1]$
(33) BB11	$\theta\min(u,v)+(1-\theta)uv$	$\theta \in [0,1]$
(34) C_Ω in Junker and May (2002)	$\beta C^s_{(\bar\theta,\bar\delta)}(u,v)-(1-\beta)C_{(\theta,\delta)}(u,v)$ with Archim. generator $\psi_{(\theta,\delta)}(t) = \left(-\log\frac{e^{-\theta t}-1}{e^{-\theta}-1}\right)^{\delta}$ $C^s_{(\bar\theta,\bar\delta)}$ is the survival copula with param. $(\bar\theta,\bar\delta)$	$\theta,\bar\theta \in \mathbb{R}\backslash\{0\}$ $\delta,\bar\delta \geq 1$ $\beta \in [0,1]$

3.4 Estimating the Tail-dependence Coefficient

Suppose X, $X^{(1)},\dots,X^{(m)}$ are i.i.d. bivariate random vectors with distribution function F and copula C. We assume continuous marginal distribution functions F_i, $i=1,2$. Tests for tail dependence or tail independence are given for example in Ledford and Tawn (1996) or Draisma et al. (2004).

We consider the following three (non-)parametric estimators for the lower and upper tail-dependence coefficients λ_U and λ_L. These estimators have been discussed in Huang (1992) and Schmidt and Stadtmüller (2003). Let C_m be the

Table 3.5: Tail-dependence coefficients (TDCs) for various copulae. Copulae BBx are provided in Joe (1997).

Number & Type	Parameters	upper-TDC	lower-TDC
(28) Raftery	$\theta \in [0,1]$	0	$\frac{2\theta}{1+\theta}$
(29) BB1	$\theta \in (0,\infty)$ $\delta \in [1,\infty)$	$2-2^{1/\delta}$	$2^{-1/(\theta\delta)}$
(30) BB4	$\theta \in [0,\infty)$ $\delta \in (0,\infty)$	$2^{-1/\delta}$	$(2-$ $2^{-1/\delta})^{-1/\theta}$
(31) BB7	$\theta \in [1,\infty)$ $\delta \in (0,\infty)$	$2-2^{1/\theta}$	$2^{-1/\delta}$
(32) BB8	$\theta \in [1,\infty)$ $\delta \in [0,1]$	$2-$ $-2(1-\delta)^{\theta-1}$	0
(33) BB11	$\theta \in [0,1]$	θ	θ
(34) C_Ω in Junker and May (2002)	$\theta,\bar{\theta} \in \mathbb{R}\backslash\{0\}$ $\delta,\bar{\delta} \geq 1$ $\beta \in [0,1]$	$(1-\beta)\cdot$ $\cdot(2-2^{1/\delta})$	$\beta(2-2^{1/\bar{\delta}})$

empirical copula defined by:

$$C_m(u,v) = F_m(F_{1m}^{-1}(u), F_{2m}^{-1}(v)), \tag{3.7}$$

with F_m and F_{im} denoting the empirical distribution functions corresponding to F and F_i, $i = 1,2$, respectively. Let $R_{m1}^{(j)}$ and $R_{m2}^{(j)}$ be the rank of $X_1^{(j)}$ and $X_2^{(j)}$, $j = 1,\dots,m$, respectively. The first estimators are based on formulas (3.1) and (3.2):

$$\begin{aligned}\hat{\lambda}^{(1)}_{U,m} &= \frac{m}{k}C_m\Big(\Big(1-\frac{k}{m},1\Big]\times\Big(1-\frac{k}{m},1\Big]\Big)\\ &= \frac{1}{k}\sum_{j=1}^{m} I(R^{(j)}_{m1} > m-k, R^{(j)}_{m2} > m-k)\end{aligned} \tag{3.8}$$

and

$$\hat{\lambda}^{(1)}_{L,m} = \frac{m}{k}C_m\Big(\frac{k}{m},\frac{k}{m}\Big) = \frac{1}{k}\sum_{j=1}^{m} I(R^{(j)}_{m1} \le k, R^{(j)}_{m2} \le k), \tag{3.9}$$

where $k = k(m) \to \infty$ and $k/m \to 0$ as $m \to \infty$, and the first expression in (3.8) has to be understood as the empirical copula-measure of the interval $(1-k/m, 1] \times (1-k/m, 1]$. The second type of estimator is already well known in multivariate extreme-value theory (Huang, 1992). We only provide the estimator for the upper TDC.

$$\begin{aligned}\hat{\lambda}^{(2)}_{U,m} &= 2-\frac{m}{k}\Big\{1-C_m\Big(1-\frac{k}{m},1-\frac{k}{m}\Big)\Big\}\\ &= 2-\frac{1}{k}\sum_{j=1}^{m} I(R^{(j)}_{m1} > m-k \text{ or } R^{(j)}_{m2} > m-k),\end{aligned} \tag{3.10}$$

with $k = k(m) \to \infty$ and $k/m \to 0$ as $m \to \infty$. The optimal choice of k is related to the usual variance-bias problem and we refer the reader to Peng (1998) for more details. Strong consistency and asymptotic normality for both types of nonparametric estimators are also addressed in the latter three reference.

Now we focus on an elliptically-contoured bivariate random vector X. In the presence of tail dependence, previous arguments justify a sole consideration of elliptical distributions having a regularly-varying density generator with regular variation index α. This implies that the distribution function of $||X||_2$ has also a regularly-varying tail with index α. Formula (3.6) shows that the upper and lower tail-dependence coefficients λ_U and λ_L depend only on the regular variation index α and the "correlation" coefficient ρ. Hence, we propose the following parametric estimator for λ_U and λ_L:

$$\hat{\lambda}^{(3)}_{U,m} = \hat{\lambda}^{(3)}_{L,m} = \lambda^{(3)}_U(\hat{\alpha}_m, \hat{\rho}_m). \tag{3.11}$$

Several robust estimators $\hat{\rho}_m$ for ρ are provided in the literature such as estimators based on techniques of multivariate trimming (Hahn, Mason, and Weiner, 1991), minimum-volume ellipsoid estimators (Rousseeuw and van Zomeren, 1990), and least square estimators (Frahm et al., 2002).

For more details regarding the relationship between the regular variation index α, the density generator, and the random variable $||X||_2$ we refer to Schmidt (2002b). Observe that even though the estimator for the regular variation index α might be unbiased, the TDC estimator $\hat{\lambda}_{U,m}^{(3)}$ is biased due to the integral transform.

3.5 Comparison of TDC Estimators

In this section we investigate the finite-sample properties of the introduced TDC estimators. One thousand independent copies of $m = 500, 1000$, and 2000 i.i.d. random vectors (m denotes the sample length) of a bivariate standard t-distribution with $\theta = 1.5, 2$, and 3 degrees of freedom are generated and the upper TDCs are estimated. Note that the parameter θ equals the regular variation index α which we discussed in the context of elliptically-contoured distributions. The empirical bias and root-mean-squared error (RMSE) for all three introduced TDC estimation methods are derived and presented in Tables 3.6, 3.7, and 3.8, respectively.

Table 3.6: Bias and RMSE for the nonparametric upper TDC estimator $\hat{\lambda}_U^{(1)}$ (multiplied by 10^3). The sample length is denoted by m.

Original parameters	$\theta = 1.5$ $\lambda_U = 0.2296$	$\theta = 2$ $\lambda_U = 0.1817$	$\theta = 3$ $\lambda_U = 0.1161$
Estimator	$\hat{\lambda}_U^{(1)}$ Bias (RMSE)	$\hat{\lambda}_U^{(1)}$ Bias (RMSE)	$\hat{\lambda}_U^{(1)}$ Bias (RMSE)
$m = 500$	25.5 (60.7)	43.4 (72.8)	71.8 (92.6)
$m = 1000$	15.1 (47.2)	28.7 (55.3)	51.8 (68.3)
$m = 2000$	8.2 (38.6)	19.1 (41.1)	36.9 (52.0)

Table 3.7: Bias and RMSE for the nonparametric upper TDC estimator $\hat{\lambda}_U^{(2)}$ (multiplied by 10^3). The sample length is denoted by m.

Original parameters	$\theta = 1.5$ $\lambda_U = 0.2296$	$\theta = 2$ $\lambda_U = 0.1817$	$\theta = 3$ $\lambda_U = 0.1161$
Estimator	$\hat{\lambda}_U^{(2)}$ Bias (RMSE)	$\hat{\lambda}_U^{(2)}$ Bias (RMSE)	$\hat{\lambda}_U^{(2)}$ Bias (RMSE)
$m = 500$	53.9 (75.1)	70.3 (88.1)	103.1 (116.4)
$m = 1000$	33.3 (54.9)	49.1 (66.1)	74.8 (86.3)
$m = 2000$	22.4 (41.6)	32.9 (47.7)	56.9 (66.0)

Table 3.8: Bias and RMSE for the parametric upper TDC estimator $\hat{\lambda}_U^{(3)}$ (multiplied by 10^3). The sample length is denoted by m.

Original parameters	$\theta = 1.5$ $\lambda_U = 0.2296$	$\theta = 2$ $\lambda_U = 0.1817$	$\theta = 3$ $\lambda_U = 0.1161$
Estimator	$\hat{\lambda}_U^{(3)}$ Bias (RMSE)	$\hat{\lambda}_U^{(3)}$ Bias (RMSE)	$\hat{\lambda}_U^{(3)}$ Bias (RMSE)
$m = 500$	1.6 (30.5)	3.5 (30.8)	16.2 (33.9)
$m = 1000$	2.4 (22.4)	5.8 (23.9)	15.4 (27.6)
$m = 2000$	2.4 (15.5)	5.4 (17.0)	12.4 (21.4)

Regarding the parametric approach we apply the procedure introduced in Section 3.4 and estimate ρ by a trimmed empirical correlation coefficient with trimming proportion 0.05% and α ($= \theta$) by a Hill estimator. For the latter we choose the optimal threshold value k according to Drees and Kaufmann (1998). The empirical bias and RMSE corresponding to the estimation of ρ and α are provided in Tables 3.9 and 3.10. Observe that Pearson's correlation coefficient ρ does not exist for $\theta < 2$. In this case, ρ denotes some dependence parameter and a more robust estimation procedure should be used (Frahm et al., 2002).

Table 3.9: Bias and RMSE for the estimator of the regular variation index α (multiplied by 10^3). The sample length is denoted by m.

Original parameters	$\theta = 1.5$ $\alpha = 1.5$	$\theta = 2$ $\alpha = 2$	$\theta = 3$ $\alpha = 3$
Estimator	$\hat{\alpha}$ Bias (RMSE)	$\hat{\alpha}$ Bias (RMSE)	$\hat{\alpha}$ Bias (RMSE)
$m = 500$	2.2 (211.9)	−19.8 (322.8)	−221.9 (543.7)
$m = 1000$	−14.7 (153.4)	−48.5 (235.6)	−242.2 (447.7)
$m = 2000$	−15.7 (101.1)	−60.6 (173.0)	−217.5 (359.4)

Table 3.10: Bias and RMSE for the "correlation" coefficient estimator $\hat{\rho}$ (multiplied by 10^3). The sample length is denoted by m.

Original parameters	$\theta = 1.5$ $\rho = 0$	$\theta = 2$ $\rho = 0$	$\theta = 3$ $\rho = 0$
Estimator	$\hat{\rho}$ Bias (RMSE)	$\hat{\rho}$ Bias (RMSE)	$\hat{\rho}$ Bias (RMSE)
$m = 500$	0.02 (61.6)	−2.6 (58.2)	2.1 (56.5)
$m = 1000$	−0.32 (44.9)	1.0 (42.1)	0.6 (39.5)
$m = 2000$	0.72 (32.1)	−1.2 (29.3)	−1.8 (27.2)

Finally, Figures 3.4 and 3.5 illustrate the (non-)parametric estimation results of the upper TDC estimator $\hat{\lambda}_U^{(i)}$, $i = 1, 2, 3$. Presented are 3×1000 TDC estimations with sample lengths $m = 500, 1000$ and 2000. The plots visualize the decreasing empirical bias and variance for increasing sample length.

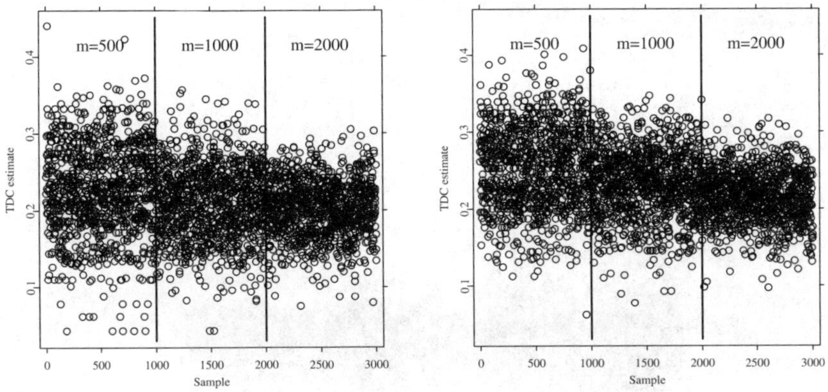

Figure 3.4: Nonparametric upper TDC estimates $\hat{\lambda}_U^{(1)}$ (left panel) and $\hat{\lambda}_U^{(2)}$ (right panel) for 3×1000 i.i.d. samples of size $m = 500, 1000, 2000$ from a bivariate t-distribution with parameters $\theta = 2$, $\rho = 0$, and $\lambda_U^{(1)} = \lambda_U^{(2)} = 0.1817$. STFtail04.xpl

The empirical study shows that the TDC estimator $\hat{\lambda}_U^{(3)}$ outperforms the other two estimators. For $m = 2000$, the bias (RMSE) of $\hat{\lambda}_U^{(1)}$ is three (two and a half) times larger than the bias (RMSE) of $\hat{\lambda}_U^{(3)}$, whereas the bias (RMSE) of $\hat{\lambda}_U^{(2)}$ is two (ten percent) times larger than the bias (RMSE) of $\hat{\lambda}_U^{(1)}$. More empirical and statistical results regarding the estimators $\hat{\lambda}_U^{(1)}$ and $\hat{\lambda}_U^{(2)}$ are given in Schmidt and Stadtmüller (2003). However, note that the estimator $\hat{\lambda}_U^{(3)}$ was especially developed for bivariate elliptically-contoured distributions. Thus, the estimator $\hat{\lambda}_U^{(1)}$ is recommended for TDC estimations of non-elliptical or unknown bivariate distributions.

3.6 Tail Dependence of Asset and FX Returns

Tail dependence is indeed often found in financial data series. Consider two scatter plots of daily negative log-returns of a tuple of financial securities and the corresponding upper TDC estimate $\hat{\lambda}_U^{(1)}$ for various k (for notational convenience we drop the index m).

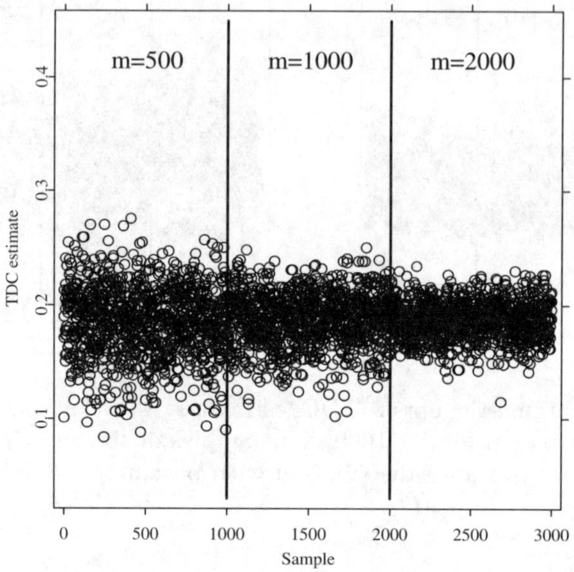

Figure 3.5: Nonparametric upper TDC estimates $\hat{\lambda}_U^{(3)}$ for 3×1000 i.i.d. samples of size $m = 500, 1000, 2000$ from a bivariate t-distribution with parameters $\theta = 2$, $\rho = 0$, and $\lambda_U^{(3)} = 0.1817$. `STFtail05.xpl`

The first data set (D_1) contains negative daily stock log-returns of BMW and Deutsche Bank for the time period 1992–2001. The second data set (D_2) consists of negative daily exchange rate log-returns of DEM/USD and JPY/USD (so-called FX returns) for the time period 1989–2001. For modelling reasons we assume that the daily log-returns are i.i.d. observations. Figures 3.6 and 3.7 show the presence of tail dependence and the order of magnitude of the tail-dependence coefficient. Tail dependence is present if the plot of TDC estimates $\hat{\lambda}_U^{(1)}$ against the thresholds k shows a characteristic plateau for small k. The existence of this plateau for tail-dependent distributions is justified by a regular variation property of the tail distribution; we refer the reader to Peng (1998) or Schmidt and Stadtmüller (2003) for more details. By contrast, the characteristic plateau is not observable if the distribution is tail independent.

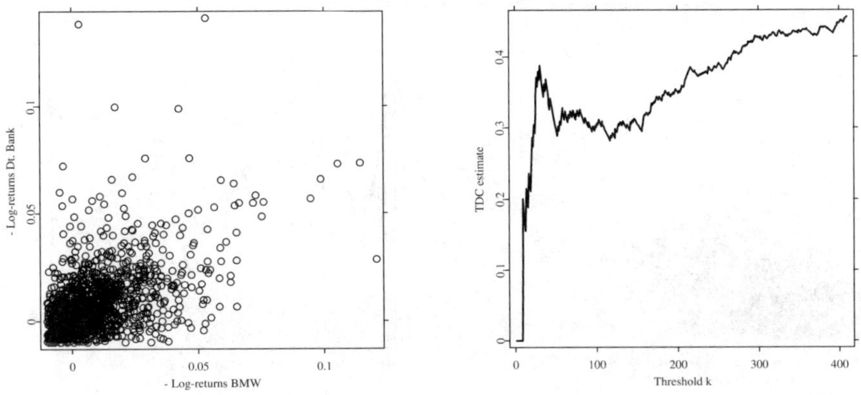

Figure 3.6: Scatter plot of BMW versus Deutsche Bank negative daily stock log-returns (2347 data points) and the corresponding TDC estimate $\hat{\lambda}_U^{(1)}$ for various thresholds k. STFtail06.xpl

The typical variance-bias problem for various thresholds k can be also observed in Figures 3.6 and 3.7. In particular, a small k comes along with a large variance of the TDC estimator, whereas increasing k results in a strong bias. In the presence of tail dependence, k is chosen such that the TDC estimate $\hat{\lambda}_U^{(1)}$ lies on the plateau between the decreasing variance and the increasing bias. Thus for the data set D_1 we take k between 80 and 110 which provides a TDC estimate of $\hat{\lambda}_{U,D_1}^{(1)} = 0.31$, whereas for D_2 we choose k between 40 and 90 which yields $\hat{\lambda}_{U,D_2}^{(1)} = 0.17$.

The importance of the detection and the estimation of tail dependence becomes clear in the next section. In particular, we show that the Value at Risk estimation of a portfolio is closely related to the concept of tail dependence. A proper analysis of tail dependence results in an adequate choice of the portfolio's loss distribution and leads to a more precise assessment of the Value at Risk.

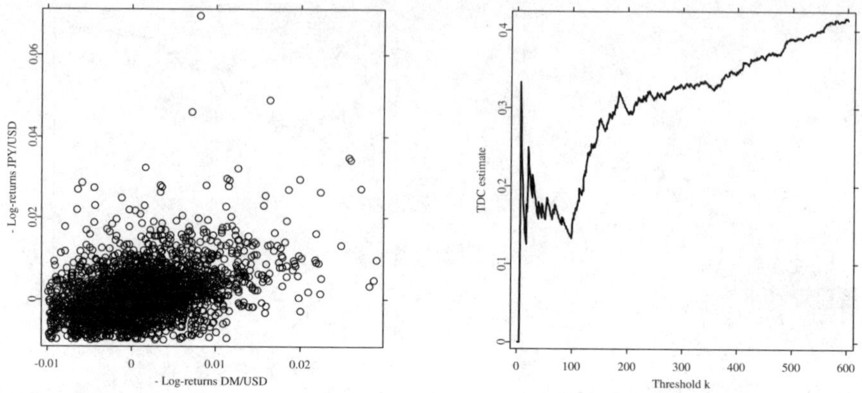

Figure 3.7: Scatter plot of DEM/USD versus JPY/USD negative daily exchange rate log-returns (3126 data points) and the corresponding TDC estimate $\hat{\lambda}_U^{(1)}$ for various thresholds k. STFtail07.xpl

3.7 Value at Risk – a Simulation Study

Value at Risk (VaR) estimations refer to the estimation of high target quantiles of single asset or portfolio loss distributions. Thus, VaR estimations are very sensitive towards the tail behavior of the underlying distribution model.

On the one hand, the VaR of a portfolio is affected by the tail distribution of each single asset. On the other hand, the general dependence structure and especially the tail-dependence structure among all assets have a strong impact on the portfolio's VaR, too. With the concept of tail dependence, we supply a methodology for measuring and modelling one particular type of dependence of extreme events.

What follows, provides empirical justification that the portfolio's VaR estimation depends heavily on a proper specification of the (tail-)dependence structure of the underlying asset-return vector. To illustrate our assertion we consider three financial data sets: The first two data sets D_1 and D_2 refer again to the daily stock log-returns of BMW and Deutsche Bank for the time period 1992–2001 and the daily exchange rate log-returns of DEM/USD and JPY/USD

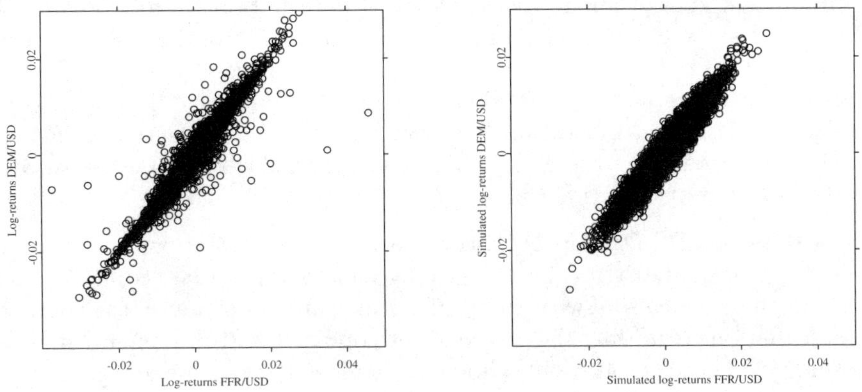

Figure 3.8: Scatter plot of foreign exchange data (left panel) and simulated normal pseudo-random variables (right panel) of FFR/USD versus DEM/USD negative daily exchange rate log-returns (5189 data points). STFtail08.xpl

for the time period 1989–2001, respectively. The third data set (D_3) contains exchange rate log-returns of FFR/USD and DEM/USD for the time period 1984–2002.

Typically, in practice, either a multivariate normal distribution or multivariate t-distribution is fitted to the data in order to describe the random behavior (market riskiness) of asset returns. Especially multivariate t-distributions have recently gained the attraction of practitioners due to their ability to model heavy tails while still having the advantage of being in the class of elliptically-contoured distributions. Recall that the multivariate normal distribution has thin tailed marginals which exhibit no tail-dependence, and the t-distribution possesses heavy tailed marginals which are tail dependent (see Section 3.3.2). Due to the different tail behavior, one might pick one of the latter two distribution classes if the data are elliptically contoured. However, elliptically-contoured distributions require a very strong symmetry of the data and might not be appropriate in many circumstances.

For example, the scatter plot of the data set D_3 in Figure 3.8 reveals that its distributional structure does not seem to be elliptically contoured at all.

To circumvent this problem, one could fit a distribution from a broader distribution class, such as a generalized hyperbolic distribution (Eberlein and Keller, 1995; Bingham and Kiesel, 2002). Alternatively, a split of the dependence structure and the marginal distribution functions via the theory of copulae (as described in Section 3.2) seems to be also attractive. This split exploits the fact that statistical (calibration) methods are well established for one-dimensional distribution functions.

For the data sets D_1, D_2, and D_3, one-dimensional t-distributions are utilized to model the marginal distributions. The choice of an appropriate copula function turns out to be delicate. Two structural features are important in the context of VaR estimations regarding the choice of the copula. First, the general structure (symmetry) of the chosen copula should coincide with the dependence structure of the real data. We visualize the dependence structure of the sample data via the respective empirical copula (Figure 3.9), i.e. the marginal distributions are standardized by the corresponding empirical distribution functions. Second, if the data show tail dependence than one must utilize a copula which comprises tail dependence. Especially VaR estimations at a small confidence level are very sensitive towards tail dependence. Figure 3.9 indicates that the FX data set D_3 has significantly more dependence in the lower tail than the simulated data from a fitted bivariate normal copula. The data clustering in the lower left corner of the scatter plot of the empirical copula is a strong indication for tail dependence.

Based on the latter findings, we use a t-copula (which allows for tail dependence, see Section 3.3.2) and t-distributed marginals (which are heavy tailed). Note, the resulting common distribution is only elliptically contoured if the degrees of freedom of the t-copula and the t-margins coincide, since in this case the common distribution corresponds to a multivariate t-distribution. The parameters of the marginals and the copula are separately estimated in two consecutive steps via maximum likelihood. For statistical properties of the latter procedure, which is called Inference Functions for Margins method (IFM), we refer to Joe and Xu (1996).

Tables 3.11, 3.12, and 3.13 compare the historical VaR estimates of the data sets D_1, D_2, and D_3 with the average of 100 VaR estimates which are simulated from different distributions. The fitted distribution is either a bivariate normal, a bivariate t-distribution or a bivariate distribution with t-copula and t-marginals. The respective standard deviation of the VaR estimations are provided in parenthesis. For a better exposition, we have multiplied all numbers by 10^5.

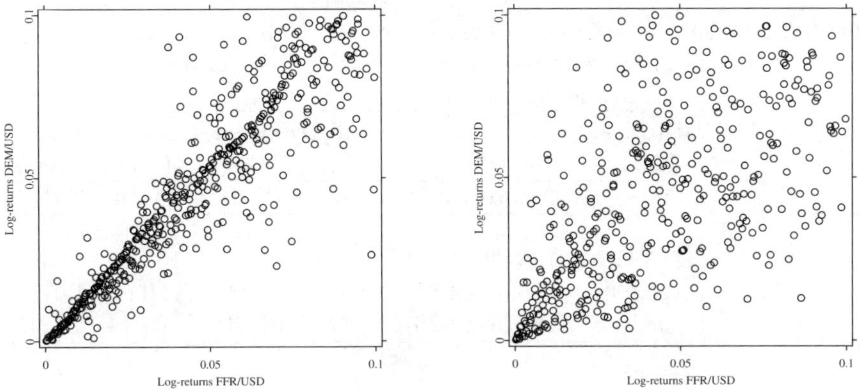

Figure 3.9: Lower left corner of the empirical copula density plots of real data (left panel) and simulated normal pseudo-random variables (right panel) of FFR/USD versus DEM/USD negative daily exchange rate log-returns (5189 data points). STFtail09.xpl

Table 3.11: Mean and standard deviation of 100 VaR estimations (multiplied by 10^5) from simulated data following different distributions which are fitted to the data set D_1.

Quantile	Historical VaR	Normal distribution Mean (Std)	t-distribution Mean (Std)	t-copula & t-marginals Mean (Std)
0.01	489.93	397.66 (13.68)	464.66 (39.91)	515.98 (36.54)
0.025	347.42	335.28 (9.67)	326.04 (18.27)	357.40 (18.67)
0.05	270.41	280.69 (7.20)	242.57 (10.35)	260.27 (11.47)

The results of the latter tables clearly show that the fitted bivariate normal-distribution does not yield an overall satisfying estimation of the VaR for all data sets D_1, D_2, and D_3. The poor estimation results for the 0.01– and 0.025–quantile VaR (i.e. the mean of the VaR estimates deviate strongly from the historical VaR estimate) are mainly caused by the thin tails of the normal

Table 3.12: Mean and standard deviation of 100 VaR estimations (multiplied by 10^5) from simulated data following different distributions which are fitted to the data set D_2.

Quantile	Historical VaR	Normal distribution	t-distribution	t-copula & t-marginals
		Mean (Std)	Mean (Std)	Mean (Std)
0.01	155.15	138.22 (4.47)	155.01 (8.64)	158.25 (8.24)
0.025	126.63	116.30 (2.88)	118.28 (4.83)	120.08 (4.87)
0.05	98.27	97.56 (2.26)	92.35 (2.83)	94.14 (3.12)

Table 3.13: Mean and standard deviation of 100 VaR estimations (multiplied by 10^5) from simulated data following different distributions which are fitted to the data set D_3.

Quantile	Historical VaR	Normal distribution	t-distribution	t-copula & t-marginals
		Mean (Std)	Mean (Std)	Mean (Std)
0.01	183.95	156.62 (3.65)	179.18 (9.75)	179.41 (6.17)
0.025	141.22	131.54 (2.41)	124.49 (4.43)	135.21 (3.69)
0.05	109.94	110.08 (2.05)	91.74 (2.55)	105.67 (2.59)

distribution. By contrast, the bivariate t-distribution provides good estimations of the historical VaR for the data sets D_1 and D_2 over all quantiles. However, both data sets are approximately elliptically-contoured distributed since the estimated parameters of the copula and the marginals are almost equal. For example for the data set D_1, the estimated degree of freedom of the t-copula is 3.05 whereas the estimated degrees of freedom of the t-marginals are 2.99 and 3.03, respectively. We have already discussed that the distribution of the data set D_3 is not elliptically contoured. Indeed, the VaR estimation improves with a splitting of the copula and the marginals. The corresponding estimated degree of freedom of the t-copula is 1.11 whereas the estimated degrees of freedom of the t-marginals are 4.63 and 5.15. Finally, note that the empirical standard deviations do significantly differ between the VaR estimation based on the multivariate t-distribution and the t-copula, respectively.

Bibliography

Bingham, N. H., Goldie, C. M. and Teugels, J. L. (1987). *Regular Variation*, Cambridge University Press, Cambridge.

Bingham, N. H. and Kiesel, R. (2002). Semi-parametric modelling in Finance: Theoretical foundation, *Quantitative Finance* **2**: 241–250.

Bingham, N. H., Kiesel, R. and Schmidt, R. (2002). Semi-parametric modelling in Finance: Econometric applications, *Quantitative Finance* **3** (6): 426–441.

Cambanis, S., Huang, S. and Simons, G. (1981). On the theory of elliptically contoured distributions, *Journal of Multivariate Analysis* **11**: 368-385.

Draisma, G., Drees, H., Ferreira, A. and de Haan, L. (2004). Bivariate tail estimation: dependence in asymptotic independence, *Bernoulli* **10** (2): 251-280.

Drees, H. and Kaufmann, E. (1998). Selecting the optimal sample fraction in univariate extreme value estimation, *Stochastic Processes and their Applications* **75**: 149-172.

Eberlein, E. and Keller, U. (1995). Hyperbolic distributions in finance, *Bernoulli* **1**: 281–299.

Embrechts, P., Klüppelberg, C. and Mikosch, T. (1997). *Modelling Extremal Events*, Springer Verlag, Berlin.

Embrechts, P., Lindskog, F. and McNeil, A. (2001). Modelling Dependence with Copulas and Applications to Risk Management, in S. Rachev (Ed.) *Handbook of Heavy Tailed Distributions in Finance*, Elsevier: 329–384.

Embrechts, P., McNeil, A. and Straumann, D. (1999). Correlation and Dependency in Risk Management: Properties and Pitfalls, in M.A.H. Dempster (Ed.) *Risk Management: Value at Risk and Beyond*, Cambridge University Press, Cambridge: 176–223.

Fang, K., Kotz, S. and Ng, K. (1990). *Symmetric Multivariate and Related Distributions*, Chapman and Hall, London.

Frahm, G., Junker, M. and Schmidt, R. (2002). Estimating the Tail Dependence Coefficient, CAESAR Center Bonn, Technical Report **38** *http://stats.lse.ac.uk/schmidt.*

Härdle, W., Kleinow, T. and Stahl, G. (2002). *Applied Quantitative Finance - Theory and Computational Tools*, Springer Verlag, Berlin.

Hahn, M.G., Mason, D.M. and Weiner D.C. (1991). *Sums, trimmed sums and extremes*, Birkhäuser, Boston.

Hauksson, H., Dacorogna, M., Domenig, T., Mueller, U. and Samorodnitsky, G. (2001). Multivariate Extremes, Aggregation and Risk Estimation, *Quantitative Finance* **1**: 79–95.

Huang, X., (1992). *Statistics of Bivariate Extreme Values.* Thesis Publishers and Tinbergen Institute.

Joe, H. (1997). *Multivariate Models and Dependence Concepts*, Chapman and Hall, London.

Joe, H. and Xu, J. J. (1996). The Estimation Method of Inference Function for Margins for Multivariate Models, British Columbia, Dept. of Statistics, Technical Report **166**.

Junker, M. and May, A. (2002). Measurement of aggregate risk with copulas, Research Center CAESAR Bonn, Dept. of Quantitative Finance, Technical Report **2**.

Kiesel, R. and Kleinow, T. (2002). Sensitivity analysis of credit portfolio models, in W. Härdle, T. Kleinow and G. Stahl (Eds.) *Applied Quantitative Finance.*, Springer Verlag, New York.

Ledford, A. and Tawn, J. (1996). Statistics for Near Independence in Multivariate Extreme Values, *Biometrika* **83**: 169–187.

Nelsen, R. (1999). *An Introduction to Copulas*, Springer Verlag, New York.

Peng, L. (1998). *Second Order Condition and Extreme Value Theory*, Tinbergen Institute Research Series **178**, Thesis Publishers and Tinbergen Institute.

Rousseeuw, P.J. and van Zomeren B.C. (2002). Unmasking multivariate outliers and leverage points, *Journal of the American Statistical Association* **85**: 633–639.

Schmidt, R. (2002a). Credit Risk Modelling and Estimation via Elliptical Copulae, in G. Bohl, G. Nakhaeizadeh, S.T. Rachev, T. Ridder and K.H. Vollmer (Eds.) *Credit Risk: Measurement, Evaluation and Management*, Physica Verlag, Heidelberg.

Schmidt, R. (2002b). Tail Dependence for Elliptically Contoured Distributions, *Math. Methods of Operations Research* **55** (2): 301–327.

Schmidt, R. (2003). *Dependencies of Extreme Events in Finance*, Dissertation, University of Ulm, *http://stats.lse.ac.uk/schmidt.*

Schmidt, R. and Stadtmüller, U. (2002). Nonparametric Estimation of Tail Dependence, The London School of Economics, Department of Statistics, Research report **101**, *http://stats.lse.ac.uk/schmidt.*

4 Pricing of Catastrophe Bonds

Krzysztof Burnecki, Grzegorz Kukla, and David Taylor

4.1 Introduction

Catastrophe (CAT) bonds are one of the more recent financial derivatives to be traded on the world markets. In the mid-1990s a market in catastrophe insurance risk emerged in order to facilitate the direct transfer of reinsurance risk associated with natural catastrophes from corporations, insurers and reinsurers to capital market investors. The primary instrument developed for this purpose was the CAT bond.

CAT bonds are more specifically referred to as insurance-linked securities (ILS) The distinguishing feature of these bonds is that the ultimate repayment of principal depends on the outcome of an insured event. The basic CAT bond structure can be summarized as follows (Lane, 2004):

1. The sponsor establishes a special purpose vehicle (SPV) as an issuer of bonds and as a source of reinsurance protection.

2. The issuer sells bonds to investors. The proceeds from the sale are invested in a collateral account.

3. The sponsor pays a premium to the issuer; this and the investment of bond proceeds are a source of interest paid to investors.

4. If the specified catastrophic risk is triggered, the funds are withdrawn from the collateral account and paid to the sponsor; at maturity, the remaining principal – or if there is no event, 100% of principal – is paid to investors.

There are three types of ILS triggers: indemnity, index and parametric. An indemnity trigger involves the actual losses of the bond-issuing insurer. For example the event may be the insurer's losses from an earthquake in a certain area of a given country over the period of the bond. An industry index trigger involves, in the US for example, an index created from property claim service (PCS) loss estimates. A parametric trigger is based on, for example, the Richter scale readings of the magnitude of an earthquake at specified data stations. In this chapter we address the issue of pricing CAT bonds with indemnity and index triggers.

4.1.1 The Emergence of CAT Bonds

Until fairly recently, property reinsurance was a relatively well understood market with efficient pricing. However, naturally occurring catastrophes, such as earthquakes and hurricanes, are beginning to have a dominating impact on the industry. In part, this is due to the rapidly changing, heterogeneous distribution of high-value property in vulnerable areas. A consequence of this has been an increased need for a primary and secondary market in catastrophe related insurance derivatives. The creation of CAT bonds, along with allied financial products such as catastrophe insurance options, was motivated in part by the need to cover the massive property insurance industry payouts of the early- to mid-1990s. They also represent a "new asset class" in that they provide a mechanism for hedging against natural disasters, a risk which is essentially uncorrelated with the capital market indices (Doherty, 1997). Subsequent to the development of the CAT bond, the class of disaster referenced has grown considerably. As yet, there is almost no secondary market for CAT bonds which hampers using arbitrage-free pricing models for the derivative.

Property insurance claims of approximately USD 60 billion between 1990 and 1996 (Canter, Cole, and Sandor, 1996) caused great concern to the insurance industry and resulted in the insolvency of a number of firms. These bankruptcies were brought on in the wake of hurricanes Andrew (Florida and Louisiana affected, 1992), Opal (Florida and Alabama, 1995) and Fran (North Carolina, 1996), which caused combined damage totalling USD 19.7 billion (Canter, Cole, and Sandor, 1996). These, along with the Northridge earthquake (1994) and similar disasters (for the illustration of the US natural catastrophe data see Figure 4.1), led to an interest in alternative means for underwriting insurance. In 1995, when the CAT bond market was born, the primary and secondary (or reinsurance) industries had access to approximately USD 240 billion in capital (Canter, Cole, and Sandor, 1996; Cummins and Danzon, 1997). Given the capital level constraints necessary for the reinsuring of property losses and the potential for single-event losses in excess of USD 100 billion, this was clearly insufficient. The international capital markets provided a potential source of security for the (re-)insurance market. An estimated capitalisation of the international financial markets, at that time, of about USD 19 trillion underwent an average daily fluctuation of approximately 70 basis points or USD 133 billion (Sigma, 1996). The undercapitalisation of the reinsurance industry (and their consequential default risk) meant that there was a tendency for CAT reinsurance prices to be highly volatile. This was reflected in the traditional insurance market, with rates on line being significantly higher in the years following catastrophes and dropping off in the intervening years (Froot and O'Connell, 1997; Sigma, 1997). This heterogeneity in pricing has a very strong damping effect, forcing many re-insurers to leave the market, which in turn has adverse consequences for the primary insurers. A number of reasons for this volatility have been advanced (Winter, 1994; Cummins and Danzon, 1997).

CAT bonds and allied catastrophe related derivatives are an attempt to address these problems by providing effective hedging instruments which reflect long-term views and can be priced according to the statistical characteristics of the dominant underlying process(es). Their impact, since a period of standardisation between 1997 and 2003, has been substantial. As a consequence the rise in prices associated with the uppermost segments of the CAT reinsurance programs has been dampened. The primary market has developed and both issuers and investors are now well-educated and technically adept. In the years 2000 to 2003, the average total issue exceeded USD 1 billion per annum (McGhee, 2004). The catastrophe bond market witnessed yet another record year in 2003, with total issuance of USD 1.73 billion, an impressive 42 percent year-on-year increase from 2002s record of USD 1.22 billion. During the year, a total of eight transactions were completed, with three originating from first-time issuers. The year also featured the first European corporate-sponsored transaction (and only the third by any non-insurance company). Electricité de France, the largest electric utility in Europe, sponsored a transaction to address a portion of the risks facing its properties from French windstorms. Since 1997, when the market began in earnest, 54 catastrophe bond issues have been completed with total risk limits of almost USD 8 billion. It is interesting to note that very few of the issued bonds receive better than "non-investment grade" BB ratings and that almost no CAT bonds have been triggered, despite an increased reliance on parametric or index based payout triggers.

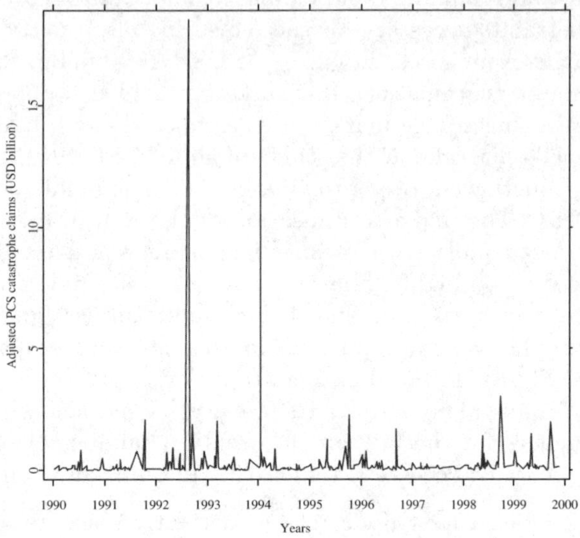

Figure 4.1: Graph of the PCS catastrophe loss data, 1990–1999.

STFcat01.xpl

4.1.2 Insurance Securitization

Capitalisation of insurance and consequential risk spreading through share issue, is well established and the majority of primary and secondary insurers are public companies. Investors in these companies are thus de facto bearers of risk for the industry. This however relies on the idea of risk pooling through the law of large numbers, where the loss borne by each investor becomes highly predictable. In the case of catastrophic natural disasters, this may not be possible as the losses incurred by different insurers tend to be correlated. In this situation a different approach for hedging the risk is necessary. A number of such products which realize innovative methods of risk spreading already exist and are traded (Litzenberger, Beaglehole, and Reynolds, 1996; Cummins and Danzon, 1997; Aase, 1999; Sigma, 2003). They are roughly divided into reinsurance share related derivatives, including Post-loss Equity Issues and Catastrophe Equity Puts, and asset–liability hedges such as Catastrophe Futures, Options and CAT Bonds.

In 1992, the Chicago Board of Trade (CBOT) introduced the CAT futures. In 1995, the CAT future was replaced by the PCS option. This option was based on a loss index provided by PCS. The underlying index represented the development of specified catastrophe damages, was published daily and eliminated the problems of the earlier ISO index. The options traded better, especially the call option spreads where insurers would appear on both side of the transaction, i.e. as buyer and seller. However, they also ceased trading in 2000. Much work in the reinsurance industry concentrated on pricing these futures and options and on modelling the process driving their underlying indices (Canter, Cole, and Sandor, 1996; Embrechts and Meister, 1997; Aase, 1999). CAT bonds are allied but separate instruments which seek to ensure capital requirements are met in the specific instance of a catastrophic event.

4.1.3 CAT Bond Pricing Methodology

In this chapter we investigate the pricing of CAT Bonds. The methodology developed here can be extended to most other catastrophe related instruments. However, we are concerned here only with CAT specific instruments, e.g. California Earthquake Bonds (Sigma, 1996; Sigma, 1997; Sigma, 2003; McGhee, 2004), and not reinsurance shares or their related derivatives.

In the early market for CAT bonds, the pricing of the bonds was in the hands of the issuer and was affected by the equilibrium between supply and demand only. Consequently there was a tendency for the market to resemble the traditional reinsurance market. However, as CAT bonds become more popular, it is reasonable to expect that their price will begin to reflect the fair or arbitrage-free price of the bond, although recent discussions of alternative pricing methodologies have contradicted this expectation (Lane, 2003). Our pricing approach assumes that this market already exists.

Some of the traditional assumptions of derivative security pricing are not correct when applied to these instruments due to the properties of the underlying contingent stochastic processes. There is evidence that certain catastrophic natural events have (partial) power-law distributions associated with their loss statistics (Barton and Nishenko, 1994). This overturns the traditional lognormal assumption of derivative pricing models. There are also well-known statistical difficulties associated with the moments of power-law distributions, thus rendering it impossible to employ traditional pooling methods and consequently the central limit theorem. Given that heavy-tailed or large deviation results assume, in general, that at least the first moment of the distribution exists, there will be difficulties with applying extreme value theory to this problem (Embrechts, Resnick, and Samorodnitsky, 1999). It would seem that these characteristics may render traditional actuarial or derivatives pricing approaches ineffective.

There are additional features to modelling the CAT bond price which are not to be found in models of ordinary corporate or government issue (although there is some similarity with pricing defaultable bonds). In particular, the trigger event underlying CAT bond pricing is dependent on both the frequency and severity of natural disasters. In the model described here, we attempt to reduce to a minimum any assumptions about the underlying distribution functions. This is in the interests of generality of application. The numerical examples will have to make some distributional assumptions and will reference some real data. We will also assume that loss levels are instantaneously measurable and updatable. It is straightforward to adjust the underlying process to accommodate a development period.

There is a natural similarity between the pricing of catastrophe bonds and the pricing of defaultable bonds. Defaultable bonds, by definition, must contain within their pricing model a mechanism that accounts for the potential (partial or complete) loss of their principal value. Defaultable bonds yield higher returns, in part, because of this potential defaultability. Similarly, CAT bonds are offered at high yields because of the unpredictable nature of the catastrophe process. With this characteristic in mind, a number of pricing models for defaultable bonds have been advanced (Jarrow and Turnbull, 1995; Zhou, 1997; Duffie and Singleton, 1999). The trigger event for the default process has similar statistical characteristics to that of the equivalent catastrophic event pertaining to CAT bonds. In an allied application to mortgage insurance, the similarity between catastrophe and default in the log-normal context has been commented on (Kau and Keenan, 1996).

With this in mind, we have modelled the catastrophe process as a compound doubly stochastic Poisson process. The underlying assumption is that there is a Poisson point process (of some intensity, in general varying over time) of *potentially* catastrophic events. However, these events may or may not result in economic losses. We assume the economic losses associated with each of the potentially catastrophic events to be independent and to have a certain common probability distribution. This is justifiable for the Property Claim Loss indices used as the triggers for the CAT bonds. Within this model, the threshold time can be seen as a point of a Poisson point process with a stochastic intensity depending on the instantaneous index position. We make this model precise later in the chapter.

In the article of Baryshnikov, Mayo, and Taylor (1998) the authors presented an arbitrage-free solution to the pricing of CAT bonds under conditions of continuous trading. They modelled the stochastic process underlying the CAT bond as a compound doubly stochastic Poisson process. Burnecki and Kukla (2003) applied their results in order to determine no-arbitrage prices of a zero-coupon and coupon bearing CAT bond. In Section 4.2 we present the doubly stochastic Poisson pricing model. In Section 4.3 we study 10-year catastrophe loss data provided by Property Claim Services. We find a distribution function which fits the observed claims in a satisfactory manner and estimate the intensity of the non-homogeneous Poisson process governing the flow of the natural events. In Section 4.4 we illustrate the values of different CAT bonds associated with this loss data with respect to the threshold level and maturity time. To this end we apply Monte Carlo simulations.

4.2 Compound Doubly Stochastic Poisson Pricing Model

The CAT bond we are interested in is described by specifying the region, type of events, type of insured properties, etc. More abstractly, it is described by the aggregate loss process L_s and by the threshold loss D. Set a probability space $(\Omega, \mathcal{F}, \mathcal{F}_t, \nu)$ and an increasing filtration $\mathcal{F}_t \subset \mathcal{F}$, $t \in [0, T]$. This leads to the following assumptions:

- There exists a doubly stochastic Poisson process (Bremaud, 1981) M_s describing the flow of (potentially catastrophic) natural events of a given type in the region specified in the bond contract. The intensity of this Poisson point process is assumed to be a predictable bounded process m_s. This process describes the estimates based on statistical analysis and scientific knowledge about the nature of the catastrophe causes. We will denote the instants of these potentially catastrophic natural events as $0 \leq t_1 \leq \ldots \leq t_i \leq \ldots \leq T$.
- The losses incurred by each event in the flow $\{t_i\}$ are assumed to be independent, identically distributed random values $\{X_i\}$ with distribution function $F(x) = \mathrm{P}(X_i < x)$.
- A progressive process of discounting rates r. Following the traditional practice, we assume the process is continuous almost everywhere. This

process describes the value at time s of USD 1 paid at time $t > s$ by

$$\exp\{-R(s,t)\} = \exp\left\{-\int_s^t r(\xi)\,d\xi\right\}.$$

Therefore, one has

$$L_t = \sum_{t_i<t} X_i = \sum_{i=1}^{M_t} X_i.$$

The definition of the process implies that L is left-continuous and predictable. We assume that the threshold event is the time when the accumulated losses exceed the threshold level D, that is $\tau = \inf\{t : L_t \geq D\}$. Now define a new process $N_t = I(L_t \geq D)$. Baryshnikov et al. (1998) show that this is also a doubly stochastic Poisson process with the intensity

$$\lambda_s = m_s \{1 - F(D - L_s)\} I(L_s < D). \tag{4.1}$$

In Figure 4.2 we see a sample trajectory of the aggregate loss process L_t ($0 \leq t \leq T = 10$ years) generated under the assumption of log-normal loss amounts with $\mu = 18.3806$ and $\sigma = 1.1052$ and a non-homogeneous Poisson process M_t with the intensity function $m_s^1 = 35.32 + 2.32 \cdot 2\pi \sin\{2\pi(s - 0.20)\}$, a real-life catastrophe loss trajectory (which will be analysed in detail in Section 4.3), the mean function of the process L_t and two sample 0.05- and 0.95-quantile lines based on 5000 trajectories of the aggregated loss process, see Chapter 14 and Burnecki, Härdle, and Weron (2004). It is evident that in the studied log-normal case, the historical trajectory falls outside even the 0.05-quantile line. This may suggest that "more heavy-tailed" distributions such as the Pareto or Burr distributions would be better for modelling the "real" aggregate loss process. In Figure 4.2 the black horizontal line represents a threshold level of $D = 60$ billion USD.

4.3 Calibration of the Pricing Model

We conducted empirical studies for the PCS data obtained from Property Claim Services. ISO's Property Claim Services unit is the internationally recognized authority on insured property losses from catastrophes in the United States, Puerto Rico and the U.S. Virgin Islands. PCS investigates reported disasters

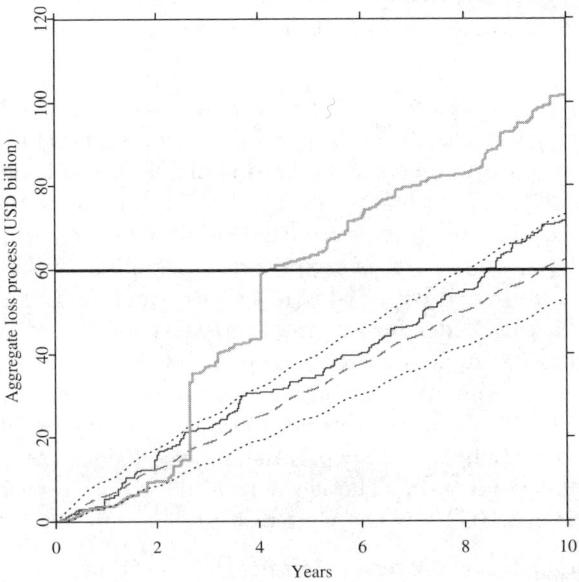

Figure 4.2: A sample trajectory of the aggregate loss process L_t (thin blue solid line), a real-life catastrophe loss trajectory (thick green solid line), the analytical mean of the process L_t (red dashed line) and two sample 0.05- and 0.95-quantile lines (brown dotted line). The black horizontal line represents the threshold level $D = 60$ billion USD.

`STFcat02.xpl`

and determines the extent and type of damage, dates of occurrence and geographic areas affected (Burnecki, Kukla, and Weron, 2000). The data, see Figure 4.1, concerns the US market's loss amounts in USD, which occurred between 1990 and 1999 and adjusted for inflation using the Consumer Price Index provided by the U.S. Department of Labor. Only natural perils like hurricane, tropical storm, wind, flooding, hail, tornado, snow, freezing, fire, ice and earthquake were taken into consideration. We note that peaks in Figure 4.1 mark the occurrence of Hurricane Andrew (the 24th August 1992) and the Northridge Earthquake (the 17th January 1994).

In order to calibrate the pricing model we have to fit both the distribution function of the incurred losses F and the process M_t governing the flow of natural events.

The claim size distributions, especially describing property losses, are usually heavy-tailed. In the actuarial literature for describing such claims, continuous distributions are often proposed (with the domain $\mathbb{R}_+$), see Chapter 13. The choice of the distribution is very important because it influences the bond price. In Chapter 14 the claim amount distributions were fitted to the PCS data depicted in Figure 4.1. The log-normal, exponential, gamma, Weibull, mixture of two exponentials, Pareto and Burr distributions were analysed. The parameters were estimated via the Anderson-Darling statistical minimisation procedure. The goodness-of-fit was checked with the help of Kolmogorov-Smirnov, Kuiper, Cramér-von Mises and Anderson-Darling non-parametric tests. The test statistics were compared with the critical values obtained through Monte Carlo simulations. The Burr distribution with parameters $\alpha = 0.4801$, $\lambda = 3.9495 \cdot 10^{16}$ and $\tau = 2.1524$ passed all tests. The log-normal distribution with parameters $\mu = 18.3806$ and $\sigma = 1.1052$ was the next best fit.

A doubly stochastic Poisson process governing the occurrence times of the losses was fitted by Burnecki and Kukla (2003). The simplest case with the intensity m_s equal to a nonnegative constant m was considered. Studies of the quarterly number of losses and the inter-occurence times of the catastrophes led to the conclusion that the flow of the events may be described by a Poisson process with an annual intensity of $m = 34.2$.

The claim arrival process is also analysed in Chapter 14. The statistical tests applied to the annual waiting times led to a renewal process. Finally, the rate function $m_s^1 = 35.32 + 2.32 \cdot 2\pi \sin\{2\pi(s - 0.20)\}$ was fitted and the claim arrival process was treated as a non-homogeneous Poisson process. Such a choice of the intensity function allows modelling of an annual seasonality present in the natural catastrophe data.

Baryshnikov, Mayo, and Taylor (1998) proposed an intensity function of the form $m_s^2 = a + b\sin^2\{2\pi(s + S)\}$. Using the least squares procedure (Ross, 2001), we fitted the cumulative intensity function (mean value function) given by $\mathrm{E}(M_s) = \int_0^s m_z dz$ to the accumulated quarterly number of PCS losses. We concluded that $a = 35.22$, $b = 0.224$, and $S = -0.16$. This choice of the rate function allows the incorporation of both an annual cyclic component and a trend which is sometimes observed in natural catastrophe data.

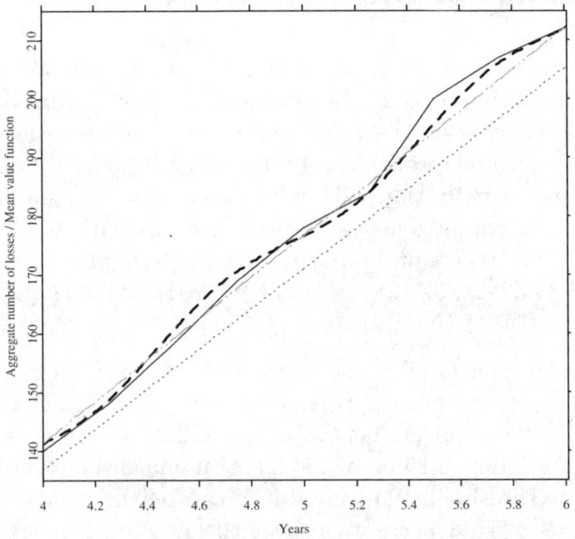

Figure 4.3: The aggregate quarterly number of PCS losses (blue solid line) together with the mean value functions $E(M_t)$ corresponding to the HP (red dotted line), NHP1 (black dashed line) and NHP2 (green dashed-dotted line) cases.

STFcat03.xpl

It appears that both the mean squared error (MSE) and the mean absolute error (MAE) favour the rate function m_s^1. In this case MSE = 13.68 and MAE = 2.89, whereas m_s^2 yields MSE = 15.12 and MAE = 3.22. Finally the homogeneous Poisson process with the constant intensity gives MSE = 55.86 and MAE = 6.1. All three choices of the intensity function m_s are illustrated in Figure 4.3, where the accumulated quarterly number of PCS losses and the mean value functions on the interval [4, 6] years are depicted. This interval was chosen to best illustrate the differences.

4.4 Dynamics of the CAT Bond Price

In this section, we present prices for different CAT bonds. We illustrate them while focusing on the influence of the choice of the loss amount distribution and the claim arrival process on the bond price. We analyse cases using the Burr distribution with parameters $\alpha = 0.4801$, $\lambda = 3.9495 \cdot 10^{16}$ and $\tau = 2.1524$, and the log-normal distribution with parameters $\mu = 18.3806$ and $\sigma = 1.1052$. We also analyse the homogeneous Poisson process with an annual intensity $m = 34.2$ (HP) and the non-homogeneous Poisson processes with the rate functions $m_s^1 = 35.32 + 2.32 \cdot 2\pi \sin\{2\pi(s - 0.20)\}$ (NHP1) and $m_s^2 = 35.22 + 0.224 \sin^2\{2\pi(s - 0.16)\}$ (NHP2).

Consider a zero-coupon CAT bond defined by the payment of an amount Z at maturity T, contingent on a threshold time $\tau > T$. Define the process $Z_s = \mathrm{E}(Z|\mathcal{F}_s)$. We require that Z_s is a predictable process. This can be interpreted as the independence of payment at maturity from the occurrence and timing of the threshold. The amount Z can be the principal plus interest, usually defined as a fixed percentage over the London Inter-Bank Offer Rate (LIBOR).

The no-arbitrage price of the zero-coupon CAT bond associated with a threshold D, catastrophic flow M_s, a distribution function of incurred losses F, and paying Z at maturity is given by Burnecki and Kukla (2003):

$$\begin{aligned} V_t^1 &= \mathrm{E}\left[Z \exp\{-R(t,T)\}(1 - N_T)|\mathcal{F}_t\right] \\ &= \mathrm{E}\Bigg[Z \exp\{-R(t,T)\} \\ &\quad \cdot \left\{1 - \int_t^T m_s\{1 - F(D - L_s)\} I(L_s < D) ds\right\} |\mathcal{F}_t\Bigg]. \end{aligned} \tag{4.2}$$

We evaluate this CAT bond price at $t = 0$, and apply appropriate Monte Carlo simulations. We assume for the purposes of illustration that the annual continuously-compounded discount rate $r = \ln(1.025)$ is constant and corresponds to LIBOR, $T \in [1/4, 2]$ years, $D \in [2.54, 30]$ billion USD (quarterly – 3*annual average loss).

Furthermore, in the case of the zero-coupon CAT bond we assume that $Z = 1.06$ USD. Hence, the bond is priced at 3.5% over LIBOR when $T = 1$ year. Figure 4.4 illustrates the zero-coupon CAT bond values (4.2) with respect

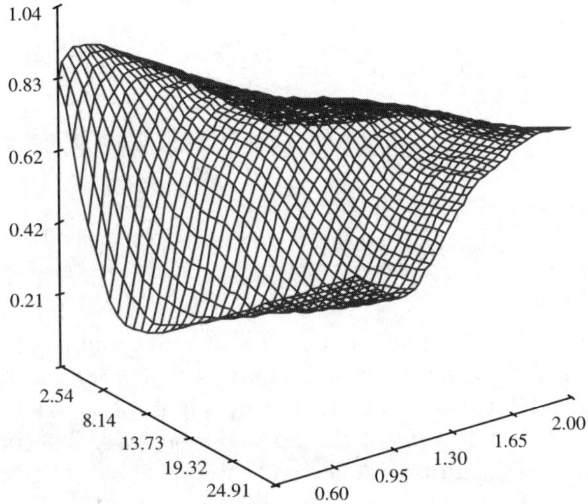

Figure 4.4: The zero-coupon CAT bond price with respect to the threshold level (left axis) and time to expiry (right axis) in the Burr and NHP1 case.

STFcat04.xpl

to the threshold level and time to expiry in the Burr and NHP1 case. We can see that as the time to expiry increases, the price of the CAT bond decreases. Increasing the threshold level leads to higher bond prices. When T is a quarter and $D = 30$ billion USD the CAT bond price approaches the value $1.06 \exp\{-\ln(1.025)/4\} \approx 1.05$ USD. This is equivalent to the situation when the threshold time exceeds the maturity ($\tau \geqslant T$) with probability one.

Consider now a CAT bond which has only coupon payments C_t, which terminate at the threshold time τ. The no-arbitrage price of the CAT bond associated with a threshold D, catastrophic flow M_s, a distribution function of incurred losses F, with coupon payments C_s which terminate at time τ is given by Burnecki and Kukla (2003):

$$\begin{aligned} V_t^2 &= \mathrm{E}\left[\int_t^T \exp\{-R(t,s)\}\, C_s(1-N_s)ds|\mathcal{F}_t\right] \\ &= \mathrm{E}\left[\int_t^T \exp\{-R(t,s)\}\, C_s\right. \\ &\quad \cdot \left.\left\{1-\int_t^s m_\xi\left\{1-F(D-L_\xi)\right\} I(L_\xi<D)d\xi\right\}ds|\mathcal{F}_t\right]. \end{aligned} \tag{4.3}$$

We evaluate this CAT bond price at $t = 0$ and assume that $C_t \equiv 0.06$. The value of V_0^2 as a function of time to maturity (expiry) and threshold level in the Burr and NHP1 case is illustrated by Figure 4.5. We clearly see that the situation is different to that of the zero-coupon case. The price increases with both time to expiry and threshold level. When $D = 30$ USD billion and $T = 2$ years the CAT bond price approaches the value $0.06\int_0^2 \exp\{-\ln(1.025)t\}\, dt \approx 0.12$ USD. This is equivalent to the situation when the threshold time exceeds the maturity ($\tau \geqslant T$) with probability one.

Finally, we consider the case of the coupon-bearing CAT bond. Fashioned as floating rate notes, such bonds pay a fixed spread over LIBOR. Loosely speaking, the fixed spread may be analogous to the premium paid for the underlying insured event, and the floating rate, LIBOR, is the payment for having invested cash in the bond to provide payment against the insured event, should a payment to the insured be necessary. We combine (4.2) with Z equal to par value (PV) and (4.3) to obtain the price for the coupon-bearing CAT bond.

The no-arbitrage price of the CAT bond associated with a threshold D, catastrophic flow M_s, a distribution function of incurred losses F, paying PV at maturity, and coupon payments C_s which cease at the threshold time τ is

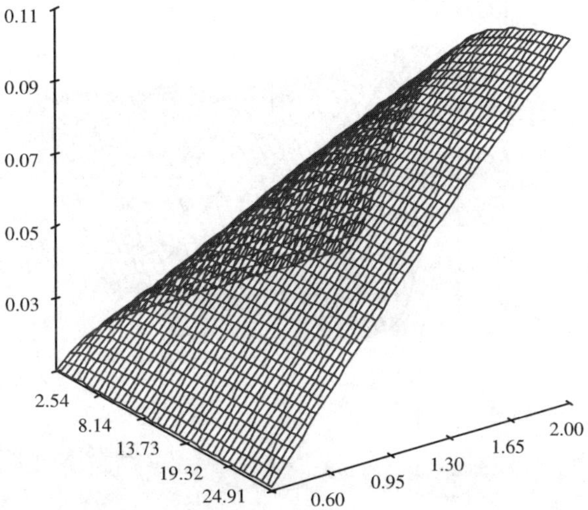

Figure 4.5: The CAT bond price, for the bond paying only coupons, with respect to the threshold level (left axis) and time to expiry (right axis) in the Burr and NHP1 case.

STFcat05.xpl

given by Burnecki and Kukla (2003):

$$\begin{aligned}
V_t^3 &= \mathrm{E}\left[PV \exp\{-R(t,T)\}(1-N_T) \right. \\
&+ \left. \int_t^T \exp\{-R(t,s)\} C_s (1-N_s) ds | \mathcal{F}_t \right] \\
&= \mathrm{E}\left[PV \exp\{-R(t,T)\} \right. \\
&+ \int_t^T \exp\{-R(t,s)\} \left\{ C_s \left(1 - \int_t^s m_\xi \{1 - F(D-L_\xi)\} I(L_\xi < D) d\xi \right) \right. \\
&- \left. \left. PV \exp\{-R(s,T)\} m_s \{1 - F(D - L_s)\} I(L_s < D) \right\} ds | \mathcal{F}_t \right]. \qquad (4.4)
\end{aligned}$$

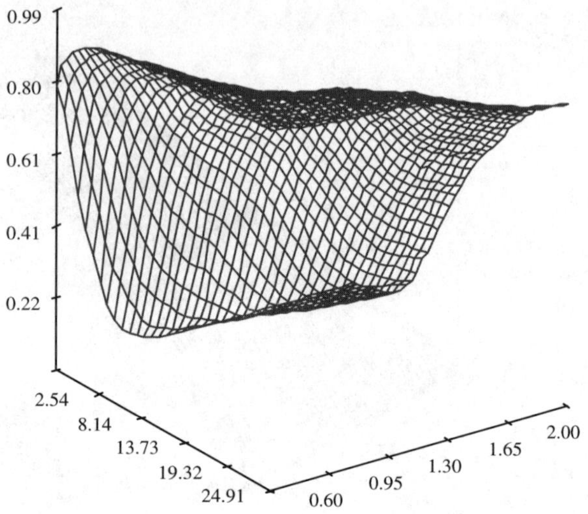

Figure 4.6: The coupon-bearing CAT bond price with respect to the threshold level (left axis) and time to expiry (right axis) in the Burr and NHP1 case.

STFcat06.xpl

We evaluate this CAT bond price at $t = 0$ and assume that $PV = 1$ USD, and again $C_t \equiv 0.06$. Figure 4.6 illustrates this CAT bond price in the Burr and NHP1 case. The influence of the threshold level D on the bond value is clear but the effect of increasing the time to expiry is not immediately clear. As T increases, the possibility of receiving more coupons increases but so does the possibility of losing the principal of the bond. In this example (see Figure 4.6) the price decreases with respect to the time to expiry but this is not always true. We also notice that the bond prices in Figure 4.6 are lower than the corresponding ones in Figure 4.4. However, we recall that in the former case $PV = 1.06$ USD and here $PV = 1$ USD.

The choice of the fitted loss distribution affects the price of the bond. Figure 4.7 illustrates the difference between the zero-coupon CAT bond prices calculated under the two assumptions of Burr and log-normal loss sizes in the NHP1 case.

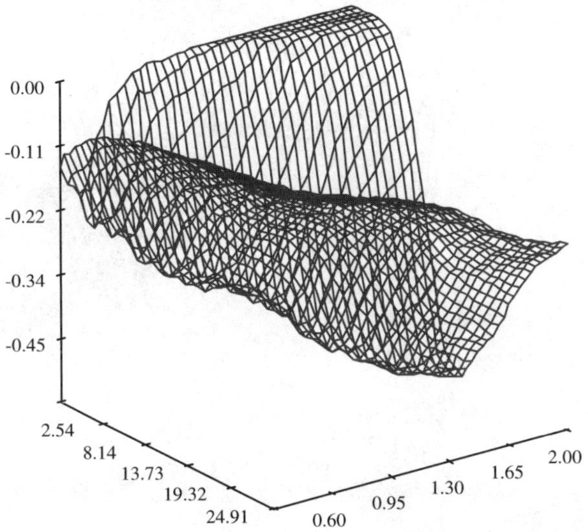

Figure 4.7: The difference between zero-coupon CAT bond prices in the Burr and log-normal cases with respect to the threshold level (left axis) and time to expiry (right axis) under the NHP1 assumption.

STFcat07.xpl

It is clear that taking into account heavier tails (the Burr distribution), which can be more appropriate when considering catastrophic losses, leads to higher prices (the maximum difference in this example reaches 50% of the principal).

Figures 4.8 and 4.9 show how the choice of the fitted Poisson point process influences the CAT bond value. Figure 4.8 illustrates the difference between the zero-coupon CAT bond prices calculated in the NHP1 and HP cases under the assumption of the Burr loss distribution. We see that the differences vary from -14% to 3% of the principal. Finally, Figure 4.9 illustrates the difference between the zero-coupon CAT bond prices calculated in the NHP1 and NHP2 cases under the assumption of the Burr loss distribution. The difference is always below 12%.

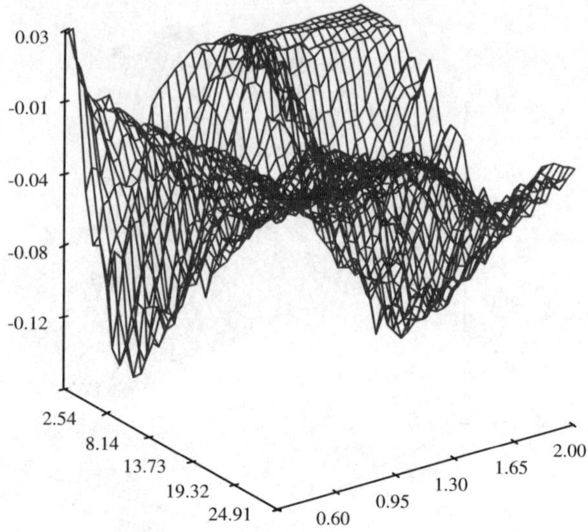

Figure 4.8: The difference between zero-coupon CAT bond prices in the NHP1 and HP cases with respect to the threshold level (left axis) and time to expiry (right axis) under the Burr assumption.

STFcat08.xpl

In our examples, equations (4.2) and (4.4), we have assumed that in the case of a trigger event the bond principal is completely lost. However, if we would like to incorporate a partial loss in the contract it is sufficient to multiply PV by the appropriate constant.

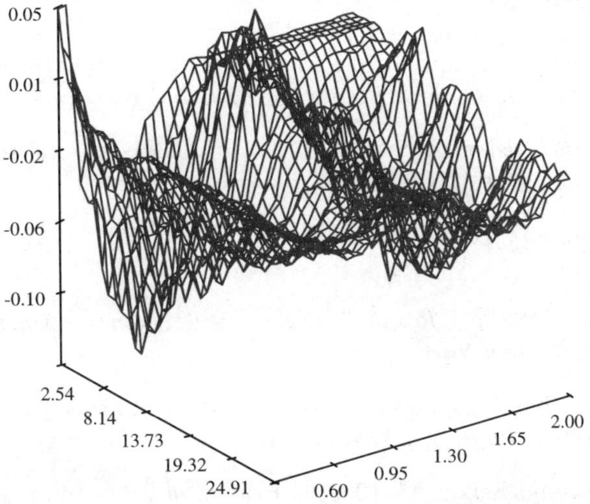

Figure 4.9: The difference between zero-coupon CAT bond prices in the NHP1 and NHP2 cases with respect to the threshold level (left axis) and time to expiry (right axis) under the Burr assumption.

STFcat09.xpl

Bibliography

Aase, K. (1999). An Equilibrium Model of Catastrophe Insurance Futures and Spreads, *The Geneva Papers on Risk and Insurance Theory* **24**: 69–96.

Barton, C. and Nishenko, S. (1994). Natural Disasters – Forecasting Economic and Life Losses, SGS special report.

Baryshnikov, Yu., Mayo, A. and Taylor, D.R. (1998). Pricing of CAT bonds, preprint.

Bremaud, P. (1981). *Point Processes and Queues: Martingale Dynamics*, Springer, New York.

Burnecki, K., Kukla, G. and Weron R. (2000). Property Insurance Loss Distributions, *Phys. A* **287**: 269–278.

Burnecki, K. and Kukla, G. (2003). Pricing of Zero-Coupon and Coupon Cat Bonds, *Appl. Math. (Warsaw)* **30(3)**: 315–324.

Burnecki, K., Härdle, W. and Weron, R. (2004). Simulation of Risk Processes, in *Encyclopedia of Actuarial Science*, J. L. Teugels and B. Sundt (eds.), Wiley, Chichester.

Canter, M. S., Cole, J. B. and Sandor, R. L. (1996). Insurance Derivatives: A New Asset Class for the Capital Markets and a New Hedging Tool for the Insurance Industry, *Journal of Derivatives* **4(2)**: 89–104.

Cummins, J. D. and Danzon, P. M. (1997). Price Shocks and Capital Flows in Liability Insurance, *Journal of Financial Intermediation* **6**: 3–38.

Cummins, J. D., Lo, A. and Doherty, N. A. (1999). Can Insurers Pay for the "Big One"? Measuring the Capacity of an Insurance Market to Respond to Catastrophic Losses, preprint, Wharton School, University of Pennsylvania.

D'Agostino, R.B.and Stephens, M.A. (1986). *Goodness-of-Fit Techniques*, Marcel Dekker, New York.

Doherty, N. A. (1997). Innovations in Managing Catastrophe Risk, *Journal of Risk & Insurance* **64(4)**: 713–718.

Duffie, D. and Singleton, K. J. (1999). Modelling Term Structures of Defaultable Bonds, *The Review of Financial Studies* **12(4)**: 687–720.

Embrechts, P., Resnick, S. I. and Samorodnitsky, G. (1999). Extreme Value Theory as a Risk Management Tool, *North American Actuarial Journal* **3(2)**: 30–41.

Embrechts, P. and Meister, S. (1997). Pricing Insurance Derivatives: The Case of Cat-Futures, in *Securitization of Insurance risk*, 1995 Bowles Symposium, SOA Monograph M-F197-1: 15–26.

Froot, K. and O'Connell P. (1997). On the Pricing of Intermediated Risks: Theory and Application to Catastrophe Reinsurance, NBER Working Paper No. w6011.

Jarrow, R. A. and Turnbull, S. (1995). Pricing Options on Financial Securities Subject to Default Risk, *Journal of Finance* **50**: 53–86.

Kau, J. B. and Keenan, D. C. (1996). An Option-Theoretic Model of Catastrophes Applied to Mortgage Insurance, *Journal of Risk and Insurance* **63(4)**: 639–656.

Lane, M.N. (2001). Rationale and Results with the LFC CAT Bond Pricing Model, Lane Financial L.L.C.

Lane, M.N. (2004). The Viability and Likely Pricing of "CAT Bonds" for Developing Countries, Lane Financial L.L.C.

Litzenberger, R.H., Beaglehole, D. R. and Reynolds, C. E. (1996). Assessing Catastrophe Reinsurance-Linked Securities as a New Asset Class, *Journal of Portfolio Management* (December): 76–86.

McGhee, C. (2004). Market Update: The Catastrophe Bond Market at Year-End 2003, Guy Carpenter & Company, Inc.

Ross, S. (2001). *Simulation, 3rd ed.*, Academic Press, Boston.

Sigma (1996). Insurance Derivatives and Securitization: New Hedging Perspectives for the US Catastrophe Insurance Market?, Report Number **5**, Swiss Re.

Sigma (1997). Too Little Reinsurance of Natural Disasters in Many Markets, Report Number **7**, Swiss Re.

Sigma (2003). The Picture of ART, Report Number **1**, Swiss Re.

Winter, R. A. (1994). The dynamics of competitive insurance markets, *Journal of Financial Intermediation* **3**: 379–415.

Zhou, C. (1994). A Jump Diffusion Approach to Modelling Credit Risk and Valuing Defaultable Securities, preprint, Federal Board.

5 Common Functional Implied Volatility Analysis

Michal Benko and Wolfgang Härdle

5.1 Introduction

Trading, hedging and risk analysis of complex option portfolios depend on accurate pricing models. The modelling of implied volatilities (IV) plays an important role, since volatility is the crucial parameter in the Black-Scholes (BS) pricing formula. It is well known from empirical studies that the volatilities implied by observed market prices exhibit patterns known as volatility smiles or smirks that contradict the assumption of constant volatility in the BS pricing model. On the other hand, the IV is a function of two parameters: the strike price and the time to maturity and it is desirable in practice to reduce the dimension of this object and characterize the IV surface through a small number of factors. Clearly, a dimension reduced pricing-model that should reflect the dynamics of the IV surface needs to contain factors and factor loadings that characterize the IV surface itself and their movements across time.

A popular dimension reduction technique is the principal components analysis (PCA), employed for example by Fengler, Härdle, and Schmidt (2002) in the IV surface analysis. The discretization of the strike dimension and application of PCA yield suitable factors (weight vectors) in the multivariate framework. Noting that the IVs of fixed maturity could also be viewed as random functions, we propose to use the functional analogue of PCA. We utilize the truncated functional basis expansion described in Ramsay and Silverman (1997) to the IVs of the European options on the German stock index (DAX). The standard functional PCA, however, yields weight functions that are too rough, hence a smoothed version of functional PCA is proposed here.

Like Fengler, Härdle, and Villa (2003) we discover similarities of the resulting weight functions across maturity groups. Thus we propose an estimation procedure based on the Flury-Gautschi algorithm, Flury (1988), for the simultaneous estimation of the weight functions for two different maturities. This procedure yields common weight functions with the level, slope, and curvature interpretation known from the financial literature. The resulting common factors of the IV surface are the basic elements to be used in applications, such as simulation based pricing, and deliver a substantial dimension reduction.

The chapter is organized as follows. In Section 5.2 the basic financial framework is presented, while in Section 5.3 we introduce the notation of the functional data analysis. In the following three sections we analyze the IV functions using functional principal components, smoothed functional principal components and common estimation of principal components, respectively.

5.2 Implied Volatility Surface

Implied volatilities are derived from the BS pricing formula for European options. Recall that European call and put options are derivatives written on an underlying asset S driven by the price process S_t, which yield the pay-off $\max(S_T - K, 0)$ and $\max(K - S_T, 0)$ respectively, at a given expiry time T and for a prespecified strike price K. The difference $\tau = T - t$ between the day of trade and day of expiration (maturity) is called time to maturity. The pricing formula for call options, Black and Scholes (1973), is:

$$
\begin{aligned}
C_t(S_t, K, \tau, r, \sigma) &= S_t \Phi(d_1) - K e^{-r\tau} \Phi(d_2) \\
d_1 &= \frac{\ln(S_t/K) + (r + 1/2\sigma^2)\tau}{\sigma\sqrt{\tau}}, \quad d_2 = d_1 - \sigma\sqrt{\tau},
\end{aligned}
\tag{5.1}
$$

where $\Phi(\cdot)$ is the cumulative distribution function of the standard normal distribution, r is the riskless interest rate, and σ is the (unknown and constant) volatility parameter. The put option price P_t can be obtained from the put-call parity $P_t = C_t - S_t + e^{-\tau r} K$.

For a European option the implied volatility $\hat{\sigma}$ is defined as the volatility – σ, which yields the BS price C_t equal to the price $\tilde{C}_t$ observed on the market. For a single asset, we obtain at each time point t a two-dimensional function – the IV surface $\hat{\sigma}_t(K, \tau)$. In order to standardize the volatility functions in time, one

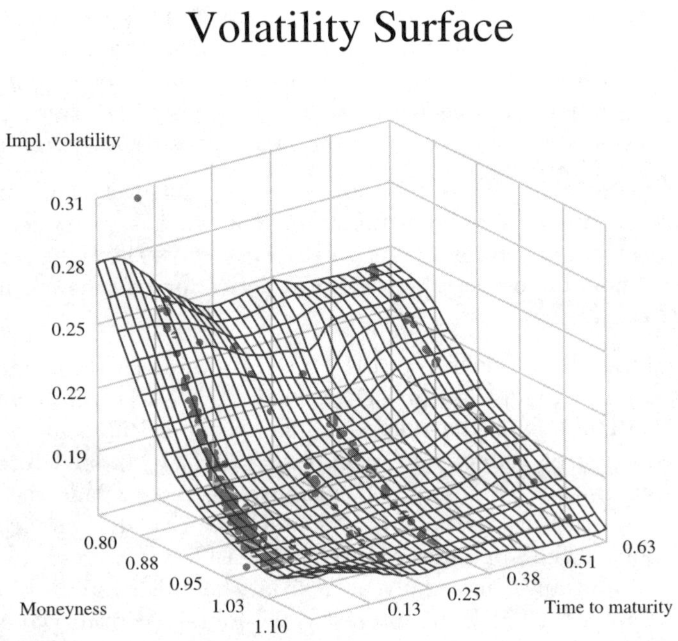

Figure 5.1: Implied volatility surface of ODAX on May 24, 2001.
STFfda01.xpl

may rescale the strike dimension by dividing K by the future price $F_t(\tau)$ of the underlying asset with the same maturity. This yields the so-called moneyness $\kappa = K/F_t(\tau)$. Note that some authors define moneyness simply as $\kappa = K/S_t$. In contrast to the BS assumptions, empirical studies show that IV surfaces are significantly curved, especially across the strikes. This phenomenon is called a volatility smirk or smile. Smiles stand for U-shaped volatility functions and smirks for decreasing volatility functions.

We focus on the European options on the German stock index (ODAX). Figure 5.1 displays the ODAX implied volatilities computed from the BS formula (red points) and the IV surface on May 24, 2001 estimated using a local polynomial estimator for $\tau \in [0, 0.6]$ and $\kappa \in [0.8, 1.2]$. We can clearly observe the "strings" of the original data on maturity grid $\tau \in \{0.06111, 0.23611, 0.33333, 0.58611\}$, which corresponds to 22, 85, 120, and 211 days to maturity. This maturity grid is structured by market conventions and changes over time. The fact that the number of transactions with short maturity is much higher than those with longer maturity is also typical for the IVs observed on the market.

The IV surface is a high-dimensional object – for every time point t we have to analyze a two-dimensional function. Our goal is to reduce the dimension of this problem and to characterize the IV surface through a small number of factors. These factors can be used in practice for risk management, e.g. with vega-strategies.

The analyzed data, taken from MD*Base, contains EUREX intra-day transaction data for DAX options and DAX futures (FDAX) from January 2 to June 29, 2001. The IVs are calculated by the Newton-Raphson iterative method. The correction of Hafner and Wallmeier (2001) is applied to avoid influence of the tax-scheme in the DAX. For robustness, we exclude the contracts with time to maturity of less than 7 days and maturity strings with less than 100 observations. The approximation of the "riskless" interest rate with a given maturity is obtained on a daily basis from the linear interpolation of the 1, 3, 6, and 12 month EURIBOR interest rates (obtained from Datastream).

The resulting data set is analyzed using the functional data analysis framework. One advantage of this approach, as we will see later in this chapter, is the possibility of introducing smoothness in the functional sense and using it for regularization. The notation of the functional data analysis is rather complex, therefor the theoretical motivation and the basic notation will be introduced in the next section.

5.3 Functional Data Analysis

In the functional data framework, the objects are usually modelled as realizations of a stochastic process $X(t), t \in J$, where J is a bounded interval in $\mathbb{R}$. Thus, the set of functions

$$x_i(t),\ i = 1, 2, \ldots n,\ t \in J,$$

represents the data set. We assume the existence of the mean, variance, and covariance functions of the process $X(t)$ and denote these by $\mathrm{E}X(t)$, $\mathrm{Var}(t)$ and $\mathrm{Cov}(s, t)$ respectively.

For the functional sample we can define the sample-counterparts of $\mathrm{E}X(t)$, $\mathrm{Var}(t)$ and $\mathrm{Cov}(s,t)$ in a straightforward way:

$$\begin{aligned}\bar{X}(t) &= \frac{1}{n}\sum_{i=1}^{n} x_i(t),\\ \widehat{\mathrm{Var}}(t) &= \frac{1}{n-1}\sum_{i=1}^{n}\left\{x_i(t)-\bar{X}(t)\right\}^2,\\ \widehat{\mathrm{Cov}}(s,t) &= \frac{1}{n-1}\sum_{i=1}^{n}\left\{x_i(s)-\bar{X}(s)\right\}\left\{x_i(t)-\bar{X}(t)\right\}.\end{aligned}$$

In practice, we observe the function values $\mathcal{X} \stackrel{\mathrm{def}}{=} \{x_i(t_{i1}), x_i(t_{i2}), \ldots, x_i(t_{ip_i}); i = 1, \ldots, n\}$ only on a discrete grid $\{t_{i1}, t_{i2}, \ldots, t_{ip_i}\} \in J$, where p_i is the number of grid points for the ith observation. One may estimate the functions $x_1, \ldots, x_n$ via standard nonparametric regression methods, Härdle (1990). Another popular way is to use a truncated functional basis expansion. More precisely, let us denote a functional basis on the interval J by $\{\Theta_1, \Theta_2, \ldots,\}$ and assume that the functions x_i are approximated by the first L basis functions Θ_l, $l = 1, 2, \ldots, L$:

$$x_i(t) = \sum_{l=1}^{L} c_{il}\Theta_l(t) = \mathbf{c}_i^\top \boldsymbol{\Theta}(t), \tag{5.2}$$

where $\boldsymbol{\Theta} = (\Theta_1, \ldots, \Theta_L)^\top$ and $\mathbf{c}_i = (c_{i1}, \ldots, c_{iL})^\top$. The number of basis functions L determines the tradeoff between data fidelity and smoothness. The analysis of the functional objects will be implemented through the coefficient matrix

$$\mathbf{C} = \{c_{il},\ i = 1, \ldots, n,\ l = 1, \ldots, L\}.$$

The mean, variance, and covariance functions are calculated by:

$$\begin{aligned}\bar{X}(t) &= \bar{\mathbf{c}}^\top \boldsymbol{\Theta}(t),\\ \widehat{\mathrm{Var}}(t) &= \boldsymbol{\Theta}(t)^\top \mathrm{Cov}(\mathbf{C})\boldsymbol{\Theta}(t),\\ \widehat{\mathrm{Cov}}(s,t) &= \boldsymbol{\Theta}(s)^\top \mathrm{Cov}(\mathbf{C})\boldsymbol{\Theta}(t),\end{aligned}$$

where $\bar{\mathbf{c}}_l \stackrel{\mathrm{def}}{=} \frac{1}{n}\sum_{i=1}^{n} c_{il}$, $l = 1, \ldots, L$ and $\mathrm{Cov}(\mathbf{C}) \stackrel{\mathrm{def}}{=} \frac{1}{n-1}\sum_{i=1}^{n}(\mathbf{c}_i - \bar{\mathbf{c}})(\mathbf{c}_i - \bar{\mathbf{c}})^\top$.
The scalar product in the functional space is defined by:

$$\langle x_i, x_j\rangle \stackrel{\mathrm{def}}{=} \int_J x_i(t)x_j(t)dt = \mathbf{c}_i^\top \mathbf{W}\mathbf{c}_j,$$

where

$$\mathbf{W} \stackrel{\text{def}}{=} \int_J \mathbf{\Theta}(t)\mathbf{\Theta}(t)^\top dt. \tag{5.3}$$

In practice, the coefficient matrix **C** needs to be estimated from the data set $\mathcal{X}$.

An example for a functional basis is the Fourier basis defined on J by:

$$\Theta_l(t) = \begin{cases} 1, & l = 0, \\ \sin(r\omega t), & l = 2r - 1, \\ \cos(r\omega t), & l = 2r, \end{cases}$$

where the frequency ω determines the period and the length of the interval $|J| = 2\pi/\omega$. The Fourier basis defined above can be easily transformed to the orthonormal basis, hence the scalar-product matrix in (5.3) is simply the identity matrix.

Our aim is to estimate the IV-functions for fixed $\tau = 1$ month (1M) and 2 months (2M) from the daily-specific grid of the maturities. We estimate the Fourier coefficients on the moneyness-range $\kappa \in [0.9, 1.1]$ for maturities observed on particular day i. For $\tau^* =$ 1M, 2M we calculate $\hat{\sigma}_i(\kappa, \tau^*)$ by linear interpolation of the closest observable IV string with $\tau \leq \tau^*$, $\widehat{\sigma}_i(\kappa, \tau^*_{i-})$ and $\tau \geq \tau^*$, $\widehat{\sigma}_i(\kappa, \tau^*_{i+})$:

$$\hat{\sigma}_i(\kappa, \tau^*) = \hat{\sigma}_i(\kappa, \tau^*_{i-}) \left(1 - \frac{\tau^* - \tau^*_{i-}}{\tau^*_{i+} - \tau^*_{i-}}\right) + \hat{\sigma}_i(\kappa, \tau^*_{i+}) \left(\frac{\tau^* - \tau^*_{i-}}{\tau^*_{i+} - \tau^*_{i-}}\right),$$

for i where τ^*_{i-} and τ^*_{i-} exist. In Figure 5.2 we show the situation for τ^* =1M on May 30, 2001. The blue points and the blue finely dashed curve correspond to the transactions with τ^*_- =16 days and the green points and the green dashed curve to the transactions with $\tau^*_+ = 51$ days. The solid black line is the linear interpolation at $\tau^* = 30$ days.

The choice of $L = 9$ delivers a good tradeoff between flexibility and smoothness of the strings. At this moment we exclude from our analysis those days, where this procedure cannot be performed due to the complete absence of the needed maturities, and strings with poor performance of estimated coefficients, due to the small number of contracts in a particular string or presence of strong outliers. Using this procedure we obtain 77 "functional" observations $x^{1M}_{i_1}(\kappa) \stackrel{\text{def}}{=} \hat{\sigma}_{i_1}(\kappa, 1M)$, $i_1 = 1, \ldots, 77$, for the 1M-maturity and 66 observations $x^{2M}_{i_2}(\kappa) \stackrel{\text{def}}{=} \hat{\sigma}_{i_2}(\kappa, 2M)$, $i_2 = 1, \ldots, 66$, for the 2M-maturity, as displayed in Figure 5.3.

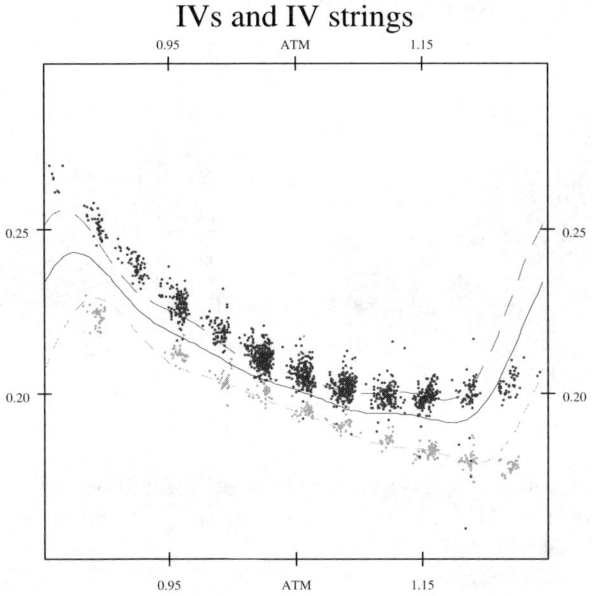

Figure 5.2: Linear interpolation of IV strings on May 30, 2001 with $L = 9$.
STFfda02.xpl

5.4 Functional Principal Components

Principal Components Analysis yields dimension reduction in the multivariate framework. The idea is to find normalized weight vectors $\gamma_m \in \mathbb{R}^p$, for which the linear transformations of a p-dimensional random vector $\mathbf{x}$, with $\mathrm{E}[\mathbf{x}] = 0$:

$$f_m = \gamma_m^\top \mathbf{x} = \langle \gamma_m, \mathbf{x} \rangle, \; m = 1, \ldots, p, \tag{5.4}$$

have maximal variance subject to:

$$\gamma_l^\top \gamma_m = \langle \gamma_l, \gamma_m \rangle = I(l = m) \text{ for } l \leq m.$$

Where I denotes the identificator function. The solution is the Jordan spectral decomposition of the covariance matrix, Härdle and Simar (2003).

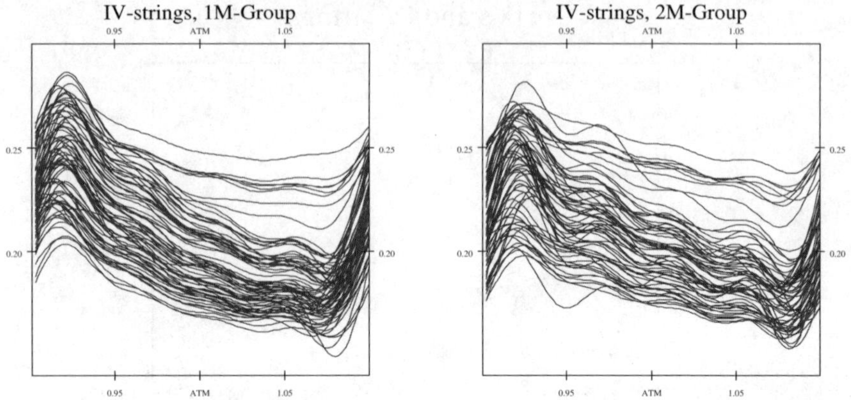

Figure 5.3: Functional observations estimated using Fourier basis with $L = 9$, $\hat{\sigma}_{i_1}(\kappa, 1M)$, $i_1 = 1, \ldots, 77$, in the left panel, $\hat{\sigma}_{i_2}(\kappa, 2M)$ $i_2 = 1, \ldots, 66$ in the right panel.

STFfda03.xpl

In the Functional Principal Components Analysis (FPCA) the dimension reduction can be achieved via the same route, i.e. by finding orthonormal weight functions $\gamma_1, \gamma_2, \ldots$, such that the variance of the linear transformation is maximal. In order to keep notation simple we assume $\mathrm{E}X(t) = 0$. The weight functions satisfy:

$$\begin{aligned} ||\gamma_m||^2 &= \int \gamma_m(t)^2 dt = 1, \\ \langle \gamma_l, \gamma_m \rangle &= \int \gamma_l(t)\gamma_m(t)dt = 0, \; l \neq m. \end{aligned}$$

The linear transformation is:

$$f_m = \langle \gamma_m, X \rangle = \int \gamma_m(t)X(t)dt,$$

and the desired weight functions solve:

$$\underset{\langle \gamma_l, \gamma_m \rangle = I(l=m), l \leq m}{\arg\max} \quad \mathrm{Var}\langle \gamma_m, X \rangle, \tag{5.5}$$

or equivalently:

$$\arg\max_{\langle\gamma_l,\gamma_m\rangle=I(l=m),l\leq m} \int\int \gamma_m(s)\mathrm{Cov}(s,t)\gamma_m(t)dsdt.$$

The solution is obtained by solving the Fredholm functional eigenequation

$$\int \mathrm{Cov}(s,t)\gamma(t)dt = \lambda\gamma(s). \tag{5.6}$$

The eigenfunctions $\gamma_1, \gamma_2, \ldots$ sorted with respect to the corresponding eigenvalues $\lambda_1 \geq \lambda_2 \geq \ldots$ solve the FPCA problem (5.5). The following link between eigenvalues and eigenfunctions holds:

$$\lambda_m = \mathrm{Var}(f_m) = \mathrm{Var}\left[\int \gamma_m(t)X(t)dt\right] = \int\int \gamma_m(s)\mathrm{Cov}(s,t)\gamma_m(t)dsdt.$$

In the sampling problem, the unknown covariance function $\mathrm{Cov}(s,t)$ needs to be replaced by the sample covariance function $\widehat{\mathrm{Cov}}(s,t)$. Dauxois, Pousse, and Romain (1982) show that the eigenfunctions and eigenvalues are consistent estimators for λ_m and γ_m and derive some asymptotic results for these estimators.

5.4.1 Basis Expansion

Suppose that the weight function γ has expansion

$$\gamma = \sum_{l=1}^{L} \mathbf{b}_l\Theta_l(t) = \boldsymbol{\Theta}^\top \mathbf{b}.$$

Using this notation we can rewrite the left hand side of eigenequation (5.6):

$$\begin{aligned}\int \mathrm{Cov}(s,t)\gamma(t)dt &= \int \boldsymbol{\Theta}(s)^\top \mathrm{Cov}(\mathbf{C})\boldsymbol{\Theta}(t)\boldsymbol{\Theta}(t)^\top \mathbf{b}dt \\ &= \boldsymbol{\Theta}^\top \mathrm{Cov}(\mathbf{C})\mathbf{W}\mathbf{b},\end{aligned}$$

so that:

$$\mathrm{Cov}(\mathbf{C})\mathbf{W}\mathbf{b} = \lambda\mathbf{b}.$$

The functional scalar product $\langle\gamma_l, \gamma_k\rangle$ corresponds to $\mathbf{b}_l^\top \mathbf{W}\mathbf{b}_k$ in the truncated basis framework, in the sense that if two functions γ_l and γ_k are orthogonal, the corresponding coefficient vectors $\mathbf{b}_l, \mathbf{b}_k$ satisfy $\mathbf{b}_l^\top \mathbf{W}\mathbf{b}_k = 0$. Matrix $\mathbf{W}$ is

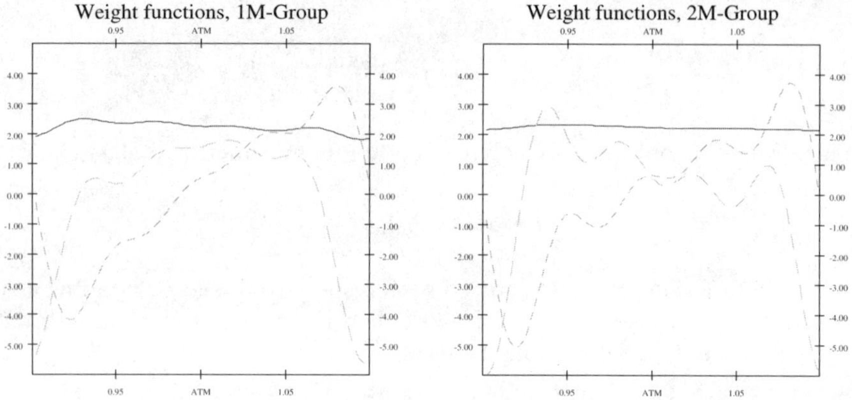

Figure 5.4: Weight functions for $1M$ and $2M$ maturity groups. Blue solid lines, $\hat{\gamma}_1^{1M}$ and $\hat{\gamma}_1^{2M}$, are the first eigenfunctions, green finely dashed lines, $\hat{\gamma}_2^{1M}$ and $\hat{\gamma}_2^{2M}$, are the second eigenfunctions, and cyan dashed lines, $\hat{\gamma}_3^{1M}$ and $\hat{\gamma}_3^{2M}$, are the third eigenfunctions.

STFfda04.xpl

symmetric by definition. Thus, defining $\mathbf{u} = \mathbf{W}^{1/2}\mathbf{b}$, one needs to solve finally a symmetric eigenvalue problem:

$$\mathbf{W}^{1/2}\mathrm{Cov}(\mathbf{C})\mathbf{W}^{1/2}\mathbf{u} = \lambda\mathbf{u},$$

and to compute the inverse transformation $\mathbf{b} = \mathbf{W}^{-1/2}\mathbf{u}$. For the orthonormal functional basis (i.e. also for the Fourier basis) $\mathbf{W} = \mathbf{I}$, i.e. the problem of FPCA is reduced to the multivariate PCA performed on the matrix $\mathbf{C}$.

Using the FPCA method on the IV-strings for 1M and 2M maturities we obtain the eigenfunctions plotted in Figure 5.4. It can be seen, that the eigenfunctions are too rough. Intuitively, this roughness is caused by the flexibility of the functional basis. In the next section we present a way of incorporating the smoothing directly into the PCA problem.

5.5 Smoothed Principal Components Analysis

As we can see in Figure 5.4, the resulting eigenfunctions are often very rough. Smoothing them could result in a more natural interpretation of the obtained weight functions. Here we apply a popular approach known as roughness penalty. The downside of this technique is that we loose orthogonality in the L^2 sense.

Assume that the underlying eigenfunctions of the covariance operator have a continuous and square-integrable second derivative. Let $\mathcal{D}\gamma = \gamma'(t)$ be the first derivative operator and define the roughness penalty by $\Psi(\gamma) = ||\mathcal{D}^2\gamma||^2$. Moreover, suppose that γ_m has square-integrable derivatives up to degree four and that the second and the third derivatives satisfy one of the following conditions:

1. $\mathcal{D}^2\gamma$, $\mathcal{D}^3\gamma$ are zero at the ends of the interval J,
2. the periodicity boundary conditions of γ,$\mathcal{D}\gamma$, $\mathcal{D}^2\gamma$, and $\mathcal{D}^3\gamma$ on J.

Then we can rewrite the roughness penalty in the following way:

$$
\begin{aligned}
||\mathcal{D}^2\gamma||^2 &= \int \mathcal{D}^2\gamma(s)\mathcal{D}^2\gamma(s)ds \\
&= \mathcal{D}\gamma(u)\mathcal{D}^2\gamma(u) - \mathcal{D}\gamma(d)\mathcal{D}^2\gamma(d) - \int \mathcal{D}\gamma(s)\mathcal{D}^3\gamma(s)ds \quad (5.7)\\
&= \gamma(u)\mathcal{D}^3\gamma(u) - \gamma(d)\mathcal{D}^3\gamma(d) - \int \gamma(s)\mathcal{D}^4\gamma(s)ds \quad (5.8)\\
&= \langle \gamma, \mathcal{D}^4\gamma \rangle, \quad (5.9)
\end{aligned}
$$

where d and u are the boundaries of the interval J and the first two elements in (5.7) and (5.8) are both zero under any of the conditions mentioned above.

Given a eigenfunction γ with norm $||\gamma||^2 = 1$, we can penalize the sample variance of the principal component by dividing it by $1 + \alpha\langle\gamma, \mathcal{D}^4\gamma\rangle$:

$$
PCAPV \stackrel{\text{def}}{=} \frac{\int\int \gamma(s)\widehat{\text{Cov}}(s,t)\gamma(t)dsdt}{\int \gamma(t)(\mathcal{I} + \alpha\mathcal{D}^4)\gamma(t)dt}, \quad (5.10)
$$

where $\mathcal{I}$ denotes the identity operator. The maximum of the penalized sample variance (PCAPV) is an eigenfunction γ corresponding to the largest eigenvalue of the generalized eigenequation:

$$
\int \widehat{\text{Cov}}(s,t)\gamma(t)dt = \lambda(\mathcal{I} + \alpha\mathcal{D}^4)\gamma(s). \quad (5.11)
$$

As already mentioned above, the resulting weight functions (eigenfunctions) are no longer orthonormal in the L^2 sense. Since the weight functions are used as smoothed estimators of principal components functions, we need to rescale them to satisfy $||\gamma_l||^2 = 1$. The weight functions γ_l can be also interpreted as orthogonal in the modified scalar product of the Sobolev type

$$(f, g) \stackrel{\text{def}}{=} \langle f, g \rangle + \alpha \langle \mathcal{D}^2 f, \mathcal{D}^2 g \rangle.$$

A more extended theoretical discussion can be found in Silverman (1991).

5.5.1 Basis Expansion

Define $\mathbf{K}$ to be a matrix whose elements are $\langle \mathcal{D}^2 \Theta_j, \mathcal{D}^2 \Theta_k \rangle$. Then the generalized eigenequation (5.11) can be transformed to:

$$\mathbf{W} \operatorname{Cov}(\mathbf{C}) \mathbf{W} \mathbf{u} = \lambda (\mathbf{W} + \alpha \mathbf{K}) \mathbf{u}. \tag{5.12}$$

Using Cholesky factorization $\mathbf{L}\mathbf{L}^\top = \mathbf{W} + \alpha \mathbf{K}$ and defining $\mathbf{S} = \mathbf{L}^{-1}$ we can rewrite (5.12) as:

$$\{\mathbf{S}\mathbf{W} \operatorname{Cov}(\mathbf{C}) \mathbf{W} \mathbf{S}^\top\}(\mathbf{L}^\top \mathbf{u}) = \lambda \mathbf{L}^\top \mathbf{u}.$$

Applying Smoothed Functional PCA (SPCA) to the IV-strings, we get the smooth-eigenfunctions plotted in Figure 5.5. We use $\alpha = 10^{-7}$, the aim is to use a rather small degree of smoothing, in order to replace the high frequency fluctuations only. Some popular methods, like cross-validation, could be employed as well, Ramsay and Silverman (1997).

The interpretation of the weight functions displayed in Figure 5.5 is as follows: The first weight function (solid blue) represents clearly the level of the volatility – weights are almost constant and positive. The second weight function (finely dashed green) changes sign near the at-the-money point, i.e. can be interpreted as the in-the-money/out-of-the-money identification factor or slope. The third (dashed cyan) weight function may play the part of the measure for a deep in-the-money or out-of-the-money factor or curvature. It can be seen that the weight functions for the 1M ($\widetilde{\gamma}_1^{1M}, \widetilde{\gamma}_2^{1M}, \widetilde{\gamma}_3^{1M}$) and 2M maturities ($\widetilde{\gamma}_1^{2M}, \widetilde{\gamma}_2^{2M}, \widetilde{\gamma}_3^{2M}$) have a similar structure. From a practical point of view it can be interesting to try to get common estimated eigenfunctions (factors in the further analysis) for both groups. In the next section, we introduce the estimation motivated by the Common Principal Component Model.

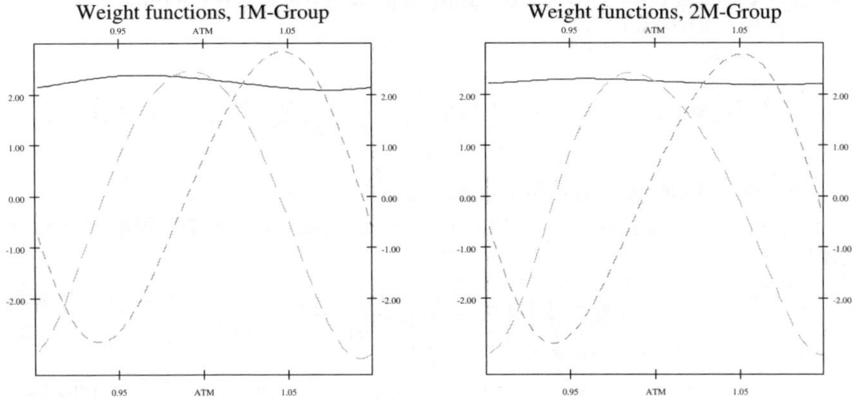

Figure 5.5: Smoothed weight functions with $\alpha = 10^{-7}$. Blue solid lines, $\hat{\gamma}_1^{1M}$ and $\hat{\gamma}_1^{2M}$, are the first eigenfunctions, green finely dashed lines, $\hat{\gamma}_2^{1M}$ and $\hat{\gamma}_2^{2M}$, are the second eigenfunctions, and cyan dashed lines, $\hat{\gamma}_3^{1M}$ and $\hat{\gamma}_3^{2M}$, are the third eigenfunctions.

STFfda05.xpl

5.6 Common Principal Components Model

The Common Principal Components model (CPC) in the multivariate setting can be motivated as the model for similarity of the covariance matrices in the k-sample problem, Flury (1988). Having k random vectors, $\mathbf{x}_{(1)}, \mathbf{x}_{(2)}, \ldots, \mathbf{x}_{(k)} \in \mathbb{R}^p$ the CPC-Model can be written as:

$$\boldsymbol{\Psi}_j \stackrel{\text{def}}{=} \text{Cov}(\mathbf{x}_{(j)}) = \boldsymbol{\Gamma}\boldsymbol{\Lambda}_{\mathbf{j}}\boldsymbol{\Gamma}^\top,$$

where $\boldsymbol{\Gamma}$ is an orthogonal matrix and $\boldsymbol{\Lambda}_j = \text{diag}(\lambda_{i1}, \ldots, \lambda_{ip})$. This means that eigenvectors are the same across samples and just the eigenvalues – variances of the principal component scores (5.4) differ.

Using the normality assumption, the sample covariance matrices $\mathbf{S}_j, j = 1, \ldots, k$, are Wishart-distributed:

$$\mathbf{S}_j \sim W_p(n_j, \boldsymbol{\Psi}_j/n_j),$$

and the CPC model can be estimated using maximum likelihood estimation with likelihood-function:

$$\mathrm{L}(\boldsymbol{\Psi}_1, \boldsymbol{\Psi}_2, \ldots, \boldsymbol{\Psi}_k) = C \prod_{j=1}^{k} \exp\left\{\mathrm{tr}\left(-\frac{n_j}{2}\boldsymbol{\Psi}_j^{-1}\mathbf{S}_j\right)\right\}(\det\boldsymbol{\Psi}_\mathbf{j})^{-n_j/2}.$$

Here C is a factor that does not depend on the parameters and n_j is the number of observations in group j. The maximization of this likelihood function is equivalent to:

$$\prod_{j=1}^{k}\left\{\frac{\det \mathrm{diag}(\boldsymbol{\Gamma}^\top\mathbf{S_j}\boldsymbol{\Gamma})}{\det(\boldsymbol{\Gamma}^\top\mathbf{S_j}\boldsymbol{\Gamma})}\right\}^{n_j}, \tag{5.13}$$

and the maximization of this criterion is performed by the so-called Flury-Gautschi(FG)-algorithm, Flury (1988).

As shown in Section 5.4, using the functional basis expansion, the FPCA and SPCA are basically implemented via the spectral decomposition of the "weighted" covariance matrix of the coefficients. In view of the minimization property of the FG algorithm, the diagonalization procedure optimizing the criterion (5.13) can be employed. However, the obtained estimates may not be maximum likelihood estimates.

Using this procedure for the IV-strings of 1M and 2M maturity we get "common" smoothed eigenfunctions. The first three common eigenfunctions ($\widetilde{\gamma}_1^c, \widetilde{\gamma}_2^c, \widetilde{\gamma}_3^c$) are displayed in Figures 5.6–5.8. The solid blue curve represents the estimated eigenfunction for the 1M maturity, the finely dashed green curve for the 2M maturity and the dashed black curve is the common eigenfunction estimated by the FG-algorithm.

Assuming that $\hat{\sigma}_i(\kappa, \tau)$ are centered for $\tau = 1M$ and $2M$ (we subtract the sample mean of corresponding group from the estimated functions), we may use the obtained weight functions in the factor model of the IV dynamics of the form:

$$\widetilde{\sigma}_i(\kappa, \tau) = \sum_{j=1}^{R} \widetilde{\gamma}_j^c(\kappa)\langle\widetilde{\gamma}_j^c(\kappa), \hat{\sigma}_i(\kappa, \tau)\rangle, \tag{5.14}$$

where $\tau \in \{1M, 2M\}$ and R is the number of factors. Thus $\widetilde{\sigma}_i$ is an alternative estimation of σ_i. This factor model can be used for simulation applications like Monte Carlo VaR. Especially the usage of Common Principal Components $\widetilde{\gamma}_j^c(\kappa)$ reduces the high-dimensional IV-surface problem to a small number of functional factors.

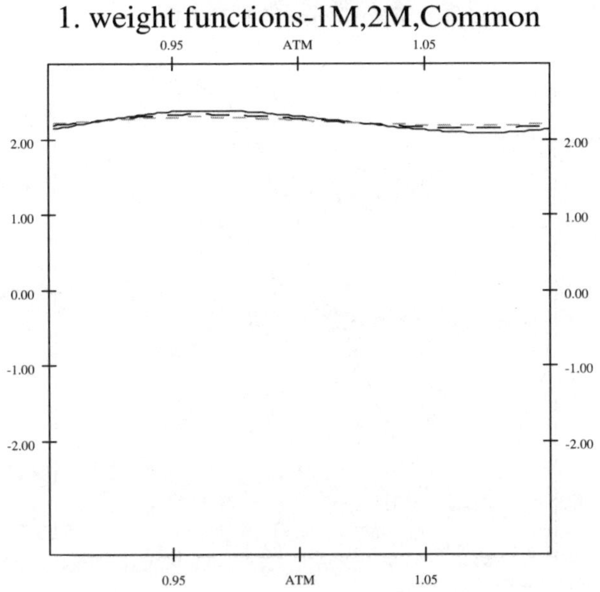

Figure 5.6: First weight functions, $\alpha = 10^{-7}$, solid blue line is the weight function of the 1M maturity group ($\hat{\gamma}_1^{1M}$), finely dashed green line of the 2M maturity group ($\hat{\gamma}_1^{2M}$), and dashed black line is the common eigenfunction ($\widetilde{\gamma}_1^c$), estimated from both groups.

In addition, an econometric approach, successfully employed by Fengler, Härdle, and Mammen (2004) can be employed. It consists of fitting an appropriate model to the time series of the estimated principal component scores, $\widetilde{f}_{ij}^c(\tau) = \langle \widetilde{\gamma}_j^c(\kappa), \hat{\sigma}_i(\kappa, \tau) \rangle$, as displayed in Figure 5.9. Note that $\hat{\sigma}_i(\kappa, \tau)$ are centered again (sample means are zero). The fitted time series model can be used for forecasting future IV functions.

There are still some open questions related to this topic. First of all, the practitioner would be interested in a good automated choice of the parameters of our method (dimension of the truncated functional basis L and smoothing parameter α). The application of the Fourier coefficients in this framework seems to be reasonable for the volatility smiles (U-shaped strings), however for the volatility smirks (typically monotonically decreasing strings) the performance

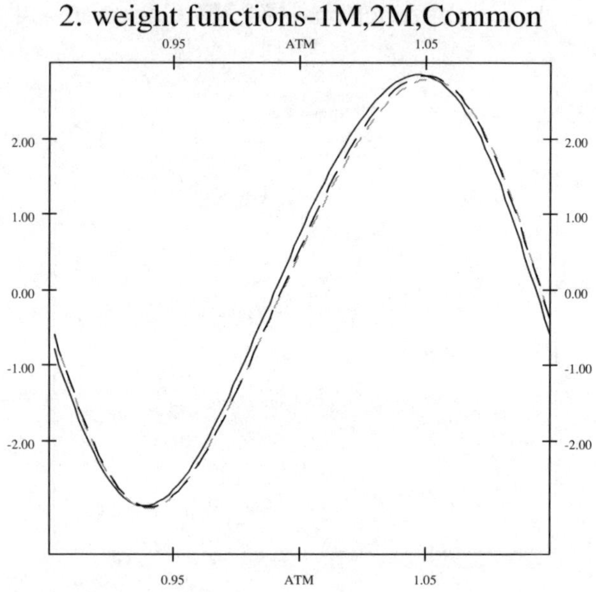

Figure 5.7: Second eigenfunctions, $\alpha = 10^{-7}$, solid blue line is the weight function of the 1M maturity group ($\hat{\gamma}_2^{1M}$), finely dashed green line of the 2M maturity group ($\hat{\gamma}_2^{2M}$), and dashed black line is the common eigenfunction ($\widetilde{\gamma}_2^{c}$), estimated from both groups.

is rather bad. In particular, the variance of our functional objects and the shape of our weight functions at the boundaries is affected. The application of regression splines in this setting seems to be promising, but it increases the number of smoothing parameters by the number and the choice of the knots – problems which are not generally easy to deal with. The next natural question, which is still open concerns the statistical properties of the technique and the testing procedure for the Functional Common PCA model. Finally, using the data for a longer time period one may also analyze the longer maturities like 3 months or 6 months.

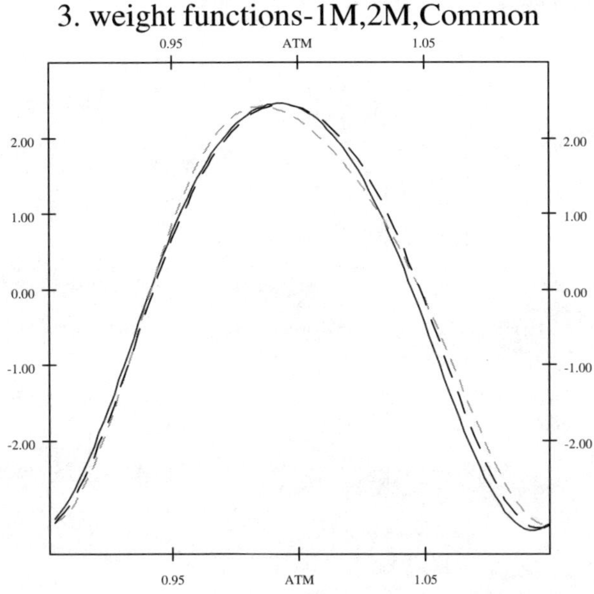

Figure 5.8: Third eigenfunctions, $\alpha = 10^{-7}$, solid blue line is the weight function of the 1M maturity group ($\hat{\gamma}_3^{1M}$), finely dashed green line of the 2M maturity group ($\hat{\gamma}_3^{2M}$), and dashed black line is the common eigenfunction ($\widetilde{\gamma}_3^c$), estimated from both groups.

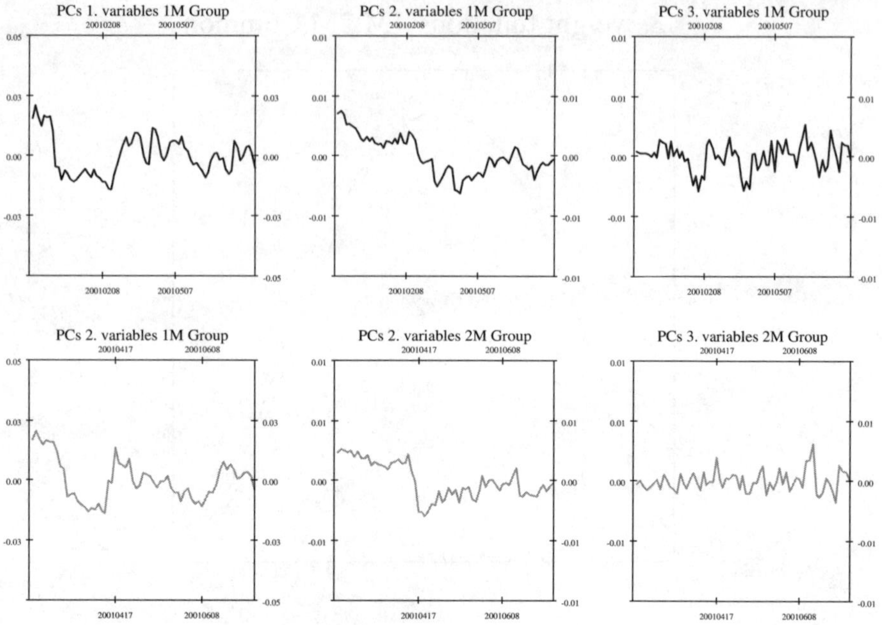

Figure 5.9: Estimated principal component scores, $\widetilde{f}^c_{i1}(1M)$, $\widetilde{f}^c_{i2}(1M)$, and $\widetilde{f}^c_{i3}(1M)$ for 1M maturity – first row, and $\widetilde{f}^c_{i1}(2M)$, $\widetilde{f}^c_{i2}(2M)$, and $\widetilde{f}^c_{i3}(2M)$ for 2M maturity – second row; $\alpha = 10^{-7}$.

Bibliography

Black, F. and Scholes, M. (1973). The pricing of options and corporate liabilities, *Journal of Political Economy*, **81**: 637:654.

Dauxois, J., Pousse, A., and Romain, Y. (1982). Asymptotic Theory for the Principal Component Analysis of a Vector Random Function: Some Applications to Statistical Inference, *Journal of Multivariate Analysis* **12**: 136-154.

Flury, B. (1988). *Common Principal Components and Related Models*, Wiley, New York.

Fengler, M., Härdle, W., and Schmidt, P. (2002). Common Factors Governing VDAX Movements and the Maximum Loss, *Journal of Financial Markets and Portfolio Management* **16(1)**: 16-29.

Fengler, M., Härdle, W., and Villa, P. (2003). The Dynamics of Implied Volatilities: A common principle components approach, *Review of Derivative Research* **6**: 179-202.

Fengler, M., Härdle, W., and Mammen, E. (2004). Implied Volatility String Dynamics, CASE Discussion Paper, http://www.case.hu-berlin.de.

Föllmer, H. and Schied A. (2002). *Stochastic Finance*, Walter de Gruyter.

Härdle, W. (1990). *Applied Nonparametric Regression*, Cambridge University Press.

Hafner, R. and Wallmeier, M. (2001). The Dynamics of DAX Implied Volatilities, *International Quarterly Journal of Finance* **1(1)**: 1-27.

Härdle, W. and Simar, L. (2003). *Applied Multivariate Statistical Analysis*, Springer-Verlag Berlin Heidelberg.

Kneip, A. and Utikal, K. (2001). Inference for Density Families Using Functional Principal Components Analysis, *Journal of the American Statistical Association* **96**: 519-531.

Ramsay, J. and Silverman, B. (1997). *Functional Data Analysis*, Springer, New York.

Rice, J. and Silverman, B. (1991). Estimating the Mean and Covariance Structure Nonparametrically when the Data are Curves, *Journal of Royal Statistical Society, Series B* **53**: 233-243.

Silverman, B. (1996). Smoothed Functional Principal Components Analysis by Choice of Norm, *Annals of Statistics* **24**: 1-24.

6 Implied Trinomial Trees

Pavel Čížek and Karel Komorád

Options are financial derivatives that, conditional on the price of an underlying asset, constitute a right to transfer the ownership of this underlying. More specifically, a *European call* and *put options* give their owner the right to buy and sell, respectively, at a fixed strike price at a given date. Options are important financial instruments used for hedging since they can be included into a portfolio to reduce risk. Corporate securities (e.g., bonds or stocks) may include option features as well. Last, but not least, some new financing techniques, such as contingent value rights, are straightforward applications of options. Thus, option pricing has become one of the basic techniques in finance.

The boom in research on the use of options started after Black and Scholes (1973) published an option-pricing formula based on geometric Brownian motion. Option prices computed by the Black-Scholes formula and the market prices of options exhibit a discrepancy though. Whereas the volatility of market option prices varies with the price (or moneyness) – the dependency referred to as the *volatility smile*, the Black-Scholes model is based on the assumption of a constant volatility. Therefore, to model option prices consistent with the market many new approaches were proposed. Probably the most commonly used and rather intuitive procedure for option pricing is based on binomial trees, which represent a discrete form of the Black-Scholes model. To fit the market data, Derman and Kani (1994) proposed an extension of binomial trees: the so-called implied binomial trees, which are able to model the market volatility smile.

Implied trinomial trees (ITTs) present an analogous extension of trinomial trees proposed by Derman, Kani, and Chriss (1996). Like their binomial counterparts, they can fit the market volatility smile and actually converge to the same continuous limit as binomial trees. In addition, they allow for a free choice of the underlying prices at each node of a tree, the so-called state space.

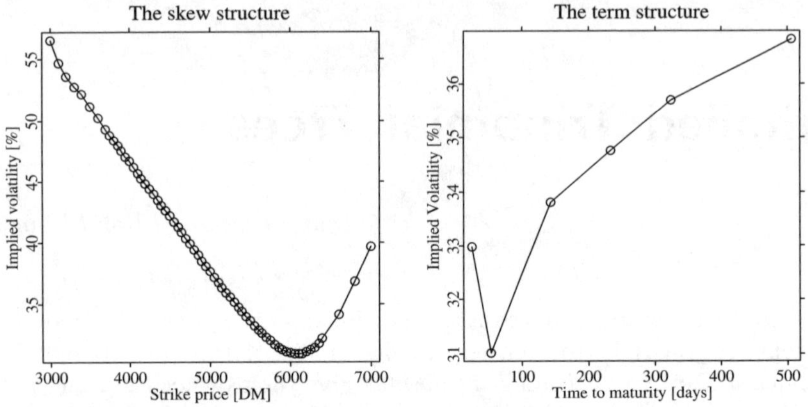

Figure 6.1: Implied volatilities of DAX put options on January 29, 1999.

This feature of ITTs allows to improve the fit of the volatility smile under some circumstances such as inconsistent, arbitrage-violating, or other market prices leading to implausible or degenerated probability distributions in binomial trees. We introduce ITTs in several steps. We first review main concepts regarding option pricing (Section 6.1) and implied models (Section 6.2). Later, we discuss the construction of ITTs (Section 6.3) and provide some illustrative examples (Section 6.4).

6.1 Option Pricing

The option-pricing model by Black and Scholes (1973) is based on the assumptions that the underlying asset follows a geometric Brownian motion with a constant volatility σ:

$$\frac{dS_t}{S_t} = \mu dt + \sigma dW_t, \tag{6.1}$$

where S_t denotes the underlying-price process, μ is the expected return, and W_t stands for the standard Wiener process. As a consequence, the distribution of S_t is lognormal. More importantly, the volatility σ is the only parameter of the Black-Scholes formula which is not explicitly observable on the market. Thus,

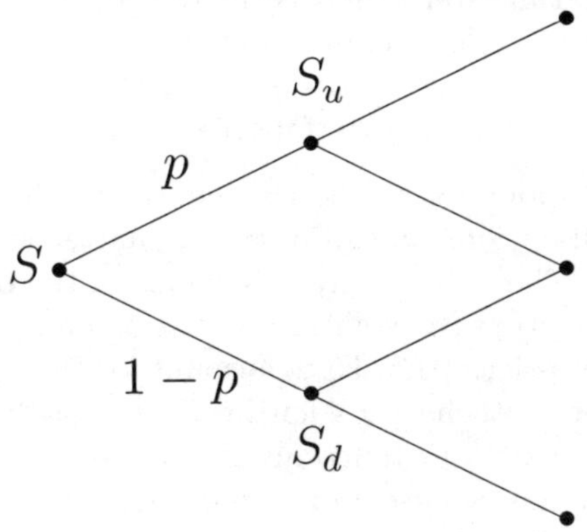

Figure 6.2: Two levels of a CRR binomial tree.

we infer on σ by matching the observed option prices. A solution σ_I, "implied" by options prices, is called the *implied volatility* (or Black-Scholes equivalent). In general, implied volatilities vary both with respect to the exercise price (the skew structure) and expiration time (the term structure). Both dependencies are illustrated in Figure 6.1, with the first one representing the volatility smile. Let us add that the implied volatility of an option is the market's estimate of the average future underlying volatility during the life of that option. We refer to the market's estimate of an underlying volatility at a particular time and price point as the *local volatility*.

Binomial trees, as a discretization of the Black-Scholes model, can be constructed in several alternative ways. Here we recall the classic Cox, Ross, and Rubinstein's (1979) scheme (CRR), which has a constant logarithmic spacing between nodes on the same level (this spacing represents the future price volatility). A standard CRR tree is depicted in Figure 6.2. Starting at a node S, the price of an underlying asset can either increase to S_u with probability p or decrease to S_d with probability $1-p$:

$$S_u = Se^{\sigma\sqrt{\Delta t}}, \tag{6.2}$$

$$S_d = Se^{-\sigma\sqrt{\Delta t}}, \tag{6.3}$$

$$p = \frac{F - S_d}{S_u - S_d}, \tag{6.4}$$

where Δt refers to the time step and σ is the (constant) volatility. The forward price $F = e^{r\Delta t}S$ in the node S is determined by the the continuous interest rate r (for the sake of simplicity, we assume that the dividend yield equals zero; see Cox, Ross, and Rubinstein, 1979, for treatment of dividends).

A binomial tree corresponding to the risk-neutral underlying evaluation process is the same for all options on this asset, no matter what the strike price or time to expiration is. There are many extensions of the original Black-Scholes approach that try to capture the volatility variation and to price options consistently with the market prices (that is, to account for the volatility smile). Some extensions incorporate a stochastic volatility factor or discontinuous jumps in the underlying price; see for instance Franke, Härdle, and Hafner (2004) and Chapters 5 and 7. In the next section, we discuss an extension of the Black-Scholes model developed by Derman and Kani (1994) – the implied trees.

6.2 Trees and Implied Trees

While the Black-Scholes model assumes that an underlying asset follows a geometric Brownian motion (6.1) with a constant volatility, more complex models assume that the underlying follows a process with a price- and time-varying volatility $\sigma(S,t)$. See Dupire (1994) and Fengler, Härdle, and Villa (2003) for details and related evidence. Such a process can be expressed by the following stochastic differential equation:

$$\frac{dS_t}{S_t} = \mu dt + \sigma(S,t) dW_t. \tag{6.5}$$

This approach ensures that the valuation of an option remains preference-free, that is, all uncertainty is in the spot price, and thus, we can hedge options using the underlying.

Derman and Kani (1994) show that it is possible to determine $\sigma(S,t)$ directly from the market prices of liquidly traded options. Further, they use this volatility $\sigma(S,t)$ to construct an implied binomial tree (IBT), which is a natural discrete representation of a non-lognormal evolution process of the underlying prices. In general, we can use – instead of an IBT – any (higher-order) multinomial tree for the discretization of process (6.5). Nevertheless, as the time step tends towards zero, all of them converge to the same continuous process (Hull and White, 1990). Thus, IBTs are among all implied multinomial trees minimal in the sense that they have only one degree of freedom – the arbitrary

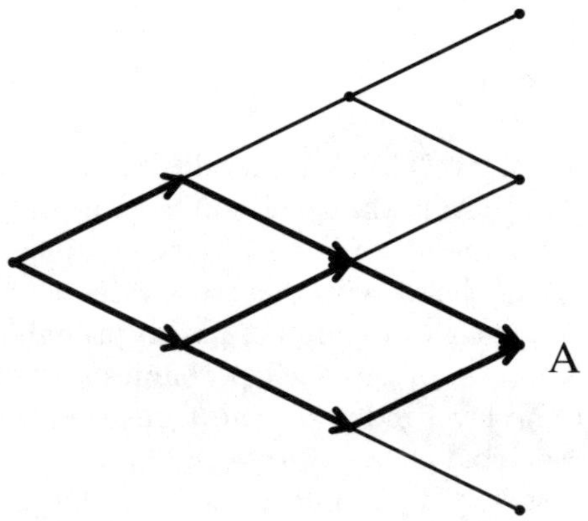

Figure 6.3: Computing the Arrow-Debreu price in a binomial tree. The bold lines with arrows depict all (three) possible path from the root of the tree to point A.

choice of the central node at each level of the tree. Although one may feel now that binomial trees are sufficient, some higher-order trees could be more useful because they allow for a more flexible discretization in the sense that transition probabilities and probability distributions can vary as smoothly as possible across a tree. This is especially important when the market option prices are inaccurate because of inefficiency, market frictions, and so on.

At the end of this section, let us to recall the concept of Arrow-Debreu prices, which is closely related to multinomial trees and becomes very useful in subsequent derivations (Section 6.3). Let (n, i) denote the ith (highest) node in the nth time level of a tree. The Arrow-Debreu price $\lambda_{n,i}$ at node (n, i) of a tree is computed as the sum of the product of the risklessly discounted transition probabilities over all paths starting in the root of the tree and leading to node (n, i). Hence, the Arrow-Debreu price of the root is equal to one and the Arrow-Debreu prices at the final level of a (multinomial) tree form a discrete approximation of the state price density. Notice that these prices are discounted, and thus, the risk-neutral probability corresponding to each node (at the final level) should be calculated as the product of the Arrow-Debreu price and the capitalizing factor e^{rT}.

6.3 Implied Trinomial Trees

6.3.1 Basic Insight

A trinomial tree with N levels is a set of nodes $s_{n,i}$ (representing the underlying price), where $n = 1, \ldots, N$ is the level number and $i = 1, \ldots, 2n-1$ indexes nodes within a level. Being at a node $s_{n,i}$, one can move to one of three nodes (see Figure 6.4a): (i) to the upper node with value $s_{n+1,i}$ with probability p_i; (ii) to the lower node with value $s_{n+1,i+2}$ with probability q_i; and (iii) to the middle node with value $s_{n+1,i+1}$ with probability $1 - p_i - q_i$. For the sake of brevity, we omit the level index n from transition probabilities unless they refer to a specific level; that is, we write p_i and q_i instead of $p_{n,i}$ and $q_{n,i}$ unless the level has to be specified. Similarly, let us denote the nodes in the new level with capital letters: $S_i(=s_{n+1,i})$, $S_{i+1}(=s_{n+1,i+1})$ and $S_{i+2}(=s_{n+1,i+2})$, respectively (see Figure 6.4b).

Starting from a node $s_{n,i}$ at time t_n, there are five unknown parameters: two transition probabilities p_i and q_i and three prices S_i, S_{i+1}, and S_{i+2} at new nodes. To determine them, we need to introduce the notation and main requirements a tree should satisfy. First, let F_i denote the known forward price of the spot price $s_{n,i}$ and $\lambda_{n,i}$ the known Arrow-Debreu price at node (n, i). The Arrow-Debreu prices for a trinomial tree can be obtained by the following iterative formulas:

$$\lambda_{1,1} = 1, \tag{6.6}$$

$$\lambda_{n+1,1} = e^{-r\Delta t}\lambda_{n,1}p_1, \tag{6.7}$$

$$\lambda_{n+1,2} = e^{-r\Delta t}\{\lambda_{n,1}(1-p_1-q_1) + \lambda_{n,2}p_2\}, \tag{6.8}$$

$$\lambda_{n+1,i+1} = e^{-r\Delta t}\{\lambda_{n,i-1}q_{i-1} + \lambda_{n,i}(1-p_i-q_i) + \lambda_{n,i+1}p_{i+1}\}, \tag{6.9}$$

$$\lambda_{n+1,2n} = e^{-r\Delta t}\{\lambda_{n,2n-1}(1-p_{2n-1}-q_{2n-1}) + \lambda_{n,2n-2}q_{2n-2}\}, \tag{6.10}$$

$$\lambda_{n+1,2n+1} = e^{-r\Delta t}\lambda_{n,2n-1}q_{2n-1}. \tag{6.11}$$

An implied tree provides a discrete representation of the evolution process of underlying prices. To capture and model the underlying price correctly, we desire that an implied tree:

1. reproduces correctly the volatility smile,
2. is risk-neutral,
3. uses transition probabilities from interval $(0, 1)$.

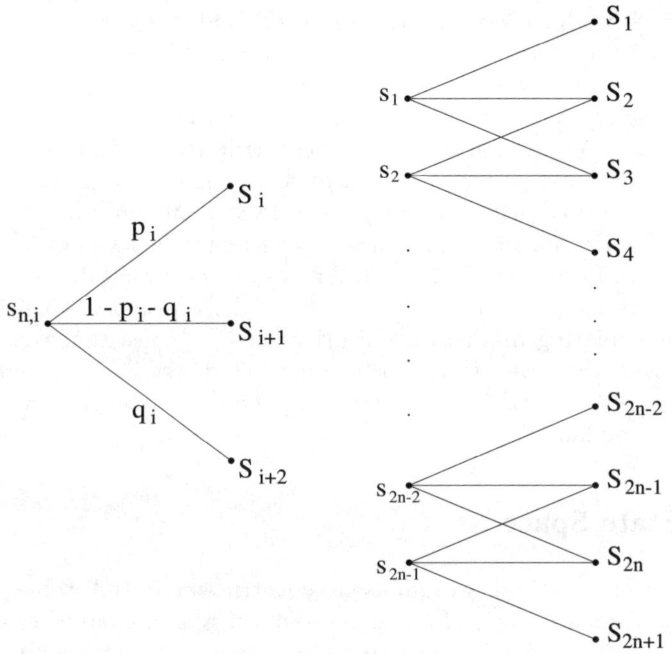

Figure 6.4: Nodes in a trinomial tree. *Left panel:* a single node with its branches. *Right panel:* the nodes of two consecutive levels $n-1$ and n.

To fulfill the risk-neutrality condition, the expected value of the underlying price $s_{n+1,i}$ in the following time period t_{n+1} has to equal its known forward price:

$$\mathrm{E}s_{n+1,i} = p_i S_i + (1 - p_i - q_i) S_{i+1} + q_i S_{i+2} = F_i = e^{r\Delta t} s_{n,i}, \tag{6.12}$$

where r denotes the continuous interest rate and Δt is the time step from t_n to t_{n+1}. Additionally, one can specify such a condition also for the second moments of $s_{n,i}$ and F_i. Hence, one obtains a second constraint on the node prices and transition probabilities:

$$p_i(S_i - F_i)^2 + (1 - p_i - q_i)(S_{i+1} - F_i)^2 + q_i(S_{i+2} - F_i)^2 = F_i^2 \sigma_i^2 \Delta t + \mathcal{O}(\Delta t), \tag{6.13}$$

where σ_i is the stock or index price volatility during the time period.

Consequently, we have two constraints (6.12) and (6.13) for five unknown parameters, and therefore, there is no unique implied trinomial tree. On the other hand, all trees satisfying these constraints are equivalent in the sense that as the time spacing Δt tends to zero, all these trees converge to the same continous process. A common method for constructing an ITT is to choose first freely the underlying prices and then to solve equations (6.12) and (6.13) for the transition probabilities p_i and q_i. Afterwards one only has to ensure that these probabilities do not violate the above mentioned Condition 3. Apparently, using an ITT instead of an IBT gives us additional degrees of freedom. This allows us to better fit the volatility smile, especially when inconsistent or arbitrage-violating market option prices make a consistent tree impossible. Note, however, that even though the constructed tree is consistent, other difficulties can arise when its local volatility and probability distributions are jagged and "implausible."

6.3.2 State Space

There are several methods we can use to construct an initial state space. Let us first discuss a construction of a constant-volatility trinomial tree, which forms a base for an implied trinomial tree. As already mentioned, binomial and trinomial discretization of the constant-volatility Black-Scholes model have the same continous limit, and therefore, are equivalent. Hence, we can start from a constant-volatility CRR binomial tree and then combine two steps of this tree into a single step of a new trinomial tree. This is illustrated in Figure 6.5, where thin lines correspond to the original binomial tree and the thick lines to the constructed trinomial tree.

Consequently, using formulas (6.2) and (6.3), we can derive the following expressions for the nodes of the constructed trinomial tree:

$$S_i = s_{n+1,i} = s_{n,i}\, e^{\sigma\sqrt{2\Delta t}}, \tag{6.14}$$

$$S_{i+1} = s_{n+1,i+1} = s_{n,i}, \tag{6.15}$$

$$S_{i+2} = s_{n+1,i+2} = s_{n,i}\, e^{-\sigma\sqrt{2\Delta t}}, \tag{6.16}$$

where σ is a constant volatility (e.g., an estimate of the at-the-money volatility at maturity T). Next, summing the transition probabilities in the binomial tree given in (6.4), we can also derive the up and down transition probabilities in

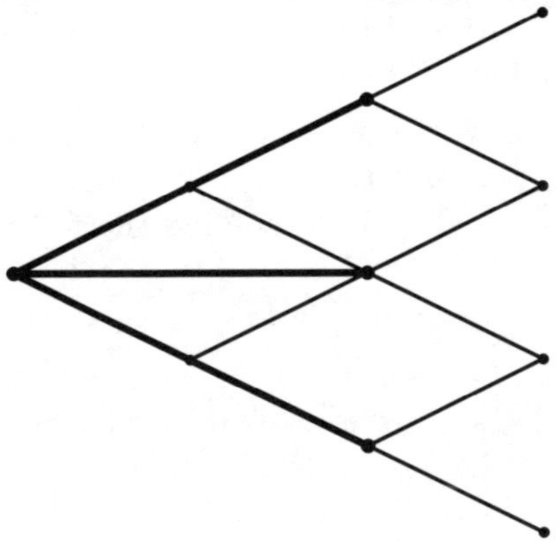

Figure 6.5: Constructing a constant-volatility trinomial tree (thick lines) by combining two steps of a CRR binomial tree (thin lines).

the trinomial tree (the "middle" transition probability is equal to $1 - p_i - q_i$):

$$p_i = \left(\frac{e^{r\Delta t/2} - e^{-\sigma\sqrt{\Delta t/2}}}{e^{\sigma\sqrt{\Delta t/2}} - e^{-\sigma\sqrt{\Delta t/2}}} \right)^2,$$

$$q_i = \left(\frac{e^{\sigma\sqrt{\Delta t/2}} - e^{r\Delta t/2}}{e^{\sigma\sqrt{\Delta t/2}} - e^{-\sigma\sqrt{\Delta t/2}}} \right)^2.$$

Note that there are more methods for building a constant-volatility trinomial tree such as combining two steps of a Jarrow and Rudd's (1983) binomial tree; see Derman, Kani, and Chriss (1996) for more details.

When the implied volatility varies only slowly with strike and expiration, the regular state space with a uniform mesh size, as described above, is adequate for constructing ITT models. On the other hand, if the volatility varies significantly with strike or time to maturity, we should choose a state space reflecting these properties. Assuming that the volatility is separable in time and stock price, $\sigma(S,t) = \sigma(S)\sigma(t)$, an ITT state space with a proper skew and term structure can be constructed in four steps.

First, we build a regular trinomial lattice with a constant time spacing Δt and a constant price spacing ΔS as described above. Additionally, we assume that all interest rates and dividends are equal to zero.

Second, we modify Δt at different time points. Let us denote the original equally spaced time points $t_0 = 0, t_1, \ldots, t_n = T$. We can then find the unknown scaled times $\tilde{t}_0 = 0, \tilde{t}_1, \ldots, \tilde{t}_n = T$ by solving the following set of non-linear equations:

$$\tilde{t}_k \sum_{i=1}^{n-1} \frac{1}{\sigma^2(\tilde{t}_i)} + \tilde{t}_k \frac{1}{\sigma^2(T)} = T \sum_{i=1}^{k} \frac{1}{\sigma^2(\tilde{t}_i)}, \qquad k = 1, \ldots, n-1. \tag{6.17}$$

Next, we change ΔS at different levels. Denoting by $S_1, \ldots, S_{2n+1}$ the original (known) underlying prices, we solve for rescaled underlying prices $\tilde{S}_1, \ldots, \tilde{S}_{2n+1}$ using

$$\frac{\tilde{S}_k}{\tilde{S}_{k-1}} = \exp\left\{ \frac{c}{\sigma(S_k)} \ln \frac{S_k}{S_{k-1}} \right\}, \qquad k = 2, \ldots, 2n+1, \tag{6.18}$$

where c is a constant. It is recommended to set c to an estimate of the local volatility. Since there are $2n$ equations for $2n+1$ unknown parameters, an additional equation is needed. Here we always suppose that the new central node equals the original central node: $\tilde{S}_{n+1} = S_{n+1}$. See Derman, Kani, and Chriss (1996) for a more elaborate explanation of the theory behind equations (6.17) and (6.18).

Finally, one can increase all node prices by a sufficiently large growth factor, which removes forward prices violations, see Section 6.3.4. Multiplying all zero-rate node prices at time $\tilde{t}_i$ by $e^{r\tilde{t}_i}$ should be always sufficient.

6.3.3 Transition Probabilities

Once the state space of an ITT is fixed, we can compute the transition probabilities for all nodes (n, i) at each tree level n. Let $C(K, t_{n+1})$ and $P(K, t_{n+1})$ denote today's price of a standard European call and put option, respectively, struck at K and expiring at t_{n+1}. These values can be obtained by interpolating the smile surface at various strike and time points. The values of these options given by the trinomial tree are the discounted expectations of the pay-off functions: $\max(S_j - K, 0) = (S_j - K)^+$ for the call option and $\max(K - S_j, 0)$ for the put option at the node $(n+1, j)$. The expectation is taken with respect to the probabilities of reaching each node, that is, with respect to transition probabilities:

$$C(K, t_{n+1}) = e^{-r\Delta t} \sum_j \{p_j \lambda_{n,j} + (1 - p_{j-1} - q_{j-1})\lambda_{n,j-1} + q_{j-2}\lambda_{n,j-2}\} (S_j - K)^+, \tag{6.19}$$

$$P(K, t_{n+1}) = e^{-r\Delta t} \sum_j \{p_j \lambda_{n,j} + (1 - p_{j-1} - q_{j-1})\lambda_{n,j-1} + q_{j-2}\lambda_{n,j-2}\} (K - S_j)^+. \tag{6.20}$$

If we set the strike price K to S_{i+1} (the stock price at node $(n+1, i+1)$), rearrange the terms in the sum, and use equation (6.12), we can express the transition probabilities p_i and q_i for all nodes above the central node from formula (6.19):

$$p_i = \frac{e^{r\Delta t} C(S_{i+1}, t_{n+1}) - \sum_{j=1}^{i-1} \lambda_{n+1,j}(F_j - S_{i+1})}{\lambda_{n+1,i}(S_i - S_{i+1})}, \tag{6.21}$$

$$q_i = \frac{F_i - p_i(S_i - S_{i+1}) - S_{i+1}}{S_{i+2} - S_{i+1}}. \tag{6.22}$$

Similarly, we compute from formula (6.20) the transition probabilities for all nodes below (and including) the center node $(n+1, n)$ at time t_n:

$$q_i = \frac{e^{r\Delta t} P(S_{i+1}, t_{n+1}) - \sum_{j=i+1}^{2n-1} \lambda_{n+1,j}(S_{i+1} - F_j)}{\lambda_{n+1,i}(S_{i+1} - S_{i+2})}, \tag{6.23}$$

$$p_i = \frac{F_i - q_i(S_{i+2} - S_{i+1}) - S_{i+1}}{S_i - S_{i+1}}. \tag{6.24}$$

A detailed derivation of these formulas can be found in Komorád (2002). Finally, the implied local volatilities are approximated from equation (6.13):

$$\sigma_i^2 \approx \frac{p_i(S_i - F_i)^2 + (1 - p_i - q_i)(S_{i+1} - F_i)^2 + q_i(S_{i+2} - F_i)^2}{F_i^2 \Delta t}. \tag{6.25}$$

6.3.4 Possible Pitfalls

Formulas (6.21)–(6.24) can unfortunately result in transition probabilities which are negative or greater than one. This is inconsistent with rational option prices

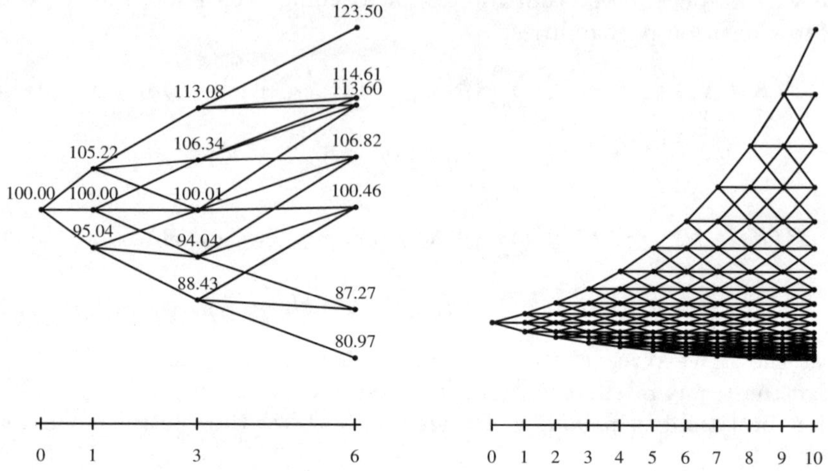

Figure 6.6: Two kinds of the forward price violation. *Left panel:* forward price outside the range of its daughter nodes. *Right panel:* sharp increase in option prices leading to an extreme local volatility.

and allows arbitrage. We actually have to face two forms of this problem, see Figure 6.6 for examples of such trees. First, we have to check that no forward price $F_{n,i}$ at node (n, i) falls outside the range of its daughter nodes at the level $n+1$: $F_{n,i} \in (s_{n+1,i+2}, s_{n+1,i})$. This inconsistency is not difficult to overcome since we are free to choose the state space. Thus, we can overwrite the nodes causing this problem.

Second, extremely small or large values of option prices, which would imply an extreme value of local volatility, can also result in probabilities that are negative or larger than one. In such a case, we have to overwrite the option prices which led to the unacceptable probabilities. Fortunately, the transition probabilities can be always corrected providing that the corresponding state space does not violate the forward price condition $F_{n,i} \in (s_{n+1,i+2}, s_{n+1,i})$. Derman, Kani, and Chriss (1996) proposed to reduce the troublesome nodes to binomial ones or to set

$$p_i = \frac{1}{2}\left(\frac{F_i - S_{i+1}}{S_i - S_{i+1}} + \frac{F_i - S_{i+2}}{S_i - S_{i+2}}\right), \quad q_i = \frac{1}{2}\left(\frac{S_i - F_i}{S_i - S_{i+2}}\right), \tag{6.26}$$

for $F_i \in (S_{i+1}, S_i)$ and

$$p_i = \frac{1}{2}\left(\frac{F_i - S_{i+2}}{S_i - S_{i+2}}\right), \quad q_i = \frac{1}{2}\left(\frac{S_{i+1} - F_i}{S_{i+1} - S_{i+2}} + \frac{S_i - F_i}{S_i - S_{i+2}}\right), \tag{6.27}$$

for $F_i \in (S_{i+2}, S_{i+1})$. In both cases, the "middle" transition probability is equal to $1 - p_i - q_i$.

6.4 Examples

To illustrate the construction of an implied trinomial tree and its use, we consider here ITTs for two artificial implied-volatility functions and an implied-volatility function constructed from real data.

6.4.1 Pre-specified Implied Volatility

Let us consider a case where the volatility varies only slowly with respect to the strike price and time to expiration (maturity). Assume that the current index level is 100 points, the annual riskless interest rate is $r = 12\%$, and the dividend yield equals $\delta = 4\%$. The annualized Black-Scholes implied volatility is assumed to be $\sigma = 11\%$, and additionally, it increases (decreases) linearly by 10 basis points (i.e., 0.1%) with every 10 unit drop (rise) in the strike price K; that is, $\sigma_I = 0.11 - \Delta K * 0.001$. To keep the example simple, we consider three one-year steps.

First, we construct the state space: a constant-volatility trinomial tree as described in Section 6.3.2. The first node at time $t_0 = 0$, labeled A in Figure 6.7, has the value of $s_A = 100$, today's spot price. The next three nodes at time t_1, are computed from equations (6.14)–(6.16) and take values $S_1 = 116.83$, $S_2 = 100.00$, and $S_3 = 85.59$, respectively. In order to determine the transition probabilities, we need to know the price $P(S_2, t_1)$ of a put option struck at $S_2 = 100$ and expiring one year from now. Since the implied volatility of this option is 11%, we calculate its price using a constant-volatility trinomial tree with the same state space and find it to be 0.987 index points. Further, the forward price corresponding to node A is $F_A = Se^{(r^* - \delta^*)\Delta t} = 107.69$, where $r^* = \log(1+r)$ denotes the continuous interest rate and $\delta^* = \log(1+\delta)$ the continuous dividend rate. Hence, the transition probability of a down movement

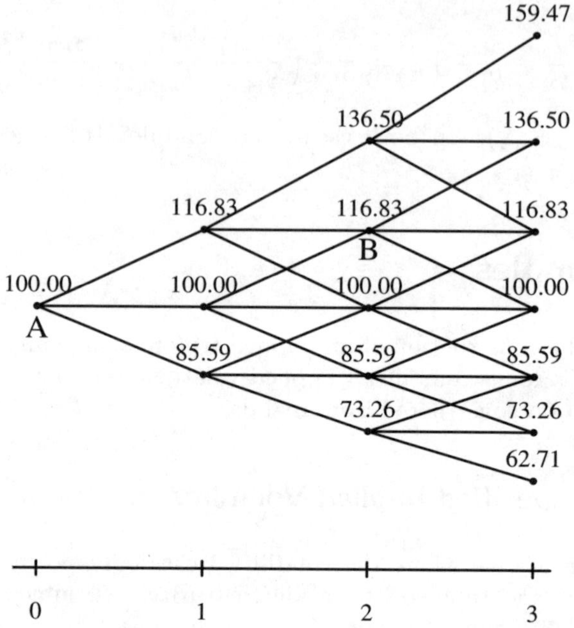

Figure 6.7: The state space of a trinomial tree with constant volatility $\sigma = 11\%$. Nodes A and B are reference points for which we demonstrate constructing of an ITT and estimating of the implied local volatility.

STFitt01.xpl

computed from equation (6.23) is

$$q_A = \frac{e^{\log(1+0.12)\cdot 1} 0.987 - \Sigma}{1 \cdot (100.00 - 85.59)} = 0.077,$$

where the summation term Σ in the numerator is zero because there are no nodes with price lower than S_3 at time t_1. Similarly, the transition probability of an upward movement p_A computed from equation (6.24) is

$$p_A = \frac{107.69 + 0.077 \cdot (100.00 - 85.59) - 100}{116.83 - 100.00} = 0.523.$$

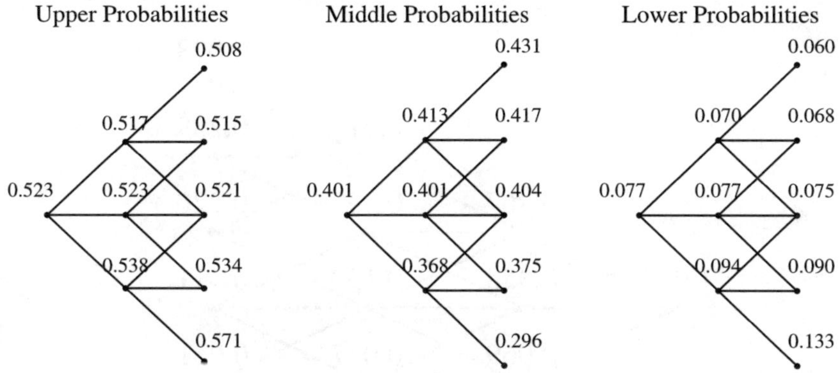

Figure 6.8: Transition probabilities for $\sigma_I = 0.11 - \Delta K \cdot 0.001$.

STFitt02.xpl

Finally, the middle transition probability equals $1 - p_A - q_A = 0.4$. As one can see from equations (6.6)–(6.11), the Arrow-Debreu prices turn out to be just discounted transition probabilities: $\lambda_{1,1} = e^{-\log(1+0.12)\cdot 1} \cdot 0.523 = 0.467$, $\lambda_{1,2} = 0.358$, and $\lambda_{1,3} = 0.069$. Finally, we can estimate the value of the implied local volatility at node A from equation (6.25), obtaining $\sigma_A = 9.5\%$.

Let us demonstrate the computation of one further node. Starting from node B in year $t_2 = 2$ of Figure 6.7, the index level at this node is $s_B = 116.83$ and its forward price one year later is $F_B = e^{(r^*-\delta^*)\cdot 1} \cdot 116.83 = 125.82$. From this node, the underlying can move to one of three future nodes at time $t_3 = 3$, with prices $s_{3,2} = 136.50$, $s_{3,3} = 116.83$, and $s_{3,4} = 100.00$. The value of a call option struck at 116.83 and expiring at time $t_3 = 3$ is $C(s_{3,3}, t_3) = 8.87$, corresponding to the implied volatility of 10.83% interpolated from the smile. The Arrow-Debreu price computed from equation (6.8) is

$$\lambda_{2,2} = e^{-\log(1+0.12)\cdot 1}\{0.467 \cdot (1 - 0.517 - 0.070) + 0.358 \cdot 0.523\} = 0.339.$$

The numerical values used here are already known from the previous level at time t_1. Now, using equations (6.21) and (6.22) we can find the transition

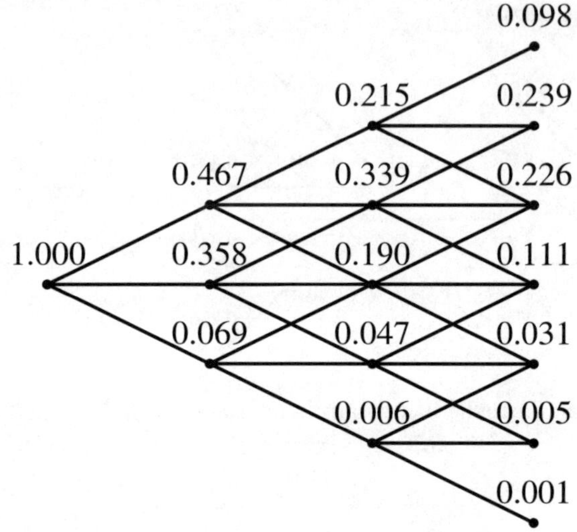

Figure 6.9: Arrow-Debreu prices for $\sigma_I = 0.11 - \Delta K \cdot 0.001$.

STFitt03.xpl

probabilities:

$$p_{2,2} = \frac{e^{\log(1+0.12)\cdot 1} \cdot 8.87 - \Sigma}{0.339 \cdot (136.50 - 116.83)} = 0.515,$$

$$q_{2,2} = \frac{125.82 - 0.515 \cdot (136.50 - 116.83) - 116.83}{100 - 116.83} = 0.068,$$

where Σ contributes only one term $0.215 \cdot (147 - 116.83)$, that is, there is one single node above S_B whose forward price is equal to 147. Finally, employing (6.25) again, we find that the implied local volatility at this node is $\sigma_B = 9.3\%$.

The complete trees of transition probabilities, Arrow-Debreu prices, and local volatilities for this example are shown in Figures 6.8–6.10.

As already mentioned in Section 6.3.4, the transition probabilities may fall out of the interval $(0, 1)$. For example, let us slightly modify our previous example and assume that the Black-Scholes volatility increases (decreases) linearly 0.5

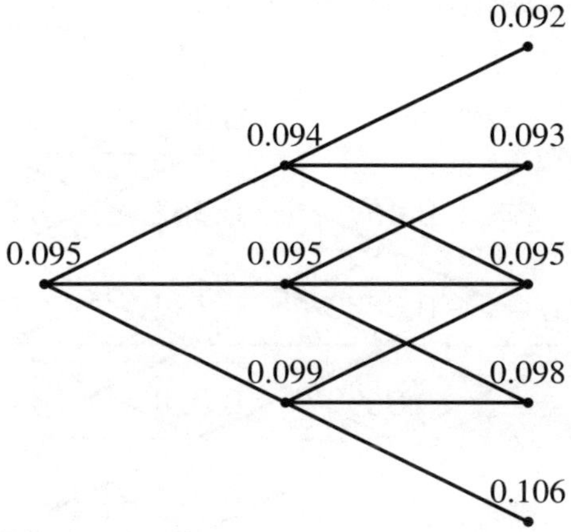

Figure 6.10: Implied local volatilities for $\sigma_I = 0.11 - \Delta K \cdot 0.001$.
STFitt04.xpl

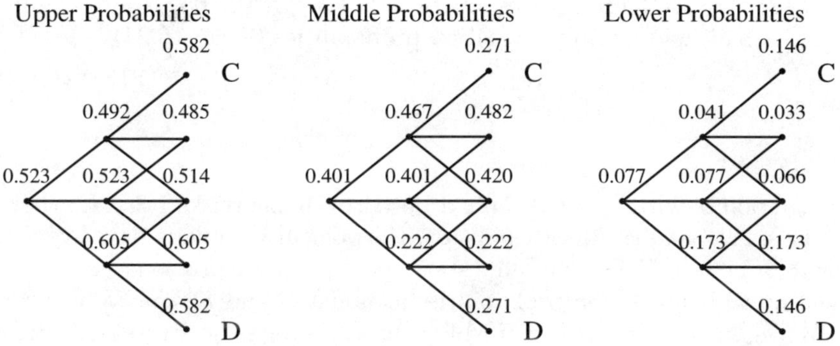

Figure 6.11: Transition probabilities for $\sigma_I = 0.11 - \Delta K \cdot 0.005$. Nodes C and D had inadmissible transition probabilities (6.21)–(6.24).
STFitt05.xpl

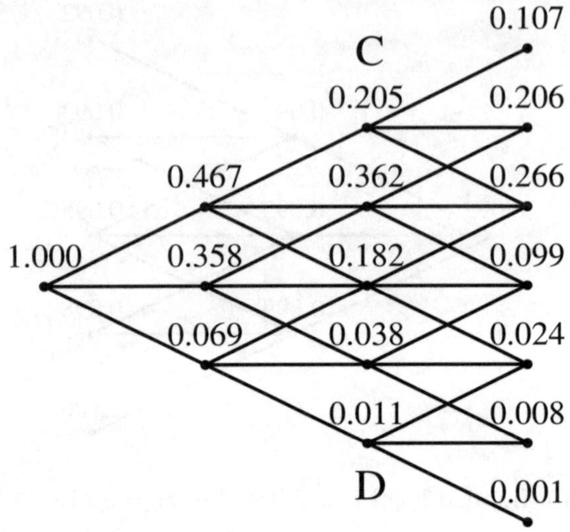

Figure 6.12: Arrow-Debreu prices for $\sigma_I = 0.11 - \Delta K \cdot 0.005$. Nodes C and D had inadmissible transition probabilities (6.21)–(6.24).

STFitt06.xpl

percentage points with every 10 unit drop (rise) in the strike price K; that is, $\sigma_I = 0.11 - \Delta K \cdot 0.005$. In other words, the volatility smile is now five times steeper than before. Using the same state space as in the previous example, we find inadmissable transition probabilities at nodes C and D, see Figures 6.11–6.13. To overwrite them with plausible values, we used the strategy described by (6.26) and (6.27) and obtained reasonable results in the sense of the three conditions stated on page 140.

6.4.2 German Stock Index

Following the artificial examples, let us now demonstrate the ITT modeling for a real data set, which consists of strike prices for DAX options with maturities from two weeks to two months on January 4, 1999. Given such data, we can

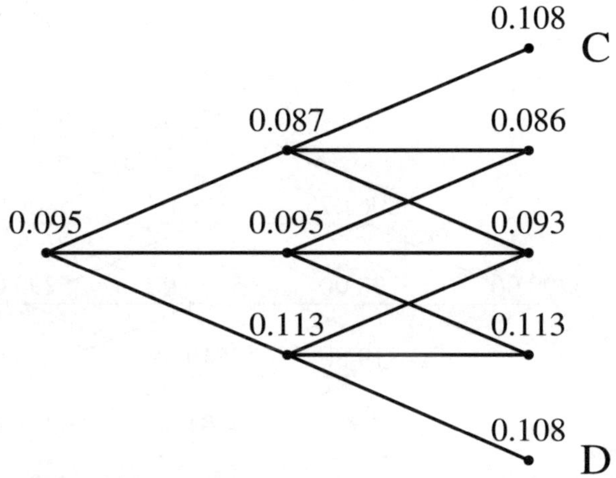

Figure 6.13: Implied local volatilities for $\sigma_I = 0.11 - \Delta K \cdot 0.005$. Nodes C and D had inadmissible transition probabilities (6.21)–(6.24).

STFitt07.xpl

firstly compute from the Black-Scholes equation (6.1) the implied volatilities at various combinations of prices and maturities, that is, we can construct the volatility smile. Next, we build and calibrate an ITT so that it fits this smile. The procedure is analogous to the examples described above – the only difference lies in replacing an artificial function $\sigma_I(K,t)$ by an estimate of implied volatility σ_I at each point (K,t).

For the purpose of demonstration, we build a three-level ITT with time step Δt of two weeks. First, we construct the state space (Section 6.3.2) starting at time $t_0 = 0$ with the spot price $S = 5290$ and riskless interest rate $r = 4\%$, see Figure 6.14. Further, we have to compute the transition probabilities. Because option contracts are not available for each combination of price and maturity, we use a nonparametric smoothing procedure to model the whole volatility surface $\sigma_I(K,t)$ as employed by Aït-Sahalia, Wang, and Yared (2001) and Fengler, Härdle, and Villa (2003), for instance. Given the data, some transition probabilities fall outside interval $(0,1)$; they are depicted by dashed lines in Figure 6.14. Such probabilities have to be corrected as described in Section 6.3.4

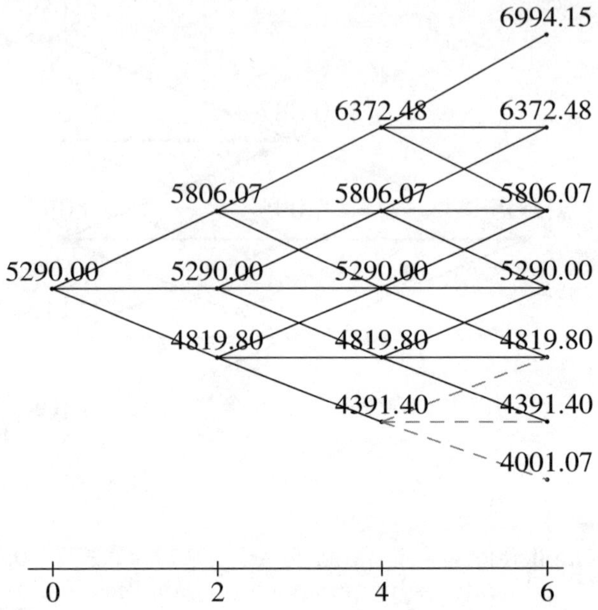

Figure 6.14: The state space of the ITT constructed for DAX on January 4, 1999. Dashed lines mark the transitions with originally inadmissible transition probabilities.

STFitt08.xpl

(there are no forward price violations). The resulting local volatilities, which reflect the volatility skew, are on Figure 6.15.

Probably the main result of this ITT model can be summarized by the state price density (the left panel of Figure 6.16). This density describes the price distribution given by the constructed ITT and smoothed by the Nadaraya-Watson estimator. Apparently, the estimated density is rather rough because we used just three steps in our tree. To get a smoother state-price density estimate, we doubled the number of steps; that is, we used six one-week steps instead of three two-week steps (see the right panel of Figure 6.16).

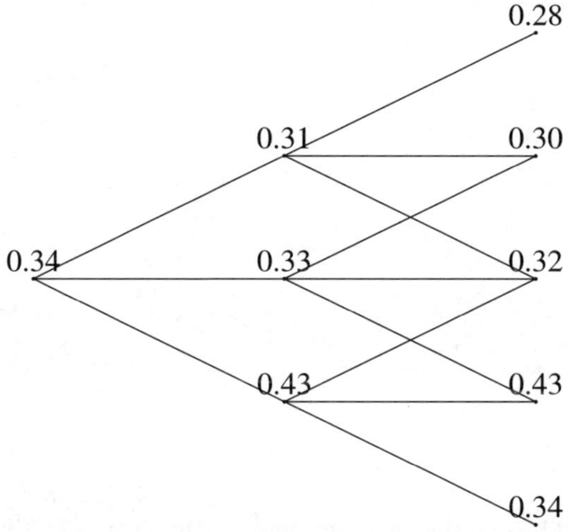

Figure 6.15: Implied local volatilities computed from an ITT for DAX on January 4, 1999.

STFitt08.xpl

Finally, it possible to use the constructed ITT to evaluate various DAX options. For example, a European knock-out option gives the owner the same rights as a standard European option as long as the index price S does not exceed or fall below some barrier B for the entire life of the knock-out option; see Härdle, Kleinow, and Stahl (2002) for details. So, let us compute the price of the knock-out-call DAX option at maturity $T = 6$ weeks, strike price $K = 5200$, and barrier $B = 4800$. The option price at time t_j ($t_0 = 0, t_1 = 2, t_2 = 4$, and $t_3 = 6$ weeks) and stock price $s_{j,i}$ will be denoted $V_{j,i}$.

At the maturity $t = T = 6$, the price is known: $V_{3,i} = \max\{0, s_{j,i} - K\}, i = 1, \dots, 7$. Thus, $V_{3,1} = \max\{0, 4001.01 - 5200\} = 0$ and $V_{3,5} = \max\{0, 5806.07 - 5200\} = 606.07$, for instance. To compute the option price at $t_j < T$, one just has to discount the conditional expectation of the option price at time t_{j+1}

$$V_{j,i} = e^{-r^* \Delta t}\{p_{j,i}V_{j+1,i+2} + (1 - p_{j,i} - q_{j,i})V_{j+1,i+1} + q_{j,i}V_{j+1,i}\} \qquad (6.28)$$

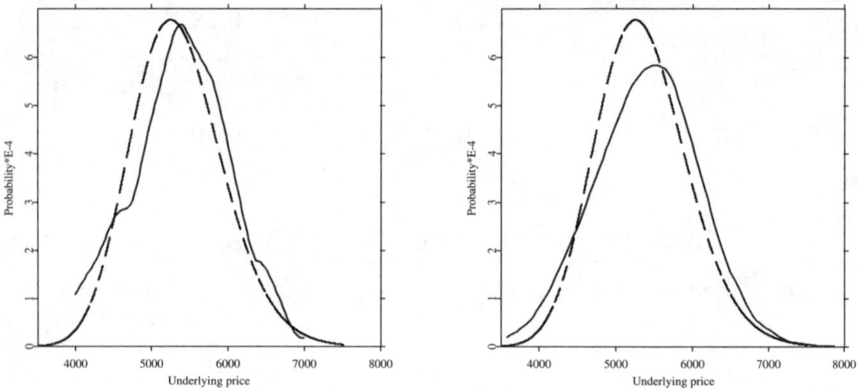

Figure 6.16: State price density estimated from an ITT for DAX on January 4, 1999. The dashed line depicts the corresponding Black-Scholes density. *Left panel:* State price density for a three-level tree. *Right panel:* State price density for a six-level tree.

STFitt08.xpl

STFitt09.xpl

provided that $s_{j,i} \geq B$, otherwise $V_{j,i} = 0$. Hence at time $t_2 = 4$, one obtains $V_{2,1} = 0$ because $s_{2,1} = 4391.40 < 4800 = B$ and

$$V_{2,3} = e^{-\log(1+0.04)\cdot 2/52}(0.22 \cdot 606.07 + 0.55 \cdot 90 + 0.23 \cdot 0) = 184.33$$

(see Figure 6.17). We can continue further and compute the option price at times $t_1 = 2$ and $t_0 = 0$ just using the standard formula (6.28) since prices no longer lie below the barrier B (see Figure 6.14). Thus, one computes $V_{1,1} = 79.7$, $V_{1,2} = 251.7$, $V_{1,3} = 639.8$, and finally, the option price at time $t_0 = 0$ and stock price $S = 5290$ equals

$$V_{0,1} = e^{-\log(1+0.04)\cdot 2/52}(0.25 \cdot 639.8 + 0.50 \cdot 251.7 + 0.25 \cdot 79.7) = 303.28.$$

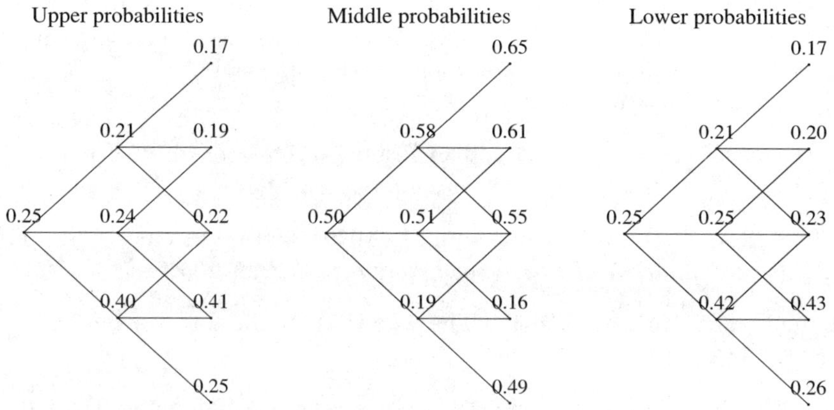

Figure 6.17: Transition probabilities of the ITT constructed for DAX on January 4, 1999.

STFitt10.xpl

Bibliography

Aït-Sahalia, Y., Wang, Y., and Yared, F. (2001). Do options markets correctly price the probabilities of movement of the underlying asset? *Journal of Econometrics* **102**, 67–110.

Black, F. and Scholes, M. (1973). The Pricing of Options and Corporate Liabilities. *Journal of Political Economy* **81**: 637–654.

Cox, J. C., Ross, S. A., and Rubinstein, M. (1979). Option Pricing: A Simplified Approach. *Journal of Financial Economics* **7**: 229–263.

Derman, E. and Kani, I. (1994). The Volatility Smile and Its Implied Tree. *RISK* **7(2)**: 139–145, 32–39.

Derman, E., Kani, I., and Chriss, N. (1996). Implied Trinomial Trees of the Volatility Smile. *The Journal of Derivatives* **3(4)**: 7–22

Dupire B. (1994). Pricing with a smile, *RISK* **7(1)**: 18–20.

Fengler, M. R., Härdle, W., and Villa, C. (2003). The dynamics of implied volatilities: a common principle components approach. *Review of Derivatives Research* **6**: 179–202.

Franke, J., Härdle, W., and Hafner, C. M. (2004). *Statistics of Financial Markets*, Springer, Heidelberg, Germany.

Härdle, W., Kleinow, T., and Stahl, G. (2002). *Applied Quantitative Finance*. Springer-Verlag, Berlin.

Hull, J. (1989). *Options, Futures and Other Derivatives*. Prentice-Hall, Englewood Cliffs, New Jersey.

Hull, J. and White, A. (1990). Valuing derivative securities using the explicit finite difference method. *The Journal of Finance and Quantitative Analysis* **25**: 87–100.

Jarrow, R. and Rudd A. (1983). *Option Pricing*, Dow Jones-Irwin Publishing, Homewood, Illinois.

Komorád, K. (2002). Implied Trinomial Trees and Their Implementation with XploRe. *Bachelor Thesis*, HU Berlin; `http://appel.rz.hu-berlin.de/Zope/ise_stat/wiwi/ise/stat/forschung/dmbarbeiten/`.

Ross, S., Westerfield, R., and Jaffe, J. (2002). *Corporate Finance.* Mc Graw-Hill.

7 Heston's Model and the Smile

Rafał Weron and Uwe Wystup

7.1 Introduction

The Black-Scholes formula, based on the assumption of log-normal stock diffusion with constant volatility, is the universal benchmark for option pricing. But as all market participants are keenly aware of, it is flawed. The model-implied volatilities for different strikes and maturities of options are not constant and tend to be smile shaped. Over the last two decades researchers have tried to find extensions of the model in order to explain this empirical fact.

A very natural approach, suggested already by Merton (1973), allows the volatilities to be a deterministic function of time. While it explains the different implied volatility levels for different times of maturity, it still does not explain the smile shape for different strikes. Dupire (1994), Derman and Kani (1994), and Rubinstein (1994) came up with the idea of allowing not only time, but also state dependence of the volatility coefficient, see Fengler (2005) and Chapter 6. This local (deterministic) volatility approach yields a complete market model. Moreover, it lets the local volatility surface to be fitted, but it cannot explain the persistent smile shape which does not vanish as time passes.

The next step beyond the local volatility approach was to allow the volatility coefficient in the Black-Scholes diffusion equation to be random. The pioneering work of Hull and White (1987), Stein and Stein (1991), and Heston (1993) led to the development of stochastic volatility models. These are two-factor models with one of the factors being responsible for the dynamics of the volatility coefficient. Different driving mechanisms for the volatility process have been proposed, including geometric Brownian motion and mean-reverting Ornstein-Uhlenbeck type processes.

Heston's model stands out from this class mainly for two reasons: (i) the process for the volatility is non-negative and mean-reverting, which is what we observe in the markets, and (ii) there exists a closed-form solution for vanilla options. It was also one of the first models that was able to explain the smile and simultaneously allow a front-office implementation and a market consistent valuation of many exotics. Hence, we concentrate in this chapter on Heston's model. First, in Section 7.2 we discuss the properties of the model, including marginal distributions and tail behavior. In Section 7.3 we adapt the original work of Heston (1993) to a foreign exchange (FX) setting. We do this because the model is particularly useful in explaining the volatility smile found in FX markets. In equity markets the typical volatility structure is an asymmetric skew (also called a smirk or grimace). Calibrating Heston's model to such a structure leads to very high, unrealistic values of the correlation coefficient. Finally, in Section 7.4 we show that the smile of vanilla options can be reproduced by suitably calibrating the model parameters.

However, we do have to say that Heston's model is not a panacea. The criticism that we might want to put forward is that the market consistency could potentially be based on a large number of market participants using it! Furthermore, while trying to calibrate short term smiles, the volatility of volatility often seems to explode along with the speed of mean reversion. This is a strong indication that the process "wants" to jump, which of course it is not allowed to do. This observation, together with market crashes, has lead researchers to consider models with jumps. Interestingly, jump-diffusion models have been investigated already in the mid-seventies (Merton, 1976), long before the advent of stochastic volatility. Jump-diffusion models are, in general, more challenging to handle numerically than stochastic volatility models. Like the latter, they result in an incomplete market. But, whereas stochastic volatility models can be made complete by the introduction of one (or a few) traded options, a jump-diffusion model typically requires the existence of a continuum of options for the market to be complete.

Recent research by Bates (1996) and Bakshi, Cao, and Chen (1997) suggests using a combination of jumps and stochastic volatility. This approach allows for even a better fit to market data, but has so many parameters, that it is hard to believe that there is enough information in the market to calibrate them. Andersen and Andreasen (2000) let the stock dynamics be described by a jump-diffusion process with local volatility. This method combines ease of modeling steep short-term volatility skews (jumps) and accurate fitting to quoted option prices (deterministic volatility function). Other alternative approaches utilize Lévy processes (Barndorff-Nielsen, Mikosch, and Resnick, 2001; Eberlein,

Kallsen, and Kristen, 2003) or mixing unconditional disturbances (Tompkins and D'Ecclesia, 2004), but it is still an open question how to price and hedge exotics using such models.

7.2 Heston's Model

Heston (1993) assumed that the spot price follows the diffusion:

$$dS_t = S_t \left(\mu \, dt + \sqrt{v_t} dW_t^{(1)} \right), \tag{7.1}$$

i.e. a process resembling geometric Brownian motion (GBM) with a non-constant instantaneous variance v_t. Furthermore, he proposed that the variance be driven by a mean reverting stochastic process of the form:

$$dv_t = \kappa(\theta - v_t) \, dt + \sigma \sqrt{v_t} dW_t^{(2)}, \tag{7.2}$$

and allowed the two Wiener processes to be correlated with each other:

$$dW_t^{(1)} dW_t^{(2)} = \rho \, dt.$$

The variance process (7.2) was originally used by Cox, Ingersoll, and Ross (1985) for modeling the short term interest rate. It is defined by three parameters: θ, κ, and σ. In the context of stochastic volatility models they can be interpreted as the long term variance, the rate of mean reversion to the long term variance, and the volatility of variance (often called the *vol of vol*), respectively.

Surprisingly, the introduction of stochastic volatility does not change the properties of the spot price process in a way that could be noticed just by a visual inspection of its realizations. In Figure 7.1 we plot sample paths of a geometric Brownian motion and the spot process (7.1) in Heston's model. To make the comparison more objective both trajectories were obtained with the same set of random numbers. Clearly, they are indistinguishable by mere eye. In both cases the initial spot rate $S_0 = 0.84$ and the domestic and foreign interest rates are 5% and 3%, respectively, yielding a drift of $\mu = 2\%$. The volatility in the GBM is constant $\sqrt{v_t} = \sqrt{4\%} = 20\%$, while in Heston's model it is driven by the mean reverting process (7.2) with the initial variance $v_0 = 4\%$, the long term variance $\theta = 4\%$, the speed of mean reversion $\kappa = 2$, and the vol of vol $\sigma = 30\%$. The correlation is set to $\rho = -0.05$.

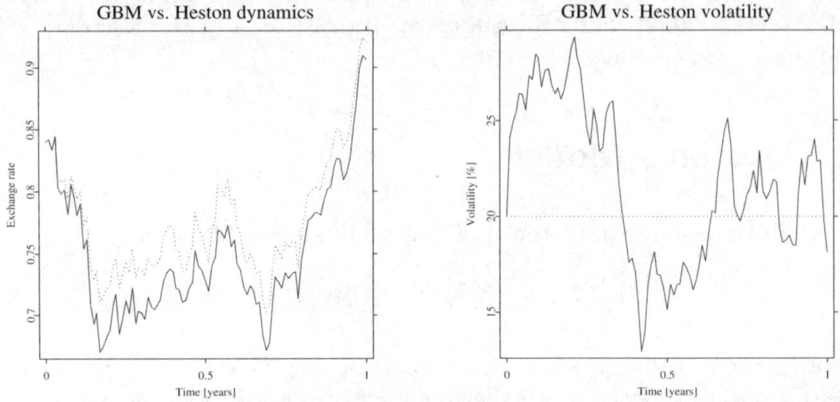

Figure 7.1: Sample paths of a geometric Brownian motion (dotted red line) and the spot process (7.1) in Heston's model (solid blue line) obtained with the same set of random numbers (*left panel*). Despite the fact that the volatility in the GBM is constant, while in Heston's model it is driven by a mean reverting process (*right panel*) the sample paths are indistinguishable by mere eye.

STFhes01.xpl

A closer inspection of Heston's model does, however, reveal some important differences with respect to GBM. For example, the probability density functions of (log-)returns have heavier tails – exponential compared to Gaussian, see Figure 7.2. In this respect they are similar to hyperbolic distributions (Weron, 2004), i.e. in the log-linear scale they resemble hyperbolas (rather than parabolas).

Equations (7.1) and (7.2) define a two-dimensional stochastic process for the variables S_t and v_t. By setting $x_t = \log(S_t/S_0) - \mu t$, we can express it in terms of the centered (log-)return x_t and v_t. The process is then characterized by the transition probability $P_t(x, v \mid v_0)$ to have (log-)return x and variance v at time t given the initial return $x = 0$ and variance v_0 at time $t = 0$. The time evolution of $P_t(x, v \mid v_0)$ is governed by the following Fokker-Planck (or forward

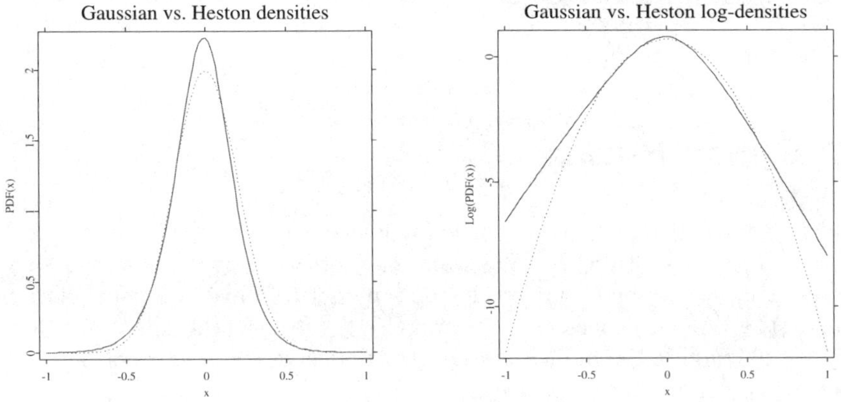

Figure 7.2: The marginal probability density function in Heston's model (solid blue line) and the Gaussian PDF (dotted red line) for the same set of parameters as in Figure 7.1 (*left panel*). The tails of Heston's marginals are exponential which is clearly visible in the *right panel* where the corresponding log-densities are plotted.

STFhes02.xpl

Kolmogorov) equation:

$$\begin{aligned}\frac{\partial}{\partial t}P &= \kappa\frac{\partial}{\partial v}\{(v-\theta)P\}+\frac{1}{2}\frac{\partial}{\partial x}(vP)+\\ &+\rho\sigma\frac{\partial^2}{\partial x\,\partial v}(vP)+\frac{1}{2}\frac{\partial^2}{\partial x^2}(vP)+\frac{\sigma^2}{2}\frac{\partial^2}{\partial v^2}(vP).\end{aligned} \tag{7.3}$$

Solving this equation yields the following analytical formula for the density of centered returns x, given a time lag t of the price changes (Dragulescu and Yakovenko, 2002):

$$P_t(x)=\frac{1}{2\pi}\int_{-\infty}^{+\infty}e^{i\xi x+F_t(\xi)}d\xi, \tag{7.4}$$

with

$$\begin{gathered}F_t(\xi)=\tfrac{\kappa\theta}{\sigma^2}\gamma t-\tfrac{2\kappa\theta}{\sigma^2}\log\left(\cosh\tfrac{\Omega t}{2}+\tfrac{\Omega^2-\gamma^2+2\kappa\gamma}{2\kappa\Omega}\sinh\tfrac{\Omega t}{2}\right),\\ \gamma=\kappa+i\rho\sigma\xi,\quad\text{and}\quad\Omega=\sqrt{\gamma^2+\sigma^2(\xi^2-i\xi)}.\end{gathered}$$

A sample marginal probability density function in Heston's model is illustrated in Figure 7.2. The parameters are the same as in Figure 7.1, i.e. $\theta = 4\%$, $\kappa = 2$, $\sigma = 30\%$, and $\rho = -0.05$. The time lag is set to $t = 1$.

7.3 Option Pricing

Consider the value function of a general contingent claim $U(t, v, S)$ paying $g(S) = U(T, v, S)$ at time T. We want to replicate it with a self-financing portfolio. Due to the fact that in Heston's model we have two sources of uncertainty (the Wiener processes $W^{(1)}$ and $W^{(2)}$) the portfolio must include the possibility to trade in the money market, the underlying and another derivative security with value function $V(t, v, S)$.

We start with an initial wealth X_0 which evolves according to:

$$dX = \Delta\, dS + \Gamma\, dV + r_d(X - \Gamma V)\, dt - (r_d - r_f)\Delta S\, dt, \tag{7.5}$$

where Δ is the number of units of the underlying held at time t and Γ is the number of derivative securities V held at time t. Since we are operating in a foreign exchange setup, we let r_d and r_f denote the domestic and foreign interest rates, respectively. The goal is to find Δ and Γ such that $X_t = U(t, v_t, S_t)$ for all $t \in [0, T]$. The standard approach to achieve this is to compare the differentials of U and X obtained via Itô's formula. After some algebra we arrive at the partial differential equation which U must satisfy:

$$\begin{aligned}\frac{1}{2}vS^2\frac{\partial^2 U}{\partial S^2} + \rho\sigma v S\frac{\partial^2 U}{\partial S \partial v} + \frac{1}{2}\sigma^2 v\frac{\partial^2 U}{\partial v^2} + (r_d - r_f)S\frac{\partial U}{\partial S} + \\ + \Big\{\kappa(\theta - v) - \lambda(t, v, S)\Big\}\frac{\partial U}{\partial v} - r_d U + \frac{\partial U}{\partial t} &= 0. \end{aligned} \tag{7.6}$$

For details on the derivation in the foreign exchange setting see Hakala and Wystup (2002). The term $\lambda(t, v, S)$ is called the *market price of volatility risk*. Without loss of generality its functional form can be reduced to $\lambda(t, v, S) = \lambda v$, Heston (1993). We obtain a solution to (7.6) by specifying appropriate boundary conditions. For a European vanilla option these are:

$$U(T, v, S) = \max\{\phi(S - K), 0\}, \tag{7.7}$$

$$U(t, v, 0) = \frac{1 - \phi}{2} K e^{-r_d \tau}, \tag{7.8}$$

$$\frac{\partial U}{\partial S}(t, v, \infty) = \frac{1 + \phi}{2} e^{-r_f \tau}, \tag{7.9}$$

$$\begin{aligned}(r_d - r_f)S\frac{\partial U}{\partial S}(t,0,S) + \\ + \kappa\theta\frac{\partial U}{\partial v}(t,0,S) + \frac{\partial U}{\partial t}(t,0,S) &= r_d U(t,0,S), &(7.10)\\ U(t,\infty,S) &= \begin{cases} Se^{-r_f\tau}, & \text{for } \phi = +1, \\ Ke^{-r_d\tau}, & \text{for } \phi = -1, \end{cases} &(7.11)\end{aligned}$$

where ϕ is a binary variable taking value $+1$ for call options and -1 for put options, K is the strike in units of the domestic currency, $\tau = T - t$, T is the expiration time in years, and t is the current time. In this case, PDE (7.6) can be solved analytically using the method of characteristic functions (Heston, 1993). The price of a European vanilla option is hence given by:

$$\begin{aligned} h(t) &= \text{HestonVanilla}(\kappa,\theta,\sigma,\rho,\lambda,r_d,r_f,v_0,S_0,K,\tau,\phi) \\ &= \phi\{e^{-r_f\tau}S_tP_+(\phi) - Ke^{-r_d\tau}P_-(\phi)\}, &(7.12)\end{aligned}$$

where $a = \kappa\theta$, $u_1 = \frac{1}{2}$, $u_2 = -\frac{1}{2}$, $b_1 = \kappa + \lambda - \sigma\rho$, $b_2 = \kappa + \lambda$, $x = \log S_t$, $d_j = \sqrt{(\rho\sigma\varphi i - b_j)^2 - \sigma^2(2u_j\varphi i - \varphi^2)}$, $g_j = (b_j - \rho\sigma\varphi i + d_j)/(b_j - \rho\sigma\varphi i - d_j)$, and

$$\begin{aligned} D_j(\tau,\varphi) &= \frac{b_j - \rho\sigma\varphi i + d_j}{\sigma^2}\left(\frac{1 - e^{d_j\tau}}{1 - g_je^{d_j\tau}}\right), &(7.13)\\ C_j(\tau,\varphi) &= (r_d - r_f)\varphi i\tau + &(7.14)\\ &+ \frac{a}{\sigma^2}\left\{(b_j - \rho\sigma\varphi i + d)\tau - 2\log\left(\frac{1 - g_je^{d_j\tau}}{1 - e^{d_j\tau}}\right)\right\}, \\ f_j(x,v,t,\varphi) &= \exp\{C_j(\tau,\varphi) + D_j(\tau,\varphi)v + i\varphi x\}, &(7.15)\\ P_j(x,v,\tau,y) &= \frac{1}{2} + \frac{1}{\pi}\int_0^\infty \Re\left\{\frac{e^{-i\varphi y}f_j(x,v,\tau,\varphi)}{i\varphi}\right\} d\varphi, &(7.16)\\ p_j(x,v,\tau,y) &= \frac{1}{\pi}\int_0^\infty \Re\left\{e^{-i\varphi y}f_j(x,v,\tau,\varphi)\right\} d\varphi. &(7.17)\end{aligned}$$

The functions P_j are the cumulative distribution functions (in the variable y) of the log-spot price after time $\tau = T - t$ starting at x for some drift μ. The functions p_j are the respective densities. The integration in (7.17) can be done with the Gauss-Legendre algorithm using 100 for ∞ and 100 abscissas. The best is to let the Gauss-Legendre algorithm compute the abscissas and weights once and reuse them as constants for all integrations. Finally:

$$P_+(\phi) = \frac{1-\phi}{2} + \phi P_1(\log S_t, v_t, \tau, \log K), \tag{7.18}$$

$$P_-(\phi) = \frac{1-\phi}{2} + \phi P_2(\log S_t, v_t, \tau, \log K). \tag{7.19}$$

Apart from the above closed-form solution for vanilla options, alternative approaches can be utilized. These include finite difference and finite element methods. The former must be used with care since high precision is required to invert scarce matrices. The Crank-Nicholson, ADI (Alternate Direction Implicit), and Hopscotch schemes can be used, however, ADI is not suitable to handle nonzero correlation. Boundary conditions must be also set appropriately. For details see Kluge (2002). Finite element methods can be applied to price both the vanillas and exotics, as explained for example in Apel, Winkler, and Wystup (2002).

7.3.1 Greeks

The Greeks can be evaluated by taking the appropriate derivatives or by exploiting homogeneity properties of financial markets (Reiss and Wystup, 2001). In Heston's model the *spot delta* and the so-called *dual delta* are given by:

$$\Delta = \frac{\partial h(t)}{\partial S_t} = \phi e^{-r_f \tau} P_+(\phi) \quad \text{and} \quad \frac{\partial h(t)}{\partial K} = -\phi e^{-r_d \tau} P_-(\phi), \tag{7.20}$$

respectively. *Gamma*, which measures the sensitivity of delta to the underlying has the form:

$$\Gamma = \frac{\partial \Delta}{\partial S_t} = \frac{e^{-r_f \tau}}{S_t} p_1(\log S_t, v_t, \tau, \log K). \tag{7.21}$$

Theta $= \partial h(t)/\partial t$ can be computed from (7.6). The formulas for *rho* are the following:

$$\frac{\partial h(t)}{\partial r_d} = \phi K e^{-r_d \tau} \tau P_-(\phi), \tag{7.22}$$

$$\frac{\partial h(t)}{\partial r_f} = -\phi S_t e^{-r_f \tau} \tau P_+(\phi). \tag{7.23}$$

Note that in a foreign exchange setting there are two *rho*'s – one is a derivative of the option price with respect to the domestic interest rate and the other is a derivative with respect to the foreign interest rate.

The notions of *vega* and *volga* usually refer to the first and second derivative with respect to volatility. In Heston's model we use them for the first and second derivative with respect to the *initial variance*:

$$\begin{aligned}\frac{\partial h(t)}{\partial v_t} &= e^{-r_f\tau}S_t\frac{\partial}{\partial v_t}P_1(\log S_t, v_t, \tau, \log K) - \\ &- Ke^{-r_d\tau}\frac{\partial}{\partial v_t}P_2(\log S_t, v_t, \tau, \log K), \qquad (7.24)\\ \frac{\partial^2 h(t)}{\partial v_t^2} &= e^{-r_f\tau}S_t\frac{\partial^2}{\partial v_t^2}P_1(\log S_t, v_t, \tau, \log K) - \\ &- Ke^{-r_d\tau}\frac{\partial^2}{\partial v_t^2}P_2(\log S_t, v_t, \tau, \log K), \qquad (7.25)\end{aligned}$$

where

$$\begin{aligned}\frac{\partial}{\partial v_t}P_j(x, v_t, \tau, y) &= \frac{1}{\pi}\int_0^\infty \Re\left[\frac{D(\tau,\varphi)e^{-i\varphi y}f_j(x, v_t, \tau, \varphi)}{i\varphi}\right] d\varphi, \quad (7.26)\\ \frac{\partial^2}{\partial v_t^2}P_j(x, v_t, \tau, y) &= \frac{1}{\pi}\int_0^\infty \Re\left[\frac{D^2(\tau,\varphi)e^{-i\varphi y}f_j(x, v_t, \tau, \varphi)}{i\varphi}\right] d\varphi. \quad (7.27)\end{aligned}$$

7.4 Calibration

Calibration of stochastic volatility models can be done in two conceptually different ways. One way is to look at a time series of historical data. Estimation methods such as Generalized, Simulated, and Efficient Methods of Moments (respectively GMM, SMM, and EMM), as well as Bayesian MCMC have been extensively applied, for a review see Chernov and Ghysels (2000). In the Heston model we could also try to fit empirical distributions of returns to the marginal distributions specified in (7.4) via a minimization scheme. Unfortunately, all historical approaches have one common flaw – they do not allow for estimation of the market price of volatility risk $\lambda(t, v, S)$. However, multiple studies find evidence of a nonzero volatility risk premium, see e.g. Bates (1996). This implies in turn that one needs some extra input to make the transition from the physical to the risk neutral world. Observing only the underlying spot price and estimating stochastic volatility models with this information will not deliver correct derivative security prices. This leads us to the second estimation approach. Instead of using the spot data we calibrate the model to derivative prices.

We follow the latter approach and take the smile of the current vanilla options market as a given starting point. As a preliminary step, we have to retrieve the strikes since the smile in foreign exchange markets is specified as a function of the deltas. Comparing the Black-Scholes type formulas (in the foreign exchange market setting we have to use the Garman and Kohlhagen (1983) specification) for delta and the option premium yields the relation for the strikes K_i. From a computational point of view this stage requires only an inversion of the cumulative normal distribution.

Next, we fit the five parameters: initial variance v_0, volatility of variance σ, long-run variance θ, mean reversion κ, and correlation ρ for a fixed time to maturity and a given vector of market Black-Scholes implied volatilities $\{\hat{\sigma}_i\}_{i=1}^n$ for a given set of delta pillars $\{\Delta_i\}_{i=1}^n$. Since we are calibrating the model to derivative prices we do not need to worry about estimating the market price of volatility risk as it is already embedded in the market smile. Furthermore, it can easily be verified that the value function (7.12) satisfies:

$$\begin{aligned} &\text{HestonVanilla}(\kappa, \theta, \sigma, \rho, \lambda, r_d, r_f, v_0, S_0, K, \tau, \phi) = \\ &= \text{HestonVanilla}\left(\kappa + \lambda, \frac{\kappa}{\kappa + \lambda}\theta, \sigma, \rho, 0, r_d, r_f, v_0, S_0, K, \tau, \phi\right), \end{aligned} \tag{7.28}$$

which means that we can set $\lambda = 0$ by default and just determine the remaining five parameters.

After fitting the parameters we compute the option prices in Heston's model using (7.12) and retrieve the corresponding Black-Scholes model implied volatilities $\{\sigma_i\}_{i=1}^n$ via a standard bisection method (a Newton-Raphson method could be used as well). The next step is to define an objective function, which we choose to be the Sum of Squared Errors (SSE):

$$\text{SSE}(\kappa, \theta, \sigma, \rho, v_0) = \sum_{i=1}^{n} \{\hat{\sigma}_i - \sigma_i(\kappa, \theta, \sigma, \rho, v_0)\}^2. \tag{7.29}$$

We compare volatilities (rather than prices), because they are all of comparable magnitude. In addition, one could introduce weights for all the summands to favor at-the-money (ATM) or out-of-the-money (OTM) fits. Finally we minimize over this objective function using a simplex search routine to find the optimal set of parameters.

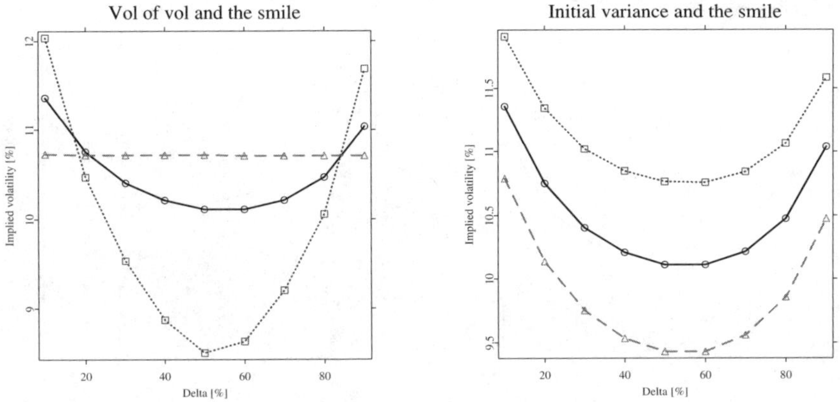

Figure 7.3: *Left panel*: Effect of changing the volatility of variance (vol of vol) on the shape of the smile. For the red dashed "smile" with triangles $\sigma = 0.01$, and for the blue dotted smile with squares $\sigma = 0.6$. *Right panel*: Effect of changing the initial variance on the shape of the smile. For the red dashed smile with triangles $v_0 = 0.008$ and for the blue dotted smile with squares $v_0 = 0.012$.

STFhes03.xpl

7.4.1 Qualitative Effects of Changing Parameters

Before calibrating the model to market data we will show how changing the input parameters affects the shape of the fitted smile curve. This analysis will help in reducing the dimensionality of the problem. In all plots of this subsection the solid black curve with circles is the smile obtained for $v_0 = 0.01$, $\sigma = 0.25$, $\kappa = 1.5$, $\theta = 0.015$, and $\rho = 0.05$.

First, to take a look at the volatility of variance (vol of vol), see the left panel of Figure 7.3. Clearly, setting σ equal to zero produces a deterministic process for the variance and hence volatility which does not admit any smile. The resulting fit is a constant curve. On the other hand, increasing the volatility of variance increases the convexity of the fit. The initial variance has a different impact on the smile. Changing v_0 allows adjustments in the height of the smile curve rather than the shape. This is illustrated in the right panel of Figure 7.3.

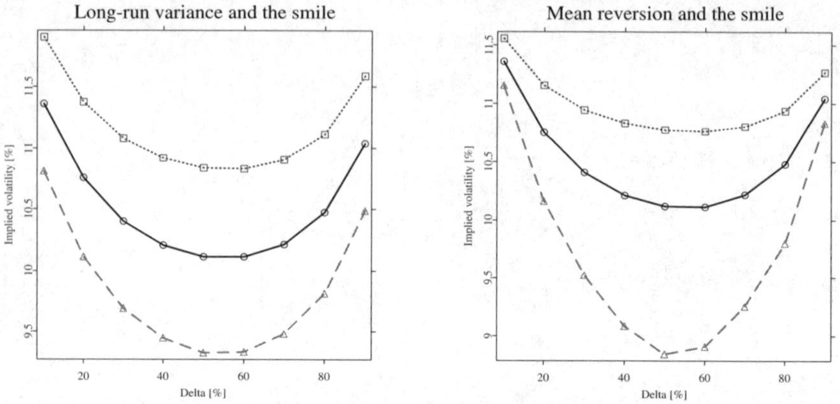

Figure 7.4: *Left panel*: Effect of changing the long-run variance on the shape of the smile. For the red dashed smile with triangles $\theta = 0.01$, and for the blue dotted smile with squares $\theta = 0.02$. *Right panel*: Effect of changing the mean reversion on the shape of the smile. For the red dashed smile with triangles $\kappa = 0.01$, and for the blue dotted smile with squares $\kappa = 3$.

STFhes04.xpl

Effects of changing the long-run variance θ are similar to those observed by changing the initial variance, see the left panel of Figure 7.4. This requires some attention in the calibration process. It seems promising to choose the initial variance a priori and only let the long-run variance vary. In particular, a different initial variance for different maturities would be inconsistent.

Changing the mean reversion κ affects the ATM part more than the extreme wings of the smile curve. The low deltas remain almost unchanged whereas increasing the mean reversion lifts the center. This is illustrated in the right panel of Figure 7.4. Moreover, the influence of mean reversion is often compensated by a stronger volatility of variance. This suggests fixing the mean reversion parameter and only calibrating the remaining parameters.

Finally, let us look at the influence of correlation. The uncorrelated case produces a fit that looks like a symmetric smile curve centered at-the-money. How-

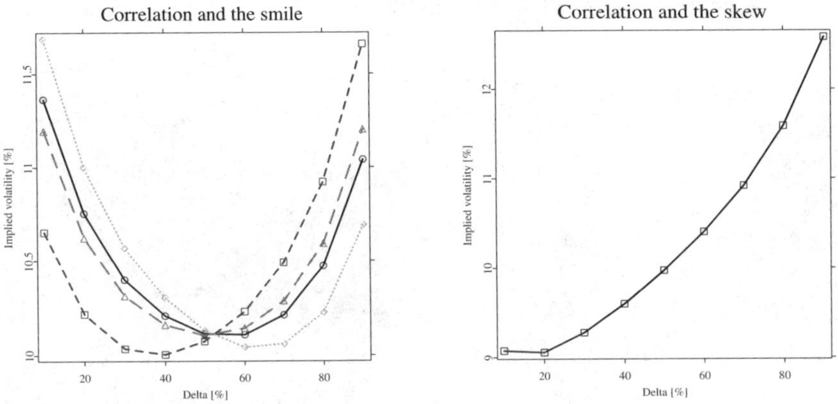

Figure 7.5: *Left panel*: Effect of changing the correlation on the shape of the smile. For the red dashed smile with triangles $\rho = 0$, for the blue dashed smile with squares $\rho = -0.15$, and for the green dotted smile with rhombs $\rho = 0.15$. *Right panel*: In order for the model to yield a volatility skew, a typically observed volatility structure in equity markets, the correlation must be set to an unrealistically high value (with respect to the absolute value; here $\rho = -0.5$).

STFhes05.xpl

ever, it is not exactly symmetric. Changing ρ changes the degree of symmetry. In particular, positive correlation makes calls more expensive, negative correlation makes puts more expensive. This is illustrated in Figure 7.5. Note that for the model to yield a volatility skew, a typically observed volatility structure in equity markets, the correlation must be set to an unrealistically high value.

7.4.2 Calibration Results

We are now ready to calibrate Heston's model to market data. We take the EUR/USD volatility surface on July 1, 2004 and fit the parameters in Heston's model according to the calibration scheme discussed earlier. The results are shown in Figures 7.6–7.8. Note that the fit is very good for maturities between three and eighteen months. Unfortunately, Heston's model does not perform

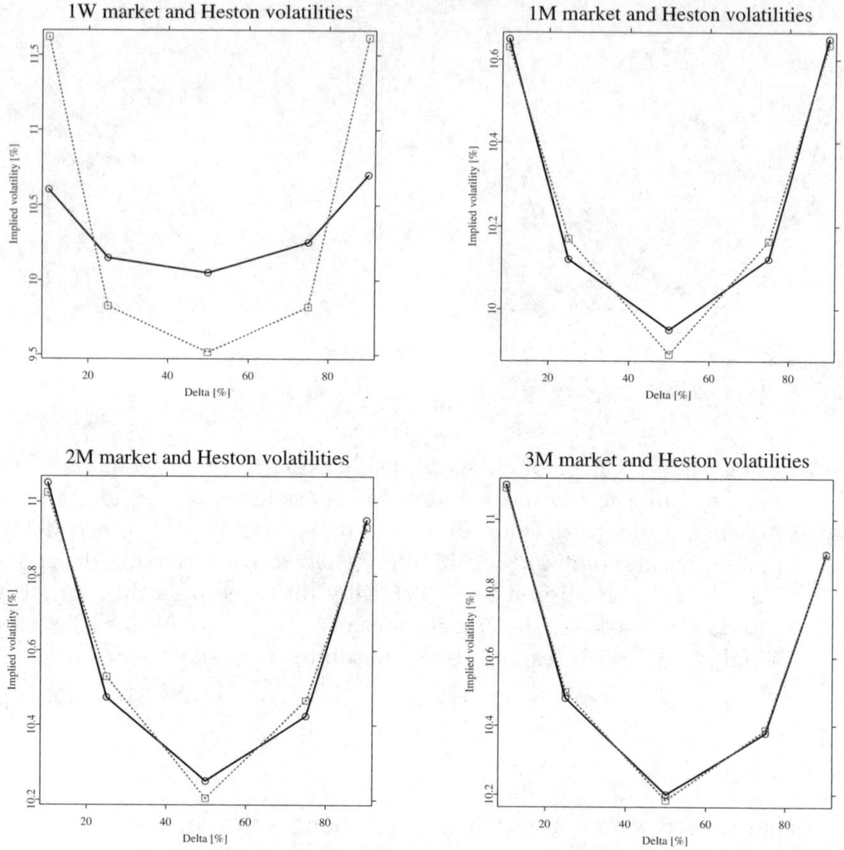

Figure 7.6: The market smile (solid black line with circles) on July 1, 2004 and the fit obtained with Heston's model (dotted red line with squares) for $\tau = 1$ week (*top left*), 1 month (*top right*), 2 months (*bottom left*), and 3 months (*bottom right*).

STFhes06.xpl

satisfactorily for short maturities and extremely long maturities. For the former we recommend using a jump-diffusion model (Cont and Tankov, 2003; Martinez and Senge, 2002), for the latter a suitable long term FX model (Andreasen, 1997).

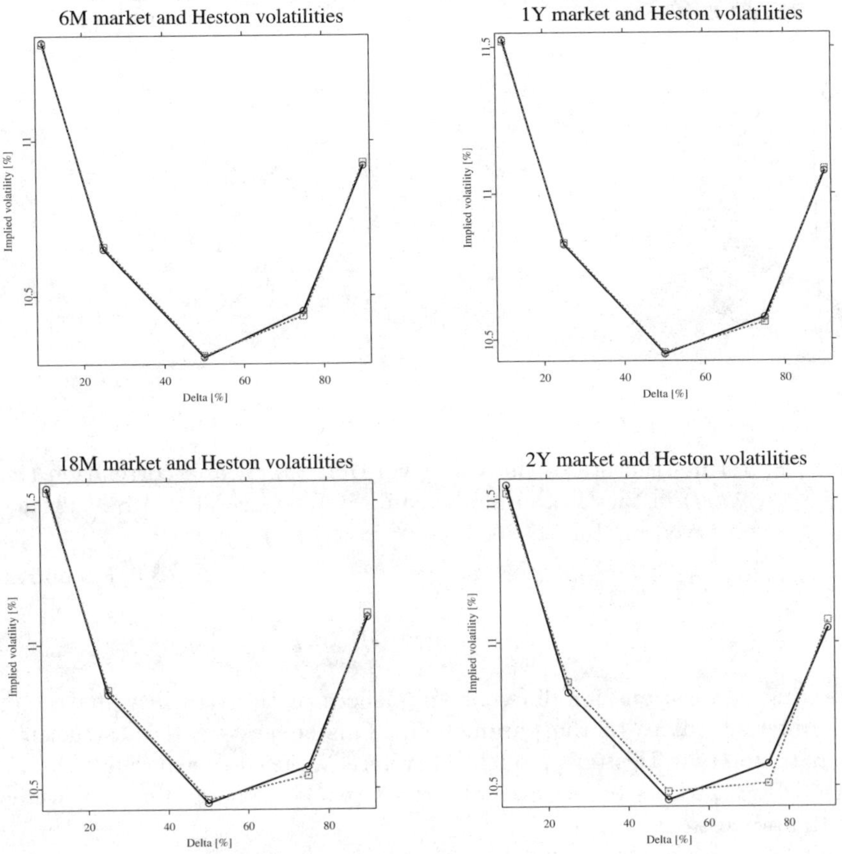

Figure 7.7: The market smile (solid black line with circles) on July 1, 2004 and the fit obtained with Heston's model (dotted red line with squares) for $\tau = 6$ months (*top left*), 1 year (*top right*), 18 months (*bottom left*), and 2 years (*bottom right*).

`STFhes06.xpl`

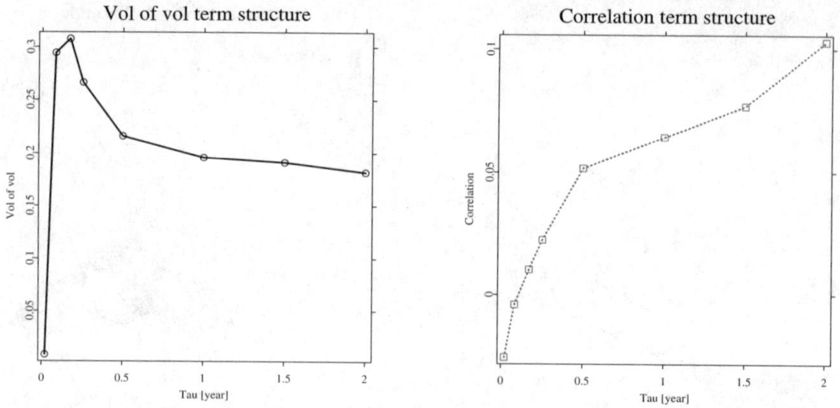

Figure 7.8: Term structure of the vol of vol (*left panel*) and correlation (*right panel*) in the Heston model calibrated to the EUR/USD surface as observed on July 1, 2004.

STFhes06.xpl

Performing calibrations for different time slices of the volatility matrix produces different values of the parameters. This suggests a term structure of some parameters in Heston's model. Therefore, we need to generalize the Cox-Ingersoll-Ross process to the case of time-dependent parameters, i.e. we consider the process:

$$dv_t = \kappa(t)\{\theta(t) - v_t\}\, dt + \sigma(t)\sqrt{v_t}\, dW_t \tag{7.30}$$

for some nonnegative deterministic parameter functions $\sigma(t)$, $\kappa(t)$, and $\theta(t)$. The formula for the mean turns out to be:

$$\mathrm{E}(v_t) = g(t) = v_0 e^{-K(t)} + \int_0^t \kappa(s)\theta(s)e^{K(s)-K(t)}\, ds, \tag{7.31}$$

with $K(t) = \int_0^t \kappa(s)\, ds$. The result for the second moment is:

$$\mathrm{E}(v_t^2) = v_0^2 e^{-2K(t)} + \int_0^t \{2\kappa(s)\theta(s) + \sigma^2(s)\}g(s)e^{2K(s)-2K(t)}\, ds, \tag{7.32}$$

and hence for the variance (after some algebra):

$$\mathrm{Var}(v_t) = \int_0^t \sigma^2(s) g(s) e^{2K(s)-2K(t)}\, ds. \tag{7.33}$$

The formula for the variance allows us to compute forward volatilities of variance explicitly. Assuming known values σ_{T_1} and σ_{T_2} for some times $0 < T_1 < T_2$, we want to determine the forward volatility of variance σ_{T_1,T_2} which matches the corresponding variances, i.e.

$$\int_0^{T_2} \sigma_{T_2}^2 g(s) e^{2\kappa(s-T_2)}\, ds = \tag{7.34}$$

$$= \int_0^{T_1} \sigma_{T_1}^2 g(s) e^{2\kappa(s-T_2)}\, ds + \int_{T_1}^{T_2} \sigma_{T_1,T_2}^2 g(s) e^{2\kappa(s-T_2)}\, ds.$$

The resulting forward volatility of variance is thus:

$$\sigma_{T_1,T_2}^2 = \frac{\sigma_{T_2}^2 H(T_2) - \sigma_{T_1}^2 H(T_1)}{H(T_2) - H(T_1)}, \tag{7.35}$$

where

$$H(t) = \int_0^t g(s) e^{2\kappa s}\, ds = \frac{\theta}{2\kappa} e^{2\kappa t} + \frac{1}{\kappa}(v_0 - \theta) e^{\kappa t} + \frac{1}{\kappa}\left(\frac{\theta}{2} - v_0\right). \tag{7.36}$$

Assuming known values ρ_{T_1} and ρ_{T_2} for some times $0 < T_1 < T_2$, we want to determine the forward correlation coefficient ρ_{T_1,T_2} to be active between times T_1 and T_2 such that the covariance between the Brownian motions of the variance process and the exchange rate process agrees with the given values ρ_{T_1} and ρ_{T_2}. This problem has a simple answer, namely:

$$\rho_{T_1,T_2} = \rho_{T_2}, \quad T_1 \le t \le T_2. \tag{7.37}$$

This can be seen by writing the Heston model in the form:

$$dS_t = S_t\left(\mu\, dt + \sqrt{v_t}\, dW_t^{(1)}\right) \tag{7.38}$$

$$dv_t = \kappa(\theta - v_t)\, dt + \rho\sigma\sqrt{v_t}\, dW_t^{(1)} + \sqrt{1-\rho^2}\sigma\sqrt{v_t}\, dW_t^{(2)} \tag{7.39}$$

for a pair of independent Brownian motions $W^{(1)}$ and $W^{(2)}$. Observe that choosing the forward correlation coefficient as stated does not conflict with the computed forward volatility.

As we have seen, Heston's model can be successfully applied to modeling the volatility smile of vanilla currency options. There are essentially three parameters to fit, namely the long-run variance, which corresponds to the at-the-money level of the market smile, the vol of vol, which corresponds to the convexity of the smile (in the market often quoted as butterflies), and the correlation, which corresponds to the skew of the smile (in the market often quoted as risk reversals). It is this direct link of the model parameters to the market that makes the Heston model so attractive to front office users.

The key application of the model is to calibrate it to vanilla options and afterward employ it for pricing exotics, like one-touch options, in either a finite difference grid or a Monte Carlo simulation (Hakala and Wystup, 2002; Wystup, 2003). Surprisingly, the results often coincide with the traders' rule of thumb pricing method. This might also simply mean that a lot of traders are using the same model. After all, it is a matter of belief which model reflects the reality most suitably.

Bibliography

Andersen, L. and Andreasen, J. (2000). Jump-Diffusion Processes: Volatility Smile Fitting and Numerical Methods for Option Pricing, *Review of Derivatives Research* **4**: 231–262.

Andreasen, J. (1997). A Gaussian Exchange Rate and Term Structure Model, *Essays on Contingent Claim Pricing* **97/2**, PhD thesis.

Apel, T., Winkler, G., and Wystup, U. (2002). Valuation of options in Heston's stochastic volatility model using finite element methods, *in* J. Hakala, U. Wystup (eds.) *Foreign Exchange Risk*, Risk Books, London.

Bakshi, G., Cao, C. and Chen, Z. (1997). Empirical Performance of Alternative Option Pricing Models, *Journal of Finance* **52**: 2003–2049.

Barndorff-Nielsen, O.E., Mikosch, T., and Resnick, S. (2001). *Levy processes: Theory and Applications*, Birkhäuser.

Bates, D. (1996). Jumps and Stochastic Volatility: Exchange Rate Processes Implicit in Deutsche Mark Options, *Review of Financial Studies* **9**: 69–107.

Chernov, M. and Ghysels, E. (2000). Estimation of the Stochastic Volatility Models for the Purpose of Options Valuation, *in* Y. S. Abu-Mostafa, B. LeBaron, A. W. Lo, and A. S. Weigend (eds.) *Computational Finance - Proceedings of the Sixth International Conference*, MIT Press, Cambridge.

Cont, R., and Tankov, P. (2003). *Financial Modelling with Jump Processes*, Chapman & Hall/CRC.

Cox, J. C., Ingersoll, J. E. and Ross, S. A. (1985). A Theory of the Term Structure of Interest Rates, *Econometrica* **53**: 385–407.

Derman, E. and Kani, I. (1994). Riding on a Smile, *RISK* **7(2)**: 32–39.

Dragulescu, A. A. and Yakovenko, V. M. (2002). Probability distribution of returns in the Heston model with stochastic volatility, *Quantitative Finance* **2**: 443–453.

Dupire, B. (1994). Pricing with a Smile, *RISK* **7(1)**: 18–20.

Eberlein, E., Kallsen, J., and Kristen, J. (2003). Risk Management Based on Stochastic Volatility, *Journal of Risk* **5(2)**: 19–44.

Fengler, M. (2005). *Semiparametric Modelling of Implied Volatility*, Springer.

Garman, M. B. and Kohlhagen, S. W. (1983). Foreign currency option values, *Journal of International Monet & Finance* **2**: 231–237.

Hakala, J. and Wystup, U. (2002). Heston's Stochastic Volatility Model Applied to Foreign Exchange Options, *in* J. Hakala, U. Wystup (eds.) *Foreign Exchange Risk*, Risk Books, London.

Heston, S. (1993). A Closed-Form Solution for Options with Stochastic Volatility with Applications to Bond and Currency Options, *Review of Financial Studies* **6**: 327–343.

Hull, J. and White, A. (1987). The Pricing of Options with Stochastic Volatilities, *Journal of Finance* **42**: 281–300.

Kluge, T. (2002). *Pricing derivatives in stochastic volatility models using the finite difference method*, Diploma thesis, Chemnitz Technical University.

Martinez, M. and Senge, T. (2002). A Jump-Diffusion Model Applied to Foreign Exchange Markets, *in* J. Hakala, U. Wystup (eds.) *Foreign Exchange Risk*, Risk Books, London.

Merton, R. (1973). The Theory of Rational Option Pricing, *Bell Journal of Economics and Management Science* **4**: 141–183.

Merton, R. (1976). Option Pricing when Underlying Stock Returns are Discontinuous, *Journal of Financial Economics* **3**: 125–144.

Reiss, O. and Wystup, U. (2001). Computing Option Price Sensitivities Using Homogeneity, *Journal of Derivatives* **9(2)**: 41–53.

Rubinstein, M. (1994). Implied Binomial Trees, *Journal of Finance* **49**: 771–818.

Stein, E. and Stein, J. (1991). Stock Price Distributions with Stochastic Volatility: An Analytic Approach, *Review of Financial Studies* **4(4)**: 727–752.

Tompkins, R. G. and D'Ecclesia, R. L. (2004). Unconditional Return Disturbances: A Non-Parametric Simulation Approach, *Journal of Banking and Finance*, to appear.

Weron, R. (2004). Computationally intensive Value at Risk calculations, *in* J.E. Gentle, W. Härdle, Y. Mori (eds.) *Handbook of Computational Statistics*, Springer.

Wystup, U. (2003). The market price of one-touch options in foreign exchange markets, *Derivatives Week*, **12(13)**.

8 FFT-based Option Pricing

Szymon Borak, Kai Detlefsen, and Wolfgang Härdle

8.1 Introduction

The Black-Scholes formula, one of the major breakthroughs of modern finance, allows for an easy and fast computation of option prices. But some of its assumptions, like constant volatility or log-normal distribution of asset prices, do not find justification in the markets. More complex models, which take into account the empirical facts, often lead to more computations and this time burden can become a severe problem when computation of many option prices is required, e.g. in calibration of the implied volatility surface. To overcome this problem Carr and Madan (1999) developed a fast method to compute option prices for a whole range of strikes. This method and its application are the theme of this chapter.

In Section 8.2, we briefly discuss the Merton, Heston, and Bates models concentrating on aspects relevant for the option pricing method. In the following section, we present the method of Carr and Madan which is based on the fast Fourier transform (FFT) and can be applied to a variety of models. We also consider briefly some further developments and give a short introduction to the FFT algorithm. In the last section, we apply the method to the three analyzed models, check the results by Monte Carlo simulations and comment on some numerical issues.

8.2 Modern Pricing Models

The geometric Brownian motion (GBM) is the building block of modern finance. In particular, in the Black-Scholes model the underlying stock price is assumed to follow the GBM dynamics:

$$dS_t = rS_t dt + \sigma S_t dW_t, \tag{8.1}$$

which, applying Itô's lemma, can be written as:

$$S_t = S_0 \exp\left\{\left(r - \frac{\sigma^2}{2}\right)t + \sigma W_t\right\}. \tag{8.2}$$

The empirical facts, however, do not confirm model assumptions. Financial returns exhibit much fatter tails than the Black-Scholes model postulates, see Chapter 1. The common big returns that are larger than six-standard deviations should appear less than once in a million years if the Black-Scholes framework were accurate. Squared returns, as a measure of volatility, display positive autocorrelation over several days, which contradicts the constant volatility assumption. Non-constant volatility can be observed as well in the option markets where "smiles" and "skews" in implied volatility occur. These properties of financial time series lead to more refined models. We introduce three such models in the following paragraphs.

8.2.1 Merton Model

If an important piece of information about the company becomes public it may cause a sudden change in the company's stock price. The information usually comes at a random time and the size of its impact on the stock price may be treated as a random variable. To cope with these observations Merton (1976) proposed a model that allows discontinuous trajectories of asset prices. The model extends (8.1) by adding jumps to the stock price dynamics:

$$\frac{dS_t}{S_t} = rdt + \sigma dW_t + dZ_t, \tag{8.3}$$

where Z_t is a compound Poisson process with a log-normal distribution of jump sizes. The jumps follow a (homogeneous) Poisson process N_t with intensity λ (see Chapter 14), which is independent of W_t. The log-jump sizes $Y_i \sim N(\mu, \delta^2)$ are i.i.d random variables with mean μ and variance δ^2, which are independent of both N_t and W_t.

The model becomes incomplete which means that there are many possible ways to choose a risk-neutral measure such that the discounted price process is a martingale. Merton proposed to change the drift of the Wiener process and to leave the other ingredients unchanged. The asset price dynamics is then given by:

$$S_t = S_0 \exp\left(\mu^M t + \sigma W_t + \sum_{i=1}^{N_t} Y_i\right),$$

where $\mu^M = r - \sigma^2 - \lambda\{\exp(\mu + \frac{\delta^2}{2}) - 1\}$. Jump components add mass to the tails of the returns distribution. Increasing δ adds mass to both tails, while a negative/positive μ implies relatively more mass in the left/right tail.

For the purpose of Section 8.4 it is necessary to introduce the characteristic function (cf) of $X_t = \ln \frac{S_t}{S_0}$:

$$\phi_{X_t}(z) = \exp\left[t\left\{-\frac{\sigma^2 z^2}{2} + i\mu^M z + \lambda\left(e^{-\delta^2 z^2/2 + i\mu z - 1}\right)\right\}\right], \tag{8.4}$$

where $X_t = \mu^M t + \sigma W_t + \sum_{i=1}^{N_t} Y_i$.

8.2.2 Heston Model

Another possible modification of (8.1) is to substitute the constant volatility parameter σ with a stochastic process. This leads to the so-called "stochastic volatility" models, where the price dynamics is driven by:

$$\frac{dS_t}{S_t} = r dt + \sqrt{v_t} dW_t,$$

where v_t is another unobservable stochastic process. There are many possible ways of choosing the variance process v_t. Hull and White (1987) proposed to use geometric Brownian motion:

$$\frac{dv_t}{v_t} = c_1 dt + c_2 dW_t. \tag{8.5}$$

However, geometric Brownian motion tends to increase exponentially which is an undesirable property for volatility. Volatility exhibits rather a mean reverting behavior. Therefore a model based on an Ornstein-Uhlenbeck-type process:

$$dv_t = \kappa(\theta - v_t)dt + \beta dW_t, \tag{8.6}$$

was suggested by Stein and Stein (1991). This process, however, admits negative values of the variance v_t.

These deficiencies were eliminated in a stochastic volatility model introduced by Heston (1993):

$$\begin{aligned} \frac{dS_t}{S_t} &= rdt + \sqrt{v_t} dW_t^{(1)}, \\ dv_t &= \kappa(\theta - v_t)dt + \sigma\sqrt{v_t} dW_t^{(2)}, \end{aligned} \tag{8.7}$$

where the two Brownian components $W_t^{(1)}$ and $W_t^{(2)}$ are correlated with rate ρ:

$$\text{Cov}\left(dW_t^{(1)}, dW_t^{(2)}\right) = \rho dt, \tag{8.8}$$

for details see Chapter 7. The term $\sqrt{v_t}$ in equation (8.7) simply ensures positive volatility. When the process touches the zero bound the stochastic part becomes zero and the non-stochastic part will push it up.

Parameter κ measures the speed of mean reversion, θ is the average level of volatility, and σ is the volatility of volatility. In (8.8) the correlation ρ is typically negative, which is consistent with empirical observations (Cont, 2001). This negative dependence between returns and volatility is known in the market as the "leverage effect."

The risk neutral dynamics is given in a similar way as in the Black-Scholes model. For the logarithm of the asset price process $X_t = \ln \frac{S_t}{S_0}$ one obtains the equation:

$$dX_t = \left(r - \frac{1}{2}v_t\right) dt + \sqrt{v_t} dW_t^{(1)}.$$

The cf is given by:

$$
\begin{aligned}
\phi_{X_t}(z) &= \frac{\exp\{\frac{\kappa\theta t(\kappa - i\rho\sigma z)}{\sigma^2} + iztr + izx_0\}}{(\cosh\frac{\gamma t}{2} + \frac{\kappa - i\rho\sigma z}{\gamma}\sinh\frac{\gamma t}{2})^{\frac{2\kappa\theta}{\sigma^2}}} \\
&\cdot \exp\left\{-\frac{(z^2 + iz)v_0}{\gamma\coth\frac{\gamma t}{2} + \kappa - i\rho\sigma z}\right\},
\end{aligned} \tag{8.9}
$$

where $\gamma = \sqrt{\sigma^2(z^2 + iz) + (\kappa - i\rho\sigma z)^2}$, and x_0 and v_0 are the initial values for the log-price process and the volatility process, respectively.

8.2.3 Bates Model

The Merton and Heston approaches were combined by Bates (1996), who proposed a model with stochastic volatility and jumps:

$$
\begin{aligned}
\frac{dS_t}{S_t} &= rdt + \sqrt{v_t}dW_t^{(1)} + dZ_t, \qquad (8.10) \\
dv_t &= \kappa(\theta - v_t)dt + \sigma\sqrt{v_t}dW_t^{(2)}, \\
\text{Cov}(dW_t^{(1)}, dW_t^{(2)}) &= \rho\, dt.
\end{aligned}
$$

As in (8.3) Z_t is a compound Poisson process with intensity λ and log-normal distribution of jump sizes independent of $W_t^{(1)}$ (and $W_t^{(2)}$). If J denotes the jump size then $\ln(1 + J) \sim N(\ln(1 + \bar{k}) - \frac{1}{2}\delta^2, \delta^2)$ for some $\bar{k}$. Under the risk neutral probability one obtains the equation for the logarithm of the asset price:

$$
dX_t = (r - \lambda\bar{k} - \frac{1}{2}v_t)dt + \sqrt{v_t}dW_t^{(1)} + \tilde{Z}_t,
$$

where $\tilde{Z}_t$ is a compound Poisson process with normal distribution of jump magnitudes.

Since the jumps are independent of the diffusion part in (8.10), the characteristic function for the log-price process can be obtained as:

$$
\phi_{X_t}(z) = \phi_{X_t}^D(z)\phi_{X_t}^J(z),
$$

where:

$$\phi^D_{X_t}(z) = \frac{\exp\left\{\frac{\kappa\theta t(\kappa - i\rho\sigma z)}{\sigma^2} + izt(r - \lambda\overline{k}) + izx_0\right\}}{\left(\cosh\frac{\gamma t}{2} + \frac{\kappa - i\rho\sigma z}{\gamma}\sinh\frac{\gamma t}{2}\right)^{\frac{2\kappa\theta}{\sigma^2}}} \cdot \exp\left\{-\frac{(z^2+iz)v_0}{\gamma\coth\frac{\gamma t}{2} + \kappa - i\rho\sigma z}\right\} \tag{8.11}$$

is the diffusion part cf and

$$\phi^J_{X_t}(z) = \exp\{t\lambda(e^{-\delta^2 z^2/2 + i(\ln(1+\overline{k}) - \frac{1}{2}\delta^2)z} - 1)\}, \tag{8.12}$$

is the jump part cf. Note that (8.9) and (8.11) are very similar. The difference lies in the shift $\lambda\overline{k}$ (risk neutral correction). Formula (8.12) has a similar structure as the jump part in (8.4), however, μ is substituted with $\ln(1+\overline{k}) - \frac{1}{2}\delta^2$.

8.3 Option Pricing with FFT

In the last section, three asset price models and their characteristic functions were presented. In this section, we describe a numerical approach for pricing options which utilizes the characteristic function of the underlying instrument's price process. The approach has been introduced by Carr and Madan (1999) and is based on the FFT. The use of the FFT is motivated by two reasons. On the one hand, the algorithm offers a speed advantage. This effect is even boosted by the possibility of the pricing algorithm to calculate prices for a whole range of strikes. On the other hand, the cf of the log price is known and has a simple form for many models considered in literature, while the density is often not known in closed form.

The approach assumes that the cf of the log-price is given analytically. The basic idea of the method is to develop an analytic expression for the Fourier transform of the option price and to get the price by Fourier inversion. As the Fourier transform and its inversion work for square-integrable functions (see Plancherel's theorem, e.g. in Rudin, 1991) we do not consider directly the option price but a modification of it.

Let $C_T(k)$ denote the price of a European call option with maturity T and strike $K = \exp(k)$:

$$C_T(k) = \int_k^{\infty} e^{-rT}(e^s - e^k) q_T(s) ds,$$

where q_T is the risk-neutral density of $s_T = \log S_T$. The function C_T is not square-integrable because $C_T(k)$ converges to S_0 for $k \to -\infty$. Hence, we consider a modified function:

$$c_T(k) = \exp(\alpha k) C_T(k), \tag{8.13}$$

which is square-integrable for a suitable $\alpha > 0$. The choice of α may depend on the model for S_t. The Fourier transform of c_T is defined by:

$$\psi_T(v) = \int_{-\infty}^{\infty} e^{ivk} c_T(k) dk.$$

The expression for ψ_T can be computed directly after an interchange of integrals:

$$\begin{aligned}
\psi_T(v) &= \int_{-\infty}^{\infty} e^{ivk} \int_k^{\infty} e^{\alpha k} e^{-rT}(e^s - e^k) q_T(s) ds dk \\
&= \int_{-\infty}^{\infty} e^{-rT} q_T(s) \int_{-\infty}^{s} (e^{\alpha k + s} - e^{(\alpha+1)k}) e^{ivk} dk ds \\
&= \int_{-\infty}^{\infty} e^{-rT} q_T(s) (\frac{e^{(\alpha+1+iv)s}}{\alpha + iv} - \frac{e^{(\alpha+1+iv)s}}{\alpha + 1 + iv}) ds \\
&= \frac{e^{-rT} \phi_T(v - (\alpha+1)i)}{\alpha^2 + \alpha - v^2 + i(2\alpha+1)v},
\end{aligned}$$

where ϕ_T is the Fourier transform of q_T. A sufficient condition for c_T to be square-integrable is given by $\psi_T(0)$ being finite. This is equivalent to

$$E(S_T^{\alpha+1}) < \infty.$$

A value $\alpha = 0.75$ fulfills this condition for the models of Section 8.2. With this choice, we follow Schoutens et al. (2003) who found in an empirical study that this value leads to stable algorithms, i.e. the prices are well replicated for many model parameters.

Now, we get the desired option price in terms of ψ_T using Fourier inversion

$$C_T(k) = \frac{\exp(-\alpha k)}{\pi} \int_0^{\infty} e^{-ivk} \psi(v) dv.$$

This integral can be computed numerically as:

$$C_T(k) \approx \frac{\exp(-\alpha k)}{\pi} \sum_{j=0}^{N-1} e^{-iv_j k} \psi(v_j)\eta, \tag{8.14}$$

where $v_j = \eta j$, $j = 0, \ldots, N-1$, and $\eta > 0$ is the distance between the points of the integration grid.

Lee (2004) has developed bounds for the sampling and truncation errors of this approximation. Formula (8.14) suggests to calculate the prices using the FFT, which is an efficient algorithm for computing the sums

$$w_u = \sum_{j=0}^{N-1} e^{-i\frac{2\pi}{N}ju} x_j, \text{ for } u = 0, \ldots, N-1. \tag{8.15}$$

To see why this is the case see Example 1 below, which illustrates the basic idea of the FFT. In general, the strikes near the spot price are of interest because such options are traded most frequently. We consider thus an equidistant spacing of the log-strikes around the log spot price s_0:

$$k_u = -\frac{1}{2}N\zeta + \zeta u + s_0, \text{ for } u = 0, \ldots, N-1, \tag{8.16}$$

where $\zeta > 0$ denotes the distance between the log strikes. Substituting these log-strikes yields for $u = 0, \ldots, N-1$:

$$C_T(k_u) \approx \frac{\exp(-\alpha k)}{\pi} \sum_{j=0}^{N-1} e^{-i\zeta\eta j u} e^{i\{(\frac{1}{2}N\zeta - s_0)v_j\}} \psi(v_j)\eta.$$

Now, the FFT can be applied to

$$x_j = e^{i\{(\frac{1}{2}N\zeta - s_0)v_j\}} \psi(v_j), \text{ for } j = 0, \ldots, N-1,$$

provided that

$$\zeta\eta = \frac{2\pi}{N}. \tag{8.17}$$

This constraint leads, however, to the following trade-off: the parameter N controls the computation time and thus is often determined by the computational setup. Hence the right hand side may be regarded as given or fixed.

One would like to choose a small ζ in order to get many prices for strikes near the spot price. But the constraint implies then a big η giving a coarse grid for integration. So we face a trade-off between accuracy and the number of interesting strikes.

Example 1

The FFT is an algorithm for computing (8.15). Its popularity stems from its remarkable speed: while a naive computation needs N^2 operations the FFT requires only $N \log(N)$ steps. The algorithm was first published by Cooley and Tukey (1965) and since then has been continuously refined. We illustrate the original FFT algorithm for $N = 4$. Writing u and j as binary numbers:

$$u = 2u_1 + u_0, \;\; j = 2j_1 + j_0,$$

with $u_1, u_0, j_1, j_0 \in \{0, 1\}$ $u = (u_1, u_0)$, $j = (j_1, j_0)$ the formula (8.15) is given as:

$$w_{(u_1,u_0)} = \sum_{j_0=0}^{1} \sum_{j_1=0}^{1} x_{(j_1,j_0)} W^{(2u_1+u_0)(2j_1+j_0)},$$

where $W = e^{-2\pi i/N}$. Because of

$$W^{(2u_1+u_0)(2j_1+j_0)} = W^{2u_0 j_1} W^{(2u_1+u_0)j_0},$$

we get

$$w_{(u_1,u_0)} = \sum_{j_0=0}^{1} (\sum_{j_1=0}^{1} x_{(j_1,j_0)}, W^{2u_0 j_1}) W^{(2u_1+u_0)j_0}.$$

Now, the FFT can be described by the following three steps

$$w^1_{(u_0,j_0)} = \sum_{j_1=0}^{1} x_{(j_1,j_0)} W^{2u_0 j_1},$$

$$w^2_{(u_0,u_1)} = \sum_{j_0=0}^{1} w^1_{(u_0,j_0)} W^{(2u_1+u_0)j_0},$$

$$w_{(u_1,u_0)} = w^2_{(u_0,u_1)}.$$

While a naive computation of (8.15) requires $4^2 = 16$ complex multiplications the FFT needs only $4 \log(4) = 8$ complex multiplications. This explains the speed of the FFT because complex multiplications are the most time consuming operations in this context.

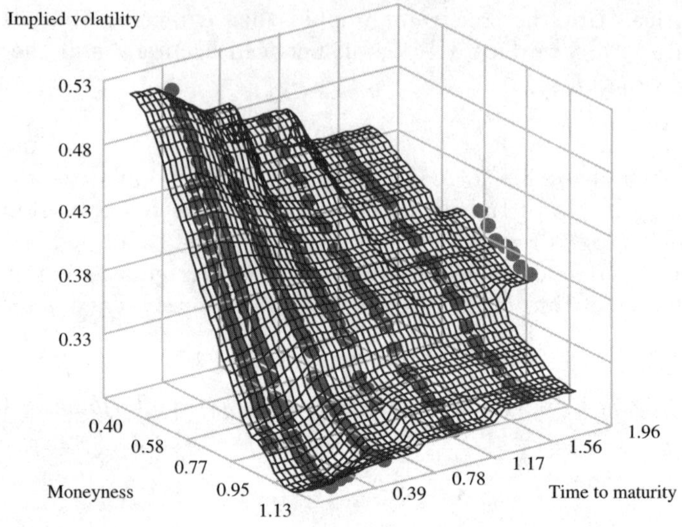

Figure 8.1: Implied volatility surface of DAX options on January 4, 1999.
STFfft01.xpl

8.4 Applications

In this section, we apply the FFT option pricing algorithm of Section 8.3 to the models described in Section 8.2. Our aim is to demonstrate the remarkable speed of the FFT algorithm by comparing it to Monte Carlo simulations. Moreover, we present an application of the fast option pricing algorithm to the calibration of implied volatility (IV) surfaces. In Figure 8.1 we present the IV surface of DAX options on January 4, 1999 where the red points are the observed implied volatilities and the surface is fitted with the Nadaraya-Watson kernel estimator. For analysis of IV surfaces consult Fengler et al. (2002) and Chapter 5.

In order to apply the FFT-based algorithm we need to know the characteristic function of the risk neutral density which has been described in Section 8.2 for the Merton, Heston, and Bates models. Moreover, we have to decide on the parameters α, N, and η of the algorithm. Schoutens et al. (2003) used $\alpha = 0.75$ in a calibration procedure for the Eurostoxx 50 index data. We follow their approach and set α to this value. The computation time depends on the parameter N which we set to 512. As the number of grid points of the numerical integration is also given by N, this parameter in addition determines the accuracy of the prices. For parameter η, which determines the distance of the points of the integration grid, we use 0.25. A limited simulation study showed that the FFT algorithm is not sensitive to the choice of η, i.e. small changes in η gave similar results. In Section 8.3, we have already discussed the relation between these parameters.

For comparison, we computed the option prices also by Monte Carlo simulations with 500 time steps and 5000 repetitions. Such simulations are a convenient way to check the results of the FFT-based algorithm. The calculations are based on the following parameters: the price of the underlying asset is $S_0 = 100$, time to maturity $T = 1$, and the interest rate $r = 0.02$. For demonstration we choose the Heston model with parameters: $\kappa = 10$, $\theta = 0.2$, $\sigma = 0.7$, $\rho = -0.5$, and $v_0 = 0.2$. To make our comparison more sound we also calculate prices with the analytic formula given in Chapter 7. In the left panel of Figure 8.2 we show the prices of European call options as a function of the strike price K. As the prices obtained with the analytical formula are close to the prices obtained with the FFT-based method and the Monte Carlo prices oscillate around them, this figure confirms that the pricing algorithm works correctly. The different values of the Monte Carlo prices are mainly due to the random nature of this technique. One needs to use even more time steps and repetitions to get better results. The minor differences between the analytical and FFT-based prices come form the fact that the latter method gives the exact values only on the grid (8.16) and between the grid points one has to use some interpolation method to approximate the price of the option. This problem can be more clearly observed in the right panel of Figure 8.2, where percentage differences between the analytical and FFT prices are presented. In order to preserve the great speed of the algorithm we simply use linear interpolation between the grid points. This approach, however, slightly overestimates the true prices since the call option price is a convex function of the strike. It can be clearly seen that near the grid points the prices obtained by both methods coincide, while between the grid points the FFT-based algorithm generates higher prices than the analytical solution.

Although these methods yield similar results they need different computation time. In Table 8.1 we compare the speed of C++ implementations of the Monte Carlo and FFT methods. We calculate Monte Carlo prices for 20 different

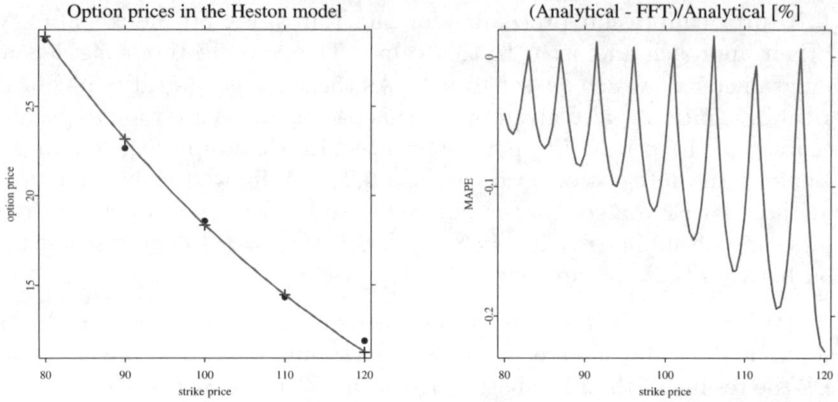

Figure 8.2: *Left panel:* European call option prices obtained by Monte Carlo simulations (filled circles), analytical formula (crosses) and the FFT method (solid line) for the Heston model. *Right panel:* Percentage differences between analytical and FFT prices.

STFfft02.xpl

Table 8.1: The computation times in seconds for the FFT method and the Monte Carlo method for three different models. Monte Carlo prices were calculated for 20 different strikes, with 500 time steps and 5000 repetitions.

Model	FFT	MC
Merton	0.01	31.25
Heston	0.01	34.41
Bates	0.01	37.53

strikes for each of the three models. The speed superiority of the FFT-based method is clearly visible. It is more than 3000 times faster than the Monte Carlo approach.

As an application of the fast pricing algorithm we consider the problem of model calibration. Given option prices observed in the market we look for model parameters that can reproduce the data well. Normally, the market prices are given by an implied volatility surface which represents the implied volatility of option prices for different strikes and maturities. The calibration can then be done for the implied volatilities or for the option prices. This decision depends on the problem considered. As a measure of fit one can use the Mean Squared Error (MSE):

$$MSE = \frac{1}{\text{number of options}} \sum_{\text{options}} \frac{(\text{market price - model price})^2}{\text{market price}^2}, \tag{8.18}$$

but other choices like the Mean Absolute Percentage Error (MAPE) or Mean Absolute Error (MAE) are also possible:

$$MAPE = \frac{1}{\text{number of options}} \sum_{\text{options}} \frac{\mid \text{market price - model price} \mid}{\text{market price}},$$

$$MAE = \frac{1}{\text{number of options}} \sum_{\text{options}} \mid \text{market price - model price} \mid .$$

Moreover, the error function can be modified by weights if some regions of the implied volatility surface are more important or some observations should be ignored completely.

The calibration results in a minimization problem of the error function MSE. This optimization can be carried out by different algorithms like simulated annealing, the Broyden-Fletcher-Goldfarb-Shanno-algorithm, the Nelder-Mead simplex algorithm or Monte Carlo Markov Chain methods. An overview of optimization methods can be found in Čížková (2003). As minimization algorithms normally have to compute the function to be minimized many times an efficient algorithm for the option prices is essential. The FFT-based algorithm is fairly efficient as is shown in Table 8.1. Moreover, it returns prices for a whole range of strikes at one maturity. This is an additional advantage because for the calibration of an implied volatility surface one needs to calculate prices for many different strikes and maturities.

As an example we present the results for the Bates model calibrated to the IV surface of DAX options on January 4, 1999. The data set, which can be found in MD*Base, contains 236 option prices for 7 maturities (for each maturity there is a different number of strikes). We minimize (8.18) with respect to 8 parameters of the Bates model: $\lambda, \delta, \overline{k}, \kappa, \theta, \sigma, \rho, v_0$. Since the function (8.18)

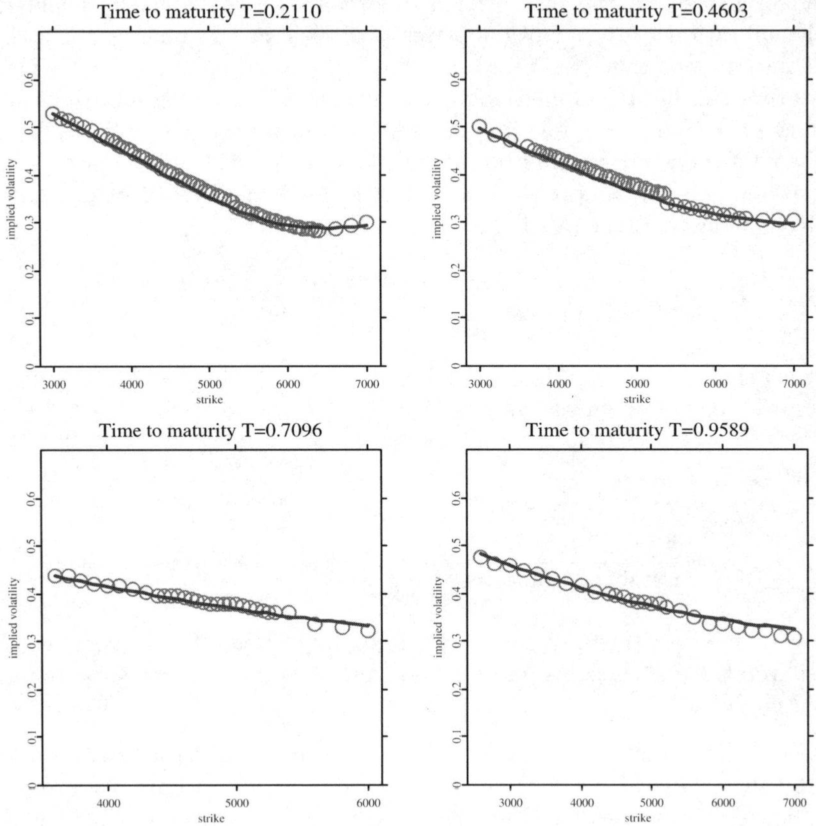

Figure 8.3: The observed implied volatilities of DAX options on January 4, 1999 (circles) and fitted Bates model (line) for 4 different maturity strings.

STFfft03.xpl

has many local minima, we use the simulated annealing minimization method, which offers the advantage to search for a global minimum, combined with the Nelder-Mead simplex algorithm. As a result we obtaine the following estimates for the model parameters: $\widehat{\lambda} = 0.13$, $\widehat{\delta} = 0.0004$, $\widehat{\overline{k}} = -0.03$, $\widehat{\kappa} = 4.23$, $\widehat{\theta} =$

0.17, $\widehat{\sigma} = 1.39$, $\widehat{\rho} = -0.55$, $\widehat{v_0} = 0.10$, and the value of MSE is 0.00381. In Figure 8.3 we show the resulting fits of the Bates model to the data for 4 different maturities. The red circles are implied volatilities observed in the market on the time to maturities $T = 0.21, 0.46, 0.71, 0.96$ and the blue lines are implied volatilities calculated from the Bates model with the calibrated parameters. In the calibration we used all data points. As the FFT-based algorithm computes prices for the whole range of strikes the biggest impact on the speed of calibration has the number of used maturities, while the total number of observations has only minor influence on the speed.

On the one hand, the Carr-Madan algorithm offers a great speed advantage but on the other hand its applications are restricted to European options. The Monte Carlo approach instead works for a wider class of derivatives including path dependent options.

Thus, this approach has been modified in different ways. The accuracy can be improved by using better integration rules. Carr and Madan (1999) considered also the Simpson rule which leads – taking (8.17) into account – to the following formula for the option prices:

$$C_T(k_u) \approx \frac{\exp(-\alpha k)}{\pi} \sum_{j=0}^{N-1} e^{-i\zeta\eta j u} e^{i\{(\frac{1}{2}N\zeta - s_0)v_j\}} \psi(v_j) \frac{\eta}{3} \{3 + (-1)^j - I(-j = 0)\}.$$

This representation again allows a direct application of the FFT to compute the sum.

An alternative to the original Carr-Madan approach is to consider instead of (8.13) other modifications of the call prices. For example, Cont and Tankov (2004) used the (modified) time value of the options:

$$\tilde{c}_T(k) = C_T(k) - \max(1 - e^{k-rT}, 0).$$

Although this method also requires the existence of α satisfying $E(S_T^{\alpha+1}) < \infty$ the parameter does not enter into the final pricing formula. Thus, it is not necessary to choose any value for α. This freedom of choice of α makes the approach easier to implement. On the other hand, option price surfaces that are obtained with this method often have a peak for small maturities and strikes near the spot. This special form differs from the surfaces typically observed in the market. The peak results from the non-differentiability of the intrinsic value at the spot. Hence, other modifications of the option prices have been considered that make the modified option prices differentiable (Cont and Tankov, 2004).

The calculation of option prices by the FFT-based algorithm leads to different errors. The truncation error results from substituting the infinite upper integration limit by a finite number. The sampling error comes from evaluating the integrand only at grid points. Lee (2004) gives bounds for these errors and discusses error minimization strategies. Moreover, he presents and unifies extensions of the original Carr-Madan approach to other payoff classes. Besides the truncation and the sampling error, the implementation of the algorithm often leads to severe roundoff errors because of the complex form of the characteristic function for some models. To avoid this problem, which often occurs for long maturities, it is necessary to transform the characteristic function.

Concluding, we can say that the FFT-based option pricing method is a technique that can be used whenever time constraints are important. However, in order to avoid severe pricing errors its application requires careful decisions regarding the choice of the parameters and the particular algorithm steps used.

Bibliography

Bates, D. (1996). Jump and Stochastic Volatility: Exchange Rate Processes Implicit in Deutsche Mark Options, *Review of Financial Studies* **9**: 69–107.

Carr, P. and Madan, D. (1999). Option valuation using the fast Fourier transform, *Journal of Computational Finance* **2**: 61–73.

Čížková, L. (2003). Numerical Optimization Methods in Econometrics, *in* J.M. Rodriguez Poo (ed.) *Computer-Aided Introduction to Econometrics*, Springer-Verlag, Berlin.

Cooley, J. and Tukey, J. (1965). An algorithm for the machine calculation of complex Fourier series, *Math. Comput.* **19**: 297–301.

Cont, R. (2001). Empirical properties of assets returns: Stylized facts and statistical issues, *Quant. Finance* **1**: 1-14.

Cont, R. and Tankov, P. (2004). *Financial Modelling With Jump Processes*, Chapman & Hall/CRC.

Fengler, M., Härdle, W. and Schmidt, P. (2002). The Analysis of Implied Volatilities, *in* W. Härdle, T. Kleinow, G. Stahl (eds.) *Applied Quantitative Finance*, Springer-Verlag, Berlin.

Heston, S. (1993). A closed-form solution for options with stochastic volatility with applications to bond and currency options, *Review of Financial Studies* **6**: 327-343.

Hull, J. and White, A. (1987). The pricing of Options on Assets with Stochastic Volatilities, *Journal of Finance* **42**: 281–300.

Lee, R. (2004). Option pricing by transform methods: extensions, unification and error control, *Journal of Computational Finance* **7**.

Merton, R. (1976). Option pricing when underlying stock returns are discontinuous, *J. Financial Economics* **3**: 125-144.

Rudin, W. (1991). *Functional Analysis*, McGrawHill.

Schoutens, W., Simons, E., and Tistaert, J. (2003). A Perfect Calibration! Now What? *UCS Technical Report*, Catholic University Leuven.

Stein, E. and Stein, J. (1991). Stock price distribution with stochastic volatility: An analytic approach, *Review of Financial Studies* **4**: 727–752.

9 Valuation of Mortgage Backed Securities: from Optimality to Reality

Nicolas Gaussel and Julien Tamine

9.1 Introduction

Mortgage backed securities (MBS) are financial assets backed by a pool of mortgages. Investors buy a part of the pool's principal and receive the corresponding mortgages cash flows. The pooled mortgages generally offer the borrower the opportunity to prepay part or all of the remaining principal before maturity. This prepayment policy is the key point for pricing and hedging MBS.

In the existing literature, two broad directions have been explored. On the one hand, the mainstream approach relies on statistical inference. The observed prepayment policy is statistically explained by the level of interest rates and some parameters of the underlying mortgage portfolio, see Schwartz and Torous (1989), Boudhouk et al. (1997). Dedicated to pricing and hedging, these approaches do not address the rationality behind the observed prepayment policy.

On the other hand, authors like Nielsen and Poulsen (2002) directly address the problem of optimal prepayment within consumption based models. This normative approach gives insights into the determinants of prepayments and relies on macro-economic variables. However, this approach appears to be of poor practical use due to the numerous economic variables involved.

In this chapter, we propose a third way. The optimality problem is addressed from an unconstrained, financial point of view. Using arguments similar to those of early exercise of American derivatives, we identify the optimal interest rate level for prepayment. Building on this frontier, we construct a family of prepayment policies based on the spread between interest rates and the optimal prepayment level. The MBS are then priced as the expected value of their forthcoming discounted cash flows, which is in line with classical methodology for flow product valuation.

Mortgages specific characteristics

Mortgage cash flows differ from those of a classical bond since their coupon is partly made of interest and partly of principal refunding. Despite this difference in cash flow structure, the prepayment option enclosed in the mortgage is very similar to the callability feature of a bond. Under classical assumptions on the bond market, an optimal time of early exercise can be exhibited, depending on the term structure and on the volatility of interest rates. Such models predict a rise in exercise probability during low interest rate periods, increasing the value of the callability option attached to the bond. These conclusions are supported by empirical evidence. Historical values of the market price of a non-callable and a callable General Electric bond with the same maturity and coupon are displayed on Figure 9.1.

The 10-year US government rate is displayed on the secondary axis. During this period of a sharp decrease of interest rates, the value of the non-callable bond rose much more than the value of the callable one. It may be tempting to adapt callable bonds pricing framework to mortgages. Nevertheless, statistical results prevent such a direct extrapolation. Though most mortgagors prepay for low interest rate levels, a significant percentage chooses to go on refunding their loan, no matter how interesting the refinancing conditions are. This phenomenon is often called *burnout*, Schwartz and Torous (1989). Conversely, some mortgagors choose to exercise their prepayment right at high interest rate levels. Such observations reveal that mortgagors are individuals whose behavior is in part determined by exogenous factors.

Economic studies suggest that major motivations for early prepayment can be classified within three broad categories, Hayre (1999):

- structural motivations accounting for occurrence of prepayment during high interest rate periods: unexpected heritage; professional move involving house sale (if residential mortgages are considered); insurance prepayment after mortgagor death;

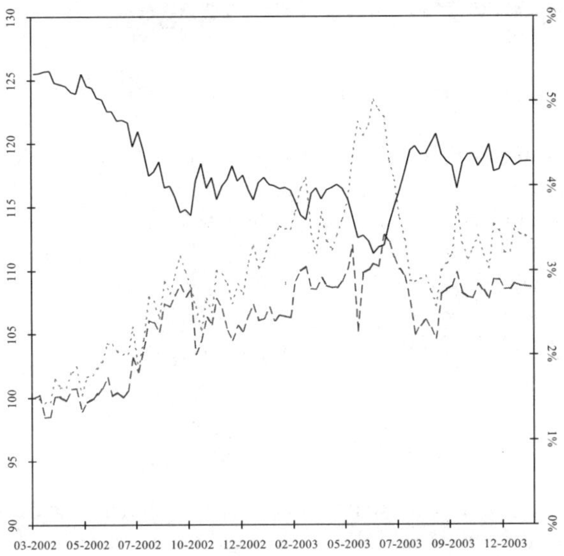

Figure 9.1: Historical prices of the 10-year US goverment bond (solid line, right axis) and a non-callable (dotted line, left axis) and a callable (dashed line, left axis) General Electric bonds. STFmbs01.xpl

- specific characteristics explaining burnout: lack of access to interest rate information;
- refunding motivations in accordance with classical financial theory.

Based on these considerations, the subsequent analysis is divided into three parts. Section 2 is concerned with the determination of the optimal time for prepaying a mortgage in an ideal market where interest rates would be the only variable of decision. This section sheds light on the influence of interest rates on refinancing incentive. In Section 3, the MBS price is expressed as the expected value of its future cash-flows, under some prepayment policy. A numerical procedure based on the resolution of a two-dimensional partial differential equation is put forward. The insights provided by our approach are illustrated through numerical examples.

9.2 Optimally Prepaid Mortgage

9.2.1 Financial Characteristics and Cash Flow Analysis

For the sake of simplicity, all cash flows are assumed to be paid continuously in time. Given a maturity T, the mortgage is defined by a fixed actuarial coupon rate c and a principal N. If the mortgagor chooses not to prepay, he refunds a continuous flow ϕdt, related to the maturity T and the coupon rate c through the initial parity condition

$$N = \int_0^T \phi \exp(-cs)\, ds, \tag{9.1}$$

where

$$\phi = N \frac{c}{1 - \exp(-cT)}.$$

As opposed to *in fine* bonds where intermediary cashflows are only made of interest and the principal is fully redeemed at maturity, this flow includes payments of both interest and principal. At time $t \in [0, T]$ the remaining principal K_t is contractually defined as the forthcoming cash flows discounted at the initial actuarial coupon rate

$$\begin{aligned} K_t &\stackrel{\text{def}}{=} \int_t^T \phi \exp\{-c(s-t)\}\, ds \\ &= \frac{\phi}{c}\left[1 - \exp\{-c(T-t)\}\right] \\ &= N \frac{1 - \exp\{-c(T-t)\}}{1 - \exp(-cT)} \end{aligned}$$

Early prepayment at date t means paying K_t to the bank. In financial terms, the mortgagor owns an American prepayment option with strike K_t. The varying proportion between interest and capital in the flow ϕ is displayed in Figure 9.2.

9.2.2 Optimal Behavior and Price

The financial model

Given its callability feature, the mortgage is a fixed income derivative product. Its valuation must therefore be grounded on the definition of a particular

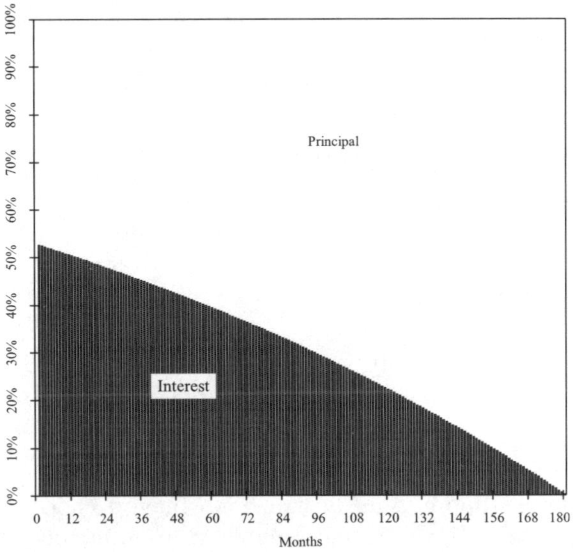

Figure 9.2: The proportion between interest and principal varying in time.

interest rate model. Since many models can be seen as good candidates, we need to specify some additional features. First, this model should be arbitrage free and consistent with the observed forward term structure. This amounts to selecting a standard Heath-Jarrow-Morton (HJM) type approach. Second, we specify an additional Markovian structure for tractability purposes. While our theoretical analysis is valid for any Markovian HJM model, all (numerical) results will be presented, for simplicity, using a one factor enhanced Vasicek model (Priaulet, 2000); see Martellini and Priaulet (2000) for practical uses or Björk (1998) for more details on theoretical grounds. Let us quickly recap its characteristics.

Assumption A The short rate process r_t is defined via an Ornstein-Uhlenbeck process:

$$dr_t = \lambda \{\theta(t) - r_t\} dt + \sigma dW_t, \tag{9.2}$$

with

$$\theta(t) = \frac{\partial}{\partial t} f(0,t) + f(0,t) + \sigma^2 \frac{1 - \exp(-2\lambda t)}{2\lambda},$$

and $f(0,t)$ being the initial instantaneous forward term curve. The parameters

σ and λ control the volatility $\sigma(\tau)$ of forward rates of maturity τ

$$\sigma(\tau) = \frac{\sigma}{\lambda}\{1 - \exp(-\lambda\tau)\},$$

and allow for a rough calibration to derivative prices. Note that in this enhanced Vasicek framework, all bond prices can be written in closed form, Martellini and Priaulet (2000).

The optimal stopping problem

The theory of optimal stopping is well known, Pham (2003). It is widely used in mathematical finance for the valuation of American contracts, Musiela and Rutkowski (1997). In the sequel, the optimally prepaid mortgage price is explicitly calculated as a solution of an optimal stopping problem.

Let $\tau \in [t, T]$ be the stopping time at which mortgagors choose to prepay. Cash flows are of two kinds. If $\tau < T$, mortgagors keep on paying continuously ϕdt at any time, with discounted (random) value equal to

$$\int_t^{\min(\tau,T)} \phi \exp\left(-\int_t^s r_u du\right) ds.$$

At date τ, if $\tau < T$, the remaining capital K_t must be paid, implying a discounted cash flow equal to

$$I(\tau < T) \exp\left(-\int_t^\tau r_u du\right) K_\tau,$$

The mortgagor will choose his prepayment time τ in order to minimize the risk neutral expected value of these future discounted cashflows. The value of the optimally prepaid mortgage is then obtained as

$$\begin{aligned} V_t &= \inf_{t<\tau<T} \mathrm{E}\left[\left\{\int_t^{\min(\tau,T)} \phi \exp\left(-\int_t^s r_u du\right) ds \right.\right. \\ &\qquad \left.\left. + I(\tau < T) \exp\left(-\int_t^\tau r_u du\right) K_\tau \right\} \middle| \mathcal{F}_t \right], \end{aligned} \tag{9.3}$$

where $\mathcal{F}_t$ is the relevant filtration. Since r_t is Markovian, V_t can be expressed as a function of the current level of the state variables and reduces to $V(t, r_t)$. The problem in (9.3) is therefore a standard Markovian optimal stopping problem (Pham, 2003).

At time t, the mortgagor's decision whether to prepay or not is made on the following arbitrage: the cost of prepaying immediately ($\tau = t$) is equal to the current value of the remaining mortgage principal K_t. This cost has to be compared to the expected cost $V(t, r_t)$ of going on refunding the continuous flow ϕdt and keeping the option to prepay until later. Obviously, the optimal mortgagor should opt for prepayment if

$$V(t, r_t) \geqslant K_t. \tag{9.4}$$

Conversely, within the non-prepayment region, the mortgage can be sold or bought: its price must be the solution of the standard Black-Scholes partial differential equation. The following proposition sums up these intuitions. Its proof uses the link between conditional expectation and partial differential equations called the "Feynman-Kac analysis."

PROPOSITION 9.1 *Under Assumption A, $V(t, r_t)$ is solution of the partial differential equation :*

$$\max \left\{ \begin{array}{c} \dfrac{\partial V(t,r)}{\partial t} + \mu(t,r) \dfrac{\partial V(t,r)}{\partial r} + \dfrac{1}{2}\sigma^2 \dfrac{\partial^2 V(t,r)}{\partial r^2} - rV(t,r) + \phi, \\ V(t,r) - K_t \end{array} \right\} = 0 \tag{9.5}$$

$$V(T, r) = 0 \tag{9.6}$$

where $\mu(t,r) \stackrel{\text{def}}{=} \lambda(\theta(t) - r)$ and σ are fixed by Assumption A.

Proof: We only give a sketch for constructing a solution. The optimal stopping time problem at time t is given by

$$V_t = \left\{ \inf_{\tau<T} \mathrm{E} \int_t^{\min(\tau,T)} \phi \exp\left(-\int_t^s r_u du\right) ds \right. \tag{9.7}$$

$$\left. + I(\tau < T) \exp\left(-\int_t^{\min(\tau,T)} r_u du\right) K_\tau \right\} \Bigg| \mathcal{F}_t \tag{9.8}$$

The Markovian property allows to change the conditioning by $\mathcal{F}_t$ by a conditioning by r_t. Thus, V_t is a function of (t, r_t). If the mortgagor does not prepay during the time interval $[t, t+h]$, $h > 0$, the discounted cashflows refunded in the interval $[t, t+h]$ equal to

$$\int_t^T \exp\left(-\int_t^s r_u du\right) \phi ds$$

The value at time $t+h$ of the remaining cash flows to be paid by the mortgagor is equal to $V(t+h, r_{t+h})$. Its discounted value, at time t is:

$$\exp\left(-\int_t^{t+h} r_u du\right) V(t+h, r_{t+h}).$$

Finally, the expected value of the cash flows to be paid for a mortgage not prepaid on the interval $[t, t+h]$ equals to

$$\mathrm{E}\left\{\int_t^T \exp\left(-\int_t^s r_u du\right) \phi ds + \exp\left(-\int_t^{t+h} r_u du\right) V(t+h, r_{t+h})\right\}.$$

Not prepaying on the time interval $[t, t+h]$ may not be optimal so that

$$V(t, r_t) \leq \mathrm{E}\left\{\int_t^T \exp\left(-\int_t^s r_u du\right) \phi ds + \exp\left(-\int_t^{t+h} r_u du\right) V(t+h, r_{t+h})\right\}.$$

Assuming regularity conditions on V, classical Taylor expansion yields

$$0 \leq \frac{\partial V(t, r_t)}{\partial t} + \mu(t, r) \frac{\partial V(t, r_t)}{\partial r} + \frac{1}{2}\sigma^2 \frac{\partial^2 V(t, r_t)}{\partial r^2} - rV(t, r_t) + \phi. \quad (9.9)$$

Furthermore, using the definition (9.7), the inequality

$$V(t, r_t) \leq K_t$$

is satisfied. Assuming this inequality to be strictly satisfied, the stopping time τ is defined by

$$\tau = \inf\{s \geq t : V(s, r_s) = K_s\}.$$

On the time interval $[t, \min\{t+h, \tau\}]$, the non-prepayment strategy is optimal since $V(s, r_s) < K_s$. As a consequence:

$$V(t, r_t) = \mathrm{E}\left\{\int_t^T \exp\left(-\int_t^s r_u du\right) \phi ds + \exp\left(-\int_t^{t+h} r_u du\right) V(t+h, r_{t+h})\right\}.$$

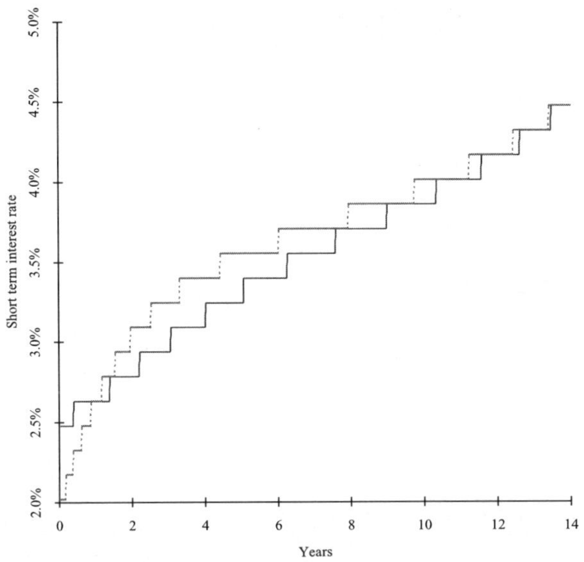

Figure 9.3: The sensitivity of the optimal prepayment-frontier to forward-rates slope: steeper forward-rate curve leads to the dotted frontier, less steep forward-rate curve to solid frontier.

Letting $h \to 0$ and applying Itô's lemma, as previously yields

$$0 = \frac{\partial V(t, r_t)}{\partial t} + \mu(t, r) \frac{\partial V(t, r_t)}{\partial r} + \frac{1}{2}\sigma^2(t, r) \frac{\partial^2 V(t, r_t)}{\partial r^2} - rV(t, r_t) + \phi \quad (9.10)$$

as long as $V(t, r_t) < K_t$.

Formula (9.9) combined with (9.10) implies

$$\max\left\{\frac{\partial V_t}{\partial t} + \mu(t, r)\frac{\partial V_t}{\partial r} + \frac{1}{2}\sigma^2\frac{\partial^2 V_t}{\partial r^2} - rV_t + \phi, V_t - K_t\right\} = 0.$$

□

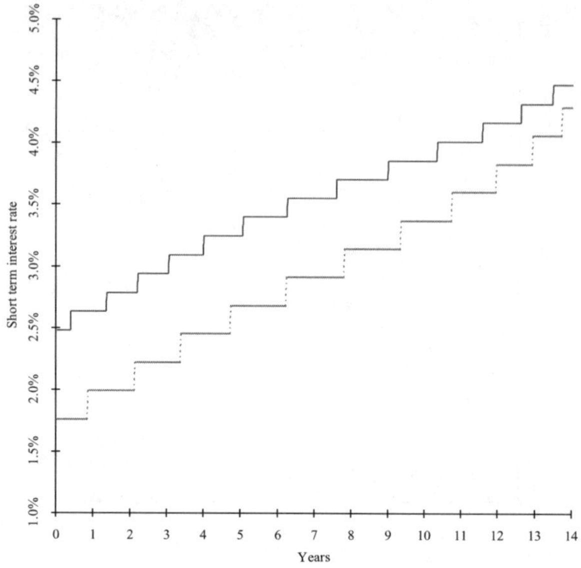

Figure 9.4: The sensitivity of the optimal prepayment frontier to interest-rates volatility: volatilities of the 1-year and 10-year bonds are 90 bps and 37 bps (solid line) and 135 bps and 55 bps (dotted line), respectively.

Discussion and visualization

In this one-dimensional framework, the prepayment condition (9.4) defines a two-dimensional no prepayment region

$$D = \{(t,r) : V_t < K_t\}\,.$$

In particular, it includes the set

$$\{(t,r) : r_t \geq c\}\,.$$

The optimal stopping theory provides characterization of D, Pham (2003). In fact, there exists an optimal, time-dependent, stopping frontier r_t^{opt} such that

$$D = \left\{(t,r) : r_t > r_t^{opt}\right\}.$$

The price V_t and the optimal frontier r_t^{opt} are jointly determined: this is a so-called *free boundary* problem. It can only be calculated via a standard

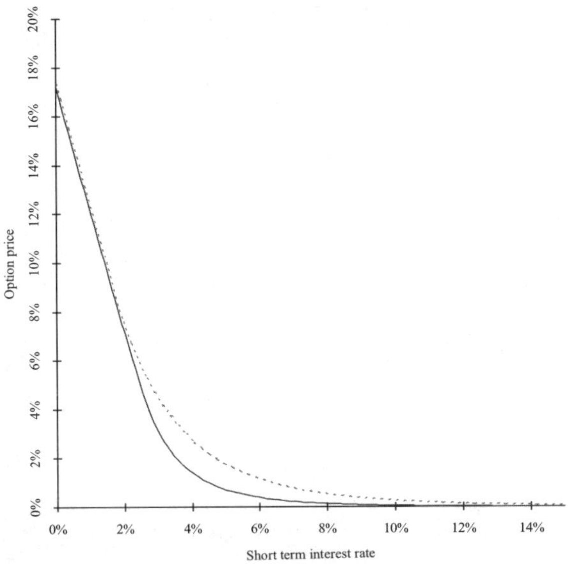

Figure 9.5: The sensitivity of the time value of the embbeded option to interest-rate volatility: volatilities of the 1-year and 10-year bonds are 90 bps and 37 bps (solid line) and 135 bps and 55 bps (dotted line), respectively.

finite difference approach, Wilmott (2000). An example is displayed in Figure 9.3. Interestingly enough, the optimal frontier heavily depends on the time to maturity and it may be far away from the mortgage coupon c. Both its shape and its level r_t^{opt} strongly depend on market conditions.

Figure 9.3 illustrates the positive impact of the slope of the curve on to the slope of the optimal frontier. The influence of implicit market volatility on the optimal prepayment frontier is displayed in Figure 9.4. As expected, the more randomness σ around future rates moves, the stronger the incentive for mortgagors to delay their prepayment in time. In the language of derivatives, the time value of the embedded option increases, see Figure 9.5. All these effects are summed up in one key indicator: the duration of the optimally prepaid mortgage. Defined as the sensitivity to the variation of interest rates, this indicator has two interesting interpretations. From an actuarial point of view, it represents the average expected maturity of the future discounted cash flows. From a hedging point of view, duration may be interpreted as the "delta" of the mortgage with respect to interest rates.

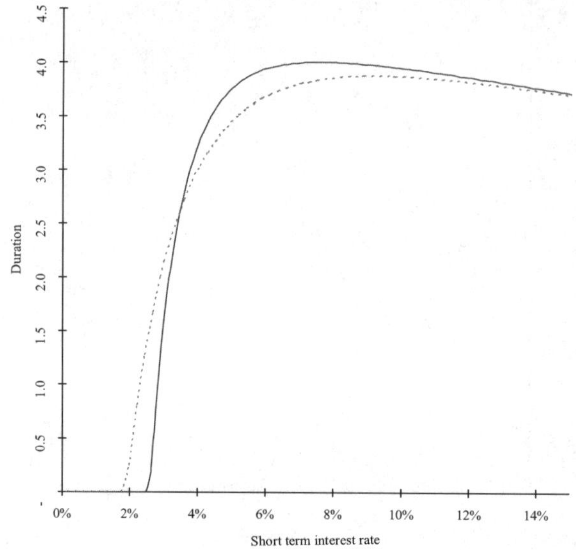

Figure 9.6: The sensitivity of the duration to interest-rate volatility: volatilities of the 1-year and 10-year bonds are 90 bps and 37 bps (solid line) and 135 bps and 55 bps (dotted line), respectively.

If interest rate is deep inside the continuing region, the expected time before prepayment is large and the duration increases. As displayed in Figure 9.6, the higher the volatility, the higher the duration. The preceeding discussion indicates that the optimally prepaid mortgage can be understood as a standard interest rate derivative, allowing one to get asymmetric exposure to future interest rates shifts.

9.3 Valuation of Mortgage Backed Securities

As confirmed by empirical evidence, mortgagors do not prepay optimally, Hayre (1999). Nielsen and Poulsen (2002) provide important insights on the constraints and information asymmetries faced by mortgagors. Although being bound by these constraints, individuals aim at minimizing their expected future cash flows. Thus, it is natural to root their prepayment policy into the optimal one. Let $d_t \stackrel{\text{def}}{=} r_t^{opt} - r_t$ be the distance between the interest rate and the optimal prepayment frontier. The optimal policy leads to a 100% prepayment of the mortgage if $d_t > 0$ and a 0% prepayment if not: it can thus be seen as a Heaviside function of d_t.

When determinants of mortgagors' behavior cannot be observed, this behavior can be modelled as a noisy version of the optimal one. It is thus natural to look for the effective prepayment policy under the form of a characteristic distribution function of d_t, which introduces dispersion around the optimal frontier.

9.3.1 Generic Framework

A pool of mortgages with similar financial characteristics is now considered. This homogeneity assumption of the pool is in accordance with market practice. For the ease of monitoring and investors' analysis, mortgages with the same coupon rate and the same maturity are chosen for pooling. Without loss of generality, the MBS can be assimilated into a single loan with coupon c and maturity T, issued with principal N normalized at 1.

Let F_t be the proportion of unprepaid shares at date t. In the optimal approach, the prepayment policy follows an "all or nothing" type strategy, with F_t being worth 0 or 1. When practical policies are involved, F_t is a positive process decreasing in time from 1 to 0. One can look for

$$\begin{aligned} F_t &\stackrel{\text{def}}{=} \exp(-\Pi_t) \\ F_0 &= 1, \end{aligned}$$

where, in probabilistic terms, Π_t is the hazard process associated with the refunding dynamics. The size of the underlying mortgage gives incentives to model Π_t as an absolutely continuous process. In mathematical terms, this amounts to assuming the existence of an intensity process π_t such that

$$d\Pi_t = \pi_t dt,$$

or equivalently

$$F_t = \exp\left(-\int_0^t \pi_u du\right). \tag{9.11}$$

In this framework, the main point lies in the functional form of the refunding intensity π_t. As it will be precised in the next subsection, π_t must be seen as a function of d_t instead of directly r_t. The valuation consists in discounting a continuous sequence of cash flows. Given the prepayment policy π_t, the MBS cashflows during $[t,T]$ can be divided in two parts. Firstly,

$$\int_t^T \exp\left(-\int_t^s r_u du\right) F_s \phi ds$$

is the discounted value of the continuous flows ϕ refunded on the outstanding MBS principal F_s. Secondly,

$$\int_t^T \exp\left(-\int_t^s r_u du\right) \pi_s K(s)\, dF_s$$

is the discounted value of the principal prepaid at time s. The MBS value equals the risk neutral expectation of these cash flows

$$P(t, r_t, F_t) = \mathrm{E}\left[\int_t^T \exp\left(-\int_t^s r_u du\right) \cdot \{F_s\phi + \pi_s F_s K(s)\}\, ds\right]. \tag{9.12}$$

Because π_t is chosen as a function of d_t, the explicit computation of P involves the knowledge of r_t^{opt}. As opposed to the classical approach, a simple Monte Carlo technique cannot do the job. P can be characterized as a solution of a standard two dimensional partial differential equation. In our one dimensional framework, this means that:

PROPOSITION 9.2 *Under Assumption A, the MBS price $P(t, r_t, F_t)$ solves the partial differential equation*

$$\begin{aligned} \frac{\partial P(t,r,F)}{\partial t} + \mu(t,r)\frac{\partial P(t,r,F)}{\partial r} - \pi(t,r)\, F\frac{\partial P(t,r,F)}{\partial F} & \\ +\frac{1}{2}\sigma^2\frac{\partial^2 P(t,r,F)}{\partial r^2} + F(\phi + \pi(t,r)\, K(t)) - rP(t,r,F) &= 0. \quad (9.13) \\ P(T,r,F) &= 0 \end{aligned}$$

where $\mu(t,r) \stackrel{\text{def}}{=} \lambda\{\theta(t) - r\}$ and σ are fixed by assumption A and π_t has to be properly determined.

9.3.2 A Parametric Specification of the Prepayment Rate

We now come to a particular specification of π_t. For simplicity, we choose an *ad hoc* parametric form for π in order to analyze its main sensitivities. In accordance with stylized facts on prepayment, the prepayment rate π_t is split in two distinct components

$$\pi_t = \pi_t^S + \pi_t^R,$$

where π_t^S represents the structural component of prepayment and π_t^R, as a function of d_t, accounts for both the refunding decision and burnout.

Structural prepayment

Structural prepayment can involve many different reasons for prepaying, including:

- professional changes,
- natural disasters followed by insurance prepayment,
- death or default of the mortgagor also followed by insurance prepayment.

Such prepayment characteristics appear to be stationary in time, Hayre (1999). Their average effect can be captured reasonably well through a deterministic model.

The Public Securities Association (PSA) recommends the use of a piecewise linear structural prepayment rate:

$$\pi_t^S = k\left(atI(0 \le t \le 30 \text{ months}) + bI(30 \text{ months} \le t)\right). \qquad (9.14)$$

This piecewise linear specification takes into account the influence of the age of the mortgage on prepayment.

According to the PSA, the mean annualized values for a and b are 2% and 6%, respectively. This implies that the prepayment starts from 0% at the issuance date of the mortgage, growing by 0.2% per month during the first 30 months, and being equal to 6% afterwards. This curve is accepted by the market practice as the benchmark structural prepayment rate, see Figure 9.7. It is known as the 100% PSA curve. The parameter k sets the desired translation level of this benchmark curve. The PSA regularly publishes statistics on the level of k according to the geographical region, in the US, of mortgage issuance.

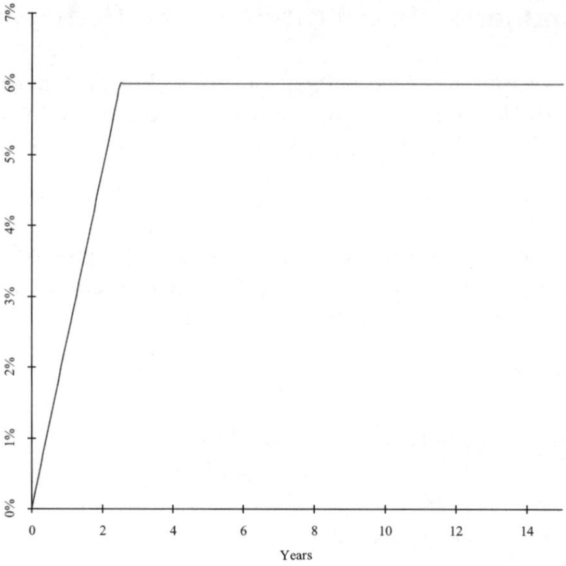

Figure 9.7: The 100% PSA curve.

Refinancing prepayment

The refinancing prepayment rate has to account for both the effect of interest rates and individual characteristics such as burnout. Refinancing incentives linked to interest rate level can be captured through the optimal prepayment framework of Section 2. This framework implies a 1 to 0 rule for MBS principal evolution, depending on the optimal short term interest rate level for prepaying, r_t^{opt}. As soon as

$$d_t > 0,$$

if the mortgagors were optimal, the whole MBS principal would be prepaid. In order to reflect the effect of individual characteristics on prepayment rate causing dispersion around the optimal level $d_t = 0$, we introduce the standard Weibull cumulative distribution function

$$\pi_t^R = \overline{\pi} \cdot \left[1 - \exp\left\{-\left(\frac{d_t}{\overline{d}}\right)^{\alpha}\right\}\right]. \tag{9.15}$$

We do not claim that this parametric form is better than other found in the literature. Its main advantage comes from the easy determination of parameters

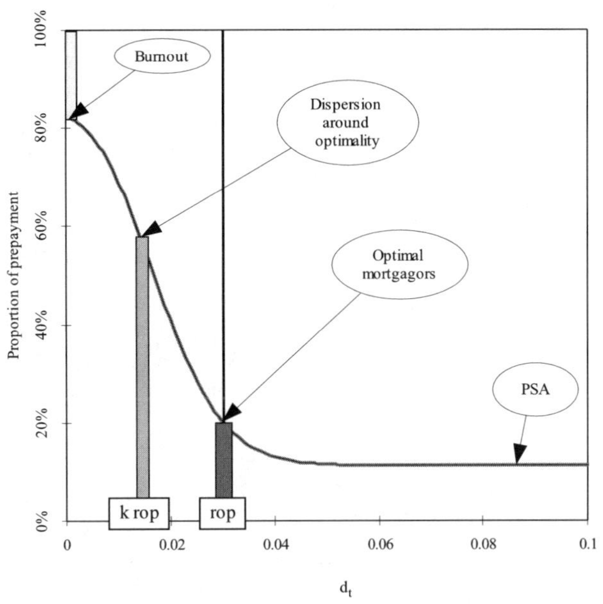

Figure 9.8: Prepayment policy.

thanks to an analytic inversion of its quantile function. In fact, as suggested by Figure 9.8, the determination of quantile ensures that this parametric specification can easily be interpreted.

Parameter $\overline{d}$ is a scale parameter. In this form, being far into the prepayment zone means that $d_t/\overline{d} \gg 0$ so that $\pi_t^R \sim \overline{\pi}$. Parameter $\overline{\pi}$ directly accounts for the magnitude of the burnout effect since it represents the instantaneous fraction of mortgagors who chose not to prepay even for very low values of r_t. More precisely, if r_t was to stay very low during a time period $[0, h]$ and if the refinancing prepayment was the only prepayment component to be considered, using expression (9.11), the proportion of unprepaid shares at date h would be equal to

$$F_h = \exp\left(-\overline{\pi} h\right).$$

This proportion is the burnout rate during the time horizon h. Parameter α controls the speed at which prepayment is made, linking the PSA regime to the burnout regime.

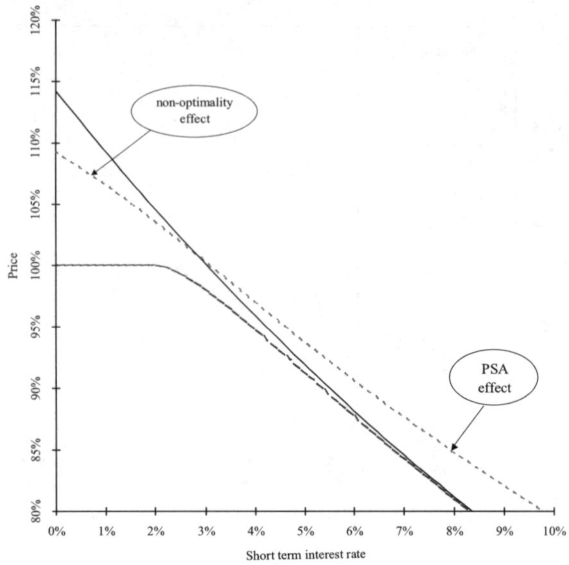

Figure 9.9: The relation between MBS and prepayment policy: MBS without prepayment (solid line), mortgage with prepayment (dashed line), and MBS (dotted line).

9.3.3 Sensitivity Analysis

In order to analyze the main effects of our model, we choose the 100% PSA curve for the structural prepayment rate; the burnout is set equal to 20%. This means that, whatever the market conditions are, 20% of the mortgagors will never repay their loan. The time horizon h for this burnout effect is fixed equal to 2 years. Parameters $\overline{d}$ and α are calibrated in such a way that when $d_t = 0$, ten percent of mortgagors prepay their loan after horizon h, and half of the mortgage is prepaid if half the distance to optimal prepayment rate is reached.

Market conditions are set as of December 2003 in the EUR zone. The short rate equals to 2.3% and the long term rate is 5%. The volatility of the short rate σ is taken equal to 0.8% and λ is such that the volatility of the 10 year forward rate equals to 0.5%. The facial coupon of the pool of mortgage is $c = 5\%$, its remaining maturity is set to $T = 15$ years and no prepayment has been made ($F_0 = 1$).

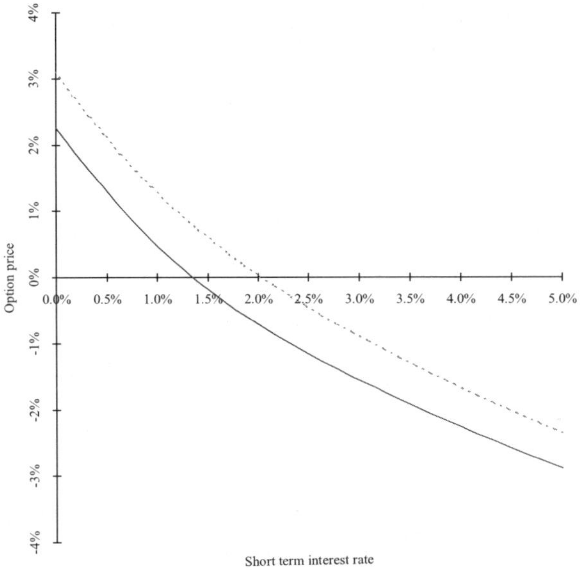

Figure 9.10: Embedded option price in MBS for a steeper forward-rate curve (dotted line) and a less steep forward-rate curve (solid line).

With such parameters, the price of the MBS is displayed in Figure 9.9 as a function of interest rates, together with the optimally prepaid mortgage (OPM) and the mortgage without callability feature (NPM). When interest rates go down, the behavior of the MBS is intermediate between the OPM and the NPM. The value at $r_t = 0$ is controlled by the burnout level. The transition part is controlled by parameters $\overline{d}$ and α. When interest rates increase, the MBS price is higher than the NPM's due to the PSA effect. In fact, by prepaying in the optimal region, mortgagors offer the holder of MBS a positive NPV. This appears clearly when displaying the value of the option embedded in MBS. Recall that in the case of the optimally prepaid mortgage, this value was always positive (Figure 9.5). This is no longer the case for MBS as indicated in Figure 9.10. As a consequence, the sensitivity of MBS to interest rates moves is reduced. Duration is computed in Figure 9.11. It is always less than the underlying pool duration. Its behavior resembles a smoothed version of the optimally prepaid one.

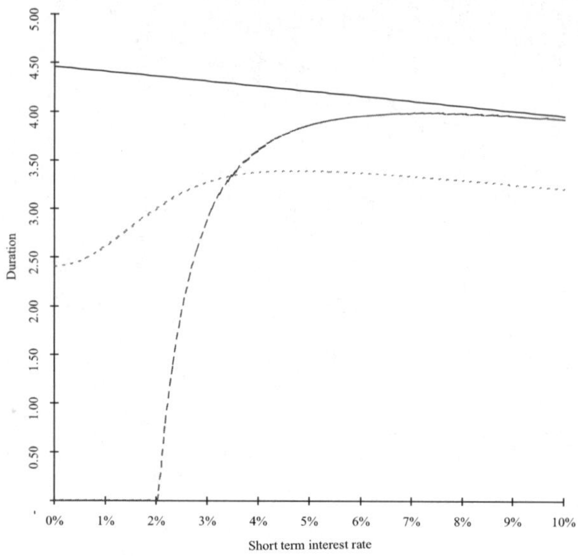

Figure 9.11: Duration of the MBS: MBS without prepayment (solid line), mortgage with prepayment (dashed line), and MBS (dotted line).

Let us now increase the implied volatility of the underlying derivatives market. The embedded option value increases, translating the negative sensitivity of the MBS price to market volatilities, see Figure 9.12. In hedging terms, MBS are "vega negative". A long position in MBS is "short volatility". This is also well indicated in the variation of duration. Figure 9.13 shows how higher volatility increases the duration when the MBS is "in the money" (low interest rates) and decreases for "out of the money" MBS. This is not surprising when one thinks of the duration as the "delta" of the MBS with respect to interest rates. The effect of volatility on the delta for a standard vanilla put option is known to be opposite, depending on the moneyness of the option.

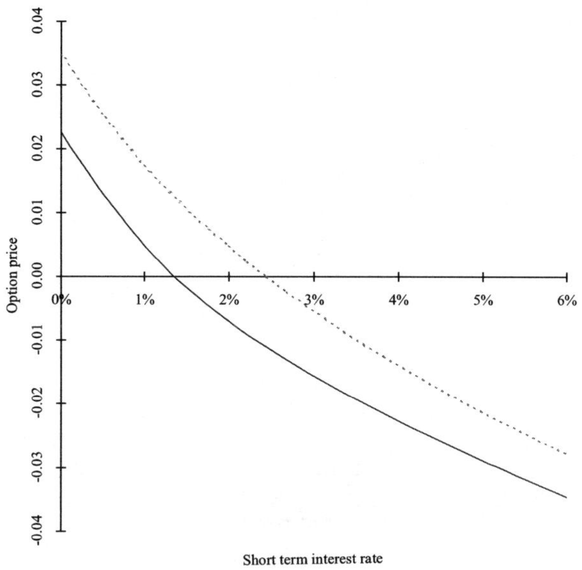

Figure 9.12: The sensitivity of the MBS price to interest-rates volatility: volatilities of the 1-year and 10-year bonds are 90 bps and 37 bps (solid line) and 135 bps and 55 bps (dotted line), respectively.

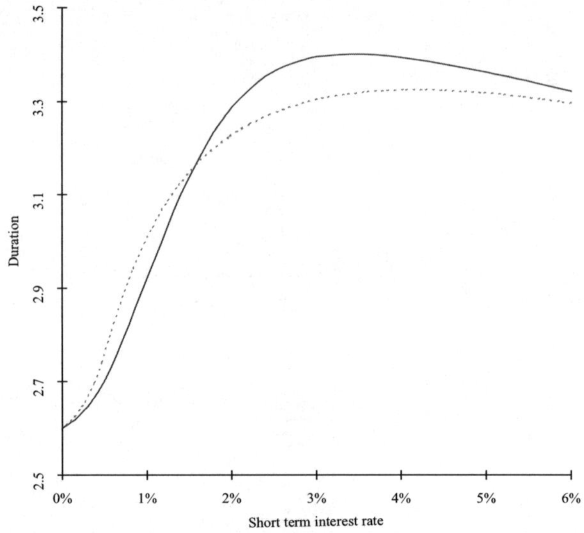

Figure 9.13: The sensitivity of the MBS duration to interest-rates volatility: volatilities of the 1-year and 10-year bonds are 90 bps and 37 bps (solid line) and 135 bps and 55 bps (dotted line), respectively.

Bibliography

Björk, T. (1998) *Arbitrage Theory in Continuous Time*, Oxford University Press.

Boudhouk, J., Richardson, M., Stanton, R., and Whitelaw, R. (1997) Pricing Mortgage Backed Securities in a Multifactor Interest Rate Environment : a Multivariate Density Estimation Approach. *Review of Financial Studies* **10:** 405–446.

Hayre, L. (1999) Guide to Mortgage Backed Securities. *Technical report*, Salomon Smith Barney Fixed Income Research.

Longstaff, F. A., and Whitelaw, E. (2001) Valuing American Options by Simulation : a Simple Least Square Approach. *Review of Financial Studies* **10:** 405–446.

Martellini, L. and Priaulet, P. (2000) *Fixed Income Securities: Dynamic Methods for Interest Rate Risk Pricing and Hedging*, Wiley.

Musiela, M. and Rutkowsky, M. (1997) *Martingal Methods in Financial Modeling*, Springer.

Nielsen, S. and Poulsen, R. (2002) A Two Factor Stochastic Programming of Danish Mortgage Backed Securities. *Technical report*, University of Copenhagen, Department of Statistics and Operation Research.

Pham, H. (2003) Contrôle Optimal Stochastique etApplications en Finance, *Lecture Notes.*

Schwartz, E. and Torous, E. S. (1989) Prepayment and the Valuation of Mortgage Backed Securities, *Journal of Finance* **44:** 375–392.

Schwartz, E. and Torous, E. S. (1993) Mortgage Prepayment and Default Decision, *Journal of the American Real Estate and Urban Economic Association* **21:** 431–449.

Wilmott, P. (2000) *On Quantitative Finance*, Wiley.

10 Predicting Bankruptcy with Support Vector Machines

Wolfgang Härdle, Rouslan Moro, and Dorothea Schäfer

The purpose of this work is to introduce one of the most promising among recently developed statistical techniques – the support vector machine (SVM) – to corporate bankruptcy analysis. An SVM is implemented for analysing such predictors as financial ratios. A method of adapting it to default probability estimation is proposed. A survey of practically applied methods is given. This work shows that support vector machines are capable of extracting useful information from financial data, although extensive data sets are required in order to fully utilize their classification power.

The support vector machine is a classification method that is based on statistical learning theory. It has already been successfully applied to optical character recognition, early medical diagnostics, and text classification. One application where SVMs outperformed other methods is electric load prediction (EUNITE, 2001), another one is optical character recognition (Vapnik, 1995). SVMs produce better classification results than parametric methods and such a popular and widely used nonparametric technique as neural networks, which is deemed to be one of the most accurate. In contrast to the latter they have very attractive properties. They give a single solution characterized by the global minimum of the optimized functional and not multiple solutions associated with the local minima as in the case of neural networks. Moreover, SVMs do not rely so heavily on heuristics, i.e. an arbitrary choice of the model and have a more flexible structure.

10.1 Bankruptcy Analysis Methodology

Although the early works in bankruptcy analysis were published already in the 19th century (Dev, 1974), statistical techniques were not introduced to it until the publications of Beaver (1966) and Altman (1968). Demand from financial institutions for investment risk estimation stimulated subsequent research. However, despite substantial interest, the accuracy of corporate default predictions was much lower than in the private loan sector, largely due to a small number of corporate bankruptcies.

Meanwhile, the situation in bankruptcy analysis has changed dramatically. Larger data sets with the median number of failing companies exceeding 1000 have become available. 20 years ago the median was around 40 companies and statistically significant inferences could not often be reached. The spread of computer technologies and advances in statistical learning techniques have allowed the identification of more complex data structures. Basic methods are no longer adequate for analysing expanded data sets. A demand for advanced methods of controlling and measuring default risks has rapidly increased in anticipation of the New Basel Capital Accord adoption (BCBS, 2003). The Accord emphasises the importance of risk management and encourages improvements in financial institutions' risk assessment capabilities.

In order to estimate investment risks one needs to evaluate the default probability (PD) for a company. Each company is described by a set of variables (predictors) x, such as financial ratios, and its class y that can be either $y = -1$ ('successful') or $y = 1$ ('bankrupt'). Initially, an unknown classifier function $f : x \to y$ is estimated on a training set of companies (x_i, y_i), $i = 1, ..., n$. The training set represents the data for companies which are known to have survived or gone bankrupt. Finally, f is applied to computing default probabilities (PD) that can be uniquely translated into a company rating.

The importance of financial ratios for company analysis has been known for more than a century. Among the first researchers applying financial ratios for bankruptcy prediction were Ramser (1931), Fitzpatrick (1932) and Winakor and Smith (1935). However, it was not until the publications of Beaver (1966) and Altman (1968) and the introduction of univariate and multivariate discriminant analysis that the systematic application of statistics to bankruptcy analysis began. Altman's linear Z-score model became the standard for a decade to come and is still widely used today due to its simplicity. However, its assumption of equal normal distributions for both failing and successful companies with the same covariance matrix has been justly criticized. This approach was further developed by Deakin (1972) and Altman et al. (1977).

Later on, the center of research shifted towards the logit and probit models. The original works of Martin (1977) and Ohlson (1980) were followed by (Wiginton, 1980), (Zavgren, 1983) and (Zmijewski, 1984). Among other statistical methods applied to bankruptcy analysis there are the gambler's ruin model (Wilcox, 1971), option pricing theory (Merton, 1974), recursive partitioning (Frydman et al., 1985), neural networks (Tam and Kiang, 1992) and rough sets (Dimitras et al., 1999) to name a few.

There are three main types of models used in bankruptcy analysis. The first one is structural or parametric models, e.g. the option pricing model, logit and probit regressions, discriminant analysis. They assume that the relationship between the input and output parameters can be described *a priori*. Besides their fixed structure these models are fully determined by a set of parameters. The solution requires the estimation of these parameters on a training set.

Although structural models provide a very clear interpretation of modelled processes, they have a rigid structure and are not flexible enough to capture information from the data. The non-structural or nonparametric models (e.g. neural networks or genetic algorithms) are more flexible in describing data. They do not impose very strict limitations on the classifier function but usually do not provide a clear interpretation either.

Between the structural and non-structural models lies the class of semiparametric models. These models, like the RiskCalc private company rating model developed by Moody's, are based on an underlying structural model but all or some predictors enter this structural model after a nonparametric transformation. In recent years the area of research has shifted towards non-structural and semi-parametric models since they are more flexible and better suited for practical purposes than purely structural ones.

Statistical models for corporate default prediction are of practical importance. For example, corporate bond ratings published regularly by rating agencies such as Moody's or S&P strictly correspond to company default probabilities estimated to a great extent statistically. Moody's RiskCalc model is basically a probit regression estimation of the cumulative default probability over a number of years using a linear combination of non-parametrically transformed predictors (Falkenstein, 2000). These non-linear transformations f_1, f_2, ..., f_d are estimated on univariate models. As a result, the original probit model:

$$E[y_{i,t}|x_{i,t}] = \Phi\left(\beta_1 x_{i1,t} + \beta_2 x_{i2,t} + \ldots + \beta_d x_{id,t}\right), \qquad (10.1)$$

is converted into:

$$E[y_{i,t}|x_{i,t}] = \Phi\{\beta_1 f_1(x_{i1,t}) + \beta_2 f_2(x_{i2,t}) + ... + \beta_d f_d(x_{id,t})\}, \quad (10.2)$$

where $y_{i,t}$ is the cumulative default probability within the prediction horizon for company i at time t. Although modifications of traditional methods like probit analysis extend their applicability, it is more desirable to base our methodology on general ideas of statistical learning theory without making many restrictive assumptions.

The ideal classification machine applying a classifying function f from the available set of functions $\mathcal{F}$ is based on the so called expected risk minimization principle. The expected risk

$$R(f) = \int \frac{1}{2} |f(x) - y| \, dP(x,y), \quad (10.3)$$

is estimated under the distribution $P(x,y)$, which is assumed to be known. This is, however, never true in practical applications and the distribution should also be estimated from the training set (x_i, y_i), $i = 1, 2, ..., n$, leading to an ill-posed problem (Tikhonov and Arsenin, 1977).

In most methods applied today in statistical packages this problem is solved by implementing another principle, namely the principle of the empirical risk minimization, i.e. risk minimization over the training set of companies, even when the training set is not representative. The empirical risk defined as:

$$\hat{R}(f) = \frac{1}{n} \sum_{i=1}^{n} \frac{1}{2} |f(x_i) - y_i|, \quad (10.4)$$

is nothing else but an average value of loss over the training set, while the expected risk is the expected value of loss under the true probability measure. The loss for i.i.d. observations is given by:

$$\frac{1}{2} |f(x) - y| = \begin{cases} 0, & \text{if classification is correct,} \\ 1, & \text{if classification is wrong.} \end{cases}$$

The solutions to the problems of expected and empirical risk minimization:

$$f_{opt} = \arg\min_{f \in \mathcal{F}} R(f), \quad (10.5)$$

$$\hat{f}_n = \arg\min_{f \in \mathcal{F}} \hat{R}(f), \quad (10.6)$$

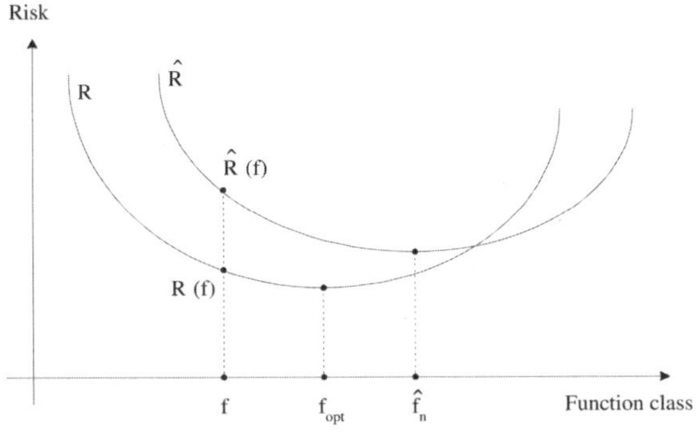

Figure 10.1: The minima f_{opt} and $\hat{f}_n$ of the expected (R) and empirical ($\hat{R}$) risk functions generally do not coincide.

generally do not coincide (Figure 10.1), although they converge to each other as $n \to \infty$ if $\mathcal{F}$ is not too large.

We cannot minimize expected risk directly since the distribution $P(x, y)$ is unknown. However, according to statistical learning theory (Vapnik, 1995), it is possible to estimate the Vapnik-Chervonenkis (VC) bound that holds with a certain probability $1 - \eta$:

$$R(f) \leq \hat{R}(f) + \phi\left(\frac{h}{n}, \frac{\ln(\eta)}{n}\right). \tag{10.7}$$

For a linear indicator function $g(x) = \text{sign}(x^\top w + b)$:

$$\phi\left(\frac{h}{n}, \frac{\ln(\eta)}{n}\right) = \sqrt{\frac{h\left(\ln \frac{2n}{h}\right) - \ln \frac{\eta}{4}}{n}}, \tag{10.8}$$

where h is the VC dimension.

The VC dimension of the function set $\mathcal{F}$ in a d-dimensional space is h if some function $f \in \mathcal{F}$ can shatter h objects $\left\{x_i \in \mathbb{R}^d, i = 1, ..., h\right\}$, in all 2^h possible configurations and no set $\left\{x_j \in \mathbb{R}^d, j = 1, ..., q\right\}$, exists where $q > h$ that satisfies this property. For example, three points on a plane ($d = 2$) can be shattered by linear indicator functions in $2^h = 2^3 = 8$ ways, whereas 4 points cannot be

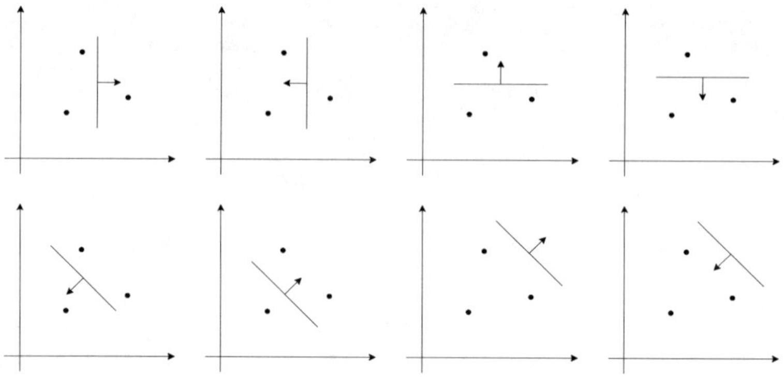

Figure 10.2: Eight possible ways of shattering 3 points on the plane with a linear indicator function.

shattered in $2^q = 2^4 = 16$ ways. Thus, the VC dimension of the set of linear indicator functions in a two-dimensional space is three, see Figure 10.2.

The expression for the VC bound (10.7) is a regularized functional where the VC dimension h is a parameter controlling complexity of the classifier function. The term $\phi\left(\frac{h}{n}, \frac{\ln(\eta)}{n}\right)$ introduces a penalty for the excessive complexity of a classifier function. There is a trade-off between the number of classification errors on the training set and the complexity of the classifier function. If the complexity were not controlled, it would be possible to find such a classifier function that would make no classification errors on the training set notwithstanding how low its generalization ability would be.

10.2 Importance of Risk Classification in Practice

In most countries only a small percentage of firms has been rated to date. The lack of rated firms is mainly due to two factors. Firstly, an external rating is an extremely costly procedure. Secondly, until the recent past most banks decided on their loans to small and medium sized firms (SME) without asking for the client's rating figure or applying an own rating procedure to estimate the client's default risk. At best, banks based their decision on rough scoring models. At worst, the credit decision was completely left to the loan officer.

Table 10.1: Rating grades and risk premia. Source: (Damodaran, 2002) and (Füser, 2002)

Rating Class (S&P)	One year PD (%)	Risk Premia (%)
AAA	0.01	0.75
AA	0.02 – 0.04	1.00
A+	0.05	1.50
A	0.08	1.80
A-	0.11	2.00
BBB	0.15 – 0.40	2.25
BB	0.65 – 1.95	3.50
B+	3.20	4.75
B	7.00	6.50
B-	13.00	8.00
CCC	> 13	10.00
CC		11.50
C		12.70
D		14.00

Since learning to know its own risk is costly and, until recently, the lending procedure of banks failed to set the right incentives, small and medium sized firms shied away from rating. However, the regulations are about to change the environment for borrowing and lending decisions. With the implementation of the New Basel Capital Accord (Basel II) scheduled for the end of 2006 not only firms that issue debt securities on the market are in need of rating but also any ordinary firm that applies for a bank loan. If no external rating is available, banks have to employ an internal rating system and deduce each client's specific risk class. Moreover, Basel II puts pressure on firms and banks from two sides.

First, banks have to demand risk premia in accordance to the specific borrower's default probability. Table 10.1 presents an example of how individual risk classes map into risk premiums (Damodaran, 2002) and (Füser, 2002). For small US-firms a one-year default probability of 0.11% results in a spread of 2%. Of course, the mapping used by lenders will be different if the firm type or the country in which the bank is located changes. However, in any case future loan pricing has to follow the basic rule. The higher the firm's default risk is the more risk premium the bank has to charge.

Table 10.2: Rating grades and capital requirements. Source: (Damodaran, 2002) and (Füser, 2002). The figures in the last column were estimated by the authors for a loan to an SME with a turnover of 5 million euros with a maturity of 2.5 years using the data from column 2 and the recommendations of the Basel Committee on Banking Supervision (BCBS, 2003).

Rating Class (S&P)	One-year PD (%)	Capital Requirements (%) (Basel I)	Capital Requirements (%) (Basel II)
AAA	0.01	8.00	0.63
AA	0.02 – 0.04	8.00	0.93 – 1.40
A+	0.05	8.00	1.60
A	0.08	8.00	2.12
A-	0.11	8.00	2.55
BBB	0.15 – 0.40	8.00	3.05 – 5.17
BB	0.65 – 1.95	8.00	6.50 – 9.97
B+	3.20	8.00	11.90
B	7.00	8.00	16.70
B-	13.00	8.00	22.89
CCC	> 13	8.00	> 22.89
CC		8.00	
C		8.00	
D		8.00	

Second, Basel II requires banks to hold client-specific equity buffers. The magnitudes of these buffers are determined by a risk weight function defined by the Basel Committee and a solvability coefficient (8%). The function maps default probabilities into risk weights. Table 10.2 illustrates the change in the capital requirements per unit of a loan induced by switching from Basel I to Basel II. Apart from basic risk determinants such as default probability (PD), maturity and loss given default (LGD) the risk weights depend also on the type of the loan (retail loan, loan to an SME, mortgages, etc.) and the annual turnover. Table 10.2 refers to an SME loan and assumes that the borrower's annual turnover is 5 million EUR (BCBS, 2003). Since the lock-in of the bank's equity affects the provision costs of the loan, it is likely that these costs will be handed over directly to an individual borrower.

Basel II will affect any firm that is in need for external finance. As both the risk premium and the credit costs are determined by the default risk, the firms' rating will have a deeper economic impact on banks as well as on firms themselves than ever before. Thus in the wake of Basel II the choice of the right rating method is of crucial importance. To avoid friction of a large magnitude the employed method must meet certain conditions. On the one hand, the rating procedure must keep the amount of misclassifications as low as possible. On the other, it must be as simple as possible and, if employed by the borrower, also provide some guidance to him on how to improve his own rating.

SVMs have the potential to satisfy both demands. First, the procedure is easy to implement so that any firm could generate its own rating information. Second, the method is suitable for estimating a unique default probability for each firm. Third, the rating estimation done by an SVM is transparent and does not depend on heuristics or expert judgements. This property implies objectivity and a high degree of robustness against user changes. Moreover, an appropriately trained SVM enables the firm to detect the specific impact of all rating determinants on the overall classification. This property would enable the firm to find out prior to negotiations what drawbacks it has and how to overcome its problems. Overall, SVMs employed in the internal rating systems of banks will improve the transparency and accuracy of the system. Both improvements may help firms and banks to adapt to the Basel II framework more easily.

10.3 Lagrangian Formulation of the SVM

Having introduced some elements of statistical learning and demonstrated the potential of SVMs for company rating we can now give a Lagrangian formulation of an SVM for the linear classification problem and generalize this approach to a nonlinear case.

In the linear case the following inequalities hold for all n points of the training set:

$$
\begin{aligned}
x_i^\top w + b &\geq 1 - \xi_i \quad \text{for} \quad y_i = 1, \\
x_i^\top w + b &\leq -1 + \xi_i \quad \text{for} \quad y_i = -1, \\
\xi_i &\geq 0,
\end{aligned}
$$

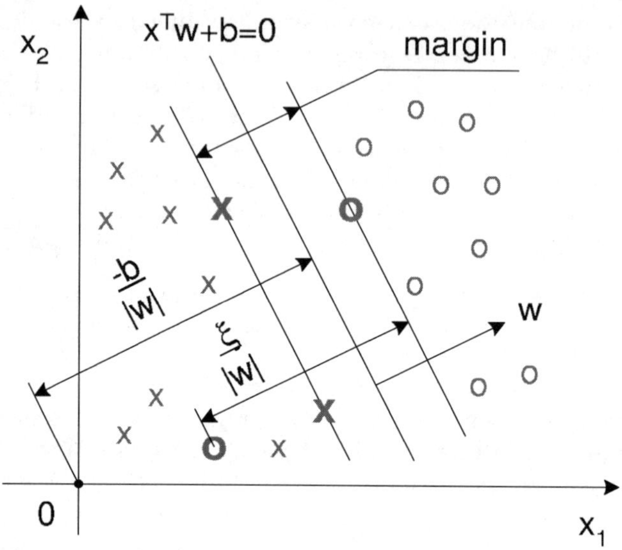

Figure 10.3: The separating hyperplane $x^\top w + b = 0$ and the margin in a non-separable case.

which can be combined into two constraints:

$$y_i(x_i^\top w + b) \geq 1 - \xi_i \tag{10.9}$$

$$\xi_i \geq 0. \tag{10.10}$$

The basic idea of the SVM classification is to find such a separating hyperplane that corresponds to the largest possible margin between the points of different classes, see Figure 10.3. Some penalty for misclassification must also be introduced. The classification error ξ_i is related to the distance from a misclassified point x_i to the canonical hyperplane bounding its class. If $\xi_i > 0$, an error in separating the two sets occurs. The objective function corresponding to penalized margin maximization is formulated as:

$$\frac{1}{2}\|w\|^2 + C\left(\sum_{i=1}^{n}\xi_i\right)^{\upsilon}, \tag{10.11}$$

where the parameter C characterizes the generalization ability of the machine and $\upsilon \geq 1$ is a positive integer controlling the sensitivity of the machine to outliers. The conditional minimization of the objective function with constraint (10.9) and (10.10) provides the highest possible margin in the case when classification errors are inevitable due to the linearity of the separating hyperplane. Under such a formulation the problem is convex. One can show that margin maximization reduces the VC dimension.

The Lagrange functional for the primal problem for $\upsilon = 1$ is:

$$L_P = \frac{1}{2}\|w\|^2 + C\sum_{i=1}^{n}\xi_i - \sum_{i=1}^{n}\alpha_i\{y_i\left(x_i^\top w + b\right) - 1 + \xi_i\} - \sum_{i=1}^{n}\mu_i\xi_i, \quad (10.12)$$

where $\alpha_i \geq 0$ and $\mu_i \geq 0$ are Lagrange multipliers. The primal problem is formulated as:

$$\min_{w_k,b,\xi_i}\max_{\alpha_i} L_P.$$

After substituting the Karush-Kuhn-Tucker conditions (Gale et al., 1951) into the primal Lagrangian, we derive the dual Lagrangian as:

$$L_D = \sum_{i=1}^{n}\alpha_i - \frac{1}{2}\sum_{i=1}^{n}\sum_{j=1}^{n}\alpha_i\alpha_j y_i y_j x_i^\top x_j, \quad (10.13)$$

and the dual problem is posed as:

$$\max_{\alpha_i} L_D,$$

subject to:

$$0 \leq \alpha_i \leq C,$$
$$\sum_{i=1}^{n}\alpha_i y_i = 0.$$

Those points i for which the equation $y_i(x_i^\top w + b) \leq 1$ holds are called support vectors. After training the support vector machine and deriving Lagrange multipliers (they are equal to 0 for non-support vectors) one can classify a company described by the vector of parameters x using the classification rule:

$$g(x) = \operatorname{sign}\left(x^\top w + b\right), \quad (10.14)$$

where $w = \sum_{i=1}^{n} \alpha_i y_i x_i$ and $b = \frac{1}{2}(x_{+1} + x_{-1})\,w$. x_{+1} and x_{-1} are two support vectors belonging to different classes for which $y(x^\top w + b) = 1$. The value of the classification function (the score of a company) can be computed as

$$f(x) = x^\top w + b. \tag{10.15}$$

Each value of $f(x)$ uniquely corresponds to a default probability (PD).

The SVMs can also be easily generalized to the nonlinear case. It is worth noting that all the training vectors appear in the dual Lagrangian formulation only as scalar products. This means that we can apply kernels to transform all the data into a high dimensional Hilbert feature space and use linear algorithms there:

$$\Psi : \mathbb{R}^d \mapsto \mathbb{H}. \tag{10.16}$$

If a kernel function K exists such that $K(x_i, x_j) = \Psi(x_i)^\top \Psi(x_j)$, then it can be used without knowing the transformation Ψ explicitly. A necessary and sufficient condition for a symmetric function $K(x_i, x_j)$ to be a kernel is given by Mercer's (1909) theorem. It requires positive definiteness, i.e. for any data set $x_1, ..., x_n$ and any real numbers $\lambda_1, ..., \lambda_n$ the function K must satisfy

$$\sum_{i=1}^{n}\sum_{j=1}^{n} \lambda_i \lambda_j K(x_i, x_j) \geq 0. \tag{10.17}$$

Some examples of kernel functions are:

- $K(x_i, x_j) = e^{-\|x_i - x_j\|/2\sigma^2}$ – the isotropic Gaussian kernel;
- $K(x_i, x_j) = e^{-(x_i - x_j)^\top r^{-2} \Sigma^{-1} (x_i - x_j)/2}$ – the stationary Gaussian kernel with an anisotropic radial basis; we will apply this kernel in our study taking Σ equal to the variance matrix of the training set; r is a constant;
- $K(x_i, x_j) = (x_i^\top x_j + 1)^P$ – the polynomial kernel;
- $K(x_i, x_j) = \tanh(k x_i^\top x_j - \delta)$ – the hyperbolic tangent kernel.

10.4 Description of Data

For our study we selected the largest bankrupt companies with the capitalization of no less than $1 billion that filed for protection against creditors under

Chapter 11 of the US Bankruptcy Code in 2001–2002 after the stock marked crash of 2000. We excluded a few companies due to incomplete data, leaving us with 42 companies. They were matched with 42 surviving companies with the closest capitalizations and the same US industry classification codes available through the Division of Corporate Finance of the Securities and Exchange Commission (SEC, 2004).

From the selected 84 companies 28 belonged to various manufacturing industries, 20 to telecom and IT industries, 8 to energy industries, 4 to retail industries, 6 to air transportation industries, 6 to miscellaneous service industries, 6 to food production and processing industries and 6 to construction and construction material industries. For each company the following information was collected from the annual reports for 1998–1999, i.e. 3 years prior to defaults of bankrupt companies (SEC, 2004): (i) S – sales; (ii) COGS – cost of goods sold; (iii) EBIT – earnings before interest and taxes, in most cases equal to the operating income; (iv) Int – interest payments; (v) NI – net income (loss); (vi) Cash – cash and cash equivalents; (vii) Inv – inventories; (viii) CA – current assets; (ix) TA – total assets; (x) CL – current liabilities; (xi) STD – current maturities of the long-term debt; (xii) TD – total debt; (xiii) TL – total liabilities; (xiv) Bankr – bankruptcy (1 if a company went bankrupt, −1 otherwise).

The information about the industry was summarized in the following dummy variables: (i) Indprod – manufacturing industries; (ii) Indtelc – telecom and IT industries; (iii) Indenerg – energy industries; (iv) Indret – retail industries; (v) Indair – air transportation industries; (vi) Indserv – miscellaneous service industries; (vii) Indfood – food production and processing industries; (viii) Indconst – construction and construction material industries.

Based on these financial indicators the following four groups of financial ratios were constructed and used in our study: (i) profit measures: EBIT/TA, NI/TA, EBIT/S; (ii) leverage ratios: EBIT/Int, TD/TA, TL/TA; (iii) liquidity ratios: QA/CL, Cash/TA, WC/TA, CA/CL and STD/TD, where QA is quick assets and WC is working capital; (iv) activity or turnover ratios: S/TA, Inv/COGS.

10.5 Computational Results

The most significant predictors suggested by the discriminant analysis belong to profit and leverage ratios. To demonstrate the ability of an SVM to extract information from the data, we will chose two ratios from these groups: NI/TA from the profitability ratios and TL/TA from the leverage ratios. The SVMs,

Table 10.3: Descriptive statistics for the companies. All data except SIZE = log (TA) and ratios are given in billions of dollars.

Variable	Min	Max	Mean	Std. Dev.
TA	0.367	91.072	8.122	13.602
CA	0.051	10.324	1.657	1.887
CL	0.000	17.209	1.599	2.562
TL	0.115	36.437	4.880	6.537
CASH	0.000	1.714	0.192	0.333
INVENT	0.000	7.101	0.533	1.114
LTD	0.000	13.128	1.826	2.516
STD	0.000	5.015	0.198	0.641
SALES	0.036	37.120	5.016	7.141
COGS	0.028	26.381	3.486	4.771
EBIT	-2.214	29.128	0.822	3.346
INT	-0.137	0.966	0.144	0.185
NI	-2.022	4.013	0.161	0.628
EBIT/TA	-0.493	1.157	0.072	0.002
NI/TA	-0.599	0.186	-0.003	0.110
EBIT/S	-2.464	36.186	0.435	3.978
EBIT/INT	-16.897	486.945	15.094	68.968
TD/TA	0.000	1.123	0.338	0.236
TL/TA	0.270	1.463	0.706	0.214
SIZE	12.813	18.327	15.070	1.257
QA/CL	-4.003	259.814	4.209	28.433
CASH/TA	0.000	0.203	0.034	0.041
WC/TA	-0.258	0.540	0.093	0.132
CA/CL	0.041	2001.963	25.729	219.568
STD/TD	0.000	0.874	0.082	0.129
S/TA	0.002	5.559	1.008	0.914
INV/COGS	0.000	252.687	3.253	27.555

besides their Lagrangian formulation, can differ in two aspects: (i) their capacity that is controlled by the coefficient C in (10.12) and (ii) the complexity of classifier functions controlled in our case by the anisotropic radial basis in the Gaussian kernel transformation.

Triangles and squares in Figures 10.4–10.7 represent successful and failing companies from the training set, respectively. The intensity of the gray background corresponds to different score values f. The darker the area, the higher the score and the greater is the probability of default. Most successful companies lying in the bright area have positive profitability and a reasonable leverage TL/TA of around 0.4, which makes economic sense.

Figure 10.4 presents the classification results for an SVM using locally near linear classifier functions (the anisotropic radial basis is $100\Sigma^{1/2}$) with the capacity fixed at $C = 1$. The discriminating rule in this case can be approximated by a linear combination of predictors and is similar to that suggested by discriminant analysis, although the coefficients of the predictors may be different.

If the complexity of classifying functions increases (the radial basis goes down to $2\Sigma^{1/2}$) as illustrated in Figure 10.5, we get a more detailed picture. Now the areas of successful and failing companies become localized. If the radial basis is decreased further down to $0.5\Sigma^{1/2}$ (Figure 10.6), the SVM will try to track each observation. The complexity in this case is too high for the given data set.

Figure 10.7 demonstrates the effects of high capacities ($C = 300$) on the classification results. As capacity is growing, the SVM localizes only one cluster of successful companies. The area outside this cluster is associated with approximately equally high score values.

Thus, besides estimating the scores for companies the SVM also managed to learn that there always exists a cluster of successful companies, while the cluster for bankrupt companies vanishes when the capacity is high, i.e. a company must possess certain characteristics in order to be successful and failing companies can be located elsewhere. This result was obtained without using any additional knowledge besides that contained in the training set.

The calibration of the model or estimation of the mapping $f \rightarrow \text{PD}$ can be illustrated by the following example (the SVM with the radial basis $2\Sigma^{1/2}$ and capacity $C = 1$ will be applied). We can set three rating grades: safe, neutral and risky which correspond to the values of the score $f < -0.0115$, $-0.0115 < f < 0.0115$ and $f > 0.0115$, respectively, and calculate the total number of companies and the number of failing companies in each of the three groups. If the training set were representative of the whole population of companies, the ratio of failing to all companies in a group would give the estimated probability of default. Figure 10.8 shows the power (Lorenz) curve (Lorenz, 1905) – the cumulative default rate as a function of the percentile

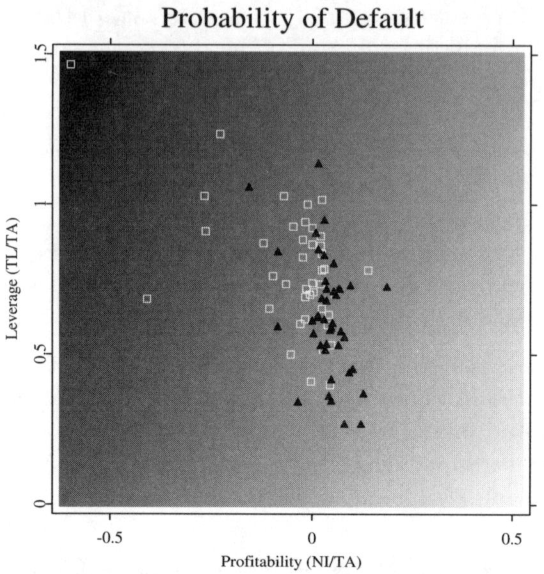

Figure 10.4: Ratings of companies in two dimensions. The case of a low complexity of classifier functions, the radial basis is $100\Sigma^{1/2}$, the capacity is fixed at $C = 1$.

STFsvm01.xpl

of companies sorted according to their score – for the training set of companies. For the abovementioned three rating grades we derive $\text{PD}_{\text{safe}} = 0.24$, $\text{PD}_{\text{neutral}} = 0.50$ and $\text{PD}_{\text{risky}} = 0.76$.

If a sufficient number of observations is available, the model can also be calibrated for finer rating grades such as AAA or BB by adjusting the score values separating the groups of companies so that the estimated default probabilities within each group equal to those of the corresponding rating grades. Note, that we are calibrating the model on the grid determined by $\text{grad}(f) = 0$ or $\text{grad}(\hat{\text{PD}}) = 0$ and not on the orthogonal grid as in the Moody's RiskCalc model. In other words, we do not make a restrictive assumption of an independent influence of predictors as in the latter model. This can be important since,

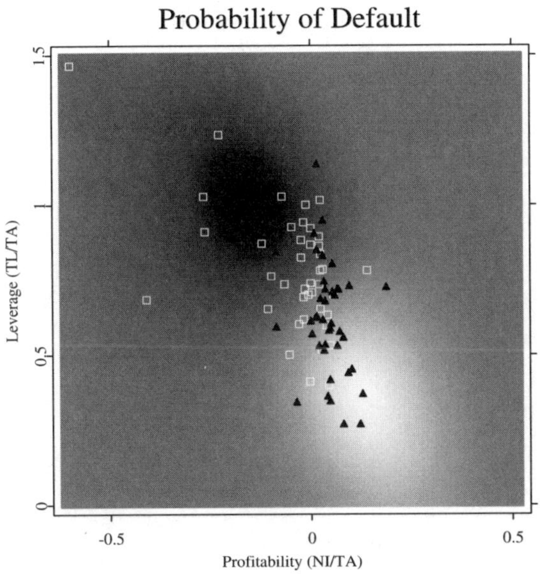

Figure 10.5: Ratings of companies in two dimensions; the case of an average complexity of classifier functions, the radial basis is $2\Sigma^{1/2}$, the capacity is fixed at $C = 1$.

STFsvm02.xpl

for example, the same decrease in profitability will have different consequences for high and low leveraged firms.

For multidimensional classification the results cannot be easily visualized. In this case we will use the cross-validation technique to compute the percentage of correct classifications and compare it with that for the discriminant analysis (DA). Note that both most widely used methods – the discriminant analysis and logit regression – choose only one significant at the 5% level predictor (NI/TA) when forward selection is used. Cross-validation has the following stages. One company is taken out of the sample and the SVM is trained on the remaining companies. Then the class of the out-of-the-sample company is evaluated by the SVM. This procedure is repeated for all the companies and the percentage of correct classifications is calculated.

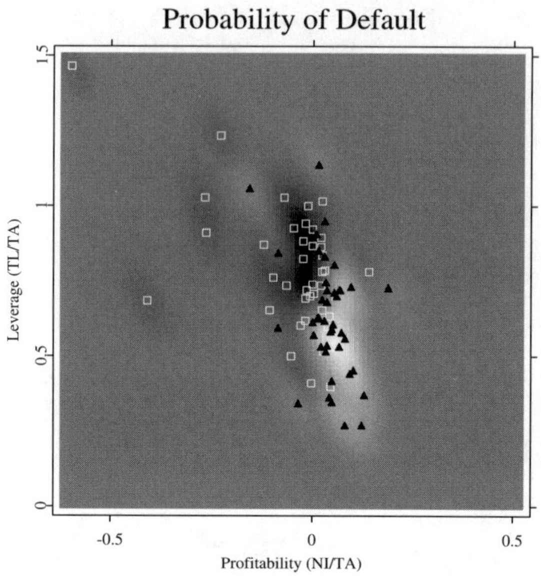

Figure 10.6: Ratings of companies in two dimensions; the case of an excessively high complexity of classifier functions, the radial basis is $0.5\Sigma^{1/2}$, the capacity is fixed at $C = 1$.

STFsvm03.xpl

The best percentage of correctly cross-validated companies (all available ratios were used as predictors) is higher for the SVM than for the discriminant analysis (62% vs. 60%). However, the difference is not significant at the 5% level. This indicates that the linear function might be considered as an optimal classifier for the number of observations in the data set we have. As for the direction vector of the separating hyperplane, it can be estimated differently by the SVM and DA without affecting much the accuracy since the correlation of underlying predictors is high.

Cluster center locations, as they were estimated using cluster analysis, are presented in Table 10.4. The results of the cluster analysis indicate that two clusters are likely to correspond to successful and failing companies. Note the

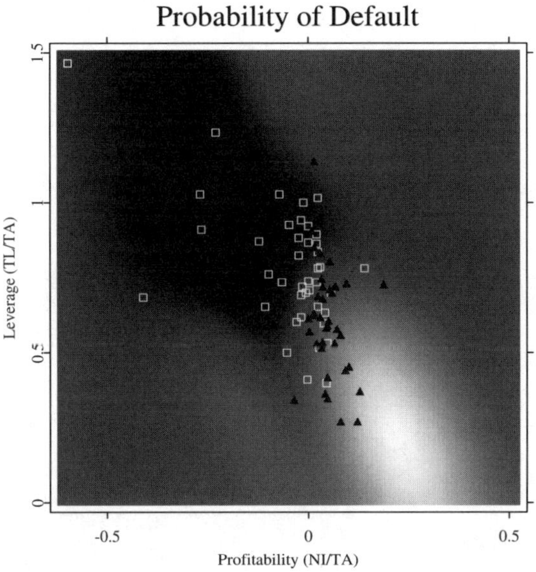

Figure 10.7: Ratings of companies in two dimensions; the case of a high capacity ($C = 300$). The radial basis is fixed at $2\Sigma^{1/2}$.

STFsvm04.xpl

substantial differences in the interest coverage ratios, NI/TA, EBIT/TA and TL/TA between the clusters.

10.6 Conclusions

As we have shown, SVMs are capable of extracting information from real life economic data. Moreover, they give an opportunity to obtain the results not very obvious at first glance. They are easily adjusted with only few parameters. This makes them particularly well suited as an underlying technique for company rating and investment risk assessment methods applied by financial institutions.

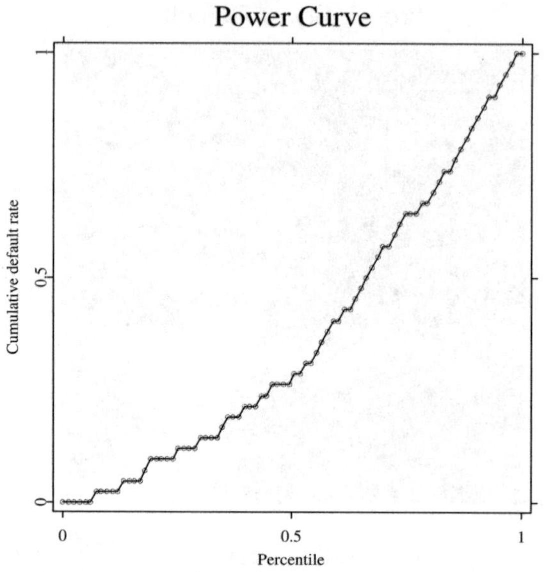

Figure 10.8: Power (Lorenz) curve (Lorenz, 1905) – the cumulative default rate as a function of the percentile of companies sorted according to their score – for the training set of companies. An SVM is applied with the radial basis $2\Sigma^{1/2}$ and capacity $C = 1$.

STFsvm05.xpl

SVMs are also based on very few restrictive assumptions and can reveal effects overlooked by many other methods. They have been able to produce accurate classification results in other areas and can become an option of choice for company rating. However, in order to create a practically valuable methodology one needs to combine an SVM with an extensive data set of companies and turn to alternative formulations of SVMs better suited for processing large data sets. Overall, we have a valuable tool for company rating that can answer the requirements of the new capital regulations.

Table 10.4: Cluster centre locations. There are 19 members in class {-1} – successful companies, and 65 members in class {1} – failing companies.

Cluster	{-1}	{1}
EBIT/TA	0.263	0.015
NI/TA	0.078	-0.027
EBIT/S	0.313	-0.040
EBIT/INT	13.223	1.012
TD/TA	0.200	0.379
TL/TA	0.549	0.752
SIZE	15.104	15.059
QA/CL	1.108	1.361
CASH/TA	0.047	0.030
WC/TA	0.126	0.083
CA/CL	1.879	1.813
STD/TD	0.144	0.061
S/TA	1.178	0.959
INV/COGS	0.173	0.155

Bibliography

Altman, E., (1968). Financial Ratios, Discriminant Analysis and the Prediction of Corporate Bankruptcy, *The Journal of Finance*, September: 589-609.

Altman, E., Haldeman, R. and Narayanan, P., (1977). ZETA Analysis: a New Model to Identify Bankruptcy Risk of Corporations, *Journal of Banking and Finance*, June: 29-54.

Basel Committee on Banking Supervision (2003). The New Basel Capital Accord, third consultative paper, *http://www.bis.org/bcbs/cp3full.pdf.*

Beaver, W., (1966). Financial Ratios as Predictors of Failures. Empirical Research in Accounting: Selected Studies, *Journal of Accounting Research*, supplement to vol. 5: 71-111.

Damodaran, A., (2002). *Investment Valuation*, second ed., John Wiley & Sons, New York, NY.

Deakin, E., (1972). A Discriminant Analysis of Predictors of Business Failure, *Journal of Accounting Research*, Spring: 167-179.

Dev, S., (1974). Ratio Analysis and the Prediction of Company Failure in Ebits, Credits, Finance and Profits, ed. H.C. Edy and B.S. Yamey, Sweet and Maxwell, London: 61-74.

Dimitras, A., Slowinski, R., Susmaga, R. and Zopounidis, C., (1999). Business Failure Prediction Using Rough Sets, *European Journal of Operational Research*, number 114: 263-280.

EUNITE, (2001). Electricity load forecast competition of the EUropean Network on Intelligent TEchnologies for Smart Adaptive Systems, *http://neuron.tuke.sk/competition/.*

Falkenstein, E., (2000). *RiskCalc for Private Companies: Moody's Default Model*, Moody's Investors Service.

Fitzpatrick, P., (2000). *A Comparison of the Ratios of Successful Industrial Enterprises with Those of Failed Companies*, The Accounting Publishing Company.

Frydman, H., Altman, E. and Kao, D.-L., (1985). Introducing Recursive Partitioning for Financial Classification: The Case of Financial Distress, *The Journal of Finance*, **40**: 269-291.

Füser, K., (2002). Basel II – was muß der Mittelstand tun?, *http://www.ey.com/global/download.nsf/Germany/Mittelstandsrating/ $file/Mittelstandsrating.pdf.*

Härdle, W. and Simar, L. (2003). *Applied Multivariate Statistical Analysis*, Springer Verlag.

Gale, D., Kuhn, H.W. and Tucker, A.W., (1951). Linear Programming and the Theory of Games, *Activity Analysis of Production and Allocation*, ed. T.C. Koopmans, John Wiley & Sons, New York, NY: 317-329.

Lorenz, M.O., (1905). Methods for Measuring the Concentration of Wealth, *Journal of American Statistical Association*, **9**: 209-219.

Martin, D., (1977). Early Warning of Bank Failure: A Logit Regression Approach, *Journal of Banking and Finance*, number 1: 249-276.

Mercer, J., (1909). Functions of Positive and Negative Type and Their Connection with the Theory of Integral Equations, *Philosophical Transactions of the Royal Society of London*, **209**: 415-446.

Merton, R., (1974). On the Pricing of Corporate Debt: The Risk Structure of Interest Rates, *The Journal of Finance*, **29**: 449-470.

Ohlson, J., (1980). Financial Ratios and the Probabilistic Prediction of Bankruptcy, *Journal of Accounting Research*, Spring: 109-131.

Ramser, J. and Foster, L., (1931). *A Demonstration of Ratio Analysis. Bulletin No. 40*, University of Illinois, Bureau of Business Research, Urbana, Illinois.

Division of Corporate Finance of the Securities and Exchange Commission, (2004). Standard industrial classification (SIC) code list, *http://www.sec.gov/info/edgar/siccodes.htm.*

Securities and Exchange Commission, (2004). Archive of historical documents, *http://www.sec.gov/cgi-bin/srch-edgar.*

Tam, K. and Kiang, M., (1992). Managerial Application of Neural Networks: the Case of Bank Failure Prediction, *Management Science*, **38**: 926-947.

Tikhonov, A.N. and Arsenin, V.Y., (1977). *Solution of Ill-posed Problems*, W.H. Winston, Washington, DC.

Vapnik, V., (1995). *The Nature of Statistical Learning Theory*, Springer Verlag, New York, NY.

Wiginton, J., (1980). A Note on the Comparison of Logit and Discriminant Models of Consumer Credit Behaviour, *Journal of Financial and Quantitative Analysis*, **15**: 757-770.

Wilcox, A., (1971). A Simple Theory of Financial Ratios as Predictors of Failure, *Journal of Accounting Research*: 389-395.

Winakor, A. and Smith, R., (1935). *Changes in the Financial Structure of Unsuccessful Industrial Corporations. Bulletin No. 51*, University of Illinois, Bureau of Business Research, Urbana, Illinois.

Zavgren, C., (1983). The Prediction of Corporate Failure: The State of the Art, *Journal of Accounting Literature*, number 2: 1-38.

Zmijewski, M., (1984). Methodological Issues Related to the Estimation of Financial Distress Prediction Models, *Journal of Accounting Research*, **20**: 59-82.

11 Econometric and Fuzzy Modelling of Indonesian Money Demand

Noer Azam Achsani, Oliver Holtemöller, and Hizir Sofyan

Money demand is an important element of monetary policy analysis. Inflation is supposed to be a monetary phenomenon in the long run, and the empirical relation between money and prices is usually discussed in a money demand framework. The main purpose of money demand studies is to analyze if a *stable* money demand function exists in a specific country, especially when a major structural change has taken place. Examples for such structural changes are the monetary union of West Germany and the former German Democratic Republic in 1990 and the introduction of the Euro in 1999. There is broad evidence that money demand has been quite stable both in Germany and in the Euro area, see for example Wolters, Teräsvirta and Lütkepohl (1998) and Holtemöller (2004a).

In this chapter, we explore the M2 money demand function for Indonesia in the period 1990:1–2002:3. This period is dominated by the Asian crises, which started in 1997. In the aftermath of the crisis, a number of immense financial and economic problems have emerged in Indonesia. The price level increased by about 16 percent in 1997 compared to the previous year. In the same period, the call money rate increased temporarily from 12.85 percent to 57.10 percent and the money stock increased by about 54 percent. Additionally, Indonesia has faced a sharp decrease in real economic activity: GNP decreased by about 11 percent. Given these extraordinary economic developments, it may not be expected that a stable money demand function existed during that period.

The main contribution of this chapter is twofold. Firstly, we provide a careful analysis of Indonesian money demand, an emerging market economy for which only very few money demand studies exist. Secondly, we do not only apply the standard econometric methods but also the fuzzy Takagi-Sugeno model which allows for locally different functional relationships, for example during the Asian crisis. This is interesting and important because the assessment of monetary policy stance as well as monetary policy decisions depend on the relationship between money and other macroeconomic variables. Hence, a stable money demand function should be supported by various empirical methodologies.

In Section 11.1 we discuss money demand specification generally and in Section 11.2 we estimate a money demand function and the corresponding error-correction model for Indonesia using standard regression techniques. In Section 11.3, we exploit the fuzzy approach and its application to money demand. Section 11.4 presents conclusions and a comparison of the two approaches.

11.1 Specification of Money Demand Functions

Major central banks stress the importance of money growth analysis and of a stable money demand function for monetary policy purposes. The Deutsche Bundesbank, for example, has followed an explicit monetary targeting strategy from 1975 to 1998, and the analysis of monetary aggregates is one of the two pillars of the European Central Bank's (ECB) monetary policy strategy. Details about these central banks' monetary policy strategies, a comparison and further references can be found in Holtemöller (2002). The research on the existence and stability of a money demand function is motivated inter alia by the following two observations: (i) Money growth is highly correlated with inflation, see McCandless and Weber (1995) for international empirical evidence. Therefore, monetary policy makers use money growth as one indicator for future risks to price stability. The information content of monetary aggregates for future inflation assessment is based on a stable relationship between money, prices and other observable macroeconomic variables. This relationship is usually analyzed in a money demand framework. (ii) The monetary policy transmission process is still a "black box", see Mishkin (1995) and Bernanke and Gertler (1995). If we are able to specify a stable money demand function, an important element of the monetary transmission mechanism is revealed, which may help to learn more about monetary policy transmission.

There is a huge amount of literature about money demand. The majority of the studies is concerned with industrial countries. Examples are Hafer and Jansen (1991), Miller (1991), McNown and Wallace (1992) and Mehra (1993) for the

USA; Lütkepohl and Wolters (1999), Coenen and Vega (1999), Brand and Cassola (2000) and Holtemöller (2004b) for the Euro area; Arize and Shwiff (1993), Miyao (1996) and Bahmani-Oskooee (2001) for Japan; Drake and Chrystal (1994) for the UK; Haug and Lucas (1996) for Canada; Lim (1993) for Australia and Orden and Fisher (1993) for New Zealand.

There is also a growing number of studies analyzing money demand in developing and emerging countries, primarily triggered by the concern among central bankers and researchers around the world about the impact of moving toward flexible exchange rate regimes, globalization of capital markets, ongoing financial liberalization, innovation in domestic markets, and the country-specific events on the demand for money (Sriram, 1999). Examples are Hafer and Kutan (1994) and Tseng (1994) for China; Moosa (1992) for India; Arize (1994) for Singapore and Deckle and Pradhan (1997) for ASEAN countries.

For Indonesia, a couple of studies have applied the cointegration and error-correction framework to money demand. Price and Insukindro (1994) use quarterly data from the period 1969:1 to 1987:4. Their results are based on different methods of testing for cointegration. The two-step Engle and Granger (1987) procedure delivers weak evidence for one cointegration relationship, while the Johansen likelihood ratio statistic supports up to two cointegrating vectors. In contrast, Deckle and Pradhan (1997), who use annual data, do not find any cointegrating relationship that can be interpreted as a money demand function.

The starting point of empirical money demand analysis is the choice of variables to be included in the money demand function. It is common practice to assume that the desired level of nominal money demand depends on the price level, a transaction (or scaling) variable, and a vector of opportunity costs (e.g., Goldfeld and Sichel, 1990; Ericsson, 1999):

$$(M^*/P) = f(Y, R_1, R_2, ...), \tag{11.1}$$

where M^* is nominal money demand, P is the price level, Y is real income (the transaction variable), and R_i are the elements of the vector of opportunity costs which possibly also includes the inflation rate. A money demand function of this type is not only the result of traditional money demand theories but also of modern micro-founded dynamic stochastic general equilibrium models (Walsh, 1998). An empirical standard specification of the money demand function is the partial adjustment model (PAM). Goldfeld and Sichel (1990) show that a desired level of real money holdings $MR_t^* = M_t^*/P_t$:

$$\ln MR_t^* = \phi_0 + \phi_1 \ln Y_t + \phi_2 R_t + \phi_3 \pi_t, \tag{11.2}$$

where R_t represents one or more interest rates and $\pi_t = \ln(P_t/P_{t-1})$ is the inflation rate, and an adjustment cost function:

$$C = \alpha_1 (\ln M_t^* - \ln M_t)^2 + \alpha_2 \{(\ln M_t - \ln M_{t-1}) + \delta (\ln P_t - \ln P_{t-1})\}^2 \tag{11.3}$$

yield the following reduced form:

$$\ln MR_t = \mu\phi_0 + \mu\phi_1 \ln Y_t + \mu\phi_2 R_t + (1-\mu)\ln MR_{t-1} + \gamma\pi_t, \tag{11.4}$$

where:

$$\mu = \alpha_1/(\alpha_1 + \alpha_2) \qquad \text{and} \qquad \gamma = \mu\phi_3 + (1-\mu)(\delta - 1). \tag{11.5}$$

The parameter δ controls whether nominal money ($\delta = 0$) or real money ($\delta = -1$) adjusts. Intermediate cases are also possible. Notice that the coefficient to the inflation rate depends on the value of ϕ_3 and on the parameters of the adjustment cost function. The imposition of price-homogeneity, that is the price level coefficient in a nominal money demand function is restricted to one, is rationalized by economic theory and Goldfeld and Sichel (1990) propose that empirical rejection of the unity of the price level coefficient should be interpreted as an indicator for misspecification. The reduced form can also be augmented by lagged independent and further lagged dependent variables in order to allow for a more general adjustment process.

Rearranging (11.4) yields:

$$\begin{aligned}\Delta \ln MR_t &= \mu\phi_0 + \mu\phi_1 \Delta \ln Y_t + \mu\phi_1 \ln Y_{t-1} + \mu\phi_2 \Delta R_t \\ &\quad + \mu\phi_2 R_{t-1} - \mu \ln MR_{t-1} + \gamma\Delta\pi_t + \gamma\pi_{t-1} \\ &= \mu\phi_0 - \mu\left(\ln MR_{t-1} - \phi_1 \ln Y_{t-1} - \phi_2 R_{t-1} - \frac{\gamma}{\mu}\pi_{t-1}\right) \\ &\quad + \mu\phi_1 \Delta \ln Y_t + \mu\phi_2 \Delta R_t + \gamma\Delta\pi_t. \end{aligned} \tag{11.6}$$

Accordingly, the PAM can also be represented by an error-correction model like (11.6).

11.2 The Econometric Approach to Money Demand

11.2.1 Econometric Estimation of Money Demand Functions

Since the seminal works of Nelson and Plosser (1982), who have shown that relevant macroeconomic variables exhibit stochastic trends and are only stationary after differencing, and Engle and Granger (1987), who introduced the concept of cointegration, the (vector) error correction model, (V)ECM, is the dominant econometric framework for money demand analysis. If a certain set of conditions about the number of cointegration relations and exogeneity properties is met, the following single equation error correction model (SE-ECM) can be used to estimate money demand functions:

$$\begin{aligned}\Delta \ln MR_t &= c_t + \alpha \underbrace{(\ln MR_{t-1} - \beta_2 \ln Y_{t-1} - \beta_3 R_{t-1} - \beta_4 \pi_{t-1})}_{\text{error correction term}} \\ &\quad + \sum_{i=1}^{k} \gamma_{1i} \Delta \ln MR_{t-i} + \sum_{i=0}^{k} \gamma_{2i} \Delta \ln Y_{t-i} \\ &\quad + \sum_{i=0}^{k} \gamma_{3i} \Delta R_{t-i} + \sum_{i=0}^{k} \gamma_{4i} \Delta \pi_{t-i}.\end{aligned} \tag{11.7}$$

It can immediately be seen that (11.6) is a special case of the error correction model (11.7). In other words, the PAM corresponds to a SE-ECM with certain parameter restrictions. The SE-ECM can be interpreted as a partial adjustment model with β_2 as long-run income elasticity of money demand, β_3 as long-run semi-interest rate elasticity of money demand, and less restrictive short-run dynamics. The coefficient β_4, however, cannot be interpreted directly.

In practice, the number of cointegration relations and the exogeneity of certain variables cannot be considered as known. Therefore, the VECM is often applied. In this framework, all variables are assumed to be endogenous a priori, and the imposition of a certain cointegration rank can be justified by statistical tests. The standard VECM is obtained from a vector autoregressive (VAR) model:

$$x_t = \mu_t + \sum_{i=1}^{k} A_i x_{t-i} + u_t, \tag{11.8}$$

where x_t is a $(n \times 1)$-dimensional vector of endogenous variables, μ_t contains deterministic terms like constant and time trend, A_i are $(n \times n)$-dimensional coefficient matrices and $u_t \sim N(0, \Sigma_u)$ is a serially uncorrelated error term. Subtracting x_{t-1} and rearranging terms yields the VECM:

$$\Delta x_{t-1} = \mu_t + \Pi x_{t-1} + \sum_{i=1}^{k-1} \Gamma_i \Delta x_{t-i} + u_t, \tag{11.9}$$

where Π and Γ_i are functions of the A_i. The matrix Π can be decomposed into two $(n \times r)$-dimensional matrices α and β: $\Pi = \alpha\beta^\top$ where α is called an adjustment matrix, β comprises the cointegration vectors, and r is the number of linearly independent cointegration vectors (cointegration rank). Following Engle and Granger (1987), a variable is integrated of order d, or I(d), if it has to be differenced d-times to become stationary. A vector x_t is integrated of order d if the maximum order of integration of the variables in x_t is d. A vector x_t is cointegrated, or CI(d, b), if there exists a linear combination $\beta^\top x_t$ that is integrated of a lower order $(d - b)$ than x_t.

The cointegration framework is only appropriate if the relevant variables are actually integrated. This can be tested using unit root tests. When no unit roots are found, traditional econometric methods can by applied.

11.2.2 Modelling Indonesian Money Demand with Econometric Techniques

We use quarterly data from 1990:1 until 2002:3 for our empirical analysis. The data is not seasonally adjusted and taken from Datastream (gross national product at 1993 prices Y and long-term interest rate R) and from Bank Indonesia (money stock M2 M and consumer price index P). In the following, logarithms of the respective variables are indicated by small letters, and $mr = \ln M - \ln P$ denotes logarithmic real balances. The data is depicted in Figure 11.1.

In the first step, we analyze the stochastic properties of the variables. Table 11.1 presents the results of unit root tests for logarithmic real balances mr, logarithmic real GNP y, logarithmic price level p, and logarithmic long-term interest rate r. Note that the log interest rate is used here while in the previous section the level of the interest rate has been used. Whether interest rates should be included in logarithms or in levels is mainly an empirical question.

Because the time series graphs show that there seem to be structural breaks in real money, GNP and price level, we allow for the possibility of a mean shift and a change in the slope of a linear trend in the augmented Dickey-Fuller test regression. This corresponds to model (c) in Perron (1989), where the critical values for this type of test are tabulated. In the unit root test for the interest rate, only a constant is considered. According to the test results, real money, real GNP and price level are trend-stationary, that is they do not exhibit a unit root, and the interest rate is also stationary. These results are quite stable with respect to the lag length specification. The result of trend-stationarity is also supported by visual inspection of a fitted trend and the corresponding

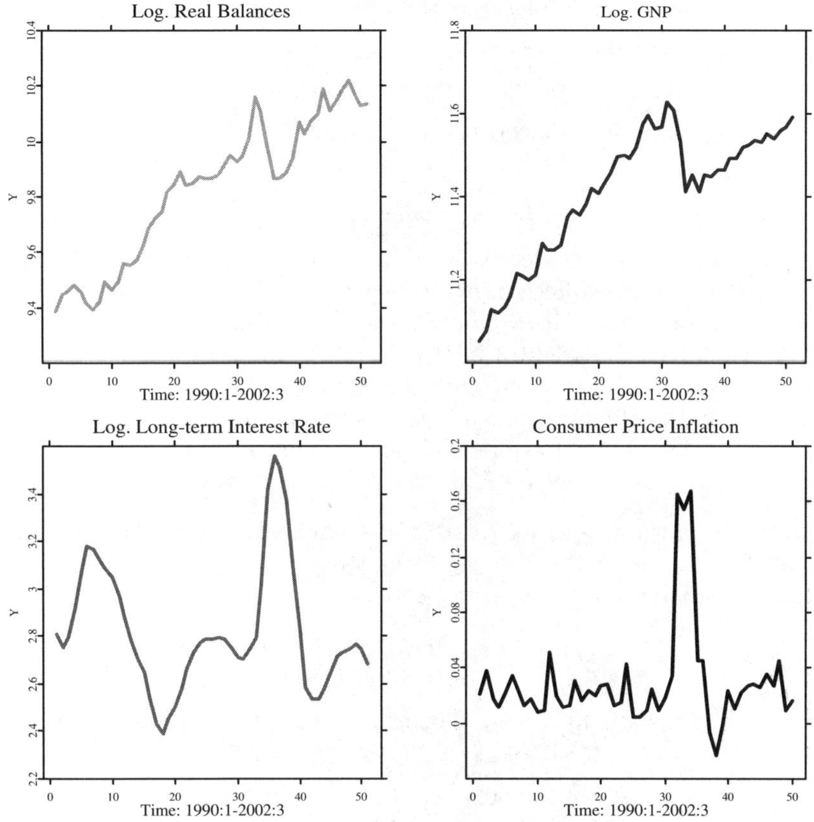

Figure 11.1: Time series plots of logarithms of real balance, GNP, interest rate, and CPI.

STFmon01.xpl

trend deviations, see Figure 11.2. In the case of real money, the change in the slope of the linear trend is not significant.

Now, let us denote centered seasonal dummies s_{it}, a step dummy switching from zero to one in the respective quarter ds, and an impulse dummy having

Table 11.1: Unit Root Tests

Variable	Deterministic terms	Lags	Test stat.	1/5/10% CV
mr	c, t, s, *P89c* (98:3)	2	-4.55^{**}	-4.75 / -4.44 / -4.18
y	c, t, s, *P89c* (98:1)	0	-9.40^{***}	-4.75 / -4.44 / -4.18
p	c, t, s, *P89c* (98:1)	2	-9.46^{***}	-4.75 / -4.44 / -4.18
r	c, s	2	-4.72^{***}	-3.57 / -2.92 / -2.60

Note: Unit root test results for the variables indicated in the first column. The second column describes deterministic terms included in the test regression: constant c, seasonal dummies s, linear trend t, and shift and impulse dummies *P89c* according to the model (c) in Perron (1989) allowing for a change in the mean and slope of a linear trend. Break points are given in parentheses. Lags denotes the number of lags included in the test regression. Column CV contains critical values. Three (two) asterisks denote significance at the 1% (5%) level.

value one only in the respective quarter *di*. Indonesian money demand is then estimated by OLS using the reduced form equation (11.4) (t- and p-values are in round and square parantheses, respectively):

$$
\begin{aligned}
mr_t = \; & \underset{(6.79)}{0.531}\, mr_{t-1} + \underset{(4.87)}{0.470}\, y_t - \underset{(-6.15)}{0.127}\, r_t \\
& - \underset{(-0.84)}{0.438} - \underset{(-2.11)}{0.029}\, s_{1t} - \underset{(-2.57)}{0.034}\, s_{2t} - \underset{(-2.77)}{0.036}\, s_{3t} \\
& + \underset{(3.54)}{0.174}\, di9802_t + \underset{(5.98)}{0.217}\, di9801_t + \underset{(5.02)}{0.112}\, ds9803_t + u_t
\end{aligned}
$$

$$
\begin{aligned}
T &= 50\ (1990:2 - 2002:3) \\
R^2 &= 0.987 \\
RESET(1) &= 0.006\ [0.941] \\
LM(4) &= 0.479\ [0.751] \\
JB &= 0.196\ [0.906] \\
ARCH(4) &= 0.970\ [0.434]
\end{aligned}
$$

Here JB refers to the Jarque-Bera test for nonnormality, RESET is the usual test for general nonlinearity and misspecification, LM(4) denotes a Lagrange-Multiplier test for autocorrelation up to order 4, ARCH(4) is a Lagrange-Multiplier test for autoregressive conditional heteroskedasticity up to order

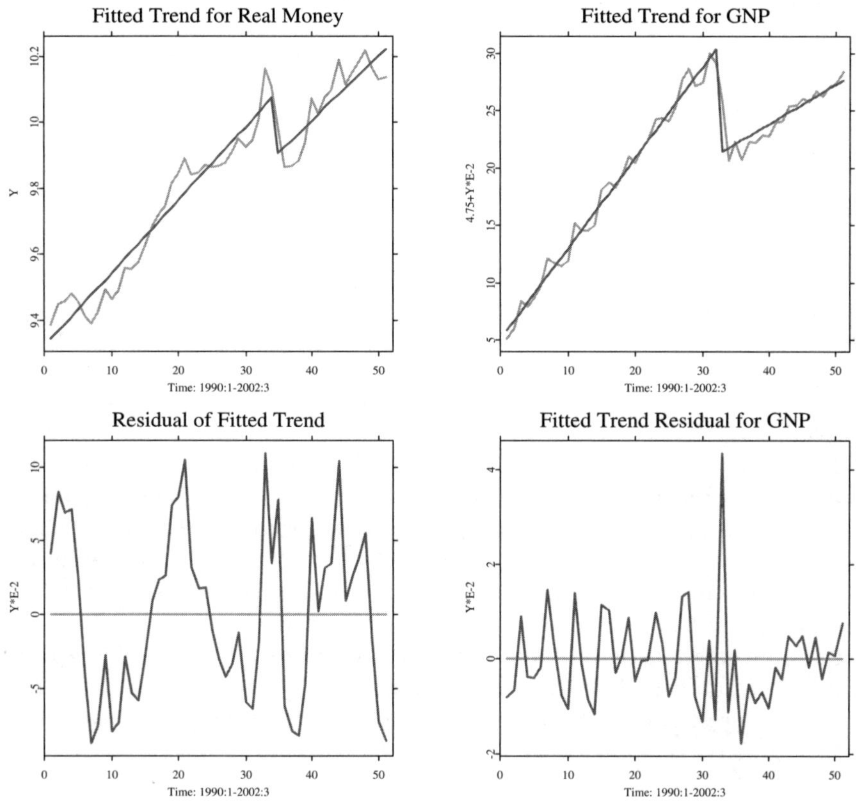

Figure 11.2: Fitted trends for real money and real GNP.

STFmon02.xpl

STFmon03.xpl

4. Given these diagnostic statistics, the regression seems to be well specified. There is a mean shift in 1998:3 and the impulse dummies capture the fact, that the structural change in GNP occurs two months before the change in real money. The inflation rate is not significant and is therefore not included in the equation.

The implied income elasticity of money demand is 0.47/(1–0.53) = 1 and the interest rate elasticity is –0.13/(1–0.53) = –0.28. These are quite reasonable magnitudes. Equation (11.10) can be transformed into the following error correction representation:

$$\begin{aligned}\Delta mr_t &= -0.47 \cdot (mr_{t-1} - y_{t-1} + 0.28 r_{t-1}) \\ &\quad + 0.47 \Delta y_t - 0.13 \Delta r_t + \text{deterministic terms} + u_t. \qquad (11.10)\end{aligned}$$

Stability tests for the real money demand equation (11.10) are depicted in Figure 11.3. The CUSUM of squares test indicates some instability at the time of the Asian crises, and the coefficients of lagged real money and GNP seem to change slightly after the crisis. A possibility to allow for a change in these coefficients from 1998 on is to introduce two additional right-hand-side variables: lagged real money multiplied by the step dummy $ds9803$ and GNP multiplied by $ds9803$. Initially, we have also included a corresponding term for the interest rate. The coefficient is negative (-0.04) but not significant (p-value: 0.29), such that we excluded the term from the regression equation. The respective coefficients for the period 1998:3-2002:3 can be obtained by summing the coefficients of lagged real money and lagged real money times step dummy and of GNP and GNP times step dummy, respectively. This reveals that the income elasticity stays approximately constant (0.28/(1–0.70)=0.93) until 1998:02 and ((0.28+0.29)/(1-0.70+0.32)=0.92) from 1998:3 to 2002:3 and that the interest rate elasticity declines in the second half of the sample from –0.13/(1–0.70)=–0.43 to –0.13/(1-0.79+0.32)=–0.21:

$$\begin{aligned} mr_t = \; & \underset{(7.09)}{0.697}\; mr_{t-1} + \underset{(2.39)}{0.281}\; y_t - \underset{(-6.81)}{0.133}\; r_t \\ & - \underset{(-2.54)}{0.322}\; mr_{t-1} \cdot ds9803_t + \underset{(2.63)}{0.288}\; y_t \cdot ds9803_t \\ & + \underset{(0.25)}{0.133} - \underset{(-2.49)}{0.032}\; s_{1t} - \underset{(-3.18)}{0.041}\; s_{2t} - \underset{(-2.76)}{0.034}\; s_{3t} \\ & + \underset{(2.04)}{0.110}\; di9802_t + \underset{(5.50)}{0.194}\; di9801_t + u_t. \end{aligned}$$

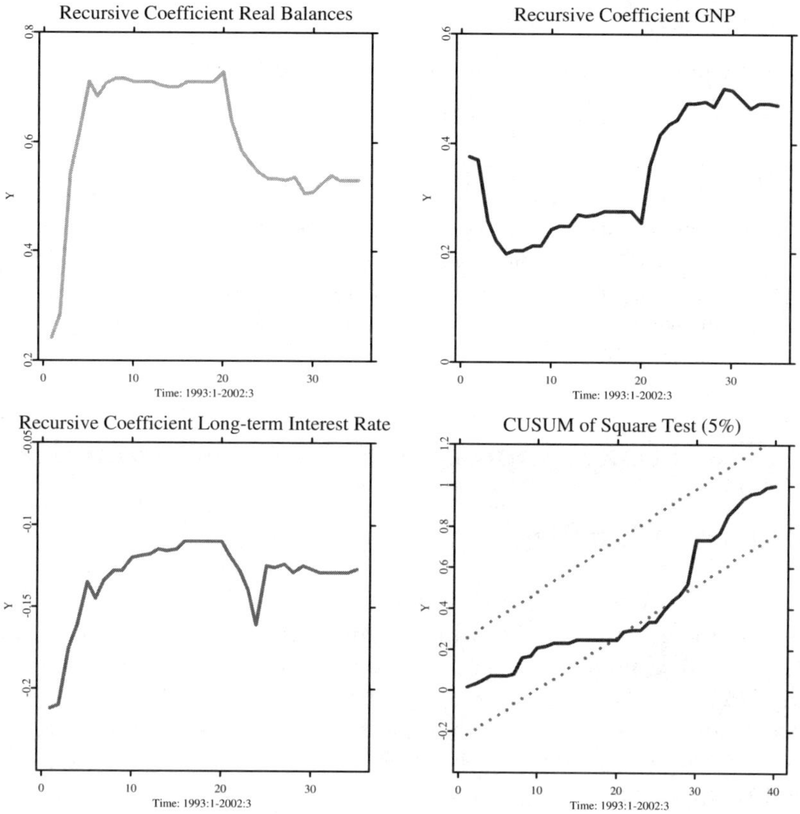

Figure 11.3: Stability test for the real money demand equation (11.10).
STFmon04.xpl

$$
\begin{aligned}
T &= 50\ (1990:2-2002:3)\\
R^2 &= 0.989\\
RESET(1) &= 4.108\ [0.050]\\
LM(4) &= 0.619\ [0.652]\\
JB &= 0.428\ [0.807]\\
ARCH(4) &= 0.408\ [0.802]
\end{aligned}
$$

Accordingly, the absolute adjustment coefficient μ in the error correction representation increases from 0.30 to 0.62.

It can be concluded that Indonesian money demand has been surprisingly stable throughout and after the Asian crisis given that the Cusum of squares test indicates only minor stability problems. A shift in the constant term and two impulse dummies that correct for the different break points in real money and real output are sufficient to yield a relatively stable money demand function with an income elasticity of one and an interest rate elasticity of –0.28. However, a more flexible specification shows that the adjustment coefficient μ increases and that the interest rate elasticity decreases after the Asian crisis. In the next section, we analyze if these results are supported by a fuzzy clustering technique.

11.3 The Fuzzy Approach to Money Demand

11.3.1 Fuzzy Clustering

Ruspini (1969) introduced fuzzy partition to describe the cluster structure of a data set and suggested an algorithm to compute the optimum fuzzy partition. Dunn (1973) generalized the minimum-variance clustering procedure to a Fuzzy ISODATA clustering technique. Bezdek (1981) used Dunn's (1973) approach to obtain an infinite family of algorithms known as the Fuzzy C-Means (FCM) algorithm. He generalized the fuzzy objective function by introducing the weighting exponent m, $1 \leq m < \infty$:

$$J_m(U,V) = \sum_{k=1}^{n} \sum_{i=1}^{c} (u_{ik})^m d^2(x_k, v_i), \qquad (11.11)$$

where $\mathcal{X} = \{x_1, x_2, \dots, x_n\} \subset \mathbb{R}^p$ is a subset of the real p-dimensional vector space $\mathbb{R}^p$ consisting of n observations, U is a random fuzzy partition matrix of $\mathcal{X}$ into c parts, v_i's are the cluster centers in $\mathbb{R}^p$, and $d(x_k, v_i) = \|x_k - v_i\| = \sqrt{(x_k - v_i)^\top (x_k - v_i)}$ is an inner product induced norm on $\mathbb{R}^p$. Finally, u_{ik} refers to the degree of membership of point x_k to the ith cluster. This degree of membership, which can be seen as a probability of x_k belonging to cluster

i, satisfies the following constraints:

$$0 \leq u_{ik} \leq 1, \quad \text{for } 1 \leq i \leq c, 1 \leq k \leq n, \tag{11.12}$$

$$0 < \sum_{k=1}^{n} u_{ik} < n, \qquad \text{for } 1 \leq i \leq c, \tag{11.13}$$

$$\sum_{i=1}^{c} u_{ik} = 1, \qquad \text{for } 1 \leq k \leq n. \tag{11.14}$$

The FCM uses an iterative optimization of the objective function, based on the weighted similarity measure between x_k and the cluster center v_i. More details on the FCM algorithm can be found in Mucha and Sofyan (2000).

In practical applications, a validation method to measure the quality of a clustering result is needed. Its quality depends on many factors, such as the method of initialization, the choice of the number of clusters c, and the clustering method. The initialization requires a good estimate of the clusters and the cluster validity problem can be reduced to the choice of an optimal number of clusters c. Several cluster validity measures have been developed in the past by Bezdek and Pal (1992).

11.3.2 The Takagi-Sugeno Approach

Takagi and Sugeno (1985) proposed a fuzzy clustering approach using the membership function $\mu_A(x) : \mathcal{X} \rightarrow [0, 1]$, which defines a degree of membership of $x \in \mathcal{X}$ in a fuzzy set A. In this context, all the fuzzy sets are associated with piecewise linear membership functions.

Based on the fuzzy-set concept, the affine Takagi-Sugeno (TS) fuzzy model consists of a set of rules $R_i, i = 1, \ldots, r$, which have the following structure:

IF x is A_i, THEN $y_i = a_i^\top x + b_i$.

This structure consists of two parts, namely the *antecedent* part "x is A_i" and the *consequent* part "$y_i = a_i^\top x + b_i$," where $x \in \mathcal{X} \subset \mathbb{R}^p$ is a crisp input vector, A_i is a (multidimensional) fuzzy set defined by the membership function $\mu_{A_i}(x) : \mathcal{X} \rightarrow [0, 1]$, and $y_i \in \mathbb{R}$ is an output of the i-th rule depending on a parameter vector $a_i \in \mathbb{R}^p$ and a scalar b_i.

Given a set of r rules and their outputs (consequents) y_i, the global output y of the Takagi-Sugeno model is defined by the fuzzy mean formula:

$$y = \frac{\sum_{i=1}^{r} \mu_{A_i}(x) y_i}{\sum_{i=1}^{r} \mu_{A_i}(x)}. \tag{11.15}$$

It is usually difficult to implement multidimensional fuzzy sets. Therefore, the antecedent part is commonly represented as a combination of equations for the elements of $x = (x_1, \ldots, x_p)^\top$, each having a corresponding one-dimensional fuzzy set $A_{ij}, j = 1, \ldots, p$. Using the conjunctive form, the rules can be formulated as:

IF x_1 is $A_{i,1}$ AND $\cdots$ AND x_p is $A_{i,p}$, THEN $y_i = a_i^\top x + b_i$,

with the degree of membership $\mu_{A_i}(x) = \mu_{A_i,1}(x_1) \cdot \mu_{A_i,2}(x_2) \cdots \mu_{A_i,p}(x_p)$. This elementwise clustering approach is also referred to as product space clustering. Note that after normalizing this degree of membership (of the antecedent part) is:

$$\phi_i(x) = \frac{\mu_{A_i}(x)}{\sum_{j=1}^{r} \mu_{A_j}(x)}. \tag{11.16}$$

We can also interpret the affine Takagi-Sugeno model as a quasilinear model with a dependent input parameter (Wolkenhauer, 2001):

$$y = \left(\sum_{i=1}^{r} \phi_i(x) a_i^\top \right) x + \sum_{i=1}^{r} \phi_i(x) b_i = a^\top(x) + b(x). \tag{11.17}$$

11.3.3 Model Identification

The basic principle of model identification by product space clustering is to approximate a nonlinear regression problem by decomposing it to several local linear sub-problems described by IF-THEN rules. A comprehensive discussion can be found in Giles and Draeseke (2001).

Let us now discuss identification and estimation of the fuzzy model in case of multivariate data. Suppose

$$y = f(x_1, x_2, ..., x_p) + \varepsilon \tag{11.18}$$

where the error term ε is assumed to be independent, identically and normally distributed around zero. The fuzzy function f represents the conditional mean of the output variable y. In the rest of the chapter, we use a linear form of f and the least squares criterion for its estimation. The algorithm is as follows.

Step 1 For each pair x_r and y, separately partition n observations of the sample into c_r fuzzy clusters by using fuzzy clustering (where $r = 1, ..., p$).

Step 2 Consider all possible combinations of c fuzzy clusters given the number of input variables p, where $c = \prod_{r=1}^{p} c_r$.

Step 3 Form a model by using data taken from each fuzzy cluster:

$$y_{ij} = \beta_{i0} + \beta_{i1}x_{1ij} + \beta_{i2}x_{2ij} + ... + \beta_{ip}x_{pij} + \varepsilon_{ij} \tag{11.19}$$

where observation index $j = 1, \ldots, n$ and cluster index $i = 1, \ldots, c$.

Step 4 Predict the conditional mean of x by using:

$$\hat{y}_k = \frac{\sum_{i=1}^{c}(b_{i0} + b_{i1}x_{1k} + ... + b_{ip}x_{pk})w_{ik}}{\sum_{i=1}^{c} w_{ik}}, \qquad k = 1, \ldots, n, \tag{11.20}$$

where $w_{ik} = \prod_{r=1}^{p} \delta_{ij}\mu_{rj}(x_k), i = 1, \ldots, c$, and δ_{ij} is an indicator equal to one if the jth cluster is associated with the ith observation.

The fuzzy predictor of the conditional mean y is a weighted average of linear predictors based on the fuzzy partitions of explanatory variables, with a membership value varying continuously through the sample observations. The effect of this condition is that the non-linear system can be effectively modelled.

The modelling technique based on fuzzy sets can be understood as a local method: it uses partitions of a domain process into a number of fuzzy regions. In each region of the input space, a rule is defined which transforms input variables into output. The rules can be interpreted as local sub-models of the system. This approach is very similar to the inclusion of dummy variables in an econometric variable. By allowing interaction of dummy-variables and independent variables, we also specify local sub-models. While the number and location of the sub-periods is determined endogenously by the data in the fuzzy approach, they have been imposed exogenously after visual data inspection in our econometric model. However, this is not a fundamental difference because the number and location of the sub-periods could also be determined automatically by using econometric techniques.

11.3.4 Modelling Indonesian Money Demand with Fuzzy Techniques

In this section, we model the M2 money demand in Indonesia using the approach of fuzzy model identification and the same data as in Section 11.2. Like

Table 11.2: Four clusters of Indonesian money demand data

Cluster	Observations	β_0 (t-value)	β_1 (y_t) (t-value)	β_2 (r_t) (t-value)
1	1-15	3.9452	0.5479	-0.2047
		(3.402)	(5.441)	(-4.195)
2	16-31	1.2913	0.7123	0.1493
		(0.328)	(1.846)	(0.638)
3	34-39	28.7063	-1.5480	-0.3177
		(1.757)	(-1.085)	(-2.377)
4	40-51	-0.2389	0.8678	0.1357
		(-0.053)	(2.183)	(0.901)

in the econometric approach logarithmic real money demand (mr_t) depends on logarithmic GNP (y_t) and the logarithmic long-term interest-rate (r_t):

$$mr_t = \beta_0 + \beta_1 \ln Y_t + \beta_2 r_t. \tag{11.21}$$

The results of the fuzzy clustering algorithm are far from being unambiguous. Fuzzy clustering with real money and output yields three clusters. However, real money and output clusters overlap, such that it is difficult to identify three common clusters. Hence, we arrange them as four clusters. On the other hand, clustering with real money and the interest rate leads to two clusters. The intersection of both clustering results gives 4 different clusters. The four local models are presented in Table 11.2. In the first cluster that covers the period 1990:1–1993:3 GNP has a positive effect on money demand, and the interest rate effect is negative. The output elasticity is substantially below one, but increases in the second cluster (1993:4–1997:3). The interest rate has no significant impact on real money in the second period. The third cluster from 1997:4 to 1998:4 covers the Asean crisis. In this period, the relationship between real money and output breaks down while the interest rate effect is stronger than before. The last cluster covers the period 1999:4–2002:3, in which the situation in Indonesia was slowly brought under control as a result of having a new government elected in October 1999. The elasticity of GNP turned back approximately to the level before the crisis. However, the effect of the interest rate is not significant.

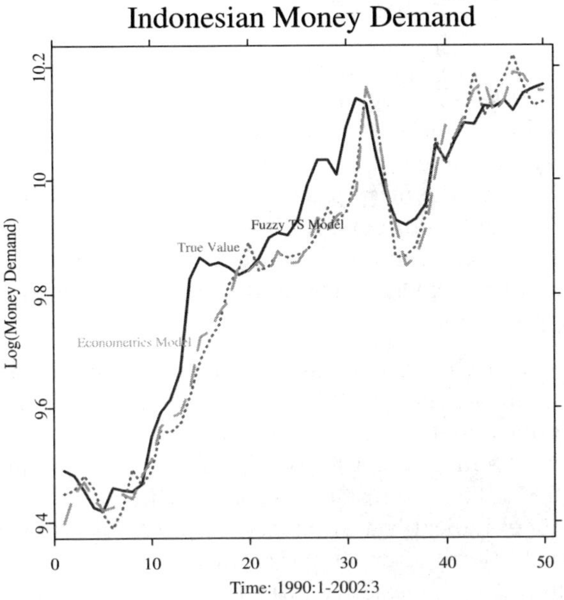

Figure 11.4: Fitted money demand (dotted line): econometric model (dashed line) and fuzzy model (solid line).

STFmon05.xpl

The fit of the local sub-models is not as good as the fit of the econometric model (Figure 11.4). The main reasons for this result are that autocorrelation and seasonality of the data have not been considered in the fuzzy approach, mainly for computational reasons. Additionally, the determination of the number of different clusters turned out to be rather difficult. Therefore, the fuzzy model for Indonesian money demand described here should be interpreted as an illustrative example for the robustness analysis of econometric models. More research is necessary to find a fuzzy specification that describes the data as well as the econometric model.

11.4 Conclusions

In this chapter, we have analyzed money demand in Indonesia in a period in which major instabilities in basic economic relations due to the Asian crises may be expected. In addition to an econometric approach we have applied fuzzy clustering in order to analyze the robustness of the econometric results. Both the econometric and the fuzzy clustering approach divide the period from 1990 to 2002 into separate sub-periods. In the econometric approach this is accomplished by inclusion of dummy variables in the regression model, and in the fuzzy clustering approach different clusters are identified in which local regression models are valid.

Both approaches reveal that there have been structural changes in Indonesian money demand during the late 1990s. A common result is that the income elasticity of money demand is quite stable before and after the crisis, the econometric estimation of the income elasticity after the crisis is about 0.93 and the fuzzy estimate is 0.87. The interest rate elasticity differs in both approaches: the econometric model indicates a absolutely smaller but still significant negative interest rate elasticity after the crisis, while the fuzzy approach yields an insignificant interest rate elasticity after the crises. A further difference is that the fuzzy approach suggests a higher number of sub-periods, namely four clusters, while the econometric model is based on only two sub-periods. However, it might well be that the results of the two approaches become even more similar when the fit of the fuzzy model is improved.

Our main conclusions are: Firstly, Indonesian money demand has been surprisingly stable in a troubled and difficult time. Secondly, the fuzzy clustering approach provides a framework for the robustness analysis of economic relationships. This framework can especially be useful if the number and location of sub-periods exhibiting structural differences in the economic relationships is not known ex-ante. Thirdly, our analysis does also reveal why the previous studies of Indonesian money demand delivered unstable results. Theses studies applied cointegration techniques. However, we show that the relevant Indonesian time series are trend-stationary such that the cointegration framework is not appropriate.

Bibliography

Arize, A. C. (1994). A Re-examination of the Demand for Money in Small Developing Economies, *Applied Economics* **26**: 217-228.

Arize, A. C. and Shwiff, S. S. (1993). Cointegration, Real Exchange Rate and Modelling the Demand for Broad Money in Japan, *Applied Economics* **25 (6)**: 717-726.

Bahmani-Oskooee, M. (2001). How Stable is M2 Money Demand Function in Japan?, *Japan and the World Economy* **13**: 455-461.

Bernanke, B. S. and Gertler, M. (1995). Inside the Black Box: the Credit Channel of Monetary Policy Transmission, *Journal of Economic Perspectives* **9**: 27–48.

Bezdek, J. C. (1981). *Pattern Recognition with Fuzzy Objective Function Algorithms*, Plenum Press, New York.

Bezdek, J. C. and Pal, S. K. (1992). *Fuzzy Models for Pattern Recognition*, IEEE Press, New York.

Brand, C. and Cassola, N. (2000). A Money Demand System for Euro Area M3, *ECB Working Paper 39.*

Coenen, G. and Vega, J. L. (1999). The Demand for M3 in the Euro Area, *ECB Working Paper 6.*

Deckle, P. and Pradhan, M. (1997). Financial Liberalization and Money Demand in ASEAN Countries: Implications for Monetary Policy. *IMF Working Paper WP/97/36.*

Drake, L. and Chrystal, K. A. (1994). Company-Sector Money Demand: New Evidence on the Existence of a Stable Long-run Relationship for the UK, *Journal of Money, Credit, and Banking* **26**: 479–494.

Dunn, J. C. (1973). A Fuzzy Relative of the ISODATA Process and its Use in Detecting Compact Well-Separated Clusters, *Journal of Cybernetics* **3**: 32–57.

Engle, R. F. and Granger, C. W. J. (1987). Co-integration and Error Correction: Representation, Estimation and Testing, *Econometrica* **55**: 251–276.

Ericsson, N. R. (1999). Empirical Modeling of Money Demand, In: Lütkepohl, H. and Wolters, J. (Eds), *Money Demand in Europe*, Physica, Heidelberg, 29-49.

Giles, D. E. A and Draeseke, R. (2001). Econometric Modelling Using Pattern Recognition via the Fuzzy c-Means Algorithm, in D.E.A. Giles (ed.), *Computer-Aided Econometrics*, Marcel Dekker, New York.

Goldfeld, S. M. and Sichel, D. E. (1990). The Demand for Money, In: Friedman, B. and Hahn, F. H. (Eds), *Handbook of Monetary Economics*, Elsevier, Amsterdam, 299-356.

Hafer, R. W. and Jansen, D. W. (1991). The Demand for Money in the United States: Evidence from Cointegration Tests, *Journal of Money, Credit, and Banking* **23**: 155-168.

Hafer, R. W. and Kutan, A. M. (1994). Economic Reforms and Long-Run Money Demand in China: Implication for Monetary Policy, *Southern Economic Journal* **60(4)**: 936–945.

Haug, A. A. and Lucas, R. F. (1996). Long-Term Money Demand in Canada: In Search of Stability, *Review of Economics and Statistics* **78**: 345–348.

Holtemöller, O. (2002). *Vector Autoregressive Analysis and Monetary Policy.* Three Essays, Shaker, Aachen.

Holtemöller, O. (2004a). Aggregation of National Data and Stability of Euro Area Money Demand, In: Dreger, Chr. and Hansen, G. (Eds), *Advances in Macroeconometric Modeling, Papers and Proceedings of the 3rd IWH Workshop in Macroeconometrics*, Nomos, Baden-Baden, 181-203.

Holtemöller, O. (2004b). A Monetary Vector Error Correction Model of the Euro Area and Implications for Monetary Policy, *Empirical Economics*, forthcoming.

Lim, G. C. (1993). The Demand for the Components of Broad Money: Error Correction and Generalized Asset Adjustment Systems, *Applied Economics* **25(8)**: 995–1004.

Lütkepohl, H. and Wolters, J. (Eds)(1999). *Money Demand in Europe*, Physica, Heidelberg.

McCandless, G. T. and Weber, W. E. (1995). Some Monetary Facts, *Federal Reserve Bank of Minneapolis Quarterly Review* **19**: 2-11.

McNown, R. and Wallace, M. S. (1992). Cointegration Tests of a Long-Run Relation between Money Demand and the Effective Exchange Rate, *Journal of International Money and Finance* **11(1)**: 107–114.

Mehra, Y. P. (1993). The Stability of the M2 Money Demand Function: Evidence from an Error-Correction Model, *Journal of Money, Credit, and Banking* **25**: 455–460.

Miller, S. M (1991). Monetary Dynamics: An Application of Cointegration and Error-Correction Modelling, *Journal of Money, Credit, and Banking* **23**: 139–168.

Mishkin, F. S. (1995). Symposium on the monetary transmission mechanism, *Journal of Economic Perspectives* **9**: 3–10.

Miyao, R. (1996). Does a Cointegrating M2 Demand Relation Really Exist in Japan?, *Journal of the Japanese and International Economics* **10**: 169–180.

Moosa, I. A. (1992). The Demand for Money in India: A Cointegration Approach, *The Indian Economic Journal* **40(1)**: 101–115.

Mucha, H. J. and Sofyan, H. (2000). Cluster Analysis, in Härdle, W., Klinke, S. and Hlavka, Z. *XploRe Application Guide*, (Eds), Springer, Heidelberg.

Nelson, C. R. and Plosser, C. I. (1982). Trends and Random Walks in Macroeconomic Time Series, *Journal of Monetary Economics* **10**: 139–162.

Orden, D. and Fisher, L. A. (1993). Financial Deregulation and the Dynamics of Money, Prices and Output in New Zealand and Australia, *Journal of Money, Credit, and Banking* **25**: 273–292.

Perron, P. (1989). The Great Crash, the Oil Price Shock, and the Unit Root Hypothesis, *Econometrica* **57**: 1361–1401.

Price, S. and Insukindro (1994). The Demand for Indonesian Narrow Money: Long-run Equilibrium, Error Correction and Forward-looking Behaviour, *The Journal of International Trade and Economic Development* **3(2)**: 147–163.

Ruspini, E. H. (1969). A New Approach to Clustering, *Information Control* **15**: 22–32.

Sriram, S. S. (1999). Demand for M2 in an Emerging-Market Economy: An Error-Correction Model for Malaysia, *IMF Working paper WP/99/173.*

Takagi, T. and Sugeno, M. (1985). Fuzzy Identification of Systems and its Application to Modelling and Control, *IEEE Transactions on Systems, Man and Cybernetics* **15(1)**: 116–132.

Tseng, W. (1994). Economic Reform in China: A New Phase, *IMF Occasional Paper 114*.

Walsh, C. E. (1998). *Monetary Theory and Policy*, MIT Press, Cambridge.

Wolkenhauer, O. (2001). *Data Engineering: Fuzzy Mathematics in System Theory and Data Analysis*, Wiley, New York.

Wolters, J., Teräsvirta, T. and Lütkepohl, H. (1998). Modeling the Demand for M3 in the Unified Germany, *The Review of Economics and Statistics* **90**: 309–409.

12 Nonparametric Productivity Analysis

Wolfgang Härdle and Seok-Oh Jeong

How can we measure and compare the relative performance of production units? If input and output variables are one dimensional, then the simplest way is to compute efficiency by calculating and comparing the ratio of output and input for each production unit. This idea is inappropriate though, when multiple inputs or multiple outputs are observed. Consider a bank, for example, with three branches A, B, and C. The branches take the number of staff as the input, and measures outputs such as the number of transactions on personal and business accounts. Assume that the following statistics are observed:

- Branch A: 60000 personal transactions, 50000 business transactions, 25 people on staff,
- Branch B: 50000 personal transactions, 25000 business transactions, 15 people on staff,
- Branch C: 45000 personal transactions, 15000 business transactions, 10 people on staff.

We observe that Branch C performed best in terms of personal transactions per staff, whereas Branch A has the highest ratio of business transactions per staff. By contrast Branch B performed better than Branch A in terms of personal transactions per staff, and better than Branch C in terms of business transactions per staff. How can we compare these business units in a fair way? Moreover, can we possibly create a virtual branch that reflects the input/output mechanism and thus creates a scale for the real branches?

Productivity analysis provides a systematic approach to these problems. We review the basic concepts of productivity analysis and two popular methods

DEA and FDH, which are given in Sections 12.1 and 12.2, respectively. Sections 12.3 and 12.4 contain illustrative examples with real data.

12.1 The Basic Concepts

The activity of production units such as banks, universities, governments, administrations, and hospitals may be described and formalized by the production set:

$$\Psi = \{(x, y) \in \mathbb{R}_+^p \times \mathbb{R}_+^q \mid x \text{ can produce } y\}.$$

where x is a vector of inputs and y is a vector of outputs. This set is usually assumed to be *free disposable*, i.e. if for given $(x, y) \in \Psi$ all (x', y') with $x' \geq x$ and $y' \leq y$ belong to Ψ, where the inequalities between vectors are understood componentwise. When y is one-dimensional, Ψ can be characterized by a function g called the *frontier function* or the production function:

$$\Psi = \{(x, y) \in \mathbb{R}_+^p \times \mathbb{R}_+ \mid y \leq g(x)\}.$$

Under free disposability condition the frontier function g is monotone nondecreasing in x. See Figure 12.1 for an illustration of the production set and the frontier function in the case of $p = q = 1$. The black curve represents the frontier function, and the production set is the region below the curve. Suppose the point A represent the input and output pair of a production unit. The performance of the unit can be evaluated by referring to the points B and C on the frontier. One sees that with less input x one could have produced the same output y (point B). One also sees that with the input of A one could have produced C. In the following we describe a systematic way to measure the efficiency of any production unit compared to the peers of the production set in a multi-dimensional setup.

The production set Ψ can be described by its sections. The input (requirement) set $X(y)$ is defined by:

$$X(y) = \{x \in \mathbb{R}_+^p \mid (x, y) \in \Psi\},$$

which is the set of all input vectors $x \in \mathbb{R}_+^p$ that yield at least the output vector y. See Figure 12.2 for a graphical illustration for the case of $p = 2$. The region over the smooth curve represents $X(y)$ for a given level y. On the other hand, the output (correspondence) set $Y(x)$ is defined by:

$$Y(x) = \{y \in \mathbb{R}_+^q \mid (x, y) \in \Psi\},$$

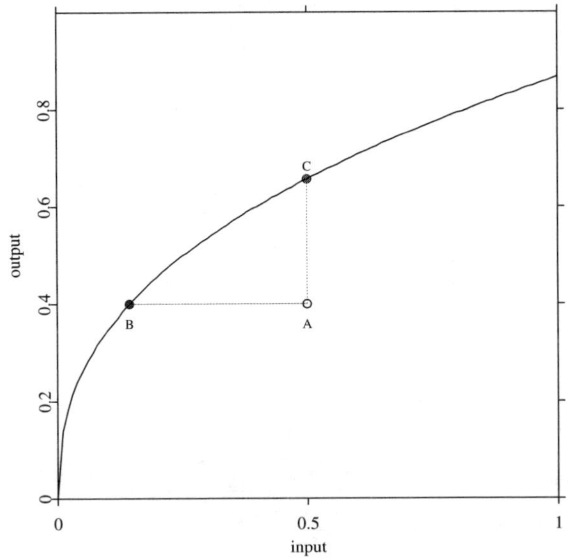

Figure 12.1: The production set and the frontier function, $p = q = 1$.

the set of all output vectors $y \in \mathbb{R}_+^q$ that is obtainable from the input vector x. Figure 12.3 illustrates $Y(x)$ for the case of $q = 2$. The region below the smooth curve is $Y(x)$ for a given input level x.

In productivity analysis one is interested in the input and output isoquants or efficient boundaries, denoted by $\partial X(y)$ and $\partial Y(x)$ respectively. They consist of the attainable boundary in a radial sense:

$$\partial X(y) = \begin{cases} \{x \mid x \in X(y),\ \theta x \notin X(y), 0 < \theta < 1\} & \text{if } y \neq 0 \\ \{0\} & \text{if } y = 0 \end{cases}$$

and

$$\partial Y(x) = \begin{cases} \{y \mid y \in Y(x),\ \lambda y \notin X(y), \lambda > 1\} & \text{if } Y(x) \neq \{0\} \\ \{0\} & \text{if } y = 0. \end{cases}$$

Given a production set Ψ with the scalar output y, the production function g can also be defined for $x \in \mathbb{R}_+^p$:

$$g(x) = \sup\{y \mid (x, y) \in \Psi\}.$$

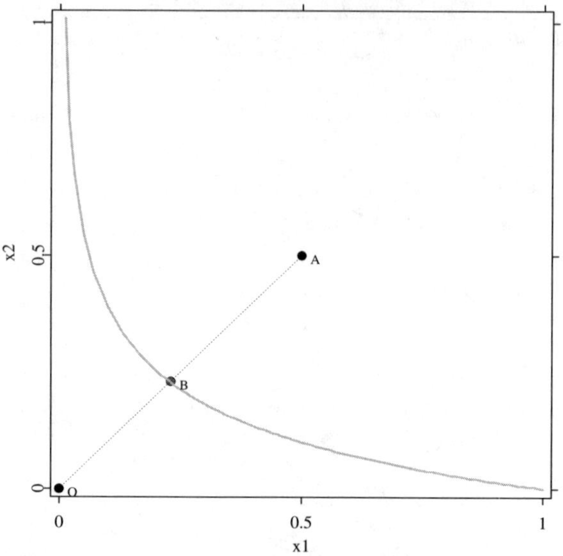

Figure 12.2: Input requirement set, $p = 2$.

It may be defined via the input set and the output set as well:

$$g(x) = \sup\{y \mid x \in X(y)\} = \sup\{y \mid y \in Y(x)\}.$$

For a given input-output point (x_0, y_0), its input efficiency is defined as

$$\theta^{\text{IN}}(x_0, y_0) = \inf\{\theta \mid \theta x_0 \in X(y_0)\}.$$

The efficient level of input corresponding to the output level y_0 is then given by

$$x^{\partial}(y_0) = \theta^{\text{IN}}(x_0, y_0)x_0. \tag{12.1}$$

Note that $x^{\partial}(y_0)$ is the intersection of $\partial X(y_0)$ and the ray θx_0, $\theta > 0$, see Figure 12.2. Suppose that the point A in Figure 12.2 represent the input used by a production unit. The point B is its efficient input level and the input efficient score of the unit is given by OB/OA. The output efficiency score $\theta^{\text{OUT}}(x_0, y_0)$ can be defined similarly:

$$\theta^{\text{OUT}}(x_0, y_0) = \sup\{\theta \mid \theta y_0 \in Y(x_0)\}. \tag{12.2}$$

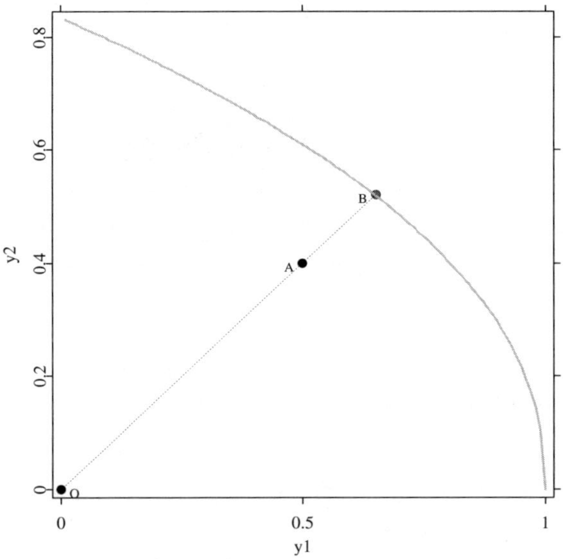

Figure 12.3: Output corresponding set, $q = 2$.

The efficient level of output corresponding to the input level x_0 is given by

$$y^{\partial}(x_0) = \theta^{\mathrm{OUT}}(x_0, y_0) y_0.$$

In Figure 12.3, let the point A be the output produced by a unit. Then the point B is the efficient output level and the output efficient score of the unit is given by OB/OA. Note that, by definition,

$$\begin{aligned} \theta^{\mathrm{IN}}(x_0, y_0) &= \inf\{\theta \mid (\theta x_0, y_0) \in \Psi\}, \\ \theta^{\mathrm{OUT}}(x_0, y_0) &= \sup\{\theta \mid (x_0, \theta y_0) \in \Psi\}. \end{aligned} \tag{12.3}$$

Returns to scale is a characteristic of the surface of the production set. The production set exhibits constant returns to scale (CRS) if, for $\alpha \geq 0$ and $P \in \Psi$, $\alpha P \in \Psi$; it exhibits non-increasing returns to scale (NIRS) if, for $0 \leq \alpha \leq 1$ and $P \in \Psi$, $\alpha P \in \Psi$; it exhibits non-decreasing returns to scale (NDRS) if, for $\alpha \geq 1$ and $P \in \Psi$, $\alpha P \in \Psi$. In particular, a convex production set exhibits non-increasing returns to scale. Note, however, that the converse is not true.

For more details on the theory and method for productivity analysis, see Shephard (1970), Färe, Grosskopf, and Lovell (1985), and Färe, Grosskopf, and Lovell (1994).

12.2 Nonparametric Hull Methods

The production set Ψ and the production function g is usually unknown, but a sample of production units or decision making units (DMU's) is available instead:

$$\mathcal{X} = \{(x_i, y_i), i = 1, \dots, n\}.$$

The aim of productivity analysis is to estimate Ψ or g from the data $\mathcal{X}$. Here we consider only the deterministic frontier model, i.e. no noise in the observations and hence $\mathcal{X} \subset \Psi$ with probability 1. For example, when $q = 1$ the structure of $\mathcal{X}$ can be expressed as:

$$y_i = g(x_i) - u_i, \ i = 1, \dots, n$$

or

$$y_i = g(x_i) v_i, \ i = 1, \dots, n$$

where g is the frontier function, and $u_i \geq 0$ and $v_i \leq 1$ are the random terms for inefficiency of the observed pair (x_i, y_i) for $i = 1, \dots, n$.

The most popular nonparametric method is Data Envelopment Analysis (DEA), which assumes that the production set is convex and free disposable. This model is an extension of Farrel (1957)'s idea and was popularized by Charnes, Cooper, and Rhodes (1978). Deprins, Simar, and Tulkens (1984), assuming only free disposability on the production set, proposed a more flexible model, say, Free Disposal Hull (FDH) model. Statistical properties of these hull methods have been studied in the literature. Park (2001), Simar and Wilson (2000) provide reviews on the statistical inference of existing nonparametric frontier models. For the nonparametric frontier models in the presence of noise, so called nonparametric stochastic frontier models, we refer to Simar (2003), Kumbhakar, Park, Simar and Tsionas (2004) and references therein.

12.2.1 Data Envelopment Analysis

The Data Envelopment Analysis (DEA) of the observed sample $\mathcal{X}$ is defined as the smallest free disposable and convex set containing $\mathcal{X}$:

$$\begin{aligned}\widehat{\Psi}_{\mathrm{DEA}} &= \{(x,y) \in \mathbb{R}_+^p \times \mathbb{R}_+^q \,|\, x \geq \sum_{i=1}^n \gamma_i x_i,\; y \leq \sum_{i=1}^n \gamma_i y_i,\\ &\quad \text{for some } (\gamma_1,\ldots,\gamma_n) \text{ such that}\\ &\quad \sum_{i=1}^n \gamma_i = 1, \gamma_i \geq 0\; \forall i = 1,\ldots,n\}.\end{aligned}$$

The DEA efficiency scores for a given input-output level (x_0, y_0) are obtained via (12.3):

$$\begin{aligned}\widehat{\theta}^{\mathrm{IN}}(x_0,y_0) &= \min\{\theta > 0 \,|\, (\theta x_0, y_0) \in \widehat{\Psi}_{\mathrm{DEA}}\},\\ \widehat{\theta}^{\mathrm{OUT}}(x_0,y_0) &= \max\{\theta > 0 \,|\, (x_0, \theta y_0) \in \widehat{\Psi}_{\mathrm{DEA}}\}.\end{aligned}$$

The DEA efficient levels for a given level (x_0, y_0) are given by (12.1) and (12.2) as:

$$\widehat{x^\partial}(y_0) = \widehat{\theta}^{\mathrm{IN}}(x_0,y_0)x_0; \quad \widehat{y^\partial}(x_0) = \widehat{\theta}^{\mathrm{OUT}}(x_0,y_0)y_0.$$

Figure 12.4 depicts 50 simulated production units and the frontier built by DEA efficient input levels. The simulated model is as follows:

$$x_i \sim \text{Uniform}[0,1],\; y_i = g(x_i)e^{-z_i},\; g(x) = 1 + \sqrt{x},\; z_i \sim \text{Exp}(3),$$

for $i = 1, \ldots, 50$, where $\text{Exp}(\nu)$ denotes the exponential distribution with mean $1/\nu$. Note that $\mathrm{E}[-z_i] = 0.75$. The scenario with an exponential distribution for the logarithm of inefficiency term and 0.75 as an average of inefficiency are reasonable in the productivity analysis literature (Gijbels, Mammen, Park, and Simar, 1999).

The DEA estimate is always downward biased in the sense that $\widehat{\Psi}_{\mathrm{DEA}} \subset \Psi$. So the asymptotic analysis quantifying the discrepancy between the true frontier and the DEA estimate would be appreciated. The consistency and the convergence rate of DEA efficiency scores with multidimensional inputs and outputs were established analytically by Kneip, Park, and Simar (1998). For $p = 1$ and $q = 1$, Gijbels, Mammen, Park, and Simar (1999) obtained its limit distribution depending on the curvature of the frontier and the density at the boundary. Jeong and Park (2004) and Kneip, Simar, and Wilson (2003) extended this result to higher dimensions.

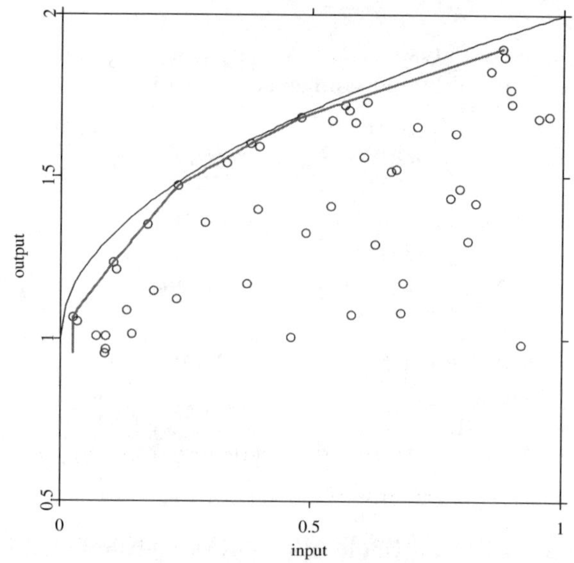

Figure 12.4: 50 simulated production units (circles), the frontier of the DEA estimate (solid line), and the true frontier function $g(x) = 1 + \sqrt{x}$ (dotted line).

STFnpa01.xpl

12.2.2 Free Disposal Hull

The Free Disposal Hull (FDH) of the observed sample $\mathcal{X}$ is defined as the smallest free disposable set containing $\mathcal{X}$:

$$\widehat{\Psi}_{\mathrm{FDH}} = \{(x, y) \in \mathbb{R}_+^p \times \mathbb{R}_+^q \mid x \geq x_i,\ y \leq y_i,\ i = 1, \ldots, n\}.$$

We can obtain the FDH estimates of efficiency scores for a given input-output level (x_0, y_0) by substituting $\widehat{\Psi}_{\mathrm{DEA}}$ with $\widehat{\Psi}_{\mathrm{FDH}}$ in the definition of DEA efficiency scores. Note that, unlike DEA estimates, their closed forms can be derived by a straightforward calculation:

$$\widehat{\theta}^{\text{IN}}(x_0, y_0) = \min_{i|y \le y_i} \max_{1 \le j \le p} x_i^j \Big/ x_0^j,$$

$$\widehat{\theta}^{\text{OUT}}(x_0, y_0) = \max_{i|x \ge x_i} \min_{1 \le k \le q} y_i^k \Big/ y_0^k,$$

where v^j is the jth component of a vector v. The efficient levels for a given level (x_0, y_0) are obtained by the same way as those for DEA. See Figure 12.5 for an illustration by a simulated example:

$$x_i \sim \text{Uniform}[1, 2], y_i = g(x_i)e^{-z_i}, g(x) = 3(x-1.5)^3+0.25x+1.125, z_i \sim \text{Exp}(3),$$

for $i = 1, \ldots, 50$. Park, Simar, and Weiner (1999) showed that the limit distribution of the FDH estimator in a multivariate setup is a Weibull distribution depending on the slope of the frontier and the density at the boundary.

12.3 DEA in Practice: Insurance Agencies

In order to illustrate a practical application of DEA we consider an example from the empirical study of Scheel (1999). This concrete data analysis is about the efficiency of 63 agencies of a German insurance company, see Table 12.1. The input $X \in \mathbb{R}_+^4$ and output $Y \in \mathbb{R}_+^2$ variables were as follows:

X_1 : Number of clients of Type A,

X_2 : Number of clients of Type B,

X_3 : Number of clients of Type C,

X_4 : Potential new premiums in EURO,

Y_1 : Number of new contracts,

Y_2 : Sum of new premiums in EURO.

Clients of an insurance company are those who are currently served by the agencies of the company. They are classified into several types which reflect, for example, the insurance coverage. Agencies should sell to the clients as many contracts with as many premiums as possible. Hence the number of clients (X_1, X_2, X_3) are included as input variables, and the number of new contracts (Y_1)

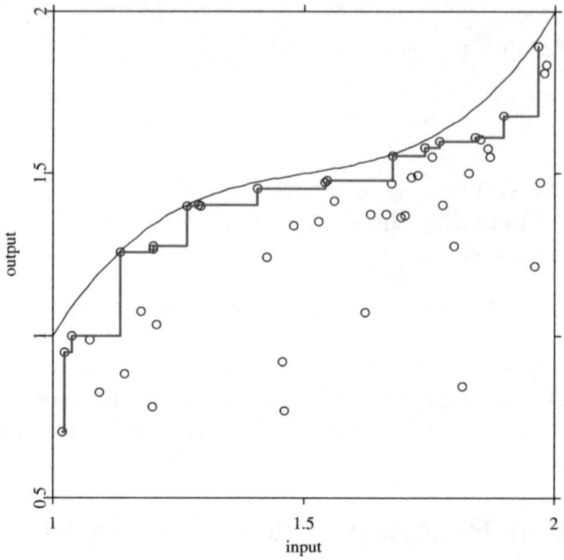

Figure 12.5: 50 simulated production units (circles) the frontier of the FDH estimate (solid line), and the true frontier function $g(x) = 3(x - 1.5)^3 + 0.25x + 1.125$ (dotted line). STFnpa02.xpl

and the sum of new premiums (Y_2) are included as output variables. The potential new premiums (X_4) is included as input variables, since it depends on the clients' current coverage.

Summary statistics for this data are given in Table 12.2. The DEA efficiency scores and the DEA efficient levels of inputs for the agencies are given in Tables 12.3 and 12.4, respectively. The input efficient score for each agency provides a gauge for evaluating its activity, and the efficient level of inputs can be interpreted as a 'goal' input. For example, agency 1 should have been able to yield its activity outputs ($Y_1 = 7$, $Y_2 = 1754$) with only 38% of its inputs, i.e., $X_1 = 53$, $X_2 = 93$, $X_3 = 4$, and $X_4 = 108960$. By contrast, agency 63, whose efficiency score is equal to 1, turned out to have used its resources 100% efficiently.

Table 12.1: Activities of 63 agencies of a German insurance company

	inputs				outputs	
Agency	X_1	X_2	X_3	X_4	Y_1	Y_2
1	138	242	10	283816.7	7	1754
2	166	124	5	156727.5	8	2413
3	152	84	3	111128.9	15	2531
.	.	.	.	.	.	.
.	.	.	.	.	.	.
.	.	.	.	.	.	.
62	83	109	2	139831.4	11	4439
63	108	257	0	299905.3	45	30545

Table 12.2: Summary statistics for 63 agencies of a German insurance company

	Minimum	Maximum	Mean	Median	Std.Error
X1	42	572	225.54	197	131.73
X2	55	481	184.44	141	110.28
X3	0	140	19.762	10	26.012
X4	73756	693820	258670	206170	160150
Y1	2	70	22.762	16	16.608
Y2	696	33075	7886.7	6038	7208

12.4 FDH in Practice: Manufacturing Industry

In order to illustrate how FDH works, the Manufacturing Industry Productivity Database from the National Bureau of Economic Research (NBER), USA is considered. This database is downloadable from the website of NBER [http://www.nber.org]. It contains annual industry-level data on output, employment, payroll, and other input costs, investment, capital stocks, and various industry-specific price indices from 1958 on hundreds of manufacturing industries (indexed by 4 digits numbers) in the United States. We selected data from the year 1996 (458 industries) with the following 4 input variables, $p = 4$, and 1 output variable, $q = 1$ (summary statistics are given in Table 12.5):

Table 12.3: DEA efficiency score of the 63 agencies

Agency	Efficiency score
1	0.38392
2	0.49063
3	0.86449
.	.
.	.
.	.
62	0.79892
63	1

STFnpa03.xpl

Table 12.4: DEA efficiency level of the 63 agencies

	Efficient level of inputs			
Agency	X_1	X_2	X_3	X_4
1	52.981	92.909	3.8392	108960
2	81.444	60.838	2.4531	76895
3	131.4	72.617	2.5935	96070
.	.	.	.	.
.	.	.	.	.
.	.	.	.	.
62	66.311	87.083	1.5978	111710
63	108	257	0	299910

STFnpa03.xpl

X_1 : Total employment,

X_2 : Total cost of material,

X_3 : Cost of electricity and fuel,

X_4 : Total real capital stock,

Y : Total value added.

Table 12.5: Summary statistics for Manufacturing Industry Productivity Database (NBER, USA)

	Minimum	Maximum	Mean	Median	Std.Error
X1	0.8	500.5	37.833	21	54.929
X2	18.5	145130	4313	1957.2	10771
X3	0.5	3807.8	139.96	49.7	362
X4	15.8	64590	2962.8	1234.7	6271.1
Y	34.1	56311	3820.2	1858.5	6392

Table 12.6 summarizes the result of the analysis of US manufacturing industries in 1996. The industry indexed by 2015 was efficient in both input and output orientation. This means that it is one of the vertices of the free disposal hull generated by the 458 observations. On the other hand, the industry 2298 performed fairly well in terms of input efficiency (0.96) but somewhat badly (0.47) in terms of output efficiency. We can obtain the efficient level of inputs (or outputs) by multiplying (or dividing) the efficiency score to each corresponding observation. For example, consider the industry 2013, which used inputs $X_1 = 88.1$, $X_2 = 14925$, $X_3 = 250$, and $X_4 = 4365.1$ to yield the output $Y = 5954.2$. Since its FDH input efficiency score was 0.64, this industry should have used the inputs $X_1 = 56.667$, $X_2 = 9600$, $X_3 = 160.8$, and $X_4 = 2807.7$ to produce the observed output $Y = 5954.2$. On the other hand, taking into account that the FDH output efficiency score was 0.70, this industry should have increased its output upto $Y = 4183.1$ with the observed level of inputs.

Table 12.6: FDH efficiency scores of 458 US industries in 1996

	Industry	Efficiency scores input	output
1	2011	0.88724	0.94203
2	2013	0.79505	0.80701
3	2015	0.66933	0.62707
4	2021	1	1
.	.	.	.
.	.	.	.
.	.	.	.
75	2298	0.80078	0.7439
.	.	.	.
.	.	.	.
.	.	.	.
458	3999	0.50809	0.47585

Q STFnpa04.xpl

Bibliography

Charnes, A., Cooper, W. W., and Rhodes, E. (1978). Measuring the Inefficiency of Decision Making Units, *European Journal of Operational Research* **2**, 429–444.

Deprins, D., Simar, L., and Tulkens, H. (1984). Measuring Labor Inefficiency in Post Offices, in Marchand, M., Pestieau, P. and Tulkens, H. (eds.) *The Performance of Public Enterprizes: Concepts and Measurements*, 243–267.

Färe, R., Grosskopf, S., and Lovell, C. A. K. (1985). *The Measurement of Efficiency of Production*, Kluwer-Nijhoff.

Färe, R., Grosskopf, S., and Lovell, C. A. K. (1994). *Production Frontiers*, Cambridge University Press.

Farrell, M. J. I.(1957). The Measurement of Productivity Efficiency, *Journal of the Royal Statistical Society, Ser. A* **120**, 253–281.

Gijbels, I., Mammen, E., Park, B. U., and Simar, L. (1999). On Estimation of Monotone and Concave Frontier Functions, *Journal of the American Statistical Association* **94**, 220–228.

Jeong, S. and Park, B. U. (2002). Limit Distributions Convex Hull Estimators of Boundaries, Discussion Paper # 0439, CASE (Center for Applieed Statistics and Economics), Humboldt-Universität zu Berlin, Germany.

Kneip, A., Park, B. U., and Simar, L. (1998). A Note on the Convergence of Nonparametric DEA Efficiency Measures, *Econometric Theory* **14**, 783–793.

Kneip, A., Simar, L., and Wilson, P. (2003). Asymptotics for DEA estimators in non-parametric frontier models, Discussion Paper # 0317, Institute de Statistique, Université catholique de Louvain, Louvain-la-Neuve, Belgium.

Kumbhakar, S. C., Park, B. U., Simar, L., and Tsionas, E. G. (2004). Nonparametric stochastic frontiers: A local maximum likelihood approach, Discussion Paper # 0417 Institut de statistique, Université catholique de Louvain, Louvain-la-Neuve, Belgium.

Park, B. U. (2001). On Nonparametric Estimation of Data Edges, *Journal of the Korean Statistical Society* **30**, 2, 265–280.

Park, B. U., Simar, L., and Weiner, Ch. (1999). The FDH Estimator for Productivity Efficiency Scores: Asymptotic Properties, *Econometric Theory* **16**, 855–877.

Scheel, H. (1999). Continuity of the BCC efficiency measure, in: Westermann (ed.), *Data Envelopment Analysis in the public and private service sector*, Gabler, Wiesbaden.

Shephard, R. W. (1970). *Theory of Cost and Production Function*, Princeton University Press.

Simar, L. (2003). How to improve the performances of DEA/FDH estimators in the presence of noise?, Discussion Paper # 0323, Institut de statistique, Université catholique de Louvain, Louvain-la-Neuve, Belgium.

Simar, L. and Wilson, P. (2000). Statistical Inference in Nonparametric Frontier Models: The State of the Art, *Journal of Productivity Analysis* **13**, 49–78.

Part II

Insurance

13 Loss Distributions

Krzysztof Burnecki, Adam Misiorek, and Rafał Weron

13.1 Introduction

The derivation of loss distributions from insurance data is not an easy task. Insurers normally keep data files containing detailed information about policies and claims, which are used for accounting and rate-making purposes. However, claim size distributions and other data needed for risk-theoretical analyzes can be obtained usually only after tedious data preprocessing. Moreover, the claim statistics are often limited. Data files containing detailed information about some policies and claims may be missing or corrupted. There may also be situations where prior data or experience are not available at all, e.g. when a new type of insurance is introduced or when very large special risks are insured. Then the distribution has to be based on knowledge of similar risks or on extrapolation of lesser risks.

There are three basic approaches to deriving the loss distribution: empirical, analytical, and moment based. The empirical method, presented in Section 13.2, can be used only when large data sets are available. In such cases a sufficiently smooth and accurate estimate of the cumulative distribution function (cdf) is obtained. Sometimes the application of curve fitting techniques – used to smooth the empirical distribution function – can be beneficial. If the curve can be described by a function with a tractable analytical form, then this approach becomes computationally efficient and similar to the second method.

The analytical approach is probably the most often used in practice and certainly the most frequently adopted in the actuarial literature. It reduces to finding a suitable analytical expression which fits the observed data well and which is easy to handle. Basic characteristics and estimation issues for the most popular and useful loss distributions are discussed in Section 13.3. Note, that sometimes it may be helpful to subdivide the range of the claim size distribution into intervals for which different methods are employed. For example, the small and medium size claims could be described by the empirical claim size distribution, while the large claims – for which the scarcity of data eliminates the use of the empirical approach – by an analytical loss distribution.

In some applications the exact shape of the loss distribution is not required. We may then use the moment based approach, which consists of estimating only the lowest characteristics (moments) of the distribution, like the mean and variance. However, it should be kept in mind that even the lowest three or four moments do not fully define the shape of a distribution, and therefore the fit to the observed data may be poor. Further details on the moment based approach can be found e.g. in Daykin, Pentikainen, and Pesonen (1994).

Having a large collection of distributions to choose from, we need to narrow our selection to a single model and a unique parameter estimate. The type of the objective loss distribution can be easily selected by comparing the shapes of the empirical and theoretical mean excess functions. Goodness-of-fit can be verified by plotting the corresponding limited expected value functions. Finally, the hypothesis that the modeled random event is governed by a certain loss distribution can be statistically tested. In Section 13.4 these statistical issues are thoroughly discussed.

In Section 13.5 we apply the presented tools to modeling real-world insurance data. The analysis is conducted for two datasets: (i) the PCS (Property Claim Services) dataset covering losses resulting from catastrophic events in USA that occurred between 1990 and 1999 and (ii) the Danish fire losses dataset, which concerns major fire losses that occurred between 1980 and 1990 and were recorded by Copenhagen Re.

13.2 Empirical Distribution Function

A natural estimate for the loss distribution is the observed (empirical) claim size distribution. However, if there have been changes in monetary values during the observation period, inflation corrected data should be used. For a sample of observations $\{x_1, \ldots, x_n\}$ the empirical distribution function (edf) is defined as:

$$F_n(x) = \frac{1}{n} \#\{i : x_i \leq x\}, \tag{13.1}$$

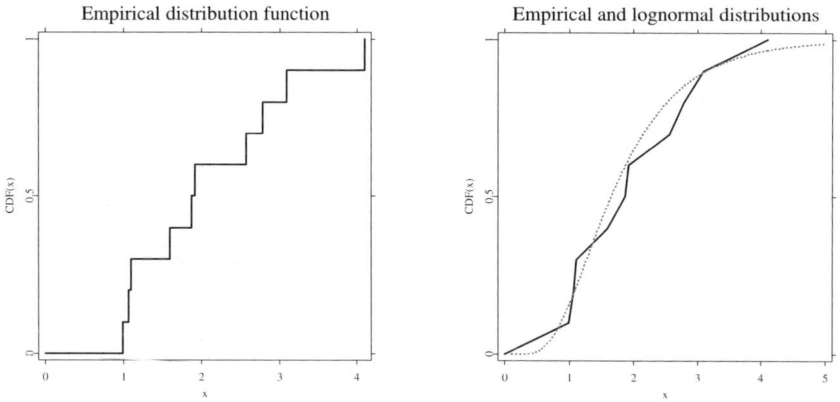

Figure 13.1: *Left panel*: Empirical distribution function (edf) of a 10-element log-normally distributed sample with parameters $\mu = 0.5$ and $\sigma = 0.5$, see Section 13.3.1. *Right panel*: Approximation of the edf by a continuous, piecewise linear function (black solid line) and the theoretical distribution function (red dotted line).

STFloss01.xpl

i.e. it is a piecewise constant function with jumps of size $1/n$ at points x_i. Very often, especially if the sample is large, the edf is approximated by a continuous, piecewise linear function with the "jump points" connected by linear functions, see Figure 13.1.

The empirical distribution function approach is appropriate only when there is a sufficiently large volume of claim data. This is rarely the case for the tail of the distribution, especially in situations where exceptionally large claims are possible. It is often advisable to divide the range of relevant values of claims into two parts, treating the claim sizes up to some limit on a discrete basis, while the tail is replaced by an analytical cdf.

13.3 Analytical Methods

It is often desirable to find an explicit analytical expression for a loss distribution. This is particularly the case if the claim statistics are too sparse to use the empirical approach. It should be stressed, however, that many standard models in statistics – like the Gaussian distribution – are unsuitable for fitting the claim size distribution. The main reason for this is the strongly skewed nature of loss distributions. The log-normal, Pareto, Burr, Weibull, and gamma distributions are typical candidates for claim size distributions to be considered in applications.

13.3.1 Log-normal Distribution

Consider a random variable X which has the normal distribution with density

$$f_N(x) = \frac{1}{\sqrt{2\pi}\sigma} \exp\left\{-\frac{1}{2}\frac{(x-\mu)^2}{\sigma^2}\right\}, \qquad -\infty < x < \infty. \tag{13.2}$$

Let $Y = e^X$ so that $X = \log Y$. Then the probability density function of Y is given by:

$$f(y) = f_N(\log y)\frac{1}{y} = \frac{1}{\sqrt{2\pi}\sigma y} \exp\left\{-\frac{1}{2}\frac{(\log y-\mu)^2}{\sigma^2}\right\}, \qquad y > 0, \tag{13.3}$$

where $\sigma > 0$ is the scale and $-\infty < \mu < \infty$ is the location parameter. The distribution of Y is termed log-normal, however, sometimes it is called the Cobb-Douglas law, especially when applied to econometric data. The log-normal cdf is given by:

$$F(y) = \Phi\left(\frac{\log y - \mu}{\sigma}\right), \qquad y > 0, \tag{13.4}$$

where $\Phi(\cdot)$ is the standard normal (with mean 0 and variance 1) distribution function. The k-th raw moment m_k of the log-normal variate can be easily derived using results for normal random variables:

$$m_k = \mathrm{E}\left(Y^k\right) = \mathrm{E}\left(e^{kX}\right) = M_X(k) = \exp\left(\mu k + \frac{\sigma^2 k^2}{2}\right), \tag{13.5}$$

where $M_X(z)$ is the moment generating function of the normal distribution. In particular, the mean and variance are

$$\mathrm{E}(X) = \exp\left(\mu + \frac{\sigma^2}{2}\right), \tag{13.6}$$

$$\mathrm{Var}(X) = \left\{\exp\left(\sigma^2\right) - 1\right\} \exp\left(2\mu + \sigma^2\right), \tag{13.7}$$

respectively. For both standard parameter estimation techniques the estimators are known in closed form. The method of moments estimators are given by:

$$\hat{\mu} = 2\log\left(\frac{1}{n}\sum_{i=1}^{n} x_i\right) - \frac{1}{2}\log\left(\frac{1}{n}\sum_{i=1}^{n} x_i^2\right), \tag{13.8}$$

$$\hat{\sigma}^2 = \log\left(\frac{1}{n}\sum_{i=1}^{n} x_i^2\right) - 2\log\left(\frac{1}{n}\sum_{i=1}^{n} x_i\right), \tag{13.9}$$

while the maximum likelihood estimators by:

$$\hat{\mu} = \frac{1}{n}\sum_{i=1}^{n} \log(x_i), \tag{13.10}$$

$$\hat{\sigma}^2 = \frac{1}{n}\sum_{i=1}^{n} \{\log(x_i) - \hat{\mu}\}^2. \tag{13.11}$$

Finally, the generation of a log-normal variate is straightforward. We simply have to take the exponent of a normal variate.

The log-normal distribution is very useful in modeling of claim sizes. It is right-skewed, has a thick tail and fits many situations well. For small σ it resembles a normal distribution (see the left panel in Figure 13.2) although this is not always desirable. It is infinitely divisible and closed under scale and power transformations. However, it also suffers from some drawbacks. Most notably, the Laplace transform does not have a closed form representation and the moment generating function does not exist.

13.3.2 Exponential Distribution

Consider the random variable with the following density and distribution functions, respectively:

$$f(x) = \beta e^{-\beta x}, \quad x > 0, \tag{13.12}$$

$$F(x) = 1 - e^{-\beta x}, \quad x > 0. \tag{13.13}$$

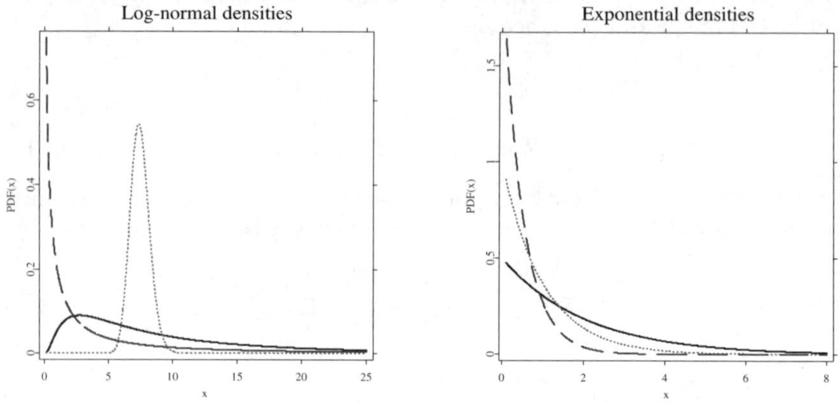

Figure 13.2: *Left panel:* Log-normal probability density functions (pdfs) with parameters $\mu = 2$ and $\sigma = 1$ (black solid line), $\mu = 2$ and $\sigma = 0.1$ (red dotted line), and $\mu = 0.5$ and $\sigma = 2$ (blue dashed line). *Right panel:* Exponential pdfs with parameter $\beta = 0.5$ (black solid line), $\beta = 1$ (red dotted line), and $\beta = 5$ (blue dashed line).

STFloss02.xpl

This distribution is termed an exponential distribution with parameter (or intensity) $\beta > 0$. The Laplace transform of (13.12) is

$$L(t) \stackrel{\text{def}}{=} \int_0^\infty e^{-tx} f(x)dx = \frac{\beta}{\beta + t}, \qquad t > -\beta, \tag{13.14}$$

yielding the general formula for the k-th raw moment

$$m_k \stackrel{\text{def}}{=} (-1)^k \frac{\partial^k L(t)}{\partial t^k}\bigg|_{t=0} = \frac{k!}{\beta^k}. \tag{13.15}$$

The mean and variance are thus β^{-1} and β^{-2}, respectively. The maximum likelihood estimator (equal to the method of moments estimator) for β is given by:

$$\hat{\beta} = \frac{1}{\hat{m}_1}, \tag{13.16}$$

where

$$\hat{m}_k = \frac{1}{n}\sum_{i=1}^{n} x_i^k, \tag{13.17}$$

is the sample k-th raw moment.

To generate an exponential random variable X with intensity β we can use the inverse transform method (L'Ecuyer, 2004; Ross, 2002). The method consists of taking a random number U distributed uniformly on the interval $(0, 1)$ and setting $X = F^{-1}(U)$, where $F^{-1}(x) = -\frac{1}{\beta}\log(1 - x)$ is the inverse of the exponential cdf (13.13). In fact we can set $X = -\frac{1}{\beta}\log U$ since $1 - U$ has the same distribution as U.

The exponential distribution has many interesting features. For example, it has the memoryless property, i.e. $\mathrm{P}(X > x + y | X > y) = \mathrm{P}(X > x)$. It also arises as the inter-occurrence times of the events in a Poisson process, see Chapter 14. The n-th root of the Laplace transform (13.14) is

$$L(t) = \left(\frac{\beta}{\beta + t}\right)^{\frac{1}{n}}, \tag{13.18}$$

which is the Laplace transform of a gamma variate (see Section 13.3.6). Thus the exponential distribution is infinitely divisible.

The exponential distribution is often used in developing models of insurance risks. This usefulness stems in a large part from its many and varied tractable mathematical properties. However, a disadvantage of the exponential distribution is that its density is monotone decreasing (see the right panel in Figure 13.2), a situation which may not be appropriate in some practical situations.

13.3.3 Pareto Distribution

Suppose that a variate X has (conditional on β) an exponential distribution with mean β^{-1}. Further, suppose that β itself has a gamma distribution (see Section 13.3.6). The unconditional distribution of X is a mixture and is called the Pareto distribution. Moreover, it can be shown that if X is an exponential random variable and Y is a gamma random variable, then X/Y is a Pareto random variable.

The density and distribution functions of a Pareto variate are given by:

$$f(x) = \frac{\alpha\lambda^\alpha}{(\lambda + x)^{\alpha+1}}, \qquad x > 0, \tag{13.19}$$

$$F(x) = 1 - \left(\frac{\lambda}{\lambda + x}\right)^\alpha, \qquad x > 0, \tag{13.20}$$

respectively. Clearly, the shape parameter α and the scale parameter λ are both positive. The k-th raw moment:

$$m_k = \lambda^k k! \frac{\Gamma(\alpha - k)}{\Gamma(\alpha)}, \tag{13.21}$$

exists only for $k < \alpha$. In the above formula

$$\Gamma(a) \stackrel{\text{def}}{=} \int_0^\infty y^{a-1} e^{-y} dy, \tag{13.22}$$

is the standard gamma function. The mean and variance are thus:

$$\mathrm{E}(X) = \frac{\lambda}{\alpha - 1}, \tag{13.23}$$

$$\mathrm{Var}(X) = \frac{\alpha\lambda^2}{(\alpha - 1)^2(\alpha - 2)}, \tag{13.24}$$

respectively. Note, that the mean exists only for $\alpha > 1$ and the variance only for $\alpha > 2$. Hence, the Pareto distribution has very thick (or heavy) tails, see Figure 13.3. The method of moments estimators are given by:

$$\hat{\alpha} = 2\frac{\hat{m}_2 - \hat{m}_1^2}{\hat{m}_2 - 2\hat{m}_1^2}, \tag{13.25}$$

$$\hat{\lambda} = \frac{\hat{m}_1 \hat{m}_2}{\hat{m}_2 - 2\hat{m}_1^2}, \tag{13.26}$$

where, as before, $\hat{m}_k$ is the sample k-th raw moment (13.17). Note, that the estimators are well defined only when $\hat{m}_2 - 2\hat{m}_1^2 > 0$. Unfortunately, there are no closed form expressions for the maximum likelihood estimators and they can only be evaluated numerically.

Like for many other distributions the simulation of a Pareto variate X can be conducted via the inverse transform method. The inverse of the cdf (13.20) has a simple analytical form $F^{-1}(x) = \lambda\left\{(1 - x)^{-1/\alpha} - 1\right\}$. Hence, we can

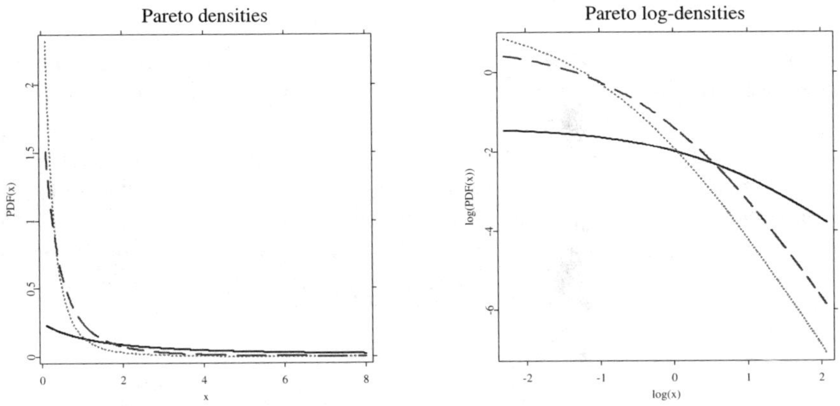

Figure 13.3: *Left panel:* Pareto pdfs with parameters $\alpha = 0.5$ and $\lambda = 2$ (black solid line), $\alpha = 2$ and $\lambda = 0.5$ (red dotted line), and $\alpha = 2$ and $\lambda = 1$ (blue dashed line). *Right panel:* The same Pareto densities on a double logarithmic plot. The thick power-law tails of the Pareto distribution are clearly visible.

STFloss03.xpl

set $X = \lambda\left(U^{-1/\alpha} - 1\right)$, where U is distributed uniformly on the unit interval. We have to be cautious, however, when α is larger but very close to one. The theoretical mean exists, but the right tail is very heavy. The sample mean will, in general, be significantly lower than $\mathrm{E}(X)$.

The Pareto law is very useful in modeling claim sizes in insurance, due in large part to its extremely thick tail. Its main drawback lies in its lack of mathematical tractability in some situations. Like for the log-normal distribution, the Laplace transform does not have a closed form representation and the moment generating function does not exist. Moreover, like the exponential pdf the Pareto density (13.19) is monotone decreasing, which may not be adequate in some practical situations.

13.3.4 Burr Distribution

Experience has shown that the Pareto formula is often an appropriate model for the claim size distribution, particularly where exceptionally large claims may occur. However, there is sometimes a need to find heavy tailed distributions which offer greater flexibility than the Pareto law, including a non-monotone pdf. Such flexibility is provided by the Burr distribution and its additional shape parameter $\tau > 0$. If Y has the Pareto distribution, then the distribution of $X = Y^{1/\tau}$ is known as the Burr distribution, see the left panel in Figure 13.4. Its density and distribution functions are given by:

$$f(x) = \tau\alpha\lambda^{\alpha}\frac{x^{\tau-1}}{(\lambda+x^{\tau})^{\alpha+1}}, \qquad x > 0, \tag{13.27}$$

$$F(x) = 1 - \left(\frac{\lambda}{\lambda+x^{\tau}}\right)^{\alpha}, \qquad x > 0, \tag{13.28}$$

respectively. The k-th raw moment

$$m_k = \frac{1}{\Gamma(\alpha)}\lambda^{k/\tau}\Gamma\left(1+\frac{k}{\tau}\right)\Gamma\left(\alpha-\frac{k}{\tau}\right), \tag{13.29}$$

exists only for $k < \tau\alpha$. Naturally, the Laplace transform does not exist in a closed form and the distribution has no moment generating function as it was the case with the Pareto distribution.

The maximum likelihood and method of moments estimators for the Burr distribution can only be evaluated numerically. A Burr variate X can be generated using the inverse transform method. The inverse of the cdf (13.28) has a simple analytical form $F^{-1}(x) = \left[\lambda\left\{(1-x)^{-1/\alpha}-1\right\}\right]^{1/\tau}$. Hence, we can set $X = \left\{\lambda\left(U^{-1/\alpha}-1\right)\right\}^{1/\tau}$, where U is distributed uniformly on the unit interval. Like in the Pareto case, we have to be cautious when $\tau\alpha$ is larger but very close to one. The theoretical mean exists, but the right tail is very heavy. The sample mean will, in general, be significantly lower than $\mathrm{E}(X)$.

13.3.5 Weibull Distribution

If V is an exponential variate, then the distribution of $X = V^{1/\tau}$, $\tau > 0$, is called the Weibull (or Frechet) distribution. Its density and distribution

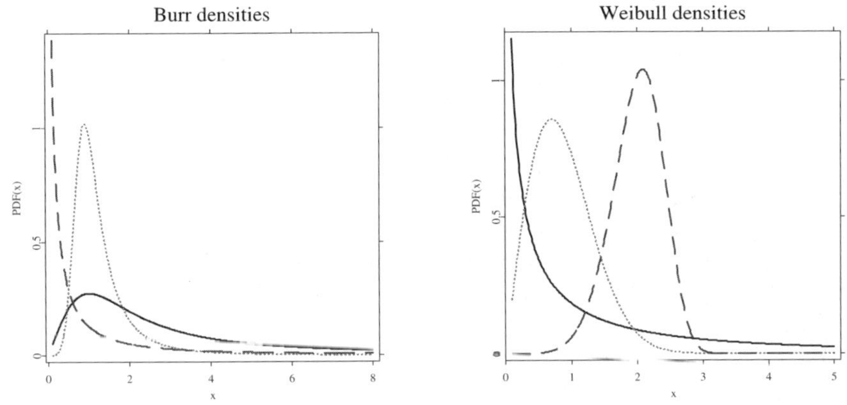

Figure 13.4: *Left panel:* Burr pdfs with parameters $\alpha = 0.5$, $\lambda = 2$ and $\tau = 1.5$ (black solid line), $\alpha = 0.5$, $\lambda = 0.5$ and $\tau = 5$ (red dotted line), and $\alpha = 2$, $\lambda = 1$ and $\tau = 0.5$ (blue dashed line). *Right panel:* Weibull pdfs with parameters $\beta = 1$ and $\tau = 0.5$ (black solid line), $\beta = 1$ and $\tau = 2$ (red dotted line), and $\beta = 0.01$ and $\tau = 6$ (blue dashed line).

STFloss04.xpl

functions are given by:

$$f(x) = \tau\beta x^{\tau-1} e^{-\beta x^{\tau}}, \qquad x > 0, \tag{13.30}$$

$$F(x) = 1 - e^{-\beta x^{\tau}}, \qquad x > 0, \tag{13.31}$$

respectively. The Weibull distribution is roughly symmetrical for the shape parameter $\tau \approx 3.6$. When τ is smaller the distribution is right-skewed, when τ is larger it is left-skewed, see the right panel in Figure 13.4. The k-th raw moment can be shown to be

$$m_k = \beta^{-k/\tau}\Gamma\left(1 + \frac{k}{\tau}\right). \tag{13.32}$$

Like for the Burr distribution, the maximum likelihood and method of moments estimators can only be evaluated numerically. Similarly, Weibull variates can be generated using the inverse transform method.

13.3.6 Gamma Distribution

The probability law with density and distribution functions given by:

$$f(x) = \beta(\beta x)^{\alpha-1}\frac{e^{-\beta x}}{\Gamma(\alpha)}, \qquad x > 0, \tag{13.33}$$

$$F(x) = \int_0^x \beta(\beta s)^{\alpha-1}\frac{e^{-\beta s}}{\Gamma(\alpha)}ds, \qquad x > 0, \tag{13.34}$$

where α and β are non-negative, is known as a gamma (or a Pearson's Type III) distribution, see the left panel in Figure 13.5. Moreover, for $\beta = 1$ the integral in (13.34):

$$\Gamma(\alpha, x) \stackrel{\text{def}}{=} \frac{1}{\Gamma(\alpha)}\int_0^x s^{\alpha-1}e^{-s}ds, \tag{13.35}$$

is called the incomplete gamma function. If the shape parameter $\alpha = 1$, the exponential distribution results. If α is a positive integer, the distribution is termed an Erlang law. If $\beta = \frac{1}{2}$ and $\alpha = \frac{\nu}{2}$ then it is termed a chi-squared (χ^2) distribution with ν degrees of freedom. Moreover, a mixed Poisson distribution with gamma mixing distribution is negative binomial, see Chapter 18.

The Laplace transform of the gamma distribution is given by:

$$L(t) = \left(\frac{\beta}{\beta + t}\right)^{\alpha}, \qquad t > -\beta. \tag{13.36}$$

The k-th raw moment can be easily derived from the Laplace transform:

$$m_k = \frac{\Gamma(\alpha + k)}{\Gamma(\alpha)\beta^k}. \tag{13.37}$$

Hence, the mean and variance are

$$\mathrm{E}(X) = \frac{\alpha}{\beta}, \tag{13.38}$$

$$\mathrm{Var}(X) = \frac{\alpha}{\beta^2}. \tag{13.39}$$

Finally, the method of moments estimators for the gamma distribution parameters have closed form expressions:

$$\hat{\alpha} = \frac{\hat{m}_1^2}{\hat{m}_2 - \hat{m}_1^2}, \tag{13.40}$$

$$\hat{\beta} = \frac{\hat{m}_1}{\hat{m}_2 - \hat{m}_1^2}, \tag{13.41}$$

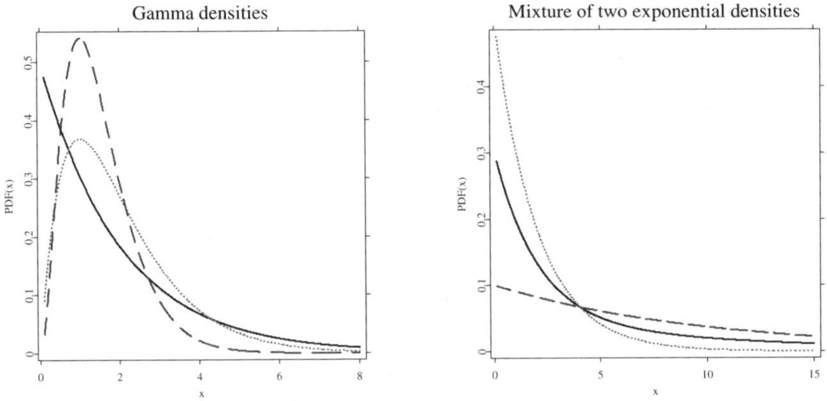

Figure 13.5: *Left panel:* Gamma pdfs with parameters $\alpha = 1$ and $\beta = 2$ (black solid line), $\alpha = 2$ and $\beta = 1$ (red dotted line), and $\alpha = 3$ and $\beta = 0.5$ (blue dashed line). *Right panel:* Densities of two exponential distributions with parameters $\beta_1 = 0.5$ (red dotted line) and $\beta_2 = 0.1$ (blue dashed line) and of their mixture with the mixing parameter $a = 0.5$ (black solid line).

`STFloss05.xpl`

but maximum likelihood estimators can only be evaluated numerically. Simulation of gamma variates is not as straightforward as for the distributions presented above. For $\alpha < 1$ a simple but slow algorithm due to Jöhnk (1964) can be used, while for $\alpha > 1$ the rejection method is more optimal (Bratley, Fox, and Schrage, 1987; Devroye, 1986).

The gamma distribution is closed under convolution, i.e. a sum of independent gamma variates with the same parameter β is again gamma distributed with this β. Hence, it is infinitely divisible. Moreover, it is right-skewed and approaches a normal distribution in the limit as α goes to infinity.

The gamma law is one of the most important distributions for modeling because it has very tractable mathematical properties. As we have seen above it is also very useful in creating other distributions, but by itself is rarely a reasonable model for insurance claim sizes.

13.3.7 Mixture of Exponential Distributions

Let $a_1, a_2, \ldots, a_n$ denote a series of non-negative weights satisfying $\sum_{i=1}^n a_i = 1$. Let $F_1(x), F_2(x), \ldots, F_n(x)$ denote an arbitrary sequence of exponential distribution functions given by the parameters $\beta_1, \beta_2, \ldots, \beta_n$, respectively. Then, the distribution function:

$$F(x) = \sum_{i=1}^{n} a_i F_i(x) = \sum_{i=1}^{n} a_i \left\{1 - \exp(-\beta_i x)\right\}, \tag{13.42}$$

is called a mixture of n exponential distributions (exponentials). The density function of the constructed distribution is

$$f(x) = \sum_{i=1}^{n} a_i f_i(x) = \sum_{i=1}^{n} a_i \beta_i \exp(-\beta_i x), \tag{13.43}$$

where $f_1(x), f_2(x), \ldots, f_n(x)$ denote the density functions of the input exponential distributions. Note, that the mixing procedure can be applied to arbitrary distributions. Using the technique of mixing, one can construct a wide class of distributions. The most commonly used in the applications is a mixture of two exponentials, see Chapter 15. In the right panel of Figure 13.5 a pdf of a mixture of two exponentials is plotted together with the pdfs of the mixing laws.

The Laplace transform of (13.43) is

$$L(t) = \sum_{i=1}^{n} a_i \frac{\beta_i}{\beta_i + t}, \qquad t > -\min_{i=1\ldots n} \{\beta_i\}, \tag{13.44}$$

yielding the general formula for the k-th raw moment

$$m_k = \sum_{i=1}^{n} a_i \frac{k!}{\beta_i^k}. \tag{13.45}$$

The mean is thus $\sum_{i=1}^n a_i \beta_i^{-1}$. The maximum likelihood and method of moments estimators for the mixture of n ($n \geq 2$) exponential distributions can only be evaluated numerically.

Simulation of variates defined by (13.42) can be performed using the composition approach (Ross, 2002). First generate a random variable I, equal to i with probability a_i, $i = 1, ..., n$. Then simulate an exponential variate with intensity β_I. Note, that the method is general in the sense that it can be used for any set of distributions F_i's.

13.4 Statistical Validation Techniques

Having a large collection of distributions to choose from we need to narrow our selection to a single model and a unique parameter estimate. The type of the objective loss distribution can be easily selected by comparing the shapes of the empirical and theoretical mean excess functions. The mean excess function, presented in Section 13.4.1, is based on the idea of conditioning a random variable given that it exceeds a certain level.

Once the distribution class is selected and the parameters are estimated using one of the available methods the goodness-of-fit has to be tested. Probably the most natural approach consists of measuring the distance between the empirical and the fitted analytical distribution function. A group of statistics and tests based on this idea is discussed in Section 13.4.2. However, when using these tests we face the problem of comparing a discontinuous step function with a continuous non-decreasing curve. The two functions will always differ from each other in the vicinity of a step by at least half the size of the step. This problem can be overcome by integrating both distributions once, which leads to the so-called limited expected value function introduced in Section 13.4.3.

13.4.1 Mean Excess Function

For a claim amount random variable X, the mean excess function or mean residual life function is the expected payment per claim on a policy with a fixed amount deductible of x, where claims with amounts less than or equal to x are completely ignored:

$$e(x) = \mathrm{E}(X - x|X > x) = \frac{\int_x^\infty \{1 - F(u)\}\, du}{1 - F(x)}. \tag{13.46}$$

In practice, the mean excess function e is estimated by $\hat{e}_n$ based on a representative sample $x_1, \ldots, x_n$:

$$\hat{e}_n(x) = \frac{\sum_{x_i > x} x_i}{\#\{i : x_i > x\}} - x. \tag{13.47}$$

Note, that in a financial risk management context, switching from the right tail to the left tail, $e(x)$ is referred to as the expected shortfall (Weron, 2004).

When considering the shapes of mean excess functions, the exponential distribution plays a central role. It has the memoryless property, meaning that whether the information $X > x$ is given or not, the expected value of $X - x$ is the same as if one started at $x = 0$ and calculated $\mathrm{E}(X)$. The mean excess function for the exponential distribution is therefore constant. One in fact easily calculates that for this case $e(x) = 1/\beta$ for all $x > 0$.

If the distribution of X is heavier-tailed than the exponential distribution we find that the mean excess function ultimately increases, when it is lighter-tailed $e(x)$ ultimately decreases. Hence, the shape of $e(x)$ provides important information on the sub-exponential or super-exponential nature of the tail of the distribution at hand.

Mean excess functions and first order approximations to the tail for the distributions discussed in Section 13.3 are given by the following formulas:

- log-normal distribution:

$$\begin{aligned} e(x) &= \frac{\exp\left(\mu + \frac{\sigma^2}{2}\right)\left\{1 - \Phi\left(\frac{\ln x - \mu - \sigma^2}{\sigma}\right)\right\}}{\left\{1 - \Phi\left(\frac{\ln x - \mu}{\sigma}\right)\right\}} - x \\ &= \frac{\sigma^2 x}{\ln x - \mu}\left\{1 + o(1)\right\}, \end{aligned}$$

  where $o(1)$ stands for a term which tends to zero as $x \to \infty$;

- exponential distribution:

$$e(x) = \frac{1}{\beta};$$

- Pareto distribution:

$$e(x) = \frac{\lambda + x}{\alpha - 1}, \qquad \alpha > 1;$$

- Burr distribution:

$$\begin{aligned} e(x) &= \frac{\lambda^{1/\tau}\Gamma\left(\alpha - \frac{1}{\tau}\right)\Gamma\left(1 + \frac{1}{\tau}\right)}{\Gamma(\alpha)} \cdot \left(\frac{\lambda}{\lambda + x^\tau}\right)^{-\alpha} \cdot \\ &\quad \cdot \left\{1 - \mathrm{B}\left(1 + \frac{1}{\tau}, \alpha - \frac{1}{\tau}, \frac{x^\tau}{\lambda + x^\tau}\right)\right\} - x \\ &= \frac{x}{\alpha\tau - 1}\left\{1 + o(1)\right\}, \qquad \alpha\tau > 1, \end{aligned}$$

where $\Gamma(\cdot)$ is the standard gamma function (13.22) and

$$B(a,b,x) \stackrel{\text{def}}{=} \frac{\Gamma(a+b)}{\Gamma(a)\Gamma(b)} \int_0^x y^{a-1}(1-y)^{b-1}dy, \tag{13.48}$$

is the beta function;

- Weibull distribution:

$$\begin{aligned} e(x) &= \frac{\Gamma(1+1/\tau)}{\beta^{1/\tau}} \left\{1 - \Gamma\left(1 + \frac{1}{\tau}, \beta x^\tau\right)\right\} \exp(\beta x^\tau) - x \\ &= \frac{x^{1-\tau}}{\beta\tau} \{1 + o(1)\}, \end{aligned}$$

where $\Gamma(\cdot,\cdot)$ is the incomplete gamma function (13.35);

- gamma distribution:

$$e(x) = \frac{\alpha}{\beta} \cdot \frac{1 - F(x, \alpha+1, \beta)}{1 - F(x, \alpha, \beta)} - x = \beta^{-1}\{1 + o(1)\},$$

where $F(x,\alpha,\beta)$ is the gamma distribution function (13.34);

- mixture of two exponential distributions:
- distribution!mixture of exponentials

$$e(x) = \frac{\frac{x}{\beta_1}\exp(-\beta_1 c) + \frac{1-x}{\beta_2}\exp(-\beta_2 c)}{x\exp(-\beta_1 c) + (1-x)\exp(-\beta_2 c)} - x.$$

Selected shapes are also sketched in Figure 13.6.

13.4.2 Tests Based on the Empirical Distribution Function

A statistics measuring the difference between the empirical $F_n(x)$ and the fitted $F(x)$ distribution function, called an edf statistic, is based on the vertical difference between the distributions. This distance is usually measured either by a supremum or a quadratic norm (D'Agostino and Stephens, 1986).

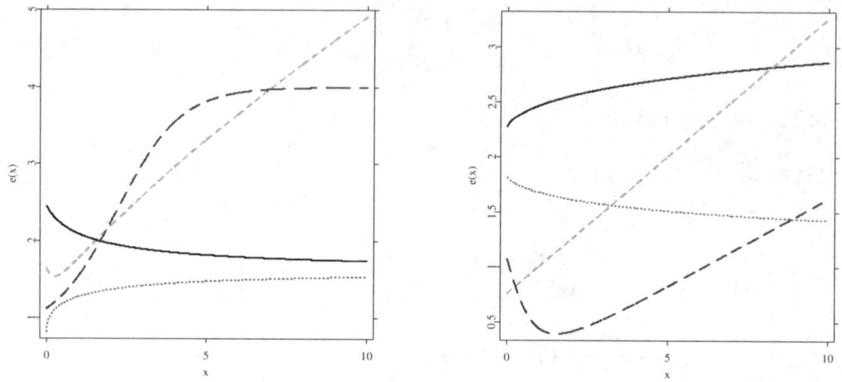

Figure 13.6: *Left panel:* Shapes of the mean excess function $e(x)$ for the log-normal (green dashed line), gamma with $\alpha < 1$ (red dotted line), gamma with $\alpha > 1$ (black solid line) and a mixture of two exponential distributions (blue long-dashed line). *Right panel:* Shapes of the mean excess function $e(x)$ for the Pareto (green dashed line), Burr (blue long-dashed line), Weibull with $\tau < 1$ (black solid line) and Weibull with $\tau > 1$ (red dotted line) distributions.

`STFloss06.xpl`

The most well-known supremum statistic:

$$D = \sup_x |F_n(x) - F(x)|, \tag{13.49}$$

is known as the Kolmogorov or Kolmogorov-Smirnov statistic. It can also be written in terms of two supremum statistics:

$$D^+ = \sup_x \{F_n(x) - F(x)\} \quad \text{and} \quad D^- = \sup_x \{F(x) - F_n(x)\},$$

where the former is the largest vertical difference when $F_n(x)$ is larger than $F(x)$ and the latter is the largest vertical difference when it is smaller. The Kolmogorov statistic is then given by $D = \max(D^+, D^-)$. A closely related statistic proposed by Kuiper is simply a sum of the two differences, i.e. $V = D^+ + D^-$.

The second class of measures of discrepancy is given by the Cramér-von Mises family

$$Q = n \int_{-\infty}^{\infty} \{F_n(x) - F(x)\}^2 \psi(x) \mathrm{d}F(x), \tag{13.50}$$

where $\psi(x)$ is a suitable function which gives weights to the squared difference $\{F_n(x) - F(x)\}^2$. When $\psi(x) = 1$ we obtain the W^2 statistic of Cramér-von Mises. When $\psi(x) = [F(x)\{1 - F(x)\}]^{-1}$ formula (13.50) yields the A^2 statistic of Anderson and Darling. From the definitions of the statistics given above, suitable computing formulas must be found. This can be done by utilizing the transformation $Z = F(X)$. When $F(x)$ is the true distribution function of X, the random variable Z is uniformly distributed on the unit interval.

Suppose that a sample $x_1, \ldots, x_n$ gives values $z_i = F(x_i)$, $i = 1, \ldots, n$. It can be easily shown that, for values z and x related by $z = F(x)$, the corresponding vertical differences in the edf diagrams for X and for Z are equal. Consequently, edf statistics calculated from the empirical distribution function of the z_i's compared with the uniform distribution will take the same values as if they were calculated from the empirical distribution function of the x_i's, compared with $F(x)$. This leads to the following formulas given in terms of the order statistics $z_{(1)} < z_{(2)} < \cdots < z_{(n)}$:

$$\begin{aligned}
D^+ &= \max_{1 \le i \le n} \left\{ \frac{i}{n} - z_{(i)} \right\}, && (13.51)\\
D^- &= \max_{1 \le i \le n} \left\{ z_{(i)} - \frac{(i-1)}{n} \right\}, && (13.52)\\
D &= \max(D^+, D^-), && (13.53)\\
V &= D^+ + D^-, && (13.54)\\
W^2 &= \sum_{i=1}^{n} \left\{ z_{(i)} - \frac{(2i-1)}{2n} \right\}^2 + \frac{1}{12n}, && (13.55)
\end{aligned}$$

$$\begin{aligned}
A^2 &= -n - \frac{1}{n} \sum_{i=1}^{n} \{\log z_{(i)} + \log(1 - z_{(n+1-i)})\} && (13.56)\\
&= -n - \frac{1}{n} \sum_{i=1}^{n} \{(2i-1) \log z_{(i)} + \\
&\quad +(2n+1-2i) \log(1 - z_{(i)})\}. && (13.57)
\end{aligned}$$

The general test of fit is structured as follows. The null hypothesis is that a specific distribution is acceptable, whereas the alternative is that it is not:

$$H_0: \quad F_n(x) = F(x;\theta),$$
$$H_1: \quad F_n(x) \neq F(x;\theta),$$

where θ is a vector of known parameters. Small values of the test statistic T are evidence in favor of the null hypothesis, large ones indicate its falsity. To see how unlikely such a large outcome would be if the null hypothesis was true, we calculate the p-value by:

$$p\text{-value} = P(T \geq t), \tag{13.58}$$

where t is the test value for a given sample. It is typical to reject the null hypothesis when a small p-value is obtained.

However, we are in a situation where we want to test the hypothesis that the sample has a common distribution function $F(x;\theta)$ with unknown θ. To employ any of the edf tests we first need to estimate the parameters. It is important to recognize, however, that when the parameters are estimated from the data, the critical values for the tests of the uniform distribution (or equivalently of a fully specified distribution) must be reduced. In other words, if the value of the test statistics T is d, then the p-value is overestimated by $P_U(T \geq d)$. Here P_U indicates that the probability is computed under the assumption of a uniformly distributed sample. Hence, if $P_U(T \geq d)$ is small, then the p-value will be even smaller and the hypothesis will be rejected. However, if it is large then we have to obtain a more accurate estimate of the p-value.

Ross (2002) advocates the use of Monte Carlo simulations in this context. First the parameter vector is estimated for a given sample of size n, yielding $\hat{\theta}$, and the edf test statistics is calculated assuming that the sample is distributed according to $F(x;\hat{\theta})$, returning a value of d. Next, a sample of size n of $F(x;\hat{\theta})$-distributed variates is generated. The parameter vector is estimated for this simulated sample, yielding $\hat{\theta}_1$, and the edf test statistics is calculated assuming that the sample is distributed according to $F(x;\hat{\theta}_1)$. The simulation is repeated as many times as required to achieve a certain level of accuracy. The estimate of the p-value is obtained as the proportion of times that the test quantity is at least as large as d.

An alternative solution to the problem of unknown parameters was proposed by Stephens (1978). The half-sample approach consists of using only half the data to estimate the parameters, but then using the entire data set to conduct the test. In this case, the critical values for the uniform distribution can be applied, at least asymptotically. The quadratic edf tests seem to converge fairly rapidly to their asymptotic distributions (D'Agostino and Stephens, 1986). Although, the method is much faster than the Monte Carlo approach it is not invariant – depending on the choice of the half-samples different test values will be obtained and there is no way of increasing the accuracy.

As a side product, the edf tests supply us with a natural technique of estimating the parameter vector θ. We can simply find such $\hat{\theta}^*$ that minimizes a selected edf statistic. Out of the four presented statistics A^2 is the most powerful when the fitted distribution departs from the true distribution in the tails (D'Agostino and Stephens, 1986). Since the fit in the tails is of crucial importance in most actuarial applications A^2 is the recommended statistic for the estimation scheme.

13.4.3 Limited Expected Value Function

The limited expected value function L of a claim size variable X, or of the corresponding cdf $F(x)$, is defined by

$$L(x) = \mathrm{E}\{\min(X, x)\} = \int_0^x y dF(y) + x\{1 - F(x)\}, \quad x > 0. \tag{13.59}$$

The value of the function L at point x is equal to the expectation of the cdf $F(x)$ truncated at this point. In other words, it represents the expected amount per claim retained by the insured on a policy with a fixed amount deductible of x. The empirical estimate is defined as follows:

$$\hat{L}_n(x) = \frac{1}{n}\left(\sum_{x_j < x} x_j + \sum_{x_j \geq x} x\right). \tag{13.60}$$

In order to fit the limited expected value function L of an analytical distribution to the observed data, the estimate $\hat{L}_n$ is first constructed. Thereafter one tries to find a suitable analytical cdf F, such that the corresponding limited expected value function L is as close to the observed $\hat{L}_n$ as possible.

The limited expected value function has the following important properties:

1. the graph of L is concave, continuous and increasing;

2. $L(x) \to E(X)$, as $x \to \infty$;
3. $F(x) = 1 - L'(x)$, where $L'(x)$ is the derivative of the function L at point x; if F is discontinuous at x, then the equality holds true for the right-hand derivative $L'(x+)$.

A reason why the limited expected value function is a particularly suitable tool for our purposes is that it represents the claim size distribution in the monetary dimension. For example, we have $L(\infty) = \mathrm{E}(X)$ if it exists. The cdf F, on the other hand, operates on the probability scale, i.e. takes values between 0 and 1. Therefore, it is usually difficult to see, by looking only at $F(x)$, how sensitive the price for the insurance – the premium – is to changes in the values of F, while the limited expected value function shows immediately how different parts of the claim size cdf contribute to the premium (see Chapter 19 for information on various premium calculation principles). Apart from curve-fitting purposes, the function L will turn out to be a very useful concept in dealing with deductibles in Chapter 19. It is also worth mentioning, that there exists a connection between the limited expected value function and the mean excess function:

$$\mathrm{E}(X) = L(x) + \mathrm{P}(X > x)e(x). \tag{13.61}$$

The limited expected value functions for all distributions considered in this chapter are given by:

- log-normal distribution:

$$L(x) = \exp\left(\mu + \frac{\sigma^2}{2}\right)\Phi\left(\frac{\ln x - \mu - \sigma^2}{\sigma}\right) + x\left\{1 - \Phi\left(\frac{\ln x - \mu}{\sigma}\right)\right\};$$

- exponential distribution:

$$L(x) = \frac{1}{\beta}\left\{1 - \exp(-\beta x)\right\};$$

- Pareto distribution:

$$L(x) = \frac{\lambda - \lambda^{\alpha}(\lambda + x)^{1-\alpha}}{\alpha - 1};$$

- Burr distribution:

$$\begin{aligned} L(x) &= \frac{\lambda^{1/\tau}\Gamma\left(\alpha-\frac{1}{\tau}\right)\Gamma\left(1+\frac{1}{\tau}\right)}{\Gamma(\alpha)}\mathrm{B}\left(1+\frac{1}{\tau},\alpha-\frac{1}{\tau};\frac{x^\tau}{\lambda+x^\tau}\right) \\ &+ x\left(\frac{\lambda}{\lambda+x^\tau}\right)^\alpha; \end{aligned}$$

- Weibull distribution:

$$L(x) = \frac{\Gamma\left(1+1/\tau\right)}{\beta^{1/\tau}}\Gamma\left(1+\frac{1}{\tau},\beta x^\alpha\right)+xe^{-\beta x^\alpha};$$

- gamma distribution:

$$L(x) = \frac{\alpha}{\beta}F(x,\alpha+1,\beta)+x\left\{1-F(x,\alpha,\beta)\right\};$$

- mixture of two exponential distributions:

$$L(x) = \frac{a}{\beta_1}\left\{1-\exp\left(-\beta_1 x\right)\right\}+\frac{1-a}{\beta_2}\left\{1-\exp\left(-\beta_2 x\right)\right\}.$$

From the curve-fitting point of view the use of the limited expected value function has the advantage, compared with the use of the cdfs, that both the analytical and the corresponding observed function $\hat{L}_n$, based on the observed discrete cdf, are continuous and concave, whereas the observed claim size cdf F_n is a discontinuous step function. Property (3) implies that the limited expected value function determines the corresponding cdf uniquely. When the limited expected value functions of two distributions are close to each other, not only are the mean values of the distributions close to each other, but the whole distributions as well.

13.5 Applications

In this section we illustrate some of the methods described earlier in the chapter. We conduct the analysis for two datasets. The first is the PCS (Property Claim Services, see Insurance Services Office Inc. (ISO) web site: www.iso.com/products/2800/prod2801.html) dataset covering losses resulting from natural catastrophic events in USA that occurred between 1990 and 1999.

The second is the Danish fire losses dataset, which concerns major fire losses in Danish Krone (DKK) that occurred between 1980 and 1990 and were recorded by Copenhagen Re. Here we consider only losses in profits. The overall fire losses were analyzed by Embrechts, Klüppelberg, and Mikosch (1997).

The Danish fire losses dataset has been already adjusted for inflation. However, the PCS dataset consists of raw data. Since the data have been collected over a considerable period of time, it is important to bring the values onto a common basis by means of a suitably chosen index. The choice of the index depends on the line of insurance. For example, an index of the cost of construction prices may be suitable for fire and other property insurance, an earnings index for life and accident insurance, and a general price index may be appropriate when a single index is required for several lines or for the whole portfolio. Here we adjust the PCS dataset using the Consumer Price Index provided by the U.S. Department of Labor. Note, that the same raw catastrophe data, however, adjusted using the discount window borrowing rate that refers to the simple interest rate at which depository institutions borrow from the Federal Reserve Bank of New York was analyzed by Burnecki, Härdle, and Weron (2004). A related dataset containing the national and regional PCS indices for losses resulting from catastrophic events in USA was studied by Burnecki, Kukla, and Weron (2000).

As suggested in the proceeding section we first look for the appropriate shape of the distribution. To this end we plot the empirical mean excess functions for the analyzed data sets, see Figure 13.7. Both in the case of PCS natural catastrophe losses and Danish fire losses the data show a super-exponential pattern suggesting a log-normal, Pareto or Burr distribution as most adequate for modeling. Hence, in the sequel we calibrate these three distributions.

We apply two estimation schemes: maximum likelihood and A^2 statistic minimization. Out of the three fitted distributions only the log-normal has closed form expressions for the maximum likelihood estimators. Parameter calibration for the remaining distributions and the A^2 minimization scheme is carried out via a simplex numerical optimization routine. A limited simulation study suggests that the A^2 minimization scheme tends to return lower values of all edf test statistics than maximum likelihood estimation. Hence, it is exclusively used for further analysis.

The results of parameter estimation and hypothesis testing for the PCS loss amounts are presented in Table 13.1. The Burr distribution with parameters $\alpha = 0.4801$, $\lambda = 3.9495 \cdot 10^{16}$, and $\tau = 2.1524$ yields the best results and passes all tests at the 2.5% level. The log-normal distribution with parameters

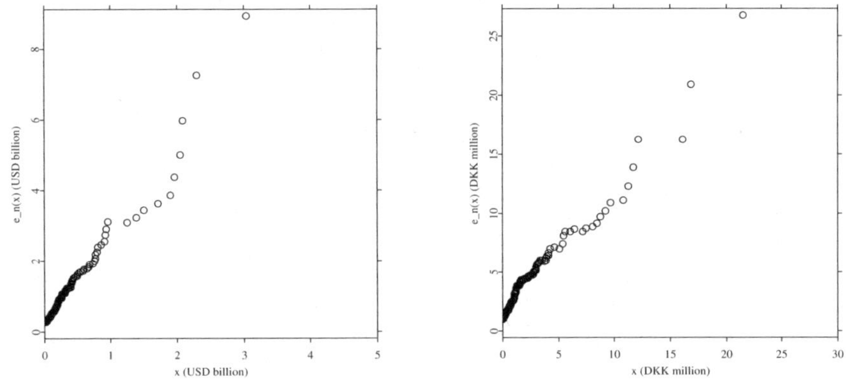

Figure 13.7: The empirical mean excess function $\hat{e}_n(x)$ for the PCS catastrophe data (*left panel*) and the Danish fire data (*right panel*).

STFloss07.xpl

$\mu = 18.3806$ and $\sigma = 1.1052$ comes in second, however, with an unacceptable fit as tested by the Anderson-Darling statistic. As expected, the remaining distributions presented in Section 13.3 return even worse fits. Thus we suggest to choose the Burr distribution as a model for the PCS loss amounts. In the left panel of Figure 13.8 we present the empirical and analytical limited expected value functions for the three fitted distributions. The plot justifies the choice of the Burr distribution.

The results of parameter estimation and hypothesis testing for the Danish fire loss amounts are presented in Table 13.2. The log-normal distribution with parameters $\mu = 12.6645$ and $\sigma = 1.3981$ returns the best results. It is the only distribution that passes any of the four applied tests (D, V, W^2, and A^2) at a reasonable level. The Burr and Pareto laws yield worse fits as the tails of the edf are lighter than power-law tails. As expected, the remaining distributions presented in Section 13.3 return even worse fits. In the right panel of Figure 13.8 we depict the empirical and analytical limited expected value functions for the three fitted distributions. Unfortunately, no definitive conclusions can be drawn regarding the choice of the distribution. Hence, we suggest to use the log-normal distribution as a model for the Danish fire loss amounts.

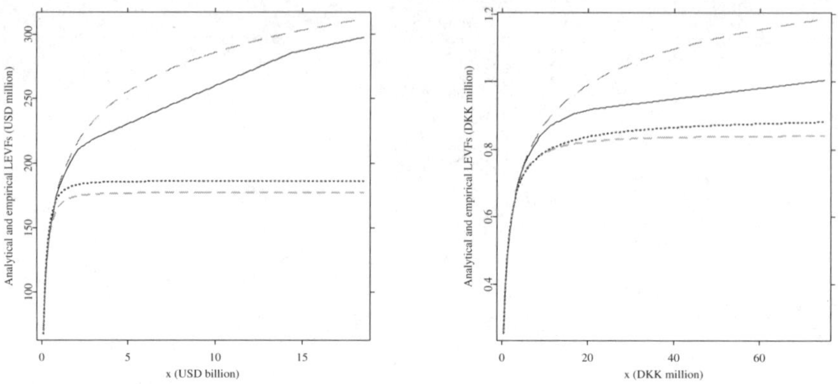

Figure 13.8: The empirical (black solid line) and analytical limited expected value functions (LEVFs) for the log-normal (green dashed line), Pareto (blue dotted line), and Burr (red long-dashed line) distributions for the PCS catastrophe data (*left panel*) and the Danish fire data (*right panel*).

STFloss08.xpl

Table 13.1: Parameter estimates obtained via the A^2 minimization scheme and test statistics for the catastrophe loss amounts. The corresponding p-values based on 1000 simulated samples are given in parentheses.

Distributions:		log-normal	Pareto	Burr
Parameters:		μ=18.3806	α=3.4081	α=0.4801
		σ=1.1052	λ=4.4767 · 10^8	λ=3.9495 · 10^{16}
				τ=2.1524
Tests:	D	0.0440	0.1049	0.0366
		(0.033)	(<0.005)	(0.077)
	V	0.0786	0.1692	0.0703
		(0.022)	(<0.005)	(0.038)
	W^2	0.1353	0.7042	0.0626
		(0.006)	(<0.005)	(0.059)
	A^2	1.8606	6.1160	0.5097
		(<0.005)	(<0.005)	(0.027)

STFloss09.xpl

Table 13.2: Parameter estimates obtained via the A^2 minimization scheme and test statistics for the fire loss amounts. The corresponding p-values based on 1000 simulated samples are given in parentheses.

Distributions:		log-normal	Pareto	Burr
Parameters:		μ=12.6645	α=1.7439	α=0.8804
		σ=1.3981	λ=6.7522 $\cdot 10^5$	λ=8.4202 $\cdot 10^6$
				τ=1.2749
Tests:	D	0.0381	0.0471	0.0387
		(0.008)	(<0.005)	(<0.005)
	V	0.0676	0.0779	0.0724
		(0.005)	(<0.005)	(<0.005)
	W^2	0.0921	0.2119	0.1117
		(0.049)	(<0.005)	(0.007)
	A^2	0.7567	1.9097	0.6999
		(0.024)	(<0.005)	(0.005)

STFloss10.xpl

Bibliography

Bratley, P., Fox, B. L., and Schrage, L. E. (1987). *A Guide to Simulation*, Springer-Verlag, New York.

D'Agostino, R. B. and Stephens, M. A. (1986). *Goodness-of-Fit Techniques*, Marcel Dekker, New York.

Burnecki, K., Härdle, W., and Weron, R. (2004). Simulation of risk processes, *in* J. Teugels, B. Sundt (eds.) *Encyclopedia of Actuarial Science*, Wiley, Chichester.

Burnecki, K., Kukla, G., and Weron, R. (2000). Property insurance loss distributions, *Physica A* **287**: 269-278.

Daykin, C.D., Pentikainen, T., and Pesonen, M. (1994). *Practical Risk Theory for Actuaries*, Chapman, London.

Devroye, L. (1986). *Non-Uniform Random Variate Generation*, Springer-Verlag, New York.

Embrechts, P., Klüppelberg, C., and Mikosch, T. (1997). *Modelling Extremal Events for Insurance and Finance*, Springer.

Hogg, R. and Klugman, S. A. (1984). *Loss Distributions*, Wiley, New York.

Jöhnk, M. D. (1964). Erzeugung von Betaverteilten und Gammaverteilten Zufallszahlen, *Metrika* **8**: 5-15.

Klugman, S. A., Panjer, H.H., and Willmot, G.E. (1998). *Loss Models: From Data to Decisions*, Wiley, New York.

L'Ecuyer, P. (2004). Random Number Generation, *in* J. E. Gentle, W. Härdle, Y. Mori (eds.) *Handbook of Computational Statistics*, Springer, Berlin, 35–70.

Panjer, H.H. and Willmot, G.E. (1992). *Insurance Risk Models*, Society of Actuaries, Chicago.

Ross, S. (2002). *Simulation*, Academic Press, San Diego.

Stephens, M. A. (1978). On the half-sample method for goodness-of-fit, *Journal of the Royal Statistical Society B* **40**: 64-70.

Weron, R. (2004). Computationally Intensive Value at Risk Calculations, *in* J. E. Gentle, W. Härdle, Y. Mori (eds.) *Handbook of Computational Statistics*, Springer, Berlin, 911–950.

14 Modeling of the Risk Process

Krzysztof Burnecki and Rafał Weron

14.1 Introduction

An actuarial risk model is a mathematical description of the behavior of a collection of risks generated by an insurance portfolio. It is not intended to replace sound actuarial judgment. In fact, a well formulated model is consistent with and adds to intuition, but cannot and should not replace experience and insight (Willmot, 2001). Even though we cannot hope to identify all influential factors relevant to future claims, we can try to specify the most important.

A typical model for insurance risk, the so-called collective risk model, has two main components: one characterizing the frequency (or incidence) of events and another describing the severity (or size or amount) of gain or loss resulting from the occurrence of an event, see also Chapter 18. The collective risk model is often used in health insurance and in general insurance, whenever the main risk components are the number of insurance claims and the amount of the claims. It can also be used for modeling other non-insurance product risks, such as credit and operational risk (Embrechts, Kaufmann, and Samorodnitsky, 2004). In the former, for example, the main risk components are the number of credit events (either defaults or downgrades), and the amount lost as a result of the credit event.

The stochastic nature of both the incidence and severity of claims are fundamental components of a realistic model. Hence, in its classical form the model for insurance risk is defined as follows (Embrechts, Klüppelberg, and Mikosch, 1997; Grandell, 1991). If $(\Omega, \mathcal{F}, \mathrm{P})$ is a probability space carrying (i) a point process $\{N_t\}_{t\geq 0}$, i.e. an integer valued stochastic process with $N_0 = 0$ a.s., $N_t < \infty$ for each $t < \infty$ and nondecreasing realizations, and (ii) an independent sequence $\{X_k\}_{k=1}^{\infty}$ of positive independent and identically distributed (i.i.d.) random variables, then the risk process $\{R_t\}_{t\geq 0}$ is given by

$$R_t = u + c(t) - \sum_{i=1}^{N_t} X_i. \tag{14.1}$$

The non-negative constant u stands for the initial capital of the insurance company. The company sells insurance policies and receives a premium according to $c(t)$. In the classical model c is constant, but in a more general setup it can be a deterministic or even a stochastic function of time. Claims form the aggregate claim loss $\{\sum_{i=1}^{N_t} X_i\}$. The claim severities are described by the random sequence $\{X_k\}$ and the number of claims in the interval $(0, t]$ is modeled by the point process N_t, often called the claim arrival process.

The modeling of the aggregate loss process consists of modeling the point process $\{N_t\}$ and the claim size sequence $\{X_k\}$. Both processes are usually assumed to be independent, hence can be treated independently of each other. The modeling of claim severities was covered in detail in Chapter 13. The focus of this chapter is therefore on modeling the claim arrival point process $\{N_t\}$.

The simplicity of the risk process (14.1) is only illusionary. In most cases no analytical conclusions regarding the time evolution of the process can be drawn. However, it is this evolution that is important for practitioners, who have to calculate functionals of the risk process like the expected time to ruin and the ruin probability, see Chapter 15. All this calls for numerical simulation schemes (Burnecki, Härdle, and Weron, 2004).

In Section 14.2 we present efficient algorithms for five classes of the claim arrival point processes. Next, in Section 14.3 we apply some of them to modeling real-world risk processes. The analysis is conducted for the same two datasets as in Chapter 13: (i) the PCS (Property Claim Services) dataset covering losses resulting from catastrophic events in USA that occurred between 1990 and 1999 and (ii) the Danish fire losses dataset, which concerns major fire losses of profits that occurred between 1980 and 1990 and were recorded by Copenhagen Re. It is important to note that the choice of the model has influence on both the ruin probability (see Chapter 15) and the reinsurance strategy of the company (see Chapter 20), hence the selection has to be made with great care.

14.2 Claim Arrival Processes

In this section we focus on efficient simulation of the claim arrival point process $\{N_t\}$. This process can be simulated either via the arrival times $\{T_i\}$, i.e. moments when the ith claim occurs, or the inter-arrival times (or waiting times) $W_i = T_i - T_{i-1}$, i.e. the time periods between successive claims. Note that in terms of W_i's the claim arrival point process is given by $N_t = \sum_{n=1}^{\infty} I(T_n \leq t)$. In what follows we discuss five prominent examples of $\{N_t\}$, namely the classical (homogeneous) Poisson process, the non-homogeneous Poisson process, the mixed Poisson process, the Cox process (also called the doubly stochastic Poisson process) and the renewal process.

14.2.1 Homogeneous Poisson Process

The most common and best known claim arrival point process is the homogeneous Poisson process (HPP) with stationary and independent increments and the number of claims in a given time interval governed by the Poisson law. While this process is normally appropriate in connection with life insurance modeling, it often suffers from the disadvantage of providing an inadequate fit to insurance data in other coverages. In particular, it tends to understate the true variability inherent in these situations.

Formally, a continuous-time stochastic process $\{N_t : t \geq 0\}$ is a (homogeneous) Poisson process with intensity (or rate) $\lambda > 0$ if (i) $\{N_t\}$ is a point process, and (ii) the waiting times W_i are independent and identically distributed and follow an exponential law with intensity λ, i.e. with mean $1/\lambda$ (see Chapter 13, where the properties and simulation scheme for the exponential distribution were discussed). This definition naturally leads to a simulation scheme for the successive arrival times $T_1, T_2, \ldots, T_n$ of the Poisson process:

Algorithm HPP1

Step 1: set $T_0 = 0$

Step 2: for $i = 1, 2, \ldots, n$ do

> **Step 2a:** generate an exponential random variable E with intensity λ
>
> **Step 2b:** set $T_i = T_{i-1} + E$

Alternatively, the homogeneous Poisson process can be simulated by applying the following property (Rolski et al., 1999). Given that $N_t = n$, the n occurrence times $T_1, T_2, \ldots, T_n$ have the same distributions as the order statistics corresponding to n i.i.d. random variables uniformly distributed on the interval $(0, t]$. Hence, the arrival times of the HPP on the interval $(0, t]$ can be generated as follows:

Algorithm HPP2

Step 1: generate a Poisson random variable N with intensity λ

Step 2: generate N random variables U_i distributed uniformly on $(0, 1)$, i.e. $U_i \sim \mathrm{U}(0, 1), i = 1, 2, \ldots, N$

Step 3: set $(T_1, T_2, \ldots, T_N) = t \cdot \mathrm{sort}\{U_1, U_2, \ldots, U_N\}$

In general, this algorithm will run faster than the previous one as it does not involve a loop. The only two inherent numerical difficulties involve generating a Poisson random variable and sorting a vector of occurrence times. Whereas the latter problem can be solved via the standard quicksort algorithm, the former requires more attention. A simple algorithm would take $N = \min\{n : U_1 \cdot \ldots \cdot U_n < \exp(-\lambda)\} - 1$, which is a consequence of the properties of the Poisson process (for a derivation see Ross, 2002). However, for large λ, this method can become slow. Faster, but more complicated methods have been proposed in the literature. Ahrens and Dieter (1982) suggested a generator which utilizes acceptance-complement with truncated normal variates whenever $\lambda > 10$ and reverts to table-aided inversion otherwise. Stadlober (1989) adapted the ratio of uniforms method for $\lambda > 5$ and classical inversion for small λ's. Hörmann (1993) advocated the transformed rejection method, which is a combination of the inversion and rejection algorithms.

Sample trajectories of homogeneous and non-homogeneous Poisson processes are plotted in Figure 14.1. The dotted green line is a HPP with intensity $\lambda = 1$ (left panel) and $\lambda = 10$ (right panel). Clearly the latter jumps more often. Since for the HPP the expected value $\mathrm{E}(N_t) = \lambda t$, it is natural to define the premium function in this case as $c(t) = ct$, where $c = (1+\theta)\mu\lambda$, $\mu = \mathrm{E}(X_k)$ and $\theta > 0$ is the relative safety loading which "guarantees" survival of the insurance company. With such a choice of the premium function we obtain the classical form of the risk process.

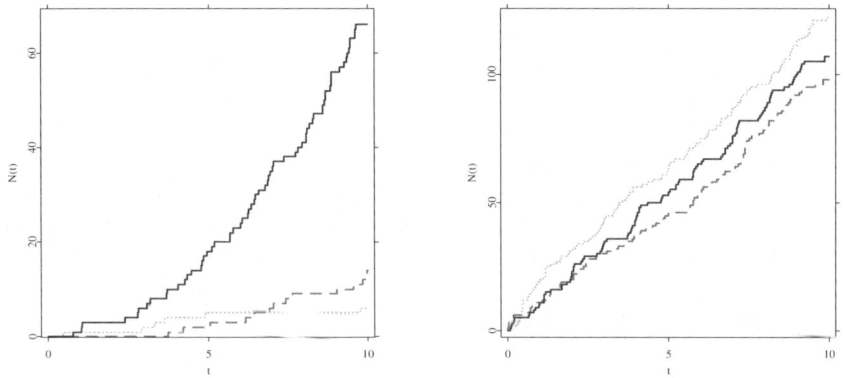

Figure 14.1: *Left panel*: Sample trajectories of a NHPP with linear intensity $\lambda(t) = a + b \cdot t$ for $a = 1$ and $b = 1$ (solid blue line), $b = 0.1$ (dashed red line), and $b = 0$ (dotted green line). Note that the latter is in fact a HPP. *Right panel*: Sample trajectories of a NHPP with periodic intensity $\lambda(t) = a + b \cdot \cos(2\pi t)$ for $a = 10$ and $b = 10$ (solid blue line), $b = 1$ (dashed red line), and $b = 0$ (dotted green line). Again, the latter is a HPP.

`STFrisk01.xpl`

14.2.2 Non-homogeneous Poisson Process

The choice of a homogeneous Poisson process implies that the size of the portfolio cannot increase or decrease. In addition, it cannot describe situations, like in motor insurance, where claim occurrence epochs are likely to depend on the time of the year or of the week. For modeling such phenomena the non-homogeneous Poisson process (NHPP) suits much better than the homogeneous one. The NHPP can be thought of as a Poisson process with a variable intensity defined by the deterministic intensity (rate) function $\lambda(t)$. Note that the increments of a NHPP do not have to be stationary. In the special case when $\lambda(t)$ takes the constant value λ, the NHPP reduces to the homogeneous Poisson process with intensity λ.

The simulation of the process in the non-homogeneous case is slightly more complicated than in the homogeneous one. The first approach, known as the thinning or rejection method, is based on the following fact (Bratley, Fox, and Schrage, 1987; Ross, 2002). Suppose that there exists a constant $\overline{\lambda}$ such that $\lambda(t) \leq \overline{\lambda}$ for all t. Let $T_1^*, T_2^*, T_3^*, \ldots$ be the successive arrival times of a homogeneous Poisson process with intensity $\overline{\lambda}$. If we accept the ith arrival time T_i^* with probability $\lambda(T_i^*)/\overline{\lambda}$, independently of all other arrivals, then the sequence $T_1, T_2, \ldots$ of the accepted arrival times (in ascending order) forms a sequence of the arrival times of a non-homogeneous Poisson process with the rate function $\lambda(t)$. The resulting algorithm reads as follows:

Algorithm NHPP1 (Thinning)

Step 1: set $T_0 = 0$ and $T^* = 0$

Step 2: for $i = 1, 2, \ldots, n$ do

- **Step 2a:** generate an exponential random variable E with intensity $\overline{\lambda}$
- **Step 2b:** set $T^* = T^* + E$
- **Step 2c:** generate a random variable U distributed uniformly on $(0, 1)$
- **Step 2d:** if $U > \lambda(T^*)/\overline{\lambda}$ then return to step 2a ($\rightarrow$ reject the arrival time) else set $T_i = T^*$ ($\rightarrow$ accept the arrival time)

As mentioned in the previous section, the inter-arrival times of a homogeneous Poisson process have an exponential distribution. Therefore steps 2a–2b generate the next arrival time of a homogeneous Poisson process with intensity $\overline{\lambda}$. Steps 2c–2d amount to rejecting (hence the name of the method) or accepting a particular arrival as part of the thinned process (hence the alternative name).

Note that in the above algorithm we generate a HPP with intensity $\overline{\lambda}$ employing the HPP1 algorithm. We can also generate it using the HPP2 algorithm, which is in general much faster.

The second approach is based on the observation (Grandell, 1991) that for a NHPP with rate function $\lambda(t)$ the increment $N_t - N_s$, $0 < s < t$, is distributed as a Poisson random variable with intensity $\widetilde{\lambda} = \int_s^t \lambda(u)du$. Hence, the cumulative distribution function F_s of the waiting time W_s is given by

$$\begin{aligned} F_s(t) &= \mathrm{P}(W_s \leq t) = 1 - \mathrm{P}(W_s > t) = 1 - \mathrm{P}(N_{s+t} - N_s = 0) = \\ &= 1 - \exp\left\{-\int_s^{s+t} \lambda(u)du\right\} = 1 - \exp\left\{-\int_0^t \lambda(s+v)dv\right\}. \end{aligned}$$

If the function $\lambda(t)$ is such that we can find a formula for the inverse F_s^{-1} for each s, we can generate a random quantity X with the distribution F_s by using the inverse transform method. The algorithm, often called the integration method, can be summarized as follows:

Algorithm NHPP2 (Integration)

Step 1: set $T_0 = 0$

Step 2: for $i = 1, 2, \ldots, n$ do

Step 2a: generate a random variable U distributed uniformly on $(0, 1)$

Step 2b: set $T_i = T_{i-1} + F_s^{-1}(U)$

The third approach utilizes a generalization of the property used in the HPP2 algorithm. Given that $N_t = n$, the n occurrence times $T_1, T_2, \ldots, T_n$ of the non-homogeneous Poisson process have the same distributions as the order statistics corresponding to n independent random variables distributed on the interval $(0, t]$, each with the common density function $f(v) = \lambda(v)/\int_0^t \lambda(u)du$, where $v \in (0, t]$. Hence, the arrival times of the NHPP on the interval $(0, t]$ can be generated as follows:

Algorithm NHPP3

Step 1: generate a Poisson random variable N with intensity $\int_0^t \lambda(u)du$

Step 2: generate N random variables $V_i, i = 1, 2, \ldots N$ with density $f(v) = \lambda(v)/\int_0^t \lambda(u)du$.

Step 3: set $(T_1, T_2, \ldots, T_N) = \text{sort}\{V_1, V_2, \ldots, V_N\}$.

The performance of the algorithm is highly dependent on the efficiency of the computer generator of random variables with density $f(v)$. Moreover, like in the homogeneous case, this algorithm has the advantage of not invoking a loop. Hence, it performs faster than the former two methods if $\lambda(u)$ is a nicely integrable function.

Sample trajectories of non-homogeneous Poisson processes are plotted in Figure 14.1. In the left panel realizations of a NHPP with linear intensity $\lambda(t) = a + b \cdot t$ are presented for the same value of parameter a. Note, that the higher the value of parameter b, the more pronounced is the increase in the intensity of the process. In the right panel realizations of a NHPP with periodic intensity $\lambda(t) = a + b \cdot \cos(2\pi t)$ are illustrated, again for the same value of parameter a. This time, for high values of parameter b the events exhibit a seasonal behavior. The process has periods of high activity (grouped around natural values of t) and periods of low activity, where almost no jumps take place. Finally, we note that since in the non-homogeneous case the expected value $\mathrm{E}(N_t) = \int_0^t \lambda(s)ds$, it is natural to define the premium function as $c(t) = (1+\theta)\mu \int_0^t \lambda(s)ds$.

14.2.3 Mixed Poisson Process

In many situations the portfolio of an insurance company is diversified in the sense that the risks associated with different groups of policy holders are significantly different. For example, in motor insurance we might want to make a difference between male and female drivers or between drivers of different age. We would then assume that the claims come from a heterogeneous group of clients, each one of them generating claims according to a Poisson distribution with the intensity varying from one group to another.

Another practical reason for considering yet another generalization of the classical Poisson process is the following. If we measure the volatility of risk processes, expressed in terms of the index of dispersion $\mathrm{Var}(N_t)/\mathrm{E}(N_t)$, then very often we obtain estimates in excess of one – a value obtained for the homogeneous and the non-homogeneous cases. These empirical observations led to the introduction of the mixed Poisson process (Ammeter, 1948).

In the mixed Poisson process the distribution of $\{N_t\}$ is given by a mixture of Poisson processes (Rolski et al., 1999). This means that, conditioning on an extrinsic random variable Λ (called a structure variable), the process $\{N_t\}$ behaves like a homogeneous Poisson process. Since for each t the claim numbers $\{N_t\}$ up to time t are Poisson variates with intensity Λt, it is now reasonable to consider the premium function of the form $c(t) = (1+\theta)\mu\Lambda t$.

The process can be generated in the following way: first a realization of a non-negative random variable Λ is generated and, conditioned upon its realization, $\{N_t\}$ as a homogeneous Poisson process with that realization as its intensity is constructed. Both the HPP1 and the HPP2 algorithm can be utilized. Making use of the former we can write:

Algorithm MPP1

Step 1: generate a realization λ of the random intensity Λ

Step 2: set $T_0 = 0$

Step 3: for $i = 1, 2, \ldots, n$ do

Step 3a: generate an exponential random variable E with intensity λ

Step 3b: set $T_i = T_{i-1} + E$

14.2.4 Cox Process

The Cox process, or doubly stochastic Poisson process, provides flexibility by letting the intensity not only depend on time but also by allowing it to be a stochastic process. Therefore, the doubly stochastic Poisson process can be viewed as a two-step randomization procedure. An intensity process $\{\Lambda(t)\}$ is used to generate another process $\{N_t\}$ by acting as its intensity. That is, $\{N_t\}$ is a Poisson process conditional on $\{\Lambda(t)\}$ which itself is a stochastic process. If $\{\Lambda(t)\}$ is deterministic, then $\{N_t\}$ is a non-homogeneous Poisson process. If $\Lambda(t) = \Lambda$ for some positive random variable Λ, then $\{N_t\}$ is a mixed Poisson process. In the doubly stochastic case the premium function is a generalization of the former functions, in line with the generalization of the claim arrival process. Hence, it takes the form $c(t) = (1+\theta)\mu \int_0^t \Lambda(s)ds$.

The definition of the Cox process suggests that it can be generated in the following way: first a realization of a non-negative stochastic process $\{\Lambda(t)\}$ is generated and, conditioned upon its realization, $\{N_t\}$ as a non-homogeneous Poisson process with that realization as its intensity is constructed. Out of the three methods of generating a non-homogeneous Poisson process the NHPP1 algorithm is the most general and, hence, the most suitable for adaptation. We can write:

Algorithm CP1

Step 1: generate a realization $\lambda(t)$ of the intensity process $\{\Lambda(t)\}$ for a sufficiently large time period

Step 2: set $\overline{\lambda} = \max\{\lambda(t)\}$

Step 3: set $T_0 = 0$ and $T^* = 0$

Step 4: for $i = 1, 2, \ldots, n$ do

Step 4a: generate an exponential random variable E with intensity $\overline{\lambda}$

Step 4b: set $T^* = T^* + E$

Step 4c: generate a random variable U distributed uniformly on $(0, 1)$

Step 4d: if $U > \lambda(T^*)/\overline{\lambda}$ then return to step 4a ($\rightarrow$ reject the arrival time) else set $T_i = T^*$ ($\rightarrow$ accept the arrival time)

14.2.5 Renewal Process

Generalizing the homogeneous Poisson process we come to the point where instead of making λ non-constant, we can make a variety of different distributional assumptions on the sequence of waiting times $\{W_1, W_2, \ldots\}$ of the claim arrival point process $\{N_t\}$. In some particular cases it might be useful to assume that the sequence is generated by a renewal process, i.e. the random variables W_i are i.i.d. and positive. Note that the homogeneous Poisson process is a renewal process with exponentially distributed inter-arrival times. This observation lets us write the following algorithm for the generation of the arrival times of a renewal process:

Algorithm RP1

Step 1: set $T_0 = 0$

Step 2: for $i = 1, 2, \ldots, n$ do

Step 2a: generate a random variable X with an assumed distribution function F

Step 2b: set $T_i = T_{i-1} + X$

An important point in the previous generalizations of the Poisson process was the possibility to compensate risk and size fluctuations by the premiums. Thus, the premium rate had to be constantly adapted to the development of the claims. For renewal claim arrival processes, a constant premium rate allows for a constant safety loading (Embrechts and Klüppelberg, 1993). Let $\{N_t\}$ be a renewal process and assume that W_1 has finite mean $1/\lambda$. Then the premium function is defined in a natural way as $c(t) = (1 + \theta)\mu\lambda t$, like for the homogeneous Poisson process.

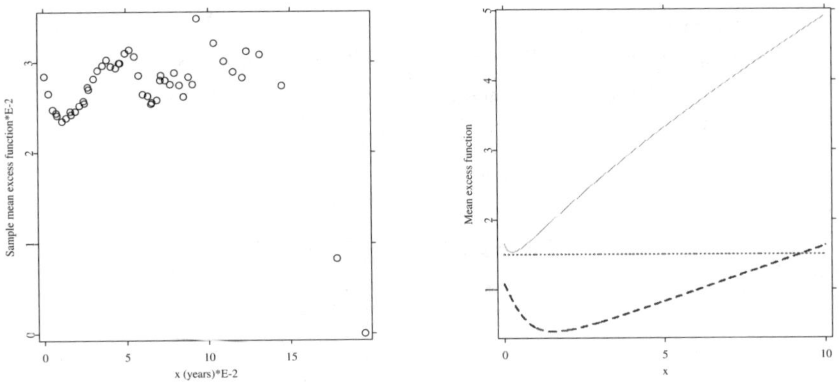

Figure 14.2: *Left panel*: The empirical mean excess function $\hat{e}_n(x)$ for the PCS waiting times. *Right panel*: Shapes of the mean excess function $e(x)$ for the log-normal (solid green line), Burr (dashed blue line), and exponential (dotted red line) distributions.

STFrisk02.xpl

14.3 Simulation of Risk Processes

14.3.1 Catastrophic Losses

In this section we apply some of the models described earlier to the PCS dataset. The Property Claim Services dataset covers losses resulting from natural catastrophic events in USA that occurred between 1990 and 1999. It is adjusted for inflation using the Consumer Price Index provided by the U.S. Department of Labor. See Chapters 4 and 13 where this dataset was analyzed in the context of CAT bonds and loss distributions, respectively. Note, that the same raw catastrophe data, however, adjusted using the discount window borrowing rate that refers to the simple interest rate at which depository institutions borrow from the Federal Reserve Bank of New York was analyzed by Burnecki, Härdle, and Weron (2004).

Table 14.1: Parameter estimates obtained via the A^2 minimization scheme and test statistics for the PCS waiting times. The corresponding p-values based on 1000 simulated samples are given in parentheses.

Distributions:	log-normal	Burr	exponential
Parameters:	μ=−3.91	α=1.3051	β=33.187
	σ=0.9051	$\lambda=1.6 \cdot 10^{-3}$	
		τ=1.7448	
Tests:			
D	0.0589	0.0492	0.1193
	(<0.005)	(<0.005)	(<0.005)
V	0.0973	0.0938	0.1969
	(<0.005)	(<0.005)	(<0.005)
W^2	0.1281	0.1120	0.9130
	(0.013)	(<0.005)	(<0.005)
A^2	1.3681	0.8690	5.8998
	(<0.005)	(<0.005)	(<0.005)

STFrisk03.xpl

Now, we study the claim arrival process and the distribution of waiting times. As suggested in Chapter 13 we first look for the appropriate shape of the approximating distribution. To this end we plot the empirical mean excess function for the waiting time data (given in years), see Figure 14.2. The initially decreasing, later increasing pattern suggests the log-normal or Burr distribution as most adequate for modeling. The empirical distribution seems, however, to have lighter tails than the two: $e(x)$ does not increase for very large x. The overall impression might be of a highly volatile but constant function, like that for the exponential distribution. Hence, we fit the log-normal, Burr, and exponential distributions using the A^2 minimization scheme and check the goodness-of-fit with test statistics. In terms of the values of the test statistics the Burr distribution seems to give the best fit. However, it does not pass any of the tests even at the very low level of 0.5% (see Chapter 13 for test definitions). The only distribution that passes any of the four applied tests, although at a very low level, is the log-normal law with parameters $\mu = -3.91$ and $\sigma = 0.9051$, see Table 14.1. Thus, if we wanted to model the claim arrival process by a renewal process then the log-normal distribution would be the best to describe the waiting times.

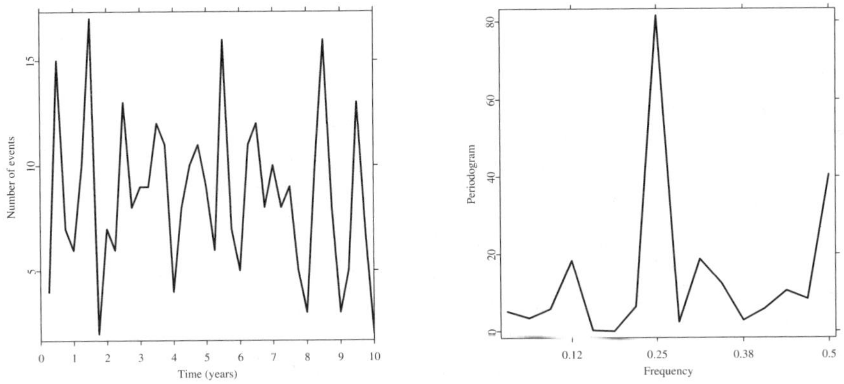

Figure 14.3: *Left panel*: The quarterly number of losses for the PCS data. *Right panel*: Periodogram of the PCS quarterly number of losses. A distinct peak is visible at frequency $\omega = 0.25$ implying a period of $1/\omega = 4$ quarters, i.e. one year.

`STFrisk04.xpl`

If, on the other hand, we wanted to model the claim arrival process by a HPP then the studies of the quarterly numbers of losses would lead us to the conclusion that the best HPP is given by the annual intensity $\lambda_1 = 34.2$. This value is obtained by taking the mean of the quarterly numbers of losses and multiplying it by four. Note, that the value of the intensity is significantly different from the parameter $\beta = 32.427$ of the calibrated exponential distribution, see Table 14.1. This, together with a very bad fit of the exponential law to the waiting times, indicates that the HPP is not a good model for the claim arrival process.

Further analysis of the data reveals its periodicity. The time series of the quarterly number of losses does not exhibit any trends but an annual seasonality can be very well observed using the periodogram, see Figure 14.3. This suggests that calibrating a NHPP with a sinusoidal rate function would give a good model. We estimate the parameters by fitting the cumulative intensity function, i.e. the mean value function $\mathrm{E}(N_t)$, to the accumulated number of PCS losses. The least squares algorithm yields the formula $\lambda_2(t) = 35.32 + 2.32 \cdot 2\pi \cdot \sin\{2\pi(t - 0.20)\}$. This choice of $\lambda(t)$ gives a reasonably good fit, see also Chapter 4.

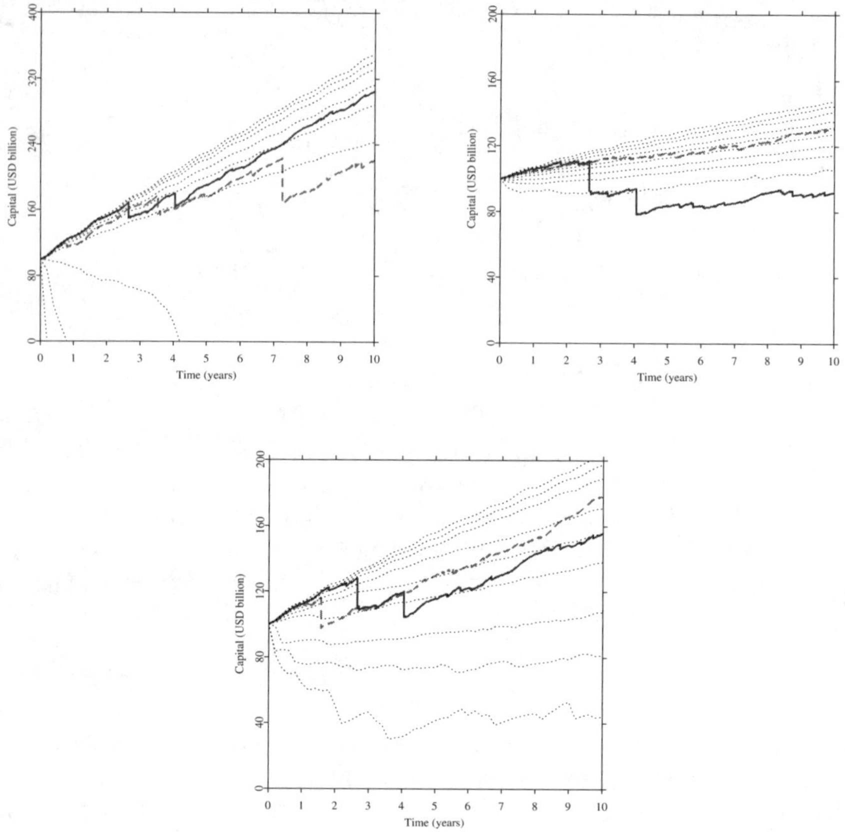

Figure 14.4: The PCS data simulation results for a NHPP with Burr claim sizes (*left panel*), a NHPP with log-normal claim sizes (*right panel*), and a NHPP with claims generated from the edf (*bottom panel*). The dotted lines are the sample 0.001, 0.01, 0.05, 0.25, 0.50, 0.75, 0.95, 0.99, 0.999-quantile lines based on 3000 trajectories of the risk process.

`STFrisk05.xpl`

To study the evolution of the risk process we simulate sample trajectories. We consider a hypothetical scenario where the insurance company insures losses resulting from catastrophic events in the United States. The company's initial capital is assumed to be $u = 100$ billion USD and the relative safety loading used is $\theta = 0.5$. We choose different models of the risk process whose application is most justified by the statistical results described above. The results are presented in Figure 14.4. In all subplots the thick solid blue line is the "real" risk process, i.e. a trajectory constructed from the historical arrival times and values of the losses. The different shapes of the "real" risk process in the subplots are due to the different forms of the premium function $c(t)$. Recall, that the function has to be chosen accordingly to the type of the claim arrival process. The dashed red line is a sample trajectory. The dotted lines are the sample 0.001, 0.01, 0.05, 0.25, 0.50, 0.75, 0.95, 0.99, 0.999-quantile lines based on 3000 trajectories of the risk process. The function $\hat{x}_p(t)$ is called a sample p-quantile line if for each $t \in [t_0, T]$, $\hat{x}_p(t)$ is the sample p-quantile, i.e. if it satisfies $F_n(x_p-) \leq p \leq F_n(x_p)$, where F_n is the edf. Quantile lines are a very helpful tool in the analysis of stochastic processes. For example, they can provide a simple justification of the stationarity (or the lack of it) of a process, see Janicki and Weron (1994). In Figure 14.4 they visualize the evolution of the density of the risk process. The periodic pattern is due to the sinusoidal intensity function $\lambda_2(t)$. We also note that we assumed in the simulations that if the capital of the insurance company drops bellow zero, the company goes bankrupt, so the capital is set to zero and remains at this level hereafter. This is in agreement with Chapter 15.

The claim severity distribution of the PCS dataset was studied in Chapter 13. The Burr distribution with parameters $\alpha = 0.4801$, $\lambda = 3.9495 \cdot 10^{16}$, and $\tau = 2.1524$ yielded the best fit. Unfortunately, such a choice of the parameters leads to an undesired feature of the claim size distribution – very heavy tails of order $x^{-\alpha\tau} \approx x^{-1.03}$. Although the expected value exists, the sample mean is, in general, significantly below the theoretical value. As a consequence, the premium function $c(t)$ cannot include the factor $\mu = \mathrm{E}(X_k)$ or the risk process trajectories will exhibit a highly positive drift. To cope with this problem, in the simulations we substitute the original factor μ with $\tilde{\mu}$ equal to the empirical mean of the simulated claims for all trajectories. Despite this change the trajectories possess a positive drift due to the large value of the relative safety loading θ. They are also highly volatile leading to a large number of ruins – the 0.05-quantile line drops to zero after five years, see the left panel in Figure 14.4. It seems that the Burr distribution overestimates the PCS losses.

In our second attempt we simulate the NHPP with log-normal claims with $\mu = 18.3806$ and $\sigma = 1.1052$, as the log-normal law was found in Chapter 13 to yield a relatively good fit to the data. The results, shown in the right panel of Figure 14.4, are not satisfactory. This time the analytical distribution largely underestimates the loss data. The "real" risk process is well outside the 0.001-quantile line. This leads us to the conclusion that none of the analytical loss distributions describes the data well enough. We either overestimate risk using the Burr distribution or underestimate it with the log-normal law. Hence, in our next attempt we simulate the NHPP with claims generated from the edf, see the bottom panel in Figure 14.4. The factor μ in the premium function $c(t)$ is set to the empirical mean. This time the "real" risk process lies close to the median and does not cross the lower and upper quantile lines. This approach seems to give the best results. However, we do have to remember that it has its shortcomings. For example, the model is tailor-made for the dataset at hand but is not universal. As the dataset will be expanded by including new losses the model may change substantially. An analytic model would, in general, be less susceptible to such modifications. Hence, it might be more optimal to use the Burr distribution after all.

14.3.2 Danish Fire Losses

We conduct empirical studies for Danish fire losses recorded by Copenhagen Re. The data concerns major Danish fire losses in Danish Krone (DKK), occurred between 1980 and 1990 and adjusted for inflation. Only losses of profits connected with the fires are taken into consideration, see Chapter 13 and Burnecki and Weron (2004), where this dataset was also analyzed.

We start the analysis with a HPP with a constant intensity λ_3. Studies of the quarterly numbers of losses and the inter-occurrence times of the fires lead us to the conclusion that the HPP with the annual intensity $\lambda_3 = 57.72$ gives the best fit. However, as we can see in the right panel of Figure 14.5, the fit is not very good suggesting that the HPP is too simplistic and forcing us to consider the NHPP. In fact, a renewal process would also give unsatisfactory results as the data reveals a clear increasing trend in the number of quarterly losses, see the left panel in Figure 14.5. We tested different exponential and polynomial functional forms, but a simple linear intensity function $\lambda_4(s) = c + ds$ gives the best fit. Applying the least squares procedure we arrive at the following values of the parameters: $c = 13.97$ and $d = 7.57$. Processes with both choices of the intensity function, λ_3 and $\lambda_4(s)$, are illustrated in the right panel of Figure

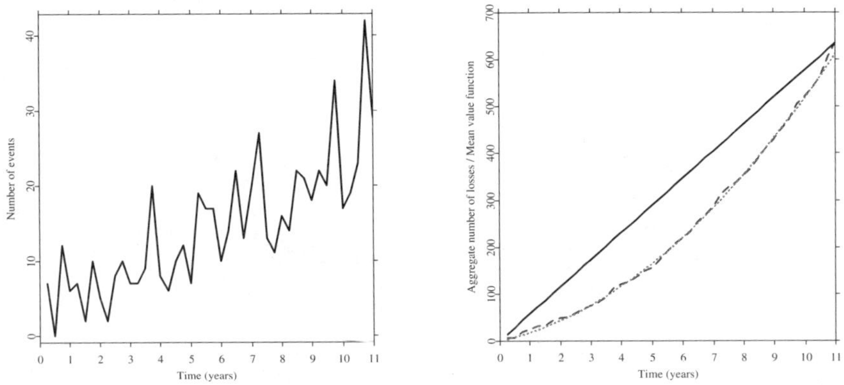

Figure 14.5: *Left panel*: The quarterly number of losses for the Danish fire data. *Right panel*: The aggregate quarterly number of losses of the Danish fire data (dashed blue line) together with the mean value function $E(N_t)$ of the calibrated HPP (solid black line) and the NHPP (dotted red line). Clearly the latter model gives a better fit to the empirical data.

STFrisk06.xpl

14.5, where the accumulated number of fire losses and mean value functions for all 11 years of data are depicted.

After describing the claim arrival process we have to find an appropriate model for the loss amounts. In Chapter 13 a number of distributions were fitted to loss sizes. The log-normal distribution with parameters $\mu = 12.6645$ and $\sigma = 1.3981$ produced the best results. The Burr distribution with $\alpha = 0.8804$, $\lambda = 8.4202 \cdot 10^6$, and $\tau = 1.2749$ overestimated the tails of the empirical distribution, nevertheless it gave the next best fit.

The simulation results are presented in Figure 14.6. We consider a hypothetical scenario where the insurance company insures losses resulting from fire damage. The company's initial capital is assumed to be $u = 400$ million DKK and the relative safety loading used is $\theta = 0.5$. We choose two models of the risk process whose application is most justified by the statistical results described above:

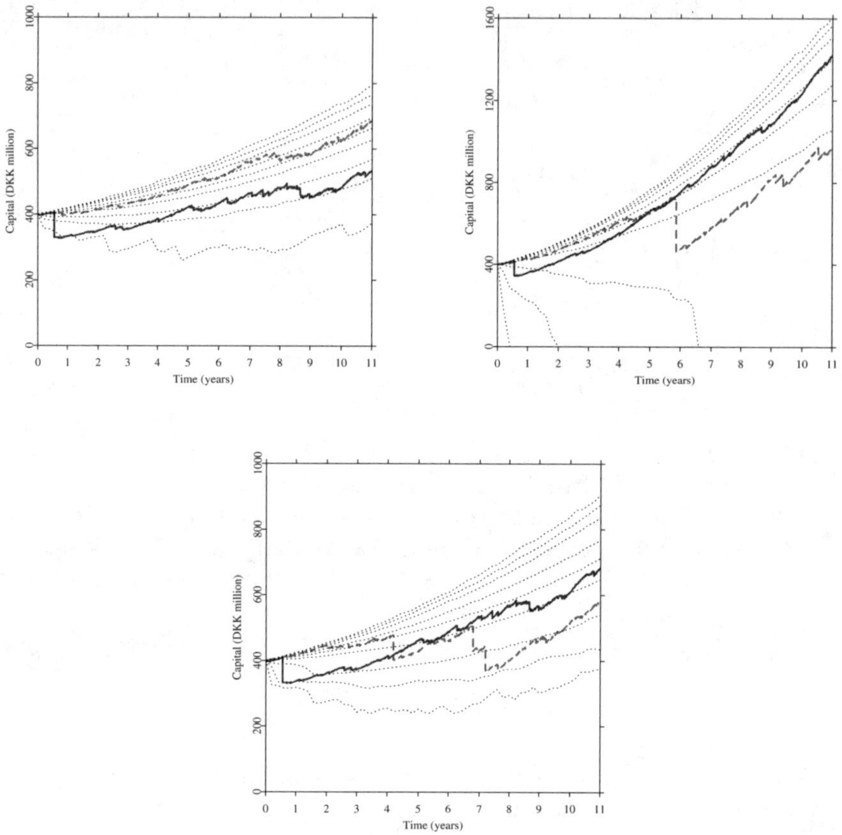

Figure 14.6: The Danish fire data simulation results for a NHPP with log-normal claim sizes (*left panel*), a NHPP with Burr claim sizes (*right panel*), and a NHPP with claims generated from the edf (*bottom panel*). The dotted lines are the sample 0.001, 0.01, 0.05, 0.25, 0.50, 0.75, 0.95, 0.99, 0.999-quantile lines based on 3000 trajectories of the risk process.

STFrisk07.xpl

a NHPP with log-normal claim sizes and a NHPP with Burr claim sizes. For comparison we also present the results of a model incorporating the empirical distribution function. Recall, that in this model the factor μ in the premium function $c(t)$ is set to the empirical mean.

In all panels of Figure 14.6 the thick solid blue line is the "real" risk process, i.e. a trajectory constructed from the historical arrival times and values of the losses. The different shapes of the "real" risk process in the subplots are due to the different forms of the premium function $c(t)$ which has to be chosen accordingly to the type of the claim arrival process. The dashed red line is a sample trajectory. The dotted lines are the sample 0.001, 0.01, 0.05, 0.25, 0.50, 0.75, 0.95, 0.99, 0.999-quantile lines based on 3000 trajectories of the risk process. Similarly as in PCS data case, we assume that if the capital of the insurance company drops bellow zero, the company goes bankrupt, so the capital is set to zero and remains at this level hereafter.

Clearly, if claim severities are Burr distributed then extreme events are more probable to happen than in the log-normal case, for which the historical trajectory falls outside the 0.001-quantile line. The overall picture is, in fact, similar to the one obtained for the PCS data. We either overestimate risk using the Burr distribution or underestimate it with the log-normal law. The empirical approach yields the "real" risk process which lies close to the median and does not cross the very low or very high quantile lines. However, as stated previously, the empirical approach has its shortcomings. Since this time we only slightly undervalue risk with the log-normal law it might be advisable to use it for further modeling.

Bibliography

Ahrens, J. H. and Dieter, U. (1982). Computer generation of Poisson deviates from modified normal distributions, *ACM Trans. Math. Software* **8**: 163–179.

Ammeter, H. (1948). A generalization of the collective theory of risk in regard to fluctuating basic probabilities, *Skand. Aktuarietidskr.* **31**: 171–198.

Bratley, P., Fox, B. L., and Schrage, L. E. (1987). *A Guide to Simulation*, Springer-Verlag, New York.

Burnecki, K. and Weron, R. (2004). Modeling the risk process in the XploRe computing environment, *Lecture Notes in Computer Science* **3039**: 868-875.

Burnecki, K., Härdle, W., and Weron, R. (2004). Simulation of risk processes, *in* J. Teugels, B. Sundt (eds.) *Encyclopedia of Actuarial Science*, Wiley, Chichester.

Embrechts, P., Kaufmann, R., and Samorodnitsky, G. (2002). Ruin theory revisited: stochastic models for operational risk, *in* C. Bernadell et al. (eds.) *Risk Management for Central Bank Foreign Reserves*, European Central Bank, Frankfurt a.M., 243–261.

Embrechts, P. and Klüppelberg, C. (1993). Some aspects of insurance mathematics, *Theory Probab. Appl.* **38**: 262–295.

Embrechts, P., Klüppelberg, C., and Mikosch, T. (1997). *Modelling Extremal Events for Insurance and Finance*, Springer.

Grandell, J. (1991). *Aspects of Risk Theory*, Springer, New York.

Hörmann, W. (1993). The transformed rejection method for generating Poisson random variables, *Insurance: Mathematics and Economics* **12**: 39–45.

Janicki, A. and Weron, A. (1994). *Simulation and Chaotic Behavior of α-Stable Stochastic Processes*, Marcel Dekker.

L'Ecuyer, P. (2004). Random Number Generation, *in* J. E. Gentle, W. Härdle, Y. Mori (eds.) *Handbook of Computational Statistics*, Springer, Berlin, 35–70.

Rolski, T., Schmidli, H., Schmidt, V., and Teugels, J. L. (1999). *Stochastic Processes for Insurance and Finance*, Wiley, Chichester.

Ross, S. (2002). *Simulation*, Academic Press, San Diego.

Stadlober, E. (1989). Sampling from Poisson, binomial and hypergeometric distributions: ratio of uniforms as a simple and fast alternative, *Math. Statist. Sektion* **303**, Forschungsgesellschaft Joanneum Graz.

Willmot, G. E. (2001). The nature of modelling insurance losses, *The Munich Re Inaugural Lecture*, December 5, 2001, Toronto.

15 Ruin Probabilities in Finite and Infinite Time

Krzysztof Burnecki, Paweł Miśta, and Aleksander Weron

15.1 Introduction

In examining the nature of the risk associated with a portfolio of business, it is often of interest to assess how the portfolio may be expected to perform over an extended period of time. One approach concerns the use of ruin theory (Panjer and Willmot, 1992). Ruin theory is concerned with the excess of the income (with respect to a portfolio of business) over the outgo, or claims paid. This quantity, referred to as insurer's surplus, varies in time. Specifically, ruin is said to occur if the insurer's surplus reaches a specified lower bound, e.g. minus the initial capital. One measure of risk is the probability of such an event, clearly reflecting the volatility inherent in the business. In addition, it can serve as a useful tool in long range planning for the use of insurer's funds.

We recall now a definition of the standard mathematical model for the insurance risk, see Grandell (1991) and Chapter 14. The initial capital of the insurance company is denoted by u, the Poisson process N_t with intensity (rate) λ describes the number of claims in $(0, t]$ interval and claim severities are random, given by i.i.d. non-negative sequence $\{X_k\}_{k=1}^{\infty}$ with mean value μ and variance σ^2, independent of N_t. The insurance company receives a premium at a constant rate c per unit time, where $c = (1+\theta)\lambda\mu$ and $\theta > 0$ is called the relative safety loading. The classical risk process $\{R_t\}_{t\geq 0}$ is given by

$$R_t = u + ct - \sum_{i=1}^{N_t} X_i.$$

We define a claim surplus process $\{S_t\}_{t\geq 0}$ as

$$S_t = u - R_t = \sum_{i=1}^{N_t} X_i - ct.$$

The time to ruin is defined as $\tau(u) = \inf\{t \geq 0 : R_t < 0\} = \inf\{t \geq 0 : S_t > u\}$. Let $L = \sup_{0\leq t<\infty}\{S_t\}$ and $L_T = \sup_{0\leq t<T}\{S_t\}$. The ruin probability in infinite time, i.e. the probability that the capital of an insurance company ever drops below zero can be then written as

$$\psi(u) = \mathrm{P}(\tau(u) < \infty) = \mathrm{P}(L > u). \tag{15.1}$$

We note that the above definition implies that the relative safety loading θ has to be positive, otherwise c would be less than $\lambda\mu$ and thus with probability 1 the risk business would become negative in infinite time. The ruin probability in finite time T is given by

$$\psi(u, T) = \mathrm{P}(\tau(u) \leq T) = \mathrm{P}(L_T > u). \tag{15.2}$$

We also note that obviously $\psi(u, T) < \psi(u)$. However, the infinite time ruin probability may be sometimes also relevant for the finite time case.

From a practical point of view, $\psi(u, T)$, where T is related to the planning horizon of the company, may perhaps sometimes be regarded as more interesting than $\psi(u)$. Most insurance managers will closely follow the development of the risk business and increase the premium if the risk business behaves badly. The planning horizon may be thought of as the sum of the following: the time until the risk business is found to behave "badly", the time until the management reacts and the time until a decision of a premium increase takes effect. Therefore, in non-life insurance, it may be natural to regard T equal to four or five years as reasonable (Grandell, 1991).

We also note that the situation in infinite time is markedly different from the finite horizon case as the ruin probability in finite time can always be computed directly using Monte Carlo simulations. We also remark that generalizations of the classical risk process, which are studied in Chapter 14, where the occurrence of the claims is described by point processes other than the Poisson process (i.e., non-homogeneous, mixed Poisson and Cox processes) do not alter the ruin probability in infinite time. This stems from the following fact. Consider a risk process $\tilde{R}_t$ driven by a Cox process $\tilde{N}_t$ with the intensity process $\tilde{\lambda}(t)$, namely $\tilde{R}_t = u + (1+\theta)\mu \int_0^t \tilde{\lambda}(s)ds - \sum_{i=1}^{\tilde{N}_t} X_i$. Define now $\Lambda_t = \int_0^t \tilde{\lambda}(s)ds$ and $R_t =$

$\tilde{R}(\Lambda_t^{-1})$. Then the point process $N_t = \tilde{N}(\Lambda_t^{-1})$ is a standard Poisson process with intensity 1, and therefore, $\tilde{\psi}(u) = \mathrm{P}(\inf_{t\geq 0}\{\tilde{R}_t\} < 0) = \mathrm{P}(\inf_{t\geq 0}\{R_t\} < 0) = \psi(u)$. The time scale defined by Λ_t^{-1} is called the operational time scale. It naturally affects the time to ruin, hence the finite time ruin probability, but not the ultimate ruin probability.

The ruin probabilities in infinite and finite time can only be calculated for a few special cases of the claim amount distribution. Thus, finding a reliable approximation, especially in the ultimate case, when the Monte Carlo method can not be utilized, is really important from a practical point of view.

In Section 15.2 we present a general formula, called Pollaczek-Khinchin formula, on the ruin probability in infinite time, which leads to exact ruin probabilities in special cases of the claim size distribution. Section 15.3 is devoted to various approximations of the infinite time ruin probability. In Section 15.4 we compare the 12 different well-known and not so well-known approximations. The finite-time case is studied in Sections 15.5, 15.6, and 15.7. The exact ruin probabilities in finite time are discussed in Section 15.5. The most important approximations of the finite time ruin probability are presented in Section 15.6. They are illustrated in Section 15.7.

To illustrate and compare approximations we use the PCS (Property Claim Services) catastrophe data example introduced in Chapter 13. The data describes losses resulting from natural catastrophic events in USA that occurred between 1990 and 1999. This data set was used to obtain the parameters of the discussed distributions.

We note that ruin theory has been also recently employed as an interesting tool in operational risk. In the view of the data already available on operational risk, ruin type estimates may become useful (Embrechts, Kaufmann, and Samorodnitsky, 2004). We finally note that all presented explicit solutions and approximations are implemented in the Insurance library of XploRe. All figures and tables were created with the help of this library.

15.1.1 Light- and Heavy-tailed Distributions

We distinguish here between light- and heavy-tailed distributions. A distribution $F_X(x)$ is said to be light-tailed, if there exist constants $a > 0$, $b > 0$ such that $\bar{F}_X(x) = 1 - F_X(x) \leq ae^{-bx}$ or, equivalently, if there exist $z > 0$, such that $M_X(z) < \infty$, where $M_X(z)$ is the moment generating function, see Chapter 13. Distribution $F_X(x)$ is said to be heavy-tailed, if for all $a > 0$,

Table 15.1: Typical claim size distributions. In all cases $x \geq 0$.

Name	Parameters	pdf
Light-tailed distributions		
Exponential	$\beta > 0$	$f_X(x) = \beta \exp(-\beta x)$
Gamma	$\alpha > 0,\ \beta > 0$	$f_X(x) = \frac{\beta^\alpha}{\Gamma(\alpha)} x^{\alpha-1} \exp(-\beta x)$
Weibull	$\beta > 0,\ \tau \geq 1$	$f_X(x) = \beta \tau x^{\tau-1} \exp(-\beta x^\tau)$
Mixed exp's	$\beta_i > 0,\ \sum_{i=1}^{n} a_i = 1$	$f_X(x) = \sum_{i=1}^{n} \{a_i \beta_i \exp(-\beta_i x)\}$
Heavy-tailed distributions		
Name	Parameters	pdf
Weibull	$\beta > 0,\ 0 < \tau < 1$	$f_X(x) = \beta \tau x^{\tau-1} \exp(-\beta x^\tau)$
Log-normal	$\mu \in \mathbb{R},\ \sigma > 0$	$f_X(x) = \frac{1}{\sqrt{2\pi}\sigma x} \exp\left\{-\frac{(\ln x - \mu)^2}{2\sigma^2}\right\}$
Pareto	$\alpha > 0,\ \lambda > 0$	$f_X(x) = \frac{\alpha}{\lambda + x}\left(\frac{\lambda}{\lambda + x}\right)^\alpha$
Burr	$\alpha > 0,\ \lambda > 0,\ \tau > 0$	$f_X(x) = \frac{\alpha \tau \lambda^\alpha x^{\tau-1}}{(\lambda + x^\tau)^{\alpha+1}}$

$b > 0$: $\bar{F}_X(x) > ae^{-bx}$, or, equivalently, if $\forall z > 0\ M_X(z) = \infty$. We study here claim size distributions as in Table 15.1.

In the case of light-tailed claims the adjustment coefficient (called also the Lundberg exponent) plays a key role in calculating the ruin probability. Let $\gamma = \sup_z \{M_X(z)\} < \infty$ and let R be a positive solution of the equation:

$$1 + (1 + \theta)\mu R = M_X(R), \qquad R < \gamma. \tag{15.3}$$

If there exists a non-zero solution R to the above equation, we call it an adjustment coefficient. Clearly, $R = 0$ satisfies the equation (15.3), but there may exist a positive solution as well (this requires that X has a moment generating function, thus excluding distributions such as Pareto and the log-normal). To see the plausibility of this result, note that $M_X(0) = 1$, $M'_X(z) < 0$, $M''_X(z) > 0$ and $M'_X(0) = -\mu$. Hence, the curves $y = M_X(z)$ and $y = 1 + (1 + \theta)\mu z$ may intersect, as shown in Figure 15.1.

An analytical solution to equation (15.3) exists only for few claim distributions. However, it is quite easy to obtain a numerical solution. The coefficient R

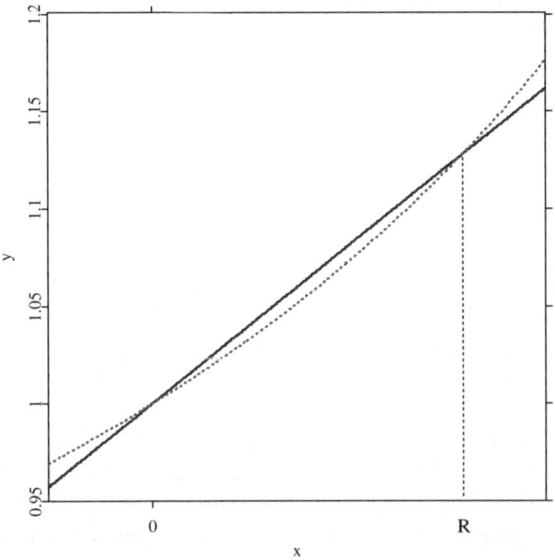

Figure 15.1: Illustration of the existence of the adjustment coefficient. The solid blue line represents the curve $y = 1 + (1+\theta)\mu z$ and the dotted red one $y = M_X(z)$.

STFruin01.xpl

satisfies the inequality:

$$R < \frac{2\theta\mu}{\mu^{(2)}}, \tag{15.4}$$

where $\mu^{(2)} = \mathrm{E}(X_i^2)$, see Asmussen (2000). Let $D(z) = 1 + (1+\theta)\mu z - M_X(z)$. Thus, the adjustment coefficient $R > 0$ satisfies the equation $D(R) = 0$. In order to get the solution one may use the Newton-Raphson formula

$$R_{j+1} = R_j - \frac{D(R_j)}{D'(R_j)}, \tag{15.5}$$

with the initial condition $R_0 = 2\theta\mu/\mu^{(2)}$, where $D'(z) = (1+\theta)\mu - M_X'(z)$.

Moreover, if it is possible to calculate the third raw moment $\mu^{(3)}$, we can obtain a sharper bound than (15.4), Panjer and Willmot (1992):

$$R < \frac{12\mu\theta}{3\mu^{(2)} + \sqrt{9(\mu^{(2)})^2 + 24\mu\mu^{(3)}\theta}},$$

and use it as the initial condition in (15.5).

15.2 Exact Ruin Probabilities in Infinite Time

In order to present a ruin probability formula we first use the relation (15.1) and express L as a sum of so-called ladder heights. Let L_1 be the value that the process $\{S_t\}$ reaches for the first time above the zero level. Next, let L_2 be the value which is obtained for the first time above the level L_1; $L_3, L_4, \ldots$ are defined in the same way. The values L_k are called ladder heights. Since the process $\{S_t\}$ has stationary and independent increments, $\{L_k\}_{k=1}^{\infty}$ is a sequence of independent and identically distributed variables with the density

$$f_{L_1}(x) = \bar{F}_X(x)/\mu. \tag{15.6}$$

One may also show that the number of ladder heights K is given by the geometric distribution with the parameter $q = \theta/(1+\theta)$. Thus, the random variable L may be expressed as

$$L = \sum_{i=1}^{K} L_i \tag{15.7}$$

and it has a compound geometric distribution. The above fact leads to the Pollaczek-Khinchin formula for the ruin probability:

$$\psi(u) = 1 - \mathrm{P}(L \leq u) = 1 - \frac{\theta}{1+\theta} \sum_{n=0}^{\infty} \left(\frac{1}{1+\theta}\right)^n F_{L_1}^{*n}(u), \tag{15.8}$$

where $F_{L_1}^{*n}(u)$ denotes the nth convolution of the distribution function F_{L_1}.

One can use it to derive explicit solutions for a variety of claim amount distributions, particularly those whose Laplace transform is a rational function. These cases will be discussed in this section. Unfortunately, heavy-tailed distributions like e.g. the log-normal or Pareto one are not included. In such a case various approximations can be applied or one can calculate the ruin probability directly via the Pollaczek-Khinchin formula using Monte Carlo simulations. This will be studied in Section 15.3.

We shall now, in Sections 15.2.1–15.2.4, briefly present a collection of basic exact results on the ruin probability in infinite time. The ruin probability $\psi(u)$ is always considered as a function of the initial capital u.

15.2.1 No Initial Capital

When $u = 0$ it is easy to obtain the exact formula:

$$\psi(u) = \frac{1}{1+\theta}.$$

Notice that the formula depends only on θ, regardless of the claim frequency rate λ and claim size distribution. The ruin probability is clearly inversely proportional to the relative safety loading.

15.2.2 Exponential Claim Amounts

One of the historically first results on the ruin probability is the explicit formula for exponential claims with the parameter β, namely

$$\psi(u) = \frac{1}{1+\theta} \exp\left(-\frac{\theta\beta u}{1+\theta}\right). \tag{15.9}$$

In Table 15.2 we present the ruin probability values for exponential claims with $\beta = 6.3789 \cdot 10^{-9}$ (see Chapter 13) and the relative safety loading $\theta = 30\%$ with respect to the initial capital u. We can observe that the ruin probability decreases as the capital grows. When $u = 1$ billion USD the ruin probability amounts to 18%, whereas $u = 5$ billion USD reduces the probability to almost zero.

15.2.3 Gamma Claim Amounts

Grandell and Segerdahl (1971) showed that for the gamma claim amount distribution with mean 1 and $\alpha \leq 1$ the exact value of the ruin probability can be

Table 15.2: The ruin probability for exponential claims with $\beta = 6.3789 \cdot 10^{-9}$ and $\theta = 0.3$ (u in USD billion).

u	0	1	2	3	4	5
$\psi(u)$	0.769231	0.176503	0.040499	0.009293	0.002132	0.000489

STFruin02.xpl

computed via the formula:

$$\psi(u) = \frac{\theta(1 - R/\alpha)\exp(-Ru)}{1 + (1+\theta)R - (1+\theta)(1 - R/\alpha)} + \frac{\alpha\theta\sin(\alpha\pi)}{\pi} \cdot I, \tag{15.10}$$

where

$$I = \int_0^\infty \frac{x^\alpha \exp\{-(x+1)\alpha u\}}{\left[x^\alpha \{1 + \alpha(1+\theta)(x+1)\} - \cos(\alpha\pi)\right]^2 + \sin^2(\alpha\pi)}\, dx. \tag{15.11}$$

The integral I has to be calculated numerically. We also notice that the assumption on the mean is not restrictive since for claims X with arbitrary mean μ we have that $\psi_X(u) = \psi_{X/\mu}(u/\mu)$. As the gamma distribution is closed under scale changes we obtain that $\psi_{G(\alpha,\beta)}(u) = \psi_{G(\alpha,\alpha)}(\beta u/\alpha)$. This correspondence enables us to calculate the exact ruin probability via equation (15.10) for gamma claims with arbitrary mean.

Table 15.3 shows the ruin probability values for gamma claims with with $\alpha = 0.9185$, $\beta = 6.1662 \cdot 10^{-9}$ (see Chapter 13) and the relative safety loading $\theta = 30\%$ with respect to the initial capital u. Naturally, the ruin probability decreases as the capital grows. Moreover, the probability takes similar values as in the exponential case but a closer look reveals that the values in the exponential case are always slightly larger. When $u = 1$ billion USD the difference is about 1%. It suggests that a choice of the fitted distribution function may have a an impact on actuarial decisions.

Table 15.3: The ruin probability for gamma claims with $\alpha = 0.9185$, $\beta = 6.1662 \cdot 10^{-9}$ and $\theta = 0.3$ (u in USD billion).

u	0	1	2	3	4	5
$\psi(u)$	0.769229	0.174729	0.039857	0.009092	0.002074	0.000473

STFruin03.xpl

15.2.4 Mixture of Two Exponentials Claim Amounts

For the claim size distribution being a mixture of two exponentials with the parameters β_1, β_2 and weights a, $1-a$, one may obtain an explicit formula by using the Laplace transform inversion (Panjer and Willmot, 1992):

$$\psi(u) = \frac{1}{(1+\theta)(r_2 - r_1)} \left\{(\rho - r_1)\exp(-r_1 u) + (r2 - \rho)\exp(-r_2 u)\right\}, \quad (15.12)$$

where

$$r_1 = \frac{\rho + \theta(\beta_1 + \beta_2) - \left[\{\rho + \theta(\beta_1 + \beta_2)\}^2 - 4\beta_1\beta_2\theta(1+\theta)\right]^{1/2}}{2(1+\theta)},$$

$$r_2 = \frac{\rho + \theta(\beta_1 + \beta_2) + \left[\{\rho + \theta(\beta_1 + \beta_2)\}^2 - 4\beta_1\beta_2\theta(1+\theta)\right]^{1/2}}{2(1+\theta)},$$

and

$$p = \frac{a\beta_1^{-1}}{a\beta_1^{-1} + (1-a)\beta_2^{-1}}, \qquad \rho = \beta_1(1-p) + \beta_2 p.$$

Table 15.4 shows the ruin probability values for mixture of two exponentials claims with $\beta_1 = 3.5900 \cdot 10^{-10}$, $\beta_2 = 7.5088 \cdot 10^{-9}$, $a = 0.0584$ (see Chapter 13) and the relative safety loading $\theta = 30\%$ with respect to the initial capital u. As before, the ruin probability decreases as the capital grows. Moreover, the increase in the ruin probability values with respect to previous cases is dramatic. When $u = 1$ billion USD the difference between the mixture of two exponentials and exponential cases reaches 240%! As the same underlying

Table 15.4: The ruin probability for mixture of two exponentials claims with $\beta_1 = 3.5900 \cdot 10^{-10}$, $\beta_2 = 7.5088 \cdot 10^{-9}$, $a = 0.0584$ and $\theta = 0.3$ (u in USD billion).

u	0	1	5	10	20	50
$\psi(u)$	0.769231	0.587919	0.359660	0.194858	0.057197	0.001447

STFruin04.xpl

data set was used in all cases to estimate the parameters of the distributions, it supports the thesis that a choice of the fitted distribution function and checking the goodness of fit is of paramount importance.

Finally, note that it is possible to derive explicit formulae for mixture of n ($n \geq 3$) exponentials (Wikstad, 1971; Panjer and Willmot, 1992). They are not presented here since the complexity of formulae grows as n increases and such mixtures are rather of little practical importance due to increasing number of parameters.

15.3 Approximations of the Ruin Probability in Infinite Time

When the claim size distribution is exponential (or closely related to it), simple analytic results for the ruin probability in infinite time exist, see Section 15.2. For more general claim amount distributions, e.g. heavy-tailed, the Laplace transform technique does not work and one needs some estimates. In this section, we present 12 different well-known and not so well-known approximations. We illustrate them on a common claim size distribution example, namely the mixture of two exponentials claims with $\beta_1 = 3.5900 \cdot 10^{-10}$, $\beta_2 = 7.5088 \cdot 10^{-9}$ and $a = 0.0584$ (see Chapter 13). Numerical comparison of the approximations is given in Section 15.4.

Table 15.5: The Cramér–Lundberg approximation for mixture of two exponentials claims with $\beta_1 = 3.5900 \cdot 10^{-10}$, $\beta_2 = 7.5088 \cdot 10^{-9}$, $a = 0.0584$ and $\theta = 0.3$ (u in USD billion).

u	0	1	5	10	20	50
$\psi_{CL}(u)$	0.663843	0.587260	0.359660	0.194858	0.057197	0.001447

STFruin05.xpl

15.3.1 Cramér–Lundberg Approximation

Cramér–Lundberg's asymptotic ruin formula for $\psi(u)$ for large u is given by

$$\psi_{CL}(u) = Ce^{-Ru}, \tag{15.13}$$

where $C = \theta\mu / \{M'_X(R) - \mu(1+\theta)\}$. For the proof we refer to Grandell (1991). The classical Cramér–Lundberg approximation yields quite accurate results, however we must remember that it requires the adjustment coefficient to exist, therefore merely the light-tailed distributions can be taken into consideration. For exponentially distributed claims, the formula (15.13) yields the exact result.

In Table 15.5 the Cramér–Lundberg approximation for mixture of two exponentials claims with β_1, β_2, a and the relative safety loading $\theta = 30\%$ with respect to the initial capital u is given. We see that the Cramér–Lundberg approximation underestimates the ruin probability. Nevertheless, the results coincide quite closely with the exact values shown by Table 15.4. When the initial capital is zero, the relative error is the biggest and exceeds 13%.

Table 15.6: The exponential approximation for mixture of two exponentials claims with $\beta_1 = 3.5900 \cdot 10^{-10}$, $\beta_2 = 7.5088 \cdot 10^{-9}$, $a = 0.0584$ and $\theta = 0.3$ (u in USD billion).

u	0	1	5	10	20	50
$\psi_E(u)$	0.747418	0.656048	0.389424	0.202900	0.055081	0.001102

STFruin06.xpl

15.3.2 Exponential Approximation

This approximation was proposed and derived by De Vylder (1996). It requires the first three moments to be finite.

$$\psi_E(u) = \exp\left\{-1 - \frac{2\mu\theta u - \mu^{(2)}}{\sqrt{(\mu^{(2)})^2 + (4/3)\theta\mu\mu^{(3)}}}\right\}. \tag{15.14}$$

Table 15.6 shows the results of the exponential approximation for mixture of two exponentials claims with β_1, β_2, a and the relative safety loading $\theta = 30\%$ with respect to the initial capital u. Comparing them with the exact values presented in Table 15.4 we see that the exponential approximation works not bad in the studied case. When the initial capital is USD 50 billion, the relative error is the biggest and reaches 24%.

15.3.3 Lundberg Approximation

The following formula, called the Lundberg approximation, comes from Grandell (2000). It requires the first three moments to be finite.

$$\psi_L(u) = \left\{1 + \left(\theta u - \frac{\mu^{(2)}}{2\mu}\right)\frac{4\theta\mu^2\mu^{(3)}}{3(\mu^{(2)})^3}\right\}\exp\left(\frac{-2\mu\theta u}{\mu^{(2)}}\right). \tag{15.15}$$

In Table 15.7 the Lundberg approximation for mixture of two exponentials claims with β_1, β_2, a and the relative safety loading $\theta = 30\%$ with respect to

Table 15.7: The Lundberg approximation for mixture of two exponentials claims with $\beta_1 = 3.5900 \cdot 10^{-10}$, $\beta_2 = 7.5088 \cdot 10^{-9}$, $a = 0.0584$ and $\theta = 0.3$ (u in USD billion).

u	0	1	5	10	20	50
$\psi_L(u)$	0.504967	0.495882	0.382790	0.224942	0.058739	0.000513

STFruin07.xpl

the initial capital u is given. We see that the Lundberg approximation works worse than the exponential one. When the initial capital is USD 50 billion, the relative error exceeds 60%.

15.3.4 Beekman–Bowers Approximation

The Beekman–Bowers approximation uses the following representation of the ruin probability:

$$\psi(u) = \mathrm{P}(L > u) = \mathrm{P}(L > 0)\mathrm{P}(L > u|L > 0). \qquad (15.16)$$

The idea of the approximation is to replace the conditional probability $1 - \mathrm{P}(L > u|L > 0)$ with a gamma distribution function $G(u)$ by fitting first two moments (Grandell, 2000). This leads to:

$$\psi_{BB}(u) = \frac{1}{1+\theta}\left\{1 - G(u)\right\}, \qquad (15.17)$$

where the parameters α, β of G are given by

$$\alpha = \left\{1 + \left(\frac{4\mu\mu^{(3)}}{3(\mu^{(2)})^2} - 1\right)\theta\right\}/(1+\theta), \beta = 2\mu\theta/\left\{\mu^{(2)} + \left(\frac{4\mu\mu^{(3)}}{3\mu^{(2)}} - \mu^{(2)}\right)\theta\right\}.$$

The Beekman–Bowers approximation gives rather accurate results, see Burnecki, Miśta, and Weron (2004). In the exponential case it becomes the exact formula. It can be used only for distributions with finite first three moments.

Table 15.8: The Beekman–Bowers approximation for mixture of two exponentials claims with $\beta_1 = 3.5900 \cdot 10^{-10}$, $\beta_2 = 7.5088 \cdot 10^{-9}$, $a = 0.0584$ and $\theta = 0.3$ (u in USD billion).

u	0	1	5	10	20	50
$\psi_{BB}(u)$	0.769231	0.624902	0.352177	0.186582	0.056260	0.001810

STFruin08.xpl

Table 15.8 shows the results of the Beekman–Bowers approximation for mixture of two exponentials claims with β_1, β_2, a and the relative safety loading $\theta =$ 30% with respect to the initial capital u. The results justify the thesis the approximation yields quite accurate results but when the initial capital is USD 50 billion, the relative error is unacceptable, reaching 25%, cf. the exact values in Table 15.4.

15.3.5 Renyi Approximation

The Renyi approximation (Grandell, 2000), may be derived from (20.5.4) when we replace the gamma distribution function G with an exponential one, matching only the first moment. Hence, it can be regarded as a simplified version of the Beekman–Bowers approximation. It requires the first two moments to be finite.

$$\psi_R(u) = \frac{1}{1+\theta} \exp\left\{ -\frac{2\mu\theta u}{\mu^{(2)}(1+\theta)} \right\}. \tag{15.18}$$

In Table 15.9 the Renyi approximation for mixture of two exponentials claims with β_1, β_2, a and the relative safety loading $\theta = 30\%$ with respect to the initial capital u is given. We see that the results compared with the exact values presented in Table 15.4 are quite accurate. The accuracy ot the approximation is similar to the Beekman–Bowers approximation but when the initial capital is USD 50 billion, the relative error exceeds 50%.

Table 15.9: The Renyi approximation for mixture of two exponentials claims with $\beta_1 = 3.5900 \cdot 10^{-10}$, $\beta_2 = 7.5088 \cdot 10^{-9}$, $a = 0.0584$ and $\theta = 0.3$ (u in USD billion).

u	0	1	5	10	20	50
$\psi_R(u)$	0.769231	0.667738	0.379145	0.186876	0.045400	0.000651

STFruin09.xpl

15.3.6 De Vylder Approximation

The idea of this approximation is to replace the claim surplus process S_t with the claim surplus process $\bar{S}_t$ with exponentially distributed claims such that the three moments of the processes coincide, namely $\mathrm{E}(S_t^k) = \mathrm{E}(\bar{S}_t^k)$ for $k = 1, 2, 3$, see De Vylder (1978). The process $\bar{S}_t$ is determined by the three parameters $(\bar{\lambda}, \bar{\theta}, \bar{\beta})$. Thus the parameters must satisfy:

$$\bar{\lambda} = \frac{9\lambda \mu^{(2)^3}}{2\mu^{(3)^2}}, \qquad \bar{\theta} = \frac{2\mu\mu^{(3)}}{3\mu^{(2)^2}}\theta, \qquad \text{and} \qquad \bar{\beta} = \frac{3\mu^{(2)}}{\mu^{(3)}}.$$

Then De Vylder's approximation is given by:

$$\psi_{DV}(u) = \frac{1}{1+\bar{\theta}} \exp\left(-\frac{\bar{\theta}\bar{\beta}u}{1+\bar{\theta}}\right). \tag{15.19}$$

Obviously, in the exponential case the method gives the exact result. For other claim amount distributions, in order to apply the approximation, the first three moments have to exist.

Table 15.10 shows the results of the De Vylder approximation for mixture of two exponentials claims with β_1, β_2, a and the relative safety loading $\theta = 30\%$ with respect to the initial capital u. The approximation gives surprisingly good results. In the considered case the relative error is the biggest when the initial capital is zero and amounts to about 13%, cf. Table 15.4.

Table 15.10: The De Vylder approximation for mixture of two exponentials claims with $\beta_1 = 3.5900 \cdot 10^{-10}$, $\beta_2 = 7.5088 \cdot 10^{-9}$, $a = 0.0584$ and $\theta = 0.3$ (u in USD billion).

u	0	1	5	10	20	50
$\psi_{DV}(u)$	0.668881	0.591446	0.361560	0.195439	0.057105	0.001424

STFruin10.xpl

15.3.7 4-moment Gamma De Vylder Approximation

The 4-moment gamma De Vylder approximation, proposed by Burnecki, Miśta, and Weron (2003), is based on De Vylder's idea to replace the claim surplus process S_t with another one $\bar{S}_t$ for which the expression for $\psi(u)$ is explicit. This time we calculate the parameters of the new process with gamma distributed claims and apply the exact formula (15.10) for the ruin probability. Let us note that the claim surplus process $\bar{S}_t$ with gamma claims is determined by the four parameters $(\bar{\lambda}, \bar{\theta}, \bar{\mu}, \bar{\mu}^{(2)})$, so we have to match the four moments of S_t and $\bar{S}_t$. We also need to assume that $\mu^{(2)}\mu^{(4)} < \frac{3}{2}(\mu^{(3)})^2$ to ensure that $\bar{\mu}, \bar{\mu}^{(2)} > 0$ and $\bar{\mu}^{(2)} > \bar{\mu}^2$, which is true for the gamma distribution. Then

$$\begin{aligned}
\bar{\lambda} &= \frac{\lambda(\mu^{(3)})^2(\mu^{(2)})^3}{\{\mu^{(2)}\mu^{(4)}-2(\mu^{(3)})^2\}\{2\mu^{(2)}\mu^{(4)}-3(\mu^{(3)})^2\}},\\
\bar{\theta} &= \frac{\theta\mu\{2(\mu^{(3)})^2-\mu^{(2)}\mu^{(4)}\}}{(\mu^{(2)})^2\mu^{(3)}},\\
\bar{\mu} &= \frac{3(\mu^{(3)})^2-2\mu^{(2)}\mu^{(4)}}{\mu^{(2)}\mu^{(3)}},\\
\bar{\mu}^{(2)} &= \frac{\{\mu^{(2)}\mu^{(4)}-2(\mu^{(3)})^2\}\{2\mu^{(2)}\mu^{(4)}-3(\mu^{(3)})^2\}}{(\mu^{(2)}\mu^{(3)})^2}.
\end{aligned}$$

When this assumption can not be fulfilled, the simpler case leads to

$$\bar{\lambda} = \frac{2\lambda(\mu^{(2)})^2}{\mu(\mu^{(3)}+\mu^{(2)}\mu)}, \quad \bar{\theta} = \frac{\theta\mu(\mu^{(3)}+\mu^{(2)}\mu)}{2(\mu^{(2)})^2}, \quad \bar{\mu} = \mu, \quad \bar{\mu}^{(2)} = \frac{\mu(\mu^{(3)}+\mu^{(2)}\mu)}{2\mu^{(2)}}.$$

Table 15.11: The 4-moment gamma De Vylder approximation for mixture of two exponentials claims with $\beta_1 = 3.5900 \cdot 10^{-10}$, $\beta_2 = 7.5088 \cdot 10^{-9}$, $a = 0.0584$ and $\theta = 0.3$ (u in USD billion).

u	0	1	5	10	20	50
$\psi_{4MGDV}(u)$	0.683946	0.595457	0.359879	0.194589	0.057150	0.001450

STFruin11.xpl

All in all, the 4-moment gamma De Vylder approximation is given by

$$\psi_{4MGDV}(u) = \frac{\bar{\theta}(1-\frac{R}{\bar{\alpha}})\exp(-\frac{\bar{\beta}R}{\bar{\alpha}}u)}{1+(1+\bar{\theta})R-(1+\bar{\theta})(1-\frac{R}{\bar{\alpha}})} + \frac{\bar{\alpha}\bar{\theta}\sin(\bar{\alpha}\pi)}{\pi}\cdot I, \tag{15.20}$$

where

$$I = \int_0^\infty \frac{x^{\bar{\alpha}}\exp\{-(x+1)\bar{\beta}u\}\,dx}{\left[x^{\bar{\alpha}}\left\{1+\bar{\alpha}(1+\bar{\theta})(x+1)\right\}-\cos(\bar{\alpha}\pi)\right]^2+\sin^2(\bar{\alpha}\pi)},$$

and $\bar{\alpha} = \bar{\mu}^2/\left(\bar{\mu}^{(2)}-\bar{\mu}^2\right)$, $\bar{\beta} = \bar{\mu}/\left(\bar{\mu}^{(2)}-\bar{\mu}^2\right)$.

In the exponential and gamma case this method gives the exact result. For other claim distributions in order to apply the approximation, the first four (or three in the simpler case) moments have to exist. Burnecki, Miśta, and Weron (2003) showed numerically that the method gives a slight correction to the De Vylder approximation, which is often regarded as the best among "simple" approximations.

In Table 15.11 the 4-moment gamma De Vylder approximation for mixture of two exponentials claims with $\beta_1 = 3.5900 \cdot 10^{-10}$, $\beta_2 = 7.5088 \cdot 10^{-9}$, $a = 0.0584$ (see Chapter 13) and the relative safety loading $\theta = 30\%$ with respect to the initial capital u is given. The most striking impression of Table 15.11 is certainly the extremely good accuracy of the simple 4-moment gamma De Vylder approximation for reasonable choices of the initial capital u. The relative error with respect to the exact values presented in Table 15.4 is the biggest for $u = 0$ and equals 11%.

Table 15.12: The heavy traffic approximation for mixture of two exponentials claims with $\beta_1 = 3.5900 \cdot 10^{-10}$, $\beta_2 = 7.5088 \cdot 10^{-9}$, $a = 0.0584$ and $\theta = 0.3$ (u in USD billion).

u	0	1	5	10	20	50
$\psi_{HT}(u)$	1.000000	0.831983	0.398633	0.158908	0.025252	0.000101

STFruin12.xpl

15.3.8 Heavy Traffic Approximation

The term "heavy traffic" comes from queuing theory. In risk theory it means that, on the average, the premiums exceed only slightly the expected claims. It implies that the relative safety loading θ is positive and small. Asmussen (2000) suggests the following approximation.

$$\psi_{HT}(u) = \exp\left(-\frac{2\theta\mu u}{\mu^{(2)}}\right). \tag{15.21}$$

This method requires the existence of the first two moments of the claim size distribution. Numerical evidence shows that the approximation is reasonable for the relative safety loading being 10 – 20% and u being small or moderate, while the approximation may be far off for large u. We also note that the approximation given by (15.21) is also known as the diffusion approximation and is further analysed and generalised to the stable case in Chapter 16, see also Furrer, Michna, and Weron (1997).

Table 15.12 shows the results of the heavy traffic approximation for mixture of two exponentials claims with β_1, β_2, a and the relative safety loading $\theta = 30\%$ with respect to the initial capital u. It is clear that the accuracy of the approximation in the considered case is extremely poor. When the initial capital is USD 50 billion, the relative error reaches 93%, cf. Table 15.4.

Table 15.13: The light traffic approximation for mixture of two exponentials claims with $\beta_1 = 3.5900 \cdot 10^{-10}$, $\beta_2 = 7.5088 \cdot 10^{-9}$, $a = 0.0584$ and $\theta = 0.3$ (u in USD billion).

u	0	1	5	10	20	50
$\psi_{LT}(u)$	0.769231	0.303545	0.072163	0.011988	0.000331	0.000000

`STFruin13.xpl`

15.3.9 Light Traffic Approximation

As for heavy traffic, the term "light traffic" comes from queuing theory, but has an obvious interpretation also in risk theory, namely, on the average, the premiums are much larger than the expected claims, or in other words, claims appear less frequently than expected. It implies that the relative safety loading θ is positive and large. We may obtain the following asymptotic formula.

$$\psi_{LT}(u) = \frac{1}{(1+\theta)\mu} \int_u^\infty \bar{F}_X(x)dx. \qquad (15.22)$$

In risk theory heavy traffic is most often argued to be the typical case rather than light traffic. However, light traffic is of some interest as a complement to heavy traffic, as well as it is needed for the interpolation approximation to be studied in the next point. It is worth noticing that this method gives accurate results merely for huge values of the relative safety loading, see Asmussen (2000).

In Table 15.13 the light traffic approximation for mixture of two exponentials claims with β_1, β_2, a and the relative safety loading $\theta = 30\%$ with respect to the initial capital u is given. The results are even worse than in the heavy case, only for moderate u the situation is better. The relative error dramatically increases with the initial capital.

Table 15.14: The heavy-light traffic approximation for mixture of two exponentials claims with $\beta_1 = 3.5900 \cdot 10^{-10}$, $\beta_2 = 7.5088 \cdot 10^{-9}$, $a = 0.0584$ and $\theta = 0.3$ (u in USD billion).

u	0	1	5	10	20	50
$\psi_{HLT}(u)$	0.769231	0.598231	0.302136	0.137806	0.034061	0.001652

STFruin14.xpl

15.3.10 Heavy-light Traffic Approximation

The crude idea of this approximation is to combine the heavy and light approximations (Asmussen, 2000):

$$\psi_{HLT}(u) = \frac{\theta}{1+\theta}\psi_{LT}\left(\frac{\theta u}{1+\theta}\right) + \frac{1}{(1+\theta)^2}\psi_{HT}(u). \tag{15.23}$$

The particular features of this approximation is that it is exact for the exponential distribution and asymptotically correct both in light and heavy traffic.

Table 15.14 shows the results of the heavy-light traffic approximation for mixture of two exponentials claims with β_1, β_2, a and the relative safety loading $\theta = 30\%$ with respect to the initial capital u. Comparing the results with Table 15.12 (heavy traffic), Table 15.13 (light traffic) and the exact values given in Table 15.4 we see that the interpolation is promising. In the considered case the relative error is the biggest when the initial capital is USD 20 billion and is over 40%, but usually the error is acceptable.

15.3.11 Subexponential Approximation

First, let us introduce the class of subexponential distributions $\mathcal{S}$ (Embrechts, Klüppelberg, and Mikosch, 1997), namely

$$\mathcal{S} = \left\{ F : \lim_{x\to\infty} \frac{\overline{F^{*2}}(x)}{\bar{F}(x)} = 2 \right\}. \tag{15.24}$$

Here $F^{*2}(x)$ is the convolution square. In terms of random variables (15.24) means $\mathrm{P}(X_1+X_2 > x) \sim 2P(X_1 > x)$, $x \to \infty$, where X_1, X_2 are independent random variables with distribution F.

The class contains log-normal and Weibull (for $\tau < 1$) distributions. Moreover, all distributions with a regularly varying tail (e.g. Pareto and Burr distributions) are subexponential. For subexponential distributions we can formulate the following approximation of the ruin probability. If $F \in \mathcal{S}$, then the asymptotic formula for large u is given by

$$\psi_S(u) = \frac{1}{\theta\mu}\left(\mu - \int_0^u \bar{F}(x)dx\right), \tag{15.25}$$

see Asmussen (2000).

The approximation is considered to be inaccurate. The problem is a very slow rate of convergence as $u \to \infty$. Even though the approximation is asymptotically correct in the tail, one may have to go out to values of $\psi(u)$ which are unrealistically small before the fit is reasonable. However, we will show in Section 15.4 that it is not always the case.

As the mixture of exponentials does not belong to the subexponential class we do not present a numerical example like in all previously discussed approximations.

15.3.12 Computer Approximation via the Pollaczek-Khinchin Formula

One can use the Pollaczek-Khinchin formula (15.8) to derive explicit closed form solutions for claim amount distributions presented in Section 15.2, see Panjer and Willmot (1992). For other distributions studied here, in order to calculate the ruin probability, the Monte Carlo method can be applied to (15.1) and (15.7). The main problem is to simulate random variables from the density $f_{L_1}(x)$. Only four of the considered distributions lead to a known density: (i) for exponential claims, $f_{L_1}(x)$ is the density of the same exponential distribution, (ii) for a mixture of exponentials claims, $f_{L_1}(x)$ is the density of the mixture of exponential distribution with the weights $\left(\frac{a_1}{\beta_1}/\left\{\sum_{i=1}^n\left(\frac{a_i}{\beta_i}\right)\right\},\cdots,\right.$ $\left.\frac{a_n}{\beta_n}/\left\{\sum_{i=1}^n\left(\frac{a_i}{\beta_i}\right)\right\}\right)$, (iii) for Pareto claims, $f_{L_1}(x)$ is the density of the Pareto distribution with the parameters $\alpha-1$ and λ, (iv) for Burr claims, $f_{L_1}(x)$ is the density of the transformed beta distribution.

Table 15.15: The Pollaczek-Khinchin approximation for mixture of two exponentials claims with $\beta_1 = 3.5900 \cdot 10^{-10}$, $\beta_2 = 7.5088 \cdot 10^{-9}$, $a = 0.0584$ and $\theta = 0.3$ (u in USD billion).

u	0	1	5	10	20	50
$\psi_{PK}(u)$	0.769209	0.587917	0.359705	0.194822	0.057173	0.001445

STFruin15.xpl

For other distributions studied here we use formula (15.6) and controlled numerical integration to generate random variables L_k (except for the Weibull distribution, $f_{L_1}(x)$ does not even have a closed form). We note that the methodology based on the Pollaczek-Khinchin formula works for all considered claim distributions.

The computer approximation via the Pollaczek-Khinchin formula will be called in short the Pollaczek-Khinchin approximation. Burnecki, Miśta, and Weron (2004) showed that the approximation can be chosen as the reference method for calculating the ruin probability in infinite time, see also Table 15.15 where the results of the Pollaczek-Khinchin approximation are presented for mixture of two exponentials claims with β_1, β_2, a and the relative safety loading $\theta = 30\%$ with respect to the initial capital u. For the Monte Carlo method purposes we generated 100 blocks of 500000 simulations.

15.3.13 Summary of the Approximations

Table 15.16 shows which approximation can be used for a particular choice of a claim size distribution. Moreover, the necessary assumptions on the distribution parameters are presented.

Table 15.16: Survey of approximations with an indication when they can be applied

Distrib. / Method	Exp.	Gamma	Weibull	Mix. Exp.	Log-normal	Pareto	Burr
Cramér-Lundberg	+	+	–	+	–	–	–
Exponential	+	+	+	+	+	$\alpha > 3$	$\alpha\tau > 3$
Lundberg	+	+	+	+	+	$\alpha > 3$	$\alpha\tau > 3$
Beekman-Bowers	+	+	+	+	+	$\alpha > 3$	$\alpha\tau > 3$
Renyi	+	+	+	+	+	$\alpha > 2$	$\alpha\tau > 2$
De Vylder	+	+	+	+	+	$\alpha > 3$	$\alpha\tau > 3$
4M Gamma De Vylder	+	+	+	+	+	$\alpha > 3$	$\alpha\tau > 3$
Heavy Traffic	+	+	+	+	+	$\alpha > 2$	$\alpha\tau > 2$
Light Traffic	+	+	+	+	+	+	+
Heavy-Light Traffic	+	+	+	+	+	$\alpha > 2$	$\alpha\tau > 2$
Subexponential	–	–	$0<\tau<1$	–	+	+	+
Pollaczek-Khinchin	+	+	+	+	+	+	+

15.4 Numerical Comparison of the Infinite Time Approximations

In this section we will illustrate all 12 approximations presented in Section 15.3. To this end we consider three claim amount distributions which were fitted to the PCS catastrophe data in Chapter 13, namely the mixture of two exponential (a running example in Section 15.3) with $\beta_1 = 3.5900 \cdot 10^{-10}$, $\beta_2 = 7.5088 \cdot 10^{-9}$ and $a = 0.0584$, log-normal with $\mu = 18.3806$ and $\sigma = 1.1052$, and Pareto with $\alpha = 3.4081$ and $\lambda = 4.4767 \cdot 10^8$ distributions.

The logarithm of the ruin probability as a function of the initial capital u ranging from USD 0 to 50 billion for the three distributions is depicted in Figure 15.2. In the case of log-normal and Pareto distributions the reference Pollaczek-Khinchin approximation is used. We see that the ruin probability values for the mixture of exponential distributions are much higher than for the log-normal and Pareto distributions. It stems from the fact that the estimated parameters of the mixture result in the mean equal to $2.88 \cdot 10^8$, whereas the mean of the fitted log-normal distribution amounts to $1.77 \cdot 10^8$ and of Pareto distribution to $1.86 \cdot 10^8$.

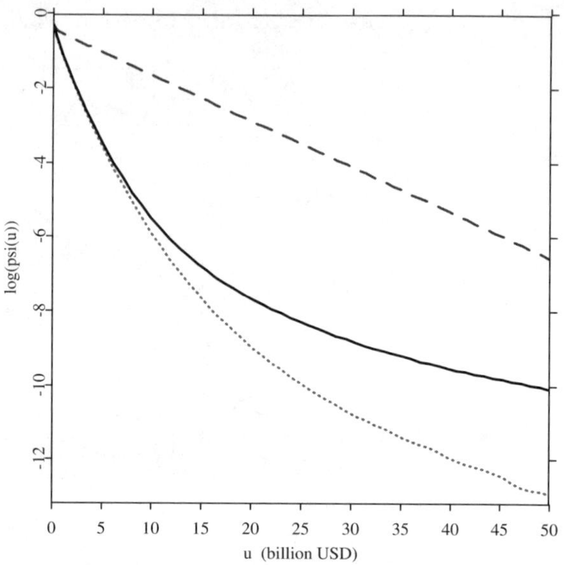

Figure 15.2: The logarithm of the exact value of the ruin probability. The mixture of two exponentials (dashed blue line), log-normal (dotted red line), and Pareto (solid black line) clam size distribution.

STFruin16.xpl

Figures 15.3–15.5 describe the relative error of the 11 approximations from Sections 15.3.1–15.3.11 with respect to exact ruin probability values in the mixture of two exponentials case and obtained via the Pollaczek-Khinchin approximation in the log-normal and Pareto cases. The relative safety loading is set to 30%. We note that for the Monte Carlo method purposes in the Pollaczek-Khinchin approximation we generate 500 blocks of 100000 simulations. First, we consider the mixture of two exponentials case already analysed in Section 15.3. Only the subexponential approximation can not be used for such a claim amount distribution, see Table 15.16. As we can clearly see in Figure 15.3 the Cramér–Lundberg, De Vylder and 4-moment gamma De Vylder approximations work extremely well. Furthermore, the heavy traffic, light traffic, Renyi,

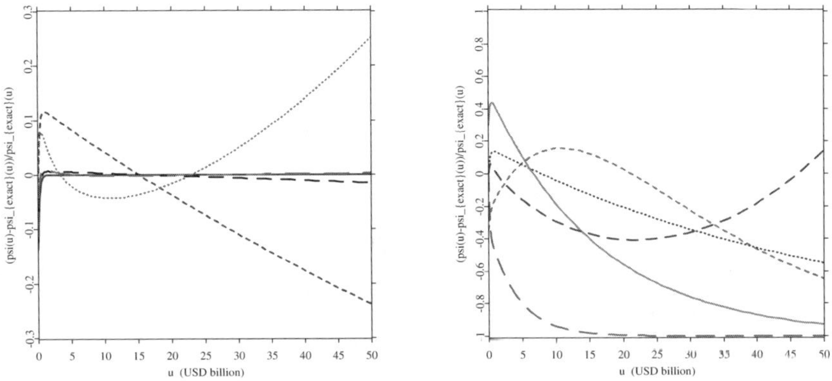

Figure 15.3: The relative error of the approximations. More effective methods (left panel): the Cramér–Lundberg (solid blue line), exponential (short-dashed brown line), Beekman–Bowers (dotted red line), De Vylder (medium-dashed black line) and 4-moment gamma De Vylder (long-dashed green line) approximations. Less effective methods (right panel): Lundberg (short-dashed red line), Renyi (dotted blue line), heavy traffic (solid magenta line), light traffic (long-dashed green line) and heavy-light traffic (medium-dashed brown line) approximations. The mixture of two exponentials case.

`STFruin17.xpl`

and Lundberg approximations show a total lack of accuracy and the rest of the methods are only acceptable.

In the case of log-normally distributed claims, the situation is different, see Figure 15.4. Only results obtained via Beekman–Bowers, De Vylder and 4-moment gamma De Vylder approximations are acceptable. The rest of the approximations are well off target. We also note that all 11 approximations can be employed in the log-normal case except the Cramér–Lundberg one.

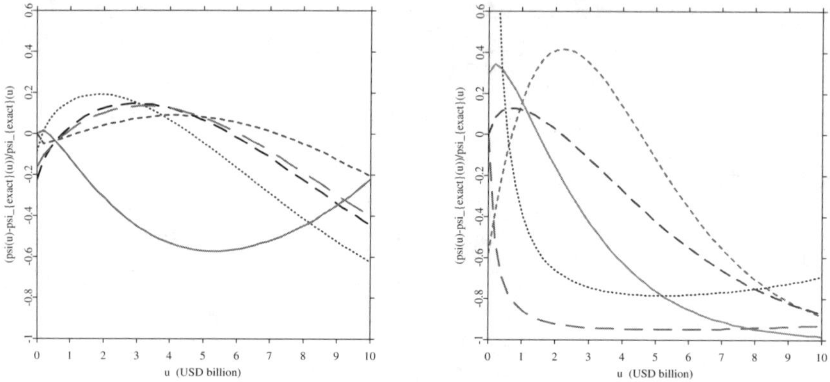

Figure 15.4: The relative error of the approximations. More effective methods (left panel): the exponential (dotted blue line), Beekman–Bowers (short-dashed brown line), heavy-light traffic (solid red line), De Vylder (medium-dashed black line) and 4-moment gamma De Vylder (long-dashed green line) approximations. Less effective methods (right panel): Lundberg (short-dashed red line), heavy traffic (solid magenta line), light traffic (long-dashed green line), Renyi (medium-dashed brown line) and subexponential (dotted blue line) approximations. The log-normal case.

STFruin18.xpl

Finally, we take into consideration the Pareto claim size distribution. Figure 15.5 depicts the relative error for 9 approximations. Only the Cramér–Lundberg and 4-moment gamma De Vylder approximations have to excluded as the moment generating function does not exist and the fourth moment is infinite for the Pareto distribution with $\alpha = 3.4081$. As we see in Figure 15.5 the relative errors for all approximations can not be neglected. There is no unanimous winner among the approximations but we may claim that the exponential approximation gives most accurate results.

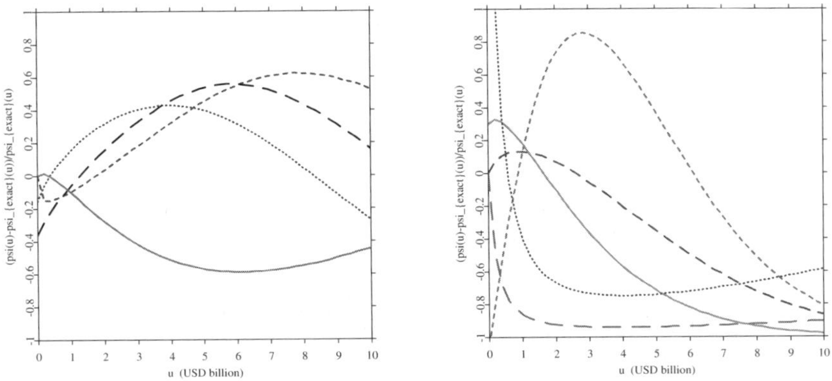

Figure 15.5: The relative error of the approximations. More effective methods (left panel): the exponential (dotted blue line), Beekman–Bowers (short-dashed brown line), heavy-light traffic (solid red line) and De Vylder (medium-dashed black line) approximations. Less effective methods (right panel): Lundberg (short-dashed red line), heavy traffic (solid magenta line), light traffic (long-dashed green line), Renyi (medium-dashed brown line) and subexponential (dotted blue line) approximations. The Pareto case.

STFruin19.xpl

15.5 Exact Ruin Probabilities in Finite Time

We are now interested in the probability that the insurer's capital as defined by (15.1) remains non-negative for a finite period T rather than permanently. We assume that the number of claims process N_t is a Poisson process with rate λ, and consequently, the aggregate loss process is a compound Poisson process. Premiums are payable at rate c per unit time. We recall that the intensity of the process N_t is irrelevant in the infinite time case provided that it is compensated by the premium, see discussion at the end of Section 15.1.

In contrast to the infinite time case there is no general formula for the ruin probability like the Pollaczek-Khinchin one given by (15.8). In the literature one can only find a partial integro-differential equation which satisfies the probability of non-ruin, see Panjer and Willmot (1992). An explicit result is merely known for the exponential claims, and even in this case a numerical integration is needed (Asmussen, 2000).

15.5.1 Exponential Claim Amounts

First, in order to simplify the formulae, let us assume that claims have the exponential distribution with $\beta = 1$ and the amount of premium is $c = 1$. Then

$$\psi(u,T) = \lambda \exp\{-(1-\lambda)u\} - \frac{1}{\pi}\int_0^{\pi} \frac{f_1(x)f_2(x)}{f_3(x)}dx, \tag{15.26}$$

where $f_1(x) = \lambda \exp\left\{2\sqrt{\lambda}T\cos x - (1+\lambda)T + u\left(\sqrt{\lambda}\cos x - 1\right)\right\}$, $f_2(x) = \cos\left(u\sqrt{\lambda}\sin x\right) - \cos\left(u\sqrt{\lambda}\sin x + 2x\right)$, and $f_3(x) = 1 + \lambda - 2\sqrt{\lambda}\cos x$.

Now, notice that the case $\beta \neq 1$ is easily reduced to $\beta = 1$, using the formula:

$$\psi_{\lambda,\beta}(u,T) = \psi_{\frac{\lambda}{\beta},1}(\beta u, \beta T). \tag{15.27}$$

Moreover, the assumption $c = 1$ is not restrictive since we have

$$\psi_{\lambda,c}(u,T) = \psi_{\lambda/c,1}(u, cT). \tag{15.28}$$

Table 15.17 shows the exact values of the ruin probability for exponential claims with $\beta = 6.3789 \cdot 10^{-9}$ (see Chapter 13) with respect to the initial capital u and the time horizon T. The relative safety loading θ equals 30%. We see that the values converge to those calculated in infinite case as T is getting larger, cf. Table 15.2. The speed of convergence decreases as the initial capital u grows.

15.6 Approximations of the Ruin Probability in Finite Time

In this section, we present 5 different approximations. We illustrate them on a common claim size distribution example, namely the mixture of two exponentials claims with $\beta_1 = 3.5900 \cdot 10^{-10}$, $\beta_2 = 7.5088 \cdot 10^{-9}$ and $a = 0.0584$ (see Chapter 13). Their numerical comparison is given in Section 15.7.

Table 15.17: The ruin probability for exponential claims with $\beta = 6.3789 \cdot 10^{-9}$ and $\theta = 0.3$ (u in USD billion).

u	0	1	2	3	4	5
$\psi(u,1)$	0.757164	0.147954	0.025005	0.003605	0.000443	0.000047
$\psi(u,2)$	0.766264	0.168728	0.035478	0.007012	0.001288	0.000218
$\psi(u,5)$	0.769098	0.176127	0.040220	0.009138	0.002060	0.000459
$\psi(u,10)$	0.769229	0.176497	0.040495	0.009290	0.002131	0.000489
$\psi(u,20)$	0.769231	0.176503	0.040499	0.009293	0.002132	0.000489

STFruin20.xpl

15.6.1 Monte Carlo Method

The ruin probability in finite time can always be approximated by means of Monte Carlo simulations. Table 15.18 shows the output for mixture of two exponentials claims with β_1, β_2, a with respect to the initial capital u and the time horizon T. The relative safety loading θ is set to 30%. For the Monte Carlo method purposes we generated 50 x 10000 simulations. We see that the values approach those calculated in infinite case as T increases, cf. Table 15.4. We note that the Monte Carlo method will be used as a reference method when comparing different finite time approximations in Section 15.7.

15.6.2 Segerdahl Normal Approximation

The following result due to Segerdahl (1955) is said to be a time-dependent version of the Cramér–Lundberg approximation given by (15.13). Under the assumption that $c = 1$, cf. relation (15.28), we have

$$\psi_S(u,T) = C\exp(-Ru)\Phi\left(\frac{T - um_L}{\omega_L\sqrt{u}}\right), \tag{15.29}$$

where $C = \theta\mu/\{M_X'(R) - \mu(1+\theta)\}$, $m_L = 1\{\lambda M_X'(R) - 1\}^{-1}$ and $\omega_L^2 = \lambda M_X''(R)m_L^3$.

Table 15.18: Monte Carlo results (50 x 10000 simulations) for mixture of two exponentials claims with $\beta_1 = 3.5900 \cdot 10^{-10}$, $\beta_2 = 7.5088 \cdot 10^{-9}$, $a = 0.0584$ and $\theta = 0.3$ (u in USD billion).

u	0	1	5	10	20	50
$\psi(u,1)$	0.672550	0.428150	0.188930	0.063938	0.006164	0.000002
$\psi(u,2)$	0.718254	0.501066	0.256266	0.105022	0.015388	0.000030
$\psi(u,5)$	0.753696	0.560426	0.323848	0.159034	0.035828	0.000230
$\psi(u,10)$	0.765412	0.580786	0.350084	0.184438	0.049828	0.000726
$\psi(u,20)$	0.769364	0.587826	0.359778	0.194262	0.056466	0.001244

STFruin21.xpl

Table 15.19: The Segerdahl approximation for mixture of two exponentials claims with $\beta_1 = 3.5900 \cdot 10^{-10}$, $\beta_2 = 7.5088 \cdot 10^{-9}$, $a = 0.0584$ and $\theta = 0.3$ (u in USD billion).

u	0	1	5	10	20	50
$\psi(u,1)$	0.663843	0.444333	0.172753	0.070517	0.013833	0.000141
$\psi(u,2)$	0.663843	0.554585	0.229282	0.092009	0.017651	0.000175
$\psi(u,5)$	0.663843	0.587255	0.338098	0.152503	0.030919	0.000311
$\psi(u,10)$	0.663843	0.587260	0.359593	0.192144	0.049495	0.000634
$\psi(u,20)$	0.663843	0.587260	0.359660	0.194858	0.057143	0.001254

STFruin22.xpl

This method requires existence of the adjustment coefficient. This implies that only light-tailed distributions can be used. Numerical evidence shows that the Segerdahl approximation gives the best results for huge values of the initial capital u, see Asmussen (2000).

In Table 15.19, the results of the Segerdahl approximation for mixture of two exponentials claims with β_1, β_2, a with respect to the initial capital u and the

Table 15.20: The diffusion approximation for mixture of two exponentials claims with $\beta_1 = 3.5900 \cdot 10^{-10}$, $\beta_2 = 7.5088 \cdot 10^{-9}$, $a = 0.0584$ and $\theta = 0.3$ (u in USD billion).

u	0	1	5	10	20	50
$\psi(u,1)$	1.000000	0.770917	0.223423	0.028147	0.000059	0.000000
$\psi(u,2)$	1.000000	0.801611	0.304099	0.072061	0.001610	0.000000
$\psi(u,5)$	1.000000	0.823343	0.370177	0.128106	0.011629	0.000000
$\psi(u,10)$	1.000000	0.829877	0.391556	0.150708	0.020604	0.000017
$\psi(u,20)$	1.000000	0.831744	0.397816	0.157924	0.024603	0.000073

STFruin23.xpl

time horizon T are presented. The relative safety loading $\theta = 30\%$. We see that the approximation in the considered case yields quite accurate results for moderate u, cf. Table 15.18.

15.6.3 Diffusion Approximation

The idea of the diffusion approximation is first to approximate the claim surplus process S_t by a Brownian motion with drift (arithmetic Brownian motion) by matching the first two moments, and next, to note that such an approximation implies that the first passage probabilities are close. The first passage probability serves as the ruin probability.

The diffusion approximation is given by:

$$\psi_D(u,T) = IG\left(\frac{T\mu_c^2}{\sigma_c^2}; -1; \frac{u|\mu_c|}{\sigma_c^2}\right), \tag{15.30}$$

where $\mu_c = -\lambda\theta\mu$, $\sigma_c^2 = \lambda\mu^{(2)}$, and $IG(\cdot;\zeta;u)$ denotes the distribution function of the passage time of the Brownian motion with unit variance and drift ζ from the level 0 to the level $u > 0$ (often referred to as the inverse Gaussian distribution function), namely $IG(x;\zeta;u) = 1 - \Phi\left(u/\sqrt{x} - \zeta\sqrt{x}\right) + \exp\left(2\zeta u\right)$ $\cdot\Phi\left(-u/\sqrt{x} - \zeta\sqrt{x}\right)$, see Asmussen (2000).

Table 15.21: The corrected diffusion approximation for mixture of two exponentials claims with $\beta_1 = 3.5900 \cdot 10^{-10}$, $\beta_2 = 7.5088 \cdot 10^{-9}$, $a = 0.0584$ and $\theta = 0.3$ (u in USD billion).

u	0	1	5	10	20	50
$\psi(u,1)$	0.521465	0.426840	0.187718	0.065264	0.007525	0.000010
$\psi(u,2)$	0.587784	0.499238	0.254253	0.104967	0.016173	0.000039
$\psi(u,5)$	0.638306	0.557463	0.321230	0.157827	0.035499	0.000251
$\psi(u,10)$	0.655251	0.577547	0.347505	0.182727	0.049056	0.000724
$\psi(u,20)$	0.660958	0.584386	0.356922	0.192446	0.055610	0.001243

STFruin24.xpl

We also note that in order to apply this approximation we need the existence of the second moment of the claim size distribution.

Table 15.20 shows the results of the diffusion approximation for mixture of two exponentials claims with β_1, β_2, a with respect to the initial capital u and the time horizon T. The relative safety loading θ equals 30%. The results lead to the conclusion that the approximation does not produce accurate results for such a choice of the claim size distribution. Only when $u = 5$ billion USD the results are acceptable, cf. the reference values in Table 15.18.

15.6.4 Corrected Diffusion Approximation

The idea presented above of the diffusion approximation ignores the presence of jumps in the risk process (the Brownian motion with drift is skip-free) and the value $S_{\tau(u)} - u$ in the moment of ruin. The corrected diffusion approximation takes this and other deficits into consideration (Asmussen, 2000). Under the assumption that $c = 1$, cf. relation (15.28), we have

$$\psi_{CD}(u,t) = IG\left(\frac{T\delta_1}{u^2} + \frac{\delta_2}{u}; -\frac{Ru}{2}; 1 + \frac{\delta_2}{u}\right), \tag{15.31}$$

where R is the adjustment coefficient, $\delta_1 = \lambda M''_X(\gamma_0)$, $\delta_2 = M'''_X(\gamma_0)/\{3M''_X(\gamma_0)\}$, and γ_0 satisfies the equation: $\kappa'(\gamma_0) = 0$, where $\kappa(s) = \lambda\{M_X(s) - 1\} - s$.

Table 15.22: The finite time De Vylder approximation for mixture of two exponentials claims with $\beta_1 = 3.5900 \cdot 10^{-10}$, $\beta_2 = 7.5088 \cdot 10^{-9}$, $a = 0.0584$ and $\theta = 0.3$ (u in USD billion).

u	0	1	5	10	20	50
$\psi(u, 1)$	0.528431	0.433119	0.189379	0.063412	0.006114	0.000003
$\psi(u, 2)$	0.594915	0.505300	0.256745	0.104811	0.015180	0.000021
$\psi(u, 5)$	0.645282	0.563302	0.323909	0.158525	0.035142	0.000215
$\psi(u, 10)$	0.662159	0.583353	0.350278	0.183669	0.048960	0.000690
$\psi(u, 20)$	0.667863	0.590214	0.359799	0.193528	0.055637	0.001218

STFruin25.xpl

Similarly as in the Segerdahl approximation, the method requires existence of the moment generating function, so we can use it only for light-tailed distributions.

In Table 15.21 the results of the corrected diffusion approximation for mixture of two exponentials claims with β_1, β_2, a with respect to the initial capital u and the time horizon T are given. The relative safety loading θ is set to 30%. It turns out that corrected diffusion method gives surprisingly good results and is vastly superior to the ordinary diffusion approximation, cf. the reference values in Table 15.18.

15.6.5 Finite Time De Vylder Approximation

Let us recall the idea of the De Vylder approximation in infinite time: we replace the claim surplus process with the one with $\theta = \bar{\theta}$, $\lambda = \bar{\lambda}$ and exponential claims with parameter $\bar{\beta}$, fitting first three moments, see Section 15.3.6. Here, the idea is the same. First, we compute

$$\bar{\beta} = \frac{3\mu^{(2)}}{\mu^{(3)}}, \qquad \bar{\lambda} = \frac{9\lambda \mu^{(2)^3}}{2\mu^{(3)^2}}, \qquad \text{and} \qquad \bar{\theta} = \frac{2\mu\mu^{(3)}}{3\mu^{(2)^2}}\theta.$$

Next, we employ relations (15.27) and (15.28) and finally use the exact, exponential case formula presented in Section 15.5.1.

Obviously, the method gives the exact result in the exponential case. For other claim distributions, the first three moments have to exist in order to apply the approximation.

Table 15.22 shows the results of the finite time De Vylder approximation for mixture of two exponentials claims with β_1, β_2, a with respect to the initial capital u and the time horizon T. The relative safety loading $\theta = 30\%$. We see that the approximation gives even better results than the corrected diffusion one, cf. the reference values presented in Table 15.18.

15.6.6 Summary of the Approximations

Table 15.23 shows which approximation can be used for each claim size distribution. Moreover, the necessary assumptions on the distribution parameters are presented.

Table 15.23: Survey of approximations with an indication when they can be applied

Distrib. / Method	Exp.	Gamma	Weibull	Mix. Exp.	Log-normal	Pareto	Burr
Monte Carlo	+	+	+	+	+	+	+
Segerdahl	+	+	–	+	–	–	–
Diffusion	+	+	+	+	+	$\alpha > 2$	$\alpha\tau > 2$
Corr. diff.	+	+	–	+	–	–	–
Fin. De Vylder	+	+	+	+	+	$\alpha > 3$	$\alpha\tau > 3$

15.7 Numerical Comparison of the Finite Time Approximations

Now, we illustrate all 5 approximations presented in Section 15.6. As in the infinite time case we consider three claim amount distributions which were best fitted to the catastrophe data in Chapter 13, namely the mixture of two exponentials (a running example in Sections 15.3 and 15.6), log-normal and Pareto distributions. The parameters of the distributions are: $\beta_1 = 3.5900 \cdot 10^{-10}$, $\beta_2 = 7.5088 \cdot 10^{-9}$, $a = 0.0584$ (mixture), $\mu = 18.3806$, $\sigma = 1.1052$

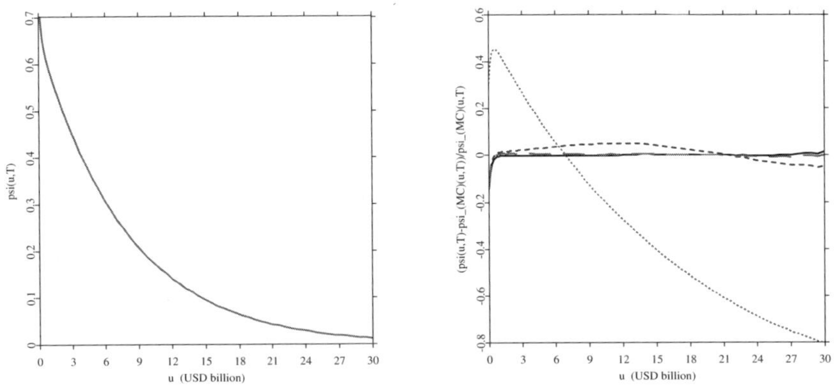

Figure 15.6: The exact ruin probability obtained via Monte Carlo simulations (left panel), the relative error of the approximations (right panel). The Segerdahl (short-dashed blue line), diffusion (dotted red line), corrected diffusion (solid black line) and finite time De Vylder (long-dashed green line) approximations. The mixture of two exponentials case with T fixed and u varying.

STFruin26.xpl

(log-normal), and $\alpha = 3.4081$, $\lambda = 4.4767 \cdot 10^8$ (Pareto). The ruin probability will be depicted as a function of u, ranging from USD 0 to 30 billion, with fixed $T = 10$ or with fixed value of $u = 20$ billion USD and varying T from 0 to 20 years. The relative safety loading is set to 30%. Figures has the same form of output. In the left panel, the exact ruin probability values obtained via Monte Carlo simulations are presented. The right panel describes the relative error with respect to the exact values. We also note that for the Monte Carlo method purposes we generated 50 x 10000 simulations.

First, we consider the mixture of two exponentials case. As we can see in Figures 15.6 and 15.7 the diffusion approximation almost for all values of u and T gives highly incorrect results. Segerdahl and corrected diffusion approximations yield similar error, which visibly decreases when the time horizon gets bigger. The finite time De Vylder method is a unanimous winner and always gives the error below 10%.

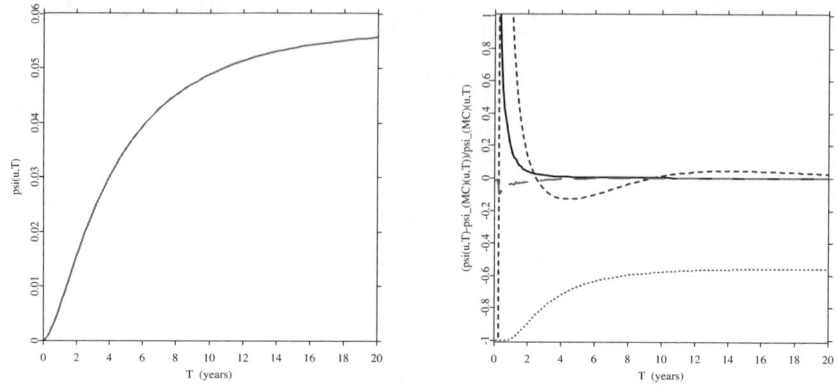

Figure 15.7: The exact ruin probability obtained via Monte Carlo simulations (left panel), the relative error of the approximations (right panel). The Segerdahl (short-dashed blue line), diffusion (dotted red line), corrected diffusion (solid black line) and finite time De Vylder (long-dashed green line) approximations. The mixture of two exponentials case with u fixed and T varying.

`STFruin27.xpl`

In the case of log-normally distributed claims, we can only apply two approximations: diffusion and finite time De Vylder ones, cf. Table 15.23. Figures 15.8 and 15.9 depict the exact ruin probability values obtained via Monte Carlo simulations and the relative error with respect to the exact values. Again, the finite time De Vylder approximation works much better than the diffusion one.

Finally, we take into consideration the Pareto claim size distribution. Figures 15.10 and 15.11 depict the exact ruin probability values and the relative error with respect to the exact values for the diffusion and finite time De Vylder approximations. We see that now we cannot claim which approximation is better. The error strongly depends on the values of u and T. We may only suspect that a combination of the two methods could give interesting results.

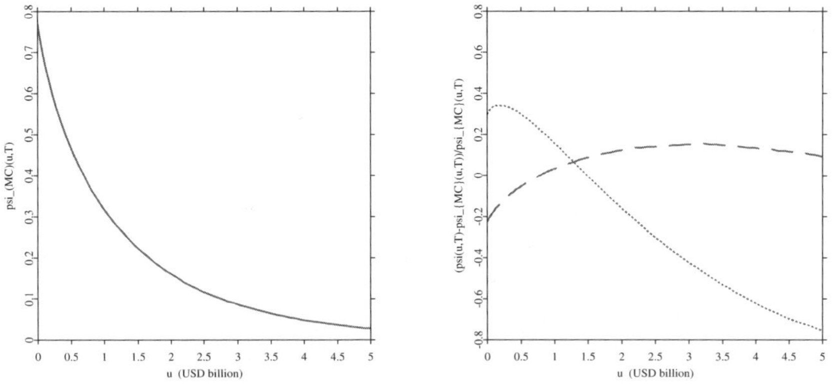

Figure 15.8: The exact ruin probability obtained via Monte Carlo simulations (left panel), the relative error of the approximations (right panel). Diffusion (dotted red line) and finite time De Vylder (long-dashed green line) approximations. The log-normal case with T fixed and u varying.

STFruin28.xpl

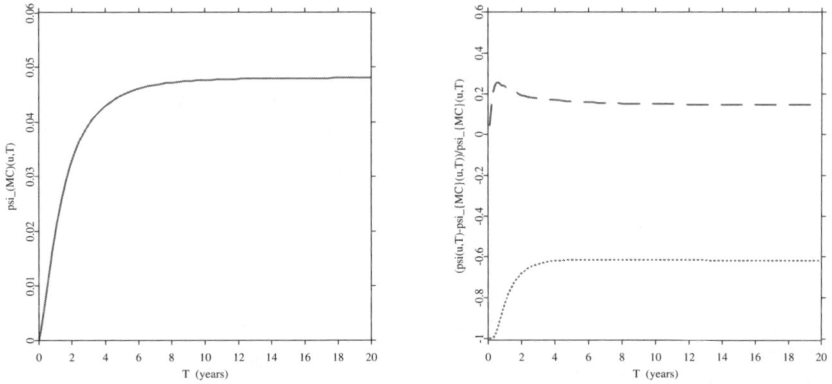

Figure 15.9: The exact ruin probability obtained via Monte Carlo simulations (left panel), the relative error of the approximations (right panel). Diffusion (dotted red line) and finite time De Vylder (long-dashed green line) approximations. The log-normal case with u fixed and T varying.

STFruin29.xpl

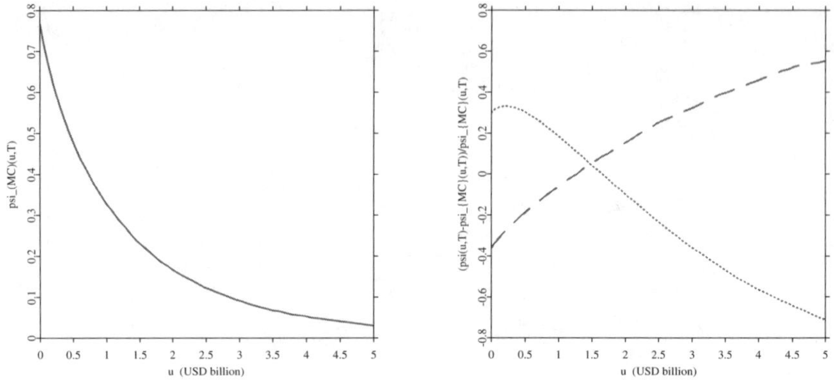

Figure 15.10: The exact ruin probability obtained via Monte Carlo simulations (left panel), the relative error of the approximations (right panel). Diffusion (dotted red line) and finite time De Vylder (long-dashed green line) approximations. The Pareto case with T fixed and u varying.

STFruin30.xpl

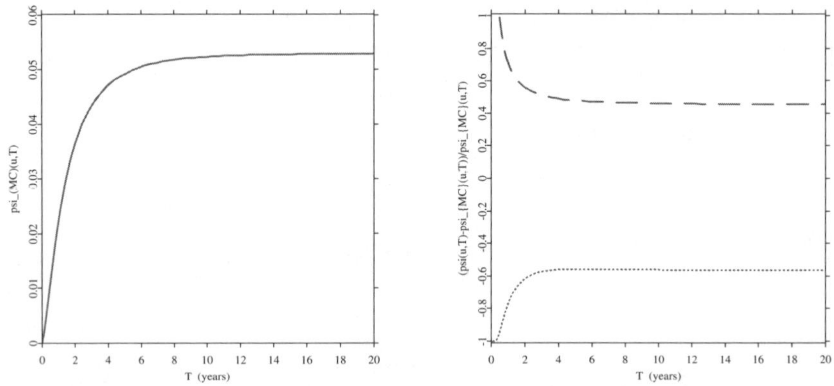

Figure 15.11: The exact ruin probability obtained via Monte Carlo simulations (left panel), the relative error of the approximations (right panel). Diffusion (dotted red line) and finite time De Vylder (long-dashed green line) approximations. The Pareto case with u fixed and T varying.

STFruin31.xpl

Bibliography

Asmussen, S. (2000). *Ruin Probabilities*, World Scientific, Singapore.

Burnecki, K., Miśta, P., and Weron A. (2003). A New De Vylder Type Approximation of the Ruin Probability in Infinite Time, Research Report HSC/03/05.

Burnecki, K., Miśta, P., and Weron A. (2005). What is the Best Approximation of Ruin Probability in Infinite Time?, *Appl. Math. (Warsaw)* **32**.

De Vylder, F.E. (1978). A Practical Solution to the Problem of Ultimate Ruin Probability, *Scand. Actuar. J.*: 114–119.

De Vylder, F.E. (1996). *Advanced Risk Theory. A Self-Contained Introduction*, Editions de l'Université de Bruxelles and Swiss Association of Actuaries.

Embrechts, P., Kaufmann, R., and Samorodnitsky, G. (2004). Ruin Theory Revisited: Stochastic Models for Operational Risk, *in* C. Bernadell et al (eds.) *Risk Management for Central Bank Foreign Reserves*, European Central Bank, Frankfurt a.M., 243-261.

Embrechts, P., Klüppelberg, C., and Mikosch, T. (1997). *Modelling Extremal Events for Insurance and Finance*, Springer, Berlin.

Furrer, H., Michna, Z., and Weron A. (1997). Stable Lévy Motion Approximation in Collective Risk Theory, *Insurance Math. Econom.* **20**: 97–114.

Grandell, J. and Segerdahl, C.-O. (1971). A Comparison of Some Approximations of Ruin Probabilities, *Skand. Aktuarietidskr.*: 144–158.

Grandell, J. (1991). *Aspects of Risk Theory*, Springer, New York.

Grandell, J. (2000). Simple Approximations of Ruin Probability, *Insurance Math. Econom.* **26**: 157–173.

Panjer, H.H. and Willmot, G.E. (1992). *Insurance Risk Models*, Society of Actuaries, Schaumburg.

Segerdahl, C.-O. (1955). When Does Ruin Occur in the Collective Theory of Risk?, *Skand. Aktuarietidskr.* **38**: 22–36.

Wikstad, N. (1971). Exemplification of Ruin Probabilities, *Astin Bulletin* **6**: 147–152.

16 Stable Diffusion Approximation of the Risk Process

Hansjörg Furrer, Zbigniew Michna, and Aleksander Weron

16.1 Introduction

Collective risk theory is concerned with random fluctuations of the total net assets – the capital of an insurance company. Consider a company which only writes ordinary insurance policies such as accident, disability, health and whole life. The policyholders pay premiums regularly and at certain random times make claims to the company. A policyholder's premium, the gross risk premium, is a positive amount composed of two components. The net risk premium is the component calculated to cover the payments of claims on the average, while the security risk premium, or safety loading, is the component which protects the company from large deviations of claims from the average and also allows an accumulation of capital. So the risk process has the Cramér-Lundberg form:

$$R(t) = u + ct - \sum_{k=1}^{N(t)} Y_k,$$

where $u > 0$ is the initial capital (in some cases interpreted as the initial risk reserve) of the company and the policyholders pay a gross risk premium of $c > 0$ per unit time, see also Chapter 14. The successive claims $\{Y_k\}$ are assumed to form a sequence of i.i.d. random variables with mean $\mathrm{E}Y_k = \mu$ and claims occur at jumps of a point process $N(t)$, $t \geq 0$.

The ruin time T is defined as the first time the company has a negative capital, see Chapter 15. One of the key problems of collective risk theory concerns calculating the ultimate ruin probability $\Psi = \mathrm{P}(T < \infty | R(0) = u)$, i.e. the probability that the risk process ever becomes negative. On the other hand, an insurance company will typically be interested in the probability that ruin occurs before time t, i.e. $\Psi(t) = \mathrm{P}(T < t | R(0) = u)$. However, many of the results available in the literature are in the form of complicated analytic expressions (for a comprehensive treatment of the theory see e.g. Asmussen, 2000; Embrechts, Klüppelberg, and Mikosch, 1997; Rolski et al., 1999). Hence, some authors have proposed to approximate the risk process by Brownian diffusion, see Iglehart (1969) and Schmidli (1994). The idea is to let the number of claims grow in a unit time interval and to make the claim sizes smaller in such a way that the risk process converges weakly to the diffusion.

In this chapter we present weak convergence theory applied to approximate the risk process by Brownian motion and α-stable Lévy motion. We investigate two different approximations. The first one assumes that the distribution of claim sizes belongs to the domain of attraction of the normal law, i.e. claims are small. In the second model we consider claim sizes belonging to the domain of attraction of the α-stable law ($1 < \alpha < 2$), i.e. large claims. The latter approximation is particularly relevant whenever the claim experience allows for heavy-tailed distributions. As the empirical results presented in Chapter 13 show, at least for the catastrophic losses the assumption of heavy-tailed severities is statistically justified. While the classical theory of Brownian diffusion approximation requires short-tailed claims, this assumption can be dropped in our approach, hence allowing for extremal events. Furthermore, employing approximations of risk processes by Brownian motion and α-stable Lévy motion we obtain formulas for ruin probabilities in finite and infinite time horizons.

16.2 Brownian Motion and the Risk Model for Small Claims

This section will be devoted to the Brownian motion approximation in risk theory and will be based on the work of Iglehart (1969). We assume that the distribution of the claim sizes belongs to the domain of attraction of the normal law. Thus, such claims attain big values with small probabilities. This assumption will cover many practical situations in which the claim size distribution possesses a finite second moment and claims constitute an i.i.d. sequence. The claims counting process does not have to be independent of the sequence of claim sizes as it is assumed in many risk models and, in general, can be a renewal process constructed from random variables having a finite first moment.

16.2.1 Weak Convergence of Risk Processes to Brownian Motion

Let us consider a sequence of risk processes $R_n(t)$ defined in the following way:

$$R_n(t) = u_n + c_n t - \sum_{k=1}^{N(nt)} Y_k^{(n)}, \tag{16.1}$$

where u_n is the initial, c_n is the premium payed by policyholders, and the sequence $\{Y_k^{(n)} : k \in \mathbb{N}\}$ describes the consecutive claim sizes. Assume also that $\mathrm{E}Y_k^{(n)} = \mu_n$ and $\mathrm{Var}Y_k^{(n)} = \sigma_n^2$. The point process $N = \{N(t) : t \geq 0\}$ counts claims appearing up to time t that is:

$$N(t) = \max\left\{k : \sum_{i=1}^{k} T_i \leq t\right\}, \tag{16.2}$$

where $\{T_k : k \in \mathbb{N}\}$ is an i.i.d. sequence of nonnegative random variables describing the times between arriving claims with $\mathrm{E}T_k = 1/\lambda > 0$. Recall that if T_k are exponentially distributed then $N(t)$ is a Poisson process with intensity λ.

To approximate the risk process by Brownian motion, we assume $n^{-1/2}u_n \to u$, $n^{-1/2}c_n \to c$, $n^{1/2}\mu_n \to \mu$, $\sigma_n^2 \to \sigma^2$, and $\mathrm{E}\left(Y_k^{(n)}\right)^{2+\varepsilon} \leq M$ for some $\varepsilon > 0$ where M is independent of n. Then:

$$\frac{1}{n^{1/2}} R_n(t) \xrightarrow{\mathcal{L}} u + (c - \mu\lambda)t + \sigma\lambda^{1/2}B(t) \tag{16.3}$$

weakly in topology U (uniform convergence on compact sets). Let us denote by $R_B(t)$ the limit process from the above approximation, i.e.:

$$R_B(t) = u + (c - \mu\lambda)t + \sigma\lambda^{1/2}B(t). \tag{16.4}$$

Property (16.3) let us approximate the risk process by $R_B(t)$ for which it is possible to derive exact formulas for ruin probabilities in finite and infinite time horizons.

16.2.2 Ruin Probability for the Limit Process

Weak convergence of stochastic processes does not imply the convergence of ruin probabilities in general. Thus, to take the advantage of the Brownian motion approximations it is necessary to show that the ruin probability in finite and infinite time horizons of risk processes converges to the ruin probabilities of Brownian motion. Let us define the ruin time:

$$T(R) = \inf\{t > 0 : R(t) < 0\}, \tag{16.5}$$

if the set is non-empty and $T = \infty$ in other cases. Then $T(R_n) \to T(R_B)$ almost surely if $R_n \to R_B$ almost surely as $n \to \infty$ and $\mathrm{P}\{T(R_n) < \infty\} \to \mathrm{P}\{T(R_B) < \infty\}$. Thus we need to find formulas for the ruin probabilities of the process R_B. Let R_B be the Brownian motion with the linear drift defined in (16.4). Then

$$\mathrm{P}\{T(R_B) < \infty\} = \exp\left\{-2\frac{u(c-\lambda\mu)}{\sigma^2\lambda}\right\} \tag{16.6}$$

and

$$\begin{aligned} \mathrm{P}\{T(R_B) \le t\} &= 1 - \Phi\left\{\frac{u+(c-\lambda\mu)t}{\sigma(\lambda t)^{1/2}}\right\} \\ &+ \exp\left\{\frac{-2u(c-\lambda\mu)}{\sigma^2\lambda}\right\}\left[1 - \Phi\left\{\frac{u-(c-\lambda\mu)t}{\sigma(\lambda t)^{1/2}}\right\}\right]. \end{aligned} \tag{16.7}$$

It is also possible to determine the density distribution of the ruin time. Let $T(R_B)$ be the ruin time of the process (16.4). Then the density f_T of the random variable $T(R_B)$ has the following form

$$f_T(t) = \frac{\beta^{-1}e^{\alpha\beta}}{(2\pi)^{2/3}} t^{-3/2} \exp\left[-\frac{1}{2}\{\beta^2 t^{-1} + (\alpha\beta)^2 t\}\right], \quad t > 0,$$

where $\alpha = (c-\lambda\mu)/\sigma\lambda^{1/2}$ and $\beta = u/\sigma\lambda^{1/2}$.

The Brownian model is an approximation of the risk process in the case when the distribution of claim sizes belongs to the domain of attraction of the normal law and the assumptions imposed on the risk process indicate that from the point of view of an insurance company the number of claims is large and the sizes of claims are small.

16.2.3 Examples

Let us consider a risk model where the distribution of claim sizes belongs to the domain of attraction of the normal law and the process counting the number of

Table 16.1: Ruin probabilities for the Brownian motion approximation. Parameters $\mu = 20, \sigma = 10$, and $t = 10$ are fixed.

u	c	λ	$\Psi(t)$	Ψ
25	50	2	8.0842e-02	8.2085e-02
25	60	2	6.7379e-03	6.7379e-03
30	60	2	2.4787e-03	2.4787e-03
35	60	2	9.1185e-04	9.1188e-04
40	60	2	3.3544e-04	3.3546e-04
40	70	3	6.5282e-02	6.9483e-02

STFdiff01.xpl

claims is a renewal counting process constructed from i.i.d. random variables with a finite first moment. Let $R(t)$ be the following risk process

$$R(t) = u + ct - \sum_{n=1}^{N(t)} Y_k \, , \tag{16.8}$$

where u is the initial capital, c is the premium income in the unit time interval and $\{Y_k : k \in \mathbb{N}\}$ are i.i.d. random variables belonging to the domain of attraction of the normal law. Moreover, $\mathrm{E}Y_k = \mu$, $\mathrm{Var}Y_k = \sigma^2$ and the intensity of arriving claims is λ (reciprocal of the expectation of claims inter-arrivals). Thus, we obtain:

$$\mathrm{P}\{T(R) \le t\} \approx \mathrm{P}\{T(R_B) \le t\} \tag{16.9}$$

and

$$\mathrm{P}\{T(R) < \infty\} \approx \mathrm{P}\{T(R_B) < \infty\} \, , \tag{16.10}$$

where

$$R_B(t) = u + (c - \mu\lambda)t + \sigma\lambda^{1/2}B(t),$$

and $B(t)$ is the standard Brownian motion. Using the formulas for ruin probabilities in finite and infinite time horizons given in (16.6) and (16.7) we compute approximate values of ruin probabilities for different levels of initial capital, premium, intensity of claims, expectation of claims and their variance, see Table 16.1. A sample path of the process $R_B(t)$ is depicted in Figure 16.1.

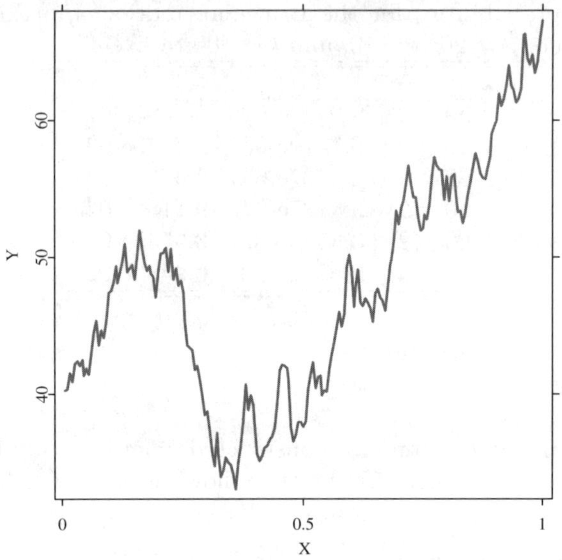

Figure 16.1: A sample path of the process R_B for $u = 40$, $c = 100$, $\mu = 20$, $\sigma = 10$, and $\lambda = 3$.

STFdiff02.xpl

16.3 Stable Lévy Motion and the Risk Model for Large Claims

In this section we present approximations of the risk process by α-stable Lévy motion. We assume that claims are large, i.e. that the distribution of their sizes is heavy-tailed. More precisely, we let the claim sizes distribution belong to the domain of attraction of the α-stable law with $1 < \alpha < 2$, see Weron (2001) and Chapter 1. This is an extension of the Brownian motion approximation approach. Note, however, that the methods and theory presented here are quite different from those used in the previous section (Weron, 1984).

We assume that claim sizes constitute an i.i.d. sequence and that the claim counting process does not have to be independent of the sequence of the claim sizes and, in general, can be a counting renewal process constructed from the random variables having a finite second moment. This model can be applied when claims are caused by earthquakes, floods, tornadoes, and other natural disasters. In fact, the catastrophic losses dataset studied in Chapter 13 reveals a very heavy-tailed nature of the severity distribution. The best fit was obtained for a Burr law with $\alpha = 0.4801$ and $\tau = 2.1524$, which indicates a power-law decay of order $\alpha\tau = 1.0334$ of the claim sizes distribution. Naturally, such a distribution belongs to the domain of attraction of the α-stable law with $1 < \alpha < 2$.

16.3.1 Weak Convergence of Risk Processes to α-stable Lévy Motion

We construct a sequence of risk processes converging weakly to the α-stable Lévy motion. Let $R_n(t)$ be a sequence of risk processes defined as follows:

$$R_n(t) = u_n + c_n t - \sum_{k=1}^{N^{(n)}(t)} Y_k^{(n)}, \tag{16.11}$$

where u_n is the initial capital, c_n is the premium rate, $\{Y_k^{(n)} : k \in \mathbb{N}\}$ is a sequence describing the sizes of the consecutive claims, and $N^{(n)}(t)$, for every $n \in \mathbb{N}$, is a point process counting the number of claims. Moreover, we assume that the random variables representing the claim sizes are of the following form

$$Y_k^{(n)} = \frac{1}{\varphi(n)} Y_k, \tag{16.12}$$

where $\{Y_k : k \in \mathbb{N}\}$ is a sequence of i.i.d. random variables with distribution F and expectation $\mathrm{E}Y_k = \mu$. The normalizing function $\varphi(n) = n^{1/\alpha} L(n)$, where L is a slowly varying function at infinity. As before it is not necessary to assume that the random variables Y_k are non-negative, however, this time we assume that they belong to the domain of attraction of an α-stable law, that is:

$$\frac{1}{\varphi(n)} \sum_{k=1}^{n} (Y_k - \mu) \xrightarrow{\mathcal{L}} Z_{\alpha,\beta}(1), \tag{16.13}$$

where $Z_{\alpha,\beta}(t)$ is the α-stable Lévy motion with scale parameter σ', skewness parameter β, and $1 < \alpha < 2$. For details see Janicki and Weron (1994) and Samorodnitsky and Taqqu (1994).

Let $R_\alpha(t)$ be the α-stable Lévy motion with a linear drift

$$R_\alpha(t) = u + ct - \lambda^{1/\alpha} Z_{\alpha,\beta}(t), \tag{16.14}$$

where u, c, and λ are positive constants. Let $\{Y_k\}$ be the sequence of the random variable defined above, $\{N^{(n)}\}$ be a sequence of point processes satisfying

$$\frac{N^{(n)}(t) - \lambda nt}{\varphi(n)} \xrightarrow{\mathcal{L}} 0, \tag{16.15}$$

where $\xrightarrow{\mathcal{L}}$ denotes weak convergence in the Skorokhod topology, and λ is a positive constant. Moreover, we assume

$$\lim_{n\to\infty} \left(c^{(n)} - \lambda n \frac{\mu}{\varphi(n)} \right) = c \tag{16.16}$$

and

$$\lim_{n\to\infty} u^{(n)} = u \,. \tag{16.17}$$

Then

$$R_n(t) = u_n + c_n t - \frac{1}{\varphi(n)} \sum_{k=1}^{N^{(n)}(t)} Y_k \xrightarrow{\mathcal{L}} R_\alpha(t) = u + ct - \lambda^{1/\alpha} Z_{\alpha,\beta}(t), \tag{16.18}$$

when $n \to \infty$, for details see Furrer, Michna, and Weron (1997).

Assumption (16.15) is satisfied for a wide class of point processes. For example, if the times between consecutive claims constitute i.i.d. sequence with the distribution possessing a finite second moment. We should also notice that the skewness parameter β equals 1 for the process $R_\alpha(t)$ if the random variables $\{Y_k\}$ are non-negative.

16.3.2 Ruin Probability in the Limit Risk Model for Large Claims

As in the Brownian motion approximation it can be shown that the finite and infinite time ruin probabilities converge to the ruin probabilities of the limit process. Thus it remains to derive ruin probabilities for the process $R_\alpha(t)$ defined in (16.18). We present asymptotic behavior for ruin probabilities in finite and infinite time horizons and an exact formula for infinite time ruin probability. An upper bound for finite time ruin probability will be shown.

First, we derive the asymptotic ruin probability for the finite time horizon. Let T be the ruin time (17.11) and $Z_{\alpha,\beta}(t)$ be the α-stable Lévy motion with $0 < \alpha < 2$, $-1 < \beta \le 1$, and scale parameter σ'. Then:

$$\lim_{u\to\infty} \frac{\mathrm{P}\{T(u+cs-\lambda^{1/\alpha}Z_{\alpha,\beta}(s)) \le t\}}{\mathrm{P}\{\lambda^{1/\alpha}Z_{\alpha,\beta}(t) > u+ct\}} = 1\,, \tag{16.19}$$

see Furrer, Michna, and Weron (1997) and Willekens (1987).

Using the asymptotic behavior of probability $\mathrm{P}\{\lambda^{1/\alpha}Z_{\alpha,\beta}(t) > u+ct\}$ when $u \to \infty$ for $1 < \alpha < 2$, we get (Samorodnitsky and Taqqu, 1994, Prop. 1.2.15) that

$$\mathrm{P}\{T(u+cs-\lambda^{1/\alpha}Z_{\alpha,\beta}(s)) \le t\} \approx C_\alpha \frac{1+\beta}{2}\lambda(\sigma')^\alpha t(u+ct)^{-\alpha}\,, \tag{16.20}$$

where

$$C_\alpha = \frac{1-\alpha}{\Gamma(2-\alpha)\cos(\pi\alpha/2)}. \tag{16.21}$$

The asymptotic ruin probability in the finite time horizon is a lower bound for the finite time ruin probability. Let $Z_{\alpha,\beta}(t)$ be the α-stable Lévy motion with $\alpha \ne 1$ and $|\beta| \le 1$ or $\alpha = 1$ and $\beta = 0$. Then for positive u, c, and λ:

$$\mathrm{P}\{T(u+cs-\lambda^{1/\alpha}Z_{\alpha,\beta}(s)) \le t\} \le \frac{\mathrm{P}\{\lambda^{1/\alpha}Z_{\alpha,\beta}(t) > u+ct\}}{P\{\lambda^{1/\alpha}Z_{\alpha,\beta}(t) > ct\}}\,. \tag{16.22}$$

Now, we consider infinite time ruin probability for the α-stable Lévy motion. It turns out that for $\beta = 1$ it is possible to give an exact formula for the ruin probability in the infinite time horizon. If $Z_{\alpha,\beta}(t)$ is the α-stable Lévy motion with $1 < \alpha < 2$, $\beta = 1$, and scale parameter σ' then for positive u, c, and λ, Furrer (1998) showed that

$$\mathrm{P}\{T(u+cs-\lambda^{1/\alpha}Z_{\alpha,\beta}(s)) < \infty\} = \sum_{n=0}^{\infty} \frac{(-a)^n}{\Gamma\{1+(\alpha-1)n\}}u^{(\alpha-1)n}\,, \tag{16.23}$$

where $a = c\lambda^{-1}(\sigma')^{-\alpha}\cos\{\pi(\alpha-2)/2\}$.

In general, for an arbitrary β we can obtain asymptotic behavior for infinite time ruin probabilities when the initial capital tends to infinity. Now, let $Z_{\alpha,\beta}(t)$ be the α-stable Lévy motion with $1 < \alpha < 2$, $-1 < \beta \le 1$, and scale parameter σ'. Then for positive u, c, and λ we have (Port, 1989, Theorem 9):

$$\mathrm{P}\{T(u+cs-\lambda^{1/\alpha}Z_{\alpha,\beta}(s)) < \infty\} = \frac{A(\alpha,\beta)\lambda(\sigma')^\alpha}{\alpha(\alpha-1)c}u^{-\alpha+1} + o(u^{-\alpha+1}) \tag{16.24}$$

when $u \to \infty$, where

$$A(\alpha,\beta) = \frac{\Gamma(1+\alpha)}{\pi}\sqrt{1+\beta^2\tan^2\left(\frac{\pi\alpha}{2}\right)}\sin\left[\frac{\pi\alpha}{2}+\arctan\{\beta\tan\left(\frac{\pi\alpha}{2}\right)\}\right].$$

For completeness it remains to consider the case $\beta = -1$, which is quite different because the right tail of the distribution of the α-stable law with $\beta = -1$ does not behave like a power function but like an exponential function (i.e. it is not a heavy tail). Let $Z_{\alpha,\beta}(t)$ be the α-stable Lévy motion with $1 < \alpha < 2$, $\beta = -1$, and scale parameter σ'. Then for positive u, c, and λ:

$$\mathrm{P}\{T(u + cs - \lambda^{1/\alpha} Z_{\alpha,\beta}(s)) < \infty\} = \exp\{-a^{1/(\alpha-1)}u\}, \tag{16.25}$$

where a is as above.

16.3.3 Examples

Let us assume that the sequence of claims is i.i.d. and their distribution belongs to the domain of attraction of the α-stable law with $1 < \alpha < 2$. Let $R(t)$ be the following risk process

$$R(t) = u + ct - \sum_{n=1}^{N(t)} Y_k, \tag{16.26}$$

where u is the initial capital, c is a premium rate payed by the policyholders, and $\{Y_k : k \in \mathbb{N}\}$ is an i.i.d. sequence with the distribution belonging to the domain of attraction of the α-stable law with $1 < \alpha < 2$, that is fulfilling (16.13). Moreover, let $\mathrm{E}Y_k = \mu$ and the claim intensity be λ. Similarly as in the Brownian motion approximation we obtain:

$$\mathrm{P}\{T(R) \le t\} \approx \mathrm{P}\{T(R_\alpha) \le t\}, \tag{16.27}$$

and

$$\mathrm{P}\{T(R) < \infty\} \approx \mathrm{P}\{T(R_\alpha) < \infty\}, \tag{16.28}$$

where

$$R_\alpha(t) = u + (c - \lambda\mu)t - \lambda^{1/\alpha} Z_\alpha(t),$$

and $Z_\alpha(t)$ is the α-stable Lévy motion with $\beta = 1$ and scale parameter σ'. The scale parameter can be calibrated using the asymptotic results of Mijnheer (1975), see also Samorodnitsky and Taqqu (1994, p. 50).

Table 16.2: Ruin probabilities for $\alpha = 1.0334$ and fixed $\mu = 20, \sigma = 10$, and $t = 10$.

u	c	λ	$\Psi(t)$	Ψ
25	50	2	0.45896	0.94780
25	60	2	0.25002	0.90076
30	60	2	0.24440	0.90022
35	60	2	0.23903	0.89976
40	60	2	0.23389	0.89935
40	70	3	0.61235	0.96404

STFdiff03.xpl

Table 16.3: Ruin probabilities for $\alpha = 1.5$ and fixed $\mu = 20, \sigma = 10$, and $t = 10$.

u	c	λ	$\Psi(t)$	Ψ
25	50	2	9.0273e-02	0.39735
25	60	2	3.7381e-02	0.23231
30	60	2	3.6168e-02	0.21461
35	60	2	3.5020e-02	0.20046
40	60	2	3.3932e-02	0.18880
40	70	3	1.1424e-01	0.44372

STFdiff04.xpl

For $\alpha = 2$, the standard deviation $\sigma = \sqrt{2}\sigma'$. Hence, it is reasonable to put $\sigma' = 2^{-1/\alpha}\sigma$ in the general case. In this way we can compare the results for the two approximations. Using (16.20) and (16.23) we compute the finite and infinite time ruin probabilities for different levels of initial capital, premium, intensity of claims, expectation of claims and their scale parameter, see Tables 16.2 and 16.3. A sample path of the process R_α is depicted in Figure 16.2.

The results in the tables show the effects of the heaviness of the claim size distribution tails on the crucial parameter for insurance companies – the ruin probability. It is clearly visible that a decrease of α increases the ruin probability. The tables also illustrate the relationship between the ruin probability and the initial capital u, premium c, intensity of claims λ, expectation of claims μ and their scale parameter σ'. For the heavy-tailed claim distributions the ruin

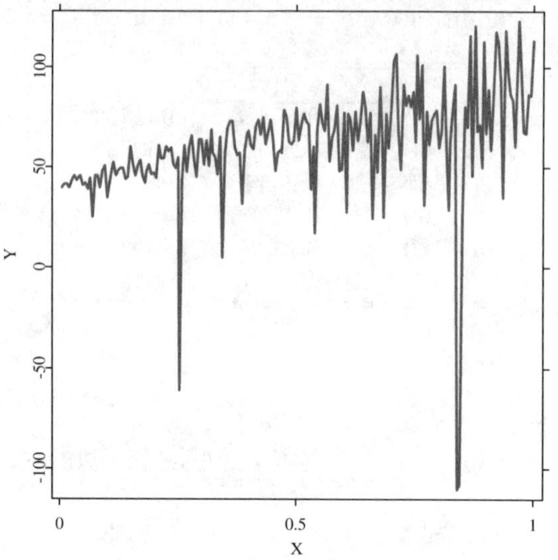

Figure 16.2: A sample path of the process R_α for $\alpha = 1.5$, $u = 40$, $c = 100$, $\mu = 20$, $\sigma = 10$, and $\lambda = 3$.

STFdiff05.xpl

probability is considerably higher than for the light-tailed claim distributions. Thus the estimation of the stability parameter α from real data is crucial for the choice of the premium c.

Bibliography

Asmussen, S. (2000). *Ruin Probabilities*, World Scientific, Singapore.

Embrechts, P., Klüppelberg, C., and Mikosch, T. (1997). *Modeling Extremal Events for Insurance and Finance*, Springer, Berlin.

Furrer, H. (1998). Risk processes perturbed by α-stable Lévy motion, *Scandinavian Actuarial Journal* **10**: 23–35.

Furrer, H., Michna, Z. and Weron A. (1997). Stable Lévy motion approximation in collective risk theory, *Insurance: Mathematics and Economics* **20**: 97–114.

Iglehart, D. L. (1969). Diffusion approximations in collective risk theory, *Journal of Applied Probability* **6**: 285–292.

Janicki, A. and Weron, A. (1994). *Simulation and Chaotic Behavior of α–Stable Stochastic Processes*, Marcel Dekker, New York.

Mijnheer, J. L. (1975). Sample path properties of stable processes, *Mathematical Centre Tracts* **59**, Mathematical Centrum Amsterdam.

Port, S. C. (1989). Stable processes with drift on the line, *Trans. Amer. Math. Soc.* **313**: 201–212.

Rolski, T., Schmidli, H., Schmidt, V. and Teugels, J. (1999). *Stochastic Processes for Insurance and Finance*, John Wiley and Sons, New York.

Samorodnitsky, G. and Taqqu, M. (1994). *Non–Gaussian Stable Processes: Stochastic Models with Infinite Variance*, Chapman and Hall, London.

Schmidli, H. (1994). Diffusion approximations for a risk process with the possibility of borrowing and investment, *Stochastic Models* **10**: 365-388.

Weron, A. (1984). Stable processes and measures: A survey. *in* Probability Theory on Vector Spaces III, D. Szynal, A. Weron (eds.), *Lecture Notes in Mathematics* **1080**: 306–364.

Weron, R. (2001). Lévy-stable distributions revisited: tail index > 2 does not exclude the Lévy-stable regime, *International Journal of Modern Physics C* **12**: 200–223.

Willekens, E. (1987). On the supremum of an infinitely divisible process, *Stoch. Proc. Appl.* **26**: 173–175.

17 Risk Model of Good and Bad Periods

Zbigniew Michna

17.1 Introduction

Classical insurance risk models rely on independent increments of the corresponding risk process. However, this assumption can be very restrictive in modeling natural events. For example, Müller and Pflug (2001) found a significant correlation of claims related to tornados in the USA. To cope with these observations we present here a risk model producing positively correlated claims. In the recent years such models have been extensively investigated by Gerber (1981; 1982), Promislov (1991), Michna (1998), Nyrhinen (1998; 1999a; 1999b), Asmussen (1999), and Müller and Pflug (2001).

We consider a model where the time of the year influences claims. For example, seasonal weather fluctuations affect the size and quantity of damages in car accidents, intensive rains can cause abnormal damage to households. We assume the existence of good and bad periods for the insurance company in the sense of different expected values for claim sizes. This structure of good and bad periods produces a dependence of claims such that the resulting risk process can be approximated by the fractional Brownian motion with a linear drift. Explicit asymptotic formulas and numerical results can be derived for different levels of the dependence structure. As we will see the dependence of claims affects a crucial parameter for the risk exposure of the insurance company – the ruin probability.

Recall that the ruin time T is defined as the first time the company has a negative capital. One of the key problems of collective risk theory concerns calculating the ultimate ruin probability $\Psi = \mathrm{P}(T < \infty)$, i.e. the probability that the risk process ever becomes negative. On the other hand, the insurance company will typically be interested in the probability that ruin occurs before time t, that is $\Psi(t) = \mathrm{P}(T \leq t)$. In the next section we present basic definitions and assumptions imposed on the model, and results which permit to approximate the risk process by fractional Brownian motion. Section 17.3 deals with bounds and asymptotic formulas for ruin probabilities. The last section is devoted to numerical results.

17.2 Fractional Brownian Motion and the Risk Model of Good and Bad Periods

In this section we describe fractional Brownian motion approximation in risk theory. We show that under suitable assumptions the risk process constructed from claims appearing in good and bad periods can be approximated by the fractional Brownian motion with a linear drift. Hence, we first introduce the definition of fractional Brownian motion and then construct the model.

A process B_H is called fractional Brownian motion if for some $0 < H \leq 1$:

1. $B_H(0) = 0$ almost surely.
2. B_H has strictly stationary increments, that is the random function $M_h(t) = B_H(t+h) - B_H(t)$, $h \geq 0$, is strictly stationary.
3. B_H is self-similar of order H denoted $H-ss$, that is $\mathcal{L}\{B_H(ct)\} = \mathcal{L}\{c^H B_H(t)\}$ in the sense of finite-dimensional distributions.
4. Finite dimensional distributions of B_H are Gaussian with $\mathrm{E}B_H(t) = 0$
5. B_H is almost surely continuous.

If not stated otherwise explicitly, we let the parameter of self-similarity satisfy $\frac{1}{2} < H < 1$. The concept of semi-stability was introduced by Lamperti (1962) and recently discussed in Embrechts and Maejima (2002). Mandelbrot and Van Ness (1968) call it self-similarity when appearing in conjunction with stationary increments, as it does here.

When we observe arriving claims we assume that we have good and bad periods (e.g. periods of good weather and periods of bad weather). These two periods alternate. Let $\{T_n^G, n \in \mathbb{N}\}$ be i.i.d. non-negative random variables representing good periods; similarly, let $\{S^B, S_n^B, n \in \mathbb{N}\}$ be i.i.d. non-negative random variables representing bad periods. The T's are assumed independent of the S's, the common distribution of good periods is F^G, and the distribution of bad periods is F^B. We assume that both F^G and F^B have finite means ν_G and ν_B, respectively, and we set $\nu = \nu_G + \nu_B$.

Consider the pure renewal sequence initiated by a good period $\{0, \sum_{i=1}^n (T_i^G + S_i^B), n \in \mathbb{N}\}$. The inter-arrival distribution is $F^G * F^B$ and the mean inter-arrival time is ν. This pure renewal process has a stationary version $\{D, D + \sum_{i=1}^n (T_i^G + S_i^B), n \in \mathbb{N}\}$, where D is a delay random variable (Asmussen, 1987). However, by defining the initial delay interval of length D this way, the interval does not decompose into a good and a bad period the way subsequent inter-arrival intervals do. Consequently, we turn to an alternative construction of the stationary renewal process to decompose the delay random variable D into a good and bad period. Define three independent random variables B, T_0^G, and S_0^B, which are independent of $(S^B, T_n^G, S_n^B, n \in \mathbb{N})$, as follows: B is a Bernoulli random variable with values in $\{0, 1\}$ and mass function

$$\mathrm{P}(B = 1) = \frac{\nu_G}{\nu} = 1 - \mathrm{P}(B = 0)$$

and

$$\mathrm{P}(T_0^G > x) = \int_x^\infty \frac{1 - F^G(s)}{\nu_G}\, ds \stackrel{\text{def}}{=} 1 - F_0^G(x),$$

$$\mathrm{P}(S_0^B > x) = \int_x^\infty \frac{1 - F^B(s)}{\nu_B}\, ds \stackrel{\text{def}}{=} 1 - F_0^B(x),$$

for $x > 0$. Define a delay random variable D_0 by

$$D_0 = (T_0^G + S^B)B + (1 - B)S_0^B$$

and a delayed renewal sequence by

$$\{S_n, n \geq 0\} \stackrel{\text{def}}{=} \left\{ D_0, D_0 + \sum_{i=1}^n (T_i^G + S_i^B), n \geq 0 \right\}.$$

One can verify that this delayed renewal sequence is stationary (Heath, Resnick, and Samorodnitsky, 1998).

We now define $L(t)$ to be 1 if t falls in a good period, and $L(t) = 0$ if t is in a bad period. More precisely, the process $\{L(t), t \geq 0\}$ is defined in terms of $\{S_n, n \geq 0\}$ as follows

$$L(t) = BI(0 \leq t < T_0^G) + \sum_{n=0}^\infty I(S_n \leq t < S_n + T_{n+1}^G). \tag{17.1}$$

The process $\{L(t), t \geq 0\}$ is strictly stationary and

$$\mathrm{P}\{L(t) = 1\} = \mathrm{E}L(t) = \frac{\nu_G}{\nu}.$$

Let $\{Y_n^G, n \geq 0\}$ be i.i.d. random variables representing claims appearing in good periods (e.g. Y_n^G describes a claim which may appear at the n-th moment in a good period). Similarly, let $\{Y_n^B, n \geq 0\}$ be i.i.d. random variables representing claims appearing in bad periods (e.g. Y_n^B describes a claim which may appear at the n-th moment in a bad period). We assume that $\{Y_n^G, n \geq 0\}$, $\{Y_n^B, n \geq 0\}$ and $\{L(t), t \geq 0\}$ are independent, $E(Y_0^G) = g < E(Y_0^B) = b$, and the second moments of Y_0^G and Y_0^B exist. Then the claim Y_n appearing at the n-th moment is

$$Y_n = L(n)Y_n^G + \{1 - L(n)\}Y_n^B, \quad n \geq 0. \tag{17.2}$$

Furthermore, the sequence $\{Y_n, n \geq 0\}$ is stationary.

Assume that

$$1 - F^G(t) = t^{-(C+1)}K(t), \tag{17.3}$$

for $t \to \infty$, $0 < C < 1$, where K is slowly varying at infinity. Moreover, assume that

$$1 - F^B(t) = o\{1 - F^G(t)\}, \tag{17.4}$$

as $t \to \infty$ and there exists an $n \geq 1$ such that $(F_G * F_B)^{*n}$ is nonsingular. Then

$$\mathrm{Cov}(Y_0, Y_n) \sim \frac{\nu_B^2(b-g)^2}{C\nu^3} n^{-C}K(n) \tag{17.5}$$

when $n \to \infty$ (Heath, Resnick, and Samorodnitsky, 1998).

We assumed that the good period dominates the bad period but one can approach the problem reversely (i.e. the bad period can dominate the good period) because of the symmetry of the good and bad period characteristics in the covariance function.

Assume that $\mathrm{E}Y_n = \mu$ and $\varphi(n) = n^H K(n)$, where K is a slowly varying function at infinity. Let the sequence $\{Y_k : k \in \mathbb{N}\}$ be as above and let $\{N^{(n)} : n \in \mathbb{N}\}$ be a sequence of point processes such that

$$\frac{N^{(n)}(t) - \lambda nt}{\varphi(n)} \xrightarrow{\mathcal{L}} 0 \tag{17.6}$$

weakly in the Skorokhod topology (Jacod and Shiryaev, 1987) for some positive constant λ. Assume also that

$$\lim_{n\to\infty}\left\{c^{(n)} - \lambda n \frac{\mu}{\varphi(n)}\right\} = c \tag{17.7}$$

and

$$\lim_{n\to\infty} u^{(n)} = u. \tag{17.8}$$

Then

$$u^{(n)} + c^{(n)}t - \frac{1}{\varphi(n)}\sum_{k=1}^{N^{(n)}(t)} Y_k \xrightarrow{\mathcal{L}} u + ct - \lambda^H B_H(t) \tag{17.9}$$

in the Skorokhod topology as $n \to \infty$. Condition (17.6) is satisfied for a wide class of point processes. For example, if the times between consecutive claims constitute an i.i.d. sequence with the distribution possessing a finite second moment.

17.3 Ruin Probability in the Limit Risk Model of Good and Bad Periods

Let us define

$$R_H(t) = u + ct - \lambda^H B_H(t), \tag{17.10}$$

where u, c, and λ are positive constants and the ruin time:

$$T(R_H) = \inf\{t > 0 : R_H(t) < 0\}, \tag{17.11}$$

if the set is non-empty and $T(R_H) = \infty$ otherwise.

The ruin probability of the process of (17.10) is given by (Michna, 1998):

$$\mathrm{P}\{T(R_H) \le t\} \le 1 - \Phi\left\{\frac{u+ct}{\sigma(\lambda t)^H}\right\} + \exp\left\{\frac{-2uct}{\sigma^2(\lambda t)^{2H}}\right\}\left[1 - \Phi\left\{\frac{u-ct}{\sigma(\lambda t)^H}\right\}\right], \tag{17.12}$$

where the functional T is given in (17.11) and $\sigma^2 = E\{B_H^2(1)\}$.

The next result enables us to approximate the ruin probability of the process $R_H(t)$ for a sufficiently large initial capital. For every $t > 0$:

$$\lim_{u\to\infty} \frac{P\{T(R_H) \le t\}}{P\{\lambda^H B_H(t) > u + ct\}} = 1, \tag{17.13}$$

where the functional T is given in (17.11).

Now, let us consider the infinite time ruin probability. The lower and upper bounds for the ruin probability are given by:

$$\mathrm{P}\{T(R_H) < \infty\} \geq 1 - \Phi\left\{\frac{u^{1-H}c^H}{\sigma(\lambda H)^H(1-H)^{1-H}}\right\}, \tag{17.14}$$

and

$$\mathrm{P}\{T(R_H) < \infty\} \leq \frac{2c}{\sqrt{8\pi}(1-H)}\int_0^\infty \exp\left\{-\frac{1}{2}\lambda^{-2H}\sigma^{-2}(ux^{-\frac{H}{1-H}} + cx)^2\right\} dx\,. \tag{17.15}$$

See Norros (1994) for the lower bound and Dębicki, Michna, and Rolski (1998) for the upper bound analysis.

The next property will show the asymptotic behavior of the infinite time ruin probability. Let the Hurst parameter satisfy $0 < H < 1$. Then (Hüsler and Piterbarg, 1999):

$$\mathrm{P}\{T(R_H) < \infty\} = \frac{P_H\sqrt{\pi}c^{1-H}H^{H-\frac{3}{2}}u^{(1-H)(\frac{1}{H}-1)}}{2^{\frac{1}{2H}-\frac{1}{2}}(1-H)^{H+\frac{1}{H}-\frac{3}{2}}\lambda^{1-H}\sigma^{\frac{1}{H}-1}}\cdot$$

$$\cdot\left[1 - \Phi\left\{\left(\frac{1-H}{H}\right)^H \frac{u^{1-H}c^H}{(1-H)\lambda^H\sigma}\right\}\right]\{1+o(1)\}, \tag{17.16}$$

as $u \to \infty$ where P_H is the Pickands constant, Piterbarg (1996). The value of the Pickands constant is known only for $H = 0.5$ and $H = 1$. Some approximations of its value can be found in Burnecki and Michna (2002) and Dębicki, Michna, and Rolski (2003). The above result permits to approximate the infinite time ruin probability in the model of good and bad periods for large values of the initial capital.

For an arbitrary value of the initial capital there exists a simulation method of the infinite time ruin probability based on the Girsanov-type theorem. To present this method we introduce the stopping time

$$\tau_a(u) = \inf\{t > 0 : B_H(t) + at > u\}\,, \tag{17.17}$$

where $a \geq 0$ and the function

$$w(t,s) = \begin{cases} c_1 s^{\frac{1}{2}-H}(t-s)^{\frac{1}{2}-H} & s \in (0,t) \\ 0, & s \notin (0,t), \end{cases} \tag{17.18}$$

where $\frac{1}{2} < H < 1$,

$$c_1 = \left\{ H(2H-1)\mathcal{B}\left(\frac{3}{2} - H, H - \frac{1}{2}\right) \right\}^{-1}, \qquad (17.19)$$

and $\mathcal{B}$ denotes the beta function. Note that $\tau_a < \infty$ almost surely for $a \geq 0$. According to Norros, Valkeila, and Virtamo (1999) the following centered Gaussian process

$$M(t) = \int_0^t w(t,s)\, dB_H(s), \qquad (17.20)$$

possesses independent increments and its variance is

$$\mathrm{E}M^2(t) = c_2^2 t^{2-2H}, \qquad (17.21)$$

where

$$c_2 = \left\{ H(2H-1)(2-2H)\mathcal{B}\left(H - \frac{1}{2}, 2 - 2H\right) \right\}^{-\frac{1}{2}}.$$

In particular $M(t)$ is a martingale. For all $a > 0$ we have

$$\mathrm{P}\{T(R_H) < \infty\} =$$

$$\mathrm{E}\exp\left\{ -\frac{c+a}{\lambda^H \sigma} \int_0^{\tau_a} w(\tau_a, s)\, dB_H(s) - \frac{1}{2\lambda^{2H}\sigma^2} c_2^2 (c+a)^2 {\tau_a}^{2-2H} \right\}.$$

The above formula enables us to simulate the infinite time ruin probability for an arbitrary value of the initial capital. Using the structure of the common distribution of $(M(t), B_H(t))$ we get the following estimator of the ruin probability valid for $0 < H < 1$:

$$\mathrm{P}\{T(R_H) < \infty\} = \mathrm{E}\exp\left\{ -\frac{(c+a)}{\lambda^{2H}\sigma^2} \tau_a^{1-2H} u + \frac{(a^2 - c^2)}{2\lambda^{2H}\sigma^2} {\tau_a}^{2-2H} \right\}. \qquad (17.22)$$

Let us note that putting $a = c$ in (17.22) we obtain a simple formula

$$\mathrm{P}\{T(R_H) < \infty\} = \mathrm{E}\exp\left\{ -\frac{2c\tau_c^{1-2H} u}{\lambda^{2H}\sigma^2} \right\}. \qquad (17.23)$$

For similar methods of simulation based on the change of measure technique applied to fluid models see Dębicki, Michna, and Rolski (2003).

Table 17.1: Ruin probabilities for $H = 0.7$ and fixed $\mu = 20, \sigma = 10$, and $t = 10$.

u	c	λ	$\Psi(t)$	Ψ
25	50	2	8.1257e-2	0.28307
25	60	2	1.3516e-2	0.03932
30	60	2	6.6638e-3	0.02685
35	60	2	3.6826e-3	0.01889
40	60	2	2.2994e-3	0.01363
40	70	3	1.0363e-1	0.38016

STFgood01.xpl

Table 17.2: Ruin probabilities for $H = 0.8$ and fixed $\mu = 20, \sigma = 10$, and $t = 10$.

u	c	λ	$\Psi(t)$	Ψ
25	50	2	0.22240	0.40728
25	60	2	0.09890	0.08029
30	60	2	0.06570	0.06583
35	60	2	0.04496	0.05471
40	60	2	0.03183	0.04646
40	70	3	0.23622	0.55505

STFgood02.xpl

17.4 Examples

Let us assume that claims appear in good and bad periods. According to (17.9) we are able to approximate the risk process by:

$$R_H(t) = u + (c - \lambda\mu)t + \lambda^H B_H(t),$$

where $B_H(t)$ is a fractional Brownian motion, c is the premium rate, μ is the expected value of claims, $\sigma^2 = \mathrm{E}B^2(1)$ is their variance, λ is the claim intensity, and u is the initial capital.

We can compute finite and infinite time ruin probabilities for different levels of the initial capital, premium, intensity of claims, expectation of claims and

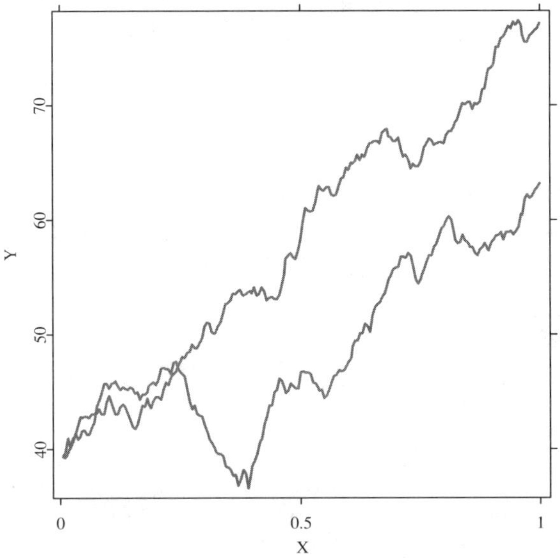

Figure 17.1: Sample paths of the process R_H for $H = 0.7$, $u = 40$, $c = 100$, $\mu = 20$, $\sigma = 10$, and $\lambda = 3$.

STFgood03.xpl

their variance (see Tables 17.1 and 17.2). We approximate the finite time ruin probabilities by formula (17.12) and the infinite time ruin probabilities using the estimator given in (17.23). Sample paths of the process R_H are depicted in Figure 17.1.

The results in the tables show the effects of dependence structures between claims on the crucial parameter for insurance companies – the ruin probability. Numerical simulations are performed for different values of the parameter of self-similarity H which defines the level of the dependence between claims. It is clearly visible that an increase of H increases the ruin probability. The tables also illustrate the relationship between the ruin probability and the initial capital u, premium c, intensity of claims λ, expectation of claims μ and their variance σ. It is shown that for dependent damage occurrences the ruin probability is considerably higher than for independent events. Thus ignoring possible dependence (existence of good and bad periods) and its level might lead to wrong choices of the premium c.

Bibliography

Asmussen, S. (1987). *Applied Probability and Queues*, John Wiley and Sons, New York.

Asmussen, S. (1999). On the ruin problems for some adapted premium rules, *MaPhySto Research Report No. 5. University of Aarhus, Denmark.*

Burnecki, K. and Michna, Z. (2002). Simulation of Pickands constants, *Probability and Mathematical Statistics* **22**: 193–199.

Dębicki, K., Michna, Z. and Rolski, T. (1998). On the supremum from Gaussian processes over infinite horizon, *Probability and Mathematical Statistics* **18**: 83–100.

Dębicki, K., Michna, Z. and Rolski T. (2003). Simulation of the asymptotic constant in some fluid models, *Stochastic Models* **19**: 407–423.

Embrechts, P. and Maejima, M. (2002). *Selfsimilar Processes*, Princeton University Press, Princeton and Oxford.

Gerber, H. U. (1981). On the probability of ruin in an autoregressive model, *Mitteilung der Vereinigung Schweiz. Versicherungsmathematiker* **2**: 213–219.

Gerber, H. U. (1982). Ruin theory in a linear model, *Insurance: Mathematics and Economics* **1**: 177–184.

Heath, D., Resnick, S. and Samorodnitsky, G. (1998). Heavy tails and long range dependence in on/off processes and associated fluid models, *Mathematics and Operations Research* **23**: 145–165.

Hüsler, J. and Piterbarg, V. (1999). Extremes of certain class of Gaussian processes, *Stochastic Processes and their Applications* **83**: 338–357.

Embrechts, P. and Maejima, M. (1987). *Limit Theorems for Stochastic Processes*, Springer, Berlin Heidelberg.

Lamperti, J. (1962). Semi-stable stochastic processes, *Transection of the American Mathematical Society.* **104**: 62–78.

Mandelbrot, B. B. and Van Ness, J. W. (1968). Fractional Brownian motions, fractional noises and applications, *SIAM Review* **10**: 422–437.

Michna, Z. (1998). Self-similar processes in collective risk theory, *Journal of Applied Mathematics and Stochastic Analysis* **11**: 429–448.

Müller, A. and Pflug, G. (2001). Asymptotic ruin probabilities for risk processes with dependent increments, *Insurance: Mathematics and Economics* **28**: 381–392.

Norros, I. (1994). A storage model with self-similar input, *Queueing Systems* **16**: 387–396.

Norros, I., Valkeila, E. and Virtamo, J. (1999). A Girsanov type theorem for the fractional Brownian motion, *Bernoulli* **5**: 571–587.

Nyrhinen, H. (1998). Rough description of ruin for general class of surplus process, *Adv. Appl. Probab.* **30**: 107–119.

Nyrhinen, H. (1999a). On the ruin probabilities in a general economic environment, *Stoch. Proc. Appl.* **83**: 319–330.

Nyrhinen, H. (1999b). Large deviations for the time of ruin, *J. Appl. Probab.* **36**: 733–746.

Piterbarg, V. I. (1996). *Asymptotic methods in the theory of Gaussian processes and fields*, Translations of Mathematical Monographs 148, AMS, Providence.

Promislow, S. D. (1991). The probability of ruin in a process with dependent increments, *Insurance: Mathematics and Economics* **10**: 99–107.

18 Premiums in the Individual and Collective Risk Models

Jan Iwanik and Joanna Nowicka-Zagrajek

The premium is the price for the good "insurance" sold by an insurance company. The right pricing is vital since too low a price level results in a loss, while with too high prices a company can price itself out of the market. It is the actuary's task to find methods of premium calculation (also called premium calculation principles), i.e. rules saying what premium should be assigned to a given risk.

We present the most important types of premiums in Section 18.1; for more premium calculation principles, that are not considered here, see Straub (1988) and Young (2004). We focus on the monetary payout made by the insurer in connection with insurable losses and we ignore premium loading for expenses and profit.

The goal of insurance modeling is to develop a probability distribution for the total amount paid in benefits. This allows the insurance company to manage its capital account and honor its commitments. Therefore, we describe two standard models: the individual risk model in Section 18.2 and the collective risk model in Section 18.3. In both cases, we determine the expectation and variance of the portfolio, consider the approximation of the distribution of the aggregate claims, and present formulae for the considered premiums. It is worth mentioning here that the collective risk model can also be applied to quantifying regulatory capital for operational risk, for example to model a yearly operational risk variable (Embrechts, Furrer, and Kaufmann, 2003).

18.1 Premium Calculation Principles

Let X denote a non-negative random variable describing the size of claim (risk, loss) with the distribution function $F_X(t)$. Moreover, we assume that the expected value $\mathrm{E}(X)$, the variance $\mathrm{Var}(X)$ and the moment generating function $M_X(z) = \mathrm{E}(e^{zX})$ exist.

The simplest premium (calculation principle) is called *pure risk premium* and it is equal to the expectation of claim size variable:

$$P = \mathrm{E}(X). \tag{18.1}$$

This premium is often applied in life and some mass lines of business in non-life insurance. As it is known from the ruin theory, the pure risk premium without any kind of loading is insufficient since, in the long run, the ruin is inevitable even in the case of substantial (though finite) initial reserves. Nevertheless, the pure risk premium can be – and still is – of practical use because, for one thing, in practice the planning horizon is always limited, and for another, there are indirect ways of loading a premium, e.g. by neglecting interest earnings (Straub, 1988).

The future claims cost X may be different from its expected value $\mathrm{E}(X)$ and the estimator $\widehat{\mathrm{E}(X)}$ drawn from past may be different from the true $\mathrm{E}(X)$. To reflect this fact, the insurer can impose the risk loading on the pure risk premium.

The pure risk *premium with safety (security) loading* given by

$$P_{SL}(\theta) = (1+\theta)\,\mathrm{E}(X), \quad \theta \geq 0, \tag{18.2}$$

where θ and $\theta\,\mathrm{E}(X)$ are the relative and total safety loadings, respectively, is very popular in practical applications. This premium is an increasing linear function of θ and it is equal to the pure risk premium for $\theta = 0$.

The pure risk premium and the premium with safety loading are sometimes criticised because they do not depend on the degree of fluctuation of X. Thus, two other rules have been proposed. The first one, denoted here by $P_V(a)$ and given by

$$P_V(a) = \mathrm{E}(X) + a\,\mathrm{Var}(X), \quad a \geq 0, \tag{18.3}$$

is called the σ^2*-loading principle* or the *variance principle*. In this case the premium depends not only on the expectation but also on the variance of the loss. The premium given by (18.3) is an increasing linear function of a and it is obvious that for $a = 0$ it is equal to the pure risk premium.

The other one, denoted here by $P_{SD}(b)$ and given by

$$P_{SD}(b) = \mathrm{E}(X) + b\sqrt{\mathrm{Var}(X)}, \quad b \geq 0, \tag{18.4}$$

is called the *σ-loading principle* or the *standard deviation principle.* In this case the premium depends on the expectation and also on the standard deviation of the loss. The premium given by (18.4) is an increasing linear function of b and clearly for $b = 0$ it reduces to the pure risk premium. Both the σ^2- and σ-loading principles are widely used in practice, but there is a discussion which one is better. If we consider two risks X_1 and X_2, the σ-loading is additive and the σ^2-loading not in case X_1 and X_2 are totally dependent, whereas the contrary is true for independent risks X_1 and X_2. Although in many cases the additivity is required from premium calculation principles, there are also strong arguments against additivity based on the idea that the price of insurance ought to be the lower the larger number of the risk carriers are sharing the risk.

The rules described so far are sometimes called "empirical" or "pragmatic". Another approach employs the notion of utility (Straub, 1988). The so-called zero utility principle states that the premium P_U for a risk X should be calculated such that the expected utility is (at least) equal to the zero utility. This principle yields a technical minimum premium in the sense that the risk X should not be accepted at a premium below P_U. In the trivial case zero utility premium equals the pure risk premium. A more interesting case is the exponential utility which leads to a premium, denoted here by $P_E(c)$ and called the *exponential premium,* given by

$$P_E(c) = \frac{\ln M_X(c)}{c} = \frac{\ln \mathrm{E}(e^{cX})}{c}, \quad c > 0. \tag{18.5}$$

This premium is an increasing function of the parameter c that measures the risk aversion and $\lim_{c \to 0} P_E(c) = \mathrm{E}(X)$. It is worth noticing that the zero utility principle yields additive premiums only in the trivial and the exponential utility cases (Gerber, 1980). As the trivial utility is just a special case of exponential utility corresponding to the limit $c \to 0$, additivity characterizes the exponential utility.

Another interesting approach to the problem of premium calculations is the *quantile premium,* denoted here by $P_Q(\varepsilon)$, is given by

$$P_Q(\varepsilon) = F_X^{-1}(1 - \varepsilon), \tag{18.6}$$

where $\varepsilon \in (0,1)$ is small enough. As it can be easily seen, it is just the quantile of order $(1-\varepsilon)$ of the loss distribution and this means that the insurer wants to get the premium that covers $(1-\varepsilon) \cdot 100\%$ of the possible loss. A reasonable range of the parameter ε is usually from 1% to 5%.

18.2 Individual Risk Model

We consider here a certain portfolio of insurance policies and the total amount of claims arising from it during a given period (usually a year). Our aim is to determine the joint premium for the whole portfolio that will cover the accumulated risk connected with all policies.

In the individual risk model, which is widely used in applications, especially in life and health insurance, we assume that the portfolio consists of n insurance policies and the claim made in respect of the policy k is denoted by X_k. Then the total, or aggregate, amount of claims is

$$S = X_1 + X_2 + \ldots + X_n, \tag{18.7}$$

where X_k is the loss on insured unit k and n is the number of risk units insured (known and fixed at the beginning of the period). The X_k's are usually postulated to be independent random variables (but not necessarily identically distributed), so we will make such assumption in this section. Moreover, the individual risk model discussed here will not recognize the time value of money because we will consider only models for short periods.

The claim amount variable X_k for each policy is usually presented as

$$X_k = I_k B_k, \tag{18.8}$$

where random variables $I_1, \ldots, I_n, B_1, \ldots, B_n$ are independent. The random variable I_k indicates whether or not the kth policy produced a payment. If the claim has occurred, then $I_k = 1$; if there has not been any claim, $I_k = 0$. We denote $q_k = \mathrm{P}(I_k = 1)$ and $1 - q_k = \mathrm{P}(I_k = 0)$. The random variable B_k can have an arbitrary distribution and represents the amount of the payment in respect of the kth policy given that the payment was made.

In Section 18.2.1 we present general formulae for the premiums introduced in Section 18.1. In Section 18.2.2 we apply the normal approximation to obtain closed-form formulae for both the exponential and quantile premiums. Finally in Section 18.2.3, we illustrate the behavior of these premiums on a real-life data describing losses resulting from catastrophic events in the USA.

18.2.1 General Premium Formulae

In order to find formulae for the "pragmatic" premiums, let us assume that the expectations and variances of B_k's exist and denote $\mu_k = \mathrm{E}(B_k)$ and $\sigma_k^2 = \mathrm{Var}(B_k)$, $k = 1, 2, \ldots, n$. Then

$$\mathrm{E}(X_k) = \mu_k q_k, \tag{18.9}$$

and the mean of the total loss in the individual risk model is given by

$$\mathrm{E}(S) = \sum_{k=1}^{n} \mu_k q_k. \tag{18.10}$$

The variance of X_k can be calculated as follows:

$$\begin{aligned} \mathrm{Var}(X_k) &= \mathrm{Var}\{\mathrm{E}(X_k|I_k)\} + \mathrm{E}\{\mathrm{Var}(X_k|I_k)\} \\ &= \mathrm{Var}\{I_k\,\mathrm{E}(B_k)\} + \mathrm{E}\{I_k\,\mathrm{Var}(B_k)\} \\ &= \{\mathrm{E}(B_k)\}^2\,\mathrm{Var}(I_k) + \mathrm{Var}(B_k)\,\mathrm{E}(I_k) \\ &= \mu_k^2 q_k(1-q_k) + \sigma_k^2 q_k. \end{aligned} \tag{18.11}$$

Applying the assumption of independent X_k's, the variance of S is of the form:

$$\mathrm{Var}(S) = \sum_{k=1}^{n} \left\{\mu_k^2 q_k(1-q_k) + \sigma_k^2 q_k\right\}. \tag{18.12}$$

Now we can easily obtain the following formulae for the individual risk model:

- *pure risk premium*

$$P = \sum_{k=1}^{n} \mu_k q_k, \tag{18.13}$$

- *premium with safety loading*

$$P_{SL}(\theta) = (1+\theta)\sum_{k=1}^{n} \mu_k q_k, \quad \theta \geq 0, \tag{18.14}$$

- *premium with variance loading*

$$P_V(a) = \sum_{k=1}^{n} \mu_k q_k + a\sum_{k=1}^{n} \left\{\mu_k^2 q_k(1-q_k) + \sigma_k^2 q_k\right\}, \quad a \geq 0, \tag{18.15}$$

- *premium with standard deviation loading*

$$P_{SD}(b) = \sum_{k=1}^{n} \mu_k q_k + b \sqrt{\sum_{k=1}^{n} \{\mu_k^2 q_k (1 - q_k) + \sigma_k^2 q_k\}}, \quad b \geq 0. \quad (18.16)$$

If we assume that for each $k = 1, 2, \ldots, n$ the moment generating function $M_{B_k}(t)$ exists, then

$$M_{X_k}(t) = 1 - q_k + q_k M_{B_k}(t), \quad (18.17)$$

and hence

$$M_S(t) = \prod_{k=1}^{n} \{1 - q_k + q_k M_{B_k}(t)\}. \quad (18.18)$$

This leads to the following formula for the exponential premium:

$$P_E(c) = \frac{1}{c} \sum_{k=1}^{n} \ln \{1 - q_k + q_k M_{B_k}(c)\}, \quad c > 0. \quad (18.19)$$

In the individual risk model, claims of an insurance company are modeled as a sum of the claims of many insured individuals. Therefore, in order to find the quantile premium given by

$$P_Q(\varepsilon) = F_S^{-1}(1 - \varepsilon), \quad \varepsilon \in (0, 1), \quad (18.20)$$

the distribution of the sum of independent random variables has to be determined. There are methods to solve this problem, see Bowers et al. (1997) and Panjer and Willmot (1992). For example, one can use the convolution of the probability distributions of $X_1, X_2, \ldots, X_n$. However in practice it can be a very complex task that involves numerous calculations. In many cases the result cannot be represented by a simple formula. Therefore, approximations for the distribution of the sum are often used.

18.2.2 Premiums in the Case of the Normal Approximation

The distribution of the total claim in the individual risk model can be approximated by means of the central limit theorem (Bowers et al., 1997). In such case it is sufficient to evaluate means and variances of the individual loss random variables, sum them to obtain the mean and variance of the aggregate loss of the insurer and apply the normal approximation. However, it is important to remember that the quality of this approximation depends not only on the size of the portfolio, but also on its homogeneity.

The approximation of the distribution of the total loss S in the individual risk model can be applied to find a simple expression for the quantile premium. If the distribution of S is approximated by a normal distribution with mean $\mathrm{E}(S)$ and variance $\mathrm{Var}(S)$, the quantile premium can be written as

$$P_Q(\varepsilon) = \sum_{k=1}^{n} \mu_k q_k + \Phi^{-1}(1-\varepsilon)\sqrt{\sum_{k=1}^{n} \{\mu_k^2 q_k(1-q_k) + \sigma_k^2 q_k\}}, \qquad (18.21)$$

where $\varepsilon \in (0,1)$ and $\Phi(\cdot)$ denotes the standard normal distribution function. It is the same premium as the premium with standard deviation loading with $b = \Phi^{-1}(1-\varepsilon)$.

Moreover, in the case of this approximation, it is possible to express the exponential premium as

$$P_E(c) = \sum_{k=1}^{n} \mu_k q_k + \frac{c}{2}\sum_{k=1}^{n} \left\{\mu_k^2 q_k(1-q_k) + \sigma_k^2 q_k\right\}, \quad c > 0, \qquad (18.22)$$

and it is easy to notice, that this premium is equal to the premium with variance loading with $a = c/2$.

Since the distribution of S is approximated by the normal distribution with the same mean value and variance, premiums defined in terms of the expected value of the aggregate claims are given by the same formulae as in Section 18.2.1.

18.2.3 Examples

Quantile premium for the individual risk model with B_k's log-normally distributed. The insurance company holds $n = 500$ policies X_k. The claims arising from policies can be represented as independent identically distributed random variables. The actuary estimates that each policy generates a claim with probability $q_k = 0.05$ and the claim size, given that the claim happens, is log-normally distributed. The parameters of the log-normal distribution correspond to the real-life data describing losses resulting from catastrophic events in the USA, i.e. $\mu_k = 18.3806$ and $\sigma_k = 1.1052$ (see Chapter 13).

As the company wants to assure that the probability of losing any money is less than a specific value ε, the actuary is asked to calculate the quantile premium. The actuary wants to compare the quantile premium given by the general formula (18.20) with the one (18.21) obtained from the approximation of the aggregate claims.

The distribution of the total claim in this model can be approximated by the normal distribution with mean $4.4236 \cdot 10^9$ and variance $2.6160 \cdot 10^{18}$.

Figure 18.1 shows the quantile premium in the individual risk model framework for $\varepsilon \in (0.01, 0.1)$. The exact premium is drawn with the solid blue line whereas the premium calculated on the base of the normal approximation is marked with the dashed red line. Because of the complexity of analytical formulae, the exact quantile premium for the total claim amount was obtained using numerical simulations. The simulation-based approach is the reason for the line being jagged. A better smoothness can be achieved by performing a larger number of Monte Carlo simulations (here we performed 10000 simulations).

We can observe now that the approximation seems to fit well for larger ε and worse for small ε. This is specific for the quantile premium. The effect is caused by the fact that even if two distribution functions $F_1(x), F_2(x)$ are very close to each other, their inverse functions $F_1^{-1}(y), F_2^{-1}(y)$ may differ significantly for y close to 1.

Exponential premium for the individual risk model with B_k's gamma distributed. Because the company has a specific risk strategy described by the exponential utility function, the actuary is asked to determine the premium for the same portfolio of 500 independent policies once again but now with respect to the risk aversion parameter c. The actuary is also asked to use a method of calculation that provides direct results and does not require Monte Carlo simulations.

This time the actuary has decided to describe the claim size, given that the claim happens, by the gamma distribution with $\alpha = 0.9185$ and $\beta = 5.6870 \cdot 10^{-9}$, see Chapter 13. The choice of the gamma distribution guarantees a simple analytical form of the premium, namely

$$P_E(c) = \frac{1}{c} \sum_{k=1}^{n} \ln \left\{ 1 - q_k + q_k \left(\frac{\beta}{\beta - c} \right)^{\alpha} \right\}, \quad c > 0. \tag{18.23}$$

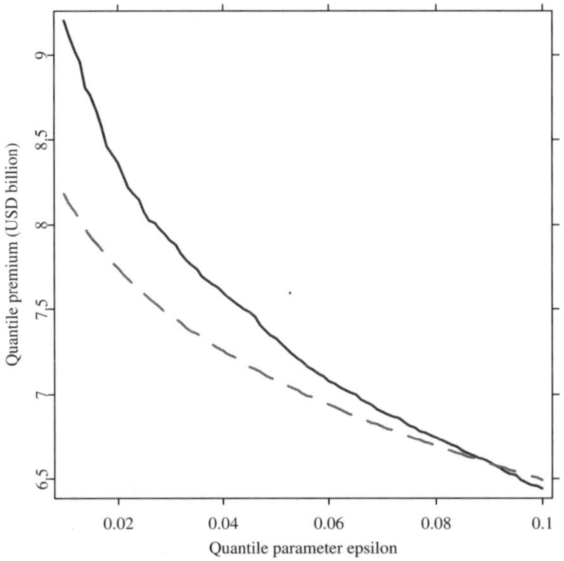

Figure 18.1: Quantile premium for the individual risk model with B_k's log-normally distributed. The exact premium (solid blue line) and the premium resulting for the normal approximation of the aggregate claims (dashed red line). STFprem01.xpl

On the other hand, the actuary can use formula (18.22) applying the normal approximation of the aggregate claims with mean $4.0377 \cdot 10^9$ and variance $1.3295 \cdot 10^{18}$.

Figure 18.2 shows the exponential premiums resulting from both approaches with respect to the risk aversion parameter c. A simple pattern can be observed – the more risk averse the customer is, the more he or she is willing to pay for the risk protection. Moreover, the normal approximation gives better results for smaller values of c.

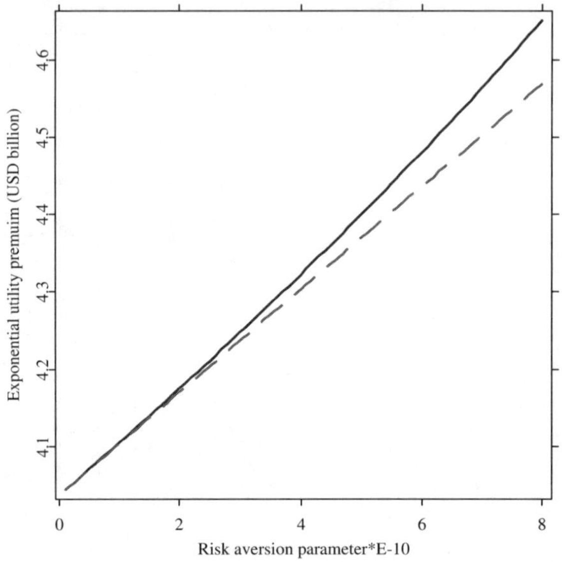

Figure 18.2: Exponential premium for the individual risk model with B_k's generated from the gamma distribution. The exact premium (solid blue line) and the premium resulting for the normal approximation of the aggregate claims (dashed red line). STFprem02.xpl

18.3 Collective Risk Model

We consider now an alternative model describing the total claim amount in a fixed period in a portfolio of insurance contracts.

Let N denote the number of claims arising from policies in a given time period. Let X_1 denote the amount of the first claim, X_2 the amount of the second claim and so on. In the collective risk model, the random sum

$$S = X_1 + X_2 + \ldots + X_N \tag{18.24}$$

represents the aggregate claims generated by the portfolio for the period under study. The number of claims N is a random variable and is associated with the frequency of claim. The individual claims $X_1, X_2, \ldots$ are also random variables and are said to measure the severity of claims. There are two fundamental assumptions that we will make in this section: $X_1, X_2, \ldots$ are identically distributed random variables and the random variables $N, X_1, X_2, \ldots$ are mutually independent.

In Section 18.3.1 we present formulae for the considered premiums in the collective risk model. In Section 18.3.2 we apply the normal and translated gamma approximations to obtain closed formulae for premiums. Since for the number of claims N, a Poisson or a negative binomial distribution is often selected, we discuss these cases in detail in Section 18.3.3 and 18.3.4, respectively. Finally, we illustrate the behavior of the premiums on examples in Section 18.3.5.

18.3.1 General Premium Formulae

In order to find formulae for premiums based on the expected value of the total claim, let us assume that $\mathrm{E}(X)$, $\mathrm{E}(N)$, $\mathrm{Var}(X)$ and $\mathrm{Var}(N)$ exist. For the collective risk model, the expected value of aggregate claims is the product of the expected individual claim amount and the expected number of claims,

$$\mathrm{E}(S) = \mathrm{E}(N)\,\mathrm{E}(X), \tag{18.25}$$

while the variance of aggregate claims is the sum of two components where the first is attributed to the variability of individual claim amounts and the other to the variability of the number of claims:

$$\mathrm{Var}(S) = \mathrm{E}(N)\,\mathrm{Var}(X) + \{\mathrm{E}(X)\}^2\,\mathrm{Var}(N). \tag{18.26}$$

Thus it is easy to obtain the following premium formulae in the collective risk model:

- *pure risk premium*

$$P = \mathrm{E}(N)\,\mathrm{E}(X), \tag{18.27}$$

- *premium with safety loading*

$$P_{SL}(\theta) = (1+\theta)\,\mathrm{E}(N)\,\mathrm{E}(X), \quad \theta \ge 0, \tag{18.28}$$

- *premium with variance loading*

$$\begin{aligned} P_V(a) &= \mathrm{E}(N)\,\mathrm{E}(X) \\ &+ a[\mathrm{E}(N)\,\mathrm{Var}(X) + \{\mathrm{E}(X)\}^2\,\mathrm{Var}(N)], \quad a \ge 0, \end{aligned} \tag{18.29}$$

- *premium with standard deviation loading*

$$\begin{aligned} P_{SD}(b) &= \mathrm{E}(N)\,\mathrm{E}(X) \\ &+ b\sqrt{\mathrm{E}(N)\,\mathrm{Var}(X) + \{\mathrm{E}(X)\}^2\,\mathrm{Var}(N)}, \quad b \geq 0. \end{aligned} \tag{18.30}$$

If we assume that $M_N(t)$ and $M_X(t)$ exist, the moment generating function of S can be derived as

$$M_S(t) = M_N\{\ln M_X(t)\}, \tag{18.31}$$

and thus the exponential premium is of the form

$$P_E(c) = \frac{\ln[M_N\{\ln M_X(c)\}]}{c}, \quad c > 0. \tag{18.32}$$

It is often difficult to determine the distribution of the aggregate claims and this fact causes problems with calculating the quantile premium given by

$$P_Q(\varepsilon) = F_S^{-1}(1-\varepsilon), \quad \varepsilon \in (0,1). \tag{18.33}$$

Although the distribution function of S can be expressed by means of the distribution of N and the convolution of the claim amount distribution, this is too complicated in practical applications, see e.g. Klugman, Panjer, and Willmot (1998). Therefore, approximations for the distribution of the aggregate claims are usually considered.

18.3.2 Premiums in the Case of the Normal and Translated Gamma Approximations

In Section 18.2.2 the normal approximation was employed as an approximation for the distribution of aggregate claims in the individual risk model. This approach can also be used in the case of the collective model when the expected number of claims is large (Bowers et al., 1997; Daykin, Pentikainen, and Pesonen, 1994).

The normal approximation simplifies the calculations. If the distribution of S can be approximated by a normal distribution with mean $\mathrm{E}(S)$ and variance $\mathrm{Var}(S)$, the quantile premium is given by the formula

$$P_Q(\varepsilon) = \mathrm{E}(N)\,\mathrm{E}(X) + \Phi^{-1}(1-\varepsilon)\sqrt{\mathrm{E}(N)\,\mathrm{Var}(X) + \{\mathrm{E}(X)\}^2\,\mathrm{Var}(N)}, \tag{18.34}$$

where $\varepsilon \in (0,1)$ and $\Phi(\cdot)$ denotes the standard normal distribution function. It is easy to notice, that this premium is equal to the standard deviation-loaded premium with $b = \Phi^{-1}(1-\varepsilon)$.

Moreover, in the case of the normal approximation, it is possible to express the exponential premium as

$$P_E(c) = \mathrm{E}(N)\,\mathrm{E}(X) + \frac{c}{2}\left[\mathrm{E}(N)\,\mathrm{Var}(X) + \{\mathrm{E}(X)\}^2\,\mathrm{Var}(N)\right], \quad c > 0, \tag{18.35}$$

which is the same premium as resulting from the variance principle with $a = c/2$.

Let us also mention that since the mean and variance in the case of the normal approximation are the same as for the distribution of S, the premiums based on the expected value are given by the general formulae presented in Section 18.3.1.

Unfortunately, the normal approximation is not usually sufficiently accurate. The disadvantage of this approximation lies in the fact that the skewness of the normal distribution is always zero, as it has a symmetric probability density function. Since the distribution of aggregate claims is often skewed, another approximation of the distribution of aggregate claims that accommodates skewness is required. In this section we describe the translated gamma approximation. For more approaches and discussion of their applicability see, for example, Daykin, Pentikainen, and Pesonen (1994).

The distribution function of the translated (shifted) gamma distribution is given by

$$G^{tr}(x;\alpha,\beta,x_0) = F(x - x_0;\alpha,\beta), \quad x,\alpha,\beta > 0, \tag{18.36}$$

where $F(x;\alpha,\beta)$ denotes the distribution function of the gamma distribution (described in Chapter 13) with parameters α and β:

$$F(x;\alpha,\beta) = \int_0^x \frac{\beta^\alpha}{\Gamma(\alpha)} t^{\alpha-1} e^{-\beta t} dt, \quad x,\alpha,\beta > 0. \tag{18.37}$$

To apply the approximation, the parameters α, β, and x_0 have to be selected so that the first, second, and third central moments of S equal the corresponding items for the translated gamma distribution. This procedure leads to the following result:

$$\alpha = 4\frac{\{\mathrm{Var}(S)\}^3}{(\mathrm{E}[\{S - \mathrm{E}(S)\}^3])^2}, \tag{18.38}$$

$$\beta = 2\frac{\mathrm{Var}(S)}{\mathrm{E}[\{S - \mathrm{E}(S)\}^3]}, \tag{18.39}$$

$$x_0 = \mathrm{E}(S) - 2\frac{\{\mathrm{Var}(S)\}^2}{\mathrm{E}[\{S - \mathrm{E}(S)\}^3]}. \tag{18.40}$$

In the case of the translated gamma distribution, it is impossible to give a simple analytical formula for the quantile premium. Therefore, in order to find this premium a numerical approximation must be used. However, it is worth noticing that the exponential premium can be presented as

$$P_E(c) = x_0 + \frac{\alpha}{c}\ln\left(\frac{\beta}{\beta - c}\right), \quad c > 0, \tag{18.41}$$

while the premiums given in terms of the expected value of the aggregate claims are the same as given in Section 18.3.1 (since the distribution of S is approximated by the translated gamma distribution with the same mean value and variance).

18.3.3 Compound Poisson Distribution

In many applications, the number of claims N is assumed to be described by the Poisson distribution with the probability function given by

$$\mathrm{P}(N = n) = \frac{\lambda^n e^{-\lambda}}{n!}, \quad n = 0, 1, 2, \ldots, \tag{18.42}$$

where $\lambda > 0$. With this choice of the distribution of N, the distribution of S is called a compound Poisson distribution.

The compound Poisson distribution has a number of useful properties. Formulae for the exponential premium and for the premiums based on the expectation of the aggregate claims simplify because $\mathrm{E}(N) = \mathrm{Var}(N) = \lambda$ and $M_N(t) = \exp\{\lambda(e^t - 1)\}$.

Moreover, for large λ, the distribution of the compound Poisson can be approximated by a normal distribution with mean $\lambda\,\mathrm{E}(X)$ and variance $\lambda\,\mathrm{E}(X^2)$, and the quantile premium is given by

$$P_Q(\varepsilon) = \lambda\,\mathrm{E}(X) + \Phi^{-1}(1 - \varepsilon)\sqrt{\lambda\,\mathrm{E}(X^2)}, \quad \varepsilon \in (0, 1), \tag{18.43}$$

and the exponential premium is of the form

$$P_E(c) = \lambda \mathrm{E}(X) + \frac{c}{2} \lambda \mathrm{E}(X^2), \quad c > 0. \tag{18.44}$$

If the first three central moments of the individual claim distribution exist, the compound Poisson distribution can be approximated by the translated gamma distribution with the following parameters

$$\alpha = 4\lambda \frac{\{\mathrm{E}(X^2)\}^3}{\{(\mathrm{E}(X^3)\}^2}, \tag{18.45}$$

$$\beta = 2 \frac{\mathrm{E}(X^2)}{\mathrm{E}(X^3)}, \tag{18.46}$$

$$x_0 = \lambda \mathrm{E}(X) - 2\lambda \frac{\{\mathrm{E}(X^2)\}^2}{\mathrm{E}(X^3)}. \tag{18.47}$$

Substituting these parameters in (18.41) one can obtain the formula for the exponential premium.

It is worth mentioning that the compound Poisson distribution has many attractive features (Bowers et al., 1997; Panjer and Willmot, 1992), for example, the combination of a number of portfolios, each of which has a compound Poisson distribution of aggregate claims, also has a compound Poisson distribution of aggregate claims. Moreover, this distribution can be used to approximate the distribution of total claims in the individual model. Although the compound Poisson distribution is normally appropriate in life insurance modeling, it sometimes does not provide an adequate fit to insurance data in other coverages (Willmot, 2001).

18.3.4 Compound Negative Binomial Distribution

When the variance of the number of claims exceeds its mean, the Poisson distribution is not appropriate – in this situation the use of the negative binomial distribution with the probability function given by

$$\mathrm{P}(N = n) = \binom{r+n-1}{n} p^r q^n, \quad n = 0, 1, 2, \ldots, \tag{18.48}$$

where $r > 0$, $0 < p < 1$, and $q = 1 - p$, is suggested. In many cases it provides a significantly improved fit to that of the Poisson distribution. When a negative binomial distribution is selected for N, the distribution of S is called a compound negative binomial distribution.

Since for the negative binomial distribution we have

$$\mathrm{E}(N) = \frac{rq}{p}, \quad \mathrm{Var}(N) = \frac{rq}{p^2}, \tag{18.49}$$

and

$$M_N(t) = \left(\frac{p}{1-qe^t}\right)^r, \tag{18.50}$$

the formulae for the exponential premium and for the premiums based on the expectation of the aggregate claims simplify.

For large r, the distribution of the compound negative binomial can be approximated by a normal distribution with the mean $\frac{rq}{p}\,\mathrm{E}(X)$ and variance $\frac{rq}{p}\,\mathrm{Var}(X) + \frac{rq}{p^2}\{\mathrm{E}(X)\}^2$. In this case the quantile premium is given by

$$P_Q(\varepsilon) = \frac{rq}{p}\,\mathrm{E}(X) + \Phi^{-1}(1-\varepsilon)\sqrt{\frac{rq}{p}\,\mathrm{Var}(X) + \frac{rq}{p^2}\{\mathrm{E}(X)\}^2}, \; \varepsilon \in (0,1), \tag{18.51}$$

and the exponential premium is of the form

$$P_E(c) = \frac{rq}{p}\,\mathrm{E}(X) + \frac{c}{2}\left[\frac{rq}{p}\,\mathrm{Var}(X) + \frac{rq}{p^2}\{\mathrm{E}(X)\}^2\right], \quad c > 0. \tag{18.52}$$

It is worth mentioning that the negative binomial distribution arises as a mixed Poisson variate. More precisely, various distributions for the number of claims can be generated by assuming that the Poisson parameter Λ is a random variable with probability distribution function $u(\lambda)$, $\lambda > 0$, and that the conditional distribution of N, given $\Lambda = \lambda$, is Poisson with parameter λ. In such case the distribution of S is called a compound mixed Poisson distribution, see also Chapter 14. This choice might be useful for example when we consider a population of insureds where various classes of insureds within the population generate numbers of claims according to the Poisson distribution, but the Poisson parameters may be different for the various classes. The negative binomial distribution can be derived in this fashion when $u(\lambda)$ is the gamma probability density function.

18.3.5 Examples

Quantile premium for the collective risk model with log-normal claim distribution. As the number of policies sold by the insurance company grows, the actuary has decided to try to fit a collective risk model to the portfolio. The log-normal distribution with the parameters $\mu = 18.3806$ and $\sigma = 1.1052$ (these parameters are again estimated on the base of the real-life data describing losses resulting from catastrophic events in the USA, see Chapter 13) is chosen to describe the amount of claims. The number of claims is assumed to be Poisson distributed with parameter $\lambda = 34.2$. Moreover, the claim amounts and the number of claims are believed to be independent. The actuary wants to compare the behavior of the quantile premium for the whole portfolio of policies given by the general formula (18.34) and in the case of the translated gamma approximation.

Figure 18.3 illustrates how the premium based on the translated gamma approximation (dashed red line) fits the premium determined by the exact compound Poisson distribution (solid blue line). The premium for the original compound distribution has to be determined on the base of numerical simulations. This is the reason why the line is jagged. Better smoothness can be achieved by performing a larger number of Monte Carlo simulations (here we again performed 10000 simulations).

The actuary notices that the approximation fits better for the larger values of ε and worse for its smaller values. In fact the compound distribution functions of the original distribution and its transformed gamma approximation lay close to each other, but both are increasing and tend to one in infinity. This explains why the quantile premiums – understood as inverse functions of the distribution functions – differ so much for ε close to zero.

Exponential premium for the collective risk model with gamma claim distribution. The actuary considers again the collective risk model where the number of claims is described by the Poisson distribution with parameter $\lambda = 34.2$, i.e. the compound Poisson model. But this time the claims are described by the gamma distribution with the parameters $\alpha = 0.9185$ and $\beta = 5.6870 \cdot 10^{-9}$ (parameters are based on the same catastrophic data as in the previous example).

Now the actuary considers the exponential premium for the aggregate claims in this model. The exponential premium in the case of the translated gamma

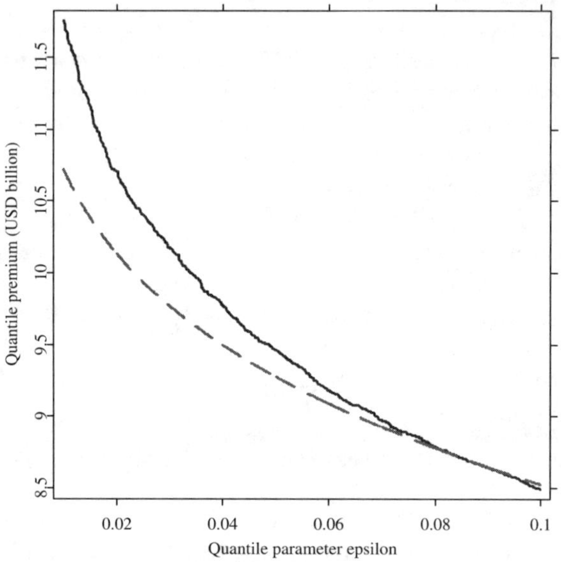

Figure 18.3: Quantile premium for the log-normal claim distribution and its translated gamma approximation in the collective risk model. The exact premium (solid blue line) and the premium in the case of the approximation (dashed red line) are plotted.

STFprem03.xpl

approximation (dashed red line) and the exact premium (solid blue line) are plotted in Figure 18.4. Both premiums – for the original and the approximating distribution – are calculated analytically while it is easy to perform the calculations in this case. Both presented functions increase with the risk aversion parameter. We see that the translated gamma approximation can be a useful and precise tool for calculating the premiums in the collective risk model.

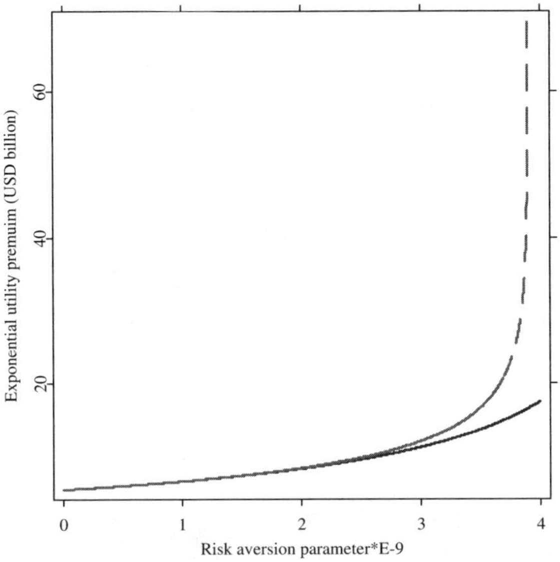

Figure 18.4: Exponential premium for the gamma claim distribution in the collective risk model. The exact premium (solid blue line) and the translated gamma approximation premium (dashed red line) are plotted. STFprem04.xpl

Bibliography

Bowers, N. L. JR., Gerber H. U., Hickman, J. C., Jones, D. A. and Nesbitt, C. J. (1997). *Actuarial Mathematics*, 2nd edition, The Society of Actuaries, Schaumburg.

Daykin, C. D., Pentikainen, T. and Pesonen, M. (1994). *Practical Risk Theory for Actuaries*, Chapman&Hall, London.

Embrechts, P., Furrer, H. and Kaufmann, R. (2003). Quantifying regulatory capital for operational risk, *Trading & Regulation* **9(3)**: 217-233.

Embrechts, P., Klüppelberg, C. and Mikosch, T. (1997). *Modelling Extremal Events for Insurance and Finance*, Springer, Berlin.

Gerber, H.U. (1980). *An introduction to mathematical risk theory*, Huebner, Philadelphia.

Klugman, S. A., Panjer, H. H. and Willmot, G. E. (1998). *Loss Models: From Data to Decisions*, Wiley, New York.

Panjer, H. H. and Willmot, G. E. (1992). *Insurance Risk Models*, Society of Actuaries, Schaumburg.

Straub, E. (1988). *Non-Life Insurance Mathematics*, Springer, Berlin.

Willmot, G. E. (2001). *The nature of modelling insurance losses*, Inaugural Lecture, Munich Reinsurance, Toronto.

Young, V. R. (2004). Premium calculation principles, to appear in *Encyclopedia of Actuarial Science*, J. L. Teugels and B. Sundt eds., Wiley, Chichester.

19 Pure Risk Premiums under Deductibles

Krzysztof Burnecki, Joanna Nowicka-Zagrajek, and Agnieszka Wyłomańska

19.1 Introduction

It is a common practice in most insurance lines for the coverage to be restricted by a deductible. For example, it is often incorporated in motor, health, disability, life, and business insurance. The main idea of a deductible is, firstly, to reduce claim handling costs by excluding coverage for the often numerous small claims and, secondly, to provide some motivation to the insured to prevent claims through a limited degree of participation in claim costs (Daykin, Pentikainen, and Pesonen, 1994; Sundt, 1994; Klugman, Panjer, and Willmot, 1998). We mention the following properties of a deductible:

(i) loss prevention – as the compensation is reduced by a deductible the retention of the insured is positive; This makes out a good case for avoiding the loss;

(ii) loss reduction – the fact a deductible puts the policyholder at risk of obtaining only partial compensation provides an economic incentive to reduce the extend of the damage;

(iii) avoidance of small claims where administration costs are dominant – for small losses, the administration costs will often exceed the loss itself, and hence the insurance company would want the policyholder to pay it himself;

(iv) premium reduction – premium reduction can be an important aspect for the policyholders, they may prefer to take a higher deductible to get a lower premium.

There are two types of deductibles: an annual deductible and a per occurrence deductible, the latter being more common. We quote now an example from the American market. Blue Shield of California, an independent member of the Blue Shield Association, is California's second largest not-for-profit health care company, with 2 million members and USD 3 billion annual revenue. Blue Shield of California offers 4 Preferred Provider Organization (PPO) Plans, each offering similar levels of benefits with a different deductible option: USD 500, 750, 1500, and 2000, respectively. For example, the Blue Shield USD 500 Deductible PPO Plan has a USD 500 annual deductible for most covered expenses. This is just the case of the fixed amount deductible, which is exploited in Section 19.2.2. The annual deductible does not apply to office visits or prescription medications. Office visits and most lab and x-ray services are provided at a USD 30 copayment. This is also the case of the fixed amount deductible. For other covered services, after the annual deductible has been met, you pay 25% up to an annual maximum of USD 3500. This is a case of the limited proportional deductible, which is examined in Section 19.2.4.

In Section 19.2 we present formulae for pure risk premiums under franchise, fixed amount, proportional, limited proportional, and disappearing deductibles in terms of the limited expected value function (levf), which was introduced and exploited in Chapter 13. Using the specific form of levf for different loss distributions, we present in Section 19.3 formulae for pure risk premiums under the deductibles for the log-normal, Pareto, Burr, Weibull, gamma, and mixture of two exponential distributions. The formulae can be used to obtain annual pure risk premiums under the deductibles in the individual and collective risk model framework analysed in Chapter 18. We illustrate graphically the influence of the parameters of the discussed deductibles on the premiums considering the Danish fire loss example, which was studied in Chapter 13. It gives an insight into an important issue of choosing an optimal deductible and its level for a potential insured and a proper pricing of the accepted risk for an insurer.

19.2 General Formulae for Premiums Under Deductibles

Let X denote a non-negative continuous random variable describing the size of claim (risk, loss), $F(t)$ and $f(t)$ its distribution and probability density functions, respectively, and $h(x)$ the payment function corresponding to a deductible. We consider here the simplest premium which is called the pure risk premium, see Chapter 18. The pure risk premium P (as we consider only pure risk premium we will henceforth use the term *premium* meaning *pure risk premium*) is equal to the expectation, i.e.

$$P = \mathrm{E}(X), \tag{19.1}$$

and we assume that the expected value $\mathrm{E}(X)$ exists.

In the case of no deductible the payment function is obviously of the form $h(x) = x$. This means that if the loss is equal to x, the insurer pays the whole claim amount and $P = \mathrm{E}(X)$.

We express formulae for premiums under deductibles in terms of the so-called limited expected value function (levf), namely

$$L(x) = \mathrm{E}\{\min(X, x)\} = \int_0^x yf(y)dy + x\{1 - F(x)\}, \quad x > 0. \tag{19.2}$$

The value of this function at a point x is equal to the expected value of the random variable X truncated at the point x. The function is a very useful tool for testing the goodness of fit an analytic distribution function to the observed claim size distribution function and was already discussed in Chapter 13.

In the following sections we illustrate premium formulae for the most important types of deductibles. All examples were created with the insurance library of XploRe.

19.2.1 Franchise Deductible

One of the deductibles that can be incorporated in the contract is the so-called franchise deductible. In this case the insurer pays the whole claim, if the agreed deductible amount is exceeded. More precisely, under the franchise deductible of a, if the loss is less than a the insurer pays nothing, but if the loss equals or exceeds a claim is paid in full. This means that the payment function can be described as (Figure 19.1)

$$h_{FD(a)}(x) = \begin{cases} 0, & x < a, \\ x, & \text{otherwise.} \end{cases} \tag{19.3}$$

It is worth noticing that the franchise deductible satisfies properties (i), (iii) and (iv), but not property (ii). This deductible can even work against property

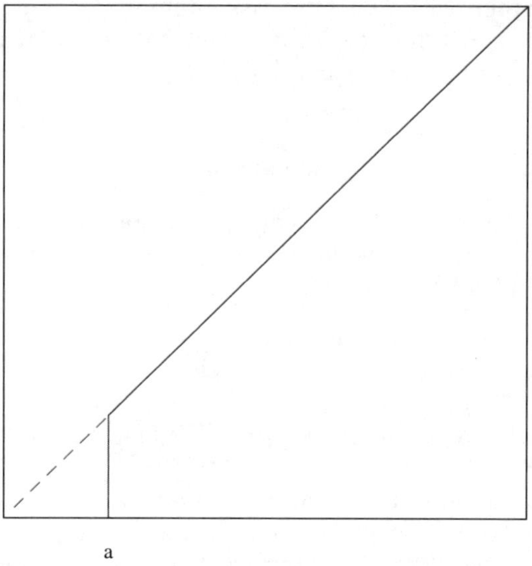

Figure 19.1: The payment function under the franchise deductible (solid blue line) and no deductible (dashed red line). STFded01.xpl

(ii). Since if a loss occurs, the policyholder would prefer it to be greater than or equal to the deductible.

The pure risk premium under the franchise deductible can be expressed in terms of the premium in the case of no deductible and the corresponding limited expected value function:

$$P_{FD(a)} = P - L(a) + a\{1 - F(a)\}. \tag{19.4}$$

It can be easily noticed that this premium is a decreasing function of a. When $a = 0$ the premium is equal to the no deductible case and if a tends to infinity the premium tends to zero.

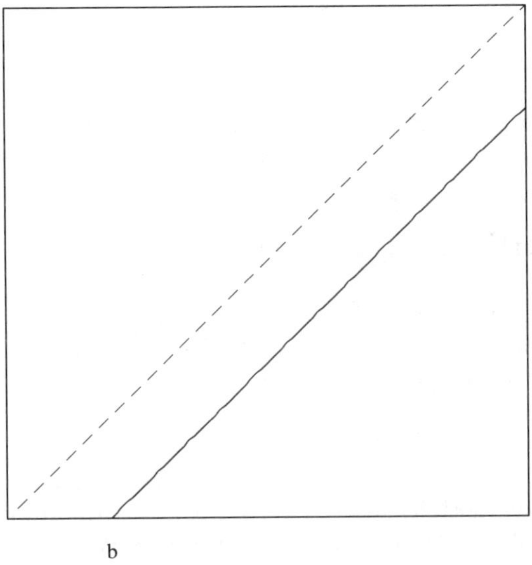

Figure 19.2: The payment function under the fix amount deductible (solid blue line) and no deductible (dashed red line). STFded02.xpl

19.2.2 Fixed Amount Deductible

An agreement between the insured and the insurer incorporating a deductible b means that the insurer pays only the part of the claim which exceeds amount b. If the size of the claim falls below this amount, the claim is not covered by the contract and the insured receives no indemnification. The payment function is thus given by

$$h_{FAD(b)}(x) = \max(0, x - b), \qquad (19.5)$$

see Figure 19.2. The fixed amount deductible satisfies all the properties (i)-(iv).

The premium in the case of the fixed amount deductible has the following form in terms of the premium under the franchise deductible.

$$P_{FAD(b)} = P - L(b) = P_{FD(b)} - b\{1 - F(b)\}. \qquad (19.6)$$

As previously, this premium is a decreasing function of b, for $b = 0$ it gives the premium in the case of no deductible and if b tends to infinity, it tends to zero.

19.2.3 Proportional Deductible

In the case of the proportional deductible with $c \in (0, 1)$, each payment is reduced by $c \cdot 100\%$ (the insurer pays $100\%(1-c)$ of the claim). Consequently, the payment function is given by (Figure 19.3)

$$h_{PD(c)}(x) = (1 - c)x. \qquad (19.7)$$

The proportional deductible satisfies properties (i), (ii), and (iv), but not property (iii), as it implies some compensation for even very small claims.

The relation between the premium under the proportional deductible and the premium in the case of no deductible has the following form.

$$P_{PD(c)} = (1 - c)\,\mathrm{E}(X) = (1 - c)P. \qquad (19.8)$$

Clearly, the premium is a decreasing function of c, $P_{PD(0)} = P$ and $P_{PD(1)} = 0$.

19.2.4 Limited Proportional Deductible

The proportional deductible is usually combined with a minimum amount deductible so the insurer does not need to handle small claims and with a maximum amount deductible to limit the retention of the insured. For the limited proportional deductible of c with a minimum amount m_1 and maximum amount m_2 $(0 \le m_1 < m_2)$ the payment function is given by

$$h_{LPD(c,m_1,m_2)}(x) = \begin{cases} 0, & x \le m_1, \\ x - m_1, & m_1 < x \le m_1/c, \\ (1-c)x, & m_1/c < x \le m_2/c, \\ x - m_2, & \text{otherwise}, \end{cases} \qquad (19.9)$$

see Figure 19.4. The limited proportional deductible satisfies all the properties.

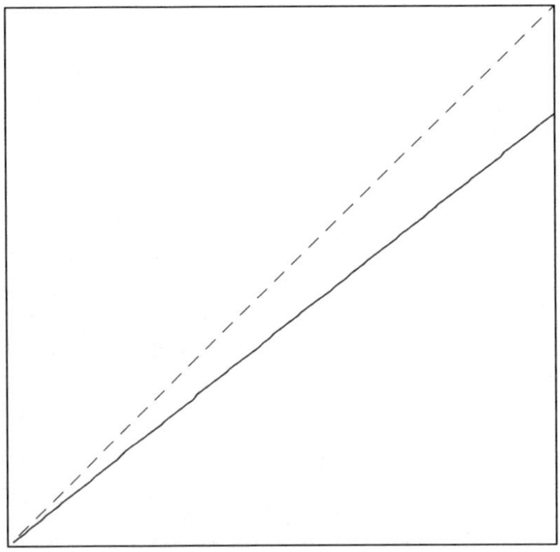

Figure 19.3: The payment function under the proportional deductible (solid blue line) and no deductible (dashed red line). STFded03.xpl

The following formula expresses the premium under the limited proportional deductible in terms of the premium in the case of no deductible and the corresponding limited expected value function.

$$P_{LPD(c,m_1,m_2)} = P - L(m_1) + c\left\{L\left(\frac{m_1}{c}\right) - L\left(\frac{m_2}{c}\right)\right\}. \qquad (19.10)$$

Sometimes only one limitation is incorporated in the contract, i.e. $m_1 = 0$ or $m_2 = \infty$. It is easy to check that the limited proportional deductible with $m_1 = 0$ and $m_2 = \infty$ reduces to the proportional deductible.

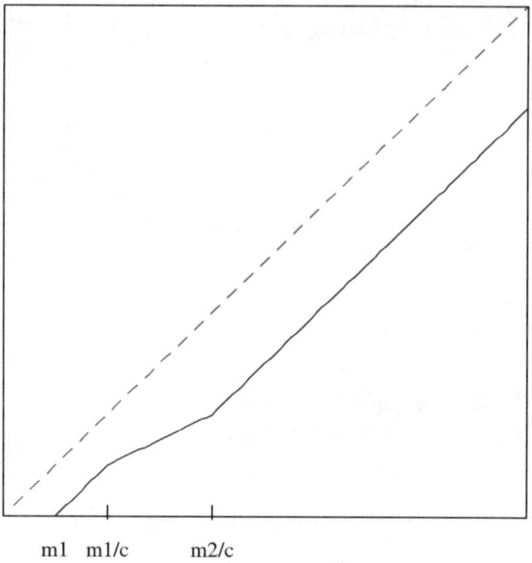

Figure 19.4: The payment function under the limited proportional deductible (solid blue line) and no deductible (dashed red line).

STFded04.xpl

19.2.5 Disappearing Deductible

There is another type of deductible that is a compromise between the franchise and fixed amount deductible. In the case of disappearing deductible the payment depends on the loss in the following way: if the loss is less than an amount of $d_1 > 0$, the insurer pays nothing; if the loss exceeds d_2 ($d_2 > d_1$) amount, the insurer pays the loss in full; if the loss is between d_1 and d_2, then the deductible is reduced linearly between d_1 and d_2. Therefore, the larger the claim, the less of the deductible becomes the responsibility of the policyholder.

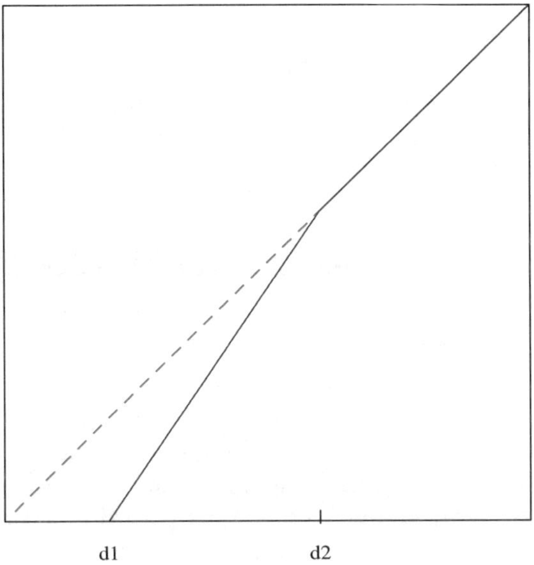

Figure 19.5: The payment function under the disappearing deductible (solid blue line) and no deductible (dashed red line). STFded05.xpl

The payment function is given by (Figure 19.5)

$$h_{DD(d_1,d_2)}(x) = \begin{cases} 0, & x \le d_1, \\ \frac{d_2(x-d_1)}{d_2-d_1}, & d_1 < x \le d_2, \\ x, & \text{otherwise}. \end{cases} \tag{19.11}$$

This kind of deductible satisfies properties (i), (iii), and (iv), but similarly to the franchise deductible it works against (ii).

The following formula shows the premium under the disappearing deductible in terms of the premium in the case of no deductible and the corresponding limited expected value function

$$P_{DD(d_1,d_2)} = P + \frac{d_1}{d_2 - d_1} L(d_2) - \frac{d_2}{d_2 - d_1} L(d_1). \tag{19.12}$$

If $d_1 = 0$, the premium does not depend on d_2 and it becomes the premium in the case of no deductible. If d_2 tends to infinity, then the disappearing deductible reduces to the fix amount deductible of d_1.

19.3 Premiums Under Deductibles for Given Loss Distributions

In the preceding section we showed a relation between the pure risk premium under several deductibles and a limited expected value function. Now, we use the relation to present formulae for premiums in the case of deductibles for a number of loss distributions often used in non-life actuarial practice, see Burnecki, Nowicka-Zagrajek, and Weron (2004). To this end we apply the formulae for levf for different distributions given in Chapter 13. The log-normal, Pareto, Burr, Weibull, gamma, and mixture of two exponential distributions are typical candidates when looking for a suitable analytic distribution, which fits the observed data well, see Aebi, Embrechts, and Mikosch (1992), Burnecki, Kukla, and Weron (2000), Embrechts, Klüppelberg, and Mikosch (1997), Mikosch (1997), Panjer and Willmot (1992), and Chapter 13. In the log-normal and Burr case the premium formulae will be illustrated on a real-life example, namely on the fire loss data, already analysed in Chapter 13. For illustrative purposes, we assume that the total amount of risk X simply follows one of the fitted distributions, whereas in practice, in the individual and collective risk model framework (see Chapter 18), in order to obtain an annual premium under a per occurrence deductible we would have to multiply the premium by a number of policies and mean number of losses per year, respectively, since in the individual risk model

$$\mathrm{E}\left\{\sum_{k=1}^{n} h(X_k)\right\} = n\,\mathrm{E}\left\{h(X_k)\right\},$$

provided that the claim amount variables are identically distributed, and in the collective risk model

$$\mathrm{E}\left\{\sum_{k=1}^{N} h(X_k)\right\} = \mathrm{E}(N)\,\mathrm{E}\{h(X_k)\}.$$

19.3.1 Log-normal Loss Distribution

Consider a random variable Z which has the normal distribution. Let $X = e^Z$. The distribution of X is called the log-normal distribution and its distribution function is given by

$$F(t) = \Phi\left(\frac{\ln t - \mu}{\sigma}\right) = \int_0^t \frac{1}{\sqrt{2\pi}\sigma y} \exp\left\{-\frac{1}{2}\left(\frac{\ln y - \mu}{\sigma}\right)^2\right\} dy,$$

where $t, \sigma > 0$, $\mu \in R$ and $\Phi(.)$ is the standard normal distribution function, see Chapter 13. For the log-normal distribution the following formulae hold:

(a) *franchise deductible premium*

$$P_{FD(a)} = \exp\left(\mu + \frac{\sigma^2}{2}\right)\left\{1 - \Phi\left(\frac{\ln a - \mu - \sigma^2}{\sigma}\right)\right\},$$

(b) *fixed amount deductible premium*

$$\begin{aligned} P_{FAD(b)} &= \exp\left(\mu + \frac{\sigma^2}{2}\right) \cdot \\ &\cdot \left\{1 - \Phi\left(\frac{\ln b - \mu - \sigma^2}{\sigma}\right)\right\} - b\left\{1 - \Phi\left(\frac{\ln b - \mu}{\sigma}\right)\right\}, \end{aligned}$$

(c) *proportional deductible premium*

$$P_{PD(c)} = (1 - c)\exp\left(\mu + \frac{\sigma^2}{2}\right),$$

(d) *limited proportional deductible premium*

$$\begin{aligned} P_{LPD(c,m_1,m_2)} &= \exp\left(\mu + \frac{\sigma^2}{2}\right)\left\{1 - \Phi\left(\frac{\ln m_1 - \mu - \sigma^2}{\sigma}\right)\right\} \\ &+ m_1\left\{\Phi\left(\frac{\ln m_1 - \mu}{\sigma}\right) - \Phi\left(\frac{\ln(m_1/c) - \mu}{\sigma}\right)\right\} \\ &+ \left\{\Phi\left(\frac{\ln(m_1/c) - \mu - \sigma^2}{\sigma}\right) - \Phi\left(\frac{\ln(m_2/c) - \mu - \sigma^2}{\sigma}\right)\right\} \cdot \\ &\cdot\ c\exp\left(\mu + \frac{\sigma^2}{2}\right) + m_2\left\{\Phi\left(\frac{\ln(m_2/c) - \mu}{\sigma}\right) - 1\right\}, \end{aligned}$$

(e) *disappearing deductible premium*

$$
\begin{aligned}
P_{DD(d_1,d_2)} &= \frac{\exp\left(\mu+\sigma^2/2\right)}{d_2-d_1} \cdot \\
&\cdot \left\{ d_2 - d_1 + d_1 \Phi\left(\frac{\ln d_2 - \mu - \sigma^2}{\sigma}\right) - d_2 \Phi\left(\frac{\ln d_1 - \mu - \sigma^2}{\sigma}\right)\right\} \\
&+ \frac{d_1 d_2}{d_2 - d_1}\left\{\Phi\left(\frac{\ln d_1 - \mu}{\sigma}\right) - \Phi\left(\frac{\ln d_2 - \mu}{\sigma}\right)\right\}.
\end{aligned}
$$

We now illustrate the above formulae using the Danish fire loss data. We study the log-normal loss distribution with parameters $\mu = 12.6645$ and $\sigma = 1.3981$, which best fitted the data. Figure 19.6 depicts the premium under franchise and fixed amount deductibles in the log-normal case.

Figure 19.7 shows the effect of parameters c, m_1, and m_2 of the limited proportional deductible. Clearly, $P_{LPD(c,m_1,m_2)}$ is a decreasing function of these parameters.

Finally, Figure 19.8 depicts the influence of parameters d_1 and d_2 of the disappearing deductible. Markedly, $P_{DD(d_1,d_2)}$ is a decreasing function of the parameters and we can observe that the effect of increasing d_2 is rather minor.

19.3.2 Pareto Loss Distribution

The Pareto distribution function is defined by

$$
F(t) = 1 - \left(\frac{\lambda}{\lambda + t}\right)^{\alpha},
$$

where $t, \alpha, \lambda > 0$, see Chapter 13. The expectation of the Pareto distribution exists only for $\alpha > 1$. For the Pareto distribution with $\alpha > 1$ the following formulae hold:

(a) *franchise deductible premium*

$$
P_{FD(a)} = \frac{1}{\alpha - 1}(a\alpha + \lambda)\left(\frac{\lambda}{a + \lambda}\right)^{\alpha},
$$

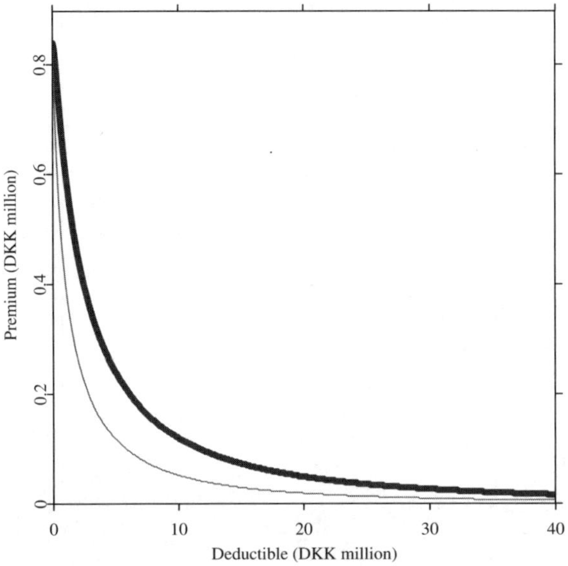

Figure 19.6: The premium under the franchise deductible (thick blue line) and fixed amount deductible (thin red line). The log-normal case.

STFded06.xpl

(b) *fixed amount deductible premium*

$$P_{FAD(b)} = \frac{1}{\alpha - 1}(b + \lambda)\left(\frac{\lambda}{b + \lambda}\right)^{\alpha},$$

(c) *proportional deductible premium*

$$P_{PD(c)} = (1 - c)\frac{\lambda}{\alpha - 1},$$

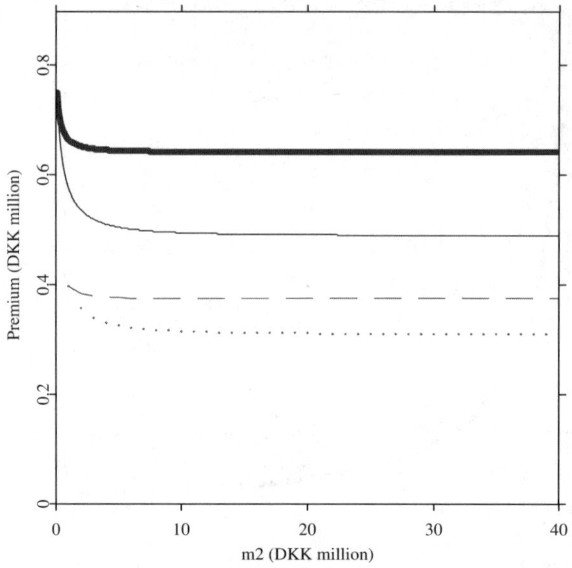

Figure 19.7: The premium under the limited proportional deductible with respect to the parameter m_2. The thick blue solid line represents the premium for $c = 0.2$ and $m_1 = 100\ 000$ DKK, the thin blue solid line for $c = 0.4$ and $m_1 = 100\ 000$ DKK, the dashed red line for $c = 0.2$ and $m_1 = 1$ million DKK, and the dotted red line for $c = 0.4$ and $m_1 = 1$ million DKK. The log-normal case.

STFded07.xpl

(d) *limited proportional deductible premium*

$$
\begin{aligned}
P_{LPD(c,m_1,m_2)} &= \frac{1}{\alpha-1}(m_1+\lambda)\left(\frac{\lambda}{m_1+\lambda}\right)^{\alpha} \\
&+ \frac{c}{\alpha-1}\left\{\left(\frac{m_2}{c}+\lambda\right)\left(\frac{\lambda}{m_2/c+\lambda}\right)^{\alpha}\right. \\
&\left. -\left(\frac{m_1}{c}+\lambda\right)\left(\frac{\lambda}{m_1/c+\lambda}\right)^{\alpha}\right\},
\end{aligned}
$$

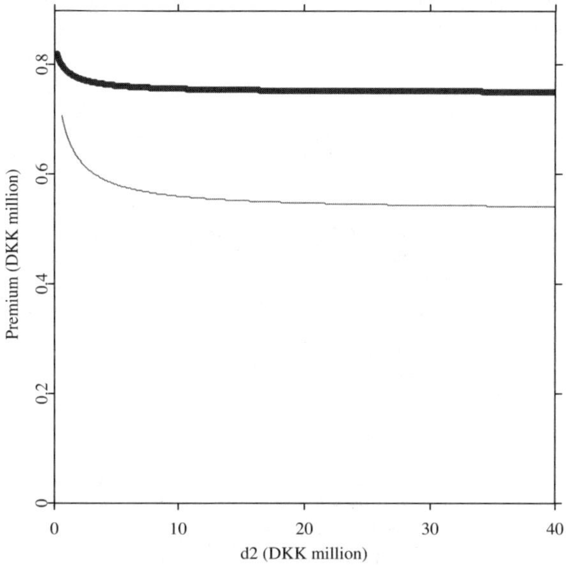

Figure 19.8: The premium under the disappearing deductible with respect to the parameter d_2. The thick blue line represents the premium for $d_1 = 100\ 000$ DKK and the thin red line the premium for $d_1 = 500\ 000$ DKK. The log-normal case. STFded08.xpl

(e) *disappearing deductible premium*

$$P_{DD(d_1,d_2)} = \frac{1}{(\alpha-1)(d_2-d_1)} \cdot \left\{ d_2(d_1+\lambda)\left(\frac{\lambda}{d_1+\lambda}\right)^{\alpha} - d_1(d_2+\lambda)\left(\frac{\lambda}{d_2+\lambda}\right)^{\alpha} \right\}.$$

19.3.3 Burr Loss Distribution

Experience has shown that the Pareto formula is often an appropriate model for the claim size distribution, particularly where exceptionally large claims may occur. However, there is sometimes a need to find heavy tailed distributions which offer greater flexibility than the Pareto law. Such flexibility is provided by the Burr distribution which distribution function is given by

$$F(t) = 1 - \left(\frac{\lambda}{\lambda + t^\tau}\right)^\alpha,$$

where t, α, λ, $\tau > 0$, see Chapter 13. Its mean exists only for $\alpha\tau > 1$. For the Burr distribution with $\alpha\tau > 1$ the following formulae hold:

(a) *franchise deductible premium*

$$P_{FD(a)} = \frac{\lambda^{1/\tau}\Gamma\left(\alpha - 1/\tau\right)\Gamma\left(1 + 1/\tau\right)}{\Gamma(\alpha)} \left\{1 - \mathrm{B}\left(1 + \frac{1}{\tau}, \alpha - \frac{1}{\tau}, \frac{a^\tau}{\lambda + a^\tau}\right)\right\},$$

(b) *fixed amount deductible premium*

$$P_{FAD(b)} = \frac{\lambda^{1/\tau}\Gamma\left(\alpha - 1/\tau\right)\Gamma\left(1 + 1/\tau\right)}{\Gamma(\alpha)} \cdot \left\{1 - \mathrm{B}\left(1 + \frac{1}{\tau}, \alpha - \frac{1}{\tau}, \frac{b^\tau}{\lambda + b^\tau}\right)\right\} - b\left(\frac{\lambda}{\lambda + b^\tau}\right)^\alpha,$$

(c) *proportional deductible premium*

$$P_{PD(c)} = (1 - c)\frac{\lambda^{1/\tau}\Gamma(\alpha - 1/\tau)\Gamma(1 + 1/\tau)}{\Gamma(\alpha)},$$

(d) *limited proportional deductible premium*

$$
\begin{aligned}
P_{LPD(c,m_1,m_2)} &= \frac{\lambda^{1/\tau}\Gamma(\alpha-1/\tau)\Gamma(1+1/\tau)}{\Gamma(\alpha)} \cdot \\
&\cdot \left\{1 - \mathrm{B}\left(1+\frac{1}{\tau}, \alpha-\frac{1}{\tau}, \frac{m_1^\tau}{\lambda+m_1^\tau}\right)\right. \\
&+c\mathrm{B}\left(1+\frac{1}{\tau}, \alpha-\frac{1}{\tau}, \frac{(m_1/c)^\tau}{\lambda+(m_1/c)^\tau}\right) \\
&\left.-c\mathrm{B}\left(1+\frac{1}{\tau}, \alpha-\frac{1}{\tau}, \frac{(m_2/c)^\tau}{\lambda+(m_2/c)^\tau}\right)\right\} \\
&- m_1\left(\frac{\lambda}{\lambda+m_1^\tau}\right)^\alpha + m_1\left(\frac{\lambda}{\lambda+(m_1/c)^\tau}\right)^\alpha \\
&- m_2\left(\frac{\lambda}{\lambda+(m_2/c)^\tau}\right)^\alpha,
\end{aligned}
$$

(e) *disappearing deductible premium*

$$
\begin{aligned}
P_{DD(d_1,d_2)} &= \frac{\lambda^{1/\tau}\Gamma(\alpha-1/\tau)\Gamma(1+1/\tau)}{\Gamma(\alpha)} \cdot \\
&\cdot \left[\frac{d_2 - d_1 + d_1\mathrm{B}\left\{1+1/\tau, \alpha-1/\tau, d_2^\tau/(\lambda+d_2^\tau)\right\}}{d_2-d_1}\right. \\
&\left.-\frac{d_2\mathrm{B}\left\{1+1/\tau, \alpha-1/\tau, d_1^\tau/(\lambda+d_1^\tau)\right\}}{d_2-d_1}\right] \\
&+ \frac{d_2 d_1}{d_2-d_1}\left\{\left(\frac{\lambda}{\lambda+d_2^\tau}\right)^\alpha - \left(\frac{\lambda}{\lambda+d_1^\tau}\right)^\alpha\right\},
\end{aligned}
$$

where the functions $\Gamma(\cdot)$ and $\mathrm{B}(\cdot,\cdot,\cdot)$ are defined as: $\Gamma(a) = \int_0^\infty y^{a-1}e^{-y}dy$ and $\mathrm{B}(a,b,x) = \frac{\Gamma(a+b)}{\Gamma(a)\Gamma(b)}\int_0^x y^{a-1}(1-y)^{b-1}dy$.

In order to illustrate the preceding formulae we consider the fire loss data. analysed in Chapter 13. The analysis showed that the losses can be well mod-

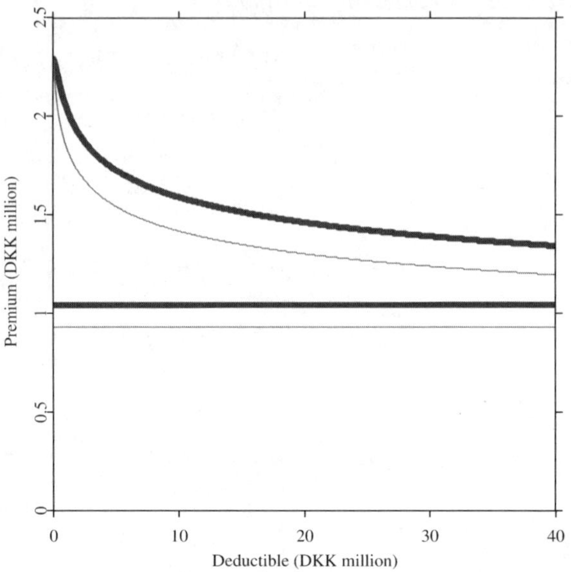

Figure 19.9: The premium under the franchise deductible (thick blue line) and fixed amount deductible (thin red line). The Burr case.

STFded09.xpl

elled by the Burr distribution with parameters $\alpha = 0.8804$, $\lambda = 8.4202 \cdot 10^6$ and $\tau = 1.2749$. Figure 19.9 depicts the premium under franchise and fixed amount deductibles for the Burr loss distribution.

In Figure 19.10 the influence of the parameters c, m_1, and m_2 of the limited proportional deductible is illustrated. Figure 19.11 shows the effect of the parameters d_1 and d_2 of the disappearing deductible.

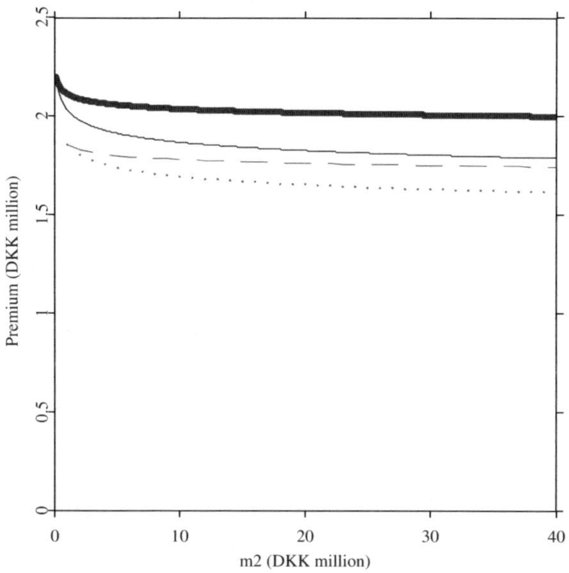

Figure 19.10: The premium under the limited proportional deductible with respect to the parameter m_2. The thick solid blue line represents the premium for $c = 0.2$ and $m_1 = 100\ 000$ DKK, the thin solid blue line for $c = 0.4$ and $m_1 = 100\ 000$ DKK, the dashed red line for $c = 0.2$ and $m_1 = 1$ million DKK, and the dotted red line for $c = 0.4$ and $m_1 = 1$ million DKK. The Burr case.

STFded10.xpl

19.3.4 Weibull Loss Distribution

Another frequently used analytic claim size distribution is the Weibull distribution which is defined by

$$F(t) = 1 - \exp\left(-\beta t^{\tau}\right),$$

where t, τ, $\beta > 0$, see Chapter 13.

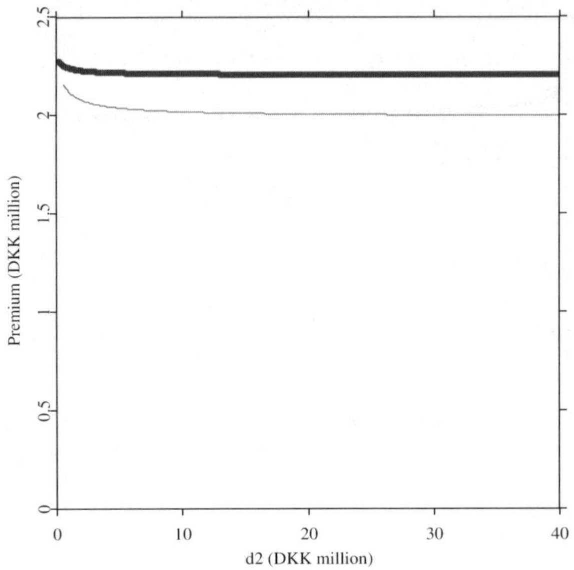

Figure 19.11: The premium under the disappearing deductible with respect to the parameter d_2. The thick blue line represents the premium for $d_1 = 100\ 000$ DKK and the thin red line the premium for $d_1 = 500\ 000$ DKK. The Burr case. STFded11.xpl

For the Weibull distribution the following formulae hold:

(a) *franchise deductible premium*

$$P_{FD(a)} = \frac{\Gamma(1+1/\tau)}{\beta^{1/\tau}} \left\{1 - \Gamma\left(1 + \frac{1}{\tau}, \beta a^{\tau}\right)\right\},$$

(b) *fixed amount deductible premium*

$$P_{FAD(b)} = \frac{\Gamma(1+1/\tau)}{\beta^{1/\tau}} \left\{1 - \Gamma\left(1 + \frac{1}{\tau}, \beta b^{\tau}\right)\right\} - b \exp\left(-\beta b^{\tau}\right),$$

(c) *proportional deductible premium*

$$P_{PD(c)} = \frac{(1-c)}{\beta^{1/\tau}}\Gamma\left(1+\frac{1}{\tau}\right),$$

(d) *limited proportional deductible premium*

$$\begin{aligned}
P_{LPD(c,m_1,m_2)} &= \frac{\Gamma(1+1/\tau)}{\beta^{1/\tau}}\left\{1-\Gamma\left(1+\frac{1}{\tau},\beta m_1^\tau\right)\right\} \\
&+ \frac{c\Gamma(1+1/\tau)}{\beta^{1/\tau}}\Gamma\left\{1+\frac{1}{\tau},\beta\left(\frac{m_1}{c}\right)^\tau\right\} \\
&- \frac{c\Gamma(1+1/\tau)}{\beta^{1/\tau}}\Gamma\left\{1+\frac{1}{\tau},\beta\left(\frac{m_2}{c}\right)^\tau\right\} \\
&- m_1\exp(-\beta m_1^\tau) + m_1\exp\left\{-\beta\left(\frac{m_1}{c}\right)^\tau\right\} \\
&- m_2\exp\left\{-\beta\left(\frac{m_2}{c}\right)^\tau\right\},
\end{aligned}$$

(e) *disappearing deductible premium*

$$\begin{aligned}
P_{DD(d_1,d_2)} &= \frac{\Gamma(1+1/\tau)}{\beta^{1/\tau}(d_2-d_1)}\left\{d_2-d_1+d_1\Gamma\left(1+\frac{1}{\tau},\beta d_2^\tau\right)\right. \\
&\left. -d_2\Gamma\left(1+\frac{1}{\tau},\beta d_1{}^\tau\right)\right\} \\
&+ \frac{d_1d_2}{d_2-d_1}\left\{\exp(-\beta d_2^\tau)-\exp(-\beta d_1^\tau)\right\},
\end{aligned}$$

where the incomplete gamma function $\Gamma(\cdot,\cdot)$ is defined as

$$\Gamma(a,x) = \frac{1}{\Gamma(a)}\int_0^x y^{a-1}e^{-y}dy.$$

19.3.5 Gamma Loss Distribution

All four presented above distributions suffer from some mathematical drawbacks such as lack of a closed form representation for the Laplace transform and nonexistence of the moment generating function. The gamma distribution given by

$$F(t) = F(t, \alpha, \beta) = \int_0^t \frac{\beta^\alpha}{\Gamma(\alpha)} y^{\alpha-1} e^{-\beta y} dy,$$

for $t, \alpha, \beta > 0$ does not have these drawbacks, see Chapter 13. For the gamma distribution the following formulae hold:

(a) *franchise deductible premium*

$$P_{FD(a)} = \frac{\alpha}{\beta} \{1 - F(a, \alpha + 1, \beta)\},$$

(b) *fixed amount deductible premium*

$$P_{FAD(b)} = \frac{\alpha}{\beta} \{1 - F(b, \alpha + 1, \beta)\} - b \{1 - F(b, \alpha, \beta)\},$$

(c) *proportional deductible premium*

$$P_{PD(c)} = \frac{(1-c)\alpha}{\beta},$$

(d) *limited proportional deductible premium*

$$\begin{aligned} P_{LPD(c,m_1,m_2)} &= \frac{\alpha}{\beta} \{1 - F(m_1, \alpha + 1, \beta)\} \\ &+ \frac{c\alpha}{\beta} \left\{ F\left(\frac{m_1}{c}, \alpha + 1, \beta\right) - F\left(\frac{m_2}{c}, \alpha + 1, \beta\right) \right\} \\ &+ m_1 \left\{ F(m_1, \alpha, \beta) - F\left(\frac{m_1}{c}, \alpha, \beta\right) \right\} \\ &- m_2 \left\{ 1 - F\left(\frac{m_2}{c}, \alpha, \beta\right) \right\}, \end{aligned}$$

(e) *disappearing deductible premium*

$$\begin{aligned} P_{DD(d_1,d_2)} &= \frac{\alpha}{\beta(d_2 - d_1)} \Big[d_2 \{1 - F(d_1, \alpha + 1, \beta)\} \\ &\quad - d_1 \{1 - F(d_2, \alpha + 1, \beta)\} \Big] \\ &+ \frac{d_1 d_2}{d_2 - d_1} \{F(d_1, \alpha, \beta) - F(d_2, \alpha, \beta)\}. \end{aligned}$$

19.3.6 Mixture of Two Exponentials Loss Distribution

The mixture of two exponentials distribution function is defined by

$$F(t) = 1 - a\exp(-\beta_1 t) - (1-a)\exp(-\beta_2 t),$$

where $0 \leq a \leq 1$ and $\beta_1, \beta_2 > 0$, see Chapter 13. For the mixture of exponentials distribution the following formulae hold:

(a) *franchise deductible premium*

$$\begin{aligned} P_{FD(c)} &= \frac{a}{\beta_1}\exp(-\beta_1 c) + \frac{1-a}{\beta_2}\exp(-\beta_2 c) \\ &+ c\{a\exp(-\beta_1 c) + (1-a)\exp(-\beta_2 c)\}, \end{aligned}$$

(b) *fixed amount deductible premium*

$$P_{FAD(b)} = \frac{a}{\beta_1}\exp(-\beta_1 b) + \frac{1-a}{\beta_2}\exp(-\beta_2 b),$$

(c) *proportional deductible premium*

$$P_{PD(c)} = (1-c)\left(\frac{a}{\beta_1} + \frac{1-a}{\beta_2}\right),$$

(d) *limited proportional deductible premium*

$$\begin{aligned} P_{LPD(c,m_1,m_2)} &= \frac{a}{\beta_1}\exp(-\beta_1 m_1) + \frac{1-a}{\beta_2}\exp(-\beta_2 m_1) \\ &+ \frac{ca}{\beta_1}\left\{\exp\left(-\beta_1\frac{m_2}{c}\right) - \exp\left(-\beta_1\frac{m_1}{c}\right)\right\} \\ &+ \frac{c(1-a)}{\beta_2}\left\{\exp\left(-\beta_2\frac{m_2}{c}\right) - \exp\left(-\beta_2\frac{m_1}{c}\right)\right\}, \end{aligned}$$

(e) *disappearing deductible premium*

$$\begin{aligned} P_{DD(d_1,d_2)} &= \frac{a}{\beta_1}\left\{\frac{d_2}{d_2-d_1}\exp(-\beta_1 d_1) - \frac{d_1}{d_2-d_1}\exp(-\beta_1 d_2)\right\} \\ &+ \frac{1-a}{\beta_2}\left\{\frac{d_2}{d_2-d_1}\exp(-\beta_2 d_1) - \frac{d_1}{d_2-d_1}\exp(-\beta_2 d_2)\right\}. \end{aligned}$$

19.4 Final Remarks

Let us first concentrate on the franchise and fixed amount deductibles. Figures 19.6 and 19.9 depict the comparison of the two corresponding premiums and the effect of increasing the parameters a and b. Evidently $P \geqslant P_{FD} \geqslant P_{FAD}$. Moreover, we can see that the deducible of about DKK 2 million in the log-normal case and DKK 40 million in the Burr case reduces P_{FAD} by half. Figures corresponding to the two loss distributions are similar, however we note that the differences do not lie in shifting or scaling. The same is true for the rest of considered deductibles. We also note that the premiums under no deductible for log-normal and Burr loss distributions do not tally because the parameters were estimated via the Anderson-Darling statistic minimization procedure which in general does not yield the same moments, cf. Chapter 13. For the considered distributions the mean, and consequently the pure risk premium, is even 3 times bigger in the Burr case.

The proportional deductible influences the premium in an obvious manner, that is pro rata (e.g. $c = 0.25$ results in cutting the premium by a quarter). Figures 19.7 and 19.10 show the effect of parameters c, m_1 and m_2 of the limited proportional deductible. It is easy to see that $P_{LPD(c,m_1,m_2)}$ is a decreasing function of these parameters. Figures 19.8 and 19.11 depict the influence of parameters d_1 and d_2 of the disappearing deductible. Clearly, $P_{DD(d_1,d_2)}$ is a decreasing function of the parameters and we can observe that the effect of increasing d_2 is rather minor.

It is clear that the choice of a distribution and a deductible has a great impact on the pure risk premium. For an insurer the choice can be crucial in reasonable quoting of a given risk. A potential insured should take into account insurance options arising from appropriate types and levels of self-insurance (deductibles). Insurance premiums decrease with increasing levels of deductibles. With adequate loss protection, a property owner can take some risk and accept a large deductible which might reduce the total cost of insurance.

We presented here a general approach to calculating pure risk premiums under deductibles. In Section 19.2 we presented a link between the pure risk premium under several deductibles and a limited expected value function. We used this link in Section 19.3 to calculate the pure risk premium in the case of the deductibles for different claim amount distributions. The results can be applied to derive annual premiums in the individual and collective risk model on a per occurrence deductible basis.

The approach can be easily extended to other distributions. One has only to calculate levf for a particular distribution. This also includes the case of right-truncated distributions which would reflect the maximum limit of liability set in a contract. Moreover, the idea can be extended to other deductibles. Once we express the pure risk premium in terms of the limited expected value function, it is enough to apply a form of levf for a specific distribution. Finally, one can also use the formulae to obtain the premium with safety loading which is discussed in Chapter 18.

Bibliography

Aebi, M., Embrechts, P., and Mikosch, T. (1992). A large claim index, *Mitteilungen SVVM*: 143–156.

Burnecki, K., Kukla, G., and Weron, R. (2000). Property insurance loss distributions, *Physica A* **287**: 269–278.

Burnecki, K., Nowicka-Zagrajek, J., and Weron, A. (2004). Pure risk premiums under deductibles. A quantitative management in actuarial practice, Research Report HSC/04/5, Hugo Steinhaus Center, Wroclaw University of Technology.

Daykin, C.D., Pentikainen, T., and Pesonen, M. (1994). *Practical Risk Theory for Actuaries*, Chapman&Hall, London.

Embrechts, P., Klüppelberg, C., and Mikosch, T. (1997). *Modelling Extremal Events for Insurance and Finance*, Springer, Berlin.

Klugman, S. A., Panjer, H.H., and Willmot, G.E. (1998). *Loss Models: From Data to Decisions*, Wiley, New York.

Mikosch, T. (1997). Heavy-tailed modelling in insurance, *Commun. Statist.-Stochastic Models* **13**: 799–815.

Panjer, H.H. and Willmot, G.E. (1992). *Insurance Risk Models*, Society of Actuaries, Schaumburg.

Sundt, B. (1994). *An Introduction to Non-Life Insurance Mathematics (3rd ed.)*, Verlag Versicherungswirtschaft e.V., Karlsruhe.

20 Premiums, Investments, and Reinsurance

Paweł Miśta and Wojciech Otto

20.1 Introduction

In this chapter, setting the appropriate level of insurance premium is considered in a broader context of business decisions, concerning also risk transfer through reinsurance, and the rate of return on capital required to ensure solvability. Furthermore, the long term dividend policy, i.e. the rule of subdividing the financial result between the company and shareholders, is analyzed.

The problem considered throughout this chapter can be illustrated by a simple example.

Example 1

Let us consider the following model of a risk process describing a capital of an insurer:

$$R_t = u + (c - du)t - S_t, \qquad t \geq 0,$$

where R_t denotes the current capital at time t, $u = R_0$ stands for initial capital, c is the intensity of premium inflow, and S_t is the aggregate loss process – amount of claim's outlays over the period $(0, t]$. The term du represents the intensity of outflow of dividends paid to shareholders with d being the dividend rate. Let us assume that increments of the amount of claims process $S_{t+h} - S_t$ are for any $t, h > 0$ normally distributed $N(\mu h, \sigma^2 h)$ and mutually independent. Below we consider premium calculation under two cases.

First case: $d = 0$. In this case the probability of ruin is an exponential function of the initial capital:

$$\psi(u) = \exp(-Ru), \qquad u \geq 0,$$

where the adjustment coefficient R exists for $c > \mu$, and equals then $2(c-\mu)\sigma^{-2}$. The above formula can be easily inverted to render the intensity of premium c for a given capital u and predetermined level ψ of ruin probability:

$$c = \mu + \frac{-\log(\psi)}{2u}\sigma^2.$$

Given the safety standard ψ, the larger the initial capital u of the company is, the more competitive it is (since it can offer the insurance cover at a lower price c). However, a more realistic result is considered when we assume positive cost of capital.

Second case: $d > 0$. Now the problem of competitiveness is reduced to the problem of minimizing the premium by choosing the optimal level of capital backing insurance risk:

$$c = \mu + \frac{-\log(\psi)}{2u}\sigma^2 + du.$$

The solution reads:

$$u_{opt} = \sigma\sqrt{\frac{-\log(\psi)}{2d}},$$

$$c_{opt} = \mu + \sigma\sqrt{-2d\log\psi},$$

where exactly one half of the loading $(c_{opt} - \mu)$ serves to finance dividends and the other half serves as a safety loading (retained in the company).

Having already calculated the total premium, we face the problem of decomposing it into premiums for individual risks. In order to do that we should first identify the random variable $W = S_{t+1} - S_t$ as a sum of independent risks $X_1, \ldots, X_n$, and the intensity of premium c as a whole-portfolio premium $\Pi(W)$, which has to be decomposed into individual premiums $\Pi(X_i)$. The decomposition is straightforward when the total premium is calculated as in the first case above:

$$\Pi(X_i) = \mathrm{E}(X_i) + \frac{-\log(\psi)}{2u}\sigma^2(X_i),$$

which is due to additivity of variance for independent risks. The premium formula in the second case contains the safety loading proportional to the standard deviation and thus is no more additive. This does not mean that reasonable decomposition rules do not exist – rather that their derivation is not so straightforward.

In this chapter, various generalizations of the basic problem presented in the Example 1 are considered. These generalizations make the basic problem more complex on the one hand, but closer to real-life situations on the other. Additionally, these generalizations do not yield analytical results and, therefore, we demonstrate in several examples how to obtain numerical solutions.

First of all, Example 1 assumes that the safety standard is expressed in terms of an acceptable level of ruin probability. On the contrary, Sections 2, 3, and 4 are devoted to the approach based on the distribution of the single-year loss function. Section 2 presents the basic problem of joint decisions on premium and capital needed to ensure safety in terms of shareholder's choice of the level of expected rate of return and risk. Section 3 presents in more details the problem of decomposition of the whole-portfolio premium into individual risks premiums. Section 4 presents the problem extended by allowing for reinsurance, where competitiveness is a result of simultaneous choice of the amount of capital and retention level. This problem has not been illustrated in Example 1, as in the case of the normal distribution of the aggregate loss and usual market conditions there is no room to improve competitiveness through reinsurance.

Sections 5, 6, and 7 are devoted again to the approach based on ruin probability. However, Section 5 departs from the simplistic assumptions of Example 1 concerning the risk process. It is shown there how to invert various approximate formulas for the ruin probability in order to calculate premium for the whole portfolio as well as to decompose it into individual risks. Section 6 exploits results of Section 5 in the context of positive cost of capital. In that section a kind of flexible dividend policy is also considered, and the possibility to improve competitiveness this way is studied. Finally, Section 7 presents an extension of the decision problem by allowing for reinsurance cession.

Throughout this chapter we assume that we typically have at our disposal incomplete information on the distribution of the aggregate loss, and this incomplete information set consists of cumulants of order 1, 2, 3, and possibly 4. The rationale is that sensible empirical investigation of frequency and severity distributions could be done only separately for sub-portfolios of homogeneous risks. Cumulants for the whole portfolio are then obtained just by summing up figures over the collection of sub-portfolios, provided that sub-portfolios are mutually independent. The existence of cumulants of higher orders is assured by the common practice of issuing policies with limited cover exclusively (which in many countries is even enforced by law). Consequences of the assumption are that both the quantile of the current year loss and the probability of ruin in the long run will be approximated by formulas based on cumulants of the one-year aggregate loss W.

The chapter is based on Otto (2004), a book on non-life insurance mathematics. However, general ideas are heavily borrowed from the seminal paper of Bühlmann (1985).

20.2 Single-period Criterion and the Rate of Return on Capital

In this section the problem of joint decisions on premium and required capital is considered in terms of shareholder's choice of the level of expected rate of return and risk. It is assumed that typically the single-year loss (when it happens) is covered by the insurance company through reduction of its own assets. This assumption can be justified by the fact that in most developed countries state supervision agencies efficiently prevent companies to undertake too risky insurance business without own assets being large enough. As shareholders are unable to externalize the loss, they are enforced to balance the required expected rate of return with the possible size of the loss. The risk based capital concept (RBC) formalizes the assumption that premium loading results from the required expected rate of return on capital invested by shareholders and the admitted level of risk.

20.2.1 Risk Based Capital Concept

Let us denote by RBC the amount of capital backing risk borne by the insurance portfolio. It is assumed that the capital has a form of assets invested in securities. Shareholders will accept risk borne by the insurance portfolio provided it yields expected rate of return larger than the rate of return on riskless investments offered by the financial market. Let us denote by r the required expected rate of return, and by r_f the riskless rate. The following equality holds:

$$\Pi(W) - \mathrm{E}(W) = (r - r_f) \cdot RBC. \tag{20.1}$$

For simplicity it is assumed that all assets are invested in riskless securities. This means that we neglect shareholder's capital locked-up in fixed assets necessary to run the insurance operations of the company, and we also assume prudent investment policy, at least with respect to those assets, which are devoted for backing the insurance risk. It is also assumed that all amounts are expressed in terms of their value at the end of year (accumulated when spent or received earlier, discounted when spent or received after the year end).

Let us also assume that company management is convinced that the rate of return r is large enough to admit the risk of technical loss in amount, let us say, ηRBC, $\eta \in (0,\ 1)$ with a presumed small probability ε. The total loss of capital amounts then to $(\eta - r_f)\, RBC$. The assumption could be expressed in the following form:

$$F_W^{-1}(1-\varepsilon) = \Pi(W) + \eta RBC, \tag{20.2}$$

where F_W denotes the cdf of random variable W.

Combining equations (20.1) and (20.2), one obtains the desired amount of capital backing risk of the insurance portfolio:

$$RBC = \frac{F_W^{-1}(1-\varepsilon) - \mathrm{E}(W)}{r - r_f + \eta}, \tag{20.3}$$

and the corresponding premium:

$$\Pi^{RBC}(W) = \mathrm{E}(W) + \frac{r - r_f}{r - r_f + \eta} \left\{ F_W^{-1}(1-\varepsilon) - \mathrm{E}(W) \right\}. \tag{20.4}$$

In both formulas, only the difference $r - r_f$ is relevant. We denote it by r^*. The obtained premium formula is just a simple generalization of the well-known quantile formula based on the one-year loss criterion. This standard formula is obtained by replacing the coefficient $r^*\,(r^* + \eta)^{-1}$ by one. Now it is clear that the standard formula could be interpreted as a result of the assumption $\eta = 0$, so that shareholders are not ready to suffer a technical loss at all (at least with probability higher than ε).

20.2.2 How to Choose Parameter Values?

Parameters r^*, η, and ε of the formula are subject to managerial decision. However, an actuary could help reducing the number of redundant decision parameters. This is because parameters reflect not only subjective factors (shareholder's attitude to risk), but also objective factors (rate of substitution between expected return and risk offered by the capital market). The latter could be deduced from capital market quotations. In terms of the Capital Asset Pricing Model (CAPM), the relationship between expectation $\mathrm{E}(\Delta R)$ and standard deviation $\sigma(\Delta R)$ of the excess ΔR of the rate of return over the riskless rate is reflected by the so-called capital market line (CML). The slope coefficient $\mathrm{E}(\Delta Rt)\sigma^{-1}(\Delta R)$ of the CML represents just a risk premium (in terms of an increase in expectation) per unit increase of standard deviation. Let us denote the reciprocal of the slope coefficient by $s \stackrel{\text{def}}{=} \{\mathrm{E}(\Delta R)\}^{-1} \sigma(\Delta R)$. We will now consider shareholder's choice between two alternatives: investment of the amount RBC in a well diversified portfolio of equities and bonds versus investment in the insurance company's capital. In the second case the total loss $W - \Pi(W) - r_f RBC$ exceeds the amount $(\eta - r_f) RBC$ with probability ε. The equally probable loss in the first case equals:

$$\{u_\varepsilon \sigma(\Delta R) - \mathrm{E}(\Delta R) - r_f\} RBC,$$

where u_ε denotes the quantile of order $(1 - \varepsilon)$ of the standard normal variable. This is justified by the fact that the CAPM is based on assumption of normality of fluctuations of rates of return. The shareholder is indifferent when the following equation holds:

$$\eta - r_f = u_\varepsilon \sigma(\Delta R) - \mathrm{E}(\Delta R) - r_f,$$

provided that expected rates of return in both cases are the same: $r = r_f + \mathrm{E}(\Delta R)$. Making use of our knowledge of the substitution rate s and putting the above results together we obtain: $\eta = r^* (u_\varepsilon s - 1)$.

In the real world the required rate of return could depart (*ceteris paribus*) from the above equation. On the one hand, required expected rate of return could be larger, because direct investments in strategic portions of the insurance company capital are not as liquid as investments in securities traded on the stock exchange. On the other hand, there is empirical evidence that fluctuations in profits in the insurance industry are uncorrelated with the business cycle. This means that having a portion of insurance company shares in the portfolio improves diversification of risk to which a portfolio investor is exposed. Hence, there are reasons to require smaller risk premium.

The reasonable range of the parameter ε is from 1% to 5%. The rate of return depends on shareholder's attitude to risk and market conditions, but it is customary to assume that the range of the risk premium r^* is from 5% to 15%. A reference point for setting the parameter η could also be deduced from regulatory requirements, as the situation when the capital falls below the solvency margin needs undertaking troublesome actions enforced by supervision authority that could be harmful for company managers. A good summary of the CAPM and related models is given in Panjer et al. (1998), Chapters 4 and 8.

20.3 The Top-down Approach to Individual Risks Pricing

As it has been pointed out in the introduction, some premium calculation formulas are additive for independent risks, and then the decomposition of the whole-portfolio premium into individual risks premiums is straightforward. However, sometimes a non-additive formula for pricing the whole portfolio is well justified, and then the decomposition is no more trivial. This is exactly the case of the RBC formula (and also other quantile-based formulas) derived in the previous section. This section is devoted to showing the range, interpretation and applications of some solutions to this problem.

20.3.1 Approximations of Quantiles

In the case of the RBC formula decomposition means answering the question what is the share of a particular risk in the demand for capital backing the portfolio risk that in turn entails the premium. In order to solve the problem one can make use of approximations of the quantile by the normal power expansions. The most general version used in practice of the normal power formula for the quantile w_ε of order $(1-\varepsilon)$ of the variable W reads:

$$w_\varepsilon \approx \mu_W + \sigma_W \left(u_\varepsilon + \frac{u_\varepsilon^2 - 1}{6}\gamma_W + \frac{u_\varepsilon^3 - 3u_\varepsilon}{24}\gamma_{2,W} - \frac{2u_\varepsilon^3 - 5u_\varepsilon}{36}\gamma_W^2 \right),$$

where $\mu_W, \sigma_W, \gamma_W, \gamma_{2,W}$ denotes expectation, standard deviation, skewness, and kurtosis of the variable W and u_ε is the quantile of order $(1-\varepsilon)$ of a $N(0,1)$ variable. Now the premium can be expressed by:

$$\Pi^{RBC}(W) = \mu_W + \sigma_W \left(a_0 + a_1\gamma_W + a_2\gamma_{2,W} - a_3\gamma_W^2 \right), \tag{20.5}$$

where coefficients a_0, a_1, a_2, a_3 are simple functions of parameters ε, η, r^*, and the quantile u_ε of the standard normal variable. The above formula was proposed by Fisher and Cornish, see Hill and Davis (1968), so it will be referred to as FC20.5. The formula reduced by neglecting the last two components (by taking $a_2 = a_3 = 0$) will be referred to as FC20.6:

$$\Pi^{RBC}(W) = \mu_W + \sigma_W \left(a_0 + a_1\gamma_W \right), \tag{20.6}$$

and the formula neglecting also the skewness component as normal approximation:

$$\Pi^{RBC}(W) = \mu_W + a_0\sigma_W. \tag{20.7}$$

More details on normal power approximation can be found in Kendall and Stuart (1977).

20.3.2 Marginal Cost Basis for Individual Risk Pricing

Premium for the individual risk X could be set on the basis of marginal cost. This means that we look for such a price at which the insurer is indifferent whether to accept the risk or not. Calculation of the marginal cost can be based on standards of differential calculus. In order to do that, we should first write the formula explicitly in terms of a function of cumulants of first four orders:

$$\Pi\left(\mu, \sigma^2, \mu_3, c_4\right) = \mu + a_0\sigma + a_1\frac{\mu_3}{\sigma^2} + a_2\frac{c_4}{\sigma^3} - a_3\frac{\mu_3^2}{\sigma^5}.$$

This allows expressing the increment $\Delta\Pi(W) \stackrel{\text{def}}{=} \Pi(W+X) - \Pi(W)$ due to extend of the basic portfolio W by additional risk X in terms of linear approximation:

$$\Delta\Pi(W) \approx \frac{\partial\Pi}{\partial\mu}(W)\,\Delta\mu_W + \frac{\partial\Pi}{\partial\sigma^2}(W)\,\Delta\sigma_W^2 + \frac{\partial\Pi}{\partial\mu_3}(W)\,\Delta\mu_{3,W} + \frac{\partial\Pi}{\partial c_4}(W)\,\Delta c_{4,W},$$

where $\frac{\partial\Pi}{\partial\mu}(W)$, $\frac{\partial\Pi}{\partial\sigma^2}(W)$, $\frac{\partial\Pi}{\partial\mu_3}(W)$, $\frac{\partial\Pi}{\partial c_4}(W)$ denote partial derivatives of the function $\Pi\left(\mu, \sigma^2, \mu_3, c_4\right)$ calculated at the point $\left(\mu_W, \sigma_W^2, \mu_{3,W}, c_{4,W}\right)$. By virtue of additivity of cumulants for independent random variables we replace increments $\left(\Delta\mu_W, \Delta\sigma_W^2, \Delta\mu_{3,W}, \Delta c_{4,W}\right)$ by cumulants of the additional risk $\left(\mu_X, \sigma_X^2, \mu_{3,X}, c_{4,X}\right)$. As a result the following formula is obtained:

$$\Pi_M(X) = \frac{\partial\Pi}{\partial\mu}(W)\,\mu_X + \frac{\partial\Pi}{\partial\sigma^2}(W)\,\sigma_X^2 + \frac{\partial\Pi}{\partial\mu_3}(W)\,\mu_{3,X} + \frac{\partial\Pi}{\partial c_4}(W)\,c_{4,X}.$$

Respective calculations lead to the marginal premium formula:

$$\begin{aligned}\Pi_M(X) &= \mu_X + a_0\frac{\sigma_X^2}{2\sigma_W} + \sigma_W a_1\gamma_W\left(\frac{\mu_{3,X}}{\mu_{3,W}} - \frac{\sigma_X^2}{\sigma_W^2}\right) + \\ &+\sigma_W\left\{a_2\gamma_{2,W}\left(\frac{c_{4,X}}{c_{4,W}} - \frac{3\sigma_X^2}{2\sigma_W^2}\right) - a_3\gamma_W^2\left(2\frac{\mu_{3,X}}{\mu_{3,W}} - \frac{5\sigma_X^2}{2\sigma_W^2}\right)\right\}.\end{aligned}$$

First two components coincide with the result obtained when the whole premium is based on the normal approximation. Setting additionally $a_1 \neq 0$ we obtain the premium for the case when skewness of the portfolio in non-neglectible (making use of FC20.6 approximation), including last two components means we regard also portfolio kurtosis (approximation based on formula FC20.5).

20.3.3 Balancing Problem

For each component the problem of balancing the premium on the whole portfolio level arises. Should all risks composing the portfolio $W = X_1 + X_2 + ... + X_n$ be charged their marginal premiums, the portfolio premium amounts to:

$$\sum_{i=1}^{n} \Pi_M (X_i) = \mu_W + \sigma_W \left(\frac{1}{2} a_0 - \frac{1}{2} a_2 \gamma_{2,W} + \frac{1}{2} a_3 \gamma_W^2 \right),$$

that is evidently underestimated by:

$$\Pi (W) - \sum_{i=1}^{n} \Pi_M (X_i) = \sigma_W \left(\frac{1}{2} a_0 + a_1 \gamma_W + \frac{3}{2} a_2 \gamma_{2,W} - \frac{3}{2} a_3 \gamma_W^2 \right).$$

The last figure represents a diversification effect obtained by composing the portfolio of a large number of individual risks, which could be also treated as an example of "positive returns to scale".

Balancing correction made so as to preserve sensitivity of premium on cumulants of order 1, 3, and 4 leads to the formula for the basic premium:

$$\begin{aligned} \Pi_B (X) &= \mu_X + \sigma_W a_0 \tfrac{\sigma_X^2}{\sigma_W^2} + \\ &+ \sigma_W \left\{ a_1 \gamma_W \tfrac{\mu_{3,X}}{\mu_{3,W}} + a_2 \gamma_{2,W} \tfrac{c_{4,X}}{c_{4,W}} - a_3 \gamma_W^2 \left(2 \tfrac{\mu_{3,X}}{\mu_{3,W}} - \tfrac{\sigma_X^2}{\sigma_W^2} \right) \right\}. \end{aligned}$$

Obviously, several alternative correction rules exist. For example, in the case of the kurtosis component any expression of the form:

$$a_2 \sigma_W \gamma_{2,W} \left\{ \frac{c_{4,X}}{c_{4,W}} + \delta \left(\frac{c_{4,X}}{c_{4,W}} - \frac{\sigma_X^2}{\sigma_W^2} \right) \right\}$$

satisfies the requirement of balancing the whole portfolio premium for arbitrary number δ. In fact, any particular choice is more or less arbitrary. Some common sense can be expressed by the requirement that a basic premium formula should not produce smaller figures than marginal formula for any risk in the portfolio. Of course this requirement is insufficient to point out a unique solution. Here, the balancing problem results from the lack of additivity of the *RBC* formula, as it is a nonlinear function of cumulants.

20.3.4 A Solution for the Balancing Problem

It seems that only in the case of the variance component $a_0\sigma_X^2/2\sigma_W$ some more or less heuristic argument for the correction can be found. The essence of the basic premium for individual risks is that it is a basis of an open market offer. Once the cover is offered to the public, clients decide whether to buy the cover or not. Thus the price should not depend on how many risks out of the portfolio W have been insured before, and how many after the risk in question. Let us imagine a particular ordering of the basic set of n risks amended by the additional risk X in a form of a sequence $\{X_1, ..., X_j, X, X_{j+1}, ...X_n\}$. Given this ordering, the respective component of the marginal cost of risk X takes the form:

$$a_0\left(\sqrt{\sum\nolimits_{k=1}^{j}\sigma^2\left(X_k\right)+\sigma_X^2}-\sqrt{\sum\nolimits_{k=1}^{j}\sigma^2\left(X_k\right)}\right).$$

We can now consider the expected value of this component, provided that each of $(n+1)!$ orderings is equally probable (as it was proposed Shapley (1953)). However, calculations are much simpler if we assume that the share U of the aggregated variance of all risks preceeding the risk X in the total aggregate variance σ_W^2 is a random variable uniformly distributed over the interval $(0,\ 1)$. The error of the simplification is neglectible as the share of each individual risk in the total variance is small. The result:

$$a_0\,\mathrm{E}\left(\sqrt{U\sigma_W^2+\sigma_X^2}-\sqrt{U\sigma_W^2}\right)=a_0\int\limits_0^1\left(\sqrt{u\sigma_W^2+\sigma_X^2}-\sqrt{u\sigma_W^2}\right)du$$

$$\approx a_0\sigma_W 2\left(\sqrt{1+\frac{\sigma_X^2}{\sigma_W}}-1\right)\approx a_0\frac{\sigma_X^2}{\sigma_W}$$

is exactly what we need to balance the premium on the portfolio level. The reader easily verifies that the analogous argumentation does not work any more in the case of components of higher orders of the premium formula.

20.3.5 Applications

Results presented in this section have three possible fields of application. The first is just passive premium calculation for the whole portfolio. In this respect several more accurate formulas exist, especially when our information on the distribution of the variable W extends its first four cumulants.

The second application concerns pricing individual risks. In this respect it is hard to find a better approach (apart from that based on long-run solvability criteria, which is a matter of consideration in next sections), which consistently links the risk relevant to the company (on the whole portfolio level) with risk borne by an individual policy. Of course open market offer should be based on basic valuation $\Pi_B(\cdot)$, whereas the marginal cost valuation $\Pi_M(\cdot)$ could serve as a lower bound for contracts negotiated individually.

The third field of applications opens when a portfolio, characterized by substantial skewness and kurtosis, is inspected in order to localize these risks (or groups of risks), that distort the distribution of the whole portfolio. Too high (noncompetitive) general premium level could be caused though by few influential risks. Such localization could help in decisions concerning underwriting limits and reinsurance program. Applying these measures could help "normalize" the distribution of the variable W. Thus in the preliminary stage, when the basis for underwriting policy and reinsurance is considered, extended pricing formulas (involving higher order cumulants) should be used. Paradoxically, once the prudent underwriting and ceding policy has been elaborated, simple normal approximation suffices to price as well the portfolio as individual risks. Clearly, such prices concern only retained portions of risk, and should be complemented by reinsurance costs.

20.4 Rate of Return and Reinsurance Under the Short Term Criterion

This section is devoted to extending the decision problem considered in previous sections by allowing for reinsurance. Then the pricing obey the form:

$$\Pi(W) = \Pi_I(W_I) + \Pi_R(W_R),$$

where the whole aggregate loss W is subdivided into the share of the insurer W_I and that of reinsurer W_R. $\Pi_I(\cdot)$ denotes the premium formula applied by the insurer to price his share, set in accordance with *RBC* concept. $\Pi_R(\cdot)$ symbolizes the pricing formula used by the reinsurer. Provided formula $\Pi_R(\cdot)$ is accurate enough to reflect the existing offer of the reinsurance market, we could compare various variants of subdivision of the variable W into components W_I and W_R, looking for such subdivision which optimizes some objective function.

20.4.1 General Considerations

No matter which particular objective function is chosen, the space of possible subdivisions of the variable W has to be reduced somehow. One of the most important cases is when the variable W has a compound Poisson distribution, and the excess of loss reinsurance is chosen. Denoting by N the number of claims, we could define for each claim amount Y_i, $i = 1, 2, ...N$ its subdivision into the truncated loss $\underline{Y}_{M,i} \stackrel{\text{def}}{=} \min\{Y_i, M\}$ and the excess of loss $\overline{Y}_{M,1} \stackrel{\text{def}}{=} \max\{Y_i - M, 0\}$ and then define variables representing subdivision of the whole portfolio:

$$W_I = \underline{Y}_{M,1} + ... + \underline{Y}_{M,N},$$

$$W_R = \overline{Y}_{M,1} + ... + \overline{Y}_{M,N},$$

both having compound Poisson distributions too, with characteristics being functions of the subdivision parameter M.

Assuming that capital of the insurer is not flexible, and that the current amount u of capital is smaller than the amount $RBC(W)$ necessary to accept solely the whole portfolio, we could simply find such value of M, for which $RBC(W_I) = u$. In the case when the current amount of capital is in excess, it is still relevant to assess such portion of the capital, which should serve as a protection for insurance operations. The excess of capital over this amount can be treated separately, as being free of prudence requirements when investment decisions are undertaken.

It is more interesting to assume that the amount of capital is flexible, and to choose the retention limit M to minimize the total premium $\Pi(W)$ given parameters r^*, s, and ε. The objective function reflects the aim of maximizing competitiveness of the company. If the resulting premium (after being charged by respective cost loadings) is lower than that acceptable by the market, we can revise assumptions. Revised problem could consist in maximizing expected rate of return given the premium level and parameters η and ε. This would mean getting higher risk premium than that offered by the capital market. Reasonable solutions could be expected in the case when reinsurance premium formula $\Pi_R(\cdot)$ contains loadings proportional primarily to the expected value, and its sensitivity to the variance (more so as to skewness and kurtosis) is small. This could be expected as a result of transaction costs on the one hand, and larger capital assets of reinsurers on the other. Also the possibility to diversify risk on the world-wide scale work in the same direction, increasing transaction costs and at the same time reducing the reinsurer's exposure to risk.

20.4.2 Illustrative Example

Example 2

Aggregate loss W has a compound Poisson distribution with truncated-Pareto severity distribution, with cdf given for $y \geqslant 0$ by the formula:

$$F_Y(y) = \begin{cases} 1 - \left(1 + \frac{y}{\lambda}\right)^{-\alpha} & \text{when} \quad y < M_0 \\ 1 & \text{when} \quad y \geqslant M_0 \end{cases}$$

Variable W is subdivided into retained part $\underline{W}_M$ and ceded part $\overline{W}_M$, that given the subdivision parameter $M \in (0, M_0]$ have a form:

$$\underline{W}_M = \underline{Y}_{M,1} + \ldots + \underline{Y}_{M,N},$$

$$\overline{W}_M = \overline{Y}_{M,1} + \ldots + \overline{Y}_{M,N}.$$

We assume that reinsurance pricing rule can be reflected by the formula:

$$\Pi_R\left(\overline{W}_M\right) = (1 + re_0)\,\mathrm{E}\left(\overline{W}_M\right) + re_1 \mathrm{Var}\left(\overline{W}_M\right),$$

and that insurer's own pricing formula is:

$$\Pi_I\left(\underline{W}_M\right) = \mathrm{E}\left(\underline{W}_M\right) + \frac{r^*}{r^* + \eta}\left\{F^{-1}_{\underline{W}_M}(1 - \varepsilon) - \mathrm{E}\left(\underline{W}_M\right)\right\},$$

with a respective approximation of the quantile of the variable $\underline{W}_M$.

For expository purposes we take the following values of parameters:

(i) Parameters of the Pareto distribution $(\alpha, \lambda) = \left(\frac{5}{2}, \frac{3}{2}\right)$, with truncation point $M_0 = 500$;

(ii) Expected value of the number of claims $\mathrm{E}(N) = \lambda_P = 1000$;

(iii) Substitution rate $s = 2$;

(iv) Remaining parameters (in the basic variant of the problem) $\varepsilon = 2\%$, $r^* = 10\%$, $re_0 = 100\%$, $re_1 = 0.5\%$.

Problem consists in choosing the retention limit $M \in (0, M_0]$ that minimize the total premium $\Pi(W) = \Pi_I\left(\underline{W}_M\right) + \Pi_R\left(\overline{W}_M\right)$.

Solution.

First step is to express moments of first four orders of variables $\underline{Y}_M$ and $\overline{Y}_M$ as functions of parameters (α, λ, M_0) and the real variable M. Expected value of the truncated-Pareto variable with parameters (α, λ, M) equals by definition:

$$\int_0^M y \frac{\alpha\lambda^\alpha}{(\lambda+y)^{\alpha+1}} dy + M\{1-F(M)\} = \int_1^{1+\frac{M}{\lambda}} (x-1)\frac{\alpha\lambda}{x^{\alpha+1}} dx + M\left(1+\frac{M}{\lambda}\right)^{-\alpha} =$$

$$= \alpha\lambda \int_1^{1+\frac{M}{\lambda}} \left(x^{-\alpha} - x^{-\alpha-1}\right) dx + M\left(1+\frac{M}{\lambda}\right)^{-\alpha}$$

that, after integration and reordering of components produces the following formula:

$$m_1 = \frac{\lambda}{\alpha-1}\left\{1 - \left(1+\frac{M}{\lambda}\right)^{1-\alpha}\right\}.$$

Similar calculations made for moments of higher order yield the recursive equation:

$$m_{k,\alpha} = \frac{\lambda}{\alpha-1}\left\{\alpha m_{k-1,\alpha-1} - (\alpha-1)\, m_{k-1,\alpha} - M^{k-1}\left(1+\frac{M}{\lambda}\right)^{1-\alpha}\right\}, \quad k = 2, 3, ...$$

where the symbol $m_{\mathrm{K,A}}$ means for $\mathrm{A} > 0$ just the moment of order K of the truncated-Pareto variable with parameters (A, λ, M). No matter whether A is positive or not, in order to start the recursion we take:

$$m_{1,\mathrm{A}} = \begin{cases} \frac{\lambda}{\mathrm{A}-1}\left\{1-\left(1+\frac{M}{\lambda}\right)^{1-\mathrm{A}}\right\} & \text{when } \mathrm{A} \neq 1 \\ \lambda \ln\left(1+\frac{M}{\lambda}\right) & \text{when } \mathrm{A} = 1 \end{cases}$$

The above formulas could serve to calculate raw moments as well of the variable $\underline{Y}_M$ as the variable Y, provided we replace M by M_0. Having calculated moments for both variables $\underline{Y}_M$ and Y already, we make use of the relation:

$$\mathrm{E}(Y^k) = \sum_{j=0}^{k} \binom{k}{j} \mathrm{E}\left(\underline{Y}_M^{k-j}\overline{Y}_M^{j}\right), \tag{20.8}$$

to calculate moments of the variable $\overline{Y}_M$. In the above formula we read $\underline{Y}_M^0$ and $\overline{Y}_M^0$ as equal one with probability one. Mixed moments appearing on the RHS of formula (20.8) can be calculated easily as positive values of the variable $\overline{Y}_M$ happen only when $\underline{Y}_M = M$. So mixed moments equal simply:

$$\mathrm{E}\left(\underline{Y}_M^m \overline{Y}_M^n\right) = M^m E\left(\overline{Y}_M^n\right)$$

for arbitrary $m, n > 0$.

The second step is to express cumulants of both variables $\underline{W}_M$ and $\overline{W}_M$ as a product of the parameter λ_P and respective raw moments of variables $\underline{Y}_M$ and $\overline{Y}_M$. Finally, both components $\Pi_I\left(\underline{W}_M\right)$ and $\Pi_R\left(\overline{W}_M\right)$ of the total premium are expressed as a function of parameters $(\lambda_P, \alpha, \lambda, M_0, \varepsilon, r^*, s, re_0, re_1)$ and the decision parameter $M \in (0, M_0]$. Now the search of such a value of M that minimizes the total premium $\Pi(W)$ is a quite feasible numerical task. Optimal retention level and related minimal premium entail optimal amount of capital $u_{opt} = (r^*)^{-1}\{\Pi(W_I) - \mathrm{E}(W_I)\}$.

20.4.3 Interpretation of Numerical Calculations in Example 2

The problem described in Example 2 has been solved in several different variants of assumptions on parameters. Variants 1–5 consist in minimization of the total premium, in variant 1 the parameters are $(s, \varepsilon, r^*, re_0, re_1) = (2, 2\%, 10\%, 100\%, 0.5\%)$. In variants 2, 3, 4 and 5 value of one of parameters $(\varepsilon, r^*, re_0, re_1)$ is modified and in variant 6 there is no reinsurance, (s, ε, r^*) are as in variant 1. Variant 7 consists in maximization of r^* where $(\varepsilon, \eta, re_0, re_1)$ are as in variant 1, and premium loading equals 4.47%. Results are presented in Table 20.1.

Reinsurance reduces the required level of *RBC*, which coincides either with premium reduction (compare variant 1 and 6) or with increase of the expected rate of return (compare variant 7 and 6). Reinsurance also reduces difference between results obtained on the basis of two different approximation methods (FC20.6 and FC20.5). In variant 6 (no reinsurance) the difference is quite large, which is caused by the fairly long right tail of the distribution of the variable Y.

Comparison of variants 2 and 1 confirms that the choice of a smaller expected rate of return (given substitution rate) automatically raises the need for capital, leaving the premium level unchanged (and therefore also the optimal retention level).

Table 20.1: Optimal choice of retention limit M. Basic characteristics of the variable W: $\mathrm{E}(W) = 999.8$, $\sigma(W) = 74.2$, $\gamma(W) = 0.779$, $\gamma_2(W) = 2.654$

Optimization variants	Quantile approx. method for $\underline{W}_M$	Retention Limit M	RBC	Loading $\left(\frac{\Pi(W)}{\mathrm{E}(W)} - 1\right)$
V.1: (basic)	FC20.6	114.5	386.6	4.11%
	FC20.5	106.5	385.2	4.13%
V.2: $r^* = 8\%$	FC20.6	114.5	483.3	4.11%
	FC20.5	106.5	481.5	4.13%
V.3: $\varepsilon = 4\%$	FC20.6	129.7	382.3	4.03%
	FC20.5	134.7	382.1	4.01%
V.4: $re_0 = 50\%$	FC20.6	79.8	373.3	4.03%
	FC20.5	76.3	372.1	4.03%
V.5: $re_1 = 0.25\%$	FC20.6	95.5	380.0	4.05%
	FC20.5	90.9	379.0	4.06%
V.6: (no reinsurance)	FC20.6	500.0	446.6	4.47%
	FC20.5	500.0	475.1	4.75%
V.7: $r^* = 11.27\%$	FC20.6	106.0	372.3	4.47%
V.7: $r^* = 11.22\%$	FC20.5	99.6	371.5	4.47%

STFrein01.xpl

Comparison of variants 3 and 1 shows that admission of greater loss probability ε causes reduction of premium, which coincides with substantial reduction of the need for reinsurance cover, and slight reduction in the need for capital. It is worthwhile to notice that replacement of $\varepsilon = 2\%$ by $\varepsilon = 4\%$ entails reversing the relation of results obtained by two approximation methods. Formula FC20.5 leads to smaller retention limits when safety standard is high (small ε), and to larger retention limits when safety standard is relaxed (large ε).

Comparison of variants 4 and 5 with variant 1 illustrates the obvious rule that it does pay off to reduce retention limits when reinsurance is cheap, and to increase them when reinsurance is expensive.

It could happen in practice that pricing rules applied by reinsurers differ by lines of business. When the portfolio $W = W_1 + ... + W_n$ consists of n business lines, for which the market offers reinsurance cover priced on the basis of different formulas $\Pi_{1,R}(\cdot)$, ..., $\Pi_{n,R}(\cdot)$, the natural generalization of the problem lies in minimization of the premium (or maximization of the rate r^*) made by choosing n retention limits M_1, ..., M_n, for each of business lines separately. Separation of business lines makes it feasible to assume different severity distributions, too.

20.5 Ruin Probability Criterion when the Initial Capital is Given

Presuming long-run horizon for premium calculation we turn back to ruin theory. Our aim is now to obtain such a level of premium for the portfolio yielding each year the aggregate loss W, which results from a presumed level of ruin probability ψ and initial capital u. This is done by inverting various approximate formulae for the probability of ruin. Information requirements of different methods are emphasized. Special attention is paid also to the problem of decomposition of the whole portfolio premium.

20.5.1 Approximation Based on Lundberg Inequality

This is a simplest (and crude) approximation method, simply assuming replacement of the true function $\psi(u)$ by:

$$\psi_{Li}(u) = e^{-Ru}.$$

At first we obtain the approximation $R_{(Li)}$ of the desired level of the adjustment coefficient R:

$$R_{(Li)} = \frac{-\ln \psi}{u}.$$

In the next step we make use of the definition of the adjustment coefficient for the portfolio:

$$\mathrm{E}\left(e^{RW}\right) = e^{R\Pi(W)},$$

to obtain directly the premium formula:

$$\Pi(W) = R^{-1} \ln \left\{\mathrm{E}\left(e^{RW}\right)\right\} = R^{-1} C_W(R),$$

where C_W denotes the cumulant generating function. The result is well known as the exponential premium formula. It possesses several desirable properties – not only that it is derivable from ruin theory. First of all, by the virtue of properties of the cumulant generating function, it is additive for independent risks. So there is no need to distinguish between marginal and basic premiums for individual risks. By the same reason the formula does not reflect the cross-sectional diversification effect when the portfolio is composed of large number of risks, each of them being small. The formula can be practically applied once we replace the adjustment coefficient R by its approximation $R_{(Li)}$.

Under certain conditions we could rely on truncating higher order terms in the expansion of the cumulant generating function:

$$\Pi(W) = \frac{1}{R} C_W(R) = \mu_W + \frac{1}{2!} R \sigma_W^2 + \frac{1}{3!} R^2 \mu_{3,W} + \frac{1}{4!} R^3 c_{4,W} + ..., \quad (20.9)$$

and use for the purpose of individual risk pricing the formula (where higher order terms are truncated as well):

$$\Pi(X) = \frac{1}{R} C_X(R) = \mu_X + \frac{1}{2!} R \sigma_X^2 + \frac{1}{3!} R^2 \mu_{3,X} + \frac{1}{4!} R^3 c_{4,X} + ... \quad (20.10)$$

Some insight into the nature of the long-run criteria for premium calculation could be gained by re-arrangement of the formula (20.9). At first we could express the initial capital in units of standard deviation of the aggregate loss: $U = u\sigma_W^{-1}$. Now the adjustment coefficient could be expressed as:

$$R = \frac{-\ln \psi}{U \sigma_W},$$

and premium formula (20.9) as:

$$\Pi(W) = \mu_W + \sigma_W \left\{ \frac{1}{2!} \frac{-\ln \psi}{U} + \frac{1}{3!} \left(\frac{-\ln \psi}{U} \right)^2 \gamma_W + \frac{1}{4!} \left(\frac{-\ln \psi}{U} \right)^3 \gamma_{2,W} + ... \right\} \quad (20.11)$$

where in the brackets appear only unit-less figures, that form together the pricing formula for the standardized risk $(W - \mu_W)\sigma_W^{-1}$. Let us notice that the contribution of higher order terms in the expansion is neglectible when initial capital is large enough. The above phenomenon could be interpreted as a result of risk diversification in time (as opposed to cross-sectional risk diversification). Provided the initial capital is large, the ruin (if it happens at all) will rather appear as a result of aggregation of poor results over many periods of time. However, given the skewness and kurtosis of one-year increment of the risk process, the sum of increments over n periods has skewness of order $n^{-\frac{1}{2}}$, kurtosis of order n^{-1} etc. Hence the larger initial capital, the smaller importance of the difference between the distribution of the yearly increment and the normal distribution. In a way this is how the diversification of risk in time works (as opposed to cross-sectional diversification). In the case of a cross-sectional diversification the assumption of mutual independency of risks plays the crucial role. Analogously, diversification of risk in time works effectively when subsequent increments of the risk process are independent.

20.5.2 "Zero" Approximation

The "zero" approximation is a kind of naive approximation, assuming replacement of the function $\psi(u)$ by:

$$\psi_0(u) = (1+\theta)^{-1} \exp(-Ru),$$

where θ denotes the relative security loading, which means that $(1+\theta) = \frac{\Pi(W)}{\mathrm{E}(W)}$. The "zero" approximation is applicable to the case of Poisson claim arrivals (as opposed to Lundberg inequality, which is applicable under more general assumptions). Relying on "zero" approximation leads to the system of two equations:

$$\Pi(W) = R^{-1} C_W(R)$$

$$R = \tfrac{1}{u} \ln \tfrac{\mathrm{E}(W)}{\psi \Pi(W)}.$$

The system could be solved by assuming at first:

$$R^{(0)} = \frac{-\ln \psi}{u},$$

and next by executing iterations:

$$\Pi^{(n)}(W) = \tfrac{1}{R^{(n-1)}} C_W\left(R^{(n-1)}\right)$$

$$R^{(n)} = \tfrac{1}{u} \ln \tfrac{\mathrm{E}(W)}{\psi \Pi^{(n)}(W)},$$

that under reasonable circumstances converge quite quickly to the solution $R_{(0)} = \lim_{n\to\infty} R^{(n)}$, which allows applying formula (20.9) for the whole portfolio and formula (20.10) for individual risks, provided the coefficient R is replaced by its approximation $R_{(0)}$.

20.5.3 Cramér–Lundberg Approximation

Premium calculation could also be based on the Cramér-Lundberg approximation. In this case the problem can be reduced also to the system of equations (three this time):

$$\begin{aligned}\Pi(W) &= R^{-1}C_W(R)\\ R &= \frac{1}{u}\left\{-\ln\psi + \ln\frac{\mu_Y\theta}{M_Y'(R)-\mu_Y(1+\theta)}\right\}\\ (1+\theta) &= \frac{\Pi(W)}{\mathrm{E}(W)}.\end{aligned}$$

where $M_Y'(\cdot)$ and μ_Y denote respectively the first order derivative of the moment generating function and the expectation of the severity distribution. Solution of the system in respect of unknowns $\Pi(W)$, θ and R requires now a bit more complex calculations. Obtained result $R_{(CL)}$ could be used then to replace R in formulas (20.9) and (20.10). The method is applicable to the case of Poisson claim arrivals. Moreover, severity distribution has to be known in this case. It can be expected that the method will produce accurate results for large u.

20.5.4 Beekman–Bowers Approximation

This method is often recommended as the one which produces relatively accurate approximations, especially for moderate amounts of initial capital. The problem consists in solving the system of three equations:

$$\begin{aligned}\psi &= (1+\theta)^{-1}\{1-G_{\alpha,\beta}(u)\}\\ \frac{\alpha}{\beta} &= (1+\theta)\frac{m_{2,Y}}{2\theta m_{1,Y}}\\ \frac{\alpha(\alpha+1)}{\beta^2} &= (1+\theta)\left\{\frac{m_{3,Y}}{3\theta m_{1,Y}} + 2\left(\frac{m_{2,Y}}{2\theta m_{1,Y}}\right)^2\right\},\end{aligned}$$

where $G_{\alpha,\beta}$ denotes the cdf of the gamma distribution with parameters (α, β), and $m_{k,Y}$ denotes the raw moment of order k of the severity distribution. Last two equations arise from equating moments of the gamma distribution to conditional moments of the maximal loss distribution (provided the maximal loss is positive). Solving this system of equation is a bit cumbersome, as it involves multiple numerical evaluations of the cdf of the gamma distribution. The admissible solution exists provided $m_{3,Y}m_{1,Y} > m_{2,Y}^2$, that is always satisfied for arbitrary severity distribution with support on the positive part of the axis. Denoting the solution for the unknown θ by θ_{BB}, we can write the latter as a function:

$$\theta_{BB} = \theta_{BB}\left(u, \psi, m_{1,Y}, m_{2,Y}, m_{2,Y}\right),$$

and obtain the whole portfolio premium from the equation:

$$\Pi_{BB}\left(W\right) = \left(1 + \theta_{BB}\right) \mathrm{E}(W).$$

Formally, application of the method requires only moments of first three orders of the severity distribution to be finite. However, the problem arises when we wish to price individual risks. Then we have to know the moment generating function of the severity distribution, and it should obey conditions for adjustment coefficient to exist. If this is a case, we can replace the coefficient θ of the equation:

$$M_Y(r) = 1 + (1 + \theta)\, m_{1,Y} r$$

by its approximation θ_{BB}, and thus obtain the approximation $R_{(BB)}$ of the adjustment coefficient R. It allows calculating premiums according to formulas (20.9) and (20.10). It is easy to verify that there is no danger of contradiction, as both formulas for the premium $\Pi_{BB}\left(W\right)$ produce the same result $\left(1 + \theta_{BB}\right) \mathrm{E}(W) = R_{(BB)}^{-1} C_W\left(R_{(BB)}\right)$.

20.5.5 Diffusion Approximation

This approximation method requires the scarcest information. It suffices to know the first two moments of the increment of the risk process, to invert the formula:

$$\psi_D(u) = \exp\left(-R_{(D)} u\right),$$

where:

$$R_{(D)} = 2\left\{\Pi(W) - \mu_W\right\} \sigma_W^{-2},$$

in order to obtain the premium:

$$\Pi_D(W) = \mu_W + \frac{\sigma_W^2}{2} \frac{-\log \psi}{u},$$

that again is easily decomposable for individual risks. The formula is equivalent to the exponential formula (20.9), where all terms except the first two are omitted.

20.5.6 De Vylder Approximation

The method requires information on moments of the first three orders of the increment of the risk process. According to the method, ruin probability could be expressed as:

$$\psi_{dV}(u) = \frac{1}{1+R_{(D)}\rho} \exp\left(-\frac{R_{(D)}u}{1+R_{(D)}\rho}\right),$$

where for simplicity the abbreviated notation $\rho \stackrel{\text{def}}{=} \frac{1}{3}\sigma_W\gamma_W$ is used. Setting $\psi_{dV}(u)$ equal to ψ and rearranging the equation we obtain another form of it:

$$\left\{-\log\psi - \log\left(1+R_{(D)}\rho\right)\right\}\left(1+R_{(D)}\rho\right) = R_{(D)}u$$

that can be solved numerically in respect of $R_{(D)}$, to yield as a result premium formula:

$$\Pi_{dV}(W) = \mu_W + \frac{\sigma_W^2}{2}R_{(D)},$$

which again is directly decomposable.

When the analytic solution is needed, we can make some further simplifications. Namely, the equation entangling the unknown coefficient $R_{(D)}$ could be transformed to a simplified form on the basis of the following approximation:

$$\left(1+R_{(D)}\rho\right)\log\left(1+R_{(D)}\rho\right) =$$

$$= \left(1+R_{(D)}\rho\right)\left\{R_{(D)}\rho - \frac{1}{2}\left(R_{(D)}\rho\right)^2 + \frac{1}{3}\left(R_{(D)}\rho\right)^3 - \ldots\right\} \approx R_{(D)}\rho.$$

Provided the error of omission of higher order terms is small, we obtain the approximation:

$$R_{(D)} \approx \frac{-\log\psi}{u+\rho(\log\psi+1)}.$$

The error of the above solution is small, provided the initial capital u is several times greater than the product $\rho\,|\log\psi+1|$. Under this condition we obtain the explicit (approximated) premium formula:

$$\Pi_{dV^*}(W) = \mu_W + \frac{\sigma_W^2}{2}\left\{\frac{-\log\psi}{u+\rho(\log\psi+1)}\right\},$$

where the star symbolizes the simplification made. Applying now the method of linear approximation of marginal cost $\Pi_{dV^*}(W+X) - \Pi_{dV^*}(W)$ presented in Section 20.3 yields the result:

$$\Pi_{dV^*}(X) = \mu_X + \frac{-\log\psi\{u + 2\rho(\log\psi + 1)\}}{2\{u + \rho(\log\psi + 1)\}^2}\sigma_X^2 + \frac{\log\psi(\log\psi + 1)}{6\{u + \rho(\log\psi + 1)\}^2}\mu_{3,X}.$$

The reader can verify that the formula $\Pi_{dV^*}(\cdot)$ is additive for independent risks, and so it can serve for marginal as well as for basic valuation.

20.5.7 Subexponential Approximation

This method applies to the classical model (Poisson claim arrivals) with thick-tailed severity distribution. More precisely, when the severity cdf F_Y possesses the finite expectation μ_Y, then the integrated tail distribution cdf F_{L_1} (interpreted as the cdf of the variable L_1, being the "ladder height" of the claim surplus process) is defined as follows:

$$1 - F_{L_1}(x) = \frac{1}{\mu_Y}\int_x^{\infty}\{1 - F_Y(y)\}dy.$$

Assuming now that the latter distribution is subexponential (see Chapter 15), we could obtain (applying the Pollaczek-Khinchin formula) the approximation, which should work for large values of initial capital:

$$\Pi_S(W) = \mu_W\left[1 + \frac{1}{\psi}\{1 - F_{L_1}(u)\}\right].$$

The extended study of consequences of thick-tailed severity distributions can be found in Embrechts, Klüppelberg, and Mikosch (1997).

20.5.8 Panjer Approximation

The Pollaczek-Khinchin formula could be also used in combination with the Panjer recursion algorithm, to produce quite accurate (at the cost of time-consuming calculations) answers in the case of the classical model (Poisson claim arrivals). The method consists of two basic steps. In the first step the integrated tail distribution $F_{L_1}(x)$ is calculated and discretized. Once this step is executed, we have a distribution of a variable $\tilde{L}_1$ (discretized version of the "ladder height" L_1):

$$f_j = \mathrm{P}\left(\tilde{L}_1 = jh\right), \qquad j = 0, 1, 2, \dots$$

The second step is based on the fact that the maximal loss $L = L_1 + \cdots + L_N$ has a compound geometric distribution. Thus the distribution of the discretized version $\tilde{L}$ of the variable L is obtained by making use of the Panjer recursion formula:

$$\mathrm{P}\left(\tilde{L} = 0\right) = (1-q)\sum_{j=0}^{\infty}(qf_0)^j,$$

and for $k = 1, 2, \dots$:

$$\mathrm{P}\left(\tilde{L} = kh\right) = \frac{q}{1-qf_0}\sum_{j=1}^{k} f_j \mathrm{P}\left\{\tilde{L} = (k-j)h\right\},$$

where $q \stackrel{\mathrm{def}}{=} (1+\theta)^{-1}$. Iterations should be stopped when for some k_ψ the cumulated probability $F_{\tilde{L}}(k_\psi h)$ exceeds for the first time the predetermined value $1-\psi$. The approximated value of the capital u at which the ruin probability attains the value ψ could be set then on the basis of interpolation, taking into account that the ruin probability function is approximately exponential:

$$u_\psi \stackrel{\mathrm{def}}{=} k_\psi h - h\frac{\log\psi - \log\{1 - F_{\tilde{L}}(k_\psi h)\}}{\log\{1 - F_{\tilde{L}}(k_\psi h - h)\} - \log\{1 - F_{\tilde{L}}(k_\psi h)\}}.$$

Calculations should be repeated for different values of θ in order to find such value $\theta_{Panjer}(\psi, u)$, at which the resulting capital u_ψ approaches the predetermined value of capital u. Then the resulting premium is given by the formula:

$$\Pi_{Panjer}(W) = (1 + \theta_{Panjer})\mu_W.$$

It should be noted, that it is only the second step of calculations which has to be repeated many times under the search procedure, as the distribution of the variable $\tilde{L}_1$ remains the same for various values of θ being tested. The advantage of the method is that the range of the approximation error is under control, as it is a simple consequence of the width of the discretization interval h and the discretization method used. The disadvantage already mentioned is a time-consuming algorithm. Moreover, the method produces only numerical results, and therefore, provides no rule for decomposition of the whole portfolio premium for individual risk premiums. Nevertheless, the method could be used to obtain quite accurate approximations, and thus, a reference point to estimate approximation errors produced by simpler methods.

All approximation methods presented in this section are more or less standard, and more detailed information on them can be found in any actuarial textbook, as for example in "Actuarial Mathematics" by Bowers et al. (1986, 1997). More advanced analysis can be found in a book "Ruin probabilities" by Asmussen (2000) and numerical comparison of this and other approximations are given in Chapter 15.

20.6 Ruin Probability Criterion and the Rate of Return

This section is devoted to considering the problem of balancing profitability and solvency requirements. In Section 20.2 a similar problem has already been studied. However, we have considered there return on capital on the single-period basis. Therefore neither the allocation of returns (losses) nor the long run consequences of decision rules applied in this respect were considered. The problem was already illustrated in Example 1. Section 20.6.1 is devoted to presenting the same problem under more general assumptions about the risk process, making use of some of approximations presented in Section 20.5. Section 20.6.2 is devoted to another generalization, where more flexible dividend policy allows for sharing risk between the company and shareholders.

20.6.1 Fixed Dividends

First we consider a reinterpretation of the model presented in Example 1. Now the discrete-time version of the model is assumed:

$$R_n = u + (c - du)\,n - (W_1 + ... + W_n)\,, \qquad n = 0, 1, 2, \ldots$$

where all events are assumed to be observed once a year, and notations are obviously adapted. The question is the same: to choose the optimal level of initial capital u that minimizes the premium c given the ruin probability ψ and the dividend rate d. The solution depends on how much information we have on the distribution of the variable W, and how precise result is required. Provided our information is restricted to the expectation and variance of W, we can use the diffusion approximation. This produces exactly the same results as in Example 1, although now we interpret them as an approximated solution. Let us remind that the resulting premium formula reads:

$$\Pi(W) = \mu_W + \sigma_W \sqrt{-2d \log \psi},$$

with the accompanying result for the optimal level of capital:

$$u_{opt} = \sigma\sqrt{-\log\psi(2d)^{-1}}.$$

Despite the fact that the premium formula is not additive, we can follow arguments presented in Section 20.3.4, to propose the individual basic premium formula:

$$\Pi_B(X) = \mu_X + \sigma_X^2\sigma_W^{-1}\sqrt{-2d\log\psi},$$

and obviously the marginal premium containing loading twice as small as the basic one.

The basic idea presented above can be generalized to cases when richer information on the distribution of the variable W allows for more sophisticated methods. For illustrative purposes only the method of De Vylder (in a simplified version) is considered.

Example 3

Our information encompasses also skewness (which is positive), so premium is calculated on the basis of the De Vylder approximation. Allowing for simplification proposed in the previous section, we obtain the minimized function:

$$c = \mu_W + \frac{\sigma_W^2}{2}\left\{\frac{-\ln\psi}{u+\rho\,(\ln\psi+1)}\right\} + du.$$

Almost as simply as in the Example 1 we get the solutions:

$$\begin{aligned} u_{opt} &= \sigma_W\sqrt{\frac{-\ln\psi}{2d}} - \rho\,(\ln\psi+1)\,, \\ c_{opt} &= \mu_W + \sigma_W\left\{\sqrt{-2d\ln\psi} - \tfrac{1}{3}d\,(\ln\psi+1)\,\gamma_W\right\}, \end{aligned}$$

where again the safety loading amounts to $\frac{1}{2}\sigma_W\sqrt{-2d\ln\psi}$. However, in this case the safety loading is smaller than a half of the total premium loading. This time the capital (and so the dividend loading) is larger, because of component proportional to $\sigma_W\gamma_W$. This complicates also individual risks pricing, as (analogously to formulas considered in Section 20.3.3), the basic premium in respect of this component has to be set arbitrarily.

Comparing problems presented above with those considered in Section 20.5 we can conclude that premium calculation based on ruin theory are easily decomposable as far as the capital backing risk is considered as fixed. Once the cost of capital is explicitly taken into account, we obtain premium calculation formulas much more similar to those derived on the basis of one-year considerations, what leads to similar obstacles when the decomposition problem is considered.

20.6.2 Flexible Dividends

So far we have assumed that shareholders are paid a fixed dividend irrespective of the current performance of the company. It is not necessarily the case, as shareholders would accept some share in risk provided they will get a suitable risk premium in exchange. The more general model which encompasses the previous examples as well as the case of risk sharing can be formulated as follows:

$$R_n = u + cn - (W_1 + ... + W_n) - (D_1 + ... + D_n)$$

where D_n is a dividend due to the year n, defined as such a function of the variable W_n that $\mathrm{E}(D_n) = du$. As dividend is a function of the current year result, it preserves independency of increments of the risk process. Of course, only such definitions of D_n are sensible, which reduce in effect the range of fluctuations of the risk process. The example presented below assumes one of possible (and sensible) choices in this respect.

Example 4

Let us assume that W_n has a gamma (α, β) distribution, and the dividend is defined as:

$$D_n = \max\{0, \delta(c - W_n)\}, \quad \delta \in (0,1),$$

which means that shareholders' share in profits amounts to $\delta 100\%$, but they do not participate in losses. Problem is to choose a value of the parameter δ and amount of capital u so as to minimize premium c, under the restriction $\mathrm{E}(D_n) = du$, and given parameters (α, β, d, ψ). The problem could be reformulated so as to solve it numerically, making use of the De Vylder approximation.

Solution.

Let us write the state of the process after n periods in the form:

$$R_n = u - (V_1 + ... + V_n)$$

with the increment equal $-V_n$. The variable V_n could be then defined as:

$$V_n = \begin{cases} W_n - c & \text{when} \quad W_n > c \\ (1-\delta)(W_n - c) & \text{when} \quad W_n \leqslant c \end{cases}$$

According to the De Vylder method ruin probability is approximated by:

$$\psi_{dV}(u) = \left(1 + R_{(D)}\rho\right)^{-1} \exp\left\{-R_{(D)}u\left(1 + R_{(D)}\rho\right)^{-1}\right\},$$

where $R_{(D)} = -2E(V)\sigma^{-2}(V)$, and $\rho = \frac{1}{3}\mu_3(V)\sigma^{-2}(V)$; for simplicity, the number of year n has been omitted.

In order to minimize the premium under restrictions:

$$\psi_{dV}(u) = \psi, \quad \mathrm{E}(D) = du, \quad \delta \in (0,1), \quad u > 0,$$

and under predetermined values of (α, β, d, ψ) it suffices to express the expectation of a variable D and cumulants of order 1, 2, and 3 of the variable V as functions of these parameters and variables. First we derive raw moments of order 1, 2, and 3 of the variable D. From its definition we obtain:

$$\mathrm{E}(D^k) = \delta^k \int_0^c (c-x)^k \, dF_W(x),$$

that (after some calculations) leads to the following results:

$$\begin{aligned}
\mathrm{E}(D) &= \delta\left\{cF_{\alpha,\beta}(c) - \tfrac{\alpha}{\beta}F_{\alpha+1,\beta}(c)\right\}, \\
\mathrm{E}(D^2) &= \delta^2\left\{c^2F_{\alpha,\beta}(c) - 2c\tfrac{\alpha}{\beta}F_{\alpha+1,\beta}(c) + \tfrac{\alpha(\alpha+1)}{\beta^2}F_{\alpha+2,\beta}(c)\right\}, \\
\mathrm{E}(D^3) &= \delta^3\left\{c^3F_{\alpha,\beta}(c) - 3c^2\tfrac{\alpha}{\beta}F_{\alpha+1,\beta}(c)\right\} + \\
&\quad + \delta^3\left\{3c\tfrac{\alpha(\alpha+1)}{\beta^2}F_{\alpha+2,\beta}(c) - \tfrac{\alpha(\alpha+1)(\alpha+2)}{\beta^3}F_{\alpha+3,\beta}(c)\right\},
\end{aligned}$$

where $F_{\alpha+j,\beta}$ denotes the cdf of gamma distribution with parameters $(\alpha + j, \beta)$.

In respect of the relation $V - D = W - c$, and taking into account that:

$$\mathrm{E}\left[D^m(-V)^n\right] = \delta^m(1-\delta)^n \int_0^c (c-x)^{m+n} \, dF_W(x) = \left(\frac{1-\delta}{\delta}\right)^n \mathrm{E}(D^{m+n}),$$

we easily obtain raw moments of the variable V:

$$\begin{aligned}
\mathrm{E}(V) &= \tfrac{\alpha}{\beta} - c + \mathrm{E}(D), \\
\mathrm{E}(V^2) &= \tfrac{\alpha}{\beta^2} + \left(\tfrac{\alpha}{\beta} - c\right)^2 - \left(1 + 2\tfrac{1-\delta}{\delta}\right)\mathrm{E}(D^2), \\
\mathrm{E}(V^3) &= \tfrac{2\alpha}{\beta^3} + \tfrac{3\alpha}{\beta^2}\left(\tfrac{\alpha}{\beta} - c\right) + \left(\tfrac{\alpha}{\beta} - c\right)^3 + \left\{1 + 3\tfrac{1-\delta}{\delta} + 3\left(\tfrac{1-\delta}{\delta}\right)^2\right\}\mathrm{E}(D^3),
\end{aligned}$$

so as cumulants of this variable, too. Provided we are able to evaluate numerically the cdf of the gamma distribution, all elements needed to construct the numerical procedure solving the problem are completed.

In Example 4 some specific rule of sharing risk by shareholders and the company has been applied. On the contrary, the assumption on the distribution of the variable W is of some general advantage, as the shifted gamma distribution is often used to approximate the distribution of the aggregate loss. We will make use of it in Example 6 presented in the next section.

20.7 Ruin Probability, Rate of Return and Reinsurance

In this section premium calculation is considered under predetermined ruin probability and predetermined rate of dividend, with reinsurance included. At first the example involving fixed dividend is presented.

20.7.1 Fixed Dividends

Example 5

We assume (as in Example 2), that the aggregate loss W has a compound Poisson distribution with expected number of claims $\lambda_P = 1000$, and with severity distribution being truncated-Pareto distribution with parameters $(\alpha, \lambda, M_0) = (2.5, 1.5, 500)$. We assume also that the excess of each loss over the limit $M \in (0, M_0]$ is ceded to the reinsurer using the same pricing formula:

$$\Pi_R\left(\overline{W}_M\right) = (1 + re_0)\,\mathrm{E}\left(\overline{W}_M\right) + re_1 VAR\left(\overline{W}_M\right).$$

The problem lies in choosing such a value of the retention limit M and initial capital u, which minimize the total premium paid by policyholders, under predetermined values of parameters (d, ψ, re_0, re_1). The problem could be solved with application of the De Vylder and Beekman–Bowers approximation methods. As allowing for reinsurance leads to numerical solutions anyway, there is no more reason to apply the simplified version of the De Vylder method, as in Example 3.

Solution.

Risk process can be written now as:

$$R_n = u + \left\{c - du - \Pi_R\left(\overline{W}_M\right)\right\} n - \left(\underline{W}_{M,1} + \ldots + \underline{W}_{M,n}\right).$$

The problem takes a form of minimization of the premium c under restrictions, which in the case of De Vylder metod take a form:

$$\begin{aligned}
\psi &= \left(1 + R_{(D)}\rho\right)^{-1} \exp\left\{-R_{(D)}u\left(1 + R_{(D)}\rho\right)^{-1}\right\}, \\
R_{(D)} &= 2\left(c - du - \Pi_R\left(\overline{W}_M\right)\right)\sigma^{-2}\left(\underline{W}_M\right), \\
\rho &= \tfrac{1}{3}\mu_3\left(\underline{W}_M\right)\sigma^{-2}\left(\underline{W}_M\right),
\end{aligned}$$

and in the version based on the Beekman–Bowers approximation method take a form:

$$\begin{aligned}
c - du - \Pi_R\left(\overline{W}_M\right) &= (1+\theta)\,\mathrm{E}\left(\underline{W}_M\right), \\
\psi &= (1+\theta)^{-1}\left(1 - G_{\alpha,\beta}(u)\right), \\
\alpha\beta^{-1} &= (1+\theta)\,\mathrm{E}\left(\underline{Y}_M^2\right)\left\{2\theta\,\mathrm{E}\left(\underline{Y}_M\right)\right\}^{-1}, \\
\alpha(\alpha+1)\beta^{-2} &= (1+\theta)\left\{\frac{\mathrm{E}\left(\underline{Y}_M^3\right)}{3\theta\,\mathrm{E}\left(\underline{Y}_M\right)} + 2\left(\frac{\mathrm{E}\left(\underline{Y}_M^2\right)}{2\theta\,\mathrm{E}\left(\underline{Y}_M\right)}\right)^2\right\}.
\end{aligned}$$

Moments of the first three orders of the variable $\underline{Y}_M$ as well as cumulants of variables $\underline{W}_M$ and $\overline{W}_M$ are calculated the same way as in Example 2. All these characteristics are functions of parameters $(\alpha, \lambda, \lambda_P)$ and the decision variable M.

20.7.2 Interpretation of Solutions Obtained in Example 5

Results of numerical optimization are reported in Table 20.2. In the basic variant of the problem, parameters has been set on the level $(d, \psi, re_0, re_1) = (5\%, 5\%, 100\%, 0.5\%)$. In variant 6 the value $M = M_0$ is assumed, so as this variant represents the lack of reinsurance. Variants 2, 3, 4 and 5 differ from the basic wariant by the value of one of parameters (d, ψ, re_0, re_1). In variant 2 the dividend rate d has been increased so as to obtain the same level of premium, than it is obtained in variant 6. Results could be summarized as follows:

Table 20.2: Minimization of premium c with respect to choice of capital u and retention limit M. Basic characteristics of the variable W: $\mu_W = 999.8$, $\sigma_W = 74.2$, $\gamma_W = 0.779$, $\gamma_{2,W} = 2.654$

Variants of minimization problems	Method of approx. of the ruin probability	Retention limit M	Initial capital u	Loading $\frac{c-\mu_W}{\mu_W}$
V.1: (basic)	BB	184.2	416.6	4.17%
	dV	185.2	416.3	4.16%
V.2: $d = 5.2\%$	BB	179.5	408.2	4.25%
	dV	180.5	407.9	4.25%
V.3: $\psi = 2.5\%$	BB	150.1	463.3	4.65%
	dV	156.3	461.7	4.63%
V.4: $re_0 = 50\%$	BB	126.1	406.2	4.13%
	dV	127.1	406.0	4.13%
V.5: $re_1 = 0.25\%$	BB	139.7	409.0	4.13%
	dV	140.5	408.8	4.13%
V.6: (no reinsurance)	BB	500.0	442.9	4.25%
	dV	500.0	442.7	4.25%

Q STFrein02.xpl

(i) Reinsurance results either in premium reduction under unchanged rate of dividend (compare variant 6 with wariant 1), or in increase of the rate of dividend under the same premium level (compare variant 2 with variant 1). In both cases the need for capital is also reduced. If we wish to obtain reduction of premium as a result of reinsurance introduced, then the reduction of capital is slightly smaller than in the case when reinsurance serves to enlarge the rate of dividend.

(ii) Comparison of variants 3 and 1 shows that increasing safety (reduction of parameter ψ from 5% to 2.5%) results in significant growth of the premium. This effect is caused as well by increase of capital (which burdens the premium through larger cost of dividends), as by increase of costs of reinsurance, because of reduced retention limit. It is also worthwhile to notice that predetermining $\psi = 2.5\%$ results in significant diversification of results obtained by two methods of approximation. In the case when $\psi = 5\%$ the difference is neglectible.

(iii) Results obtained in variants 4 and 5 show that the optimal level of reinsurance is quite sensitive to changes of parameters reflecting costs of reinsurance.

20.7.3 Flexible Dividends

In the next example assumptions are almost the same as in Example 5, except that the fixed dividend is replaced by the dividend dependent on financial result by the same manner, as in Example 4.

Example 6

Assumptions on the aggregate loss W are the same as in Example 5: compound Poisson truncated-Pareto distribution with parameters $(\lambda_P, \alpha, \lambda, M_0)$. Assumptions concerning available reinsurance (excess of loss over $M \in (0, M_0]$, pricing formulas characterized by parameters re_0 and re_1) are also the same. Dividend is defined as in Example 4, with a suitable correction due to reinsurance allowed:

$$D_n = \max\left\{0,\ \delta\left[c - \underline{W}_{M,n} - \Pi_R\left(\overline{W}_M\right)\right]\right\}, \quad \delta \in (0,1).$$

Now the problem lies in choosing capital u, risk-sharing parameter δ and retention limit M so as to minimize premium c under the restriction $\mathrm{E}(D_n) = du$, and predetermined values of parameters characterizing the distribution $(\lambda_P, \alpha, \lambda, M_0)$, parameters characterizing reinsurance costs $(re_0,\ re_1)$ and parameters characterizing profitability and safety (d, ψ).

Solution.

Under the predetermined values of decision variables (u, δ, M) and remaining parameters the risk process has a form:

$$R_n = u - (V_1 + \ldots + V_n),$$

with increment $-V_n$, where the variable V_n is defined as:

$$V_n = \begin{cases} \underline{W}_{M,n} - c + \Pi_R\left(\overline{W}_M\right) & \text{when } \underline{W}_{M,n} > c - \Pi_R\left(\overline{W}_M\right) \\ (1-\delta)\left(\underline{W}_{M,n} - c + \Pi_R\left(\overline{W}_M\right)\right) & \text{when } \underline{W}_{M,n} \leqslant c - \Pi_R\left(\overline{W}_M\right) \end{cases}$$

The problem differs from that presented in Example 4 by two factors: variable $\underline{W}_M$ is not gamma distributed, and the premium c is now replaced by the constant $c - \Pi_R\left(\overline{W}_M\right)$. However, variable $\underline{W}_M$ could be approximated by the shifted gamma distribution with parameters (x_0, α_0, β_0) chosen so as to match moments of order 1, 2, and 3 of the original variable $\underline{W}_M$. Suitable calculations lead to the definition of the variable $\tilde{V}$, that approximates the original variable V_n:

$$\tilde{V} = \begin{cases} X - c^* & \text{when } X > c^* \\ (1-\delta)(X - c^*) & \text{when } X \leqslant c^* \end{cases}$$

where the variable X has a gamma (α_0, β_0) distribution, and the constant c^* equals $c - \Pi_R\left(\bar{W}_M\right) - x_0$. Thus we could express moments of the variable $\tilde{V}$ as functions of parameters $(\alpha_0, \beta_0, c^*, \delta)$ exactly this way, as it is done with respect to variable V and parameters $(\alpha, \beta, c, \delta)$ in Example 4. It suffices in turn to approximate ruin probability with the De Vylder method:

$$\psi_{dV}(u) = \left(1 + R_{(D)}\rho\right)^{-1} \exp\left\{-R_{(D)}u\left(1 + R_{(D)}\rho\right)^{-1}\right\},$$

where $R_{(D)} = -2E\left(\tilde{V}\right)\sigma^{-2}\left(\tilde{V}\right)$ and $\rho = \frac{1}{3}\mu_3\left(\tilde{V}\right)\sigma^{-2}\left(\tilde{V}\right)$, and where the expected value of dividend $\mathrm{E}(D)$ satisfies the restriction:

$$c - \Pi_R\left(\overline{W}_M\right) - \mathrm{E}\left(\underline{W}_M\right) - \mathrm{E}(D) = -\mathrm{E}(\tilde{V}).$$

Hence it is clear that the problem of minimization of premium under restrictions $\psi_{dV}(u) = \psi$, $\mathrm{E}(D) = du$, $\delta \in (0,1)$, $u > 0$, $M \in (0, M_0]$ and predetermined values of parameters $(\lambda_P, \alpha, \lambda, re_0, re_1, d, \psi, M_0)$ is in essence analogous to the problem presented in Example 4, and differs only in details. The set of decision variables (u, δ) in Example 4 is now extended by additional variable M, and the variable $\underline{W}_M$ is only approximately gamma distributed.

20.7.4 Interpretation of Solutions Obtained in Example 6

Results are presented in Table 20.3. In all variants predetermined values of parameters $(\lambda_P, \alpha, \lambda, M_0, re_0, re_1) = (1000,\ 2.5,\ 1.5,\ 500,\ 100\%,\ 0.5\%)$ are the same. In variant 1 (basic) the ruin probability $\psi = 5\%$ is assumed, and reinsurance is allowed. Variant 2 differs from the basic one by higher safety standard ($\psi = 2.5\%$), whereas variant 3 differs by lack of reinsurance. In each variant three slightly different versions of the problem have been solved. Version A is a simplified one, assuming fixed dividend rate $d = 5\%$, so that $D_n = du$. Consequently the minimization of the premium is conducted with respect to (u, M) only. In fact, the results from Table 20.2 are quoted for this version. Versions B and C assume minimization with respect to (u, M, δ). Version B plays a role of a basic version, where premium c is minimized under the expected rate of dividend $d = 5\%$. In version C such a rate of dividend d has been chosen, that leads (through minimization) to the same premium level, as obtained previously in version A. So two alternative effects of the consent of shareholders to participate in risk could be observed. Effect in terms of reduction of premium (expected rate of dividend remaining unchanged) is observed

Table 20.3: Minimization of premium c under three variants of assumptions and three versions of the problem.

Variant of assumptions	Version of problem	d	M	u	$\frac{c-\mu_W}{\mu_W}$	δ	$\frac{\sigma_D}{u}$
	A	5%	185.2	416.3	4.16%	-	0
V.1: $\psi = 5\%$, reins.	B	5%	189.3	406.0	3.35%	41.7%	5.02%
	C	8.54%	143.6	305.2	4.16%	48.6%	8.14%
	A	5%	156.3	461.7	4.63%	-	0
V.2: $\psi = 2.5\%$, reins.	B	5%	157.0	447.5	3.67%	44.4%	4.94%
	C	8.96%	122.9	329.7	4.63%	52.3%	8.29%
	A	5%	500.0	442.7	4.25%	-	0
V.3: $\psi = 5\%$, no reins.	B	5%	500.0	429.8	3.45%	42.0%	4.70%
	C	8.09%	500.0	340.0	4.25%	48.2%	7.15%

STFrein03.xpl

when we compare version B and A. Effect in terms of increase of the expected rate of dividend (premium being fixed) is observed when versions C and A are compared. Results could be summarized as follows.

In each of three variants, the consent of shareholders for risk participation allows for substantial reduction of premium (loading reduced by about 20%).

It is interesting that shareholder's consent to participate in risk allows for much more radical reduction of premium than reinsurance. It results from the fact that reinsurance costs have been explicitly involved in optimization, whereas the "costs of the shareholder's consent to participate in risk" have not been accounted for.

Comparison of versions C with versions A in each variant of the problem allows us to see the outcome (increase of expected rate of dividend) of the shareholder's consent to share risk. In the last column of the table the (relative) standard deviation σ_D/u of dividends is reported; it could serve as a measure of "cost" at which the outcome, in terms of the increment of the expected dividend rate, is obtained.

Comparing versions B and C in variants 1 and 2 we could observe effects of the increment in the expected rate of dividend. Apart from the obvious effect on premium increase, also the reduction of capital could be observed (cost of capital is higher), and at the same time retention limits are reduced. Also the sharing parameter δ increases, as well as the (relative) standard deviation of dividends σ_D/u.

Comparing variants 1 and 2 (in all versions A, B, and C) we notice the substantial increase of the premium as an effect of higher safety standard (smaller ψ). Also the amount of capital needed increases and the retention limit is reduced. At the same time a slight increase of sharing parameter δ is observed (versions B and C).

20.8 Final Remarks

It should be noted that all presented models, including risk participation of reinsurers and shareholders, lead only to a modification of the distribution of the increment of the risk process. Still the mutual independence of subsequent increments and their identical distribution is preserved. There are also models where decisions concerning premiums, reinsurance, and dividends depend on current size of the capital. In general, models of this type need the stochastic control technique to be applied. Nevertheless, models presented in this chapter preserve simplicity, and allow just to have insight on long-run consequences of some decision rules, provided they remain unchanged for a long time. This insight is worthwhile despite the fact that in reality decisions are undertaken on the basis of the current situation, and no fixed strategy remains unchanged under changing conditions of the environment. On the other hand, it is always a good idea to have some reference point, when consequences of decisions motivated by current circumstances have to be evaluated.

Bibliography

Asmussen, S. (2000). *Ruin Probabilities*, World Scientific, Advanced Series on Statistical Science & Applied Probability, Vol. 2, Singapore.

Bowers, N.L., Gerber H.U., Hickman J.C., Jones D.A., and Nesbitt C.J. (1986, 1997). *Actuarial Mathematics*, Society of Actuaries, Itasca, Illinois

Bühlmann H. (1985). Premium calculation from top down, *Astin Bulletin* **15**: 89–101.

Embrechts, P., Klüppelberg, C., and Mikosch, T. (1997). *Modelling Extremal Events for Insurance and Finance*, Springer, Berlin.

Hill, G.W. and Davis, A.W. (1968). Generalized asymptotic expansions of Cornish-Fisher type, *Ann. Math. Statist.* **39**: 1264–1273.

Kendall, M. and Stuart, A. (1977). *The Advanced Theory of Statistics*, 4th ed. MacMillan.

Otto, W. (2004). *Nonlife insurance – part I – Theory of risk*, series "Mathematics in Insurance" WNT (in Polish).

Panjer, H.H. (ed.), Boyle, P.P., Cox, S.H., Dufresne, D., Gerber, H.U., Mueller, H.H., Pedersen, H.W., Pliska, S.R., Sherris, M., Shiu, E.S., and Tan, K. S. (1998). *Financial Economics with Applications to Investments, Insurance and Pensions*, The Actuarial Foundation, Schaumburg, Illinois.

Shapley, L.S.(1953). A Value for n-Person Games, in Kuhn, H.W. and Tucker, A.W. (eds.) *Contributions to the Theory of Games II*, Princeton University Press, 307–317.

Part III

General

21 Working with the XQC

Szymon Borak, Wolfgang Härdle, and Heiko Lehmann

21.1 Introduction

An enormous number of statistical methods have been developed in quantitive finance during the last decades. Nonparametric methods, bootstrapping time series, wavelets, Markov Chain Monte Carlo are now almost standard in statistical applications. To implement these new methods the method developer usually uses a programming environment he is familiar with. Thus, automatically such methods are only available for preselected software packages, but not for widely used standard software packages like MS Excel. To apply these new methods to empirical data a potential user faces a number of problems or it may even be impossible for him to use the methods without rewriting them in a different programming language. Even if one wants to apply a newly developed method to simulated data in order to understand the methodology one is confronted with the drawbacks described above. A very similar problem occurs in teaching statistics at undergraduate level. Since students (by definition!) have their preferred software and often do not have access to the same statistical software packages as their teacher, illustrating examples have to be executable with standard tools. The delayed proliferation of new statistical technology over heterogeneous platforms and the evident student/teacher software gap are examples of inefficient distribution of quantitative methodology. This chapter describes the use of a platform independent client that is the basis for e-books, transparencies and other knowledge based systems.

In general, two statisticians are on either side of the distribution process of newly implemented methods, the provider (inventor) of a new technique (algorithm) and the user who wants to apply (understand) the new technique. The aim of the XploRe Quantlet client/server architecture is to bring these statisticians closer to each other. The XploRe Quantlet Client (XQC) represents the front end – the user interface (UI) of this architecture allowing to access the XploRe server and its methods and data. The XQC is fully programmed in Java not depending on a specific computer platform. It runs on Windows and Mac platforms as well as on Unix and Linux machines.

The following sections contain a description of components and functionalities the XQC offers. Section 21.2.1 gives a short overview about possible configuration settings of the XQC, which allow influencing the behaviour of the client. Section 21.2.2 explains how to connect the XQC to an XploRe Quantlet Server. A detailed description of the XQC's components *desktop*, *Quantlet editor*, *data editor* and *method tree* is part of Sections 21.3 to 21.3.3. Section 21.3.4 finally explains graphical features offered by the XploRe Quantlet Client.

21.2 The XploRe Quantlet Client

The XploRe Quantlet Client can be initiated in two different ways. The way depends on whether the XQC is supposed to run as a standalone application or as an applet embedded within an HTML page. The XQC comes packed in a single Java Archive (JAR) file, which allows an easy usage. This JAR file allows for running the XQC as an application, as well as running it as an applet.

Running the XQC as an **application** does not require any programming skills. Provided that a Java Runtime Environment is installed on the computer the XQC is supposed to be executed on, the *xqc.jar* will automatically be recognized as an executable jar file that opens with the program *javaw*. If the XQC is embedded in a HTML page it runs as an **applet** and can be started right after showing the page.

21.2.1 Configuration

Property files allow configuring the XQC to meet special needs of the user. These files can be used to manage the appearance and behavior of the XQC. Any text editor can be used in editing the configuration files. Generally, the use of all information is optional. In its current version, the XQC works with three different configuration files. The *xqc.ini* file contains important information about the basic setup of the XploRe Quantlet Client, such as server and port information the client is supposed to connect to. It also contains information

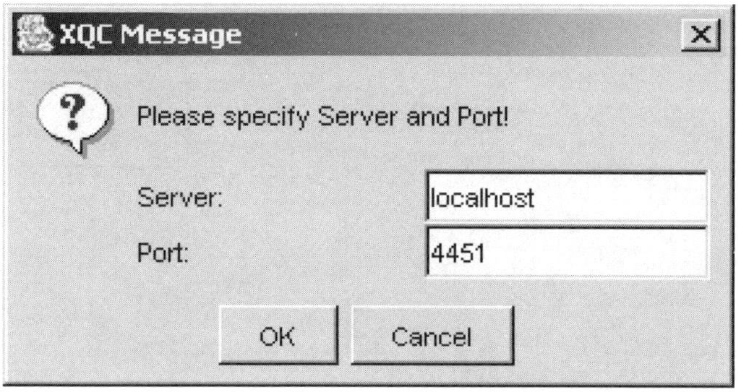

Figure 21.1: Manual input for server and port number.

about the size of the client. This information can be maintained either relative to the actual size of the screen by using a factor or by stating its exact width and height. If this information is missing, the XQC begins by using its default values.

The *xqc_language.ini* allows for setting up the XQC's language. This file contains all texts used within the XQC. To localize the client, the texts have to be translated. If no language file can be found, the client starts with its default setup, showing all menus and messages in English.

The *xqc_methodtree.ini* file finally contains information about the method tree that can be shown as part of the METHOD/DATA window, see Section 21.3.2. A detailed description of the set up of the method tree will be part of Section 21.3.3.

21.2.2 Getting Connected

After starting the XQC the client attempts to access and read information from the configuration files. If no configuration file is used error messages will pop up. If server and port information cannot be found, a pop up appears and enables a manual input of server and port number, as displayed in Figure 21.1.

The screenshot in Figure 21.2 shows the XQC after it has been started and connected to an XploRe server. A traffic light in the lower right corner of the screen indicates the actual status of the server. A green light means the client

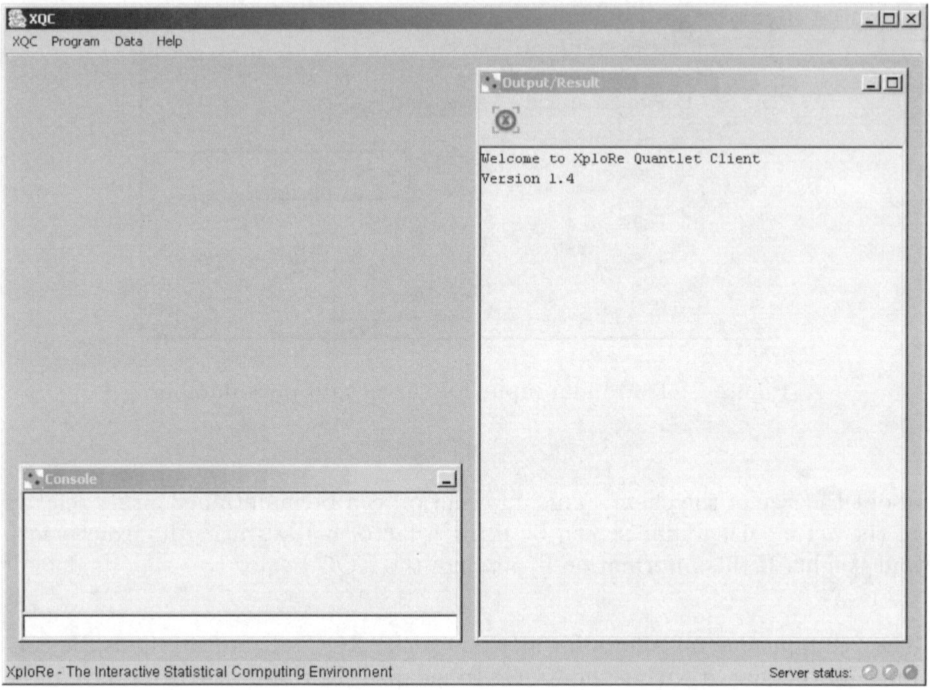

Figure 21.2: XQC connected and ready to work.

has successfully connected to the server and the server is ready to work. If the server is busy, computing previously received XploRe code, the traffic light will be set to yellow. A red light indicates that the XQC is not connected to the server.

21.3 Desktop

If no further restrictions or features are set in the configuration file (e.g. not showing any window or starting with executing a certain XploRe Quantlet) the XQC should look like shown in the screen shot. It opens with the two screen components CONSOLE and OUTPUT/RESULT window. The CONSOLE allows for the sending of single-line XploRe commands to the server to be executed immediately. It also offers a history of the last 20 commands sent to the server. To repeat a command from the history, all that is required is a mouse click on the command, and it will be copied to the command line. Pressing the 'Return' key on the keyboard executes the XploRe command.

Text output coming from the XploRe server will be shown in the OUTPUT / RESULT window. Any text that is displayed can be selected and copied for use in other applications – e.g. for presentation of results within a scientific article. At the top of the screen the XQC offers additional functions via a menu bar. These functions are grouped into four categories. The **XQC** menu contains the features *Connect*, *Disconnect*, *Reconnect* and *Quit*.

Depending on the actual server status not every feature is enabled – e.g. if the client is not connected (the server status is indicated by a red traffic light) it does not make sense to disconnect or reconnect, if the client is already connected (server status equals a green light) the connect feature is disabled.

21.3.1 XploRe Quantlet Editor

The **Program** menu contains the features *New Program*, *Open Program (local)...* and *Open Program (net)....* *New Program* opens a new and empty text editor window. This window enables the user to construct own XploRe Quantlets.

The feature *Open Program (local)* offers the possibility of accessing XploRe Quantlets stored on the local hard disk drive. It is only available if the XQC is running as an application or a certified applet. Due the Java sandbox restrictions running the XQC as an unsigned applet, it is not possible to access local programs.

If the user has access to the internet the menu item *Open Program (net)* can be useful. This feature allows the opening of Quantlets stored on a remote Web server. All it needs is the filename and the URL address at which the file is located.

Figure 21.3 shows a screen shot of the editor window containing a simple XploRe Quantlet. Two icons offer actions on the XploRe code:

- 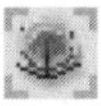 – Represents the probably most important feature – it sends the XploRe Quantlet to the server for execution.

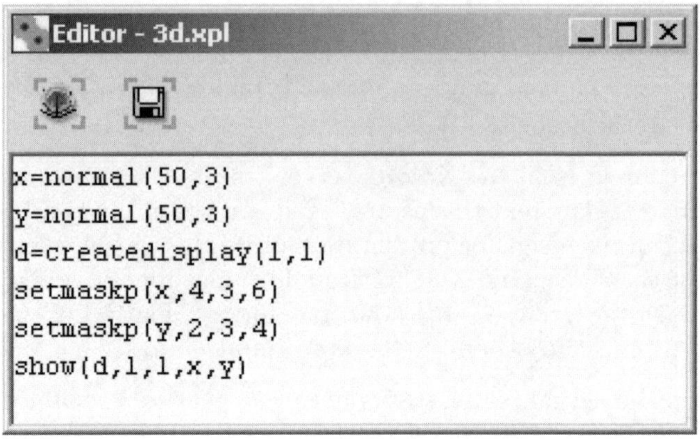

Figure 21.3: XploRe Editor window.

-  – Saves the XploRe Quantlet to your local computer (not possible if running the XQC as an unsigned applet).

The Quantlet shown in Figure 21.3 assigns two three-dimensional standard normal distributions to the variables x and y. The generated data are formatted to a certain color, shape and size using the command `setmaskp`. The result is finally shown in a single display.

21.3.2 Data Editor

The **Data** menu contains the features *New Data...*, *Open Data (local)...*, *Open Data (net)...*, *Download DataSet from Server...* and *DataSets uploaded to Server.*

New Data can be used to generate a new and empty data window. Before the data frame opens a pop-up window as shown in Figure 21.4 appears, asking for the desired dimension – the number of rows and cols – of the new data set. The XQC needs this information to create the spreadsheet. This definition does not have to be the exact and final decision, it is possible to add and delete rows and columns later on.

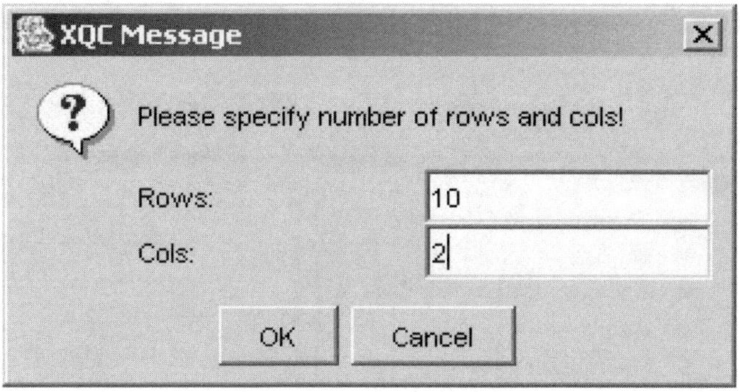

Figure 21.4: Dimension of the Data Set.

The menu item *Open Data (local)* enables the user to open data sets stored on the local hard disk. Again, access to local resources of the user's computer is only possible if the XQC is running as an application or a certified applet. The file will be interpreted as a common text format file. Line breaks within the file are considered as new rows for the data set. To recognize data belonging to a certain column the single data in one line must be separated by either using a ";" or a "tab" (separating the data by just a "space" will force the XQC to open the complete line in just on cell).

Open Data (net) lets the user open a data set that is stored on a web server by specifying the URL.

The menu item *Download DataSet from Server* offers the possibility to download data from the server. The data will automatically be opened in a new method and data window, offering all features of the method and data window (e.g. applying methods, saving, ...) to them.

A helpful feature especially for research purposes is presented with the menu item *DataSets uploaded to Server*. This item opens a window that contains a list of objects uploaded to the server using the data window or the console. Changes of these objects are documented as an object history. Due to performance reasons only uploaded data and actions on data from the CONSOLE and the TABLE MODEL are recorded.

The appearance of the data window depends on the settings in the configuration file. If a method tree is defined and supposed to be shown, the window shows

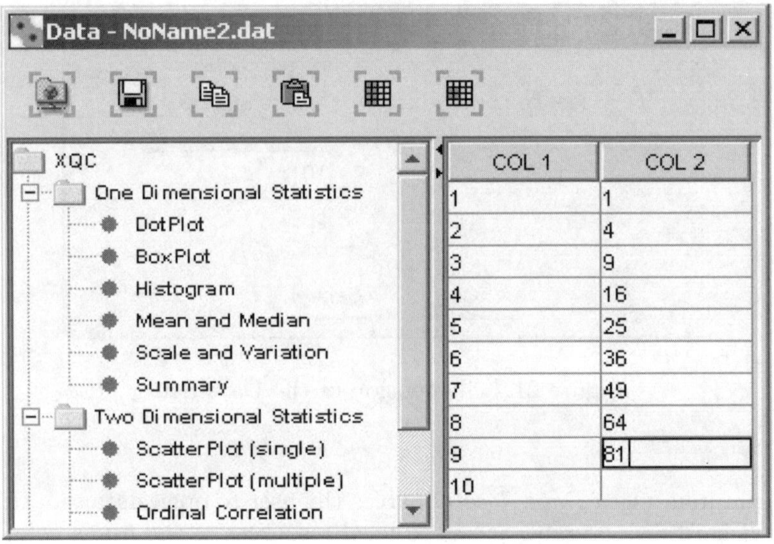

Figure 21.5: Combined Data and Method Window.

the method tree on the left part and data spreadsheet on the right part of the frame. If no method tree has been defined, only the spreadsheet will be shown. The method tree will be discussed in more detail in Section 21.3.3. Figure 21.5 shows a screen shot of the combined data and method frame.

Icons on the upper part of the data and method window offer additional functionalities:

-  – If columns or cells are selected – this specific selection, otherwise the entire data set can be uploaded to the server with specifying a variable name.
-  – Saves the data to your local computer (not possible if running the XQC as an unsigned applet).
-  /  – Copy and paste.

-  /  – Switches the column or cell selection mode on and off. Selected columns/cells can be uploaded to the server or methods can be executed on them.

The spreadsheet of the data and method window also offers a context menu containing the following items:

- Copy
- Paste
- No Selection Mode – Switches OFF the column or cell selection mode.
- Column Selection Mode – Switches ON the column selection mode.
- Cell Selection Mode – Switches ON the cell selection mode.
- Set Row as Header Line
- Set column Header
- Delete single Row
- Insert single Row
- Add single Row
- Delete single Column
- Add single Column

Most of the context menu items are self-explaining. However, there are two items that are worth taking a closer look at – *'Set Row as Header Line'* and *'Set column Header'*. The spreadsheet has the capability to specify a header for each column. This information can be used within XploRe Quantlets to name the axis within a plot, making it easier for the user to interpret graphics. A more detailed description is included in Section 21.3.3. Default values for the headers are COL1, COL2, ... as shown in Figure 21.6. Naming a single column can be performed using the menu item *'Set column Header'*. The name has to be maintained within the pop up window that appears right after choosing this menu item. It can also be used to change existing column headers. The spreadsheet also offers the possibility to set column headers all at once. If the

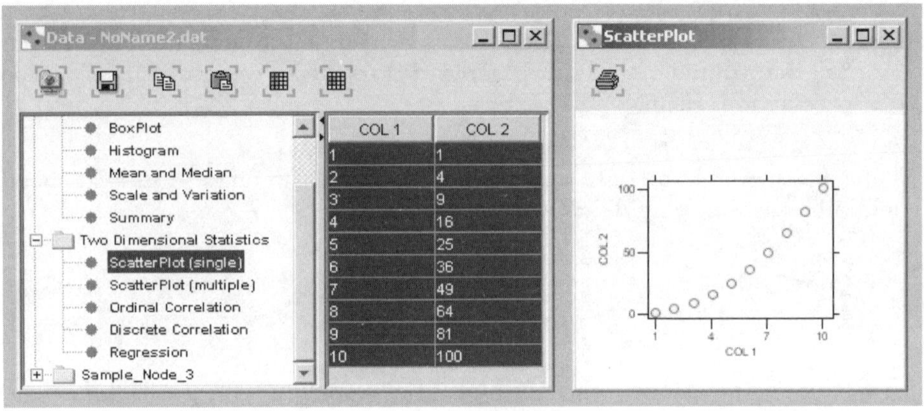

Figure 21.6: Working with the Data and Method Window.

data set already contains a row with header information – either coming from manual input or as part of an opened data set – these row can be set as header using the menu item *'Set Row as Header Line'*. The row with the cell that is active at that time will be cut out of the data set and pasted into the header line.

Setting the header is also possible while opening a data set. After choosing the data, a pop up asks whether or not the first row of the data set to be opened should be used as the header. Nevertheless, the context menu features just described above are of course still available, enabling the user to set or change headers afterwards.

Working with the XQC's method and data window does not require any XploRe programming knowledge. All it requires is a pointing device like the mouse. Applying, for example, the scatter-plot-method on the two columns would only mean to

- switch on the column selection mode
- mark both columns
- mouse click on the method "Scatter Plot"

Result will be a plot as shown in Figure 21.6. As stated above, the selected area can also be uploaded to the server using the  icon in order to be used for further investigation. This new variable can be used within XploRe Quantlets written using the EDITOR window or manipulated via the CONSOLE.

21.3.3 Method Tree

The METHOD TREE represents a tool for accessing statistical methods in an easy way. Its setup does not require any Java programming skills. All it needs is the maintenance of two configuration files.

Settings maintained within the *xqc.ini* file tell to the XQC whether there will be a method tree to be shown or not and where to get the tree information from. The client also needs to know where the methods are stored at. The `MethodPath` contains this information. Path statements can either be absolute statements or relative to the directory the XQC has been started in. For relative path information the path must start with `XQCROOT`. The settings in the example below tell the client to generate a method tree by using the file *xqc_methodtree.ini* with the XploRe Quantlets stored in the relative subdirectory `xqc_quantlets/`.

```
ShowMethodTree     = yes
MethodTreeIniFile = xqc_methodtree.ini
MethodPath         = XQCROOT/xqc_quantlets/
```

The actual method tree is set up in a separate configuration file that is given by the property of `MethodTreeIniFile`. This file contains a systematic structure of the tree – nodes and children, the method to be executed and its description to be shown within the tree frame.

```
Node_1 = path name
  Child_1.1 = method|description
  Child_1.2 = method|description
  Child_1.3 = method|description
  Node_2 = path name
    Node_2.1 = path name
      Child_2.1.1 = method|description
```

The name of the method has to be identical to the name of the XploRe program (Quantlet). The Quantlet itself has to have a procedure with the same name as the method. This procedure is called by the XQC on execution within the method tree.

Example

The following example shows how to set up a simple method tree. First of all, we choose XploRe Quantlets used within this e-book that we want to be part of the method tree. The aim of the Quantlet should be to generate graphics from selected data of the data spreadsheet or to just generate text output. Before being able to use the Quantlets within the method tree, they have to be 'wrapped' in a procedure. The name of the procedure – in our case for example 'STFstab08MT' – has to equal the name of the saved XploRe file. Our example Quantlet *STFstab08MT.xpl* is based on the original Quantlet *STFstab08.xpl* used in Chapter 1. The procedure must further have two parameters:

- `data` – Used for passing the selected data to the XploRe Quantlet.
- `names` – Contains the names of the selected columns taken from the header of the spreadsheet.

It might also be necessary to make some minor adjustments within the Quantlet in order to refer to the parameter handed over by the XQC. Those changes depend on the Quantlet itself.

```
library ("graphic")
proc() = STFstab08MT(data, names)
    ...
endp
```

Figure 21.7: STFstab08MT.xpl.

The XploRe coding within the procedure statement is not subject to any further needs or restrictions.

Once we have programmed the Quantlet it needs to be integrated into a method tree. For this purpose we define our own configuration file - *xqc_methodtree_STF* – with the following content shown in Figure 21.8.

```
Node_1 = Stable Distribution

    Node_1.1 = Estimation
       Child_1.1.1 = stabreg.xpl|Stabreg
       Child_1.1.2 = stabcull.xpl|Stabcull
       Child_1.1.3 = stabmom.xpl|Stabmom

    Node_1.2 = Examples
       Child_1.2.1 = STFstab08.xpl|STFstab08
       Child_1.2.2 = STFstab09.xpl|STFstab09
       Child_1.2.3 = STFstab10.xpl|STFstab10
```

Figure 21.8: sample_tree.ini

We create a node calling it 'Estimation'. Below this first node we set up the Quantlets *stabreg.xpl*, *stabcull.xpl* and *stabmom.xpl*. A second node – 'Examples' contains the Quantlets *STFstab08.xpl*, *STFstab09.xpl* and *STFstab10.xpl*. The text stated right beside each Quantlet (separated by the '|') represents the text we would like to be shown in the method tree.

Now that we have programmed the XploRe Quantlet(s) and set up the method tree we still need to tell the XQC to show our method tree upon opening data sets.

```
...

ShowMethodTree    = yes
MethodTreeIniFile = xqc_methodtree_STF.ini
MethodPath        = XQCROOT/xqc_quantlets/

...
```

Figure 21.9: Extract of the xqc.ini.

The settings as shown in Figure 21.9 tell the XQC to show the method tree that is set up in our *xqc_methodtree_STF.ini* file and to use our XploRe Quantlet stored in a subdirectory of the XQC itself.

Our method tree is now ready for finally being tested. Figure 21.10 shows a screenshot of the final result – the method tree, set up above.

21.3.4 Graphical Output

The previous sections contain some examples of graphical output shown within a display. The XQC's displays do not show only the graphical results received

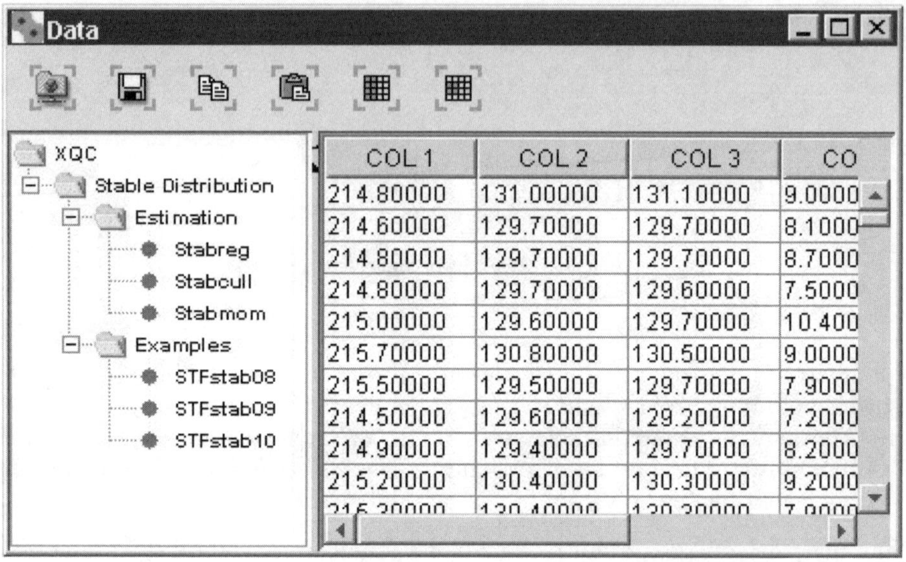

Figure 21.10: Final result of our tree example.

from the XploRe server. Besides the possibility to print out the graphic it offers additional features that can be helpful for investigating data - especially for three-dimensional plots. Those features can be accessed via the display's context menu. Figure 21.11 shows three-dimensional plot of the 236 implied volatilities and fitted implied volatility surface of DAX from January 4th 1999.

The red points in the plot represent observed implied volatilities on 7 different maturities $T = 0.13, 0.21, 0.46, 0.71, 0.96, 1.47, 1.97$. The plot shows that implied volatilities are observed in strings and there are more observations on the strings with small maturities than on the strings with larger maturities. The surface is obtained with Nadaraya-Watson kernel estimator.

For a more detailed inspection three-dimensional plots can be rotated by using a pointing device such as a mouse (with the left mouse-button pressed) or by using the keyboards arrow-keys. Figure 21.12 shows the same plot as before – it has just been rotated by some degrees. Now, one can see implied volatilities "smiles" and "smirks" and recognize different curvature for different maturities. For further research it would be helpful to know which data point belongs to which string. Here the XQC's display offers a feature to show

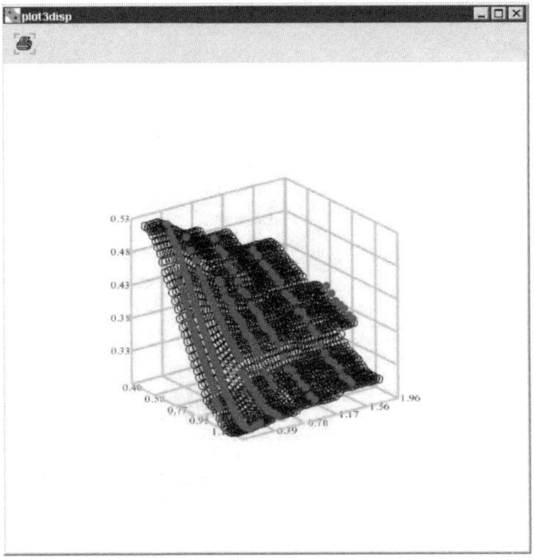

Figure 21.11: Plot of the implied volatility surface from January 4, 1999

the point's coordinates. This feature can be accessed via the display's context menu. 'Showing coordinates' is not the only option. The user could also switch between the three dimensions - 'Show X$\tilde{Y}$', 'Show X$\tilde{Z}$' and 'Show Y$\tilde{Z}$'.

After the 'Showing coordinates' has been chosen all it needs is to point the mouse arrow on a certain data point in order to get the information.

The possibility to configure the XploRe Quantlet Client for special purposes as well as its platform independence are features that recommends itself for the integration into HTML and PDF contents for visualizing statistical and mathematical coherences as already shown in this e-book.

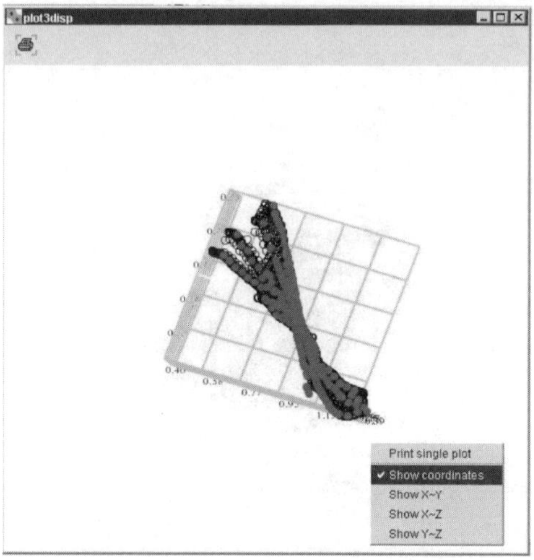

Figure 21.12: Rotating scatter plot showing the context menu.

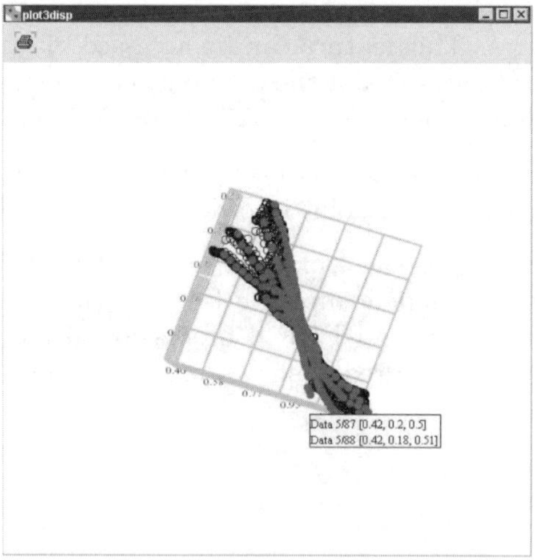

Figure 21.13: Showing the coordinates of a data point.

Index

Printing: Krips bv, Meppel
Binding: Litges & Dopf, Heppenheim

methods & data TECH*

Springer

www.mdtech.de

www.springer.de

The ebook version of

P. Cizek • W. Härdle • R. Weron
"Statistical Tools for Finance and Insurance"
ISBN 3-540-22189-1

including all data sets used in the printed edition can be downloaded from

www.xplore-stat.de

Please use the licence key

STF-DE-0383-0880